Business and Society

Stakeholders, Ethics, Public Policy

Fifteenth Edition

Anne T. Lawrence
San José State University

James Weber
Duquesne University

Mc
Graw
Hill
Education

BUSINESS AND SOCIETY: STAKEHOLDERS, ETHICS, PUBLIC POLICY, FIFTEENTH EDITION

Published by McGraw-Hill Education, 2 Penn Plaza, New York, NY 10121. Copyright © 2017 by McGraw-Hill Education. All rights reserved. Printed in the United States of America. Previous editions © 2014 and 2011. No part of this publication may be reproduced or distributed in any form or by any means, or stored in a database or retrieval system, without the prior written consent of McGraw-Hill Education, including, but not limited to, in any network or other electronic storage or transmission, or broadcast for distance learning.

Some ancillaries, including electronic and print components, may not be available to customers outside the United States.

This book is printed on acid-free paper.

1 2 3 4 5 6 7 8 9 DOW 21 20 19 18 17 16

ISBN 978-1-259-25547-2
MHID 1-259-25547-6

mheducation.com/highered

About the Authors

Anne T. Lawrence   *San José State University*

Anne T. Lawrence is a professor of management at San José State University. She holds a Ph.D. from the University of California, Berkeley, and completed two years of postdoctoral study at Stanford University. Her articles, cases, and reviews have appeared in many journals, including the *Academy of Management Review, Administrative Science Quarterly, Case Research Journal, Journal of Management Education, California Management Review, Business and Society Review, Research in Corporate Social Performance and Policy,* and *Journal of Corporate Citizenship.* Her cases in business and society have been reprinted in many textbooks and anthologies. She has served as guest editor of the *Case Research Journal* for two special issues on business ethics and human rights, and social and environmental entrepreneurship. She served as president of both the North American Case Research Association (NACRA) and the Western Casewriters Association and is a Fellow of NACRA, from which she received a Distinguished Contributor Award in 2014. She received the Emerson Center Award for Outstanding Case in Business Ethics (2004) and the Curtis E. Tate Award for Outstanding Case of the Year (1998, 2009, and 2015). At San José State University, she was named Outstanding Professor of the Year in 2005. In 2015, she received a Master Teacher in Ethics Award from The Wheatley Institution at Brigham Young University.

James Weber   *Duquesne University*

James Weber is a professor of management and business ethics at Duquesne University. He also serves as the executive director of the Institute for Ethics in Business and coordinates the Masters of Science in Leadership and Business Ethics program at Duquesne. He holds a Ph.D. from the University of Pittsburgh and has taught at the University of San Francisco, University of Pittsburgh, and Marquette University. His areas of interest and research include managerial and organizational values, cognitive moral reasoning, business ethics, ethics training and education, eastern religions' ethics, and corporate social audit and performance. His work has appeared in *Organization Science, Human Relations, Business & Society, Journal of Business Ethics, Academy of Management Perspectives,* and *Business Ethics Quarterly.* He received the SIM Sumner Marcus Award for lifetime contribution to the Social Issues in Management division of the Academy of Management in 2013 and the Best Reviewer Award from *Business & Society* in 2015. He was recognized by the Social Issues in Management division with the Best Paper Award in 1989 and 1994 and received the Best Article Award from the International Association for Business and Society (IABS) in 1998. He has served as division and program chair of the Social Issues in Management division of the Academy of Management. He has also served as president and program chair of the IABS.

Preface

In a world economy that is becoming increasingly integrated and interdependent, the relationship between business and society is becoming ever more complex. The globalization of business, the emergence of civil society organizations in many nations, and new government regulations and international agreements have significantly altered the job of managers and the nature of strategic decision making within the firm.

At no time has business faced greater public scrutiny or more urgent demands to act in an ethical and socially responsible manner than at the present. Consider the following:

- The global financial crisis—highlighted by the failure of major business firms and unprecedented intervention in the economy by many governments—and its continuing aftermath as societies have struggled to recover have focused a fresh spotlight on issues of corporate responsibility and ethics. Around the world, people and governments are demanding that executives do a better job of serving shareholders and the public. Once again, policymakers are actively debating the proper scope of government oversight in such wide-ranging arenas as health care, financial services, and manufacturing. Management educators are placing renewed emphasis on issues of business leadership and accountability.

- A host of new technologies have become part of the everyday lives of billions of the world's people. Advances in the basic sciences are stimulating extraordinary changes in agriculture, telecommunications, and pharmaceuticals, which have the potential to enhance peoples' health and quality of life. Technology has changed how we interact with others, bringing people closer together through social networking, instant messaging, and photo and video sharing. These innovations hold great promise. But they also raise serious ethical issues, such as those associated with genetically modified foods, stem cell research, or use of the Internet to exploit or defraud others, censor free expression, or invade individuals' privacy. Businesses must learn to harness new technologies, while avoiding public controversy and remaining sensitive to the concerns of their many stakeholders.

- Businesses in the United States and other nations are transforming the employment relationship, abandoning practices that once provided job security and guaranteed pensions in favor of highly flexible but less secure forms of employment. The Great Recession caused job losses across broad sectors of the economy in the United States and many other nations. Many jobs, including those in the service sector, are being outsourced to the emerging economies of China, India, and other nations. As jobs shift abroad, transnational corporations are challenged to address their obligations to workers in far-flung locations with very different cultures and to respond to initiatives, like the Bangladesh Accord on Fire and Building Safety, which call for voluntary commitment to enlightened labor standards and human rights.

- Ecological and environmental problems have forced businesses and governments to take action. An emerging consensus about the risks of climate change, for example, is leading many companies to adopt new practices, and the nations of the world have recently adopted a groundbreaking agreement designed to limit the emissions of greenhouse gases. Many businesses have cut air pollution, curbed solid waste, and designed products and buildings to be more energy-efficient. A better understanding of how human activities affect natural resources is producing a growing understanding that economic growth must be achieved in balance with environmental protection if development is to be sustainable.

- Many regions of the world and their nations are developing at an extraordinary rate. Yet, the prosperity that accompanies economic growth is not shared equally. Access to health care and education remain unevenly distributed among and within the world's nations, and inequalities of wealth and income have become greater than they have been in many years. These trends have challenged businesses to consider the impact of their compensation, recruitment, and professional development practices on the persistent—and in some cases, growing—gap between the haves and the have-nots.

- The tragic epidemic of Ebola in West Africa, as well as the continuing pandemic of AIDS in sub-Saharan Africa and the threat of a swine or avian flu outbreak have compelled drug makers to rethink their pricing policies and raised troubling questions about the commitment of world trade organizations to patent protection. Many businesses must consider the delicate balance between their intellectual property rights and the urgent demands of public health, particularly in the developing world.

- In many nations, legislators have questioned business's influence on politics. Business has a legitimate role to play in the public policy process, but it has on occasion shaded over into undue influence and even corruption. In the United States, recent court decisions have changed the rules of the game governing how corporations and individuals can contribute to and influence political parties and public officials. Technology offers candidates and political parties new ways to reach out and inform potential voters. Businesses the world over are challenged to determine their legitimate scope of influence and how to voice their interests most effectively in the public policy process.

The new Fifteenth Edition of *Business and Society* addresses this complex agenda of issues and their impact on business and its stakeholders. It is designed to be the required textbook in an undergraduate or graduate course in Business and Society; Business, Government, and Society; Social Issues in Management; or the Environment of Business. It may also be used, in whole or in part, in courses in Business Ethics and Public Affairs Management. This new edition of the text is also appropriate for an undergraduate sociology course that focuses on the role of business in society or on contemporary issues in business.

The core argument of *Business and Society* is that corporations serve a broad public purpose: to create value for society. All companies must make a profit for their owners. Indeed, if they did not, they would not long survive. However, corporations create many other kinds of value as well. They are responsible for professional development for their employees, innovative new products for their customers, and generosity to their communities. They must partner with a wide range of individuals and groups in society to advance collaborative goals. In our view, corporations have multiple obligations, and all stakeholders' interests must be taken into account.

A Tradition of Excellence

Since the 1960s, when Professors Keith Davis and Robert Blomstrom wrote the first edition of this book, *Business and Society* has maintained a position of leadership by discussing central issues of corporate social performance in a form that students and faculty have found engaging and stimulating. The leadership of the two founding authors, and later of

Professors William C. Frederick and James E. Post, helped *Business and Society* to achieve a consistently high standard of quality and market acceptance. Thanks to these authors' remarkable eye for the emerging issues that shape the organizational, social, and public policy environments in which students will soon live and work, the book has added value to the business education of many thousands of students.

Business and Society has continued through several successive author teams to be the market leader in its field. The current authors bring a broad background of business and society research, teaching, consulting, and case development to the ongoing evolution of the text. The new Fifteenth Edition of *Business and Society* builds on its legacy of market leadership by reexamining such central issues as the role of business in society, the nature of corporate responsibility and global citizenship, business ethics practices, and the complex roles of government and business in a global community.

For Instructors

For instructors, this textbook offers a complete set of supplements.

Continually evolving, McGraw-Hill Connect® has been redesigned to provide the only true adaptive learning experience delivered within a simple and easy-to-navigate environment, placing students at the very center.

- Performance Analytics—Now available for both instructors and students, easy-to-decipher data illuminates course performance. Students always know how they are doing in class, while instructors can view student and section performance at-a-glance.
- Personalized Learning—Squeezing the most out of study time, the adaptive engine within Connect creates a highly personalized learning path for each student by identifying areas of weakness and providing learning resources to assist in the moment of need.

This seamless integration of reading, practice, and assessment ensures that the focus is on the most important content for that individual.

Instructor Library

The Connect Management Instructor Library is a repository for additional resources to improve student engagement in and out of class. The instructor can select and use any asset that enhances his or her lecture. The Connect Instructor Library includes an extensive instructor's resource manual—fully revised for this edition—with lecture outlines, discussion case questions and answers, tips from experienced instructors, and extensive case teaching notes. A computerized test bank and power point slides for every chapter are also provided.

Manager's Hot Seat

Now instructors can put students in the hot seat with access to an interactive program. Students watch real managers apply their years of experience when confronting unscripted issues. As the scenario unfolds, questions about how the manager is handling the situation pop up, forcing the student to make decisions along with the manager. At the end of the scenario, students watch a postinterview with the manager and view how their responses matched up to the manager's decisions. The Manager's Hot Seat videos are now available as assignments in Connect.

Create

With McGraw-Hill Create, **www.mcgrawhillcreate.com**, the instructor can easily rearrange chapters, combine material from other content sources, and quickly upload self-developed content such as a course syllabus or teaching notes. Content may be drawn from any of the thousands of leading McGraw-Hill textbooks and arranged to fit a particular class or teaching approach. Create even allows an instructor to personalize the book's appearance by selecting the cover and adding the instructor's name, school, and course information and to select a print or eBook format.

For Students

Business and Society has long been popular with students because of its lively writing, up-to-date examples, and clear explanations of theory. This textbook has benefited greatly from feedback over the years from thousands of students who have used the material in the authors' own classrooms. Its strengths are in many ways a testimony to the students who have used earlier generations of *Business and Society.*

The new Fifteenth Edition of the text is designed to be as student-friendly as always. Each chapter opens with a list of key learning objectives to help focus student reading and study. Numerous figures, exhibits, and real-world business examples (set as blocks of colored type) illustrate and elaborate the main points. A glossary at the end of the book provides definitions for bold-faced and other important terms. Internet references and a full section-by-section bibliography guide students who wish to do further research on topics of their choice, and subject and name indexes help students locate items in the book.

LearnSmart®

The Fifteenth Edition of *Business and Society* is available with LearnSmart, the most widely used adaptive learning resource, which is proven to improve grades. (To find out more about LearnSmart, go to McGraw-Hill Connect® connect.mheducation.com.) By helping students focus on the most important information they need to learn, LearnSmart personalizes the learning experience so they can study as efficiently as possible.

SmartBook®

An extension of LearnSmart, SmartBook is an adaptive eBook that helps students focus their study time more effectively. As students read, SmartBook assesses comprehension and dynamically highlights where they need to study more.

New for the Fifteenth Edition

Over the years, the issues addressed by *Business and Society* have changed as the environment of business itself has been transformed. This Fifteenth Edition is no exception, as readers will discover. Some issues have become less compelling and others have taken their place on the business agenda, while others endure through the years.

The Fifteenth Edition has been thoroughly revised and updated to reflect the latest theoretical work in the field and the latest statistical data, as well as recent events. Among the new additions are:

- An all-new chapter for this edition on business and its suppliers, incorporating the latest thinking about social, ethical, and environmental responsibility in global supply chains.

- New discussion of theoretical advances in stakeholder theory, corporate citizenship, public affairs management, public and private regulation, corporate governance, social and environmental auditing, social investing, reputation management, business partnerships, and corporate philanthropy.

- Treatment of practical issues, such as social networking, digital medical records, bottom of the pyramid, gender diversity, political advertising and campaign contributions, as well as the latest developments in the regulatory environment in which businesses operate, including the Dodd-Frank Act and the Affordable Care Act.

- New discussion cases and full-length cases on such timely topics as worker safety in the garment industry in Bangladesh; the ignition switch recalls by General Motors; Google and the "right to be forgotten"; Uber's responsibilities toward its drivers, customers, and communities; the decision to raise wages at Gravity Payments; the regulation of e-cigarettes; security breaches that compromised customers' information at Target and other companies; the hacking of Sony Pictures' servers; the environmental impact of hydraulic fracturing; shareholder proxy access at Whole Foods; the sale of chemically tainted flooring by Lumber Liquidators; substandard wages and working conditions at nail salons; and JPMorgan Chase's reputational challenges.

Finally, this is a book with a vision. It is not simply a compendium of information and ideas. The new edition of *Business and Society* articulates the view that in a global community, where traditional buffers no longer protect business from external change, managers can create strategies that integrate stakeholder interests, respect personal values, support community development, and are implemented fairly. Most important, businesses can achieve these goals while also being economically successful. Indeed, this may be the *only* way to achieve economic success over the long term.

Anne T. Lawrence

James Weber

Acknowledgments

We are grateful for the assistance of many colleagues at universities in the United States and abroad who over the years have helped shape this book with their excellent suggestions and ideas. We also note the feedback from students in our classes and at other colleges and universities that has helped make this book as user-friendly as possible.

We especially wish to thank three esteemed colleagues who made special contributions to this edition. Cynthia E. Clark, founder and director of the Harold S. Geneen Institute of Corporate Governance and director of the Alliance for Ethics and Social Responsibility at Bentley University, generously shared with us her expertise on corporate reputation, governance, and media relations. She provided new material for and helped reorganize Chapter 19, which has greatly benefited from her insights. She also advised us on the revisions of Chapter 3 and contributed the case, "Google and the Right to Be Forgotten." Anke Arnaud of Embry-Riddle Aeronautical University provided research support for the two environmental chapters (Chapters 9 and 10), drawing on her extensive knowledge of the sustainability literature. An expert in pedagogy, she also prepared the PowerPoint slides that accompany the text. Harry J. Van Buren III of the University of New Mexico shared his expertise on technology and society and provided in-depth suggestions on how best to reorganize the two technology chapters (Chapters 11 and 12), which have been extensively revised for this edition. For all of these contributions, we are most grateful.

We also wish to express our appreciation for the colleagues who provided detailed reviews for this edition. These reviewers were Heather Elms of the Kogod School of Business at American University; Joseph A. Petrick of Wright State University; Kathleen Rehbein of Marquette University; Judith Schrempf-Stirling of the Robins School of Business at the University of Richmond; and Caterina Tantalo of San Francisco State University.

In addition, we are grateful to the many colleagues who over the years have generously shared with us their insights into the theory and pedagogy of business and society. In particular, we would like to thank Shawn Berman of University of New Mexico; Jennifer J. Griffin of George Washington University; Ronald M. Roman, Asbjorn Osland, and Marc-Charles Ingerson of San José State University; Bernie Hayen of Kansas State University; Cynthia M. Orms of Georgia College & State University; Alexia Priest of Post University; Sandra Waddock of Boston College; Mary C. Gentile of Giving Voice to Values; Margaret J. Naumes of the University of New Hampshire (retired); Michael E. Johnson-Cramer and Jamie Hendry of Bucknell University; John Mahon and Stephanie Welcomer of the University of Maine; Bradley Agle of Brigham Young University; Ann Svendsen of Simon Fraser University (retired); Robert Boutilier of Robert Boutilier & Associates; Kathryn S. Rogers of Pitzer College (retired); Anne Forrestel of the University of Oregon; Kelly Strong of Colorado State University; Daniel Gilbert of Gettysburg College; William Sodeman of Hawaii Pacific University; Gina Vega of Merrimack College; Craig Dunn and Brian Burton of Western Washington University; Lori V. Ryan of San Diego State University; Bryan W. Husted of York University; Sharon Livesey of Fordham University; Barry Mitnick of the University of Pittsburgh; Virginia Gerde, Matthew Drake, and David Wasieleski of Duquesne University; Robbin Derry of the University of Lethbridge; Linda Ginzel of the University of Chicago; Jerry Calton of the University of Hawaii–Hilo; Anthony J. Daboub of the University of Texas at Brownsville; Linda Klebe Treviño of Pennsylvania State University; Mary

Meisenhelter of York College of Pennsylvania; Stephen Payne of Georgia College and State University; Amy Hillman and Gerald Keim of Arizona State University; Jeanne Logsdon of the University of New Mexico (retired); Barbara Altman of Texas A&M University Central Texas; Craig Fleisher of the College of Coastal Georgia; Karen Moustafa Leonard of Indiana University–Purdue University Fort Wayne; Deborah Vidaver-Cohen of Florida International University; Lynda Brown of the University of Montana; Kathleen A. Getz of Loyola University–Maryland; Gordon P. Rands of Western Illinois University; Paul S. Adler of the University of Southern California; Diana Sharpe of Monmouth University; Pierre Batellier and Emmanuel Raufflet of HEC Montreal; Bruce Paton, Tom E. Thomas, Denise Kleinrichert, Geoffrey Desa, and Peter Melhus of San Francisco State University; Jacob Park of Green Mountain College; Armand Gilinsky of Sonoma State University; Tara Ceranic of the University of San Diego; and Diane Swanson of Kansas State University.

These scholars' dedication to the creative teaching of business and society has been a continuing inspiration to us.

Thanks are also due to Murray Silverman of San Francisco State University; Robyn Linde of Rhode Island College and H. Richard Eisenbeis of the University of Southern Colorado Pueblo (retired); Steven M. Cox, Bradley W. Brooks, S. Cathy Anderson, and J. Norris Frederick of Queens University of Charlotte; and Debra M. Staab, a freelance writer and researcher, who contributed cases to this edition.

A number of individuals have made research contributions to this project for which we are appreciative. Among the special contributors to this edition were Patricia Morrison of Grossmont College and Caitlin Merritt and Clare Lamperski of Duquesne University, who provided research assistance, and Debra M. Staab, who both provided research and assisted in preparing the instructor's resource manual and ancillary materials. Thanks are also due to Carolyn Roose, Nate Marsh, and Benjamin Eagle for research support. Emily Marsh, of The Sketchy Pixel, provided graphic design services.

We wish to express our continuing appreciation to William C. Frederick, who invited us into this project many years ago and who has continued to provide warm support and sage advice as the book has evolved through numerous editions. James E. Post, another former author of this book, has also continued to offer valuable intellectual guidance to this project.

We continue to be grateful to the excellent editorial and production team at McGraw-Hill. We offer special thanks to Laura Hurst Spell, our sponsoring editor, for her skillful leadership of this project. We also wish to recognize the able assistance of Diana Murphy, development editor, and MaryJane Lampe and Ligo Alex, project managers, whose ability to keep us on track and on time has been critical. Casey Keske headed the excellent marketing team. Keri Johnson, media project manager; Susan K. Culbertson, buyer; Richard Wright, copy editor; and Studio Montage, who designed the book cover, also played key roles. Each of these people has provided professional contributions that we deeply value and appreciate.

As always, we are profoundly grateful for the ongoing support of our spouses, Paul Roose and Sharon Green.

Anne T. Lawrence

James Weber

Brief Contents

Contents

PART FOUR
BUSINESS AND THE NATURAL
ENVIRONMENT   181

CHAPTER NINE
Sustainable Development and Global Business   182

CHAPTER TEN
Managing for Sustainability   205

PART FIVE
BUSINESS AND TECHNOLOGY   231

CHAPTER ELEVEN
The Role of Technology   232

PART ONE

Business in Society

CHAPTER ONE

The Corporation and Its Stakeholders

Business corporations have complex relationships with many individuals and organizations in society. The term *stakeholder* refers to all those that affect, or are affected by, the actions of the firm. An important part of management's role is to identify a firm's relevant stakeholders and understand the nature of their interests, power, and alliances with one another. Building positive and mutually beneficial relationships across organizational boundaries can help enhance a company's reputation and address critical social and ethical challenges. In a world of fast-paced globalization, shifting public expectations and government policies, growing ecological concerns, and new technologies, managers face the difficult challenge of achieving economic results while simultaneously creating value for all of their diverse stakeholders.

This Chapter Focuses on These Key Learning Objectives:

LO 1-1 Understanding the relationship between business and society and the ways in which business and society are part of an interactive system.

LO 1-2 Considering the purpose of the modern corporation.

LO 1-3 Knowing what a stakeholder is and who a corporation's market and nonmarket and internal and external stakeholders are.

LO 1-4 Conducting a stakeholder analysis and understanding the basis of stakeholder interests and power.

LO 1-5 Recognizing the diverse ways in which modern corporations organize internally to interact with various stakeholders.

LO 1-6 Analyzing the forces of change that continually reshape the business and society relationship.

Walmart has been called "a template for 21st century capitalism." In each period of history, because of its size and potential impact on many groups in society, a single company often seems to best exemplify the management systems, technology, and social relationships of its era. In 1990, this company was U.S. Steel. In 1950, it was General Motors. Now, in the 2010s, it is Walmart.[1]

In 2015, Walmart was the largest private employer in the world, with 2.2 million employees worldwide. The company operated more than 11,000 facilities in 27 countries and had annual sales of $473 billion. The retailer was enormously popular with customers, drawing them in with its great variety of products under one roof and "save money, live better" slogan; 250 million customers worldwide shopped there every week. Economists estimated that Walmart had directly through its own actions and indirectly through its impact on its supply chain saved American shoppers $287 billion annually, about $957 for every person in the United States.[2] Shareholders who invested early were richly rewarded; the share price rose from 5 cents (split adjusted) when the company went public in 1970 to around $90 a share in early 2015, its all-time high. Walmart was a major customer for tens of thousands of suppliers worldwide, ranging from huge multinationals to tiny one-person operations.

Yet, Walmart had become a lightning rod for criticism from many quarters, charged with corruption; driving down wages, benefits, and working conditions; and hurting local communities. Consider that:

- On the Friday after Thanksgiving 2014—so-called Black Friday—thousands of protesters rallied at 1,600 Walmart stores across the United States, calling on the retailer to raise its workers' pay to at least $15 an hour and offer more of them full-time work and predictable schedules. Said one part-time cashier, "It is very hard on what I earn. Right now I'm on food stamps and applying for medical assistance." A month earlier, the company had announced it would no longer provide health insurance to associates working less than 30 hours a week.[3]

- In 2012, the company confronted shocking charges that it had conducted a "campaign of bribery" to facilitate its rapid growth in Mexico. According to an investigation by *The New York Times,* Walmart had made $24 million in payments to government officials to clear the way for hundreds of new stores in what became the company's most important foreign subsidiary, in probable violation of both U.S. and Mexican law. Two years later, the company had spent more than $400 million to investigate the bribery allegations, and faced numerous lawsuits from irate shareholders and an ongoing U.S. government investigation.[4]

- In 2013, local activists protested the opening of a Walmart neighborhood market in Los Angeles's Chinatown, carrying large puppets dressed as the ghosts of small businesses. It was the latest of many incidents in which communities resisted the arrival of the retail giant, saying it would hurt local shopkeepers.[5] Economists studying Walmart's impact in Chicago, for example, found that about one-quarter of neighborhood retailers near a new Walmart had gone out of business, causing a loss of 300 jobs.[6]

In a continuing effort to improve its social performance, Walmart offered grants to small businesses, donated to wildlife habitat restoration, and announced a plan to lower

[1] Nelson Lichtenstein, "Wal-Mart: A Template for Twenty-First Century Capitalism," in *Wal-Mart: The Face of Twenty-First Century Capitalism,* ed. Nelson Lichtenstein (New York: The New Press, 2006), pp. 3–30.

[2] Global Insight, "The Price Impact of Wal-Mart: An Update through 2006," September 4, 2007.

[3] "Wal-Mart Cutting Health Benefits to Some Part-Time Employees," *Bloomberg,* October 7, 2014, and "On Black Friday, Walmart Is Pressed for Wage Increases," *The New York Times,* November 28, 2014.

[4] "Wal-Mart Hushed Up a Vast Mexican Bribery Case," *The New York Times,* April 21, 2012; "After Bribery Scandal, High-Level Departures at Walmart," *The New York Times,* June 4, 2014.

[5] "Walmart in LA's Chinatown Has Opened, Despite Major Protest," September 13, 2013, *www.huffingtonpost.com.*

[6] Julie Davis et al., "The Impact of an Urban Wal-Mart Store on Area Businesses: An Evaluation of One Chicago Neighborhood's Experience," Center for Urban Research and Learning, Loyola University Chicago, December 2009.

the salt, fat, and sugar in many of its packaged foods. The company strengthened its ethics and compliance program. It also pursued ambitious environmental goals to reduce waste, use more renewable energy, and sell more sustainable products, and began reporting to the public on its progress.[7] "Reputation is very important to Wal-Mart," said a historian who had studied the company. "They put a lot of money into building it."[8]

Walmart's experience illustrates, on a particularly large scale, the challenges of managing successfully in a complex global network of stakeholders. The company's actions affected not only itself, but also many other people, groups, and organizations in society. Customers, suppliers, employees, stockholders, creditors, business partners, governments, and local communities all had a stake in Walmart's decisions. Walmart had to learn just how difficult it could be to simultaneously satisfy multiple stakeholders with diverse and, in some respects, contradictory interests.

Every modern company, whether small or large, is part of a vast global business system. Whether a firm has 50 employees or 50,000—or, like Walmart, more than 2 million—its links to customers, suppliers, employees, and communities are certain to be numerous, diverse, and vital to its success. This is why the relationship between business and society is important for you to understand as both a citizen and a manager.

 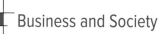

Business and Society

Business today is arguably the most dominant institution in the world. The term *business* refers here to any organization that is engaged in making a product or providing a service for a profit. Consider that in the United States today there are 6 million businesses, according to government estimates, and in the world as a whole, there are uncounted millions more. Of course, these businesses vary greatly in size and impact. They range from a woman who helps support her family by selling handmade tortillas by the side of the road in Mexico City for a few pesos, to ExxonMobil, a huge corporation that employs 75,000 workers and earns annual revenues approaching $412 billion in almost every nation in the world.

Society, in its broadest sense, refers to human beings and to the social structures they collectively create. In a more specific sense, the term is used to refer to segments of humankind, such as members of a particular community, nation, or interest group. As a set of organizations created by humans, business is clearly a part of society. At the same time, it is also a distinct entity, separated from the rest of society by clear boundaries. Business is engaged in ongoing exchanges with its external environment across these dividing lines. For example, businesses recruit workers, buy supplies, and borrow money; they also sell products, donate time, and pay taxes. This book is broadly concerned with the relationship between business and society. A simple diagram of the relationship between the two appears in Figure 1.1.

As the Walmart example that opened this chapter illustrates, business and society are highly interdependent. Business activities impact other activities in society, and actions by various social actors and governments continuously affect business. To manage these interdependencies, managers need an understanding of their company's key relationships and how the social and economic system of which they are a part affects, and is affected by, their decisions.

A Systems Perspective

General systems theory, first introduced in the 1940s, argues that all organisms are open to, and interact with, their external environments. Although most organisms have clear boundaries, they cannot be understood in isolation, but only in relationship to their surroundings.

---

[7] "2014 Global Responsibility Report," *http://corporate.walmart.com/global-responsibility/environment-sustainability/global-responsibility*.

[8] "Wal-Mart's Good-Citizen Efforts Face a Test," *The New York Times,* April 30, 2012.

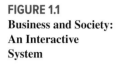

FIGURE 1.1
**Business and Society:
An Interactive
System**

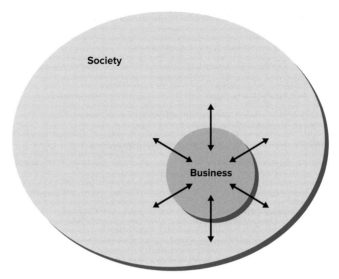

This simple but powerful idea can be applied to many disciplines. For example, in botany, the growth of a plant cannot be explained without reference to soil, light, oxygen, moisture, and other characteristics of its environment. As applied to management theory, the systems concept implies that business firms (social organisms) are embedded in a broader social structure (external environment) with which they constantly interact. Corporations have ongoing boundary exchanges with customers, governments, competitors, suppliers, communities, and many other individuals and groups. Just as good soil, water, and light help a plant grow, positive interactions with society benefit a business firm.

Like biological organisms, moreover, businesses must adapt to changes in the environment. Plants growing in low-moisture environments must develop survival strategies, like the cactus that evolves to store water in its leaves. Similarly, a long-distance telephone company in a newly deregulated market must learn to compete by changing the products and services it offers. The key to business survival is often this ability to adapt effectively to changing conditions. In business, systems theory provides a powerful tool to help managers conceptualize the relationship between their companies and their external environments.

Systems theory helps us understand how business and society, taken together, form an **interactive social system**. Each needs the other, and each influences the other. They are entwined so completely that any action taken by one will surely affect the other. They are both separate and connected. Business is part of society, and society penetrates far and often into business decisions. In a world where global communication is rapidly expanding, the connections are closer than ever before. Throughout this book we discuss examples of organizations and people that are grappling with the challenges of, and helping to shape, business–society relationships.

The Stakeholder Theory of the Firm

What is the purpose of the modern corporation? To whom, or what, should the firm be responsible?[9] No question is more central to the relationship between business and society.

[9] For summaries of contrasting theories of the purpose of the firm, see Margaret M. Blair, "Whose Interests Should Corporations Serve," in Margaret M. Blair and Bruce K. MacLaury, *Ownership and Control: Rethinking Corporate Governance for the Twenty-First Century* (Washington, DC: Brookings Institution, 1995), ch. 6, pp. 202–34; and James E. Post, Lee E. Preston, and Sybille Sachs, *Redefining the Corporation: Stakeholder Management and Organizational Wealth* (Palo Alto, CA: Stanford University Press, 2002).

In the **ownership theory of the firm** (sometimes also called property or finance theory), the firm is seen as the property of its owners. The purpose of the firm is to maximize its long-term market value, that is, to make the most money it can for shareholders who own stock in the company. Managers and boards of directors are agents of shareholders and have no obligations to others, other than those directly specified by law. In this view, owners' interests are paramount and take precedence over the interests of others.

A contrasting view, called the **stakeholder theory of the firm**, argues that corporations serve a broad public purpose: to create value for society. All companies must make a profit for their owners; indeed, if they did not, they would not long survive. However, corporations create many other kinds of value as well, such as professional development for their employees and innovative new products for their customers. In this view, corporations have multiple obligations, and all stakeholders' interests must be taken into account. This approach has been expressed well by the pharmaceutical company Novartis, which states in its code of conduct that it "places a premium on dealing fairly with employees, customers, vendors, government regulators, and the public. Novartis' success depends upon maintaining the trust of these essential stakeholders."[10]

Supporters of the stakeholder theory of the firm make three core arguments for their position: *descriptive, instrumental,* and *normative.*[11]

The *descriptive argument* says that the stakeholder view is simply a more realistic description of how companies really work. Managers have to pay keen attention, of course, to their quarterly and annual financial performance. Keeping Wall Street satisfied by managing for growth—thereby attracting more investors and increasing the stock price—is a core part of any top manager's job. But the job of management is much more complex than this. In order to produce consistent results, managers have to be concerned with producing high-quality and innovative products and services for their customers, attracting and retaining talented employees, and complying with a plethora of complex government regulations. As a practical matter, managers direct their energies toward all stakeholders, not just owners.

In what became known as the "dollar store wars," in 2014 two companies made competing bids to buy Family Dollar, a U.S. discount retail chain based in Charlotte, North Carolina—each with very different consequences for stakeholders. One suitor, Dollar Tree, offered $76.50 per share for the company, while the other, Dollar General, offered $80—seemingly a better deal for shareholders. But the Dollar General deal faced likely government antitrust scrutiny and would probably have required the closure of thousands of stores, throwing employees out of work and depriving low-income communities of access to a discount store. In the end, after considering the impact on all stakeholders, Family Dollar's management recommended the lower-priced offer, and three-quarters of its shareholders agreed.[12]

The *instrumental argument* says that stakeholder management is more effective as a corporate strategy. A wide range of studies have shown that companies that behave responsibly toward multiple stakeholder groups perform better financially, over the long run, than those that do not. (This empirical evidence is further explored in Chapter 3.) These findings make sense, because good relationships with stakeholders are themselves a source of value for the firm. Attention to stakeholders' rights and concerns can help produce

---

[10] "Code of Conduct: Values to Live By," online at *www.novartisvaccines.com*.

[11] The descriptive, instrumental, and normative arguments are summarized in Thomas Donaldson and Lee E. Preston, "The Stakeholder Theory of the Corporation: Concepts, Evidence and Implications," *Academy of Management Review* 20, no. 1 (1995), pp. 65–71. See also, Post, Preston, and Sachs, *Redefining the Corporation,* ch. 1.

[12] "Family Dollar Shareholders Approve Sale to Dollar Tree," *Charlotte Observer,* January 22, 2015.

motivated employees, satisfied customers, committed suppliers, and supportive communities, all good for the company's bottom line.

The *normative argument* says that stakeholder management is simply the right thing to do. Corporations have great power and control vast resources; these privileges carry with them a duty toward all those affected by a corporation's actions. Moreover, all stakeholders, not just owners, contribute something of value to the corporation. A skilled engineer at Microsoft who applies his or her creativity to solving a difficult programming problem has made a kind of investment in the company, even if it is not a monetary investment. Any individual or group who makes a contribution, or takes a risk, has a moral right to some claim on the corporation's rewards.[13]

A basis for both the ownership and stakeholder theories of the firm exists in law. The legal term *fiduciary* means a person who exercises power on behalf of another, that is, who acts as the other's agent. In U.S. law, managers are considered fiduciaries of the owners of the firm (its stockholders) and have an obligation to run the business in their interest. These legal concepts are clearly consistent with the ownership theory of the firm. However, other laws and court cases have given managers broad latitude in the exercise of their fiduciary duties. In the United States (where corporations are chartered not by the federal government but by the states), most states have passed laws that permit managers to take into consideration a wide range of other stakeholders' interests, including those of employees, customers, creditors, suppliers, and communities. (Benefit corporations, firms with a special legal status that obligates them to do so, are further discussed in Chapter 3.) In addition, many federal laws extend specific protections to various groups of stakeholders, such as those that prohibit discrimination against employees or grant consumers the right to sue if harmed by a product.

In other nations, the legal rights of nonowner stakeholders are often more fully developed than in the United States. For example, a number of European countries—including Germany, Norway, Austria, Denmark, Finland, and Sweden—require public companies to include employee members on their boards of directors, so that their interests will be explicitly represented. Under the European Union's so-called harmonization statutes, managers are specifically permitted to take into account the interests of customers, employees, creditors, and others.

In short, while the law requires managers to act on behalf of stockholders, it also gives them wide discretion—and in some instances requires them—to manage on behalf of the full range of stakeholder groups. The next section provides a more formal definition and an expanded discussion of the stakeholder concept.

The Stakeholder Concept

The term **stakeholder** refers to persons and groups that affect, or are affected by, an organization's decisions, policies, and operations.[14] The word *stake,* in this context, means

---

[13] Another formulation of this point has been offered by Robert Phillips, who argues for a principle of stakeholder fairness. This states that "when people are engaged in a cooperative effort and the benefits of this cooperative effort are accepted, obligations are created on the part of the group accepting the benefit" [i.e., the business firm]. Robert Phillips, *Stakeholder Theory and Organizational Ethics* (San Francisco: Berrett-Koehler, 2003), p. 9 and ch. 5.

[14] The term *stakeholder* was first introduced in 1963 but was not widely used in the management literature until the publication of R. Edward Freeman's *Strategic Management: A Stakeholder Approach* (Marshfield, MA: Pitman, 1984). For summaries of the stakeholder theory literature, see Thomas Donaldson and Lee E. Preston, "The Stakeholder Theory of the Corporation: Concepts, Evidence, Implications," *Academy of Management Review,* January 1995, pp. 71–83; Max B. E. Clarkson, ed., *The Corporation and Its Stakeholders: Classic and Contemporary Readings* (Toronto: University of Toronto Press, 1998); Abe J. Zakhem, Daniel E. Palmer, and Mary Lyn Stoll, *Stakeholder Theory: Essential Readings in Ethical Leadership and Management* (Amherst, NY: Prometheus Books, 2008); and R. Edward Freeman, *Stakeholder Theory: The State of the Art* (Cambridge, UK: Cambridge University Press, 2010).

an interest in—or claim on—a business enterprise. Those with a stake in the firm's actions include such diverse groups as customers, employees, shareholders (also called stockholders), governments, suppliers, professional and trade associations, social and environmental activists, and nongovernmental organizations. The term *stakeholder* is not the same as *stockholder,* although the words sound similar. Stockholders—individuals or organizations that own shares of a company's stock—are one of several kinds of stakeholders.

Business organizations are embedded in networks involving many participants. Each of these participants has a relationship with the firm, based on ongoing interactions. Each of them shares, to some degree, in both the risks and rewards of the firm's activities. And each has some kind of claim on the firm's resources and attention, based on law, moral right, or both. The number of these stakeholders and the variety of their interests can be large, making a company's decisions very complex, as the Walmart example illustrates.

Managers make good decisions when they pay attention to the effects of their decisions on stakeholders, as well as stakeholders' effects on the company. On the positive side, strong relationships between a corporation and its stakeholders are an asset that adds value. On the negative side, some companies disregard stakeholders' interests, either out of the belief that the stakeholder is wrong or out of the misguided notion that an unhappy customer, employee, or regulator does not matter. Such attitudes often prove costly to the company involved. Today, for example, companies know that they cannot locate a factory or store in a community that strongly objects. They also know that making a product that is perceived as unsafe invites lawsuits and jeopardizes market share.

Different Kinds of Stakeholders

Business interacts with society in many diverse ways, and a company's relationships with various stakeholders differ.

Market stakeholders are those that engage in economic transactions with the company as it carries out its purpose of providing society with goods and services. Each relationship between a business and one of its market stakeholders is based on a unique transaction, or two-way exchange. Stockholders invest in the firm and in return receive the potential for dividends and capital gains. Creditors loan money and collect payments of interest and principal. Employees contribute their skills and knowledge in exchange for wages, benefits, and the opportunity for personal satisfaction and professional development. In return for payment, suppliers provide raw materials, energy, services, finished products, and other inputs; and wholesalers, distributors, and retailers engage in market transactions with the firm as they help move the product from plant to sales outlets to customers. All businesses need customers who are willing to buy their products or services.

The puzzling question of whether or not managers should be classified as stakeholders along with other employees is discussed in Exhibit 1.A.

Nonmarket stakeholders, by contrast, are people and groups who—although they do not engage in direct economic exchange with the firm—are nonetheless affected by or can affect its actions. Nonmarket stakeholders include the community, various levels of government, nongovernmental organizations, business support groups, competitors, and the general public. Nonmarket stakeholders are not necessarily less important than others, simply because they do not engage in direct economic exchange with a business. On the contrary, interactions with such groups can be critical to a firm's success or failure, as shown in the following example.

Are managers, especially top executives, stakeholders? This has been a contentious issue in stakeholder theory.

On one hand, the answer clearly is "yes." Like other stakeholders, managers are impacted by the firm's decisions. As employees of the firm, managers receive compensation—often very generous compensation, as shown in Chapter 13. Their managerial roles confer opportunities for professional advancement, social status, and power over others. Managers benefit from the company's success and are hurt by its failure. For these reasons, they might properly be classified as employees.

On the other hand, top executives are agents of the firm and are responsible for acting on its behalf. In the stakeholder theory of the firm, their role is to integrate stakeholder interests, rather than to promote their own more narrow, selfish goals. For these reasons, they might properly be classified as representatives of the firm itself, rather than as one of its stakeholders.

Management theory has long recognized that these two roles of managers potentially conflict. The main job of executives is to act for the company, but all too often they act primarily for themselves. Consider, for example, the many top executives of Lehman Brothers, MF Global, and Merrill Lynch, who enriched themselves personally at the expense of shareholders, employees, customers, and other stakeholders. The challenge of persuading top managers to act in the firm's best interest is further discussed in Chapter 13.

In 2001, a company called Energy Management Inc. (EMI) announced a plan to build a wind farm about six miles off the shore of Cape Cod, Massachusetts, to supply clean, renewable power to New England customers. The project, called Cape Wind, immediately generated intense opposition from residents of Cape Cod and nearby islands, who were concerned that its 130 wind turbines would spoil the view and get in the way of boats. A nonprofit group called Save Our Sound filed dozens of lawsuits, charging possible harm to wildlife, increased electricity rates, and danger to aircraft. In early 2015, EMI appeared blocked on all sides, as local utilities withdrew their commitments to buy power from the wind farm, which one local newspaper called the final "death blow."[15]

In this instance, activists were able to block the company's plans for more than a decade—and possibly permanently—even though they did not have a market relationship with it.

Theorists also distinguish between **internal stakeholders** and **external stakeholders**. Internal stakeholders are those, such as employees and managers, who are employed by the firm. They are "inside" the firm, in the sense that they contribute their effort and skill, usually at a company worksite. External stakeholders, by contrast, are those who—although they may have important transactions with the firm—are not directly employed by it.

The classification of government as a nonmarket stakeholder has been controversial in stakeholder theory. Most theorists say that government is a nonmarket stakeholder (as does this book) because it does not normally conduct any direct market exchanges (buying and selling) with business. However, money often flows from business to government in the form of taxes and fees, and sometimes from government to business in the form of subsidies or incentives. Moreover, some businesses—defense contractors for example—*do*

---

[15] "Renewable Energy: Wind Power Tests the Waters," *Nature,* September 24, 2014; "Cape Wind's Future Called into Question," *The Boston Globe,* January 8, 2015; and "Cape Wind Becalmed," *Providence Journal,* January 21, 2015. The website of the project is at *www.capewind.org*. The story of the opposition to Cape Wind is told in Robert Whitcomb and Wendy Williams, *Cape Wind: Money, Celebrity, Energy, Class, Politics, and the Battle for Our Energy Future* (New York: PublicAffairs, 2008).

sell directly to the government and receive payment for goods and services rendered. For this reason, a few theorists have called government a market stakeholder of business. And, in a few cases, the government may take a direct ownership stake in a company—as the U.S. government did after the financial crisis of 2008–09 when it invested in several banks and auto companies, becoming a shareholder of these firms. Government also has special influence over business because of its ability to charter and tax corporations, as well as make laws that regulate their activities. The unique relationship between government and business is discussed throughout this book.

Other stakeholders also have some market and some nonmarket characteristics. For example, business support groups, such as the Chamber of Commerce, are normally considered a nonmarket stakeholder. However, companies may support the Chamber of Commerce with their membership dues—a market exchange. Communities are a nonmarket stakeholder, but receive taxes, philanthropic contributions, and other monetary benefits from businesses. These subtleties are further explored in later chapters.

Modern stakeholder theory recognizes that most business firms are embedded in a complex web of stakeholders, many of which have independent relationships with each other.[16] In this view, a business firm and its stakeholders are best visualized as an interconnected network. Imagine, for example, an electronics company, based in the United States, that produces smartphones, tablets, and music players. The firm employs people to design, engineer, and market its devices to customers in many countries. Shares in the company are owned by investors around the world, including many of its own employees and managers. Production is carried out by suppliers in Asia. Banks provide credit to the company, as well as to other companies. Competing firms sell their products to some of the same customers, and also contract production to some of the same Asian suppliers. Nongovernmental organizations may seek to lobby the government concerning the firm's practices, and may count some employees among their members. A visual representation of this company and its stakeholders is shown in Figure 1.2.

As Figure 1.2 suggests, some individuals or groups may play multiple stakeholder roles. Some theorists use the term *role sets* to refer to this phenomenon. For example, a person may work at a company, but also live in the surrounding community, own shares of company stock in his or her 401(k) retirement account, and even purchase the company's products from time to time. This person has several stakes in a company's actions.

Later sections of this book (especially Chapters 13 through 19) will discuss in more detail the relationship between business and its various stakeholders.

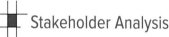

Stakeholder Analysis

An important part of the modern manager's job is to identify relevant stakeholders and to understand both their interests and the power they may have to assert these interests. This process is called **stakeholder analysis**. The organization from whose perspective the analysis is conducted is called the **focal organization**.

The first step of a stakeholder analysis is for managers of the focal organization to identify the issue at hand. For example, in the Cape Wind situation discussed earlier in this chapter, Energy Management Inc. had to analyze how best to win regulatory approval for the construction of its wind farm. Once the issue is determined, managers must ask four key questions, as discussed below and summarized in Figure 1.3.

---

[16] Timothy J. Rowley, "Moving Beyond Dyadic Ties: A Network Theory of Stakeholder Influence," *Academy of Management Review* 22, no. 4 (October 1997).

FIGURE 1.2
A Firm and Its Stakeholders

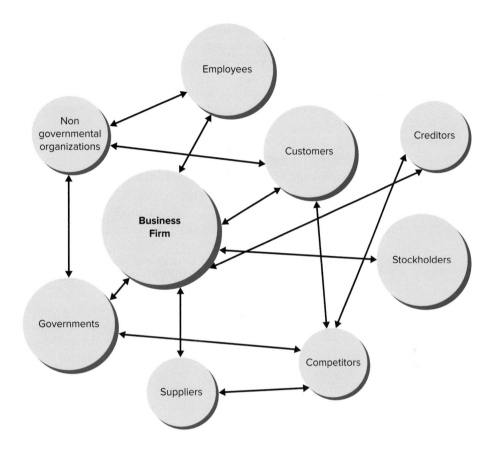

Who are the relevant stakeholders?

The first question requires management to identify and map the relevant stakeholders. Exhibit 1.B, which appears later in this chapter, provides a guide. However, not all stakeholders listed will be relevant in every management situation. For example, a privately held

FIGURE 1.3
The Four Key Questions of Stakeholder Analysis

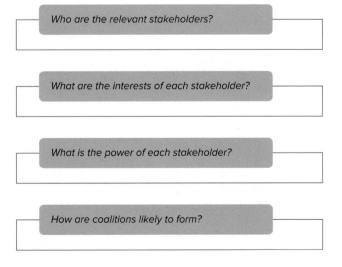

firm will not have shareholders. Some businesses sell directly to customers online, and therefore will not have retailers. In other situations, a firm may have a stakeholder—say, a creditor that has loaned money—but this group is not relevant to a particular issue that management faces.

But stakeholder analysis involves more than simply *identifying* stakeholders; it also involves understanding the nature of their interests, power, legitimacy, and links with one another.

Stakeholder Interests

What are the interests of each stakeholder?

Each stakeholder has a unique relationship to the organization, and managers must respond accordingly. **Stakeholder interests** are, essentially, the nature of each group's stake. What are their concerns, and what do they want from their relationship with the firm?[17]

Shareholders, for their part, have an ownership interest in the firm. In exchange for their investment, shareholders expect to receive dividends and, over time, capital appreciation. The economic health of the corporation affects these people financially; their personal wealth—and often, their retirement security—is at stake. They may also seek to achieve social objectives through their choice of investments. Customers, for their part, are most interested in gaining fair value and quality in exchange for the purchase price of goods and services. Suppliers wish to obtain profitable orders, use their capacity efficiently, and build stable relationships with their business customers. Employees, in exchange for their time and effort, want to receive fair compensation and an opportunity to develop their job skills. Governments, public interest groups, and local communities have another sort of relationship with the company. In general, their stake is broader than the financial stake of owners, customers, and suppliers. They may wish to protect the environment, assure human rights, or advance other broad social interests. Managers need to understand these complex and often intersecting stakeholder interests.

Stakeholder Power

What is the power of each stakeholder?

Stakeholder power means the ability to use resources to make an event happen or to secure a desired outcome. Stakeholders have five different kinds of power: *voting power, economic power, political power, legal power,* and *informational power.*

Voting power means that the stakeholder has a legitimate right to cast a vote. Shareholders typically have voting power proportionate to the percentage of the company's stock they own. They typically have an opportunity to vote on such major decisions as mergers and acquisitions, the composition of the board of directors, and other issues that may come before the annual meeting. (Shareholder voting power should be distinguished from the voting power exercised by citizens, which is discussed below.)

> For example, Starboard Value LP, a New York–based hedge fund, used its voting power as a shareholder to force change in a company it had invested in. Starboard bought more than 8 percent of the shares of Darden Restaurants, the owner of Red Lobster, Olive Garden, and other eatery chains. It called for radical change, slamming management for tolerating "lavish excess, bureaucracy, and low standards." When Darden resisted, Starboard and its allies fielded their own slate of nominees in the

---

[17] A full discussion of the interests of stakeholders may be found in R. Edward Freeman, *Ethical Theory and Business* (Englewood Cliffs, NJ: Prentice Hall, 1994).

election for the board of directors, organized support from other voting shareholders—and won. Activist investors like Starboard engaged in almost 300 such campaigns in 2014, the highest in five years, and won almost three-quarters of the time.[18]

Suppliers, customers, employees, and other stakeholders have *economic power* with the company. Suppliers, for example, can withhold supplies or refuse to fill orders if a company fails to meet its contractual responsibilities. Customers may refuse to buy a company's products or services if the company acts improperly. They can boycott products if they believe the goods are too expensive, poorly made, or unsafe. Employees, for their part, can refuse to work under certain conditions, a form of economic power known as a strike or slowdown. Economic power often depends on how well organized a stakeholder group is. For example, workers who are organized into unions usually have more economic power than do workers who try to negotiate individually with their employers.

Governments exercise *political power* through legislation, regulations, or lawsuits. While government agencies act directly, other stakeholders use their political power indirectly by urging government to use its powers by passing new laws or enacting regulations. Citizens may also vote for candidates that support their views with respect to government laws and regulations affecting business, a different kind of voting power than the one discussed above. Stakeholders may also exercise political power directly, as when social, environmental, or community activists organize to protest a particular corporate action.

Stakeholders have *legal power* when they bring suit against a company for damages, based on harm caused by the firm; for instance, lawsuits brought by customers for damages caused by defective products, brought by employees for damages caused by workplace injury, or brought by environmentalists for damages caused by pollution or harm to species or habitat. After the mortgage lender Countrywide collapsed, many institutional shareholders, such as state pension funds, sued Bank of America (which had acquired Countrywide) to recoup some of their losses.

Finally, stakeholders have *informational power* when they have access to valuable data, facts, or details and are able to bring their own information and perspectives to the attention of the public or key decision makers. With the explosive growth of technologies that facilitate the sharing of information, this kind of stakeholder power has become increasingly important.

> Consumers' ability to use social networks to express their views about businesses they like—and do not like—has given them power they did not previously have. For example, Yelp Inc. operates a website where people can search for local businesses, post reviews, and read others' comments. In 2014, a decade after its launch, Yelp attracted almost 140 million unique visitors every month. Its reviewers collectively have gained considerable influence. Restaurants, cultural venues, hair salons, and other establishments can attract customers with five-star ratings and "People Love Us on Yelp" stickers in their windows—but, by the same token, can be badly hurt when reviews turn nasty. A study in the *Harvard Business Review* reported that a one-star increase in an independent restaurant's Yelp rating led to a 5 to 9 percent increase in revenue. Some businesses have complained that Yelp reviewers have too much power. "My business just died," said the sole proprietor of a housecleaning business. "Once they locked me into the 3.5 stars, I wasn't getting any calls."[19]

---

[18] "The Hedge Fund Presentation on Olive Garden is a Masterpiece," *Business Insider,* September 13, 2014; "Activist Hedge Fund Starboard Succeeds in Replacing Darden Board," *The New York Times,* October 10, 2014; and "Taking Recipes from the Activist Cookbook," *The New York Times,* December 9, 2014.

[19] "Is Yelp Fair to Businesses?" *PC World,* November 15, 2011.

Activists often try to use all of these kinds of power when they want to change a company's policy. For example, human rights activists wanted to bring pressure on Unocal Corporation to change its practices in Burma (Myanmar), where it had entered into a joint venture with the government to build a gas pipeline. Critics charged that many human rights violations occurred during this project, including forced labor and relocations. In an effort to pressure Unocal to change its behavior, activists organized protests at stockholder meetings (*voting power*), called for boycotts of Unocal products (*economic power*), promoted local ordinances prohibiting cities from buying from Unocal (*political power*), brought a lawsuit for damages on behalf of Burmese villagers (*legal power*), and gathered information about government abuses by interviewing Burmese refugees and publicizing the results online (*informational power*). These activists increased their chances of success by mobilizing many kinds of power. This combination of tactics eventually forced Unocal to pay compensation to people whose rights had been violated and to fund education and health care projects in the pipeline region.[20]

Exhibit 1.B provides a schematic summary of some of the main interests and powers of both market and nonmarket stakeholders.

Stakeholder Coalitions

An understanding of stakeholder interests and power enables managers to answer the final question of stakeholder analysis regarding coalitions.

How are coalitions likely to form?

Not surprisingly, stakeholder interests often coincide. For example, consumers of fresh fruit and farmworkers who harvest that fruit in the field may have a shared interest in reducing the use of pesticides, because of possible adverse health effects from exposure to chemicals. When their interests are similar, stakeholders may form coalitions, temporary alliances to pursue a common interest. Companies may be both opposed and supported by stakeholder coalitions, as shown in the example of the controversial Keystone XL pipeline.

> TransCanada, a major North American energy company, sought approval to build a pipeline from Alberta, Canada, to Steele City, Nebraska, where it would connect to existing pipelines running to refineries and ports along the Gulf Coast. In opposing the Keystone XL pipeline, environmentalists argued it would enable the export of oil extracted from Canadian tar sands, an energy-intensive and dirty process. When burned, the tar sands oil would release carbon dioxide, contributing to further climate change, and spills from the pipeline could foul water supplies. They were joined in coalition by other groups, such as ranchers, farmers, and Native Americans whose land would be crossed by the pipeline. On the other side, construction unions, many local governments, and business groups supported the pipeline, saying that it would create jobs, reduce U.S. dependence on foreign oil, and provide a safer method of transport than trains or tanker trucks.[21]

Stakeholder coalitions are not static. Groups that are highly involved with a company today may be less involved tomorrow. Issues that are controversial at one time may be uncontroversial later; stakeholders that are dependent on an organization at one time may be less so at another. To make matters more complicated, the process of shifting coalitions does not occur uniformly in all parts of a large corporation. Stakeholders involved with one part of a large company often have little or nothing to do with other parts of the

---

[20] Further information about the campaign against Unocal is available at *www.earthrights.org/unocal*.

[21] "Keystone Pipeline Pros, Cons and Steps to a Final Decision," *The New York Times,* November 18, 2014.

organization. Today, stakeholder coalitions are numerous in every industry and important to every company.

The discussion case at the end of this chapter describes the coalitions that developed in favor of and opposition to new regulations that would require the ride-hailing start-up Uber to insure drivers logged onto its system to look for customers.

Stakeholder Salience and Mapping

Some scholars have suggested that managers pay the most attention to stakeholders possessing greater **salience**. (Something is *salient* when it stands out from a background, is seen as important, or draws attention.) Stakeholders stand out to managers when they have power, legitimacy, and urgency. The previous section discussed various forms of stakeholder power. *Legitimacy* refers to the extent to which a stakeholder's actions are seen as proper or appropriate by the broader society, because they are clearly affected by the company's actions. *Urgency* refers to the time-sensitivity of a stakeholder's claim, that is, the extent to which it demands immediate action. The more of these three attributes a stakeholder possesses, the greater the stakeholder's salience and the more likely that managers will notice and respond.[22]

Managers can use the salience concept to develop a **stakeholder map**, a graphical representation of the relationship of stakeholder salience to a particular issue. Figure 1.4 presents a simple example of a stakeholder map. The figure shows the position of various stakeholders on a hypothetical issue—whether or not a company should shut down an underperforming factory in a community. The horizontal axis represents each stakeholder's position on this issue—from "against" (the company should not shut the plant) to "for" (the company should shut the plant). The vertical axis represents the salience of the stakeholder, an overall measure of that stakeholder's power, legitimacy, and urgency. In this example, the company's creditors (banks) are pressuring the firm to close the plant.

FIGURE 1.4
Stakeholder Map of a Proposed Plant Closure

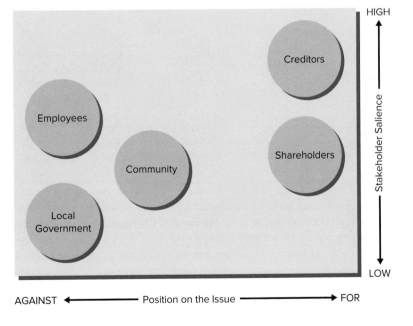

[22] Ronald K. Mitchell, Bradley R. Agle, and Donna J. Wood, "Toward a Theory of Stakeholder Identification and Salience: Defining the Principle of Who and What Really Counts," *Academy of Management Review* 22, no. 4 (1997), pp. 853–86.

Exhibit 1.B

Stakeholders: Nature of Interest and Power

Stakeholder	Nature of Interest— Stakeholder Wishes To:	Nature of Power—Stakeholder Influences Company By:
Market Stakeholders		
Employees	■ Maintain stable employment in firm ■ Receive fair pay for work and mandated benefits ■ Work in safe, comfortable environment	■ Union bargaining power ■ Work actions or strikes ■ Publicity
Shareholders	■ Receive a satisfactory return on investments (dividends) ■ Realize appreciation in stock value over time	■ Exercising voting rights based on share ownership ■ Exercising rights to inspect company books and records

Customers	■ Receive fair exchange: value and quality for money spent
	■ Receive safe, reliable products
	  ■ Receive accurate information
	  ■ Be able to voice concerns
		■ Purchasing goods from competitors
		■ Boycotting companies whose products are unsatisfactory or whose policies are unacceptable

Suppliers	■ Receive regular orders for goods
	■ Be paid promptly for supplies delivered
	  ■ Use capacity efficiently
	  ■ Build stable relationships with business customers
	  ■ Be treated ethically
		■ Refusing to meet orders if conditions of contract are breached
		■ Supplying to competitors

Retailers, Wholesalers	■ Receive quality goods in a timely fashion at reasonable cost ■ Offer reliable products that consumers trust and value	■ Buying from other suppliers if terms of contract are unsatisfactory ■ Boycotting companies whose goods or policies are unsatisfactory
Creditors	■ Receive repayment of loans ■ Collect debts and interest	■ Calling in loans if payments are not made ■ Utilizing legal authorities to repossess or take over property if loan payments are severely delinquent

They have high salience, because they control the company's credit line and are urgently demanding action. Shareholders, who are powerful and legitimate (but not as urgent in their demands), also favor the closure. On the other side, employees urgently oppose shutting the plant, because their jobs are at stake, but they do not have as much power as the creditors and are therefore less salient. Local government officials and local businesses also wish the plant to remain open, but have lower salience than the other stakeholders involved.

A stakeholder map is a useful tool, because it enables managers to see quickly how stakeholders feel about an issue and whether salient stakeholders tend to be in favor or opposed. It also helps managers see how stakeholder coalitions are likely to form, and what outcomes are likely. In this example, company executives might conclude from the

Stakeholder	Nature of Interest—Stakeholder Wishes To:	Nature of Power—Stakeholder Influences Company By:
Nonmarket Stakeholders		
Communities	■ Employ local residents in the company ■ Ensure that the local environment is protected ■ Ensure that the local area is developed	■ Refusing to extend additional credit ■ Issuing or restricting operating licenses and permits ■ Lobbying government for regulation of the company's policies or methods of land use and waste disposal
Nongovernmental organizations	■ Monitor company actions and policies to ensure that they conform to legal and ethical standards ■ Promote social and economic development	■ Gaining broad public support through publicizing the issue ■ Lobbying government for regulation of the company
Business support groups (e.g., trade associations)	■ Provide research and information which will help the company or industry perform in a changing environment	■ Using its staff and resources to assist company in business endeavors and development efforts ■ Providing legal or "group" political support beyond that which an individual company can provide for itself
Governments	■ Promote economic development ■ Encourage social improvements ■ Raise revenues through taxes	■ Adopting regulations and laws ■ Issuing licenses and permits ■ Allowing or disallowing commercial activity
The general public	■ Protect social values ■ Minimize risks ■ Achieve prosperity for society ■ Receive fair and honest communication	■ Networking with other stakeholders ■ Pressing government to act ■ Condemning or praising individual companies

Competitors	■ Compete fairly
	  ■ Cooperate on industry-wide or community issues
	  ■ Seek new customers
		■ Pressing government for fair competition policies
		  ■ Suing companies that compete unfairly

stakeholder map that those supporting the closure—creditors and shareholders—have the greatest salience. Although they are less salient, employees, local government officials, and the community all oppose the closure and may try to increase their salience by working together. Managers might conclude that the closure is likely, unless opponents organize an effective coaliton. This example is fairly simple; more complex stakeholder maps can represent network ties among stakeholders, the size of stakeholder groups, and the degree of consensus within stakeholder groups.[23]

[23] For two different approaches to stakeholder mapping, see David Saiia and Vananh Le, "A Map Leading to Less Waste," *Proceedings of the International Association for Business and Society* 20: 302–13 (2009); and Robert Boutilier, *Stakeholder Politics: Social Capital, Sustainable Development, and the Corporation* (Sheffield, UK: Greenleaf Publishing, 2009), chs. 6 and 7.

The Corporation's Boundary-Spanning Departments

How do corporations organize internally to respond to and interact with stakeholders?

Boundary-spanning departments are departments, or offices, within an organization that reach across the dividing line that separates the company from groups and people in society. Building positive and mutually beneficial relationships across organizational boundaries is a growing part of management's role.

Figure 1.5 presents a list of the corporation's market and nonmarket stakeholders, alongside the corporate departments that typically have responsibility for engaging with them. As the figure suggests, the organization of the corporation's boundary-spanning functions is complex. For example, in many companies, departments of public affairs or government relations interact with elected officials and regulators. Departments of investor relations

FIGURE 1.5 **The Corporation's Boundary-Spanning Departments**

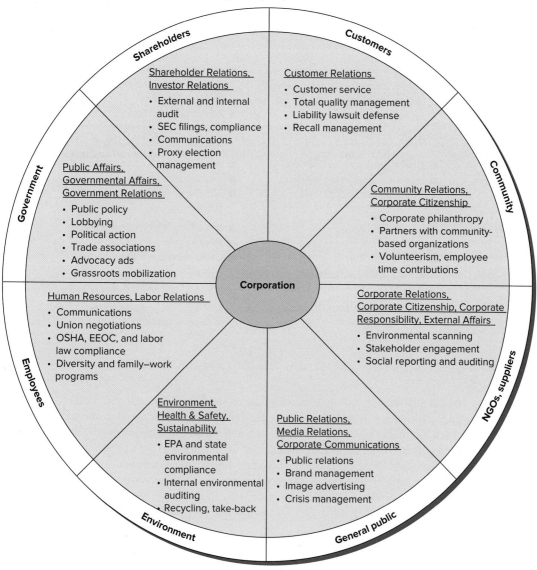

interact with stockholders; human resources with employees; customer relations with customers; and community relations with the community. Specialized departments of environment, health, and safety may deal with environmental compliance and worker health and safety, and public relations or corporate communications. Many of these specific departments will be discussed in more detail in later chapters.

The Dynamic Environment of Business

A core argument of this book is that *the external environment of business is dynamic and ever changing.* Businesses and their stakeholders do not interact in a vacuum. On the contrary, most companies operate in a swirl of social, ethical, global, political, ecological, and technological change that produces both opportunities and threats. Figure 1.6 diagrams the six dynamic forces that powerfully shape the business and society relationship. Each of these forces is introduced briefly below and will be discussed in more detail later in this book.

Changing societal expectations. Everywhere around the world, society's expectations of business are rising. People increasingly expect business to be more responsible, believing companies should pay close attention to social issues and act as good citizens in society. New public issues constantly arise that require action. Increasingly, business is faced with the daunting task of balancing its social, legal, and economic obligations, seeking to meet its commitments to multiple stakeholders. Modern businesses are increasingly exploring opportunities to act in ways that balance numerous stakeholders' needs with their multiple obligations. These changes in society's expectations of business, and how managers have responded, are described in Chapters 2 and 3.

FIGURE 1.6
Forces That Shape the Business and Society Relationship

Globalization. We live in an increasingly integrated world economy, characterized by the unceasing movement of goods, services, and capital across national borders. Large transnational corporations do business in scores of countries. Products and services people buy every day in the United States or Germany may have come from Indonesia, Haiti, or Mexico. Today, economic forces truly play out on a global stage. A financial crisis on Wall Street can quickly impact economies around the world. Societal issues—such as the race to find a cure for Ebola, the movement for women's equality, or the demands of citizens everywhere for full access to the Internet—also cut across national boundaries. Chapter 4 addresses the challenges of globalization.

Growing emphasis on ethical reasoning and actions. The public also expects business to be ethical and wants corporate managers to apply ethical principles or values—in other words, guidelines about what is right and wrong, fair and unfair, and morally correct—when they make business decisions. Fair employment practices, concern for consumer safety, contribution to the welfare of the community, and human rights protection around the world have become more prominent and important. Business has created ethics programs to help ensure that employees are aware of these issues and act in accordance with ethical standards. The ethical challenges faced by business, both domestically and abroad—and business's response—are discussed in Chapters 5 and 6.

Evolving government regulations and business response. The role of government has changed dramatically in many nations in recent decades. Governments around the world have enacted a myriad of new policies that have profoundly constrained how business is allowed to operate. Government regulation of business periodically advances and then retreats, much as a pendulum swings back and forth. Because of the dynamic nature of this force, business has developed various strategies to influence elected officials and government regulators at federal, state, and local levels. Companies may seek to be active participants in the political process, and in recent years the courts have given them more opportunities to do so. The changing role of government, its impact, and business's response are explored in Chapters 7 and 8.

Dynamic natural environment. All interactions between business and society occur within a finite natural ecosystem. Humans share a single planet, and many of our resources—oil, coal, and gas, for example—are nonrenewable. Once used, they are gone forever. Other resources, like clean water, timber, and fish, are renewable, but only if humans use them sustainably, not taking more than can be naturally replenished. Climate change now threatens all nations. The relentless demands of human society, in many arenas, have already exceeded the carrying capacity of the Earth's ecosystem. The state of the Earth's resources and changing attitudes about the natural environment powerfully impact the business–society relationship. These issues are explored in Chapters 9 and 10.

Explosion of new technology and innovation. Technology is one of the most dramatic and powerful forces affecting business and society. It has led to the world appearing to be smaller and more connected. New technological innovations harness the human imagination to create new machines, processes, and software that address the needs, problems, and concerns of modern society. In recent years, the pace of technological change has increased enormously. From genetically modified foods to social networking, change keeps coming. The extent and pace of technological innovation pose massive challenges for business, and sometimes government, as they seek to manage various privacy, security, and intellectual property issues embedded in this dynamic force. As discussed in Chapters 11 and 12, new technologies often force managers and organizations to examine seriously the ethical implications of their use.

Creating Value in a Dynamic Environment

These powerful and dynamic forces—fast-paced changes in societal and ethical expectations, the global economy, government policies, the natural environment, and new technology—establish the context in which businesses interact with their many market and nonmarket stakeholders, as discussed in Chapters 13 to 19. This means that the relationship between business and society is continuously changing in new and often unpredictable ways. Environments, people, and organizations change; inevitably, new issues will arise and challenge managers to develop new solutions. To be effective, corporations must meet the reasonable expectations of stakeholders and society in general. A successful business must meet *all* of its economic, social, and environmental objectives. A core argument of this book is that *the purpose of the firm is not simply to make a profit, but to create value for all its stakeholders.* Ultimately, business success is judged not simply by a company's financial performance but by how well it serves broad social interests.

Summary

- Business firms are organizations that are engaged in making a product or providing a service for a profit. Society, in its broadest sense, refers to human beings and to the social structures they collectively create. Business is part of society and engages in ongoing exchanges with its external environment. Together, business and society form an interactive social system in which the actions of each profoundly influence the other.

- According to the stakeholder theory of the firm, the purpose of the modern corporation is to create value for all of its stakeholders. To survive, all companies must make a profit for their owners. However, they also create many other kinds of value as well for their employees, customers, suppliers, communities, and others. For both practical and ethical reasons, corporations must take all stakeholders' interests into account.

- Every business firm has economic and social relationships with others in society. Some are intended, some unintended; some are positive, others negative. Stakeholders are all those who affect, or are affected by, the actions of the firm. Some have a market relationship with the company, and others have a nonmarket relationship with it; some stakeholders are internal, and others are external.

- Stakeholders often have multiple interests and can exercise their economic, political, and other powers in ways that benefit or challenge the organization. Stakeholders may also act independently or create coalitions to influence the company. Stakeholder mapping is a technique for graphically representing stakeholders' relationship to an issue facing a firm.

- Modern corporations have developed a range of boundary-crossing departments and offices to manage interactions with market and nonmarket stakeholders. The organization of the corporation's boundary-spanning functions is complex. Most companies have many departments specifically charged with interacting with stakeholders.

- A number of broad forces shape the relationship between business and society. These include changing societal and ethical expectations; a dynamic global economy; redefinition of the role of government; ecological and natural resource concerns; and the transformational role of technology and innovation. To deal effectively with these changes, corporate strategy must address the expectations of all of the company's stakeholders.

Key Terms

boundary-spanning
departments, *18*
business, *4*
external stakeholder, *9*
focal organization, *10*
general systems
theory, *4*
interactive social
system, *5*

internal stakeholder, *9*
ownership theory of the
firm, *6*
society, *4*
stakeholder, *7*
stakeholder analysis, *10*
stakeholder
coalitions, *14*
stakeholder interests, *12*

stakeholder (market), *8*
stakeholder (nonmarket), *8*
stakeholder map, *15*
stakeholder power, *12*
stakeholder
salience, *15*
stakeholder theory of the
firm, *6*

**Internet
Resources**

www.economist.com	The Economist
www.fortune.com	Fortune
www.nytimes.com	The New York Times
www.wsj.com	The Wall Street Journal
www.bloomberg.com	Bloomberg
www.ft.com	Financial Times (London)
www.cnnmoney.com	CNN Money

Discussion Case: *Insuring Uber's App-On Gap*

At around 8 p.m. on the evening on December 31, 2013, a mother and her two young children were walking home in San Francisco. At a busy intersection, the family waited for the "walk" signal and then started across the street. Just then, an SUV made a right turn, striking all three members of the family in the crosswalk. The mother and her 5-year-old son were seriously injured. Her 6-year-old daughter was killed. The man behind the wheel of the SUV identified himself as a driver for the ride-hailing service Uber.

Uber immediately distanced itself from the tragedy, saying that the driver was "not providing services on the Uber system at the time of the accident." The family's attorney contested this, saying that the driver was logged onto the Uber application, appeared on the system as available to accept a rider, and was interacting with his device when he struck the mother and children.

In other words, the tragic incident had apparently occurred during the *app-on gap*—the driver was on the road with his Uber application activated, but had not yet connected with or picked up a rider. So, who was responsible, the driver or the ride-hailing service?

Uber was, in the words of a *New York Times* columnist, "the hottest, most valuable technology startup on the planet." The company was founded in 2009 as "everyone's private driver," providing a premium town car service that could be summoned online. In 2012, it rolled out UberX, a service that enabled nonprofessional drivers to use their own vehicles to transport riders. Customers could use the Uber app to hail a car, connect with a willing driver, watch the vehicle approach on a map, pay their fare, and receive a receipt, all on their smartphone. Uber provided the technology and took a commission on each transaction.

Uber's disruptive business model caught on rapidly. By mid-2014, Uber's ride-sharing service had spread to more than 120 cities in 36 countries. In the United States, the service could reach 137 million people with an average pickup time of less than 10 minutes. Demand was growing so fast that Uber was scrambling to recruit 20,000 new drivers, whom Uber called "transportation entrepreneurs," every month. Private investors were enthusiastic about the company's prospects: Uber had attracted $1.2 billion in funding and was valued at $18.2 billion.

Drivers who partnered with Uber had the flexibility to drive when and as much as they wished. They could also make a decent living; the median annual income for its full-time drivers in San Francisco, for example, was about $74,000. But they also assumed risk. In the event of an accident, Uber instructed its drivers to submit a claim to their personal insurance carrier first. If it was denied, Uber's backup commercial liability insurance would go into effect, but only after the driver had been summoned by a customer or had one in the vehicle.

Traditional taxicab companies did not welcome competition from Uber. Cabdrivers in many cities across the world protested the entry of Uber into their markets, conducting strikes and "rolling rallies" charging Uber with unfair practices. Uber drivers did not have to comply with many of the rules that applied to taxicabs, such as those requiring commercial driver's licenses, regular mechanical inspections, and commercial liability insurance. Governments at city, state, and national levels had become involved, with some imposing restrictions and others even banning Uber outright.

In the wake of the 6-year-old's death in San Francisco, California, legislator Susan Bonilla introduced a bill that would require Uber and other ride-hailing companies to provide commerical liability insurance from when the driver turned on the app to when the customer got out of the car, thus filling the app-on gap.

The American Insurance Association, representing insurance companies, supported the legislation, saying that personal auto policies should not be expected to cover ride-hailing drivers once they signaled availability. "This is not someone commuting to work or going to the grocery store or stopping to pick their children up from school," a spokesperson said. The family of the girl killed on New Year's Eve also supported Bonilla's bill, as did consumer attorneys and the California App-Based Drivers Association.

But others lined up in opposition. Uber and other ride-hailing companies strenuously objected to the bill, as did trade associations representing high-technology and Internet-based firms, apparently concerned about increases in their costs of doing business. The bill, said an Uber spokesperson, was "an example of what happens when special interest groups distract lawmakers from the best interests of consumers and small businesses."

Sources: "Deadly Pedestrian Accident Driver Claimed He Drove for Uber," January 1, 2014, *www.abclocal.go.com*; "Uber and a Child's Death," *New York Times,* January 27, 2014; "An Uber Impact: 20,000 Jobs Created on the Uber Platform Every Month," Uber press release, May 27, 2014; "With Uber, Less Reason to Own a Car," *New York Times,* June 11, 2014; "Uber and Airbnb's Incredible Growth in 4 Charts," VB News, June 19, 2014, online at *www.venturebeat.com*; "In Uber vs. Taxi Companies, Local Governments Play Referee," *Christian Science Monitor,* July 7, 2014; "The Company Cities Love to Hate," *Bloomberg Businessweek,* July 7, 2014; "Uber, Lyft, Sidecar Fight to Block New California Regulations," *San Jose Mercury News,* August 13, 2014; "The Question of Coverage for Ride Service Drivers," *New York Times,* September 5, 2014; and private correspondence with the office of Assemblywoman Susan Bonilla.

Discussion Questions

1. Who are Uber's relevant market and nonmarket stakeholders in this situation?
2. What are the various stakeholders' interests? Please indicate if each stakeholder would likely support, or oppose, a requirement that Uber extend its insurance to cover the app-on gap.
3. What sources of power do the relevant stakeholders have?
4. Based on the information you have, draft a stakeholder map of this case showing each stakeholder's position on the issue and degree of salience. What conclusions can you draw from the stakeholder map?
5. What do you think Uber should do in response to the bill introduced by Susan Bonilla, and why?

CHAPTER TWO

Managing Public Issues and Stakeholder Relationships

Businesses today operate in an ever-changing external environment, where effective management requires anticipating emerging public issues and engaging positively with a wide range of stakeholders. Whether the issue is growing concerns about climate change, water scarcity, child labor, animal cruelty, or consumer safety, managers must respond to the opportunities and risks it presents. To do so effectively often requires building relationships across organizational boundaries, learning from external stakeholders, and altering practices in response. Effective management of public issues and stakeholder relationships builds value for the firm.

This Chapter Focuses on These Key Learning Objectives:

LO 2-1 Identifying public issues and analyzing gaps between corporate performance and stakeholder expectations.

LO 2-2 Applying available tools or techniques to scan an organization's multiple environments and assessing stakeholder materiality.

LO 2-3 Describing the steps in the issue management process and determining how to make the process most effective.

LO 2-4 Identifying the managerial skills required to respond to emerging issues effectively.

LO 2-5 Understanding how businesses can effectively engage with its stakeholders, what drives this engagement, and the role social media can play.

LO 2-6 Recognizing the value of creating stakeholder dialogue and networks.

For more than a decade consumer advocates and government regulators grew increasingly concerned about the widespread use of antibiotics to treat disease in animals raised for meat, milk, and eggs. The problem was that this practice contributed to the emergence of antibiotic-resistant germs that then went on to infect humans. In 2013, the Centers for Disease Control and Prevention estimated that 2 million Americans fell ill, and at least 23,000 died, because of antibiotic-resistant infections. "Up to half of antibiotic use in humans and much of the antibiotic use in animals in unnecessary and inappropriate and makes everyone less safe," said a representative of the Centers for Disease Control.

As public concern grew, many companies responded. In 2014, Perdue, one of America's largest poultry producers, announced that it would no longer use antibiotics in its egg hatcheries, completing a phase out program begun in the mid-2000s. Tyson Foods, another large American poultry producer, announced in 2015 that it would eliminate the use of human antibiotics in its chicken production by 2017. This announcement came 1 month after McDonald's, one of Tyson's largest customers, said it would no longer accept chickens treated with antibiotics. Foster Farms, another major U.S. poultry producer, also agreed to ban the use of antibiotics and pledged to introduce a line of organic poultry products. "Our company is committed to responsible growing practices that help preserve the effectiveness of antibiotics for human health and medicine," said Foster Farms' chief executive Ron Foster.[1]

In this case, consumers' and government agencies' growing concerns about the overuse of antibiotics led food producers to take positive action. This will likely improve people's health and benefit companies by increasing sales. Yet, as this chapter will show, companies often ignore or mismanage public issues.

Public Issues

A **public issue** is any issue that is of mutual concern to an organization and one or more of its stakeholders. (Public issues are sometimes also called *social issues* or *sociopolitical issues.*) They are typically broad issues, often impacting many companies and groups, and of concern to a significant number of people. Public issues are often contentious— different groups may have different opinions about what should be done about them. They often, but not always, have public policy or legislative implications.

The emergence of a new public issue—such as concerns over the presence of antibiotics in our food and its impact on our health, mentioned in the opening example of this chapter— often indicates there is a *gap* between what the firm wants to do or is doing and what stakeholders expect. Scholars have called this the **performance–expectations gap**. Stakeholder expectations are a mixture of people's opinions, attitudes, and beliefs about what constitutes reasonable business behavior. Managers and organizations have good reason to identify emergent expectations as early as possible. Failure to understand stakeholder concerns and to respond appropriately will permit the performance–expectations gap to grow: the larger the gap, the greater the risk of stakeholder backlash or of missing a major business opportunity. The performance–expectations gap is pictured in Figure 2.1.

Emerging public issues are both a risk and an opportunity. They are a risk because issues that firms do not anticipate and plan for effectively can seriously hurt a company.

---

[1] "Antibiotics Eliminated in Hatchery, Perdue Says," *The New York Times,* September 3, 2014, *www.nytimes.com*; "Meat Companies Go Antibiotics-Free as More Consumers Demand It," *The Wall Street Journal,* November 3, 2014, *online.wsj.com*; "Tyson to End Use of Human Antibiotics in Its Chickens by 2017," *The New York Times,* April 28, 2015, *www.nytimes.com*; and, "Foster Farms to Eliminate Human Antibiotics in Poultry," *The New York Times,* June 1, 2015, *www.nytimes.com*.

FIGURE 2.1
The Performance–Expectations Gap

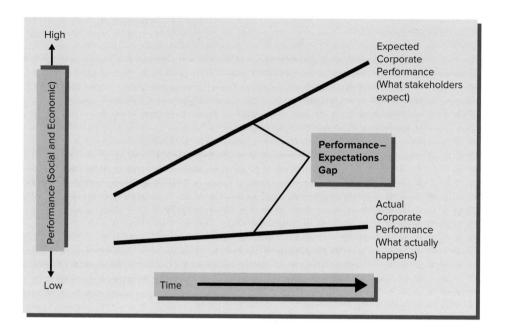

On the other hand, correctly anticipating the emergence of a public issue can confer a competitive advantage, as the following example shows.

> In the wake of serious outbreaks of *E. coli,* salmonella, listeria, and other food-borne pathogens, firms that moved quickly to address public concerns about food safety prospered. For example, a company called iFoodDecisionSciences developed mobile applications to help food producers collect and analyze data and receive instant alerts about hazards. By 2015, iFood—founded just two years earlier—had attracted more than a dozen clients, including growers that supplied Walmart and Chipotle Mexican Grill. "Food companies are hungry for help right now," said the company's chief executive.[2]

Understanding and responding to changing societal expectations is a business necessity. As Mark Moody-Stuart, former managing director of Royal Dutch/Shell, put it in an interview, "Communication with society. . . is a commercial matter, because society is your customers. It is not a soft and wooly thing, because society is what we depend on for our living. So we had better be in line with its wishes, its desires, its aspirations, its dreams."[3]

Every company faces many public issues. Some emerge over a long period of time; others emerge suddenly. Some are predictable; others are completely unexpected. Some companies respond effectively; others do not. Consider the following recent examples of public issues and companies' responses:

- *Executive compensation:* In 2013, Swiss voters passed some of the world's most severe restrictions on executive and board members' compensation. The measure was opposed by banks and other multinational companies, who argued that these actions would seriously damage the country's business-friendly climate. But advocates called for greater control over the "ridiculous backdoor deals" that characterized executive compensation

---

[2] "When E. coli Becomes a Business Opportunity," *The Wall Street Journal,* May 14, 2015, *www.wsj.com.*

[3] Interview conducted by Anne T. Lawrence, "Shell Oil in Nigeria," interactive online case published by *www.icase.co.*

in this country. Firms that violated these new rules face fines worth as much as their salaries for 6 years and up to 3 years in prison.

- *Consumer safety:* Keurig Green Mountain recalled more than 7 million hot beverage-brewing machines in the United States and Canada after the firm discovered that they could overheat and cause injury by spraying users with hot liquid. The defect occurred most often when a user attempted to brew more than two cups in quick succession. The company reported receiving 90 burn-related injury reports and about 200 reports of hot liquid escaping from the brewing machines.

- *Race relations:* Starbucks' CEO Howard Schultz was a long-time advocate of bringing discussions of social issues into his stores, from health care to gun ownership, so few were surprised when he asked his baristas to write "Race Relations" on customers' cups. Schultz hoped that this would spur conversations about racial inequality and justice in the aftermath of a number of incidents across the country involving white police officers and black citizens. A week later, after strong criticism from various community leaders, Starbucks' CEO asked his employees to stop this practice, which he said he intended to do after one week regardless of the public criticism.[4]

Whether the focus is executive compensation, consumer safety, or race relations, society has increased its demands that businesses take on important public issues and become more involved in addressing them. A survey of Millennials (people born between 1977 and 1994) was conducted in 2014 and found that four out of five Millennials "need (not just want) business to get involved in addressing social issues and believe business can make a greater impact." One Millennial from China explained: "Compared to governments, businesses have the potential and the possibility to make real change in society happen faster and more efficiently. Businesses have the resources—from financial means, collective intelligence to technology—to contribute and make a difference."[5]

Environmental Analysis

As new public issues arise, businesses must respond. Organizations need a systematic way of identifying, monitoring, and selecting public issues that warrant organizational action because of the risks or opportunities they present. Organizations rarely have full control of a public issue because of the many factors involved. But it is possible for the organization to create a management system that identifies and monitors issues as they emerge.

To identify those public issues that require attention and action, a firm needs a framework for seeking out and evaluating environmental information. (In this context, *environmental* means *outside the organization;* in Chapters 9 and 10, the term refers to the natural environment.) **Environmental analysis** is a method managers use to gather information about external issues and trends, so they can develop an organizational strategy that minimizes threats and takes advantage of new opportunities.

Environmental intelligence is the acquisition of information gained from analyzing the multiple environments affecting organizations. Acquiring this information may be done informally or as a formal management process. If done well, this environmental intelligence can help an organization avoid crises and spot opportunities.

---

[4] "Showdown on Executive Compensation in Switzerland," *The New York Times,* March 1, 2013, *www.nytimes.com*; "Keurig Recalls More Than 7 Million Brewing Machines in North America," *The New York Times,* December 23, 2014, *www.nytimes.com*; and, "Starbucks Ends Key Phase in 'Race Together' Campaign," *The Wall Street Journal,* March 22, 2015, *www.wsj.com*.
[5] *The Future of Business Citizenship,* People's Insights Magazine, *www.scribd.com*.

According to management scholar Karl Albrecht, scanning to acquire environmental intelligence should focus on eight *strategic radar screens.*[6] Radar is an instrument that uses microwave radiation to detect and locate distant objects, which are often displayed on a screen; law enforcement authorities use radar, for example, to track the speed of passing cars. Albrecht uses the analogy of radar to suggest that companies must have a way of tracking important developments that are outside of their immediate view. He identifies eight different environments that managers must systematically follow. These are shown in Figure 2.2 and described next.

- *Customer environment* includes the demographic factors, such as gender, age, marital status, and other factors, of the organization's customers as well as their social values or preferences, buying preferences, and technology usage. For example, the explosion of social media has created opportunities for creating new marketing approaches that provide potential consumers with coupons or sales information on their smartphones as they leave their car and walk toward the retail store.

- *Competitor environment* includes information on the number and strength of the organization's competitors, whether they are potential or actual allies, patterns of aggressive growth versus static maintenance of market share, and the potential for customers to become competitors if they "insource" products or services previously purchased from the organization. (This environment is discussed further in the next section of this chapter.)

FIGURE 2.2
Eight Strategic Radar Screens

Source: Karl A. Albrecht, *Corporate Radar: Tracking the Forces That Are Shaping Your Business* (New York: American Management Association, 2000).

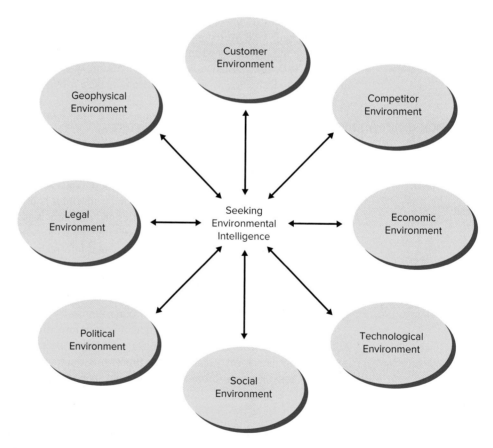

[6] Adapted from Karl Albrecht, *Corporate Radar: Tracking the Forces That Are Shaping Your Business* (New York: American Management Association, 2000).

- *Economic environment* includes information about costs, prices, international trade, and any other features of the economic environment. The severe recession that hit the world's economy in the late 2000s greatly shifted the behavior of customers, suppliers, creditors, and other stakeholders, dramatically impacting decision making in many firms.
- *Technological environment* includes the development of new technologies and their applications affecting the organization, its customers, and other stakeholder groups. Faster access to information through cell phones, tablets, and other handheld electronic devices changed how people around the world were alerted to the devastation of natural disasters or terrorist actions and how they could be contacted regarding new job openings or the launching of innovative consumer products.
- *Social environment* includes cultural patterns, values, beliefs, trends, and conflicts among the people in the societies where the organization conducts business or might conduct business. Issues of civil or human rights, family values, and the roles of special interest groups are important elements in acquiring intelligence from the social environment.
- *Political environment* includes the structure, processes, and actions of all levels of government—local, state, national, and international. Awareness of the stability or instability of governments and their inclination or disinclination to pass laws and regulations is essential environmental intelligence for the organization. The emergence of strict environmental laws in Europe—including requirements to limit waste and provide for recycling at the end of a product's life—have caused firms all over the world that sell to Europeans to rethink how they design and package their products.
- *Legal environment* includes patents, copyrights, trademarks, and considerations of intellectual property, as well as antitrust considerations and trade protectionism and organizational liability issues. China's commitment to triple its patent filings from nearly 1 million in 2013 to 3 million by 2020 sent shock waves through the global business community.
- *Geophysical environment* relates to awareness of the physical surroundings of the organization's facilities and operations, whether it is the organization's headquarters or its field offices and distribution centers, and the organization's dependency and impact on natural resources such as minerals, water, land, or air. Growing concerns about global warming and climate change, for example, have caused many firms to seek to improve their energy efficiency.

The eight strategic radar screens represent a system of interrelated segments, each one connected to and influencing the others.

Companies do not become experts in acquiring environmental intelligence overnight. New attitudes have to be developed, new routines learned, and new policies and action programs designed. Many obstacles must be overcome in developing and implementing the effective scanning of the business environments. Some are structural, such as the reporting relationships between groups of managers; others are cultural, such as changing traditional ways of doing things. In addition, the dynamic nature of the business environments requires organizations to continually evaluate their environmental scanning procedures.

Competitive Intelligence

One of the eight environments discussed by Albrecht is the competitor environment. The term **competitive intelligence** refers to the systematic and continuous process of gathering, analyzing, and managing external information about the organization's competitors that can affect the organization's plans, decisions, and operations. (As discussed in Chapter 1, competitors may be considered a nonmarket stakeholder of business.) The acquisition of this information benefits an organization by helping it better understand what other companies in its industry are doing. Competitive intelligence enables managers in companies of all sizes to make informed decisions ranging from marketing, research and development, and investing tactics to long-term business strategies. "During difficult times, excellent competitive intelligence can be the differentiating factor in the marketplace," explained Paul Meade, vice president of the research and consulting firm Best Practices. "Companies that can successfully gather and analyze competitive information, then implement strategic decisions based on that analysis, position themselves to be ahead of the pack."[7]

However, the quest for competitors' information can also raise numerous ethical issues. Businesses may overstep ethical and legal boundaries when attempting to learn as much as they can about their competitors, as the following example shows.

> ShaveLogic Inc., a Dallas company specializing in wet shaving products, was increasingly worried about new technological advances developed by one of its primary competitors, Procter & Gamble, owner of the Gillette brand of shavers. ShaveLogic often recruited and hired Gillette employees, reportedly to obtain its competitor's trade secrets. In 2015, Procter & Gamble sued four former employees and ShaveLogic, claiming that the former employees provided ShaveLogic with confidential information about future Gillette products they developed while working at Gillette. Procter & Gamble also alleged that ShaveLogic took the information provided by its former employees and received a patent based on this information.[8]

As the example above indicates, the perceived value of trade secrets or other information may be so great that businesses or their employees may be tempted to use unethical or illegal means to obtain such information (or provide it to others). However, competitive intelligence acquired ethically remains one of the most valued assets sought by businesses. A business must balance the importance of acquiring information about its competitors' practices with the need to comply with all applicable laws, domestic and international, and to follow the professional standards of fairness and honesty. Disclosure of all relevant information prior to conducting an interview and avoidance of conflicts of interest are just a few of the ethical guidelines promoted by the Strategic and Competitive Intelligence Professional's code of ethics.[9]

Stakeholder Materiality

After the many environments are scanned, a company needs to evaluate and prioritize the impact that its stakeholders and their issues may have on the company. The importance attributed to a stakeholder is often referred to as materiality. **Stakeholder materiality** is an adaptation of an accounting term that focuses on the importance or significance of something. In this case, it describes a method used to prioritize the relevance of the stakeholders and their issues to the company.

> Sonoco, a global provider of packaging products and services, completed its first stakeholder materiality assessment of economic, environmental, and social issues in 2014. The company began by identifying potential stakeholders and created a list of

---

[7] See Best Practices report at *www.benchmarkingreports.com/competitiveintelligence*.

[8] "Gillette Sues Former Employees for Allegedly Sharing Secrets," *Boston Globe,* January 16, 2015, *www.bostonglobe.com*.

[9] For information about the professional association focusing on competitive intelligence, particularly with attention to ethical considerations, see the Strategic and Competitive Intelligence Professionals' website at *www.scip.org*.

nine stakeholders: customers, suppliers, peers, shareholders, nongovernmental organizations, community leaders, government regulators, employees, and leadership. The company then searched various sources for information on each stakeholder, such as websites, corporate social responsibility reports, mission statements, and 10-K filings, to create a list of issues. They used a four-point scale to rate each stakeholder from low to high based on the significance of the issue to the stakeholder. This scoring system enabled Sonoco to identify highly influential stakeholder groups as having the greatest potential impact on the company's strategic objectives or those stakeholders most influenced by the company's operations.[10]

After the information is collected, it needs to be analyzed and placed on a matrix that shows the importance of the issue for the stakeholder and the importance of the issue assigned by the company. This evaluation allows the company to prioritize their attention on issues in the quadrant showing issues of importance to stakeholders *and* the company. An example of such a matrix representing stakeholder materiality at Symantec is shown in Figure 2.3.

The Issue Management Process

Once a company has identified a public issue and detects a gap between society's expectations and its own practices, what are its next steps? Proactive companies do not wait for something to happen; they actively manage issues as they arise. The process of doing so is called **issue management**. The **issue management process**, illustrated in Figure 2.4, has five steps or stages. Each of these steps is explained below, using the example of McDonalds's response to allegations of harming customers by using spoiled meat in its more than 2,000 restaurants in China. Although McDonald's was a key target in the Chinese

FIGURE 2.3
The Stakeholder Materiality Matrix

Source: From Symantec's website, *www.symantec.com/ corporate_responsibility/topic. jsp?id=priority_issues*. Used with permission.

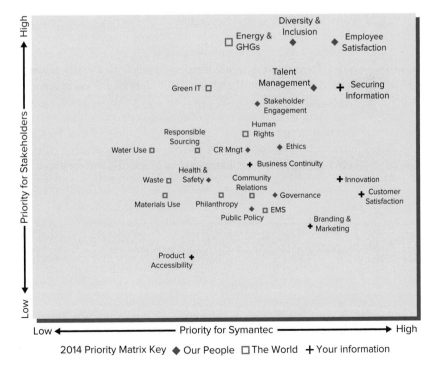

[10] Information from Sonoco's website, *www.sonoco.com/sustainability/sustainabilityoversight*.

FIGURE 2.4
The Issue
Management Process

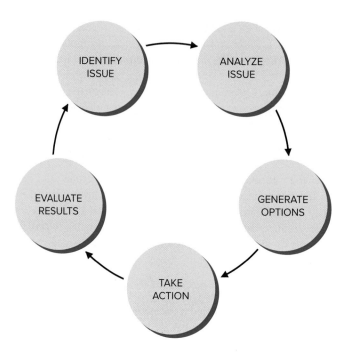

government's investigation of food safety, the firm was well positioned to take action and move ahead of its competitors. As this example also illustrates, even a strong corporate response does not completely close an issue, as it may arise again in a new form.

Identify Issue

Issue identification involves anticipating emerging concerns, sometimes called "horizon issues" because they seem to be just coming up over the horizon like the first morning sun. Sometimes managers become aware of issues by carefully tracking the media, experts' views, activist opinion, and legislative developments to identify issues of concern to the public. Normally, this requires attention to all eight of the environments described in Figure 2.2. Organizations often use techniques of data searching, media analysis, and public surveys to track ideas, themes, and issues that may be relevant to their interests all over the world. They also rely on ongoing conversations with key stakeholders. Sometimes the firm is completely unaware of the issue before it emerges and must attempt to respond to lawsuits, protests by activists, or government allegations, as McDonald's experienced in China.

> In 2014, McDonald's was surprised to learn that the Chinese government had initiated an investigation of the Shanghai Husi Food Group, which alleged supplied expired meat to McDonald's and other restaurants. McDonald's had a long-standing relationship with Shanghai Husi. In 1955, when McDonald's founder Ray Kroc wanted to expand his hamburger restaurant chain across the United States, he partnered with Otto & Sons, Inc., a family-owned meat supplier located in Chicago. This relationship continued to grow for decades as Otto & Sons became a leading meat supplier for many of the world's largest fast-food chains, eventually becoming the OSI Group, Inc. Shanghai Husi Food Company was a subsidiary of the OSI Group. Until the 2014 incident, McDonald's had known of no violations of Chinese government standards for product quality when sourcing meat from the OSI Group subsidiary.[11]

[11] "China Meat Supplier 'Appalled' by Allegations," *The Wall Street Journal*, July 21, 2014, *online.wsj.com*.

The allegations of tainted food caught McDonald's by surprise, and the company announced an immediate investigation. A McDonald's spokesperson said the company was appalled by the allegations and apologized to its customers.

Analyze Issue

Once an issue has been identified, its implications must be analyzed. Organizations must understand how the issue is likely to evolve, and how it is likely to affect them. For each company, the ramifications of the issue will be different.

Understanding how the quality of meat at McDonald's Chinese restaurants affected McDonald's global reputation was complex. On one hand, the company was concerned about the public's safety, and did not want customers to become ill if they consumed expired meat at their restaurants. On the other hand, McDonald's had a long-standing relationship with the OSI Group and relied on this company for high-quality food products for its restaurants globally. McDonald's knew it had to analyze the issue quickly and be ready to make major changes if a new supplier was needed.

> As soon as McDonald's heard of the Chinese government's investigation into Shanghai Husi Food Company, the company began a rigorous, in-house product quality comparison, analyzing meat supplied by OSI with meat provided by other suppliers for other locations. Although McDonald's never publicly reported any product quality problems with OSI-supplied meat, the company pledged to fully cooperate with the government agencies' investigations into this issue. The company's spokesperson said that if the practices described in media reports were confirmed, they would be "completely unacceptable to McDonald's." McDonald's also tried to reassure its customers. In a press release, the company said, "We reiterate that all the food sold at McDonald's restaurants conform to the food safety standards."[12]

Generate Options

An issue's public profile indicates to managers how significant an issue is for the organization, but it does not tell them what to do. The next step in the issue management process involves generating, evaluating, and selecting among possible options. This requires complex judgments that incorporate ethical considerations, the organization's reputation and good name, and other nonquantifiable factors.

> McDonald's was faced with a number of possible actions: continue using meat supplied by the Shanghai Husi Food Company until government investigations revealed that the meat failed to meet government standards, continue to use the OSI Group as its meat supplier but shift orders to other OSI facilities in China, or look for a new regional meat supplier and cancel all orders from the OSI Group.
>
> Unlike the response from other Chinese fast-food restaurants (like Yum Brands who cancelled all orders from the OSI Group), McDonald's announced that it was sticking with its long-time meat supplier. Although the company's internal inspections confirmed that its meat products met government standards, McDonald's switched its orders from the Shanghai Husi Food Company to other OSI factories in China. A retired McDonald's executive said of the OSI Group, "they were one of our most trusted suppliers. They were a model of integrity."[13]

---

[12] McDonald's Stands by Meat Supplier in Crisis," *The Wall Street Journal,* July 24, 2014, *online.wsj.com.*

[13] McDonald's Stands by Meat Supplier in Crisis," *The Wall Street Journal,* July 24, 2014, *online.wsj.com*; and "McDonald's Suspends Sales of Chicken Nuggets in Hong Kong," *The New York Times,* July 25, 2014, *www.nytimes.com.*

Selecting an appropriate response often involves a creative process of considering various alternatives and rigorously evaluating them to see how they work in practice.

Take Action

Once an option has been chosen, the organization must design and implement a plan of action. Sometimes there may be unintended consequences from the actions undertaken by the company.

> The immediate change in meat suppliers for its Chinese locations resulted in disruptions to the inventories at various McDonald's restaurants. The company reported that it had run out of hamburgers and chicken nuggets, angering its customers, and had tried to encourage customers to purchase fish sandwiches. One customer commented, "A hamburger restaurant that doesn't have hamburgers; it's pretty funny." These shortages and a delayed government investigation eventually led to McDonald's reconsidering the decision to retain its long-time relationship with the OSI Group. But, McDonald's also realized that it would take time to perform due diligence on alternative suppliers and be able to guarantee the high quality of the meat products previously provided by the OSI Group
>
> In September 2014, six weeks after the allegations of expired meat being sold to its customers in China, McDonald's announced it was overhauling its food-safety strategy in China. The company planned to review surveillance video from its suppliers' meat-production sites and boost the number of audits of its suppliers. More than half of the audits would be unannounced and conducted by third-party auditors and McDonald's management teams. Others would be conducted by the suppliers' own auditors.
>
> McDonald's also reported that it would create anonymous hotlines for suppliers and their employees to report unethical or noncompliant practices and dispatched quality-control specialists to all of McDonald's meat-production faculties in China. Finally, the company appointed Cindy Jiang, McDonald's senior director of global food safety, as the first new head of national food safety in China. Jiang reported directly to McDonald's chief executive officer.[14]

Evaluate Results

Once an organization has implemented the issue management program, it must continue to assess the results and make adjustments if necessary. Many managers see issue management as a continuous process, rather than one that comes to a clear conclusion.

> In January 2015, McDonald's chief financial officer Peter Bensen reported, "it will take at least three to six more months for business in China to return to normal." The company was hurt by growing consumer worries after a human tooth, plastic pieces, and other objects were found in food in McDonald's restaurants in Japan and lawsuits were filed against McDonald's in Russia after that country's consumer safety regulator accused McDonald's of alleged violations of consumer safety and labeling regulations. In the months following the scandal in China, McDonald's sales fell more than 12 percent in Asia, despite a slight rise in sales in the United States and Europe.[15]

[14] "McDonald's Faces Shortages at Some China Outlets," *The Wall Street Journal,* July 28, 2014, *online.wsj.com*; "McDonald's Could Reconsider Its Relationship with Supplier OSI in China," *The Wall Street Journal,* August 26, 2014, *online.wsj.com*; and "McDonald's Overhauls Food-Safety Strategy in China," *The Wall Street Journal,* September 2, 2014, *online.wsj.com*.

[15] "Food Scares Cost McDonald's in China, Japan; Sales Fall," *Yahoo! Finance,* February 9, 2015, *finance.yahoo.com*; and "Russia's Food Regulator Files Suit against McDonald's," *The Wall Street Journal,* July 25, 2014, *online.wsj.com*.

This example illustrates the complexity of the issue management process. Figure 2.4 is deliberately drawn in the form of a loop. When working well, the issue management process continuously cycles back to the beginning and repeats, pulling in more information, generating more options, and improving programmatic response. Such was the case with the concern over safety for McDonald's customers in China. McDonald's was committed to addressing the issue and knew that it needed to monitor the progress being made with its suppliers to fully address an emerging public issue.

Contemporary issue management is truly an interactive process, as forward-thinking companies must continually engage in a dialogue with their stakeholders about issues that matter, as McDonald's has learned. McDonald's reached out to government investigators, established open communications with its consumers through the media, and were engaged in extensive discussions with its suppliers. New challenges may emerge from anywhere in the world and at any time. Managers must not only implement programs, but continue to reassess their actions to be consistent with both ethical practices and long-term survival.

Organizing for Effective Issue Management

Who manages public issues? What departments and people are involved? There is no simple answer to this question. Figure 1.5, presented in Chapter 1, showed that the modern corporation has many boundary-spanning departments. Which part of the organization is mobilized to address a particular emerging issue often depends on the nature of the issue itself. For example, if the issue has implications for public policy or government regulations, the public affairs or government relations department may take a leadership role. (The public affairs department is further discussed in Chapter 8.) If the issue is an environmental one, the department of sustainability or environment, health, and safety may take on this role. Some companies combine multiple issue management functions in an office of external relations or corporate affairs. The following example illustrates how one company has organized to manage emerging public issues.

> At Publix, the largest employee-owned grocery chain in the United States, the coordination of public issues is handled by six different, yet related, teams: corporate communications, customer care, government relations, media and community relations, social media, and special projects. The corporate communications team handles a wide array of internal communications, including an eight-page monthly newsletter, *Publix News.* When customers contact the company with a potential public issue, the customer care team responds to resolve customer concerns and answer customer questions. If the public issue has a governmental element, then the government relations team is organized to communicate with federal, state, and local officials regarding matters affecting the company's ability to effectively compete in the marketplace. Each division within the company has a media and community relations team who interacts with the news media and the communities served by the company to address any public issue. A social media team at Publix uses Facebook, Twitter, and other channels to monitor and handle any emerging public issues. And, finally, the special projects team preserves and promotes the company's history as an important part of the Publix culture. The company relies on its tradition to guide responses to public issues as they arise.[16]

A corporation's issue management activities are usually linked to both the board of directors and to top management levels, because of their increasing importance. The

[16] See the Publix Company website at *corporate.publix.com.*

Foundation for Public Affairs reported the early 2010s that "70 percent of business executives say public affairs already plays an increasingly important or very important strategic role in their firms." Another 14 percent said that it was becoming more important. Despite widespread corporate budget cuts due to the recession, 80 percent of the corporate executives surveyed by the Foundation for Public Affairs reported that their firm's budgets for public issues had increased or remained the same following the economic recession of the mid-2000s.[17] One award-winning example of an exemplary corporate response to an important public issue is described in Exhibit 2.A.

What kinds of managers are best able to anticipate and respond effectively to emerging public issues? What skill sets are required? The European Academy of Business in Society (EABIS) undertook a major study of leaders in companies participating in the United Nations Global Compact. (This initiative is a set of basic principles covering labor, human rights, and environmental standards, to which companies can voluntarily commit.) The researchers were interested in the knowledge and skills required of what they called the "global leader of tomorrow."

They found that effective global leadership on these public issues required three basic capabilities. The first was an understanding of the changing business *context:* emerging environmental and social trends affecting the firm. The second was an ability to lead in the face of *complexity.* Many emerging issues, the researchers found, were surrounded by ambiguity; to deal with them, leaders needed to be flexible, creative, and willing to learn from their mistakes. The final capability was *connectedness:* the ability to engage with external stakeholders in dialogue and partnership. Although more than three-fourths of executives polled said that these skills were important, only 7 percent said their organization was developing them very effectively.[18]

Stakeholder Engagement

One of the key themes of this book is that companies that actively engage with stakeholders do a better job of managing a wide range of issues than companies that do not. The term **stakeholder engagement** is used to refer to this process of ongoing relationship building between a business and its stakeholders. In the McDonald's example presented earlier in this chapter, the company's challenge was to engage with its various stakeholder groups, consumers, the media, government agencies, suppliers, and others in addressing an emerging issue of food product quality. This section will further explore the various forms the business–stakeholder relationship takes, when stakeholder engagement is likely to occur, what drives this engagement, and the expanding role assumed by social media in stakeholder engagement.

Stages in the Business–Stakeholder Relationship

Over time, the nature of business's relationship with its stakeholders often evolves through a series of stages. Scholars have characterized these stages as *inactive, reactive, proactive,* and *interactive,* with each stage representing a deepening of the relationship. Sometimes, companies progress through this sequence from one stage to the next; other companies remain at one stage or another, or move backward in the sequence.[19]

---

[17] "Public Affairs Goes Mainstream," *Public Affairs Council,* January 13, 2012, *pac/org/blog.*

[18] European Academy of Business in Society, *Developing the Global Leader of Tomorrow* (United Kingdom: Ashridge, December 2008). Based on a global survey of 194 CEOs and senior executives in September–October 2008.

[19] This typology was first introduced in Lee Preston and James E. Post, *Private Management and Public Policy* (Englewood Cliffs, NJ: Prentice Hall, 1975). For a more recent discussion, see Sandra Waddock, *Leading Corporate Citizens: Visions, Values, and Value Added,* 2nd ed. (New York: McGraw-Hill, 2006), ch. 1.

The DuPont Company, a global leader in food production, nutrition, and safety, received the 2013 W. Howard Chase Award for its role in addressing the growing issue of global food safety. DuPont took seriously the challenge of feeding the world's population, in spite of sharp disagreements among governments, public policy leaders, and corporations about how best to do so. The firm felt "a responsibility to provide leadership and act as a catalyst for bringing together the global food security influencer community" to raise awareness of the issue and build collaborations that would help ensure global food security. DuPont adopted a set of Food Security Goals that committed, by the end of 2020, to invest $10 billion to develop 4,000 new products. These would be designed to increase food production, enhance nutrition, promote sustainability and safety, boost food availability and shelf life, and reduce waste. The company also said it would educate two million young people around the world on the importance of food safety and nutrition. Finally, DuPont set out to improve the livelihoods of at least three million farmers and their rural communities through targeted collaboration and investments to strengthen agricultural systems and make food more available, nutritious, and culturally appropriate.

Source: "The W. Howard Chase Award—2013," *Issue Management Council, www.issuemanagement.org.*

- *Inactive* companies simply ignore stakeholder concerns. These firms may believe—often incorrectly—that they can make decisions unilaterally, without taking into consideration their impact on others. Executives at Home Depot failed to listen to their employees' concerns about potential breaches of the company's data security systems and later experienced the theft of detailed consumer information from 56 million credit and debit cards. Their inactive response was costly: according to some estimates, the information from the stolen cards could be used to make $3 billion in illegal purchases.[20]

- Companies that adopt a *reactive* posture generally act only when forced to do so, and then in a defensive manner. For example, in the film *A Civil Action,* based on a true story, W. R. Grace (a company that was later bought by Beatrice Foods) allegedly dumped toxic chemicals that leaked into underground wells used for drinking water, causing illness and death in the community of Woburn, Massachusetts. The company paid no attention to the problem until forced to defend itself in a lawsuit brought by a crusading lawyer on behalf of members of the community.

- *Proactive* companies try to anticipate stakeholder concerns. These firms use environmental scanning practices to identify emerging public issues. They often have specialized departments such as those at Publix, described earlier in the chapter. These firms are much less likely to be blindsided by crises and negative surprises. Stakeholders and their concerns are still, however, considered a problem to be managed, rather than a source of competitive advantage.

- Finally, an *interactive* stance means that companies actively engage with stakeholders in an ongoing relationship of mutual respect, openness, and trust. For example, in an effort to address continuing high unemployment rates, Starbucks teamed with Opportunity Finance Network, a group of community development financial institutions, to launch "Create Jobs for USA." Donations from Starbucks customers, employees, and others were pooled into a nationwide fund to promote community business lending. In 2014 the focus expanded to include veterans with a goal of employing 10,000 veterans and active duty spouses by 2018.[21]

---

[20] See *www.welivesecurity.com/2014/09/22/home-depot-data-breach.*

[21] These programs are profiled in Starbucks' Global Responsibility Report at *globalassets.starbucks.com/assets/.*

Firms with this approach recognize that positive stakeholder relationships are a source of value and competitive advantage for the company. They know that these relationships must be nurtured over time.

Drivers of Stakeholder Engagement

When are companies most likely to engage with stakeholders, that is, to be at the interactive stage? What drives companies to go beyond an inactive or a reactive stage to a proactive or interactive stage of stakeholder engagement?

Stakeholder engagement is, at its core, a *relationship.* The participation of a business organization and at least one stakeholder organization is necessary, by definition, to constitute engagement. In one scholar's view, engagement is most likely when both the company and its stakeholders both have an urgent and important *goal,* the *motivation* to participate, and the *organizational capacity* to engage with one another. These three elements are presented in Figure 2.5.

Goals

For stakeholder engagement to occur, both the business and the stakeholder must have a problem that they want solved. The problem must be both important and urgent (the concept of stakeholder materiality was discussed earlier in this chapter). Business is often spurred to act when it recognizes a gap between its actions and public expectations, as discussed earlier. The company may perceive this gap as a reputational crisis or a threat to its license to operate in society. For their part, stakeholders are typically concerned about an issue important to them—whether child labor, animal cruelty, environmental harm, or something else—that they want to see addressed.

Motivation

Both sides must also be motivated to work with one another to solve the problem. For example, the company may realize that the stakeholder group has technical expertise to help it address an issue. Or, it needs the stakeholder's approval, because the stakeholder is in a position to influence policymakers, damage a company's reputation, or bring a lawsuit. Stakeholders may realize that the best way actually to bring about change is to help a company alter its behavior. In other words, both sides depend on each other to accomplish their goals; they cannot accomplish their objectives on their own. (Theorists sometimes refer to this as *interdependence.*)

FIGURE 2.5
Drivers of Stakeholder Engagement

Source: Adapted from Anne T. Lawrence, "The Drivers of Stakeholder Engagement: Reflections on the Case of Royal Dutch/Shell, *Journal of Corporate Citizenship,* Summer 2002, pp. 71–85.

	Company	Stakeholders(s)
Goal	To improve corporate reputation; to earn a license to operate; to win approval of society	To change corporate behavior on an issue of concern
Motivation	Needs stakeholder involvement because of their expertise or control of critical resources	Governmental campaigns, protest perceived as inadequate to change corporate behavior
Organizational capacity	Top leaders committed to engagement; well-funded department of external (stakeholder) affairs	Experienced staff; core group of activists committed to dialogue with business

Organizational Capacity

Each side must have the organizational capacity to engage the other in a productive dialogue. For the business, this may include support from top leadership and an adequately funded external affairs or comparable department with a reporting relationship to top executives. It may also include an issue management process that provides an opportunity for leaders to identify and respond quickly to shifts in the external environment. For the stakeholder, this means a leadership or a significant faction that supports dialogue and individuals or organizational units with expertise in working with the business community.

In short, engagement is most likely to occur where both companies and stakeholders perceive an important and urgent problem, see each other as essential to a solution, and have the organizational capacity to interact with one another.

The Role of Social Media in Stakeholder Engagement

Social media plays an increasingly important role in businesses' effort to address public issues and engage stakeholders. Beyond the common use of social media as an advertising tool, many companies now use social networks to identify and solve problems faster, share information better among their employees and partners, and bring customers' ideas for new product designs to market earlier. They have also redesigned all kinds of corporate software in a Facebook-like easy-to-learn style. "At a very basic level, Facebook is the most popular application ever, with a billion people who know how to use it," said Marc Benioff, chief executive at *salesforce.com,* whose Chatter social-networking tools were used by more than 150,000 companies by 2013. Forrester Research reported that sales of software to run corporate social networks grew by 61 percent from 2011 to 2012 and were projected to top $6 billion by 2016. Two-thirds of large businesses used Web 2.0 tools, such as social networks or blogs, according to a McKinsey & Company survey. These tools enabled businesses to connect with employees and serve their customers better, as the following examples show.

> When the restaurant chain Red Robin planned to introduce its new Tavern Double burger, the firm turned to social media to bring together hundreds of its store managers for speedy communication. The firm created an internal social network that resembled Facebook to teach its managers everything from the recipes to the fastest way to make the burger. Instead of mailing out spiral-bound notebooks, getting feedback during the executives' sporadic store visits, and taking six months to act on advice from the store employees, the social media network discussion and video sharing produced results in just a few days.
>
> SuperValu, a national supermarket chain, constructed a social network system to link its 11,000 executives and store managers. Nearly 200 managers joined a social media group to discuss a common problem for stores in college towns. Rather than coming together for a meeting or retreat, common in the past, these managers discussed the problem of inconsistent seasonal sales to college students and came upon a new promotion: to place $99 worth of store coupons in the $99 mini-refrigerators they sold, a popular item for college students living in dorm rooms, to bring the students back to the store to buy food and other items.[22]

As businesses and their public affairs managers have increasingly turned to social media platforms to engage with multiple stakeholders, communication has become faster and more effective.

---

[22] "Social Media Is Reinventing How Business Is Done," *USA Today,* May 16, 2012, *usatoday30.usatoday.com*. Also see "Report: 6 Ways Social Media Can Drive Business Impact," *Venture Beat,* March 12, 2013, *venturebeat.com*.

Stakeholder Dialogue

The process of engaging with stakeholders can take many forms, but it often eventually involves dialogue with stakeholders. One management theorist has defined dialogue as "the art of thinking together."[23] In **stakeholder dialogue**, a business and its stakeholders come together for face-to-face conversations about issues of common concern. There, they attempt to describe their core interests and concerns, prepare a common definition of the problem, invent innovative solutions for mutual gain, and establish procedures for implementing solutions. To be successful, the process requires that participants express their own views fully, listen carefully and respectfully to others, and open themselves to creative thinking and new ways of looking at and solving a problem. The promise of dialogue is that, together, they can draw on the understandings and concerns of all parties to develop solutions that none of them, acting alone, could have envisioned or implemented.[24]

> PacifiCorp is a major electric utility, serving customers throughout the Pacific Northwest. In the 2000s, the company initiated the process of renewing the permits for seven hydroelectric dams it operated on the Klamath River, a massive waterway that ran 250 miles from Southern Oregon into Northern California and drained a 13,000 square mile watershed before emptying into the Pacific. Renewing the permits turned out to be highly contentious, as it impacted numerous stakeholders, including state and federal agencies, Native American tribes, fishermen, environmentalists, farmers, and recreational users, all with diverse interests. Finally, in 2010, after a lengthy collaborative process, the various stakeholders hammered out an historic pact, called the Klamath Basin Restoration Agreement, to remove the dams, restore habitat, and guarantee water for local farmers. PacifiCorp agreed to the plan when it realized that bringing the dams up to modern standards (the oldest had been built in 1903) would be more expensive than removing them. By 2014, the Klamath Water Recover and Economic Restoration Act, which would enforce the terms of the three Klamath Restoration Agreements, was still being considered by the Senate Energy and Natural Resources Committee.[25]

Stakeholder Networks

Dialogue between a single firm and its stakeholders is sometimes insufficient to address an issue effectively. Corporations sometimes encounter public issues that they can address effectively only by working collaboratively with other businesses and concerned persons and organizations in **stakeholder networks**. One such issue that confronted Nike, Inc. was a growing demand by environmentally aware consumers for apparel and shoes made from organic cotton.

> Cotton, traditionally cultivated with large quantities of synthetic fertilizers, pesticides, and herbicides, is one of the world's most environmentally destructive crops. In the late 1990s, in response both to consumer pressure and to its own internal commitments, Nike began for the first time to incorporate organic cotton into its sports apparel products. Its intention was to ramp up slowly, achieving 5 percent

---

[23] William Isaacs, *Dialogue and the Art of Thinking Together* (New York: Doubleday, 1999).

[24] This section draws on the discussion in Anne T. Lawrence and Ann Svendsen, *The Clayoquot Controversy: A Stakeholder Dialogue Simulation* (Vancouver: Centre for Innovation in Management, 2002). The argument for the benefits of stakeholder engagement is fully developed in Ann Svendsen, *The Stakeholder Strategy: Profiting from Collaborative Business Relationships* (San Francisco: Berrett-Koehler, 1998).

[25] Information about the Klamath Restoration Agreements can be found at *www.klamathrestoration.org*.

organic content by 2010. However, the company soon encountered barriers to achieving even these limited objectives. Farmers were reluctant to transition to organic methods without a sure market, processors found it inefficient to shut down production lines to clean them for organic runs, and banks were unwilling to loan money for unproven technologies. The solution, it turned out, involved extensive collaboration with groups throughout the supply chain—farmers, cooperatives, merchants, processors, and financial institutions—as well as other companies that were buyers of cotton, to facilitate the emergence of a global market for organic cotton. By 2013, 88 percent of Nike's cotton-containing apparel used at least 5 percent organic cotton, down slightly from 90 percent in 2011. Nike reported in its 2013 environmental report that they are still committed to their goals, but it was taking longer than expected for their cotton suppliers to make the transition.[26]

In this instance, Nike realized that in order to reach its objective, it would be necessary to become involved in building a multiparty, international network of organizations with a shared interest in the issue of organic cotton.

The Benefits of Engagement

Engaging interactively with stakeholders—whether through dialogue, network building, or some other process—carries a number of potential benefits.[27]

Stakeholder organizations bring a number of distinct strengths. They are often aware of shifts in popular sentiment before companies are, and are thus able to alert companies to emerging issues. For example, as described earlier in this chapter, Perdue, Tyson Foods, and Foster Farms removed antibiotics from their poultry products after growing health concerns were raised by the Centers for Disease Control and Prevention. Stakeholders often operate in networks of organizations very different from the company's; interacting with them gives a firm access to information in these networks. Stakeholders often bring technical or scientific expertise in their area of concern. Finally, when a stakeholder agrees to work with a company on implementing a mutually agreed-upon solution, they can give the resulting work greater legitimacy in the eyes of the public. For example, when Coca-Cola partnered with the World Wildlife Fund and other nonprofit organizations to address stakeholder concerns about the company's impact on water quality and access—a story told in the discussion case at the end of this chapter—their efforts were more believable to many than if the company had undertaken this initiative on its own.

In short, stakeholder engagement can help companies learn about society's expectations, draw on outside expertise, generate creative solutions, and win stakeholder support for implementing them. It can also disarm or neutralize critics and improve a company's reputation for taking constructive action. On the other hand, corporations that do *not* engage effectively with those their actions affect may be hurt. Their reputation may suffer, their sales may drop, and they may be prevented from taking action. The need to respond to stakeholders has only been heightened by the increased globalization of many businesses and by the rise of technologies that facilitate fast communication on a worldwide scale.

Companies are learning that it is important to take a strategic approach to the management of public issues, both domestically and globally. This requires thinking ahead,

---

[26] Nike's description of its efforts is available online at *www.nike.com/nikebiz* and updates are available at *www.nikeresponsibility.com/report*. This case is discussed in Ann C. Svendsen and Myriam Laberge, "Convening Stakeholder Networks: A New Way of Thinking, Being, and Engaging," *Journal of Corporate Citizenship* 19 (Autumn 2005), pp. 91–104.

[27] The following paragraph is largely based on the discussion in Michael Yaziji and Jonathan Doh, *NGOs and Corporations: Conflict and Collaboration* (Cambridge, UK: Cambridge University Press, 2009), ch. 7, "Corporate-NGO Engagements: From Conflict to Collaboration," pp. 123–45.

understanding what is important to stakeholders, scanning the environment, and formulating action plans to anticipate changes in the external environment. Effective issue management requires involvement both by professional staff and leaders at top levels of the organization. It entails communicating across organizational boundaries, engaging with the public, and working creatively with stakeholders to solve complex problems.

Summary

- A public issue is an issue that is of mutual concern to an organization and one or more of the organization's stakeholders. Stakeholders expect a level of performance by businesses, and if it is not met a gap between performance and expectation emerges. The larger the gap, the greater risk of stakeholder backlash or missed business opportunity.
- The eight strategic radar screens (the customer, competitor, economic, technological, social, political, legal, and geophysical environments) enable public affairs managers to assess and acquire information regarding their business environments. Managers must also assess the importance or materiality of public issues to the firm and their stakeholders.
- The issue management process includes identification and analysis of issues, the generation of options, action, and evaluation of the results.
- In the modern corporation, the issue management process takes place in many boundary-spanning departments. Some firms have a department of external affairs or corporate relations to coordinate these activities and top management support is essential for effective issue management.
- Stakeholder engagement involves building relationships between a business firm and its stakeholders around issues of common concern and is enhanced by understanding the goals, motivations, and organizational capacities relevant to the engagement. Social media is playing a more expansive role in stakeholder engagement.
- Stakeholder dialogue is central to good stakeholder engagement, supported by network building or partnerships.

Key Terms

competitive intelligence, *29*
environmental analysis, *27*
environmental intelligence, *27*
issue management, *31*
issue management process, *31*
performance–expectations gap, *25*
public issue, *25*
stakeholder dialogue, *40*
stakeholder engagement, *36*
stakeholder materiality, *30*
stakeholder networks, *40*

Internet Resources

www.wn.com/publicissues	World News, Public Issues
www.nifi.org	National Issues Forum
www.un.org/en/globalissues	United Nations, Global Issues
www.issuemanagement.org	Issue Management Council
www.scip.org	Strategic and Competitive Intelligence Professionals
www.wfs.org	World Future Society
www.globalissues.org	Global Issues
millennium-project.org	The Millennium Project
www.cfr.org	Council on Foreign Relations

Discussion Case: *Coca-Cola's Water Neutrality Initiative*

Since the 2000s, Coca-Cola has grappled with an emerging issue: its corporate impact on water quality, availability, and access around the world.

In 2015, The Coca-Cola Company (TCCC) was the world's largest beverage company. The company operated in more than 200 countries, providing 1.8 billion servings a day of more than 500 nonalcoholic beverage brands of water, enhanced water, juices and juice drinks, ready-to-drink teas and coffees, and energy and sports drinks. The company also partnered with more than 300 bottlers, independent companies that manufactured various Coca-Cola products under franchise. Seventy percent of the company's revenue came from outside the United States.

Water was essential to Coca-Cola's business. The company and its bottlers used around 82 billion gallons of water worldwide every year. Of this, about two-fifths went into finished beverages, and the rest was used in the manufacturing process—for example, to wash bottles, clean equipment, and provide sanitation for employees. Water supplies were also essential to the production of many ingredients in its products, such as sugar, corn, citrus fruit, tea, and coffee. Coca-Cola's chairman and CEO put it bluntly when he commented that unless the communities where the company operated had access to water, "we haven't got a business."

In the mid-2000s, Coca-Cola was abruptly reminded of the impact of its water use on local communities when the Center for Science and the Environment, a think tank in India, charged that Coca-Cola products there contained dangerous levels of pesticide residues. Other activists in India charged that the company's bottling plants used too much water, depriving local villagers of supplies for drinking and irrigation. Local officials shut down a Coca-Cola bottling plant in the state of Kerala, saying it was depleting groundwater, and an Indian court issued an order requiring soft-drink makers to list pesticide residues on their labels. In the United States, the India Resource Center took up the cause, organizing a grassroots campaign to convince schools and colleges to boycott Coca-Cola products.

Water was also emerging as a major concern to the world's leaders. In the early 21st century, more than 1 billion people worldwide lacked access to safe drinking water. Water consumption was doubling every 20 years, an unsustainable rate of growth. By 2025, one-third of the world's population was expected to face acute water shortages. The secretary general of the United Nations highlighted water stress as a major cause of disease, rising food prices, and regional conflicts, and called on national governments and corporations to take steps to address the issue.

Coca-Cola undertook a comprehensive study, surveying its global operations to assess its water management practices and impacts. It also reached out to other stakeholders, including the World Wildlife Fund, the Nature Conservancy, the humanitarian organization CARE, and various academic experts, to seek their advice. As the leader of TCCC's water stewardship initiative explained, the company also "sat down with each of our top bottlers, all of our operating groups, and really walked through all aspects of water and really understood where they were coming from and reached consensus though a very deliberate process."

In 2007, TCCC announced an aspirational goal of *water neutrality,* "to safely return to nature and to communities an amount of water equal to what we use in all our beverages and their production, by the year 2020." This goal would be accomplished in three ways: reduce, recycle, and replenish. The company said it would reduce its own use of water by running its operations more efficiently. It would discharge water used in manufacturing only if it were clean enough to support aquatic life—treating its wastewater itself where

local authorities were unable to do so. Finally, the company would replenish the balance of the water it used (for example, as an ingredient in bottled beverages) by participating in various water conservation projects globally, such as river conservation, rainwater collection, and efficient irrigation.

As the water neutrality initiative proceeded, Coca-Cola moved to measure and publicly share its results. In 2011, the company reported that it had reduced its "water ratio" (the number of gallons of water used per gallons of product produced) by 13 percent from baseline levels. It estimated that 39 percent of its facilities were using recycled water, and 23 percent of the water used in finished products had been replenished through community water projects.

The company also sought to measure the benefits of more than 300 partnerships with governments and nonprofit organizations in 61 countries, ranging from building water treatment facilities in Colombia, to restoring watersheds in Thailand, to improving sugarcane irrigation in Australia. Coca-Cola estimated in 2014 that they replenished 68 percent of the volume of finished beverages to communities and nature. They also improved water use efficiency for the eleventh straight year, with an 8 percent improvement since 2010. They worked with 2030 Water Resources Group, created in 2007, to address water issues on a national level in different countries. In 2013, Coca-Cola invested $2 million in this partnership to help countries like Jordan implement solutions to conserve water by cutting costs and becoming more efficient. In 2012, Coca-Cola used the Ceres Aqua Gauge tool to track the strengths and weaknesses of its program. With this tool's help, Coca-Cola changed its sustainability goals by redoubling its efforts on water efficiency and announced in August 2015 that it expcted to meet its water replenishment goals by 2020—5 years earlier than anticipated.

Sources: *The Coca-Cola Company 2013/2014 Sustainability Report,* at *assets.coca-colacompany.com*; "Drinking It In: The Evolution of a Global Water Stewardship Program at The Coca-Cola Company," *Business for Social Responsibility,* March 2008; "Coca-Cola in India," in Michael Yaziji and Jonathan Doh, *NGOs and Corporations* (Cambridge, UK: Cambridge University Press, 2009), pp. 115–19; and "Coca-Cola Expects to Reach Its Water Replenishment Goals 5 Years Early," *The New York Times,* Augusut 25, 2015, *www.nytimes.com*.

Discussion Questions

1. What was the public issue facing The Coca-Cola Company (TCCC) in this case? Describe the "performance–expectations gap" found in the case—what were the stakeholders' concerns, and how did their expectations differ from the company's performance?

2. If you applied the strategic radar screens model to this case, which of the eight environments would be most significant, and why?

3. Apply the issue management life cycle process model to this case. Which stages of the process can you identify in this case?

4. How did TCCC use stakeholder engagement and dialogue to improve its response to this issue, and what were the benefits of engagement to the company?

5. In your opinion, did TCCC respond appropriately to this issue? Why or why not?

Corporate Social Responsibility and Citizenship

The idea that businesses bear broad responsibilities to society as they pursue economic goals is an age-old belief. Both market and nonmarket stakeholders expect businesses to act responsibly, and many companies have responded by making social goals a part of their overall business operations and adopting the goal of being a good corporate citizen. Businesses embracing these responsibilities often build positive relationships with stakeholders, discover business opportunities in serving society, and transform a concern for financial performance into a vision of integrated financial and social and environmental performance. Establishing effective structures and processes to meet a company's social and corporate citizenship responsibilities, assessing the results of these efforts, and reporting on the firm's performance to the public are important challenges facing today's managers.

This Chapter Focuses on These Key Learning Objectives:

LO 3-1   Understanding the role of big business and the responsible use of corporate power in a democratic society.

LO 3-2   Knowing when the idea of corporate social responsibility originated and investigating how a company's purpose or mission can integrate social objectives with economic and legal objectives.

LO 3-3   Examining the key arguments for and against corporate social responsibility.

LO 3-4   Defining global corporate citizenship and recognizing the rapidly evolving management practices to support global citizenship.

LO 3-5   Distinguishing among the sequential stages of global corporate citizenship.

LO 3-6   Understanding how businesses assess and report their social performance.

Do managers have a responsibility to their shareholders? Certainly they do, because the owners of the business have invested their capital in the firm, exhibiting the ownership theory of the firm presented in Chapter 1. Do managers also have a responsibility, a *social* responsibility, to their company's other market and nonmarket stakeholders—the people who live where the firm operates, who purchase the firm's product or service, or who work for the firm? Does the stakeholder theory of the firm, described in detail in Chapter 1, expand a firm's obligations to include multiple stakeholders present in an interactive social system? Generally, yes, but while managers may have a clear responsibility to respond to all stakeholders, just how far should this responsibility go? Consider the following examples:

> Starbucks Coffee Company launched a $70 million initiative to help coffee farming communities around the world mitigate their climate change impacts and promote long-term crop stability. This was just part of Starbucks' ongoing billion-dollar commitment to ethically sourcing 100 percent of its coffee by 2016. Starbucks transformed a 240-hectare farm located on the slopes of the Poas Volcano in Costa Rica into a global agronomy center, enabling the company to expand its Coffee and Farming Equity practices program (C.A.F.E.). Starbucks' chairman Howard Schultz said, "This investment, and the cumulative impact it will have when combined with programs we have put into place over the last forty years, will support the resiliency of coffee farmers and their families as well as one million people that represent our collective coffee supply chain."[1]
>
> In 2015 consumer goods giant RB, formerly known as Reckitt Benckiser, partnered with Save The Children, an international charitable organization, to help eradicate child deaths from diarrhea in India, Pakistan, and Nigeria. The company helped develop two new hygiene and sanitation products aimed at preventing, controlling, and treating the condition. The first product was a multipurpose soap bar that could be used by families for cleaning and washing hands; the second product was a toilet powder to make bathroom facilities more hygienic. RB reinvested all revenues from the sale of these products in the Stop Diarrhea program, a partnership with the World Health Organization and UNICEF. RB also insisted that the two new products be produced locally, encouraging entrepreneurship, in addition to reducing the overall carbon footprint and transport costs associated with their manufacture.[2]

Are the efforts described above examples of a corporation's social responsibility and citizenship? Do they represent a successful merger of social and economic objectives, or do they represent inappropriate uses of corporate assets—finances, personnel, and products? How far should an organization go to help those in society in need of their support? How much is too much?

This chapter describes the role business plays in society, introduces the concepts of corporate social responsibility and global citizenship, and describes how businesses implement them in practice. How organizations should balance their multiple responsibilities—economic, legal, and social—and become a valued corporate citizen is an ongoing challenge. What are the advantages and drawbacks of being socially responsible? Should the purpose or mission of the business integrate social objectives with economic objectives? How does a business become a better corporate citizen; what steps are necessary? What standards do businesses use to assess their social performance, and how do they report their performance to stakeholders?

---

[1] "Starbucks Expands $70 Million Ethical Sourcing Program with New Global Agronomy Center," *Fort Mills Times,* March 19, 2013, *www.fortmilltimes.com.*

[2] "RB and Save The Children Partner to Stop Children Dying of Diarrhoea," *Ethics Performance,* 2015, *ethicalperformance. com/article/8936.*

Corporate Power and Responsibility

Undeniably, businesses, especially large corporations—whether by intention or accident, and whether for good or evil—play a major role in all that occurs in society. The power exerted by the world's largest business organizations is obvious and enormous. This influence, termed **corporate power**, refers to the capability of corporations to influence government, the economy, and society, based on their organizational resources.

One way to get a sense of the economic power of the world's largest companies is to compare them with nations. Figure 3.1 shows some leading companies alongside countries whose total gross domestic product is about the same as these companies' revenue. The revenues of automaker Toyota Motor, for example, are about equal to the entire economic output of Hong Kong; Walmart's are about the size of the economy of Norway; and BP's are about the size of the economy of Denmark.

The size and global reach of major transnational corporations such as Walmart and the others listed in Figure 3.1 give them tremendous power. Through their ever-present marketing, they influence what people want and how they act around the world. We count on corporations for job creation; much of our community well-being; the standard of living we enjoy; the tax base for essential municipal, state, and national services; and our needs for banking and financial services, insurance, transportation, communication, utilities, entertainment, and a growing proportion of health care. These corporations have the resources to make substantial contributions to political campaigns, as discussed in Chapter 8, thus influencing the policies of governments. They dominate not only the traditional domains of product manufacture and service delivery, but also increasingly reach into such traditionally public sector activities as education, law enforcement, and the provision of social services.[3]

FIGURE 3.1

Comparison of Annual Sales Revenue and the Gross Domestic Product for Selected Transnational Corporations and Nations, 2014, in $ Billions*

Sources: *"Fortune* Global 500," *fortune.com;* and World Bank data, *databank.worldbank.org.*

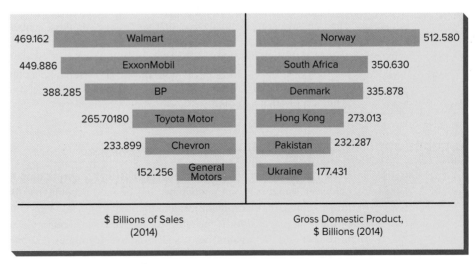

*2014 $ billions of sales compared to 2014 gross domestic product in $ billions.

[3] For two classic analyses of corporate power, see Alfred C. Neal, *Business Power and Public Policy* (New York: Praeger, 1981); and Edwin M. Epstein and Dow Votaw, eds., *Rationality, Legitimacy, Responsibility: Search for New Directions in Business and Society* (Santa Monica, CA: Goodyear, 1978). More recent treatments may be found in David C. Korten, *When Corporations Rule the World* (San Francisco, CA: Berrett-Koehler, 1996) and Steve Coll, *Private Empire: ExxonMobil and American Power* (New York: Penguin Books, 2012).

The following well-known quotation, frequently appearing in journals for business executives, challenges its readers to assume a responsible role for business in society:

> Business has become . . . the most powerful institution on the planet. The dominant institution in any society needs to take responsibility for the whole. . . . Every decision that is made, every action that is taken, must be viewed in light of that kind of responsibility.[4]

The tremendous power of the world's leading corporations has both positive and negative effects. A big company may have definite advantages over a small one. It can command more resources, produce at a lower cost, plan further into the future, and weather business fluctuations somewhat better. Globalization of markets can bring new products, technologies, and economic opportunities to developing societies, and help those in need. After two earthquakes devastated India and Nepal, Canadian-made drones (unmanned aerial vehicles) provided the American Red Cross with an-eye-in-the-sky technology to survey the region and determine where aid was needed the most. Similar technology was used after earthquakes ravaged Haiti, and relief efforts were slow in delivering needed medical supplies and other forms of aid.

Yet, the concentration of corporate power can also harm society. Huge businesses can disproportionately influence politics, shape tastes, and dominate public discourse. They can move production from one site to another, weakening unions and communities. These companies can also use their economic influence to collude to fix prices, divide markets, and quash competition in ways that can negatively affect consumer choices, employment opportunities, or the creation of new businesses. A United Nations report estimated that the world's largest 3,000 businesses were responsible for $2.2 trillion in environmental damage, equal to one-third of the firms' annual profits.[5]

The focused power found in the modern business corporation means that every action it takes can affect the quality of human life—for individuals, for communities, and for the entire globe. The obligation this gives rise to the notion of the *iron law of responsibility.* The **iron law of responsibility** says that in the long run those who do not use power in ways that society considers responsible will tend to lose it.

Given the virtually immeasurable power in the hands of the leaders of large, global corporations, stakeholders throughout the social system expect business to take great care in wielding its power responsibly for the betterment of society. As a result, social responsibility has become a worldwide expectation.

Corporate Social Responsibility and Citizenship

Corporate social responsibility (CSR) means that a corporation should act in a way that enhances society and its inhabitants and be held accountable for any of its actions that affect people, their communities, and their environment. This concept is based in the root of the term *responsibility,* meaning "to pledge back," creating a commitment to give back to society and the organization's stakeholders.[6] It implies that harm to people and society

[4] David C. Korten, "Limits to the Social Responsibility of Business," *The People-Centered Development Forum,* article 19, June 1, 1996.

[5] "World's Top Firms Cause $2.2tn of Environmental Damage, Report Estimates," *The Guardian,* February 18, 2010, *guardian .co.uk.*

[6] For a more complete discussion of the roots of corporate social responsibility and how it is practiced, see Jerry D. Goldstein and Andrew C. Wicks, "Corporate and Stakeholder Responsibility: Making Business Ethics a Two-Way Conversation," *Business Ethics Quarterly* 17 (2007), pp. 375–98.

should be acknowledged and corrected if at all possible. It may require a company to forgo some profits if its social impacts seriously hurt some of its stakeholders or if its funds can be used to have a positive social impact.

Being socially responsible does not mean that a company must abandon its other missions. As discussed later in this chapter, a business has many responsibilities: economic, legal, and social; the challenge for management is to integrate them all into a coherent and comprehensive mission. As Axel Weber, chairman of UBS, a Swiss global financial services company, explained,

> "I see it as my duty to understand the scope and scale of societal challenges. [At UBS] we consider the immediate and long-term effects of these challenges. We look at how they may impact the firm, our clients, and other stakeholders, and what action we may need to take in response. Acting responsibly, achieving a positive societal change—through our own activities as well as through the products, services and advice we offer to our clients—that's one of our key roles."[7]

At times a firm's economic, legal, and societal responsibilities will be in tension; at other times they will blend together to better the firm and actually make it more profitable. Thus, having multiple and sometimes competing responsibilities does not mean that socially responsible firms cannot be as profitable as others that are less responsible; some are and some are not.

More recently, many companies have adopted the term **corporate citizenship** to refer to the actions they take to put their commitments to corporate social responsibility into practice. This term refers not to an abstract principle or set of beliefs, but rather to actual behaviors. The term *global corporate citizenship,* similarly, refers to putting these commitments into practice worldwide, not only locally or regionally. Companies demonstrate their corporate citizenship by proactively building stakeholder partnerships, discovering business opportunities in serving society, and transforming a concern for financial performance into a vision of integrated financial *and* social performance.[8]

One way to understand the multiple dimensions of corporate social responsibility or citizenship is to ask: What are business's obligations to its various stakeholders? One scholar's answer to this question is shown in Exhibit 3.A.

The Origins of Corporate Social Responsibility

In the United States, the idea of corporate social responsibility appeared around the start of the 20th century. Corporations at that time came under attack for being too big, too powerful, and guilty of antisocial and anticompetitive practices. Critics tried to curb corporate power through antitrust laws, banking regulations, and consumer protection laws.

Faced with this social protest, a few farsighted business executives advised corporations to use their power and influence voluntarily for broad social purposes rather than for profits alone. Some of the wealthiest business leaders—steelmaker Andrew Carnegie is a good example—became great philanthropists who gave much of their wealth to educational and charitable institutions. (Today a new cohort of philanthropists is emerging, drawn from Generations X and Y. Some have predicted that these generations, composed of individuals

---

[7] "Interview with Axel Weber on Corporate Culture and Responsibility at UBS," UBS website, *www.ubs.com*.

[8] Michael S. Aßländer and Janina Curbach, "The Corporation as Citoyen? Towards a New Understanding of Corporate Citizenship," *Journal of Business Ethics,* 120 (2014), pp. 541–54; Matthias S. Fifka, "Corporate Citizenship in Germany and the United States—Differing Perceptions and Practices in Transatlantic Comparison," *Business Ethics,* 22 (2013), pp. 341–56; and, Dorothée Baumann-Pauly and Andreas Georg Scherer, "The Organizational Implementation of Corporate Citizenship: An Assessment Tool and its Application at UN Global Compact Participants," *Journal of Business Ethics,* 117 (2013), pp. 1–17.

Exhibit 3.A

Principles of Corporate Citizenship

Good corporate citizens strive to conduct all business dealings in an ethical manner, make a concerted effort to balance the needs of all stakeholders, and work to protect the environment. The principles of corporate citizenship include the following:

Ethical Business Behavior

1. Engages in fair and honest business practices in its relationship with stakeholders.
2. Sets high standards of behavior for all employees.
3. Exercises ethical oversight of the executive and board levels.

Stakeholder Commitment

4. Strives to manage the company for the benefit of all stakeholders.
5. Initiates and engages in genuine dialogue with stakeholders.
6. Values and implements dialogue.

Community

7. Fosters a reciprocal relationship between the corporation and community.
8. Invests in the communities in which the corporation operates.

Consumers

9. Respects the rights of consumers.
10. Offers quality products and services.
11. Provides information that is truthful and useful.

Employees

12. Provides a family-friendly work environment.
13. Engages in responsible human resource management.
14. Provides an equitable reward and wage system for employees.
15. Engages in open and flexible communication with employees.
16. Invests in employee development.

Investors

17. Strives for a competitive return on investment.

Suppliers

18. Engages in fair trading practices with suppliers.

Environment Commitment

19. Demonstrates a commitment to the environment.
20. Demonstrates a commitment to sustainable development.

Source: Kimberly Davenport, "Corporate Citizenship: A Stakeholder Approach for Defining Corporate Social Performance and Identifying Measures for Assessment," 1998, doctoral dissertation, Fielding Graduate University, *www.fielding.edu/library/dissertations/*. Used with permission.

born after 1965, could amass even greater wealth than their predecessors, through inheritance, entrepreneurial success, and other means. They will be in a position to transform charitable giving unlike any previous generation.[9] Corporate philanthropy is discussed in more detail in Chapter 18.) Other business leaders, like automaker Henry Ford, developed

[9] *Portraits of Young Philanthropists: How Generation X and Generation Y Are Transforming Charitable Giving* (New York, The Economist, 2014).

paternalistic programs to support the recreational and health needs of their employees. These business leaders believed that business had a responsibility to society that went beyond or worked along with their efforts to make profits.

William C. Frederick, a leading scholar and a coauthor of several earlier editions of this textbook, described how business's understanding of corporate social responsibility has evolved over the past half century. During each of four historical periods, corporate social responsibility has had a distinct focus, set of drivers, and policy instruments, as shown in Figure 3.2. Corporate social responsibility is defined in its most basic form as "learning to live with, and respect, others." In his view, corporate social responsibility evolved from a stewardship, to strategic responsiveness, to an ethics-based understanding based in culture, to what Frederick calls the most recent phase of corporate social responsibility: *corporate citizenship.*

FIGURE 3.2 Evolving Phases of Corporate Social Responsibility

	Phases of Corporate Social Responsibility	CSR Drivers	CSR Policy Instruments
CSR$_1$ Early in the 20th century but formally in the 1950s–60s	**Corporate Social Stewardship** Corporate philanthropy—acts of charity Managers as public Trustee-stewards Balancing social pressures	Executive conscience Company image/reputation	Philanthropic funding Public relations
CSR$_2$ 1960s–70s	**Corporate Social Responsiveness** Social impact analysis Strategic priority for social response Organizational redesign and training for responsiveness Stakeholder mapping and implementation	Social unrest/protest Repeated corporate misbehavior Public policy/government regulation Stakeholder pressures think tank policy papers	Stakeholder strategy Regulatory compliance Social audits Public affairs function Governance reform Political lobbying
CSR$_3$ 1980s–90s	**Corporate/Business Ethics** Foster an ethical corporate culture Establish an ethical organizational climate Recognize common ethical principles	Religious/ethnic beliefs Technology-driven value changes Human rights pressures Code of ethics Ethics committee/officer/audits Ethics training Stakeholder negotiations	Mission/vision/values Statements CEO leadership ethics
CSR$_4$ 1990s–present	**Corporate/Global Citizenship** Stakeholder partnerships Integrate financial, social, and environmental performance Identify globalization impacts Sustainability of company and environment	Global economic trade/investment High-tech communication networks Geopolitical shifts/competition Ecological awareness/concern NGO pressures	Intergovernmental compacts Global audit standards NGO dialogue Sustainability audits/ reports

Source: William C. Frederick, "Corporate Social Responsibility: Deep Roots, Flourishing Growth, Promising Future," In *The Oxford Handbook of Corporate Social Responsibility*, eds. Andrew Crane, Abagail Williams, Dirk Matten, Jeremy Moon, and Donald S. Siegel (Oxford: Oxford University Press, 2008), pp. 522–32. Used with permission.

Balancing Social, Economic, and Legal Responsibilities

Being socially responsible by meeting the public's continually changing expectations requires wise leadership at the top of the corporation. Companies with the ability to recognize profound social changes and anticipate how they will affect operations have proven to be survivors. They get along better with government regulators, are more open to the needs of the company's stakeholders, and often cooperate with legislators as new laws are developed to cope with social problems.

> Nestlé, the world's leading nutrition, health, and wellness company with its headquarters in Switzerland, launched a large-scale research project on children's nutrition leading to product modification or new product development by 2016. The global initiative focused on 10 countries, including the United States, Mexico, China, and Russia, and collaborated with over 240,000 public health opinion leaders, third-party organizations, and pediatricians around the world. The Kids Nutrition and Health Study targeted children's nutrient intake, dietary patterns, and family lifestyle factors. The aim was to help parents ensure the healthy growth and development of their children, while also giving the company insights into how to modify existing product ingredients and develop new products.[10]

The actions taken by Nestlé are an example of a business organization's leaders being guided by **enlightened self-interest**. This concept reflects the notion that providing value to stakeholders is in a business's *long run* self-interest. Nestlé's research initiative certainly cost the company money in the short run, but new product development and assistance to the families and children who used their products and the communities where they lived would also bring long-term benefits through enhanced reputation and customer loyalty.[11]

Social responsibility is not a business organization's sole responsibility. In addition, as a member of a civil society, organizations have legal obligations, as well as economic responsibilities, to their owners and other stakeholders affected by the financial well-being of the firm. Any organization or manager must seek to juggle these multiple responsibilities—economic, legal, and social. The belief that the business of business is solely to attend to shareholders' return on investment and make a profit is no longer widely held and has no legal foundation, as discussed next in the chapter. Rather, many business executives believe the key challenge facing their organizations today is to meet their multiple economic and social responsibilities simultaneously.

The Corporate Social Responsibility Debate

As we have seen, there are various views about business's social responsibilities and these views evolve over time. The arguments for and against corporate social responsibility are detailed next and summarized in Figure 3.3.

Arguments for Corporate Social Responsibility

Who favors the notion of corporate social responsibility? Many business executives believe that companies should make a profit but should balance this with their social

---

[10] "Nestle in Society: Creating Shared Value and Meeting Our Commitments, 2014," *Nestle's Annual Social Report,* 2014, *www.nestle.com/csv.*

[11] Jeff Frooman, "Socially Irresponsible and Illegal Behavior and Shareholder Wealth," *Business & Society,* September 1997, pp. 221–49, argues that the negative effects on shareholder wealth when a firm acts irresponsibly support the enlightened self-interest view: act responsibly to promote shareholders' interests.

FIGURE 3.3
The Pros and Cons of Corporate Social Responsibility

Arguments for Corporate Social Responsibility	Arguments against Corporate Social Responsibility
Balances corporate power with responsibility. Discourages government regulation. Promotes long-term profits for business. Improves stakeholder relationships. Enhance business reputation.	Lowers economic efficiency and profit. Imposes unequal costs among competitors. Imposes hidden costs passed on to stakeholders. Requires skills business may lack. Places responsibility on business rather than individuals.

responsibilities. Clearly, many stakeholder groups see the value in corporate socially responsible action, as it preserves the environment, protects consumers, safeguards the safety and health of employees, and prevents job discrimination, but shareholders also expect business to maintain a strong return on their financial investments. Government officials also support CSR in that it ensures corporate compliance with laws and regulations that protect the general public from abusive business practices. In other words, both businesspeople and stakeholders, and both supporters and critics of business, have reasons for wanting businesses to act in socially responsible ways.

Balances Corporate Power with Responsibility

Today's business enterprise possesses much power and influence. Most people believe that responsibility must accompany power, whomever holds it. This obligation, presented earlier in this chapter, is the *iron law of responsibility*. Corporations' reputations, especially in the banking industry, have taken a hit since the economic downturn of 2008–09. Half of American adults say their trust in banks has declined over the past few years, joining a growing distrust of Wall Street and mortgage lenders. This shows one example of how managers' misuse of corporate power and their lack of responsibility as trustees of the public's wealth can result in their loss of power.

Discourages Government Regulation

One of the most appealing arguments in favor of CSR is that voluntary socially responsible acts may head off increased government regulation of business. Some regulation may reduce freedom for both business and society, and freedom is a desirable public good. In the case of business, regulations tend to add economic costs and restrict flexibility in decision making. From business's point of view, freedom in decision making allows companies to maintain initiative in meeting market and social forces as the following example illustrates.

> The beer, distilled spirits, and wine industries have a long-time understanding with the Federal Trade Commission (FTC) that self-regulation and responsiveness to a series of FTC "recommendations" may prevent more aggressive and binding regulatory control over these industries' practices. They developed their own advertisement campaign to warn potential consumers over the perils of driving drunk, underage drinking, and alcoholism. Some FTC reports suggested that industry efforts have been effective and, in some instances, have involved voluntary measures that have exceeded accepted standards. Despite concerns that these initiatives have not gone far enough, these industries have generally been able to ward off strict regulatory controls.[12]

[12] "Self-regulation in the Alcohol Industry," *truthinadvertising.org,* n.d., *www.truthinadvertising.org/self-regulation-in-the-alcohol-industry.*

This view is also consistent with political philosophy that wishes to keep power as decentralized as possible in a democratic society. From this perspective, government is already a massive institution whose centralized power and bureaucracy threaten the balance of power in society. Therefore, if business by its own socially responsible behavior can discourage new government restrictions, it is accomplishing a public good as well as its own private good.

Promotes Long-Term Profits for Business

At times, social initiatives by business produce long-run business profits. In 1951 a New Jersey judge ruled in a precedent-setting case, *Barlow et al. v. A.P. Smith Manufacturing*, that a corporate donation to Princeton University was an *investment* by the firm, and thus an allowable business expense. The rationale was that a corporate gift to a school, though costly in the present, might in time provide a flow of talented graduates to work for the company. The court ruled that top executives must take "a long-range view of the matter" and exercise "enlightened leadership and direction" when it comes to using company funds for socially responsible programs.[13]

> A classic example of the long-term benefits of social responsibility was the Johnson & Johnson Tylenol incident in the 1980s, when several people died after ingesting Extra-Strength Tylenol capsules laced with the poison cyanide. To ensure the safety of its customers, Johnson & Johnson immediately recalled the product, an action that cost the firm millions of dollars in the short term. The company's production processes were never found defective. Customers rewarded Johnson & Johnson's responsible actions by continuing to buy its products, and in the long run the company once again became profitable.

Empirical evidence has supported this view. Studies generally have found that most of the time, more responsible companies also had better financial results; the statistical association has been highly to modestly positive across the range of all prior studies. According to one recent study, the association was strongest when a company pursued social responsibility initiatives that were linked to stakeholder preferences. As one group of scholars concluded, "companies need to link their CSR initiatives to the likely preferences of their stakeholders and undertake the corporate social actions that are relevant to the company's strategy."[14]

In this chapter's opening examples, Starbucks Coffee Company launched an initiative to help coffee farming communities around the world to mitigate climate change impact and promote long-term crop stability, and consumer foods company RB partnered with Save The Children to help eradicate child deaths from diarrhea in developing countries. In both instances, these companies were investing in the future, hoping that their social responsibility efforts would also indirectly help their firm's financial bottom line.

Improves Stakeholder Relationships

Managers often believe that developing a strong social agenda and series of social programs will improve the firm's stakeholder relationships. Whether it improved the quality of people it attracted as employees, or appealed to consumers to purchase the firm's

---

[13] *Barlow et al. v. A.P. Smith Manufacturing* (1951, New Jersey Supreme Court), discussed in Clarence C. Walton, *Corporate Social Responsibility* (Belmont, CA: Wadsworth, 1967), pp. 48–52.

[14] Quote is from Giovanna Michelon, Giacomo Boesso, and Kamalesh Kumar, "Examining the Link between Strategic Corporate Social Responsibility and Company Performance: An Analysis of the Best Corporate Citizens," *Corporate Social Responsibility and Environmental Management,* 20 (2013), pp. 81–94. Also see Qian Wang, Junsheng Dou, and Shenghua Jia, "A Meta-Analytic Review of Corporate Social Responsibility and Corporate Financial Performance: The Moderating Effect of Contextual Factor," *Business & Society,* available online on May 4, 2015.

product or services, or built strong ties with the community in which it operated, or persuaded investors to purchase company stock, managers felt that social action by the firm was viewed positively by stakeholders. This belief was borne out in recent research where corporate social responsibility was linked to current and prospective employees' trust in the firm and desire to work for the firm, positive consumer purchasing decisions, and investors' decisions, especially during times of economic downturn. At Coca-Cola, 60,000 employees were surveyed and reported that corporate social responsibility was the second biggest driver of their commitment and loyalty to the firm, after leadership.[15]

Enhances Business Reputation

The social reputation of the firm is often viewed as an important element in establishing trust between the firm and its stakeholders. **Reputation** refers to desirable or undesirable qualities associated with an organization or its actors that may influence the organization's relationships with its stakeholders.[16] Rating Research, a British firm, created a "reputation index" to measure a company's social reputation. The index evaluates critical intangible assets that constitute corporate reputation and broadly disseminates these ratings to interested parties.

As further explored in Chapter 19, a firm's reputation is a valuable intangible asset, as it prompts repeat purchases by loyal consumers and helps to attract and retain better employees to spur productivity and enhance profitability. Employees who have the most to offer may be attracted to work for a firm that contributes to the social good of the community, or is more sensitive to the needs and safety of its consumers, or takes better care of its employees. Research has confirmed that a firm's "good deeds" or reputation increases its attractiveness to employees.[17] An example of a company that has embraced having a solid reputation when managing their stakeholders is described next.

> Sodexo, a provider of integrated food and facilities management services throughout North America including many hospitals, senior living centers, colleges, universities, and school districts, was committed to developing a positive reputation. "Being a responsible corporate citizen is at the core of Sodexo's business," declared the company's website. "We set the benchmark in areas such as sustainability, diversity and inclusion, wellness, and the fight against hunger." Sodexo's "The Better Tomorrow Plan" impacted 80 countries at 30,600 locations and engaged the company's 380,000 employees. The program addressed 14 different issues, such as reducing the firm's carbon and water usage in all company operations and at all client's locations, providing and promoting varied and balanced food options to its clients, increasing the purchase of products sourced from fairly and responsibly certified sources, and ensuring compliance with a Global Sustainable Supply Chain Code of Conduct.[18]

[15] For additional research exploring this relationship, see R. E. Slack, S. Corlett, and R. Morris, "Exploring Employee Engagement with (Corporate) Social Responsibility: A Social Exchange Perspective on Organizational Participation," *Journal of Business Ethics* 127 (2015), pp. 537–48; Danae Manika, Victoria K. Wells, Diana Gregory-Smith, and Michael Gentry, "The Impact of Individual Attitudinal and Organizational Variables on Workplace Environmentally Friendly Behaviors," *Journal of Business Ethics* 126 (2015), pp. 663–84; and Lisa E. Bolton and Anna S. Mattila, "How Does Corporate Social Responsibility Affect Consumer Response to Service Failure in Buyer-Seller Relationships?" *Journal of Retailing* 91 (2015), pp. 140–53.

[16] The definition of reputation is adapted from John F. Mahon, "Corporate Reputation: A Research Agenda Using Strategy and Stakeholder Literature," *Business & Society* 41, no. 4 (December 2002), pp. 415–45. For the "reputation index," see Charles Fombrun, *Reputation: Realizing Value from the Corporate Image* (Cambridge, MA: Harvard University Press, 1996) and Rating Research LLC, *www.ratingresearch.com*.

[17] Turhan Erkmen and Emel Esen, "The Mediating Role of Trust to Managers on the Relationship Between Corporate Reputation Practices and Employees' Course of Actions to Customers, *Social Responsibility Journal* 10 (2014), pp. 296–82.

[18] The quotation and information about Sodexo is from the company's website, *www.sodexousa.com*.

Arguments against Corporate Social Responsibility

Who opposes corporate social responsibility? The economist Milton Friedman famously stated in 1970, "There is only one responsibility of business, namely to use its resources and engage in activities designed to increase its profits." Some people in the business world—such as the 16 percent of CEOs in the survey (shown later in Figure 3.4) who believe that the appropriate role of business is to provide the highest possible returns to shareholders while obeying all laws and regulations—clearly agree with this view. Some fear that the pursuit of social goals by business will lower firms' economic efficiency, thereby depriving society of important goods and services. Others are skeptical about trusting business with social improvements; they prefer governmental initiatives and programs. According to some of the more radical critics of the private business system, social responsibility is nothing but a clever public relations smokescreen to hide business's true intentions to make as much money as possible, often at the expense of workers, communities, and customers. See Figure 3.3 again for some of the arguments against corporate social responsibility, discussed next.

Lowers Economic Efficiency and Profits

According to one argument, when a business uses some of its resources for social purposes, it risks lowering its efficiency or even going out of business.

> Life was very good for Aaron Feuerstein in the mid-1990s. His company, Malden Mills, was flourishing, despite a sharp decline in the textile industry in the United States. Malden Mills' popular flagship product, Polarfleece, was widely used in high-performance athletic and aerobic apparel, outerwear products, and had even been adopted for military use. But on December 11, 1995, as Feuerstein was returning from his 70th birthday party, he saw his factory burn to the ground. Critics thought Feuerstein should just accept the $300 million in insurance money and relocate or dissolve the business. But Feuerstein was committed to his employers, so he vowed to keep them all on the payroll, at a cost of $1.5 million per week, and continue their benefits for at least 90 more days. The eventual cost of $25 million in employee wages, lawsuits filed by injured employees, and the $100 million cost to rebuild the factory turned out to be too much for Feuerstein's company. By 2001, Malden Mills had filed for bankruptcy, and Feuerstein eventually lost control of the company.[19]

In this example, Feuerstein's motives were admirable, his commitments to his employees eventually became too costly and threatened the survival of the firm.

Business managers and economists argue that the business of business is business. Businesses are told to concentrate on producing goods and services and selling them at the lowest competitive price. When these economic tasks are done, the most efficient firms survive. Even though corporate social responsibility is well-intended, such social activities lower business's efficiency, thereby depriving society of higher levels of economic production needed to maintain everyone's standard of living.[20]

---

[19] "The Mensch of Malden Mills: CEO Aaron Feuerstein Puts Employees First," *CBS News 60 Minutes,* July 3, 2003, *cbsnews.com*; and, David W. Gill, "Was Aaron Feuerstein Wrong?" *Ethix,* June 25, 2011, *ethix.org.*

[20] This argument is most often attributed to Milton Friedman, "The Social Responsibility of Business Is to Increase Its Profits," *The New York Times Magazine,* September 13, 1970, pp. 33, 122–26.

Imposes Unequal Costs among Competitors

Another argument against social responsibility is that it imposes greater costs on more responsible companies, putting them at a competitive disadvantage. Consider the following scenario:

> A manufacturer operating in multiple countries wishes to be more socially responsible worldwide and decides to protect its employees by installing more safety equipment at its plants than local law requires. Other manufacturers in competition with this company do not take similar steps, choosing to install only as much safety equipment as required by law. As a result their costs are lower, and their profits higher. In this case, the socially responsible firm penalizes itself and even runs the risk of going out of business, especially in a highly competitive market.

This kind of problem becomes acute when viewed from a global perspective, where laws and regulations differ from one country to the next. If one nation requires higher and more costly pollution control standards, or stricter job safety rules, or more stringent premarket testing of prescription drugs than other nations, it imposes higher costs on business. This cost disadvantage means that competition cannot be equal. Foreign competitors who are the least socially responsible will actually be rewarded because they will be able to capture a bigger share of the market.

Imposes Hidden Costs Passed on to Stakeholders

Many social proposals undertaken by business do not pay their own way in an economic sense; therefore, someone must pay for them. Ultimately, society pays all costs. Some people may believe that social benefits are costless, but socially responsible businesses will try to recover all of their costs in some way. For example, if a company chooses to install expensive pollution abatement equipment, the air may be cleaner, but ultimately someone will have to pay. Shareholders may receive lower dividends, employees may be paid less, or consumers may be charged higher prices. If the public knew that it would eventually have to pay these costs, and if it knew how high the true costs were, it might not be so insistent that companies act in socially responsible ways. The same might be true of government regulations intended to produce socially desirable business behavior. By driving up business costs, these regulations often increase prices and lower productivity, in addition to making the nation's tax bill higher.

Requires Skills Business May Lack

Businesspeople are not primarily trained to solve social problems. They may know about production, marketing, accounting, finance, information technology, and personnel work, but what do they know about inner-city issues or world poverty or violence in schools? Putting businesspeople in charge of solving such problems may lead to unnecessarily expensive and poorly conceived approaches. Thus one might question the effectiveness and efficiency of businesspeople seeking to address social issues. Business analysts might be tempted to believe that methods that succeed in normal business operations will also be applicable to complex social problems, even though different approaches may work better in the social arena.

 A related idea is that public officials who are duly elected by citizens in a democratic society should address societal issues. Business leaders are not elected by the public and therefore do not have a mandate to solve social problems. In short, businesspeople do not have the expertise or the popular support required to address what are essentially issues of public policy.

FIGURE 3.4
**Business Executives'
View of the Role of
Business in Society**

Source: For a more detailed
discussion of these views,
see "The McKinsey Global
Survey of Business Executives:
Business and Society,"
McKinsey Quarterly, January
2006, based on a survey of
4,238 executives (more than a
quarter are CEOs or other top
executives) in 116 countries.

Percentage of business executives who believe that business organizations should . . .

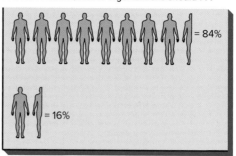

Balance their responsibility to their investors with their responsibilities to other business stakeholders = 84%

Primarily focus on maximizing their investors' returns while staying within the law of society = 16%

Places Responsibility on Business Rather Than Individuals

The entire idea of *corporate* responsibility is misguided, according to some critics. Only *individual persons* can be responsible for their actions. People make decisions; organizations do not. An entire company cannot be held liable for its actions, only those individuals who are involved in promoting or carrying out a policy. Therefore, it is wrong to talk about the social responsibility of *business* when it is the social responsibility of *individual businesspersons* that is involved. If individual business managers want to contribute their own personal money to a social cause, let them do so; but it is wrong for them to contribute their company's funds in the name of corporate social responsibility.[21] Together, the above arguments claim that the attempt to exercise corporate social responsibility places added burdens on both business and society without producing the intended effect of social improvement or produces it at excessive cost.

This view was challenged a number of years ago when a survey by the consulting firm McKinsey reported that a solid majority—84 percent—of business executives said that they believe that companies should balance their responsibility to their investors with their responsibilities of other business stakeholders. Only a minority—16 percent—felt that companies should focus primarily on maximizing their investors' returns while staying within the law of society. These results are summarized in Figure 3.4.

An emerging type of businesses, called **B Corporations**, explicitly seek to balance the interests of multiple stakeholders. B Corporations are business organizations that focus on social responsibility and citizenship by blending their social objectives with financial goals and use the power of business to solve social and environmental problems. B Corporations are further described in Exhibit 3.B.

Management Systems for Corporate Social Responsibility and Citizenship

Corporate social responsibility and citizenship require more than espoused values; they require action. Companies must establish management processes and structures to carry out their citizenship commitments. This section describes some of the ways forward-thinking companies are changing to improve their ability to act as socially responsible citizens.

BSR, a management consultancy formerly called Businesses for Social Responsibility, surveyed its more than 300 members to determine how they had organized to carry out their citizenship functions. BSR observed great variation in what they termed corporate social responsibility (CSR) or corporate citizenship management systems. BSR found that

---

[21] This argument, like the "lowers economic efficiency and profits" argument, often is attributed to Friedman, "The Social Responsibility of Business." "Social Responsibility of Business" Ibid.

To qualify for B Corporation status, an organization must meet rigorous, independent social and environmental performance standards, assessed by the nonprofit organization B Lab. The company is assessed on the impact it has on its communities, employees, consumers, and the environment. The idea is that a business cannot just claim it is socially responsible, but it must prove it by meeting the B Lab standards. By May 2015, there were 1,281 organizations in 41 countries and 121 industries that had received the B Corp certification. (Certified B Corporations are different from businesses that are chartered in a state as a "benefit corporation." Benefit corporations use the protection afforded by state-driven statues to enable the company to address social objectives, as well as financial objectives, without facing legal challenges by stockholders for shirking the firm's financial responsibilities.)

Certified B Corporations are more likely to receive various government recognitions, such as the U.S. Drug Administration's organic seal, or to qualify for a LEED certification for their buildings (designating environmental excellence), or to be certified as engaging in fair trade. B Corporations are subjected to random audits, and these reports are made public, adding a layer of transparency to the process and certification. In addition, B Corporations must modify their company's bylaws in order to formalize their social mission.

Warby Parker is a B Corporation. Four college friends started the company to design, manufacture, and distribute high-quality eyeglasses that sold for around $95 rather than the more common $500 price tag. But, its founders also wanted to have a social impact so adopted the policy that for every pair of eyeglasses sold, one pair would be donated to someone in need. Warby Parker also pledged to become one of the few carbon-neutral eyewear brands in the world. "It was important to the four of us that if we are going to dedicate our life savings and our time to building an organization, we wanted to have a positive impact," said Neil Blumenthal. This combination of economic and social objectives qualified Warby Parker for B Corporation certification.[22]

the goal of a global citizenship management system is to integrate corporate responsibility and citizenship concerns into a company's values, culture, operations, and business decisions at all levels of the organization. Many companies have taken steps to create such a system by assigning responsibility to a committee of the board, an executive-level committee, or a single executive or group of executives who can identify key CSR or corporate citizenship issues and evaluate and develop a structure for long-term integration of social values throughout the organization. One important observation is that there is no single universally accepted method for designing a global corporate citizenship management structure. This is definitely not a "one size fits all" exercise.

Corporate citizenship, as this study recognized, is a rapidly evolving area of managerial practice in many organizations. While businesses administer this corporate activity in different ways, one example is Gap Inc.'s appointment of Bobbi Silten.

> Bobbi Silten is the Executive Vice President of Global Talent & Sustainability at Gap, Inc., after previously serving as its Senior Vice President of Global Responsibility and President of Gap Foundation. In those roles, she oversaw the company's global community investments in women's advancement and jobs for youth, and volunteer programs for employees worldwide. She also served as a member of the White House Council for Community Solutions, which provided advice to President Obama on the best ways to mobilize citizens, nonprofits, businesses, and government to work more effectively together to solve specific community needs.

[22] See the B Corporation website at *www.bcorporation.net* and Warby Parker was profiled in "Vision Quest," *Entrepreneur,* January 2012, pp. 56–57.

In her current executive role, Silten oversees the company's sustainable innovations and coordinates global stakeholder partnerships.[23]

One emerging trend is the consolidation of corporate citizenship efforts, like those at Gap, into a single office that may encompass community relations, philanthropy, stakeholder engagement, social auditing and reporting, and other functions. According to a study of American companies, almost all—94 percent—of *Fortune* 250 companies (the largest corporations in the United States, published annually in *Fortune* magazine) had a department of corporate citizenship, global citizenship, corporate social responsibility, or a similar name. Many of these departments had been recently established. The heads of many of them were senior vice presidents or vice presidents.[24]

CEOs increasingly have accepted the multiple responsibilities of business notion—economic, social, and legal—that make up the citizenship profile, as described by senior Walmart executives:

> "Long-term capitalism takes a deeper view of business's role in society, recognizing that, in the long run, the interests of stakeholders converge with the interests of the broader community. The actions of any one company may reverberate throughout the various systems in which it operates, generating second- and third-order benefits. . . . Under long-term capitalism, companies recognize that fact and, through concerted actions with others of sufficient scale, work to ensure constant improvements to those systems."[25]

Visionary CEOs clearly see citizenship as an opportunity to create value for their organization, gain a competitive advantage, and help address some of the world's biggest challenges. As businesses have become more committed to citizenship, specialized consultancies and professional associations for managers with responsibility in this area have emerged. Many of these organizations, including BSR, whose study is cited earlier, are profiled in Exhibit 3.C.

Stages of Corporate Citizenship

Companies do not become socially responsible or good corporate citizens overnight. The process takes time. New attitudes have to be developed, new routines learned, new policies and action programs designed, and new relationships formed. Many obstacles must be overcome. What process do companies go through as they proceed down this path? What factors push and pull them along?

Philip H. Mirvis and Bradley K. Googins of the Center for Corporate Citizenship at Boston College developed a five-stage model of global corporate citizenship, based on their work with hundreds of practitioners in a wide range of companies.[26] In their view, firms typically pass through a sequence of five stages as they develop as corporate citizens. Each stage is characterized by a distinctive pattern of concepts, strategic intent, leadership, structure, issues management, stakeholder relationships, and transparency, as illustrated in Figure 3.5.

---

[23] See "Bobbi Silten," *The Huffington Post,* July 2, 2015, *www.huffingtonpost.com.*

[24] Anne T. Lawrence, Gordon Rands, and Mark Starik, "The Role, Career Path, Skill Set, and Reporting Relationships of the Corporate Social Responsibility/Citizenship/Sustainability Officer in Fortune 250 Firms," presented at the annual meeting of the International Association for Business and Society, 2009.

[25] "Business and Society in the Coming Decades," *McKinsey & Company,* April 2015, *www.mckinsey.com.*

[26] Philip H. Mirvis and Bradley K. Googins, *Stages of Corporate Citizenship: A Developmental Framework* (Chestnut Hill, MA: Center for Corporate Citizenship at Boston College, 2006). For a contrasting stage model, based on the experience of Nike, see Simon Zadek, "The Path to Corporate Responsibility," *Harvard Business Review,* December 2004, pp. 125–32.

As the practice of corporate citizenship has spread, so have professional associations and consultancies serving managers in this arena. Among the leading organizations are these:

- In the United States, *BSR* (formerly Business for Social Responsibility) provides consulting services to its members and works with business to create a just and sustainable world.
- *Canadian Business for Social Responsibility* seeks to be the premier network and key resource in Canada for large and small companies, researchers, opinion leaders, and the media to advance corporate social responsibility and sustainability.
- *Corporate Social Responsibility Europe* (CSR Europe) is the leading European business network with 70 corporate members and 41 national CSR organizations, representing over 10,000 companies.
- *Forum Empresa* was created an as inter-American organization (North and South America) and represents 19 countries in the region and a combined total of more than 3,300 affiliated businesses.
- The *African Institute of Corporate Citizenship* (AICC or AICC Africa) is a nongovernmental organization specializing in acting as a catalyst and facilitator of change; as a broker and initiator of multisector partnerships and platforms; and as a knowledge management hub for issues relating to the role of responsible business in African societies.
- *CSR Asia* promotes awareness of sustainable development across the region by providing cutting-edge research, strategy advisory, networking, and executive education services with an informed understanding of evolving CSR issues on the ground.
- *Asian Forum on Corporate Social Responsibility,* based in the Philippines, sponsors conferences to provide CSR practitioners in Asia an opportunity to learn, collaborate, and share insights.

Source: More information about these organizations is available online at *www.bsr.org*, *www.cbsr.ca*, *www.csreurope.org*, *empresa.org*, *www.aiccafrica.org*, *csr-asia.com*, and *www.asianforum.com*.

FIGURE 3.5   **The Stages of Global Corporate Citizenship**

	Citizenship Content	Strategic Intent	Leadership	Structure	Issues Management	Stakeholder Relationships	Transparency
Stage 5: Transforming	Change the game	Market creation or social change	Visionary, ahead of the pack	Mainstream: business driven	Defining	Multi-organization	Full disclosure
Stage 4: Integrated	Sustainability or triple bottom line	Value proposition	Champion, in front of it	Organizational alignment	Proactive, systems	Partnership alliance	Assurance
Stage 3: Innovative	Stakeholder management	Business case	Steward, on top of it	Cross-functional coordination	Responsive, programs	Mutual influence	Public reporting
Stage 2: Engaged	Philanthropy, environmental protection	License to operate	Supporter, in the loop	Functional ownership	Reactive, policies	Interactive	Public relations
Stage 1: Elementary	Jobs, profits, and taxes	Legal compliance	Lip service, out of touch	Marginal, staff-driven	Defensive	Unilateral	Flank protection

From the Boston College Center for Corporate Citizenship's "Stages of Corporate Citizenship: A Developmental Framework," by Philip Mirvis, PhD and Bradley K. Googins, PhD, 2006. Used with permission.

Elementary Stage. At this stage, citizenship is undeveloped. Managers are uninterested and uninvolved in social issues. Although companies at this stage obey the law, they do not move beyond compliance. Companies tend to be defensive; they react only when threatened. Communication with stakeholders is one-way: from the company to the stakeholder.

Engaged Stage. At this second stage, companies typically become aware of changing public expectations and see the need to maintain their license to operate. Engaged companies may adopt formal policies, such as governing labor standards or human rights. They begin to interact with and listen to stakeholders, although engagement occurs mainly through established departments. Top managers become involved. Often, a company at this stage will step up its philanthropic giving or commit to specific environmental objectives. When Home Depot announced that it would sell only environmentally certified wood products, this was an example of a company at the engaged stage of corporate citizenship.

Innovative Stage. At this third stage, organizations may become aware that they lack the capacity to carry out new commitments, prompting a wave of structural innovation. Departments begin to coordinate, new programs are launched, and many companies begin reporting their efforts to stakeholders. (Social reporting is discussed later in this chapter.) External groups become more influential. Companies begin to understand more fully the business reasons for engaging in citizenship.

Integrated Stage. As they move into the fourth stage, companies see the need to build more coherent initiatives. Mirvis and Googins cite the example of Asea Brown Boveri (ABB), a Switzerland-based multinational producer of power plants and automation systems, which carefully coordinates its many sustainability programs from the CEO level down to line officers in more than 50 countries where the company has a presence. Integrated companies may adopt triple bottom line measures turn to external audits and enter into ongoing partnerships with stakeholders.

Transforming Stage. This is the fifth and highest stage in the model. Companies at this stage have visionary leaders and are motivated by a higher sense of corporate purpose. They partner extensively with other organizations and individuals across business, industry, and national borders to address broad social problems and reach underserved markets.

Net-Works is a project that joined carpet manufacturer Interface with the Zoological Society of London to focus on the wasteful use of fishing nets in the Philippines. When fishermen were done using their nonbiodegradable fishing nets, they had simply discarded them on the beach or in the sea, posing a threat to marine life. To change this, Net-Works paid villagers living along the beaches to collect the old nets, which were then sold directly to Interface's nylon supplier. The nets were then reprocessed for use in manufacturing Interface's carpets. In just a year, more than 25 tons of waste nets were collected and 4,800 extra meals were on the tables of the local villagers due to the income they received. The visionary partnership helped the environment, the community, and the company.[27]

The model's authors emphasize that individual companies can be at more than one stage at once, if their development progresses faster in some areas than in others. For example, a company might audit its activities and disclose the findings to the public in

---

[27] "Best Business/NGO Partnership: Net-Works," *Ethical Corporation Responsible Business Awards 2014—Part 1,* Ethical Corporation, *www.ethicalcorp.com.*

social reports (transparency, stage 5), but still be interacting with stakeholders in a pattern of mutual influence (stakeholder relationships, stage 3). This is normal, the authors point out, because each organization evolves in a way that reflects the particular challenges it faces. Nevertheless, because the dimensions of global corporate citizenship are linked, they tend to become more closely aligned over time.

Assessing and Reporting Social Performance

As companies around the world expand their commitment to corporate responsibility and citizenship, they have also improved their capacity to measure performance and assess results. A **social audit** is a systematic evaluation of an organization's social, ethical, and environmental performance.[28]

In a social audit, a company's performance is evaluated relative to a set of externally imposed standards. The results of the audit are used to improve the firm's performance and to communicate with stakeholders and the public. The scholar Simon Zadek has identified six benefits of social audits. They help businesses know what is happening within their firm, understand what stakeholders think about and want from the business, tell stakeholders what the business has achieved, strengthen the loyalty and commitment of stakeholders, enhance the organization's decision making, and improve the business's overall performance.

Today, many businesses use social audits to measure the societal impact of their actions. In a world where the use of company resources must be justified, the greater the social equity documented, the stronger the argument a business can make that it is meeting its social obligations. Businesses also used their social audit results to minimize risks or capitalize on opportunities. They see the process as fostering innovation within the company. Some believe that to communicate with the organization's stakeholders in a transparent manner is simply the ethical thing to do.

Social Audit Standards

In response to the emerging efforts by governments to promote global citizenship, a number of different corporate citizenship standards have been developed that establish measures or benchmarks against which a firm's citizenship activities (or those of its suppliers or partners) can be compared in a social audit. Social audits look not only at what an organization does, but also at the results of these actions. For example, if a company supports a tutorial program at a local school, the audit might not only look at the number of hours of employee volunteerism, but also assess changes in student test scores as an indicator of the program's social impact.

Audit standards can be created in three different ways. Companies can develop standards designed to set expectations of performance for themselves or their suppliers or partners. For example, Apple developed its own supplier code of conduct. Or, companies within an industry can agree on a common industrywide standard, as several high technology companies did when they agreed on an Electronics Industry Citizenship Coalition (EICC) Code of Conduct. The EICC's attention to good corporate citizenship focused on combatting forced labor, making it a priority in 2015. The revised EICC Code prohibits the holding of passports and other key worker documents as well as unreasonable restrictions on movement and access to basic liberties, and requires that workers be provided with a written employment agreement in their native language prior to departing from their

---

[28] The concept of a social audit was first introduced in Howard R. Bowen, *Social Responsibilities of the Businessman* (New York: Harper, 1953).

Exhibit 3.D

The Global Reporting Initiative (GRI)

The GRI is based on the belief that a sustainable global economy should combine long-term profitability with ethical behavior, social justice, and environmental care. This means that when companies and organizations consider sustainability—and integrate it into how they operate—they must consider four key areas of their performance and impacts: economic, environmental, social, and governance.

GRI's Sustainability Reporting Framework is a reporting system that enables all companies and organizations to measure, understand, and communicate this information using common metrics, so performance can be compared across firms and industries. The GRI Guidelines offer an international reference for all those interested in the disclosure of the governance approach and the environmental, social, and economic performance and impacts of organizations. The GRI Guidelines are developed through a global multistakeholder process involving representatives from business, labor, civil society, and financial markets, as well as auditors and experts in various fields; and in close dialogue with regulators and governmental agencies in several countries. By 2015, nearly 7,500 organizations generated nearly 20,000 reports based on the GRI Sustainability Reporting Framework.

Source: See the Global Reporting Initiatives website at *www.globalreporting.org*.

country of origin. Both companywide and industrywide supply chain codes of conduct, as well as auditing processes, are further described in Chapter 17.

Finally, audit standards can be developed by global nongovernmental organizations or standard-setting organizations. A number of such organizations have developed standards to judge corporate performance. These include the International Organisation for Standards (ISO 14001, 14063, and 26000), Social Accountability 8000, the Institute of Social and Ethical Accountability (ISEA), AccountAbility (or AA 1000), the United Nations Global Compact, and the Global Reporting Initiative, which is profiled in Exhibit 3.D.

Social Reporting

When a company decides to publicize information collected in a social audit, this is called **corporate social reporting**. While there is a risk of incurring reputational damage from exposing any problems publicly, many companies see value in practicing **transparency**. The term *transparency* refers to a quality of complete clarity; a clear glass window, for example, is said to be transparent. When companies clearly and openly report their performance—financial, social, and environmental—to their various stakeholders, they are acting with transparency. One region where the trend toward corporate reporting and transparency has been particularly apparent in Australia and New Zealand.

In 2014, 99 percent of all Australian and New Zealand companies indicated that they would conduct an assessment of their business operations and publicly report the results that year, according to a study by the Australian Centre for Corporate Social Responsibility. They attributed their nearly unanimous preference for reporting to the International Integrated Reporting Commission's Integrated Reporting Framework and the new Global Reporting Initiative fourth generation (G4) guidelines (see Exhibit 3.D). The companies surveyed said they believed in transparent reporting because they understood it could build a reputation for responsibility, contribute to the company's brand, engage senior leadership in strategic conversations, improve stakeholder engagement, and identify opportunities for improvement. According to Victoria Whitaker, head of GRI Focal Point Australia, "businesses around the world are recognizing that reporting can help them understand the

FIGURE 3.6
Trends in Corporate Social Reporting, 1993–2013

Source: *KPMG International Corporate Responsibility Reporting Survey 2013 at www.kpmg.com.*

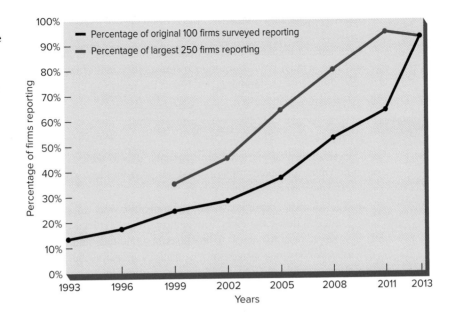

context in which they operate and the stakeholders whom they serve. Done well it informs corporate strategy and decision making."[29]

A survey of business firms by KPMG, an accounting and consulting firm, showed a steep increase in corporate social reporting in recent years, as shown in Figure 3.6.

The 2013 KPMG report declared, "The debate is over. Companies should no longer ask whether or not they should publish a CR [corporate responsibility] report. The high rates of CR reporting in all regions suggest it is now standard business practice worldwide. The leaders of N100 or G250 companies that still do not publish CR reports should ask themselves whether it benefits them to continue swimming against the tide or whether it puts them at risk." Seventy-eight percent of reporting companies worldwide referred to the GRI reporting guidelines (see Exhibit 3.D) in their CR reports, a rise of 9 percentage points since the 2011 survey (over 90 percent do so in South Korea, South Africa, Portugal, Chile, Brazil, and Sweden).[30]

An emerging trend in corporate reporting is the integration of legally required financial information with social and environmental information into a single **integrated report**. In 2013, a majority of companies (51 percent) included information of corporate responsibility in their annual financial reports. This reflected a dramatic rise in integrated reporting, from 8 percent in 2008 and 20 percent in 2011.[31]

Why do companies publish social responsibility reports? According to one study, most firms (80 percent) are motivated by ethical concerns. Ethical drivers replaced economic considerations (80 percent versus 50 percent) as the primary motivator for publishing these reports, a complete reverse from a few years ago when economic considerations were viewed as the most important. Nearly two-thirds of the 250 firms worldwide reported

---

[29] Information from "The 10th Year-Progress and Prospects for CSR in Australia and New Zealand," *Australian Centre for Corporate Social Responsibility,* 2014.

[30] See *The KPMG Survey of Corporate Social Reporting 2013* at *www.kpmg.com.*

[31] KPMG report 2013, *Ibid.*

that they engaged with their stakeholders in a structured way, up from 33 percent a decade earlier.[32]

In today's business climate, multiple stakeholders demand that businesses adopt measureable standards for corporate responsibility and citizenship, audit their organizations according to these standards, and report the results to the public.

Summary

- The world's largest corporations are capable of wielding tremendous influence, at times even more than national governments, due to their economic power. Because of this potential influence, the organizations' stakeholders expect businesses to enhance society when exercising their power.

- The idea of corporate social responsibility was adopted by business leaders in the United States in the early 20th century. It has evolved from a notion of stewardship and strategic responsiveness to an ethics-based understanding found in culture and the practice of corporate citizenship. Socially responsible businesses attempt to balance economic, legal, and social obligations. Following an enlightened self-interest approach, a firm may be economically rewarded while society benefits from the firm's actions.

- Corporate social responsibility is a debatable notion. Some argue that its benefits include discouraging government regulation, promoting long-term profitability for the firm, and enhancing the company's stakeholder relationships and business reputation. Others believe that it lowers efficiency, imposes undue costs, and shifts unnecessary obligations to business. Most executives believe that they should use their corporate power and influence to balance their response to multiple stakeholders rather than maximize stockholders' return alone.

- Global corporate citizenship refers to putting a commitment to serving various stakeholders into practice by building stakeholder partnerships, discovering business opportunities in serving society, and transforming a concern for financial performance into a vision of integrated financial *and* social performance worldwide. Global corporate citizenship programs can be considered a strategic investment by the firm.

- Companies progress through five distinct stages as they develop as global corporate citizens; these are termed the elementary, engaged, innovative, integrated, and transforming stages. A particular company may be at more than one stage at once, as it may be progressing more quickly on some dimensions than on others.

- Many companies have created systemic audits of their social, ethical, and environmental performance, measured against industrywide performance expectations as well as auditing standards developed by global standard-setting organizations. An emerging trend is the practice of communicating social, environmental, and financial results to stakeholders through an integrated corporate report.

[32]"Socially Responsible Investment Analysts Find More Large U.S. Companies Reporting on Social and Environmental Issues," Social Investment Research Analysts Network Report, *www.kld.com*.

Key Terms

B Corporation, *58*	corporate social responsibility, *48*	iron law of responsibility, *48*
corporate citizenship, *49*	enlightened self-interest, *52*	reputation, *55*
corporate power, *47*	integrated reporting, *65*	social audit, *63*
corporate social reporting, *64*		transparency, *64*

**Internet
Resources**

www.bsr.org	BSR: The business of a better world
www.businessinsociety.eu	The Business in Society Gateway
www.csr-search.net	CSR News
www.csrwire.com	The Corporate Social Responsibility Newswire
www.corporateresponsibility.net	Corporate Responsibility.Net
www.thecro.com	Corporate Responsibility Magazine
www.globalreporting.org	Global Reporting Initiative
www.unglobalcompact.org	United Nations Global Compact

Discussion Case: *Corporate Social Responsibility at Gravity Payments*

Dan Price, the founder of Gravity Payments, a small, privately owned company that provided high-service and low-cost credit card processing, surprised his 120-person staff when he announced that over the next three years he would raise the salary of all employees, even the lowest paid clerk, customer service representative, and salesperson, to a minimum of $70,000. The average annual salary at that time at Gravity was around $48,000, so the increase would nearly double some employees' salaries. Price explained that he would pay for the wage increases by cutting his own salary from nearly $1 million to $70,000 and using 75 to 80 percent of the company's anticipated $2.2 million in profit.

Price's announcement was met with mixed reactions. Some employees were thrilled, clapping and whooping when they heard the announcement. "I'm freaking out," said one employee. But, others—many from the financial services community—said that this was just a costly publicity stunt.

Price was no stranger to the spotlight. He earned the honor of Entrepreneur of the Year in 2014 from *Enterprise Magazine. GeekWire* named Price its Young Entrepreneur of the Year in 2013, and in 2010 he received the Small Business Administration's National Young Entrepreneur of the Year award. When asked about his recent awards, Price said, "I'm looking at this not as any kind of end result to celebrate, but more just a stepping stone to get our ultimate goal, which is to level the playing field and make payments and financial services and business services fair for independent business owners." Price also annually donated 10 percent of Gravity's profits to charity. The equitable employee salary announcement seemed like another step toward achieving Price's goals as a business owner.

Price launched Gravity (a name, Price explained, that was selected because "you could understand [it] on the phone") while attending college, but the firm actually grew out of a technology consulting business he created while in high school. His goal was to manage credit card transactions for small businesses, like coffeehouses, in a more affordable and transparent way. "I never intended to make a lot of money, or really any," said Price. "I was really upset at this industry for the way they were treating my [consulting] clients, and I just wanted to blow the thing up. So I was like, 'I'm going to charge a third of what everyone [else does].'"

Financial analysts recognized Gravity Payments' success; his company processed nearly $10 billion in credit card transactions and generated revenues of about $150 million annually. When asked why he did not "cash out," Price responded, "I'll ask my friends who have sold their businesses, 'Did that business get to the goal that you originally had in mind?' And they're all happy they sold because of the phenomenal financial outcome. But when I ask them, 'Did you actually accomplish the nonfinancial goal that you set out in starting a business?' . . . they almost all say no."

Price encountered hard times in 2008 when Gravity lost 20 percent of its revenue nearly overnight because customers were running less volume through the system during the economic recession. Price recalled that half of his staff was in his office asking for raises and the other half was definitely afraid they were going to lose their jobs. So, he called his employees together and explained that the company had eight months of cash in the bank. "If we hold our expenses steady and just sell the same amount every month for five months, we'll get back to break-even and not have to do any benefit cuts, any layoffs, anything like that," he told his staff. Given Price's response during the economically challenging times, it did not surprise his employees when he took the bold move of promising every employee a salary of $70,000 annually.

Price's commitment to a new company minimum wage captured national attention given the soaring disparity between executives' pay and that of their employees. In the United States, where the pay gap was the greatest for any country, chief executives earned more than 300 times what the average worker made (as discussed in more detail in Chapter 13). Some people, like Gilded Age's executive J. Pierpont Morgan and management scholar Peter Drucker, advocated a 20-to-1 executive to average employee ratio. Price's 1-to-1 ratio was unprecedented in the business community. "The market rate for me as a CEO compared to a regular person is ridiculous, it's absurd," explained Price, who admitted that his only main extravagances were snowboarding and picking up the bar bill for his friends. He drove a 12-year-old Audi, which he received in a barter for service from the local dealer. "As much as I'm a capitalist, there is nothing in the market that is making me do it," said Price, referring to paying wages that would make it possible for his employees "to go after their own American dream, buy a house and pay for their children's education." After the passage of the Dodd-Frank Act in 2010, the Securities and Exchange Commission was supposed to require all publicly held companies to disclose the ratio of CEO pay to the median pay of all other employees, but as of 2015 this legislative rule has not been put into effect. Corporate executives vigorously oppose this rule, complaining that it would be cumbersome and costly to implement.

Price admitted that hearing his employees' problems with making ends meet on wages that were well above the $7.50 per hour minimum wage or even at $40,000 a year "just eats at me inside." He wanted to address the social issue of wage inequality and felt that as a business leader he was in a position to do something, but he wanted to do something that would not result in raising prices for his customers or cutting back on services. Hayley Vogt, a 24-year-old communications coordinator at Gravity who earned $45,000 annually, said, "I'm completely blown away right now [after hearing Price's announcement]." She said she had worried about covering rent increases and a recent emergency room bill. "Everyone is talking about this $15 minimum wage in Seattle and it's nice to work someplace where someone is actually doing something about it and not just talking about it."

Sources: "Gravity Payments CEO Dan Price Named 'Entrepreneur of 2014' by Enterprise Magazine," *GeekWire*, December 17, 2014, *www.geekwire.com*; and, "One Company's New Minimum Wage: $70,000 a Year," *The New York Times*, April 13, 2015, *www.nytimes.com*.

Discussion Questions

1. Is Price demonstrating elements of corporate social responsibility by his actions in this case, or not?

2. What principles of corporate citizenship (using Exhibit 3.A) are evident in this case?

3. What arguments for and against corporate social responsibility (referring to Figure 3.3) are relevant to this case?

4. Is Price acting like an executive of a firm that could be certified as a B Corporation?

5. What stage of global corporate citizenship (using Figure 3.5) is Gravity Payments operating at, and why do you think so?

CHAPTER FOUR

Business in a Globalized World

The world economy has become increasingly integrated, and many businesses have extended their reach beyond national borders. Yet the process of globalization is controversial, and the involvement of corporations in other nations is not always welcome. Doing business in diverse political and economic systems and in societies with stark differences in wealth and income poses difficult challenges. When a transnational corporation buys resources, manufactures products, or sells goods and services in multiple countries, it is inevitably drawn into a web of global social and ethical issues. Understanding what these issues are and how to manage them through collaborative action with governments and civil society organizations is a vital skill for today's managers.

This Chapter Focuses on These Key Learning Objectives:

LO 4-1   Defining globalization and classifying the major ways in which companies enter the global marketplace.

LO 4-2   Identifying the international financial and trade institutions that have shaped the globalization process in recent decades.

LO 4-3   Analyzing the benefits and costs of the globalization of business.

LO 4-4   Identifying the major types of political and economic systems in which companies operate across the world.

LO 4-5   Understanding global inequalities of wealth and income and analyzing the special challenges of serving those at the "bottom of the pyramid."

LO 4-6   Assessing how businesses can work collaboratively with governments and the civil sector to address global social issues.

In 2015, Newmont Mining Corp.'s plans to begin production at a major gold and copper project in Peru seemed stalled indefinitely. Since 1993, in partnership with the World Bank's International Finance Corporation, Newmont had operated three open-pit gold mines high in the Andes Mountains, six miles from the city of Cajamarca. The company planned to develop a new surface mine about 15 miles away, to be called Minas Conga, in what would be Peru's biggest-ever mining operation. In 2011, the company's board of directors approved funding for the $4.8 billion project, which was scheduled to begin production in 2015. But violent protests broke out, involving thousands of local residents concerned that the new mine would require draining four natural lakes, drying up and polluting the community's water supplies. Newmont then suspended the project, saying it could not proceed without "tranquility and social peace," and noting that its global portfolio enabled it to consider alternative development sites in Ghana, Canada, Indonesia, and elsewhere. If it went forward, the Minas Conga project would employ five to seven thousand workers during its construction, in a nation that was home to 8 million people who lived in extreme poverty. In the 2010s, mining provided 60 percent of Peru's exports and 30 percent of its tax revenue. The re-election of an opponent of Minas Conga as president of the region in 2014, however, showed that the local population remained solidly against the mining development.[1]

This complex episode captures much of the turmoil and controversy that surrounds the globalization of business and its far-reaching social impacts. We live in a world that seems increasingly small, more connected, and highly interdependent. It is a world in which transnational companies such as Newmont Mining often bring much-needed technical know-how, capital, managerial experience, and jobs to poorer nations deeply in need of them. Yet, in this instance, the company failed to navigate opposition from government officials and civil society. How companies can best deal with the difficult challenges of doing business in a global world of great complexity is the subject of this chapter. It will also examine the respective roles of businesses, civil society organizations, and governments in addressing common global problems.

The Process of Globalization

Globalization refers to the increasing movement of goods, services, and capital across national borders. Globalization is a *process,* that is, an ongoing series of interrelated events. International trade and financial flows integrate the world economy, leading to the spread of technology, culture, and politics. Thomas Friedman, a columnist for *The New York Times* and a well-known commentator, has described globalization as a *system* with its own internal logic:

> Globalization is not simply a trend or a fad but is, rather, an international system. It is the system that has now replaced the old Cold War system, and, like that Cold War system, globalization has its own rules and logic that today directly or indirectly influence the politics, environment, geopolitics, and economics of virtually every country in the world.[2]

The process of globalization is so pervasive that it affects all businesses—whether they are small or large, local or multinational, or an employer of one or many.

---

[1] "Peruvian Voters Favor Anti-Mining Candidates," *The Wall Street Journal,* October 6, 2014; "Peru's Conga Mine Conflict: Cajamarca Won't Capitulate," May 1, 2014, *http://upsidedownworld.org;* and *www.newmont.com/south-america.*

[2] Thomas L. Friedman, *The Lexus and the Olive Tree* (New York: Anchor Books, 2000), p. ix.

Firms can enter and compete in the global marketplace in several ways. Many companies first build a successful business in their home country, and then export their products or services to buyers in other countries. In other words, they develop *global market channels* for their products. Nestlé, for example, began in Switzerland, but now sells its food and beverage products all over the world. Other firms begin in their home country, but realize that they can cut costs by locating some or all of their *global operations* in another country. This decision leads to establishing manufacturing plants or service operations abroad. For example, the Ford Motor Company's Fusion is manufactured in Mexico, its Mondeo in Taiwan, and its Transit Connect vans in Turkey and Romania. BMW, which is headquartered in Germany, has manufacturing facilities in 14 countries, including Brazil, Thailand, Egypt, Indonesia, and the United States. Finally, a third strategy involves subcontracting manufacturing to suppliers located abroad. In other words, these companies develop *global supply chains.* For example, in the apparel and shoe industries, companies such as Nike, Gap, and Abercrombie & Fitch have extensive networks of suppliers outside the United States—mostly in Asia—that make products of their design. Suppliers and their relationship to lead firms are further discussed in Chapter 17.

These three strategies of globalization can be summarized in three words: *sell, make,* and *source.* Today, many companies have all three elements of global business—market channels, manufacturing operations, and supply chains.

Major Transnational Corporations

According to United Nations estimates, there are almost 104,000 **transnational corporations (TNCs)** operating in the modern global economy (defined by the United Nations as firms that control assets abroad). These corporations, in turn, have about 9 times that number of *affiliates,* meaning suppliers, subcontractors, retailers, and other entities with which they have some business relationship. These affiliates collectively produce more than 10 percent of global gross domestic product (GDP) and employ 80 million workers.[3] The interconnectedness of the world's businesses is a major reason why the financial crisis that started in 2008 spread so quickly to almost all corners of the globe.

Although many firms conduct business across national boundaries, most global commerce is carried out by a small number of powerful firms. (Corporate power is further discussed in Chapter 3.) Who are these leading transnational corporations? Figure 4.1 lists the top 10 nonfinancial transnational corporations, ranked in order of the value of the foreign assets they control. Leading the list is General Electric, the American electrical equipment and electronics conglomerate. Rounding out the group are several of the world's leading oil companies, automakers, and a telecommunications firm.[4] The world's major financial institutions also extend across the globe; four of the five largest banks in the world, ranked by assets, are in China.[5] JP Morgan Chase, the largest U.S.-based bank, operates in more than 60 countries.

Although much of global commerce is carried out by a small number of large firms, globalization affects almost all businesses, whatever their size and reach. Even small, local firms use products and services that originate abroad, and they often compete with other businesses from around the world.

---

[3] United Nations Conference on Trade and Development, *World Investment Report 2011,* Web Table 34, *www.unctad.org.* Data are for 2010.

[4] United Nations Conference on Trade and Development, *World Investment Report 2014,* Web Table 298, *www.unctad.org.* Data are for 2013.

[5] "Bank Rankings: Top Banks in the World," *www.accuity.com.* Data are as of November, 2014.

FIGURE 4.1
The World's Top 10 Nonfinancial Transnational Corporations, Ranked by Foreign Assets

Source: United Nations, "The World's Top 100 Non-Financial TNCs, Ranked by Foreign Assets, 2013," *www.unctad.org.* All data are for the year 2013.

Corporation	Home Economy	Industry	Foreign Assets (in $ millions)
General Electric	United States	Electrical equipment	$331,160
Royal Dutch Shell	United Kingdom	Petroleum	301,898
Toyota Motor	Japan	Motor vehicles	274,380
ExxonMobil	United States	Petroleum	231,033
Total	France	Petroleum	226,717
BP	United Kingdom	Petroleum	202,899
Vodafone	United Kingdom	Telecommunications	182,837
Volkswagen Group	Germany	Motor vehicles	176,656
Chevron	United States	Petroleum	175,736
Eni S.p.A.	Italy	Petroleum	141,021

Another important aspect of globalization is the worldwide flow of capital. **Foreign direct investment (FDI)** occurs when a company, individual, or fund invests money in another country, for example, by buying shares of stock in or loaning money to a foreign firm. The world economy is increasingly bound together by such cross-border flows of capital. In 2013, FDI was $1.45 trillion, up somewhat from the previous year but still below its pre-crisis average.[6] An emerging trend in foreign direct investment is the rise of *sovereign wealth funds.* These are funds operated by governments to invest their foreign currency reserves. They are most commonly operated by nations that export large amounts of oil and manufactured goods; the largest are run by Norway, the United Arab Emirates (Abu Dhabi), China, Kuwait, and Singapore. In recent years, sovereign wealth funds have made significant cross-border investments.

One aspect of globalization that has received recent attention is the effort of some companies to avoid taxes in their home countries by merging with companies located in other countries and shifting their headquarters there. This phenomenon, known as *inversion,* is profiled in Exhibit 4.A.

International Financial and Trade Institutions

Global commerce is carried out in the context of a set of important **international financial and trade institutions (IFTIs)**. The most important of these are the World Bank, the International Monetary Fund, and the World Trade Organization. By setting the rules by which international commerce is transacted, these institutions increasingly determine who wins and who loses in the global economy.

The **World Bank (WB)** was set up in 1944, near the end of World War II, to provide economic development loans to its member nations. Its main motivation at that time was to help rebuild the war-torn economies of Europe. Today, the World Bank is one of the world's largest sources of economic development assistance; it provided almost $66 billion in loans, grants, equity investments and guarantees in 2014 for roads, dams, power plants, and other infrastructure projects, as well as for education, health, and social services. The bank gets its funds from dues paid by its member countries and from money it borrows in the international capital markets. Representation on the bank's governing board is based on economic power; that is, countries have voting power based on the size of their economies. Not surprisingly, the United States and other rich nations dominate the bank.

[6] UNCTAD, *World Investment Report 2014, www.unctad.org.*

Exhibit 4.A

Globalization to Cut the Tax Bill

Businesses today increasingly operate across international boundaries. But they are taxed by national governments. This reality gives rise to *inversion:* a strategy of acquiring or merging with a foreign firm in order to reduce corporate tax obligations at home. For example, in 2014 Burger King (based in the United States) acquired Tim Horton's, a Canadian coffee-and-donut chain, for $11.5 billion. After the acquisition, Burger King reincorporated in Canada and renamed itself Restaurant Brands International. According to a study by Americans for Tax Fairness, the maneuver could save the company $275 million in U.S. taxes between 2015 and 2018.

How does inversion work? By law, the U.S. corporate tax rate is 35 percent, while it is lower in many other industrial countries. (To cite just a few examples, the rate is 26.5 percent in Canada, 21 percent in the United Kingdom, and 12.5 percent in Ireland.) Companies that merge with a foreign firm can take advantage of this difference by stashing cash abroad, loading up their U.S. subsidiary with debt, buying stock internally, and other complex arrangements that enable them to avoid paying taxes on their earnings at the higher U.S. rate.

Between the 1980s, when the technique was first used, about 50 inversions have taken place—but the pace picked up in the 2010s, with half of all inversions occurring since the 2008–09 financial crisis. In response, the U.S. Department of the Treasury announced new rules in 2014 that would make inversions less attractive going forward, but would not affect companies that had already completed their mergers. In the wake of these rules, several inversions that were underway—including drugmaker AbbVie's $54 billion acquisition of Ireland's Shire—collapsed.

Some companies realized that whatever the tax benefits, inversion could hurt their public image and offend customers. Walgreen's, the drugstore chain, backed off from an inversion in 2014 after public pushback, including a letter from a U.S. senator that warned that the company's customers were "deeply patriotic and will not support Walgreen's decision to turn its back on the United States." In announcing its change of plans, Walgreen's noted that it was "mindful of the ongoing public reaction to a potential inversion" and "its unique role as an iconic American retailer."

Sources: "Walgreen Turns Down Inversion to Cut Tax Bill," *The New York Times,* August 6, 2014; "New Corporate Tax Shelter: A Merger Abroad," *The New York Times,* October 8, 2014; "AbbVie, Shire Terminate Year's Biggest Deal," *The Wall Street Journal,* October 20, 2014; and Americans for Tax Fairness, "A Whopper of a Tax Dodge: How Burger King's Inversion Could Shortchange America," December, 2014.

The World Bank's sister organization is the **International Monetary Fund (IMF)**. Founded at the same time as the bank (and today residing across the street from it in Washington, DC), the IMF has a somewhat narrower purpose: to stabilize the system of currency exchange rates and international payments to enable member countries to participate in global trade. It does this by lending foreign exchange to member countries. Like the World Bank, the IMF sometimes imposes strict conditions on governments that receive its loans. These conditions may include demands that governments cut spending, devalue their currencies, increase exports, liberalize financial markets, and reduce wages. These conditions often lead to hardship.

One country that was particularly hard hit by loan conditions was Greece, one of the poorest nations in the European Union. Beginning in 2010, the IMF, the European Central Bank, and several European countries made a series of multibillion-dollar loans to Greece to enable it to pay its bills and service its debts. In exchange, the lenders imposed severe conditions, including sharp cuts in government spending and the sale of public assets. The Greek economy shrank by a quarter, the unemployment rate rose to 27 percent, and half its young people were thrown out of work. Public pensions and salaries were slashed. The Greek people voted in a new government whose candidates had called the austerity measures

Exhibit 4.B

Vulture Funds and Heavily Indebted Nations

A "vulture fund" is a private equity fund (also called a hedge fund) that buys the debt of weak companies or heavily indebted countries with the intention of making a profit. (The term analogizes these investors to vultures, birds of prey that feed on dead or dying animals.) For example, when Argentina defaulted on about $81 billion of loans in 2001, a hedge fund called Elliott Management bought some of these defaulted loans at a deep discount. It then sued, demanding that Argentina pay back the loans at full face value with interest—about $1.3 billion, much more than it had paid. In 2012, a U.S. judge ruled in favor of the hedge fund—and said that until Argentina paid what it owed to Elliott Management, it was barred from paying *any* of its creditors (who had already agreed to accept less). In 2014, talks to settle the matter collapsed. Both the IMF and the World Bank said that the behavior of vulture funds like Elliott Management threatened the financial recovery of fragile economies. "When vulture funds sue for such exorbitant amounts, it's clearly taking away money that should be invested in health, education, infrastructure, and other social problems, and goes to line the pockets of already wealthy investors," said a representative of the nongovernmental organization (NGO) Africa Action.

Sources: "Argentina Finds Relentless Foe in Paul Singer's Hedge Fund," *The New York Times,* July 30, 2014; "Vulture Funds Prey on Poor Debtor Nations," *Inter Press Service (Johannesburg, South Africa),* August 19, 2009; and *Jubilee Network,* "Vulture Funds," *www.jubileeusa.org/ourwork/vulturefunds.*

"waterboarding" and advocated for a restructuring of the country's debt. In 2015, Greece narrowly avoided default after agreeing to another round of budget cuts and tax increases in exchange for additional aid.[7]

Significant progress has been made to reduce indebtedness by poor countries. By the mid-2000s, many developing countries had accumulated huge debts to the World Bank, the IMF, and other lenders. The total amount of money owed was almost $3 trillion. One of the unintended consequences of past loans was persistent poverty, because a large share of many nations' earnings went to pay off debt rather than to develop the economy or improve the lives of citizens. In response, many industrialized nations extended aid to heavily indebted countries to enable them to pay down loans to the World Bank, IMG, and other lenders. By 2014, more than $75 billion in **debt relief** had been extended to 35 heavily indebted countries, significantly reducing these nations' payments and enabling them to direct more resources to alleviating poverty.[8]

However, problems remained. Poor countries still owed billions more, and the world financial crisis weakened their ability to pay—and the ability of developed countries to offer aid. And, so-called *vulture funds* sought to take advantage of the indebted countries, a situation that is profiled in Exhibit 4.B.

The final member of the triumvirate of IFTIs is the **World Trade Organization (WTO)**. The WTO, founded in 1995 as a successor to the General Agreement on Tariffs and Trade (GATT), is an international body that establishes the ground rules for trade among nations. Most of the world's nations are members of the WTO, which is based in Switzerland. Its major objective is to promote free trade; that is, to eliminate barriers to trade among nations, such as quotas, duties, and tariffs. Unlike the WB and the IMF, the WTO does not lend money or foreign exchange; it simply sets the rules for international trade. The WTO conducts multiyear negotiations, called *rounds,* on various trade-related topics, rotating its

[7] "Greece's Debt Crisis Explained," *The New York Times,* [updated] September 21, 2015; "Greece's Agonized Cry to Europe," *The New York Times,* January 26, 2015; and Lionel Reynolds, "The Greek Economic Crisis, the Social Impacts of Austerity, and Debunking the Myths," February 13, 2015, *www.globalresearch.ca.*

[8] "Heavily Indebted Poor Countries Initiative and Multilateral Debt Relief Initiative, Statistical Update," *www.img.org,* December 2014.

meetings among different cities. The most recent negotiations, conducted in Bali, Indonesia, in 2013, reduced import tariffs and agricultural subsidies.

Under the WTO's most favored nation rule, member countries may not discriminate against foreign products for any reason. All import restrictions are illegal unless proven scientifically, for example, on the basis that a product is unsafe. If countries disagree about the interpretation of this or any other WTO rule, they can bring a complaint before the WTO's Dispute Settlement Body (DSB), a panel of appointed experts, which meets behind closed doors. For example, China complained to the DSB that India had tried to ban imports of Chinese toys to protect its own toy industry, a possible violation of WTO rules.[9] Usually, member countries comply voluntarily with the DSB's rulings. If they do not, the DSB can allow the aggrieved nation to take retaliatory measures, such as imposing tariffs. Rulings are binding; the only way a decision can be overruled is if every member country opposes it.

These three international financial and trade institutions are important because no business can operate across national boundaries without complying with the rules set by the WTO, and many businesses in the developing world are dependent on World Bank and IMF loans for their very lifeblood. The policies these institutions adopt, therefore, have much to do with whether or not globalization is perceived as a positive or negative force, a subject to which we turn next.

The Benefits and Costs of Globalization

Globalization has both benefits and costs, and not all countries and stakeholders are affected equally. In this section, we present some of the arguments advanced by both sides in the debate over this important issue.

Benefits of Globalization

Proponents of globalization point to its many benefits. One of the most important of these is that globalization tends to increase economic productivity. That means, simply, that more is produced with the same effort.

Why should that be? As the economist David Ricardo first pointed out, productivity rises more quickly when countries produce goods and services for which they have a natural talent. He called this the *theory of comparative advantage*. Suppose, for example, that one country had a climate and terrain ideally suited for raising sheep, giving it an advantage in the production of wool and woolen goods. A second country had a favorable combination of iron, coal, and water power that allowed it to produce high-grade steel. The first country would benefit from trading its woolen goods for the second country's steel, and vice versa; and the world's economy overall would be more productive than if both countries had tried to make everything they needed for themselves. In other words, in the context of free trade, specialization (everyone does what they are best at) makes the world economy as a whole more efficient, so living standards rise.

> Many countries today have developed a specialization in one or another skill or industry. India, with its excellent system of technical education, has become a world powerhouse in the production of software engineers. China has become expert in electronics manufacturing. France and Italy, with their strong networks of skilled craftspeople and designers, are acknowledged leaders in the world's high fashion and footwear design industries. The United States, with its concentration of actors, directors, special effects experts, and screenwriters, is the global headquarters for the movie industry.

[9] Information about this and other cases heard by the Dispute Settlement Body is available at *www.wto.org*.

Comparative advantage can come from a number of possible sources, including natural resources; the skills, education, or experience of a critical mass of people; or an existing production infrastructure.

Globalization also tends to reduce prices for consumers. If a shopper in the United States goes into Walmart to buy a shirt, he or she is likely to find one at a very reasonable price. Walmart sources its apparel from all over the world, enabling it to push down production costs. Globalization also benefits consumers by giving them access to a wide range of diverse goods and the latest "big thing." Teenagers in Malaysia can enjoy the latest Johnny Depp or Will Smith movie, while American children can play with new Nintendo Wii games from Japan.

For the developing world, globalization also brings benefits. It helps entrepreneurs the world over by giving all countries access to foreign investment funds to support economic development. Globalization also transfers technology. In a competitive world marketplace, the best ideas and newest innovations spread quickly. Multinational corporations train their employees and partners how to make the fastest computer chips, the most productive food crops, and the most efficient light bulbs. In many nations of the developing world, globalization has meant more manufacturing jobs in export sectors and training for workers eager to enhance their skills.

The futurist Allen Hammond identifies two additional benefits of globalization. First, he says that world trade has the potential of supporting the spread of democracy and freedom.

> The very nature of economic activity in free markets . . . requires broad access to information, the spread of competence, and the exercise of individual decision making throughout the workforce—conditions that are more compatible with free societies and democratic forms of government than with authoritarian regimes.[10]

Second, according to Hammond, global commerce can reduce military conflict by acting as a force that binds disparate peoples together on the common ground of business interaction. "Nations that once competed for territorial dominance," he writes, "will now compete for market share, with money that once supported military forces invested in new ports, telecommunications, and other infrastructure." In this view, global business can become both a stabilizing force and a conduit for Western ideas about democracy and freedom.

Costs of Globalization

If globalization has all these benefits, why are so many individuals and organizations so critical of it? The answer is complex. Just as some gain from globalization, others are hurt by it. From the perspective of its victims, globalization does not look nearly so attractive.

One of the costs of globalization is job insecurity. As businesses move manufacturing across national borders in search of cheaper labor, workers at home are laid off. Jobs in the domestic economy are lost as imports replace homemade goods and services. In the American South, for example, tens of thousands of jobs in the textile industry have been lost, as jobs have shifted to low-labor cost areas of the world, leaving whole communities devastated. In the past, mainly manufacturing was affected by the shift of jobs abroad; more recently, clerical, white-collar, and professional jobs have also been "offshored." Many customer service calls originating in the United States are now answered by operators in the Philippines and India. The back office operations of many banks—sorting and recording check transactions, for example—are done in India and China. Aircraft manufacturers are using aeronautical specialists in Russia to design parts for new planes. Economists have estimated that around one in four jobs in the United States may be potentially

[10] Allen Hammond, *Which World? Scenarios for the 21st Century* (Washington, DC: Island Press, 1998), p. 30.

"offshorable."[11] Even when jobs are not actually relocated, wages may be driven down because companies facing foreign competition try to keep their costs in check. Much of the opposition to globalization in affluent nations comes from people who feel their own jobs, pay, and livelihoods threatened by workers abroad who can do their work more cheaply.

> Some evidence suggests a countertrend, as some companies have moved production back to the United States—in part, as a way to gain greater control over the supply chain. Wages have increased in China and many other developing nations, while wages gains in the United States have stagnated. Productivity is considerably higher in the United States than in China. And, small businesses in particular have found that solving everyday production problems with a contractor halfway around the globe can be daunting. "If we have an issue in manufacturing, in America we can walk down to the plant floor," explained the founder of a business that made emergency lights for homeowners. "We can't do that in China." The company had recently relocated production from China to a facility near its headquarters in California.[12]

Not only workers in rich countries are affected by globalization. When workers in Indonesia began organizing for higher wages, Nike Corporation moved much of its production to Vietnam and China. Many Indonesian workers lost their jobs. Some call this feature of global capitalism the **race to the bottom**.

Another cost of globalization is that environmental and labor standards may be weakened as companies seek manufacturing sites where regulations are most lax. Just as companies may desire locations offering the cheapest labor, they may also search for locations with few environmental protections; weak regulation of occupational health and safety, hours of work, and discrimination; and few rights for unions. For example, the so-called gold coast of southeastern China has become a world manufacturing center for many products, including electronics and toys. An undercover team investigating conditions there found that many workers were paid up to a month late, were expected to work with dangerous machines without training or safety equipment, and were fined for using the toilet without permission.[13] Low wages, long hours, and weak health and safety and environmental regulations—and lax enforcement of the laws that do exist—are a major draw for the companies that manufacture in factories in China's industrial zones.

A related concern is that the World Trade Organization's most favored nation rules make it difficult for individual nations to adopt policies promoting environmental or social objectives, if these have the effect of discriminating against products from another country.

> For example, the United States banned the importation of Indonesian clove cigarettes, saying that the sweet-flavored cigarettes attracted younger smokers, drawing them into nicotine addiction and violating U.S. tobacco control laws. Indonesia brought a complaint before the WTO's dispute settlement body. In 2012, the WTO ruled in Indonesia's favor, saying that because the United States permitted the sale of another flavored cigarette—menthols—it had acted in a discriminatory way by excluding Indonesian clove cigarettes. The dispute was finally settled in 2014, after Indonesia agreed to the ban in exchange for other concessions from the United States.[14]

---

[11] "Offshoring (or Offshore Outsourcing) and Job Loss among U.S. Workers," *Congressional Research Service,* January 21, 2011.

[12] "Small U.S. Manufacturers Give Up on 'Made in China,'" *Bloomberg Businessweek,* June 21, 2012.

[13] "Revealed: True Cost of the Christmas Toys We Buy from China's Factories, *The Observer [London],* December 3, 2011.

[14] "U.S., Indonesia Settle Fight over Clove Cigarettes," *The Hill,* October 3, 2014. Details on this and other cases before the WTO's dispute settlement body are available at *www.wto.org.*

FIGURE 4.2
Benefits and Costs of
Globalization

Benefits of Globalization	Costs of Globalization
Increases economic productivity.	Causes job insecurity.
Reduces prices for consumers.	Weakens environmental and labor standards.
Gives developing countries access to foreign investment funds to support economic development.	Prevents individual nations from adopting policies promoting environmental or social objectives, if these discriminate against products from another country.
Transfers technology.	Erodes regional and national cultures and undermines cultural, linguistic, and religious diversity.
Spreads democracy and freedom, and reduces military conflict.	Is compatible with despotism.

Critics of globalization say that incidents such as this one show that free trade rules are being used to restrict the right of sovereign nations to make their own laws setting health or environmental standards for imported products.

Another cost of globalization is that it erodes regional and national cultures and undermines cultural, linguistic, and religious diversity. In other words, global commerce makes us all very much the same. Is a world in which everyone is drinking Coke, watching Hollywood movies, texting on an iPhone, and wearing Gap jeans a world we want, or not? Some have argued that the deep **anti-Americanism** present in many parts of the world reflects resentment at the penetration of the values of dominant U.S.–based transnational corporations into every corner of the world.

With respect to the point that globalization promotes democracy, critics charge that market capitalism is just as compatible with despotism as it is with freedom. Indeed, transnational corporations are often drawn to nations that are governed by antidemocratic or military regimes, because they are so effective at controlling labor and blocking efforts to protect the environment. For example, Unocal's joint-venture collaboration to build a gas pipeline with the military government of Myanmar (Burma), a notorious abuser of human rights, may have brought significant financial benefits to the petroleum company.

Figure 4.2 summarizes the major points in the discussion about the costs and benefits of globalization.

This discussion raises the very real possibility that globalization may benefit the world economy as a whole, while simultaneously hurting many individuals and localities. An ongoing challenge to business, government, and society is to find ways to extend the benefits of globalization to all, while mitigating its adverse effects.[15]

Doing Business in a Diverse World

Doing business in other nations is much more than a step across a geographical boundary; it is a step into different social, political, cultural, and economic realities. As shown in Chapters 1, 2, and 3, even businesses operating in one community or one nation cannot function successfully without considering a wide variety of stakeholder needs and

[15] For arguments for and against globalization, and on strategies to make the world's governing institutions more effective, see Jagdish Bhagwati, *In Defense of Globalization* (New York: Oxford University Press, 2007); and Joseph E. Stiglitz, *Making Globalization Work* (New York: W.W. Norton, 2007).

interests. When companies operate globally, the number of stakeholders to be considered in decision making, and the diversity of their interests, increases dramatically.

Comparative Political and Economic Systems

The many nations of the world differ greatly in their political, social, and economic systems. One important dimension of this diversity is how power is exercised, that is, the degree to which a nation's people may freely exercise their democratic rights. **Democracy** refers broadly to the presence of political freedom. Arthur Lewis, a Nobel laureate in economics, described it this way: "The primary meaning of democracy is that all who are affected by a decision should have the right to participate in making that decision, either directly or through chosen representatives." According to the United Nations, democracy has four defining features:[16]

- Fair elections, in which citizens may freely choose their leaders from among candidates representing more than one political party.
- An independent media, in which journalists and citizens may express their political views without fear of censorship or punishment.
- Separation of powers among the executive, legislative, and judicial branches of government.
- An open society where citizens have the right to form their own independent organizations to pursue social, religious, and cultural goals.

One of the truly remarkable facts about the past century has been the spread of democratic rights for the first time to many nations around the world. Consider, for example, that at the beginning of the 20th century *no* country in the world had universal suffrage (all citizens can vote); today, the majority of countries do. One hundred and forty of the world's nearly 200 countries now hold multiparty elections, the highest number ever.[17] The collapse of communist party rule in the former Soviet Union and its satellites in eastern and central Europe in the early 1990s was followed by the first open elections ever in these countries. These changes led some observers to call the end of the 20th century the "third wave of democracy."

> In an extraordinary development, popular movements that became known as the "Arab Spring" swept through much of northern Africa, the Persian Gulf region, and the Middle East in 2011 and 2012, as ordinary people demanded full political rights. In Egypt, Tunisia, and Libya, long-time strongmen were deposed, and people demanded free elections to choose their successors. Widespread civil resistance occurred in Morocco, Algeria, Bahrain, and Yemen; and Syria fell into civil war when its dictatorial leader refused to give up power. In a speech in Israel in 2012, Ban Ki Moon, secretary-general of the United Nations, declared, "It is hard not to view the dramatic events of the past year as a fulfillment of our most noble aspirations. . . . Everywhere people are experiencing a fundamental human yearning; a universal hunger for freedom, dignity, and human rights.[18]

Despite these developments, many countries still lack basic democratic rights. Single-party rule by communist parties remains a reality in China, Vietnam, Cuba, and the People's

[16] United Nations Development Programme, *Human Development Report 2000* (New York: Oxford University Press, 2000), ch. 3, "Inclusive Democracy Secures Rights," pp. 56–71. The quotation from Arthur Lewis appears on p. 56.

[17] An interactive world map showing what countries hold free elections is available at *www.democracyweb.org/new-map*.

[18] "All Hail the Arab Spring," February 2, 2012, *www.israelnationalnews.com*.

Democratic Republic of Korea (North Korea). **Military dictatorships,** that is, repressive regimes ruled by dictators who exercise total power through control of the armed forces, are in place in, among others, Zimbabwe, Uzbekistan, and Eritrea.[19] The rights of women to full societal participation—and the rights of all citizens to organize in support of cultural and religious goals—are restricted in a number of Arab states, including Egypt, Syria, and Saudi Arabia. According to United Nations estimates, 106 countries still limit important civil and political freedoms.

The degree to which human rights are protected also varies widely across nations. *Human rights,* further discussed in Chapters 5 and 17, refer broadly to the rights and privileges accorded to all people, simply by virtue of being human, for example, the rights to a decent standard of living, free speech, religious freedom, and due process of law, among others. Fundamental human rights have been codified in a number of international agreements, the most important of which is the Universal Declaration of Human Rights of 1948.[20] The second half of the 20th century was a period of great advances in human rights in many regions, and over half of the world's nations have now ratified *all* of the United Nations' human right covenants. Nonetheless, many human rights problems remain. Consider the following examples:

- More than 6 million children die each year before their fifth birthday. Most of these deaths are due to diseases such as pneumonia, diarrhea, and malaria, which are preventable with proper vaccinations, nutrition, and basic medical care. Although this number has fallen by 50 percent since 1990, it is still tragically high.[21]

- Gross violations of human rights have not been eliminated. *Genocide,* mass murder of innocent civilians, has occurred all too recently in Syria, Rwanda, Iraq, Bosnia and Herzegovina, the Congo, and Sudan.

- The International Labor Organization estimated in 2014 that 21 million people worldwide were victims of forced labor, trafficking, and human slavery. Their labor generated annual profits of $150 billion. (The topic of forced labor is further explored in Chapter 17.) More than half of them were women and girls, who had been forced into prostitution or domestic work.[22] The efforts of a major hotel chain, The Carlson Companies, to prevent the use of their facilities for prostitution or child trafficking is described in a case at the end of this book.

- Minority groups and indigenous peoples in many nations still lack basic political and social rights. In Nepal, the life expectancy of "untouchables," the lowest caste, is fully 15 years less than that of Brahmins, the highest caste.

The absence of key human rights in many nations remains a significant issue for companies transacting business there.

Another dimension of difference among nations today is how economic assets are controlled, that is, the degree of economic freedom. On one end of the continuum are societies in which assets are privately owned and exchanged in a free and open market. Such **free enterprise systems** are based on the principle of voluntary association and exchange. In such a system, people with goods and services to sell take them voluntarily to the marketplace, seeking to exchange them for money or other goods or services. Political and economic

---

[19] For profiles of the dictators of these nations, see *Parade Magazine,* "The World's 10 Worst Dictators," April 4, 2013, *www.parade.com.*

[20] For more information on the Universal Declaration of Human Rights and other United Nations agreements on human rights, see the website of the U.N. High Commissioner for Human Rights at *www.unhchr.org.*

[21] United Nations Children's Fund (UNICEF) data on child mortality are available online at *www.childinfo.org.*

[22] ILO, *Profits and Poverty: The Economics of Forced Geneva, Switzerland: International Labour Office,* 2014.

Exhibit 4.C

China: A Case of Authoritarian Capitalism?

Democracy, a *political* system in which citizens choose their own leaders and may openly express their ideas, and capitalism, an *economic* system in which the means of creating wealth are privately owned and controlled, have historically often developed in tandem. The two are not always coupled, however. During the early years of the 20th century, for example, capitalism coexisted with nondemocratic, fascist governments in Germany, Spain, and Japan. More recently, scholars have coined the term "authoritarian capitalism" to refer to modern states that combine elements of a market economy with political control by nonelected elites. A prime example is China. In its drive for economic development, the Chinese government has granted considerable freedom to private individuals to own property, invest, and innovate. The result has been very rapid growth in much of the country over the past two decades. At the same time, the Chinese communist authorities have vigorously held onto political power and suppressed dissent. As further explored in Chapter 12, the Chinese government operates one of the most sophisticated systems of Internet censorship in the world. It has also held onto ownership of some big companies, such as the China National Petroleum Corporation and China Mobile. In what direction will China and other authoritarian capitalist nations evolve in the future? "Some believe these countries could ultimately become liberal democracies through a combination of internal development, increasing affluence, and outside influence," commented the political scientist Azar Gat. "Alternatively, they may have enough weight to create a new nondemocratic but economically advanced Second World."

Sources: "The Rise of State Capitalism," *The Economist,* January 21, 2012; Azar Gat, "The Return of the Authoritarian Capitalists," *International Herald Tribune,* June 14, 2007; and "The Return of Authoritarian Great Powers," *Foreign Affairs,* July/August 2007.

freedoms are related: as people gain more control over government decisions they often press for greater economic opportunity; open markets may give people the resources to participate effectively in politics. But this is not always the case. The particular situation of China with respect to political and economic freedom is explored in Exhibit 4.C.

At the other end of the continuum are systems of **central state control**, in which economic power is concentrated in the hands of government officials and political authorities. The central government owns the property that is used to produce goods and services. Private ownership may be forbidden or greatly restricted, and most private markets are illegal. Very few societies today operate on the basis of strict central state control of the economy. More common is a system of mixed free enterprise and central state control in which some industries are state controlled, and others are privately owned. For example, in Nigeria, the oil industry is controlled by a government-owned enterprise that operates in partnership with foreign companies such as Shell and Chevron, but many other industries are privately controlled. In the social democracies of Scandinavia, such as Norway, the government operates some industries but not others. In the United States, the government temporarily took partial ownership in some banks, including Citigroup, as they faltered during the financial crisis.

The Heritage Foundation, a conservative think tank, has scored the nations of the world according to an *index of economic freedom* defined as "the fundamental rights of every human being to control his or her own labor and property." In economically free societies, governments "refrain from coercion or restraint of liberty beyond the extent necessary to protect and maintain liberty itself." Among the freest nations in 2015, by this measure, were Hong Kong, Singapore, and New Zealand; among the most repressed were Cuba, Venezuela, and—the least free in the world— North Korea. The United States ranked twelfth out of 178 countries.[23]

[23] Available at *www.heritage.org.*

FIGURE 4.3
The Global Wealth Pyramid

Source: Credit Suisse, Global Wealth Report 2014, Figure 1, p. 24. Used by permission.

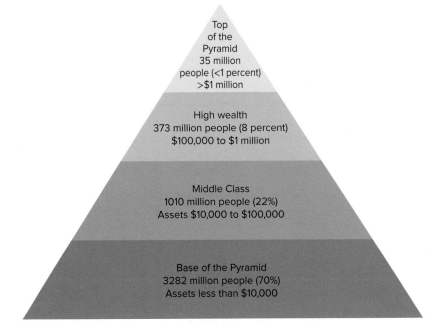

Top
of the
Pyramid
35 million
people (<1 percent)
>$1 million

High wealth
373 million people (8 percent)
$100,000 to $1 million

Middle Class
1010 million people (22%)
Assets $10,000 to $100,000

Base of the Pyramid
3282 million people (70%)
Assets less than $10,000

Global Inequality and the Bottom of the Pyramid

Nations also differ greatly in their overall levels of economic and social development. Ours is a world of great inequalities. Nations themselves differ in economic development, and individual wealth and income varies widely within and among nations.

Inequality may be measured in two ways: by wealth and income. *Wealth* refers to assets that a person accumulates and he or she owns at a point in time. Levels of wealth can be expressed as a pyramid, as shown in Figure 4.3. Most of the world's population—about 70 percent—are at the base, or bottom, of the pyramid, owning less than $10,000 worth of assets. They might own some work tools, household furnishings, and a bicycle or used car. More than 90 percent of adults in India and Africa (and only 20 percent of adults in developed countries) are at the bottom of the pyramid. Close to a quarter of the world's people are considered middle class, with assets between $10,000 and $100,000. This group is present in all countries, but is growing especially fast in China (whose share of the world's middle class has doubled since 2000). These individuals might have equity in a home and some retirement savings. High wealth individuals, with assets above $100,000, are concentrated in the United States, Europe, Japan, and Australia—with growing numbers in China. At the top of the pyramid—just over one-half of 1 percent of the world's population—are millionaires. Forty-one percent of these millionaires reside in the United States; 39 percent in Europe; 8 percent in Japan; and 3 percent in China.

Another way to conceptualize inequality is in terms of *income*—how much a person earns in a day or a year. Some theorists have defined the **bottom of the pyramid** as individuals who earn below $3000 a year in local purchasing power. This varies from place to place; for example, this would amount to less than $3.35 a day in Brazil, $2.11 in China, and $1.89 in Ghana. By this measure, about 4 billion people globally are part of this segment.[24]

[24] World Resources Institute and International Finance Corporation, "The Next 4 Billion: Market Size and Business Strategy at the Base of the Pyramid," March 2007, *www.wri.org*.

Whether measured by assets or income, historically, major transnational corporations have focused most of their attention on the top of the pyramid and, to some extent, the middle. But today, they are increasingly facing the challenge of bringing products, services, and employment to the many at the bottom of the pyramid. As the scholar C. K. Prahalad argued in his book *The Fortune at the Bottom of the Pyramid*, this group, while often overlooked, represents an incredible business opportunity. Although the poor earn little individually, collectively they represent a vast market—and they often pay a "poverty premium," creating an opening for companies able to deliver quality products at lower prices. The size of this market has been estimated at as high as $5 trillion.[25] Many businesses are learning that focusing on the bottom of the pyramid can foster social development and provide employment in underserved communities—and reap profits.

> For example, S.C. Johnson, a global manufacturer of household cleaning supplies and other consumer chemicals, launched a business called WOW in rural Ghana. In partnership with the Gates Foundation and the Center for Sustainable Global Enterprise, the company developed a packet of products specifically designed to help poor families prevent malaria, an illness spread by mosquitoes. Insect repellants and cleaning products were provided in refillable containers and sold by subscription in small amounts to groups of homemakers, village by village. "Since our initial launch of WOW, we've learned so much about what consumers in Ghana want and how to construct a sustainable business model in the process," said the company's vice president of international markets marketing in 2014.[26]

One product that people in poor countries often desperately need is loans with which to operate or expand their farms or small businesses. Commercial banks have historically been reluctant to make small loans to people with little or no collateral. In response to this need, a new system has emerged called **microfinance**. This occurs when financial organizations provide loans to low-income clients or solidarity lending groups (a community of borrowers) who traditionally lack access to banking or related services. One of the most recognized microfinance institutions is the Grameen Bank in Bangladesh. Grameen Bank and its affiliated foundation and partners have had amazing results; by 2015, 1.2 million microloans had been made, nearly 10 million people had been helped, and $225 million had been leveraged to support projects in 13 countries.[27]

> In Indonesia, a midsized bank called BTPN grew rapidly after it decided in 2008 to expand into microloans to what its executives called the "productive poor." BTPN set up numerous small branches in rural areas and equipped staff with portable devices that could scan fingerprints, to facilitate doing business with illiterate customers. Typical loans were for $4,000 or less, with a term of a year or two, made to traders and small shopkeepers. As the economy rebounded from the global financial crisis, many entrepreneurs were eager to grow their businesses. BTPN's model benefited both these customers and the bank, which by 2011 had become one of the most profitable in Indonesia.[28]

[25] C.K. Prahalad, *The Fortune at the Bottom of the Pyramid* (Philadelphia; Wharton School Publishing, 2004). See also C.K. Prahalad and Stuart L. Hart, "The Fortune at the Bottom of the Pyramid," *Strategy + Business,* No. 26, 2002.

[26] "SC Johnson Expands WOW Business Concept in Ghana," press release, October 8, 2014, and "Reality Check at the Bottom of the Pyramid," *Harvard Business Review,* June 2012.

[27] Data available at *www.grameenfoundation.org*.

[28] Gardner Bell, Ryan Nelson, and Carl Zeithaml, "BTPN (A): Banking for the Bottom of the Pyramid in Indonesia," William Davidson Institute of the University of Michigan, January 26, 2015; and *The Economist,* "Rich Pickings: Microlending Has Helped Make BTPN One of Asia's Most Profitable Banks," April 20, 2011.

Microfinance has developed into a global trend, as evidenced by the annual Global Microcredit Summit (GMS), where thousands of business leaders and government representatives from more than 100 countries have gathered to meet since 1997. At its most recent meeting, the GMS announced that its members had collectively reached over 195 million clients; assuming a family size of five, microfinance had helped more than one-seventh of the world's people.[29]

Collaborative Partnerships for Global Problem Solving

As the preceding section suggested, doing business in a diverse world is exceptionally challenging for businesses. One solution to the challenging questions facing transnational corporations is to approach them collectively, through a collaborative process. An emerging trend is the development of collaborative, multisector partnerships focused on particular social issues or problems in the global economy. These partnerships have been termed **global action networks (GANs)**.[30] This final section of Chapter 4 describes this approach.

A Three-Sector World

The term *sector* refers to broad divisions of a whole. In this context, it refers to major parts or spheres of society, such as business (the private sector), government (the public sector), and civil society. **Civil society** comprises nonprofit, educational, religious, community, family, and interest-group organizations; that is, social organizations that do not have a commercial or governmental purpose.

The process of globalization has spurred development of civil society. In recent decades, the world has witnessed the creation and growth of large numbers of **nongovernmental organizations (NGOs)** concerned with such issues as environmental risk, labor practices, worker rights, community development, and human rights. (NGOs are also called *civil society organizations* or *civil sector organizations*.) The number of NGOs accredited by the United Nations has soared in recent years, rising from 1000 in 1996 to more than 4000 in 2015. This figure counts just major organizations.[31] Worldwide, the total number of international NGOs is estimated to be around 55,000.[32] (Many more NGOs operate regionally or locally.)

Experts attribute the growth of NGOs to several factors, including the new architecture of global economic and political relationships. As the Cold War has ended, with democratic governments replacing dictatorships, greater openness has emerged in many societies. More people, with more views, are free to express their pleasure or displeasure with government, business, or one another. NGOs form around specific issues or broad concerns (environment, human rights) and become voices that must be considered in the public policy debates that ensue.

Each of the three major sectors that participate in global action networks—business, government, and civil society—has distinctive resources and competencies, as well as weaknesses. For example, businesses have access to capital, specialized technical knowledge, networks of commercial relationships, and the management skills to get projects completed on time and on budget. On the other hand, the short-term orientation of many businesses may lead them to disregard the long-term impacts of their actions on others. For their part, government agencies have knowledge of public policy, an ability to enforce rules, and revenue from taxation, but are often inflexible, slow to mobilize, and poorly

---

[29] See the Global Microcredit Summit website at *www.microcreditsummit.org*.

[30] Steve Waddell, *Global Action Networks: Creating Our Future Together* (New York: Palgrave Macmillan, 2011).

[31] Data available at *http://csonet.org/*.

[32] *Global Civil Society 2012* (London: Palgrave Macmillan, 2012).

coordinated. Finally, NGOs often enjoy strong community knowledge, volunteer assets, and inspirational leaders, but may lack financial resources and technical skill and may suffer from a narrow, parochial focus.[33] One model highlighting various attributes of actors in the business, government, and civil society sectors is presented in Figure 4.4.

Many businesses have realized that these differences across sectors can be a resource to be exploited. In this view, global action networks—alliances among organizations from the three sectors—can draw on the unique capabilities of each and overcome particular weaknesses that each has.

> One example of a global action network was the Kimberley Process, an initiative to end the trade in *conflict diamonds*—gemstones that had been mined or stolen by rebels fighting internationally recognized governments. The problem was that combatants in civil wars in Africa had seized control of diamond mines in Sierra Leone, Angola, and the Congo, and were selling uncut diamonds to fund their operations. Concerned that the image of diamonds as a symbol of romance would be tarnished, the World Diamond Congress and the international diamond company DeBeers joined forces with the governments of nations with legitimate diamond industries and NGOs campaigning to end civil violence. Together, these parties developed the Kimberley Process, a system for tracking diamonds all the way from the mine to the jewelry shop, so that consumers could be assured that their gem was "conflict-free."

In this case, although the interests of the parties were somewhat different, they were each able to bring their distinctive capabilities to bear to accomplish a common objective. A similar multiparty effort to ban conflict minerals—ones mined in war-torn areas of the Congo—is profiled in the discussion case at the end of this chapter. Other applications of the principle of cross-sector networks and collaborations are explored in Chapters 10 and 17.

The process of globalization presents today's business leaders with both great promise and great challenge. Despite periodic global economic downturns and the ever-present threat of war and terrorism, the world's economy continues to become more integrated

FIGURE 4.4   Distinctive Attributes of the Three Major Sectors

Source: Adapted from Steven Waddell, "Core Competences: A Key Force in Business-Government-Civil Society Collaborations," *Journal of Corporate Citizenship,* Autumn 2002, pp. 43–56, Tables 1 and 2. Used by permission.

	Business	Government	Civil Society
Organizational form	For-profit	Governmental	Nonprofit
Goods produced	Private	Public	Group
Primary control agent	Owners	Voters/rulers	Communities
Primary power form	Money	Laws, police, fines	Traditions, values
Primary goals	Wealth creation	Societal order	Expression of values
Assessment frame	Profitability	Legality	Justice
Resources	Capital assets, technical knowledge, production skills	Tax revenue, policy knowledge, regulatory and enforcement power	Community knowledge, inspirational leadership
Weaknesses	Short-term focus, lack of concern for external impacts	Bureaucratic, slow-moving, poorly coordinated internally	Amateurish, lack of financial resources, parochial perspective

[33] This paragraph draws on Steven Waddell, "Core Competences: A Key Force in Business-Government-Civil Society Collaborations," *Journal of Corporate Citizenship,* Autumn 2002, pp. 43–56.

and interdependent. Transnational corporations, with their financial assets and technical and managerial skills, have a great contribution to make to human betterment. Yet, they must operate in a world of great diversity, and in which their presence is often distrusted or feared. Often, they must confront situations in which political and economic freedoms are lacking and human rights are routinely violated. The challenge facing forward-looking companies today is how to work collaboratively with stakeholders to promote social and economic justice, while still achieving strong bottom-line results.

Summary

- Globalization refers to the increasing movement of goods, services, and capital across national borders. Firms can enter and compete in the global marketplace by exporting products and services; locating operations in another country; or buying raw materials, components, or supplies from sellers abroad.
- The process of globalization is driven by technological innovation, improvements in transportation, the rise of major multinational corporations, and social and political reforms.
- Globalization brings both benefits and costs. On one hand, it has the potential to pull nations out of poverty, spread innovation, and reduce prices for consumers. On the other hand, it may also produce job loss, reduce environmental and labor standards, and erode national cultures. An ongoing challenge is to extend the benefits of globalization to all, while mitigating its adverse effects.
- Multinational corporations operate in nations that vary greatly in their political, social, and economic systems. They face the challenge of deciding how to do business in other nations, while remaining true to their values.
- In a world of great inequalities of wealth and income, businesses are making progress in understanding how to serve the poor to aid social development while earning a profit.
- Businesses can work with governments and civil society organizations around the world in collaborative partnerships that draw on the unique capabilities of each to address common problems.

Key Terms

anti-Americanism, *79*
bottom of the pyramid, *83*
central state control, *82*
civil society, *85*
debt relief, *75*
democracy, *80*
foreign direct investment (FDI), *73*
free enterprise system, *81*

global action network (GAN), *85*
globalization, *71*
international financial and trade institution (IFTI), *73*
International Monetary Fund (IMF), *74*
microfinance, *84*
military dictatorships, *81*

nongovernmental organizations (NGOs), *85*
race to the bottom, *78*
transnational corporation (TNC), *72*
World Bank (WB), *73*
World Trade Organization (WTO), *75*

Internet Resources

www.wto.org
www.imf.org
www.worldbank.org

World Trade Organization
International Monetary Fund
World Bank

Discussion Case: *Intel and Conflict Minerals*

At the 2014 Consumer Electronics Show in Las Vegas, Intel's CEO Brian Krzanich announced that from then on, all microprocessors made by the company would be certified as *conflict-free*. This meant they would contain no *conflict minerals*—tantalum, tungsten, tin, or gold sourced from mines that financed horrific civil conflict in the Democratic Republic of the Congo (DRC) and nearby countries. "The solution isn't easy," the Intel CEO noted. "But nothing worthwhile ever is."

Of the four conflict minerals, the one most important to Intel and other electronics companies is tantalum. Columbite-tantalite, commonly known as "coltan," is a black metallic ore. When refined, it produces tantalum, which is used to regulate electricity in portable consumer electronics, such as smartphones, laptops, play stations, and digital cameras. The largest share of coltan comes from Africa; other sources include Australia, Brazil, and Canada.

In the late 2000s, a common goal to ban conflict minerals emerged among members of an oddly matched group—the electronics industry, the United Nations, governments, and human rights organizations. Their efforts led, ultimately, to a set of international guidelines, national laws, and voluntary initiatives whose goal was to keep the electronics industry and its customers from inadvertently supporting killing, sexual assault, and labor abuses.

The Democratic Republic of the Congo is a nation of 71 million people in central Africa, covering a vast region the size of Western Europe. Since the late 1990s, the DRC has been the site of a brutal regional conflict, in which armed militias, including some from neighboring states, have fought for control. Despite the presence of United Nations troops, as many as 5 million people have died—the most in any conflict since World War II. Warring groups have used sexual assault as a weapon to control the population; an estimated 200,000 Congolese women and girls have been raped, often in front of their husbands and families.

The United Nations and several NGOs reported that militias had systematically looted coltan and other minerals from eastern Congo, using the profits to fund their operations. According to the human rights group Global Witness:

> In the course of plundering these minerals, rebel groups and the Congolese army have used forced labor (often in extremely harsh and dangerous conditions), carried out systematic extortion, and imposed illegal "taxes" on the civilian population. They have also used violence and intimidation against civilians who attempt to resist working for them or handing over the minerals they produce.

Said a representative of The Enough Project, another human rights group, "In eastern Congo, you see child miners [with] no health or safety standards. Minerals are dug by hand, traded in sacks, smuggled across borders."

Once mined—whether in the Congo or elsewhere—raw coltan made its way through a complex, multistep global supply chain. Local traders sold to regional traders, who shipped the ore to processing companies such as H.C. Starck (Germany), Cabot Corporation (United States), and Ningxia (China). Their smelters produced refined tantalum powder, which was then sold to parts makers such as Kemet (United States), Epcos (Germany), and Flextronics (Singapore). They sold, in turn, to original equipment manufacturers such as Dell (United States), Sony (Japan), and Nokia (Finland).

By the time coltan reached the end of this convoluted supply chain, determining its source was nearly impossible. Steve Jobs, then the CEO of Apple, commented in an e-mail in 2010, "We require all of our suppliers to certify in writing that they use conflict-free materials. But honestly there is no way for them to be sure. Until someone invents a way to chemically trace minerals from the source mine, it's a very difficult problem."

As public awareness of atrocities in the Congo grew, governments began to take action. The Organization for Economic Cooperation and Development, an alliance of mostly European nations, issued guidance for companies that wished to responsibly source minerals. In 2010, the U.S. Congress passed the Wall Street Reform and Consumer Protection Act (also known as the Dodd-Frank Act, and further discussed in Chapters 7 and 13). This law included a provision, Section 1502, which required companies to disclose whether tantalum, tin, tungsten, and gold used in their products had come from the DRC or adjoining countries. Companies were required to file their first Section 1502 reports in 2014 (although some business groups had sued to overturn the requirement, saying it was too burdensome).

Companies also acted. For its part, Intel sent teams to more than 86 smelters and refiners in 21 countries, educating their partners about conflict minerals and collecting information about the origin of raw materials they processed. The company collaborated with other companies in the Electronics Industry Citizenship Coalition (EICC) to develop a Conflict-Free Smelter Assessment Program, a voluntary system in which an independent third-party auditor evaluated smelters and refiners and designated them as conflict-free. Minerals would be "bagged and tagged" and then tracked through each step of the supply chain.

Intel was particularly concerned that it exclude from its products only conflict minerals, not those coming from legitimate mines in conflict areas. To this end, it worked with government agencies and civil society organizations, including the U.S. State Department and RESOLVE, an NGO working to map the conflict mineral supply chain, to form the Public-Private Alliance for Responsible Minerals Trade. This multisector initiative worked to support responsible mines and to develop effective chain-of-custody programs in the Congo. In a statement published on its website, Intel said it "believes that an effective solution to the complex issue of conflict minerals will require coordinated efforts by governments, industry, and NGOs."

Sources: "Intel's Efforts to Achieve a Conflict-Free Supply Chain," White Paper, 2014, *www.intel.com*; "Intel Unveils Conflict-Free Processors: Will the Industry Follow Suit?" *The Guardian*, January 13, 2014; "Companies Detail Use of 'Conflict' Metals," *The Wall Street Journal*, June 4, 2014; "Where Apple Gets the Tantalum for Your iPhone," *Newsweek*, February 4, 2015; Peter Eichstaedt, *Consuming the Congo* (Chicago: Lawrence Hill, 2011); Michael Nest, *Coltan* (Cambridge, UK: Polity Press, 2011); The Enough Project, "Conflict Minerals," *www.enoughproject.org*; "Tracing a Path Forward: A Study of the Challenges of the Supply Chain for Target Markets Used in Electronics," *RESOLVE*, April 2010, *http://eicc.info/documents/RESOLVEReport4.10.10.pdf*; and Global Witness, *Faced with a Gun, What Can You Do?* July 2009, *www.globalwitness.org*.

Discussion Questions

1. How do conflict minerals, and in particular, conflict coltan get their name? What groups benefited from the trade in conflict minerals? What groups were hurt by it?

2. Consider the three sectors discussed in this chapter (business, government, and civil society). What were the interests of each, with respect to conflict coltan, and in what ways did their interests converge?

3. Why was Intel unable to eliminate conflict minerals from its supply chain unilaterally, that is, without the help of others?

4. In what ways did Intel collaborate with other sectors (governments and civil society) in its efforts to eliminate conflict minerals from its products? What strengths and weaknesses did each sector bring to the task?

5. What further steps could be taken by governments, NGOs, and companies to strengthen the process to exclude conflict minerals from the global supply chain?

PART TWO

Business and Ethics

Ethics and Ethical Reasoning

People who work in business frequently encounter and must deal with on-the-job ethical issues. Being ethical is important to the individual, the organization, and the global marketplace in today's business climate. Managers and employees alike must learn how to recognize ethical dilemmas and know why they occur. In addition, they need to be aware of the role their own ethical character plays in their decision-making process, as well as the influence of the ethical character of others. Finally, managers and employees must be able to analyze the ethical problems they encounter at work to determine an ethical resolution to these dilemmas.

This Chapter Focuses on These Key Learning Objectives:

LO 5-1   Defining ethics and business ethics.

LO 5-2   Evaluating why businesses should be ethical.

LO 5-3   Knowing why ethical problems occur in business.

LO 5-4   Identifying managerial values as influencing ethical decision making.

LO 5-5   Recognizing how people's spirituality influences their ethical behavior.

LO 5-6   Understanding stages of moral reasoning.

LO 5-7   Analyzing ethical problems using generally accepted ethics theories.

In 2014, Mathew Martoma, a securities trader for the hedge fund SAC Capital Advisors, was convicted of two counts of security fraud and one count of conspiracy for his role in insider trading at the firm. He was sentenced to 9 years in prison and ordered to forfeit a $9.38 million bonus he had earned at SAC. (SAC Capital Advisors also agreed to pay $1.8 million to resolve criminal and civil charges related to insider trading, but no other employee was charged.) The court found that Martoma had convinced two doctors to provide confidential information about clinical trial results for an experimental Alzheimer's drug developed by Elan and Wyeth, two pharmaceutical companies. SAC owned shares of stock in these two companies, valued at $700 million, which it had purchased largely based on Martoma's earlier recommendation. The firm began selling these stocks after Martoma acquired inside information from the doctors that the drugs were not performing as well as hoped in the clinical trials. The stock sale enabled SAC to avoid losses and generated profits totaling $275 million before the drug companies publicly announced the results from the clinical trials.[1]

Dov Charney founded American Apparel in 1998 as a wholesale T-shirt business, and the company grew into one of the leading American-made apparel companies. In 2014, American Apparel's board of directors voted to fire Charney. The decision was partially based on net losses of $5.5 million for a three-month period in 2014 and a $46.5 million loss reported a year earlier, but also on the executive's personal antics. Charney believed that sexuality should be used to sell clothes, and he often discussed his own sex life in public. In 2011, he reportedly permitted an employee to post naked photos of a former female employee who had sued Charney. He also was said to have wandered into his factory wearing only his underpants, causing several employees to file sexual harassment lawsuits. Other charges were also filed against Charney, including assault and battery, impersonation through the Internet, and defamation, according to the company's regulatory filing in 2014. "The company has grown a lot bigger than just one person and the liabilities Dov brought to the situation began to far outweigh his strengths," said the Board's chairman.[2]

The actions taken by Martoma and Charney were both highly unethical. What does it mean for an action to be ethical or unethical? This chapter explains the meaning of ethics, explains why businesses and managers should be ethical, identifies the different types of ethical problems that occur in business, and focuses on an ethical decision-making framework influenced by the core elements of an individual's ethical character. Then, Chapter 6 builds on this foundation with a discussion of how ethical performance in business can be improved by strengthening the organization's culture and climate and by providing organizational safeguards, such as policies, training, and reporting procedures.

The Meaning of Ethics

Ethics is a conception of right and wrong conduct. It tells us whether our behavior is moral or immoral and deals with fundamental human relationships—how we think and behave toward others and how we want them to think and behave toward us. **Ethical principles** are guides to moral behavior. For example, in most societies lying, stealing, deceiving, and

---

[1] "Ex-SAC Trader Convicted of Securities Fraud," *The New York Times,* February 6, 2014, *dealbook.nytimes.com;* and "Martoma, SAC Capital Ex-Trader, Gets 9 Years in Prison," *The New York Times,* September 8, 2014, *dealbook.nytimes.com.*

[2] "American Apparel Board Moves to Fire Founder, CEO Dov Charney," *The Wall Street Journal,* June 19, 2014, *online.wsj.com;* "For Dov Charney of American Apparel, an Abrupt Fall From Grace," *The New York Times,* June 19, 2014, *www.nytimes.com;* and, "American Apparel Ousts Its Founder, Dov Charney, Over Nude Photos," *The New York Times,* June 21, 2014, *www.nytimes.com.*

harming others are considered to be unethical and immoral. Honesty, keeping promises, helping others, and respecting the rights of others are considered to be ethically and morally desirable behavior. Such basic rules of behavior are essential for the preservation and continuation of organized life everywhere.

These notions of right and wrong come from many sources. Religious beliefs are a major source of ethical guidance for many. The family institution—whether two parents, a single parent, or a large family with brothers and sisters, grandparents, aunts, cousins, and other kin—imparts a sense of right and wrong to children as they grow up. Schools and schoolteachers, neighbors and neighborhoods, friends, admired role models, ethnic groups, and the ever-present electronic media and the Internet influence what we believe to be right and wrong in life. The totality of these learning experiences creates in each person a concept of ethics, morality, and socially acceptable behavior. This core of ethical beliefs then acts as a moral compass that helps guide a person when ethical puzzles arise.

Ethical ideas are present in all societies, organizations, and individual persons, although they may vary greatly from one to another. Your ethics may not be the same as your neighbor's; one particular religion's notion of morality may not be identical to another's; or what is considered ethical in one society may be forbidden in another society. These differences raise the important and controversial issue of **ethical relativism**, which holds that ethical principles should be defined by various periods of time in history, a society's traditions, the special circumstances of the moment, or personal opinion. In this view, the meaning given to ethics would be relative to time, place, circumstance, and the person involved. In that case, the logical conclusion would be that there would be no universal ethical standards on which people around the globe could agree. However, for companies conducting business in several societies at one time, whether or not ethics is relevant can be vitally important; we discuss these issues in more detail in Chapter 6.

For the moment, however, we can say that despite the diverse systems of ethics that exist within our own society and throughout the world, all people everywhere do depend on ethical systems to tell them whether their actions are right or wrong, moral or immoral, approved or disapproved. Ethics, in this basic sense, is a universal human trait, found everywhere.

Are ethics the same as laws? In other words, can we determine what is right or moral by asking what is legal? Some people have argued that the best way to assure ethical business conduct is to insist that business firms obey society's laws. However, laws and ethics are not quite the same. **Laws** are society's formal written rules about what constitutes right and wrong conduct in various spheres of life. For example, hydraulic fracturing in oil drilling operations is legal in many communities but some argue it is unethical due to its potential for destroying the environment. While it may be illegal for environmentalists to attempt to stop work operations by blockading a drilling location, they believe they are acting ethically by protecting the environment.

Laws are similar to ethics because both define proper and improper behavior. Yet, ethical concepts—like the people who believe in them—are more complex than written rules of law. Ethics deal with human dilemmas that frequently go beyond the formal language of law and the meanings given to legal rules.

What Is Business Ethics?

Business ethics is the application of general ethical ideas to business behavior. Business ethics is not a special set of ethical ideas different from ethics in general and applicable only to business. If dishonesty is considered to be unethical and immoral, then anyone in business who is dishonest with stakeholders—employees, customers, suppliers, stockholders, or competitors—is acting unethically and immorally. If protecting others from harm is considered to be ethical, then a company that recalls a dangerously defective product is acting in an ethical way. To be considered ethical, business must draw its ideas about what is proper behavior from the same sources as everyone else in society. Business should not try to make up its own definitions of what is right and wrong. Employees and managers may believe at times that they are permitted or even encouraged to apply special or weaker ethical rules to business situations, but society does not condone or permit such an exception.

How common are such exceptions? In a series of studies conducted by the Ethics Resource Center, researchers found that observations of unethical conduct in the workplace reached a peak in 2009 and then has dropped slightly since 2011, as shown in Figure 5.1. Yet the pressure on managers to act unethically remains a serious problem for businesses. The Institute for Leadership and Management reported in 2013 that 63 percent of managers said they were expected to behave unethically at some point in their career.[3]

Why Should Business Be Ethical?

Why should business be ethical? What prevents a business firm from piling up as much profit as it can, in any way it can, regardless of ethical considerations? Figure 5.2 lists the major reasons why business firms should promote a high level of ethical behavior.

Enhance Business Performance

Some people argue that one reason for businesses to be ethical is that it enhances the firm's performance, or simply: *ethics pays.*

Empirical studies have supported the economic benefits of being perceived as an ethical company. *Ethisphere* also found a strong link between ethics and financial performance. Companies that were on *Ethisphere*'s list of the *World's Most Ethical Companies* have returned 53 percent to shareholders since 2005, significantly better than the Standard and Poor's benchmark return of only 4 percent. This positive relationship between ethics and profits can be seen in Figure 5.3.

FIGURE 5.1
Observing Misconduct at Work, 2000–13

Source: *2013 National Business Ethics Survey of the U.S. Workforce,* Ethics Resource Center, Washington, DC, 2014.

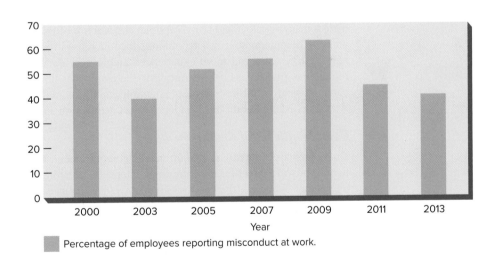

Percentage of employees reporting misconduct at work.

FIGURE 5.2
Why Should Business Be Ethical?

To enhance business performance.
To comply with legal requirements.
To prevent or minimize harm.
To meet demands of business stakeholders.
To promote personal morality.

[3]"Three Out of Five Managers Pressured to Behave Unethically at Work, According to New Research," *Institute of Leadership and Management,* June 10, 2013, press release.

FIGURE 5.3
World's Most Ethical Index versus S&P 500 and FTSE 100, 2005–10

Source: See www.ethisphere.com/2011-worlds-most-ethical-companies/.

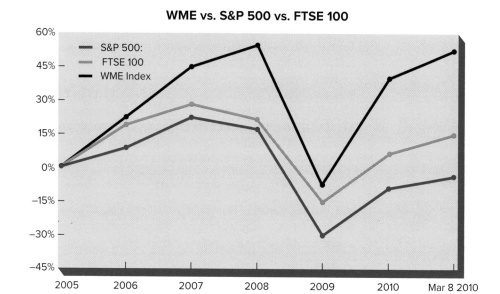

Businesses increasingly are recognizing that ethics pays and are encouraging ethical behavior by their employees. Business executives recognize that ethical actions can directly affect their organization's bottom line.

It is also clear that a lack of ethics has serious negative financial impact. Researchers have identified that costs to the company go far beyond the government's fines. In a study conducted by the University of Washington's business school, researchers found that "companies that have cooked their books [misstated accounting information] lose 41 percent of their market value after news spreads about their misdeeds." The reputational damage to the company is calculated to be 7.5 times the amount of the penalties imposed by government.[4] Companies with bad reputations face increased recruiting costs, especially when recruiting females and more experienced employees. By contrast, companies with good reputations find it easier to recruit desirable employees, lower costs to bring these candidates on board, and have greater retention among employees, according to a report by Alexander Mann Solutions, a leader of talent acquisition and management services.[5]

Comply with Legal Requirements

Doing business ethically is also often a legal requirement. Two legal requirements, in particular, provide direction for companies interested in being more ethical in their business operations. Although they apply only to U.S.–based firms, these legal requirements also provide a model for firms that operate outside the United States.

The first is the **U.S. Corporate Sentencing Guidelines**, which provide a strong incentive for businesses to promote ethics at work.[6] The sentencing guidelines come into play when an employee of a firm has been found guilty of criminal wrongdoing and the firm

---

[4] "Cooked Books, Fried Reputation: Study," *Ethics Newsline*, Institute for Global Ethics, November 20, 2006, *www.globalethics.org*. Also see Jonathan M. Karpoff, D. Scott Lee, and Gerald S. Martin, "The Cost to Firms of Cooking the Books," *Journal of Financial and Quantitative Analysis*, 2008, pp. 581–611.

[5] "The Cost of Bad Reputation," *Corporate Responsibility Magazine*, October 2014.

[6] For a thorough discussion of the U.S. Corporate Sentencing Guidelines, see Dan R. Dalton, Michael B. Metzger, and John W. Hill, "The 'New' U.S. Sentencing Commission Guidelines: A Wake-Up Call for Corporate America," *Academy of Management Executive*, 1994, pp. 7–13; and Dove Izraeli and Mark S. Schwartz, "What Can We Learn from the U.S. Federal Sentencing Guidelines for Organizational Ethics?" *Journal of Business Ethics*, 1998, pp. 1045–55.

Exhibit 5.A

Is the Sarbanes-Oxley Act Still a Potent Government Tool?

In 2012, the Sarbanes-Oxley Act (SOX) turned 10 years old. SOX was once regarded as government's "biggest hammer" to control businesses and executives through the threat of intimidation of civil penalties and jail time for transgressions. But the hammer did not seem so big after the government failed to use SOX against any of the large banks and their executives for false certification of financial reports in the wake of the financial crisis of 2008–09. "I think there's been a reluctance to prosecute the cases," said Frank Partnoy, a university law and finance professor. "I'm quite surprised they haven't, given that it was supposed to be one of the more powerful tools coming out of Enron and the other corporate debacles."

The Securities and Exchange Commission (SEC) countered by clarifying that the SEC took action on every case they believed was worthy of prosecution, according to an SEC commissioner. The SEC brought civil false-certification charges against more than 200 parties, including a handful of executives at companies involved in financial scandals such as Fannie Mae, Freddie Mac, and Countrywide. But critics pointed out that the SEC did not bring any false-certification charges against any of the large banks or their executives for their actions during the financial crisis; rather, it targeted only mid-sized or small banks whose actions were less serious. No executives at Bear Stearns or J.P. Morgan Chase were ever charged with any wrongdoing, despite being accused by their shareholders of misleading investors about hundreds of millions of dollars in losses. Professor Partnoy asked, "Could it really be the case that the number of high-level criminal actions at Wall Street firms over the last decade is zero? Could the firms really be that clean?" These questions lead some to believe that the once-powerful Sarbanes-Oxley Act has lost its influence to the point of being ineffective as a deterrent for unethical corporate behavior.

Sources: "Law's Big Weapon Sits Idle," *The Wall Street Journal,* July 29, 2012, *online.wsj.com.*

is facing sentencing for the criminal act, since the firm is responsible for actions taken by its employees. To determine the sentencing, the judge computes a culpability (degree of blame) score using the guidelines, based on whether or not the company has:

1. Established standards and procedures to reduce criminal conduct.
2. Assigned high-level officer(s) responsibility for compliance.
3. Not assigned discretionary authority to "risky" individuals.
4. Effectively communicated standards and procedures through training.
5. Taken reasonable steps to ensure compliance—monitor and audit systems, maintain and publicize reporting system.
6. Enforced standards and procedures through disciplinary mechanisms.
7. Following detection of offense, responded appropriately and prevented reoccurrence.

The U.S. Sentencing Commission reviewed and made important revisions to the Sentencing Guidelines in 2004 and each year since 2010, yet the "seven steps" described above remain the blueprint for many businesses in designing their ethics and compliance program.[7]

Another legal requirement imposed upon U.S. businesses is the **Sarbanes-Oxley Act** of 2002 (often referred to as SOX).[8] Born from the ethics scandals at Enron, WorldCom, Tyco, and others, this law seeks to ensure that firms maintain high ethical standards in how they conduct and monitor business operations. For example, the Sarbanes-Oxley Act requires executives to vouch for the accuracy of a firm's financial reports and requires them to pay back bonuses based on earnings that are later proved fraudulent. The act also established strict rules for auditing firms. Recently some questioned the powerful influence once wielded by this Act, as discussed in Exhibit 5.A.

[7] For a discussion of the most recent sentencing guidelines amendments, see *www.ussc.gov.*

[8] See Jeanette M. Franzel, "A Decade after Sarbanes-Oxley: The Need for Ongoing Vigilance, Monitoring, and Research," *Accounting Horizons,* 2014, pp. 917–30; and Parveen P. Gupta, Thomas R. Weirich, and Lynn E. Turner, "Sarbanes-Oxley and Public Reporting on Internal Control: Hasty Reaction or Delayed Action?," *Accounting Horizons,* 2013, pp. 371–408.

Despite the possibility that the SOX may be losing its punitive influence, more than one-third of all firms reported a rise in SOX compliance costs, compared to one in ten that reported a decline. These increased costs were attributed to meeting tough new compliance requirements set by the Public Company Accounting Oversight Board (PCAOB).[9]

Prevent or Minimize Harm

Another reason businesses and their employees should act ethically is to prevent harm to the general public and the corporation's many stakeholders. One of the strongest ethical principles is stated very simply: *Do no harm.* The notorious examples of outright greed and other unethical behavior by managers in the financial community contributed in part to the long-lasting Great Recession in the United States and around the world. These managers' unethical actions were responsible for significant harm to many stakeholders in society. Investors' portfolios dropped in value, retirees saw their nest eggs dwindle, hundreds of thousands of employees lost their jobs, and many small businesses failed. More recently, when Mathew Martoma committed insider trading, as described in an example at the beginning of this chapter, investors who traded stock with SAC Capital Advisors lost money because they did not have access to the same information Martoma did.

Meet Demands of Business Stakeholders

Another reason businesses should be ethical is that stakeholders demand it. As discussed in Chapter 3, organizational stakeholders expect that companies will exhibit high levels of ethical performance and social responsibility. If employees view their company as ethical, they likely take greater pride in working there, have higher overall work satisfaction, and are willing to recommend the company as a good place to work. Scholars reviewing work in this field found that consumers who considered companies as being ethical or involved in socially responsible programs are more inclined to purchase these companies' products. Socially responsible purchasing activities, such as purchasing from smaller firms or minority or women-owned firms, have benefited companies both in the United States and Europe. Finally, scholars argue that ethical and socially responsible firms are signaling a long-term concern for all stakeholders that could translate into better economic performance and therefore motivates investors to trust these companies.[10]

Some businesses know that meeting stakeholders' expectations is good business, as illustrated by the Co-operative Bank, a retail bank based in Manchester, United Kingdom:

> The Co-operative Bank first introduced its Ethics Policy in 1992. The bank's policy precluded it from lending funds to firms that were involved in animal testing, nuclear power, unfair labor practices, or weapons production. Since then it withheld billions of pounds of funding from businesses whose policies violated the bank's ethics standards. Yet, the bank reported that any losses were more than made up by income from consumers who supported the bank's strong ethical stand. During the same time period, Co-operative Bank increased its commercial lending sixteen-fold and experienced strong growth in profitability, increased customer deposits, and other positive financial measures. The Bank features on its opening web page the offer "£100 to you and £25 to charity when you switch your current account to us."[11]

[9] "SOX Compliance Costs Rise for Many Companies, Report Finds," *Journal of Accountancy,* May 15, 2013, *www.journalofac couyntancy.com.*

[10] Many of these issues are discussed in C. B. Bhattacharya, Daniel Korschun, and Sankar Sen, "Strengthening Stakeholder-Company Relationships through Mutually Beneficial Corporate Socially Responsible Initiatives," *Journal of Business Ethics,* 2009, pp. 257–72; and Henry L. Petersen and Harrie Vredenburg, "Morals or Economics? Institutional Investor Preference for Corporate Social Responsibility," *Journal of Business Ethics,* 2009, pp. 1–14.

[11] For additional information about Co-operative Bank, *see* the Bank's website at *www.co-operativebank.co.uk.*

Promote Personal Morality

A final reason for promoting ethics in business is a personal one. Most people want to act in ways that are consistent with their own sense of right and wrong. The Dov Charney example at the beginning of this chapter shows how a lack of personal morality by the firm's leader can adversely affect employees. Being pressured to contradict their personal values creates emotional stress. Knowing that one works in a supportive ethical climate contributes to one's sense of psychological security:

> According to an Ernst & Young study of employees in Asia, almost 80 percent said they would be unwilling to work for companies involved in bribery and corruption and nearly 70 percent saw a strong reputation for ethical behavior as a commercial advantage. The CEO of Gallup, an organization that annually assesses people's opinions, explained, "If I think my boss treats me ethically and honestly, that is what I think of the company. That is a pretty intense finding in all of Gallup's work in the last couple of decades."[12]

Why Ethical Problems Occur in Business

If businesses have so many reasons to be ethical, why do ethical problems occur? Although not necessarily common or universal, ethical problems occur frequently in business. Finding out what causes them is one step toward minimizing their impact on business operations and on the people affected. Some of the main reasons are summarized in Figure 5.4 and are discussed next.

Personal Gain and Selfish Interest

Desire for personal gain, or even greed, causes some ethics problems. Businesses sometimes employ people whose personal values are less than desirable, who will put their own welfare ahead of all others, regardless of the harm done to other employees, the company, or society.

A manager or an employee who puts his or her own self-interest above all other considerations is called an **ethical egoist**.[13] Self-promotion, a focus on self-interest to the point of

FIGURE 5.4
Why Ethical Problems Occur in Business

Reason	Nature of Ethical Problem	Typical Approach	Attitude
Personal gain and selfish interest	Selfish interest versus others' interests	Egotistical mentality	"I want it!"
Competitive pressures on profits	Firm's interest versus others' interests	Bottom-line mentality	"We have to beat the others at all costs!"
Conflicts of interest	Multiple obligations or loyalties	Favoritism mentality	"Help yourself and those closest to you!"
Cross-cultural contradictions	Company's interests versus diverse cultural traditions and values	Ethnocentric mentality	"Foreigners have a funny notion of what's right and wrong."

[12] "Employees Care about Ethical Practices: Survey," *Business Asia One Business,* June 12, 2015, *businessasiaone.com*; and Jim Clifton, CEO of Gallup quoted in Executive Board press release, January 17, 2013, *executiveboard.com.blogs*.

[13] For a compact discussion of ethical egoism, see Denis G. Arnold, Tom L. Beauchamp, and Norman E. Bowie, *Ethical Theory and Business,* 9th ed. (Upper Saddle River, NJ: Pearson, 2012), pp. 12–17; and Laura P. Hartman, Joe DesJardins, and Chris MacDonald, *Business Ethics: Decision-Making for Personal Integrity and Social Responsibility,* 3rd ed. (New York: McGraw-Hill, 2014), p. 108.

selfishness, and greed are traits commonly observed in an ethical egoist. The ethical egoist tends to ignore ethical principles accepted by others, believing that ethical rules are made for others. Altruism—acting for the benefit of others when self-interest is sacrificed—is seen to be sentimental or even irrational. "Looking out for number one" is the ethical egoist's motto, as demonstrated by the Martoma and Charney examples at the beginning of this chapter and the following stories:

> Gary Foster, a former Citigroup vice president, embezzled nearly $23 million from the bank by wiring company funds to his personal account at JP Morgan. Foster used the company money to purchase a Ferrari, a Maserati, and residences in Manhattan, Brooklyn, and New Jersey. "The defendant violated his employer's trust and stole a stunning amount of money over an extended period of time to finance his personal lifestyle," explained U.S. Attorney Loretta Lynch. Foster pleaded guilty to bank fraud in 2011.
>
> Former Coca-Cola executive Jeffrey Shamp was sentenced to 27 months in federal prison for diverting more than $400,000 in company funds for personal expenses. The former national account executive admitted to redirected American Express gift checks intended for a sales incentive program for Coke customers and used to pay his alimony, rent expenses, and for gifts to friends and relatives, according to authorities.[14]

Competitive Pressures on Profits

When companies are squeezed by tough competition, they sometimes engage in unethical activities to protect their profits. This may be especially true in companies whose financial performance is already substandard. Research has shown that managers of poor financial performers and companies with financial uncertainty are more prone to commit illegal acts. In addition, intense competitive pressure in the global marketplace has resulted in unethical activity, such as the practice of price fixing or falsifying documents.

> Senior executives at numerous state-run energy companies in South Korea were indicted on corruption charges in 2013. The government found that 277 documents were faked over the past decade at a majority of the country's nuclear reactors. The scandal was attributed to the intense competition in the industry and the increased demand for energy from the country's 23 commercial nuclear power plants, which provided about a third of the nation's power. These actions also dealt a blow to the country's efforts to export its nuclear power business.[15]

Conflicts of Interest

Ethical challenges in business often arise in the form of conflicts of interest. A **conflict of interest** occurs when an individual's self-interest conflicts with acting in the best interest of another, when the individual has an obligation to do so.[16] For example, if a purchasing agent directed her company's orders to a firm from which she had received a valuable gift, regardless if this firm offered the best quality or value, she would have acted unethically because of a conflict of interest. In this situation, she would have acted to benefit herself, rather than in the best interests of her employer. A failure to disclose a conflict of interest

---

[14] "Ex-Citigroup Executive Foster Pleads Guilty to Bank Fraud," *Bloomberg,* September 6, 2011, *www.bloomberg.com*; and "Former Coke Executive Sentenced to Prison for Diverting Company Funds," *The Wall Street Journal,* May 19, 2014, *online.wsj.com*.

[15] "South Korea Indicts Over Faked Nuclear Documents," *The Wall Street Journal,* October 10, 2013, *online.wsj.com*.

[16] Based on John R. Boatright, *Ethics and the Conduct of Business,* 7th ed. (Upper Saddle River, NJ: Pearson, 2011), p. 101.

may represent deception in and of itself and may hurt the person or organization on whose behalf judgment has been exercised. Many ethicists believe that even the *appearance* of a conflict of interest should be avoided, because it undermines trust:

> With the help of orthopedic surgeons from around the world, DePuy Orthopaedics, a division of Johnson & Johnson, developed three innovative devices intended to provide a more flexible hip replacement option for younger patients. More than 25,000 orthopedic surgeons implanted these devices in nearly 100,000 patients worldwide. However, according to a U.K. study, more than 10 percent of the devices failed within two years of the surgery. The study also discovered that approximately 1,000 of the surgeons involved in the development of these devices received consulting fees or royalty payments for their work, calling into question the surgeons' objectivity when recommending these devices to their patients.[17]

In this case, some doctors may have had a conflict of interest, because their financial interest in the success of the DePuy devices may have led them to promote them over other products that might have been safer.

Many cases of financial fraud illustrate conflicts of interest, in which opportunities for self-enrichment by senior managers conflict with the long-term viability of the firm and the best interests of employees, customers, suppliers, and stockholders. The case "Moody's Credit Ratings and the Subprime Mortgage Meltdown," which appears at the end of this book, describes an organizational conflict of interest in which a company was paid by the firms whose bonds it rated, rather than by the buyers of these bonds. Many firms seek to guard against the dangers inherent in conflicts of interest by including prohibitions of any such practices in their codes of ethics, as discussed in Chapter 6.

Cross-Cultural Contradictions

Some of the knottiest ethical problems occur as corporations do business in other societies where ethical standards differ from those at home. Today, policymakers and strategic planners in all multinational corporations, regardless of the nation where they are headquartered, often face this kind of ethical dilemma. Consider the following situation:

> PPG Industries, the global leader in coatings and specialty products operating in more than 60 countries around the world, has sold high lead content paint to the African nation of Cameroon for many years. The United States banned interior and exterior household paint with lead content above 600 parts per million in 1978 and tightened this standard to 90 parts per million in 2008 to reduce the risk of lead poisoning in children who can ingest paint chips, flakes, or peelings or inhale lead paint dust. But as far as international sales, the company maintained that it "initiated its own action to review its consumer coatings to ensure the lead content confirms to applicable legal requirements." Cameroon has no lead paint limits, and PPG's product on the shelves in stores in this country have lead paint levels of well above the U.S. legal limit. Studies have shown that even low-level lead exposure can significantly affect mental capacity and higher exposures can cause behavioral problems, learning disabilities, even seizures and death. PPG stopped short of requiring its newly acquired Cameroon subsidiary, Seigneurie, to recall the lead-based paint already on the market in Cameroon or label it as containing lead but has agreed to exchange lead-free paint for previously sold paint containing lead.[18]

[17] "Conflict of Interest between Surgeons and Device Manufacturers," *Drugwatch,* April 1, 2015, *www.drugwatch.com/depuy-hip/replacement.php.*

[18] "PPG Refuses to Recall Leaded Paint in Cameroon," *Pittsburgh Post-Gazette,* February 6, 2012, *www.post-gazette.com.*

This episode raises the issue of *ethical relativism,* which was defined earlier in this chapter. Although the sale of lead-based paint in Cameroon was *legal,* was it *ethical?* Is the selling of unsafe products by any measure *ethical* if it is not forbidden by the receiving nation, especially if the company knows that the products are exported to another country where others are exposed to serious health risks?

As business becomes increasingly global, with more and more corporations penetrating overseas markets where cultures and ethical traditions vary, these cross-cultural questions will occur more frequently.

The Core Elements of Ethical Character

The ethical analysis and resolution of ethical dilemmas in the workplace significantly depend on the ethical character and moral development of managers and other employees. Good ethical practices not only are possible, but also become normal with the right combination of these components.

Managers' Values

Managers are key to whether a company and its employees will act ethically or unethically. As major decision makers, they have more opportunities than others to create an ethical tone for their company. The values held by managers, especially the top-level managers, will serve as models for others who work at the company. Unfortunately, according to a 2013 opinion poll, Americans hold a dim view of business executives' and managers' values. Only a small minority—24 percent—believed that managers contribute "a lot" to society's well being, and 28 percent believed that managers contribute "not very much or nothing."[19] In an annual Gallup poll that rated 21 occupations for honesty and ethics, nurses—for the thirteenth straight year—came out on top. In 2014, only 17 percent of those surveyed saw business executives as having "very high" or "high" ethical standards or honesty. This placed executives below clergy and lawyers on this list. Advertising practitioners ranked lower than business executives, with car salespeople and members of Congress at the bottom of the list.[20]

How do executives view their own values? Studies generally show that most U.S. managers focus on themselves and place importance on values such as having a comfortable and exciting life. Researchers also found that new CEOs tend to be more self-interested and short-term focused, possibly in an effort to immediately drive up company profits, rather than valuing long-term investments in research and development or capital expenditures. However, a recent study found that today's managers place slightly more importance on moral values, such as honesty and forgiveness, than managers did in the 1980s, who focused more on competency values, like capability and independence.[21]

The challenge for many moral managers is acting effectively on their beliefs in the day-to-day life of their organizations. Educator Mary Gentile tries to empower business leaders and managers by enabling them to give voice to—and to act on—their values at work.

---

[19] "Public Esteem for Military Still High," *Pew Forum on Religion and Public Life,* July 11, 2013, *www.pewforum.org*; and "Fortune 1000 Executives Say Loss of Trust Is an Issue," *PR Newswire,* July 26, 2010, *www.prnewswire.com*.

[20] "Honesty/Ethics in the Professions," *Gallup Poll,* December 8–11, 2014, *www.gallup.com*.

[21] See Jeffrey S. Harrison and James O. Fiet, "New CEOs Pursue Their Own Self-Interests by Sacrificing Stakeholder Value," *Journal of Business Ethics,* 1999, pp. 301–8; and James Weber, "Identifying and Assessing Managerial Value Orientations: A Cross-Generational Replication Study of Key Organizational Decision-Makers' Values," *Journal of Business Ethics,* 2014, available online at *link.springer.com*.

Gentile's "Giving Voice to Values" program believes that the key is knowing how to act on your values despite opposing pressure, and she offers advice, practical exercises, and scripts for handling a wide range of ethical dilemmas through her innovative curriculum for values-driven management and leadership.[22]

Spirituality in the Workplace

A person's **spirituality**—that is, a personal belief in a supreme being, religious organization, or the power of nature or some other external, life-guiding force—has always been a part of the human makeup. In 1953, *Fortune* published an article titled "Businessmen on Their Knees" and claimed that American businessmen (women generally were excluded from the executive suite in those days) were taking more notice of God. More recently, cover stories in *Fortune, Bloomberg Businessweek,* and other business publications have documented a resurgence of spirituality or religion at work.

As far back as 1976, scholars have found a positive relationship between an organization's economic performance and attention to spiritual values. They have shown that spirituality positively affects employee and organizational performance by enhancing intuitive abilities and individual capacity for innovation, as well as increasing personal growth, employee commitment, and responsibility. Spirituality also helps employees who are dealing with workplace stress.[23]

Organizations have responded to the increased attention to spirituality and religion at work by taking action to accommodate their employees' spiritual needs.

> The chief diversity officer at PricewaterhouseCoopers found office space in their Asia-Pacific region facility to provide a prayer room for their Muslim employees. In the United States, employers are required by law to make substantial accommodations for their employees' religious practices, as long as it does not create major hardships for the organization. Ford's Interfaith Network, a group of employees focusing on religious issues, successfully lobbied the company to install sinks designed for the religious washings that Muslim employees perform.[24]

Marketplace Ministries is a nonprofit organization that provides about 2870 Protestant chaplains working in more than 3300 service locations and caring for more than 546,000 client company employees and their family members, for a reported income of about $13.5 million for 2014. Other firms, such as Tyson Foods, have found it worthwhile to have a chaplain on staff full-time. When a Tyson employee told his boss that he had a drug problem, the supervisor sent the employee to the chaplain. The employee thought, "What could he do? Offer me a prayer?" The chaplain met with the employee and over the next few months helped the employee enroll in a drug rehabilitation program, find a drug counselor, and attend Narcotics Anonymous meetings. The spread of the practice of including chaplains within the organization demonstrates the understanding that firms need to

---

[22] To learn more about Mary Gentile's "Giving Voice to Values" program, see *www.marygentile.com* or *www.GivingVoicetoValues .com* at Babson College.

[23] For a study establishing a link between spirituality and economic performance see Christopher P. Neck and John F. Milliman, "Thought Self-Leadership: Finding Spiritual Fulfillment in Organizational Life," *Journal of Managerial Psychology,* 1994, pp. 9–16; and for a study promoting spirituality as a way to reduce workplace stress, see Amal Altaf and Mohammad Atif Awan, "Moderating Affect of Workplace Spirituality on the Relationship of Job Overload and Job Satisfaction," *Journal of Business Ethics,* 2011, pp. 93–99.

[24] "When Religious Needs Test Company Policy," *The New York Times,* February 25, 2007, *www.nytimes.com*; and "More Businesses Turning to Workplace Chaplains," *PilotOnline.com,* October 30, 2011, *hamptonroads.com*.

embrace their employees' religious or spiritual characteristics as part of who they are as employees, not something relegated to places of worship alone.[25]

However, others disagree with the trend toward a stronger presence of religion in the workplace. They hold the traditional belief that business is a secular—that is, nonspiritual—institution. They believe that business is business, and spirituality is best left to churches, synagogues, mosques, and meditation rooms, not corporate boardrooms or shop floors. This, of course, reflects the separation of church and state in the United States and many other countries.

Beyond the philosophical opposition to bringing spirituality into the business environment, procedural or practical challenges arise. Whose spirituality should be promoted? The CEO's? With greater workplace diversity comes greater spiritual diversity, so which organized religion's prayers should be cited or ceremonies enacted? How should businesses handle employees who are agnostics or atheists (who do not follow any religion)?

Just as personal values and character strongly influence employee decision making and behavior in the workplace, so does personal spirituality, from all points on the religious spectrum, impact how businesses operate.

Managers' Moral Development

People's values and spirituality exert a powerful influence on the way ethical work issues are treated. Since people have different personal histories and have developed their values and spirituality in different ways, they are going to think differently about ethical problems. This is as true of corporate managers as it is of other people. In other words, the managers in a company are likely to be at various **stages of moral development**. Some will reason at a high level, others at a lower level.

A summary of the way people grow and develop morally is diagrammed in Figure 5.5. From childhood to mature adulthood, most people move steadily upward in their moral reasoning capabilities from stage 1. Over time, they become more developed and are capable of more advanced moral reasoning, although some people never use the most advanced stages of reasoning in their decision processes.

FIGURE 5.5
Stages of Moral Development and Ethical Reasoning

Source: Adapted from Lawrence Kohlberg, *The Philosophy of Moral Development* (New York: Harper & Row, 1981).

Age Group	Development Stage and Major Ethics Referent	Basis of Ethics Reasoning
Mature adulthood	**Stage 6** Universal principles: justice, fairness, universal human rights	Principle-centered reasoning
Mature adulthood	**Stage 5** Moral beliefs above and beyond specific social custom: human rights, social contract, broad constitutional principles	Principle-centered reasoning
Adulthood	**Stage 4** Society at large: customs, traditions, laws	Society- and law-centered reasoning
Early adulthood, adolescence	**Stage 3** Social groups: friends, school, coworkers, family	Group-centered reasoning
Adolescence, youth	**Stage 2** Reward seeking: self-interest, own needs, reciprocity	Ego-centered reasoning
Childhood	**Stage 1** Punishment avoidance: avoid harm, obedience to power	Ego-centered reasoning

[25] For additional information, see "Faith in the Workplace: Marketplace Chaplains Finds a $13.5M Niche," *Business Journals,* September 15, 2014, *www.bizjournals.com*. For a list of companies considered "religious," see "18 Extremely Religious Big American Companies," *Business Insider,* June 13, 2013, *www.businessinsider.com*.

At first, individuals are limited to an ego-centered focus (stage 1), fixed on avoiding punishment and obediently following the directions of those in authority. (The word *ego* means "self.") Slowly and sometimes painfully, the child learns that what is considered to be right and wrong is pretty much a matter of reciprocity: "I'll let you play with my toy, if I can play with yours" (stage 2). At both stages 1 and 2, however, the individual is mainly concerned with his or her own pleasure. The self-dealings of Gary Foster and Jeffrey Shamp, described earlier in this chapter, exemplify ego-centered reasoning. By taking money from their companies for personal use, they benefited themselves and their immediate families, without apparent concern for others.

In adolescence the individual enters a wider world, learning the give-and-take of group life among small circles of friends, schoolmates, and similar close-knit groups (stage 3). Studies have reported that interaction within groups can provide an environment that improves the level of moral reasoning. This process continues into early adulthood. At this point, pleasing others and being admired by them are important cues to proper behavior. Most people are now capable of focusing on other-directed rather than self-directed perspectives. When a manager "goes along" with what others are doing or what the boss expects, this would represent stage 3 behavior. On reaching full adulthood—the late teens to early 20s in most modern, industrialized nations—most people are able to focus their reasoning according to society's customs, traditions, and laws as the proper way to define what is right and wrong (stage 4). At this stage, a manager would seek to follow the law; for example, he or she might choose to curtail a chemical pollutant because of government regulations mandating this.

Stages 5 and 6 lead to a special kind of moral reasoning. At stage 5, individuals apply their moral beliefs above and beyond specific social custom and consider changing law based on rational reflection of social utility. Stage 6 emphasizes ethical reasoning using broad principles and relationships, such as human rights and constitutional guarantees of human dignity, equal treatment, and freedom of expression. For example, at this stage, an executive might decide to pay wages above the minimum required by law, because this is the morally just thing to do.[26]

Researchers have consistently found that most managers typically rely on criteria associated with reasoning at stages 3 and 4, although some scholars argue that these results may be slightly inflated.[27] Although they may be capable of more advanced moral reasoning that adheres to or goes beyond society's customs or law, managers' ethical horizons most often are influenced by their immediate work group, family relationships, or compliance with the law. Two studies found that senior leaders often demonstrate higher stages of moral reasoning than typical managers, giving some basis for optimism regarding the ethical leadership of businesses.[28]

The development of a manager's moral character can be crucial to a company. Some ethics issues require managers to move beyond selfish interest (stages 1 and 2), beyond company interest (stage 3 reasoning), and even beyond sole reliance on society's customs

[26] For details and research findings, see Lawrence Kohlberg, *The Philosophy of Moral Development* (San Francisco: Harper & Row, 1981); and Anne Colby and Lawrence Kohlberg, *The Measurement of Moral Judgment, Volume I: Theoretical Foundations and Research Validations* (Cambridge: Cambridge University Press, 1987).

[27] James Weber and Janet Gillespie, "Differences in Ethical Beliefs, Intentions, and Behaviors," *Business & Society,* 1998, pp. 447–67; and James Weber and David Wasieleski, "Investigating Influences on Managers' Moral Reasoning," *Business & Society,* 2001, pp. 79–111.

[28] John J. Juzbasich and Jae Uk Chun, "Effects of Moral Reasoning and Management Level on Ratings of Charismatic Leadership, In-Role and Extra-Role Performance of Managers," *Leadership Quarterly,* 2011, pp. 434–50; and James Weber, "Assessing the 'Tone at the Top': The Moral Reasoning of CEOs in the Automobile Industry," *Journal of Business Ethics,* 2010, pp. 167–82.

and laws (stage 4 reasoning). Needed is a manager whose personal character is built on a caring attitude toward all affected, recognizing others' rights and their essential humanity (a combination of stage 5 and 6 reasoning). The moral reasoning of upper-level managers, whose decisions affect companywide policies, can have a powerful and far-reaching impact both inside and outside the company.

Analyzing Ethical Problems in Business

Underlying an ethical decision framework is a set of universal ethical values or principles, notions that most people anywhere in the world would hold as important. While a list of ethical principles may be exhaustive, these values seem to be generally accepted and are present in most ethical dilemmas: do no harm; be compassionate, fair and just, and honest; respect others' rights; and, do your duty/act responsibly.[29] Business managers and employees need a set of decision guidelines that will shape their thinking when on-the-job ethics issues occur. The guidelines should help them (1) identify and analyze the nature of an ethical problem and (2) decide which course of action is likely to produce an ethical result. The following four methods of ethical reasoning can be used for these analytical purposes, as summarized in Figure 5.6.

Virtue Ethics: Pursuing a "Good" Life

Some philosophers believe that the ancient Greeks, specifically Plato and Aristotle, developed the first ethical theory, which was based on values and personal character. Commonly referred to as **virtue ethics**, it focuses on character traits that a good person should possess, theorizing that moral values will direct the person toward good behavior. Aristotle argued, "Moral virtue is a mean between two vices, one of excess and the other of deficiency, and it aims at hitting the mean in feelings, desires, and action."[30] A variety of people have suggested lists of moral values over the years as shown in Figure 5.7.

As indicated in Figure 5.7, Plato, Aristotle, Aquinas, Franklin, and Solomon have slightly different views of what guides a moral or virtuous person. This suggests that to

FIGURE 5.6
Four Methods of Ethical Reasoning

Method	Critical Determining Factor	An Action Is Ethical When . . .	Limitations
Virtues	Values and character	It aligns with good character	Subjective or incomplete set of good virtues
Utilitarian	Comparing benefits and costs	Net benefits exceed net costs	Difficult to measure some human and social costs; majority may disregard rights of the minority
Rights	Respecting entitlements	Basic human rights are respected	Difficult to balance conflicting rights
Justice	Distributing fair shares	Benefits and costs are fairly distributed	Difficult to measure benefits and costs; lack of agreement on fair shares

[29] See Rushworth Kidder, *Moral Courage* (New York: HarperCollins, 2005).

[30] For discussions of virtue ethics, see Laura P. Hartman, Joe DesJardins, and Chris MacDonald, *Business Ethics: Decision-Making for Personal Integrity and Social Responsibility,* 3rd ed. (New York: McGraw-Hill, 2014), pp. 123–27.

FIGURE 5.7
Lists of Moral Values across Time

Plato and Aristotle, 4th century BC	St Thomas Aquinas, 1225–1274	Benjamin Franklin, 1706–1790	Robert Solomon, 1942–2007
• Courage	• Faith	• Cleanliness	• Honesty
• Self-control	• Hope	• Silence	• Trust
• Generosity	• Charity	• Industry	• Toughness
• Magnificence	• Prudence	• Punctuality	
• High-mindedness	• Justice	• Frugality	
• Gentleness	• Temperance		
• Friendliness	• Fortitude		
• Truthfulness	• Humility		
• Wittiness			
• Modesty			

Sources: Plato and Aristotle's values are from Steven Mintz, "Aristotelian Virtue and Business Ethics Education," *Journal of Business Ethics,* 1996; St. Thomas Aquinas's values are from Manuel G. Velasquez, *Business Ethics: Concepts and Cases,* 9th ed. (Upper Saddle River, NJ: Pearson, 2012); Benjamin Franklin's values, from the American Industrial Revolution era, are from Peter McMylor, *Alisdair MacIntyre: Critic of Modernity* (London: Routledge, 1994); and Robert Solomon's moral values can be found in Robert C. Solomon, *Ethics and Excellence: Cooperation and Integrity in Business* (New York: Oxford University Press, 1992).

some extent what counts as a moral virtue depends on one's personal beliefs and is often influenced by an organization or a society.

> When placing virtue ethics in a business context, ethicist Robert Solomon explains, "The bottom line of the Aristotelian approach to business ethics is that we have to get away from 'bottom line' thinking and conceive of business as an essential part of the good life, living well, getting along with others, having a sense of self-respect, and being a part of something one can be proud of."[31]

However, others argue that virtue ethics is not a thoroughly developed ethical system of rules and guidelines, but rather a system of values that form good character. Virtue ethics also suffers from this challenge: whose values? Does a set of values provide a sufficient framework to resolve the most complex ethical dilemmas found in global business? Does a manager sometimes have to be or seem to be "the bad person" or do or seem to do "a bad thing" for the sake of some ultimate ethical good? Would this be virtuous or vicious?[32]

Utility: Comparing Benefits and Costs

Another approach to ethics emphasizes *utility,* or the overall amount of good that can be produced by an action or a decision. This ethical approach is called **utilitarian reasoning**. It is often referred to as cost–benefit analysis because it compares the costs and benefits of a decision, a policy, or an action, as shown in Figure 5.6. These costs and benefits can be economic (expressed in dollar amounts), social (the effect on society at large), or human (usually a psychological or an emotional impact). After business managers add up all the costs and benefits and compare them with one another, the net cost or the net benefit should be apparent. For a utilitarian, the alternative where the benefits most outweigh the costs is the ethically preferred action because it produces the greatest good for the greatest number of people in society.

The main drawback to utilitarian reasoning is the difficulty of accurately measuring both costs and benefits. Some things can be measured in monetary terms—goods produced, sales, payrolls, and profits—but others that are less tangible, such as employee

---

[31] Robert C. Solomon, *Ethics and Excellence: Cooperation and Integrity in Business* (New York: Oxford University Press, 1992), p. 104.

[32] For a critique of virtue ethics, see Boatright, *Ethics and the Conduct of Business,* pp. 58–60.

Exhibit 5.B

Do Patients Have the "Right to Try"

The emergence of "Right to Try" laws in a handful of states—Colorado, Michigan, Missouri, Louisiana, and Arizona by January 2015—catapulted this ethical question into national prominence and touches on some of the methods for ethical reasoning discussed in this chapter.

At the core of this debate is whether or not terminally ill patients have the ethical right to try therapy or experimental drugs that are still in the testing phase at pharmaceutical companies in the hope of stopping the spread of their disease or possibly saving their lives. Patients' were often naturally focused on the potential benefits of using these drugs, even if they were still under development and might be risky or ineffective. An executive at The Goldwater Institute, a libertarian group supporting Right to Try laws, explained, "The goal is for terminally ill patients to have choice when it comes to end-stage disease. Right to Try is something that will help terminally ill people all over the country." These sentiments were echoed by Larry Kutt, a 65-year-old man with an advanced blood cancer hoping to gain access to a therapy currently being tested by several pharmaceutical companies, who said, "It's my life and I want the chance to save it."

Lawmakers in Kansas, Tennessee, Texas, and Wyoming planned to introduce "Right to Try" legislation in 2015 but critics called these efforts "a cruel shame," causing more harm than good by creating false hope. Dr. David Gorski, a Michigan surgeon, argued that releasing unapproved therapies could cause untold pain in a person's final days, even hastening death. Focusing on a benefits versus harms perspective, Dr. Gorski explained, "They are far more likely to harm patients than to help them."

The formal legal position in the United States was based on a 2007 court ruling that stated patients did not have a constitutional right to medicines that were not federally approved. The Food and Drug Administration had a program under which terminally ill patients, who had exhausted their treatment options, could try to obtain therapies that had passed at least the first of three FDA investigation phases. But, the law did not require pharmaceutical companies to provide the treatment nor did it mandate that insurance companies cover these therapies. Also, the law did allow insurance companies to deny coverage to patients while they use drugs under investigation. In 2015, Johnson & Johnson created a panel of bioethicists to study patients' requests for potentially lifesaving medicines and make recommendations to the pharmaceutical firm.

Sources: "Patients Seek 'Right to Try' New Drugs," *The New York Times,* January 10, 2015, *www.nytimes.com*; and, "Company Creates Bioethics Panel on Trial Drugs," *The New York Times,* May 7, 2015, *www.nytimes.com.*

morale, psychological satisfaction, or the worth of a human life, are trickier. Human and social costs are particularly difficult to measure with precision. But unless they can be measured, the cost–benefit calculations will be incomplete, and it will be difficult to know whether the overall result is good or bad, ethical or unethical. Another limitation of utilitarian reasoning is that the majority may override the rights of those in the minority. Since utilitarian reasoning is primarily concerned with the end results of an action, managers using this reasoning process often fail to consider the means taken to reach the end. Some of these challenges are evident in Exhibit 5.B.

Despite these drawbacks, cost–benefit analysis is widely used in business. Because this method works well when used to measure economic and financial outcomes, business managers sometimes are tempted to rely on it to decide important ethical questions without being fully aware of its limitations or the availability of still other methods that may improve the ethical quality of their decisions.

Rights: Determining and Protecting Entitlements

Human rights are another basis for making ethical judgments. A right means that a person or group is entitled to something or is entitled to be treated in a certain way, as shown in Figure 5.6. The most basic human rights are the rights to life, safety, free speech, freedom, being informed, due process, and property, among others. Denying those rights or failing to protect them for other persons and groups is normally considered to be unethical and is the core of the debate over the "Right to Try" controversy profiled in Exhibit 5.B. This approach to ethical reasoning holds that individuals are to be treated as valuable ends in themselves just because they are human beings. Using others for your own purposes is unethical if, at the same time, you deny them their goals and purposes.

The main limitation of using rights as a basis of ethical reasoning is the difficulty of balancing conflicting rights. For example, an employee's right to privacy may be at odds with an employer's right to protect the firm's assets by testing the employee's honesty. Rights also clash when U.S. multinational corporations move production to a foreign nation, causing job losses at home but creating new jobs abroad. In such cases, whose job rights should be respected?[33]

Despite this kind of problem, the protection and promotion of human rights is an important ethical benchmark for judging the behavior of individuals and organizations. Surely most people would agree that it is unethical to deny a person's fundamental right to life, freedom, privacy, growth, and human dignity. By defining the human condition and pointing the way to a realization of human potentialities, such rights become a kind of common denominator of ethical reasoning, setting forth the essential conditions for ethical actions and decisions.

Justice: Is It Fair?

A fourth method of ethical reasoning concerns **justice**. As shown in Figure 5.6, a common question in human affairs is, Is it fair or just? Employees want to know if pay scales are fair. Consumers are interested in fair prices when they shop. When new tax laws are proposed, there is much debate about their fairness—where will the burden fall, and who will escape paying their fair share?[34] After the U.S. government bailed out several big banks and insurance companies in 2008–09, many people wondered if it was fair that some of their top executives continued to receive big bonuses while their employees, shareholders, and bondholders suffered—and taxpayers absorbed the cost. The Occupy Wall Street protests, which began in 2010, called attention to the perceived lack of fairness in the distribution of income and assets between wealthy bankers and ordinary Americans. (This topic is also taken up in Chapter 15.)

Justice, or fairness, exists when benefits and burdens are distributed equitably and according to some accepted rule. For society as a whole, social justice means that a society's income and wealth are distributed among the people in fair proportions. A fair distribution does not necessarily mean an equal distribution. Most societies try to consider people's needs, abilities, efforts, and the contributions they make to society's welfare. Since these factors are seldom equal, fair shares will vary from person to person and group to group.

Justice reasoning is not the same as utilitarian reasoning. A person using utilitarian reasoning adds up costs and benefits to see if one is greater than the other; if benefits exceed costs, then the action would probably be considered ethical. A person using justice reasoning considers who pays the costs and who gets the benefits; if the shares seem fair (according to society's rules), then the action is probably just.

Applying Ethical Reasoning to Business Activities

Anyone in the business world can use these four methods of ethical reasoning to gain a better understanding of ethical issues that arise at work. Usually, all four can be applied at the same time. Using only one of the four methods is risky and may lead to an incomplete understanding of all the ethical complexities that may be present. It also may produce a lopsided ethical result that will be unacceptable to others.

---

[33] For a discussion of ethical rights, see Boatright, ibid., pp. 60–61; and Velasquez, *Business Ethics: Concepts and Cases,* pp. 90–98.

[34] For an interesting discussion of "what is fair?" see Patrick Primeaux and Frank P. LeVeness, "What is Fair: Three Perspectives," *Journal of Business Ethics* 84 (2009), pp. 89–102.

Once the ethical analysis is complete, the decision maker should ask this question: Do all of the ethics approaches lead to the same decision? If so, then the decision, policy, or activity is probably ethical. If the application of all ethics theories result in a "no, this is not ethical," then it is probably unethical. The reason you cannot be *absolutely* certain is that different people and groups (1) may honestly and genuinely use different sources of information, (2) may rely on different values or definitions of what is a virtuous character, (3) may measure costs and benefits differently, (4) may not share the same meaning of justice, or (5) may rank various rights in different ways. Nevertheless, any time an analyst obtains a consistent result when using all of the approaches, it indicates that a strong case can be made for either an ethical or an unethical conclusion.

What happens when the application of the four ethical approaches does not lead to the same conclusion? A corporate manager or an employee then has to assign priorities to each method of ethical reasoning. What is most important to the manager, to the employee, or to the organization—virtue, utility, rights, or justice? What ranking should they be given? A judgment must be made, and priorities must be determined. These judgments and priorities will be strongly influenced by a company's culture and ethical climate. Some will be sensitive to people's needs and rights; others will put themselves or their company ahead of all other considerations.

The importance of being attentive to ethical issues at work and the ability to reason to an ethical resolution of these knotty dilemmas have always been important but today are essential given the increasing ethical scrutiny of business and the grave consequences for unethical behavior in the workplace. Employees do not work in a vacuum. The organization where they work and the culture that exists within any organization exert significant influence on the individual as an ethical decision maker. Businesses are making significant efforts to improve the ethical work climates in their organizations and are providing safeguards to encourage ethical behavior by their employees, as the next chapter discusses.

Summary

- Ethics is a conception of right and wrong behavior, defining for us when our actions are moral and when they are immoral. Business ethics is the application of general ethical ideas to business behavior.

- Ethical business behavior enhances business performance, complies with legal requirements, prevents or minimizes harm, is demanded by business stakeholders, and promotes personal morality.

- Ethics problems occur in business for many reasons, including the selfishness of a few, competitive pressures on profits, the clash of personal values and business goals, and cross-cultural contradictions in global business operations.

- Managers' on-the-job values tend to be company-oriented, assigning high priority to company goals. Managers often value being competent and place importance on having a comfortable or exciting life, among other values.

- Individual spirituality can greatly influence how a manager understands ethical challenges; increasingly, it is recognized that organizations must acknowledge employees' spirituality in the workplace.

- Individuals reason at various stages of moral development, with most managers focusing on personal rewards, recognition from others, or compliance with company rules as guides for their reasoning.

- People in business can analyze ethics dilemmas by using four major types of ethical reasoning: virtue ethics, utilitarian reasoning, rights reasoning, and justice reasoning.

Key Terms

business ethics, *94*
conflict of interest, *100*
ethical egoist, *99*
ethical principles, *93*
ethical relativism, *94*
ethics, *93*

human rights, *108*
justice, *109*
laws, *94*
Sarbanes-Oxley
Act, *97*
spirituality, *103*

stages of moral
development, *104*
U.S. Corporate Sentencing
Guidelines, *96*
utilitarian reasoning, *107*
virtue ethics, *106*

Internet Resources

www.ethics.org
www.ibe.org.uk
www.business-ethics.org
www.charactercounts.org
www.soxlaw.com
www.oge.gov
www.ussc.gov
www.cfsaw.org

Ethics Resource Center
Institute for Business Ethics
International Business Ethics Institute
Josephson Institute
Sarbanes-Oxley Act
U.S. Office of Government Ethics
U.S. Sentencing Commission
Center for Spirituality at Work

Discussion Case: *Chiquita Brands:* *Ethical Responsibility or Illegal Action?*

In 2014, the 11th United States Court of Appeals ruled in favor of Chiquita Brands, a Cincinnati–based multinational marketer and distributor of food products—widely known for its Chiquita banana brand—which had been accused by 4000 Colombians of supporting paramilitary soldiers who had killed or tortured their relatives. The court ruled on technical grounds that the Colombians could not sue the company under the laws they had cited. "The Alien Tort Statute does not apply extraterritorially," wrote Judge David Sentelle, and "the Torture Victim Protection Act only applies to actual people, not to corporations."

The Colombians had sought $7.86 billion in damages, on the basis that Chiquita was responsible for the deaths of 393 victims at the hands of a paramilitary group called the United Self-Defense Forces of Colombia that Chiquita had funded through their payments. The lawsuits pointed specifically to a 1997 massacre in which 49 people were tortured, dismembered, and decapitated and another incident in 2000 in which 36 more people were killed.

The lawsuit was ironic, because Chiquita had originally made the payments to the paramilitary group to protect its Colombian employees from harm—not to put people at risk. However, once the payments had been made, Chiquita had no control over what the outlaw group did with the funds—which it had apparently used to terrorize other people in the community. "The principle upon which this lawsuit is brought," said the Colombians' attorney Jonathan Reiter, "is that when you put money into the hands of terrorists, when you put guns into the hands of terrorists, then you are legally responsible for the atrocities, the murders and the tortures that those terrorists commit."

Chiquita's problems began in the early 2000s, when the United Self-Defense Forces of Colombia attempted to extort substantial payments from the company to help fund the group's operations. The paramilitary group made it clear that if the company did not make the payments Chiquita's employees would be at risk. The company's managers took these threats seriously, because they were aware that in 1995 the paramilitary group had been responsible for bombing Chiquita's operations and murdering 17 banana workers, who had been gunned down on a muddy soccer field.

Chiquita's mission emphasized a strong sense of ethical performance and social responsibility. It stated that it wanted "to help the world's consumers broaden mindsets about nutrition and bring healthy, nutritious, and convenient foods that taste great and improve people's lives." Therefore, it was not surprising that Chiquita's management also wanted to protect its employees and ensure their safety while working for the company. In a handwritten note, a Chiquita executive said that such payments were the "cost of doing business in Colombia." The company agreed to make the payments demanded by the paramilitary group, but hid the payments through a series of questionable accounting actions. From 1997 through 2004 Chiquita paid monthly "protection payments" totaling more than $1.7 million.

After the September 11, 2001, terrorist attack in the United States, the U.S. Government declared the Colombian paramilitary group to be a terrorist organization. In February 2003, a Chiquita employee informed a senior Chiquita officer that the company's protection payments were illegal under the new U.S. terrorism laws. Chiquita officials met with their attorneys in Washington, DC, and were advised to stop the payments to the terrorist group. Yet the company continued to make the protection payments, amounting to an additional $825,000.

In the minds of the Chiquita's executives, stopping the payments would risk the lives of their employees. Chiquita's executives also considered but rejected the option of withdrawing operations from Colombia. But in a surprising move in April 2003, Chiquita decided to disclose to the Department of Justice that the company was still making payments to the Colombian paramilitary group. The company told the government that the payments were made under the threat of violence against them and their employees.

The Justice Department informed Chiquita that these payments were illegal, yet the company continued to make the payments. In 2007 Chiquita Brands International pleaded guilty to one count of the criminal charge of engaging in transactions with a designated global terrorist group and agreed to pay a $25 million fine.

In explaining its actions, a company spokesperson stated that "Chiquita and its employees were victims and that the actions taken by the company were always motivated to protect the lives of our employees and their families." He added, "Our company had been forced to make protection payments to safeguard our workforce. It is absolutely untrue for anyone to suggest that these payments were made for any other purpose."

Sources: "Chiquita Brands International Pleads Guilty to Making Payments to a Designated Terrorist Organization and Agrees to Pay $25 Million Fine," *U.S. Department of Justice Press Release,* March 19, 2007, *www.justice.gov/opa/pr/2007/March/07_ nsd_161.html*; "Colombian Families' Suit Says Chiquita Liable for Torture, Murder," *CNN.com*, February 14, 2007, *www.cnn. com/2007/US/law/11/14/chiquita.lawsuit*; "Chiquita Sued Over Colombian Paramilitary Payments," *The Sacramento Bee,* May 30, 2011, *www.sacbeee.com*; and "US Appeals Court Says Colombians Cannot Sue Chiquita," BBC News, July 24, 2014, *www. bbc.com/news/world-latin-america-28469357.*

Discussion Questions

1. Do you agree with the 11th U.S. Court of Appeals ruling that cleared Chiquita of any liability for the victims killed by the paramilitary group that Chiquita funded? Construct an ethical argument that supports your view.

2. Using each of the four methods of ethical reasoning (see Figure 5.6), was it ethical or not for Chiquita to pay the terrorist organization when payments were demanded in the early 2000s?

3. Should the U.S. ban against supporting terrorist groups, imposed after the September 11, 2001, attacks in the United States, be applied in this situation? Why or why not?

4. Is there anything that Chiquita could have done to protect its employees adequately without paying the terrorists?

5. Should Chiquita be assessed a penalty that puts the firm out of business for their actions?

CHAPTER SIX

Organizational Ethics

Faced with increasing pressure to create an ethical environment at work, businesses can take tangible steps to improve their ethical performance. The organization's culture and ethical work climate play a central role in promoting ethics at work. Ethical situations arise in all areas and functions of business, and often professional associations seek to guide managers in addressing these challenges. Corporations can also implement ethical safeguards to create a comprehensive ethics program. This can become a complex challenge when facing different customs and regulations around the world.

This Chapter Focuses on These Key Learning Objectives:

LO 6-1   Classifying an organization's culture and ethical climate.

LO 6-2   Recognizing ethics challenges across the multiple functions of business.

LO 6-3   Creating effective ethics policies, ethics reporting mechanisms, ethics training programs, and similar safeguards.

LO 6-4   Assessing the strengths and weaknesses of a comprehensive ethics program.

LO 6-5   Understanding how to conduct business ethically in the global marketplace.

In 2014 Takata Corporation, a major supplier of automobile air bags, admitted a defect with their product and recalled more than 34 million vehicles—about one in every seven cars on the road—making the automotive recall the largest in U.S. history. The recalls were spawned by a series of deaths and injuries from automobile accidents in which the airbag propellant deployed with such force that it ruptured its container, shooting metal parts at the driver or front seat passenger. Eleven automakers—including Toyota, Mazda, Honda, BMW, Nissan, General Motors, and Chrysler—mandated recalls. Later it was revealed that Takata knew about the defects. The company had secretly conducted tests in 2004 after normal work hours and on weekends and holidays, and executives had ordered its engineers to delete the test results from their computers.

On January 7, 2013, a lithium-ion battery, made by the Boeing Company, exploded on a Japan Airlines Boeing Dreamliner 787 jet parked at Boston's Logan Airport, setting off an intense fire. Earlier that month, All Nippon Airlines reported unexpectedly low charges on its main battery and the pilot smelled smoke in the cockpit, causing another Boeing plane to make an emergency landing in Japan. These two incidents led to the global grounding of all Boeing 787 planes until safety investigations were conducted. Boeing knew that the batteries tended to overheat but said that this would not threaten the planes and their passengers. Nearly four months later Boeing 787s returned to the skies, only to have an internal on-board fire ignite on an Ethiopian Airlines 787 parked at Heathrow Airport in July 2013.[1]

Around the world, dozens and dozens of other companies were charged with accounting fraud, mishandling investors' funds, market improprieties, jeopardizing the safety of consumers, and many other illegal activities. *Why are business executives, managers, and employees repeatedly being caught conducting illegal and unethical activities? What can firms do to minimize or prevent the unethical activities perpetrated by their executives and employees? Could companies set in place systems or programs to monitor workplace activities to detect illegal or unethical behavior?*

Corporate Ethical Climates

Personal values and moral character play key roles in improving a company's ethical performance, as discussed in Chapter 5. However, they do not stand alone, because personal values and character can be affected by a company's culture and ethical climate.

The terms *culture* and *climate* are often used interchangeably and, in fact, are highly interrelated. **Corporate culture** is a blend of ideas, customs, traditional practices, company values, and shared meanings that help define normal behavior for everyone who works in a company. Culture is "the way we do things around here." Anne Harris, a long-time ethics and compliance offer, explained the impact of having a good corporate culture:

> "Companies with lower rates of ethical misconduct have both strong E&C [ethics and compliance] program elements and strong ethical cultures. In such companies, employees also experience less pressure to compromise standards, greater willingness to speak up internally, and less retaliation."[2]

The Ethics Resource Center (ERC) observed that a "strong ethical culture in a company has a profound impact on the kinds of workplace behavior that can put a business in jeopardy." According to an ERC study, organizations with strong ethical cultures find that fewer than 5 percent of their employees feel pressure to commit misconduct, compared with 15 percent in ones

[1] "Takata Saw and Hid Risk in Airbags in 2004, Former Workers Say," *The New York Times,* November 6, 2014, *www.nytimes. com;* "Mazda Expands Recall of Takata Airbags," *The New York Times,* December 12, 2014, *www.nytimes.com;* "Boeing 787 Battery Was a Concern before Failure," *The New York Times,* January 29, 2013, *www.nytimes.com;* and "Boeing 787 Dreamliner Catches Fire in London," *The Wall Street Journal,* July 12, 2013, *online.wsj.com.*
[2] Anne R. Harris, "Want an Ethical Company? Keys for Fostering an Ethical Culture," *CR Magazine,* May/June 2014, pp. 36–37.

FIGURE 6.1
The Components of Ethical Climates

Source: Adapted from Bart Victor and John B. Cullen, "The Organizational Bases of Ethical Work Climates," *Administrative Science Quarterly* 33 (1988), p. 104.

Ethical Criteria	Focus of Individual Person	Organization	Society
Egoism (self-centered approach)	Self-interest	Company interest	Economic efficiency
Benevolence (concern-far-others approach)	Friendship	Team interest	Social responsibility
Principle (integrity approach)	Personal morality	Company rules and procedures	Laws and professional codes

with weak ethical cultures. Nearly twice as many employees observe misconduct by coworkers in weak ethical cultures companies (76 percent) as in strong ethical cultures (39 percent).[3]

Most companies have a kind of moral atmosphere. People can feel which way the ethical winds are blowing. They pick up subtle hints and clues that tell them what behavior is approved and what is forbidden. The **ethical climate** represents an unspoken understanding among employees of what is and is not acceptable behavior based on the expected standards or norms used for ethical decision making. It is the part of broader corporate culture that sets the ethical tone in a company. One way to view ethical climates is diagrammed in Figure 6.1. Three distinct ethical criteria are *egoism* (self-centeredness), *benevolence* (concern for others), and *principle* (respect for one's own integrity, for group norms, and for society's laws). (These parallel the levels of moral development developed by Lawrence Kohlberg that are discussed in Chapter 5.) These ethical criteria can be used to describe how individuals, a company, or society at large approach various moral dilemmas.

For example, if a company approaches ethics issues with benevolence in mind, it would emphasize friendly relations with its employees, stress the importance of team play and cooperation for the company's benefit, and recommend socially responsible courses of action. However, a company using egoism would be more likely to think first of promoting the company's profit and striving for efficient operations at all costs, perhaps at the sake of others or the environment, as illustrated by the following example:

> Barrick, a Toronto-based gold-mining corporation, was listed as one of the least ethical companies according to Covalence, a Swiss research firm. Allegations against the company included charges that it participated in the burning of at least 130 homes near its Porgera Mine in Papua New Guinea and that it manipulated land titles in Australia and Chile. The company was also blamed in a toxic spill in Tanzania that left dangerous levels of arsenic in the area around its North Mara mine. Barrick's attempts to mine along the Argentina-Chile border were associated with a significant shrinking of nearby glaciers. These allegations would point to a company placing its own interests ahead of others.[4]

Researchers have found that multiple ethical climates, or subclimates, may exist within one organization. For example, one company might include managers who often interact with the public and government regulators, using a principle-based approach, compared to another group of managers, whose work is geared toward routine process tasks and whose focus is mainly egotistic—higher personal pay or company profits.[5]

[3] "A Strong Culture Is a Key to Cutting Misconduct on the Job," *Ethics Resource Center*, June 23, 2010, www.ethics.org/files/u5/CultureSup4.pdf.

[4] "The 12 Least Ethical Companies In the World: Covalence's Ranking," *The Huffington Post,* May 25, 2011, www.huffingtonpost.com.

[5] James Weber, "Influences upon Organizational Ethical Subclimates: A Multi-departmental Analysis of a Single Firm," *Organization Science* 6 (1995), pp. 509–23. For a summary of ethical climate research, see Aditya Simha and John B. Cullen, "Ethical Climates and Their Effects on Organizational Outcomes: Implications from the Past and Prophesies for the Future," *Academy of Management Perspectives,* 2012, pp. 20–34.

Corporate ethical climates can also signal to employees that ethical transgressions are acceptable. By signaling what is considered to be right and wrong, corporate cultures and ethical climates can pressure people to channel their actions in certain directions desired by the company. This kind of pressure can work both for and against good ethical practices.

Business Ethics across Organizational Functions

Not all ethics issues in business are the same. Because business operations are highly specialized, ethics issues can appear in any of the major functional areas of a business firm. Accounting, finance, marketing, information technology, and other areas of business all have their own particular brands of ethical dilemmas. In many cases, professional associations in these functional areas have attempted to define a common set of ethical standards, as discussed next.

Accounting Ethics

The accounting function is a critically important component of every business firm. By law, the financial records of publicly held companies are required to be audited by a certified professional accounting firm. Company managers, external investors, government regulators, tax collectors, and labor unions rely on such public audits to make key decisions. Honesty, integrity, and accuracy are absolute requirements of the accounting function, and the impact can be devastating for organizations when these values are absent.

> The U.S. Securities and Exchange Commission filed an administrative proceeding against five accounting firms, alleging they refused to hand over documents sought in an investigation of alleged accounting fraud at nine Chinese companies. This action, if supported by an administrative judge, could bar the four largest U.S. accounting firm's Chinese affiliates from auditing U.S.-traded companies. At the core of this inquiry was the fact that dozens of Chinese companies made billions of dollars by listing their shares of stock on U.S. stock exchanges before their share prices plummeted, raising questions about their bookkeeping and disclosures.[6]

Accountants often are faced with conflicts of interest, introduced in Chapter 5, where loyalty or obligation to the company (the client) may be divided or in conflict with self-interest (of the accounting firm) and the interests of others (shareholders and the public). For example, while conducting an audit of a company, should the auditor look for opportunities to recommend to the client consulting services that the auditor's firm can provide? Sometimes, accounting firms may be tempted to soften their audit of a company's financial statements if the accounting firm wants to attract the company's nonaudit business. For this reason, the Sarbanes–Oxley Act severely limits the offering of nonaudit consulting services by the auditing firm.

Examples of the U.S. accounting profession's efforts promoting ethics are shown in Exhibit 6.A. Spurred by a threat of liability suits filed against accounting firms and a desire to reaffirm professional integrity, these standards go far toward ensuring a high level of honest and ethical accounting behavior.[7]

Financial Ethics

Within companies, the finance department and its officers are typically responsible for managing the firm's assets and raising capital—for example, by issuing stocks and bonds. Financial institutions, such as commercial banks, securities firms, and so forth, assist in raising

---

[6] "U.S. Sues Big Firms over China Audits," *The Wall Street Journal,* December 3, 2012, *online.wsj.com.*

[7] For several excellent examples of ethical dilemmas in accounting, see Leonard J. Brooks and Paul Dunn, *Business & Professional Ethics for Directors, Executives and Accountants,* 7th ed. (Stamford, CT: Cengage Learning, 2015); and Ronald Duska, Brenda Duska, and Julie Ragatz, *Accounting Ethics,* 2nd ed. (Malden, MA: Wiley-Blackwell, 2011).

Exhibit 6.A

Professional Codes of Conduct in Accounting and Finance

AMERICAN INSTITUTE OF CERTIFIED PUBLIC ACCOUNTANTS (AICPA)

Code of Professional Conduct

These Principles of the Code of Professional Conduct of the American Institute of Certified Public Accountants express the profession's recognition of its responsibilities to the public, to clients, and to colleagues. They guide members in the performance of their professional responsibilities and express the basic tenets of ethical and professional conduct. The Principles call for an unswerving commitment to honorable behavior, even at the sacrifice of personal advantage.

- Responsibilities—In carrying out their responsibilities as professionals, members should exercise sensitive professional and moral judgments in all their activities. . . .
- The Public Interest—Members should accept the obligation to act in a way that will serve the public interest, honor the public trust, and demonstrate commitment to professionalism. . . .
- Integrity—To maintain and broaden public confidence, members should perform all professional responsibilities with the highest sense of integrity. . . .
- Objectivity and Independence—A member should maintain objectivity and be free of conflicts of interest in discharging professional responsibilities. A member in public practice should be independent in fact and appearance when providing auditing and other attestation services. . . .
- Due Care—A member should observe the profession's technical and ethical standards, strive continually to improve competence and the quality of services, and discharge professional responsibility to the best of the member's ability. . . .
- Scope and Nature of Services—A member in public practice should observe the Principles of the Code of Professional Conduct in determining the scope and nature of services to be provided.*

CHARTERED FINANCIAL ANALYST (CFA)®

Summary from CFA Institute Code of Ethics and Standards of Professional Conduct

Members of CFA Institute (including Chartered Financial Analyst® (CFA®) charterholders) and candidates for the CFA designation ("Members and Candidates") must:

- Act with integrity, competence, diligence, respect, and in an ethical manner with the public, clients, prospective clients, employers, employees, colleagues in the investment profession, and other participants in the global capital markets.
- Place the integrity of the investment profession and the interests of clients above their own personal interests.
- Use reasonable care and exercise independent professional judgment when conducting investment analysis, making investment recommendations, taking investment actions, and engaging in other professional activities.
- Practice and encourage others to practice in a professional and ethical manner that will reflect credit on themselves and the profession.
- Promote the integrity and viability of the global capital markets for the ultimate benefit of society.
- Maintain and improve their professional competence and strive to maintain and improve the competence of other investment professionals.†

capital and managing assets for both individuals and institutions. Whether working directly for a business or in a firm that provides financial services, finance professionals face a particular set of ethical issues. Consider the following ethical lapses in corporate finance:

- More than 100 former loan officers at Wells Fargo and JP Morgan Chase were accused of accepting kickbacks as part of a scheme to steer business to a now defunct title insurance company, Genuine Title. In one instance, Genuine Title reportedly paid tens of thousands of dollars to a former Wells Fargo employee's wife as kickbacks for business referrals. Wells Fargo agreed to pay a $24 million penalty and $10.8 million to consumers harmed by the scheme in a consent decree agreement. JP Morgan was fined $600,000 and must pay $300,000 to customers.

- The LIBOR financial scandal, named after the London interbank offered rate (LIBOR) benchmark, resulted in numerous large banks agreeing to settlement payments to avoid costly litigation. Traders from some of the world's largest banks were accused of colluding to influence foreign-currency rates for their own financial benefit. London-based ICAP, a British multinational operator and provider of posttrade risk mitigation and information services, agreed to pay $87 million. Settlement agreements by Barclays, Citigroup, JP Morgan Chase, and the Royal Bank of Scotland totaled more than $5 billion in combined penalties and executives at their banks plead guilty to criminal charges. UBS received immunity on some charges but pled guilty to manipulating the London interbank rate and paid $545 million in fines.[8]

These and other lapses in ethical conduct occurred despite efforts by the finance professions to foster an ethical environment. As shown in Exhibit 6.A, the highly regarded Chartered Financial Analyst Institute, which oversees financial executives performing many different types of jobs in the financial discipline, emphasizes self-regulation as the best path for ethical compliance.[9]

Marketing Ethics

Marketing refers to advertising, distributing, and selling products or services. Within firms, the marketing department is the functional area that typically interacts most directly with customers. Outside the firm, advertising agencies and other firms provide marketing services to businesses. The complex set of activities involved in marketing generates its own distinctive ethical issues.

One issue in marketing ethics emphasizes honesty and fairness in advertising, especially toward children.

In 2014, the U.S. Federal Trade Commission (FTC) sued Gerber Products Company for claiming that its Good Start Gentle formula could prevent or reduce allergies in children. The FTC argued that the claim was bogus and misleading, and demanded that Gerber pull its claim from all formula labels and its advertisements. Gerber denied the allegations, saying, "We are defending our position because we believe we have met, and will continue to meet, all legal requirements to make these product claims."[10]

---

[8] "UBS Fined $47.5 Million in Rogue Trading Scandal," *The New York Times,* November 26, 2012, *dealbook.nytimes.com;* "Wells Fargo and JP Morgan Loan Officers Accused of Taking Kickbacks," *The New York Times,* January 22, 2015, *dealbook. nytimes.com;* "Libor Scandal Shows Pressures on 'Honest Bankers,'" *Reuters,* September 25, 2013, *www.reuters.com;* "Banks to Pay $5.6 Billion in Probes, *The Wall Street Journal,* May 20, 2015, *www.wsj.com;* and "UBS Hit with $545 Million in Fines," *The Wall Street Journal,* May 20, 2015, *www.wsj.com.* For a good example of other financial ethics issues, see John B. Boatright, *Ethics in Finance,* 3rd ed. (Malden, MA: Wiley-Blackwell, 2014).

[9] For a good example of other financial ethics issues, see John B. Boatright, *Ethics in Finance,* 3rd ed. (Malden, MA: Wiley-Blackwell, 2014).

[10] "FTC Sues Gerber for False Advertising Claims," *Food Manufacturing,* October 20, 2014, *www.foodmanufacturing.com.*

AMERICAN MARKETING ASSOCIATION (AMA)

Statement of Ethics

The American Marketing Association commits itself to promoting the highest standard of professional ethical norms and values for its members (practitioners, academics, and students).

As Marketers, we must:

1. **Do no harm.** This means consciously avoiding harmful actions or omissions by embodying high ethical standards and adhering to all applicable laws and regulations in the choices we make.
2. **Foster trust in the marketing system.** This means striving for good faith and fair dealing so as to contribute toward the efficacy of the exchange process as well as avoiding deception in product design, pricing, communication, and delivery of distribution.
3. **Embrace ethical values.** This means building relationships and enhancing consumer confidence in the integrity of marketing by affirming these core values: honesty, responsibility, fairness, respect, transparency, and citizenship.

We expect AMA members to be courageous and proactive in leading and/or aiding their organizations in the fulfillment of the explicit and implicit promises made to those stakeholders.*

ASSOCIATION OF INFORMATION TECHNOLOGY PROFESSIONALS (AITP)

Code of Ethics and Standards of Conduct

This code begins with a commitment by each association's member to:

- Promote the understanding of information processing methods and procedures to management using every resource at my command,
- . . . an obligation to my fellow members . . . to uphold the ideals of AITP . . . and shall cooperate with my fellow members and treat them with honesty and respect at all times,
- . . . an obligation to society and will participate to the best of my ability in the dissemination of knowledge pertaining to the general development and understanding of information processing . . .
- . . . an obligation to my employer whose trust I hold . . . I shall endeavor to discharge this obligation to the best of my ability, to guard my employer's interests, and to advise him wisely and honestly,
- . . . an obligation to my country . . . I shall uphold my nation and shall honor the chosen way of life of my fellow citizens,
- I accept these obligations as a personal responsibility and as a member of this Association.**

* Used with permission from the American Marketing Association's Statement of Ethics, 2016, as it appears in *www.marketing.com*.

** Copyright 2011–14, Association of Information Technology Professionals. A full text of the AITP code of ethics can be found at *www.aitp.org*.

In addition to the general ethical questions that surround the marketing or advertising of products to consumers, consumer health and safety are another key ethics issue in marketing. Chapter 14 discusses several other issues in marketing ethics, including deceptive advertising, firm liability for consumer injury, and a firm's responsibility for the unethical use of products by buyers.

To improve the ethics of the marketing profession, the American Marketing Association (AMA) has adopted a code of ethics for its members, as shown in Exhibit 6.B. The AMA code advocates professional conduct guided by ethics, adherence to applicable laws, and honesty and fairness in all marketing activities. The code seeks to help marketing professionals translate general ethical principles into specific working rules.[11]

[11] The AMA Code for Market Researchers and a discussion of numerous marketing ethics issues can be found in Patrick E. Murphy, Gene R. Laczniak, and Andrea Prothero, *Ethics in Marketing: International Cases and Perspectives* (New York: Routledge, 2012).

Information Technology Ethics

One of the most complex and fast-changing areas of business ethics is in the field of information technology. Ethical challenges in this field involve invasions of privacy; the collection and storage of, and access to, personal and business information, especially through e-commerce transactions; confidentiality of electronic mail communication; copyright protection regarding software, music, and intellectual property; and numerous others.

> During one week in 2012, a Facebook scientist and two university researchers manipulated nearly 700,000 Facebook users' news feeds to gauge whether emotions spread on social media. The investigation revealed that users who saw more positive posts tended to write more positive posts themselves and vice versa. This study generated many complaints about a lack of ethical standards, since Facebook users, many of whom were younger than 18, were not notified of being manipulated in this way and were unwittingly used as "lab rats." This study shined a light on how companies and researchers can tap vast amounts of data created online.[12]

As discussed in later chapters of this book, the explosion of information technology has raised serious questions of trust between individuals and businesses. In response to calls by businesspeople and academics for an increase in ethical responsibility in the information technology field, professional organizations have developed or revised professional codes of ethics, as shown in Exhibit 6.B.[13]

Other Functional Areas

Production and operations functions, which may seem remote from ethics considerations, have also been at the center of some ethics storms.

> Mylan Inc., the world's third largest manufacturer of generic pharmaceuticals, abruptly halted production at its Morgantown, West Virginia, plant and privately informed workers that two employees had violated government-mandated quality control procedures. These procedures were intended to ensure the safety and effectiveness of their manufactured prescription drugs. A confidential internal report leaked to a local newspaper said that workers routinely overrode computer-generated warnings about potential problems with the medications they were producing. The report said that this practice was "pervasive," occurring on all three shifts at the plant for at least two years.[14]

Similar to the other professional associations, whose codes of ethical conduct are presented in Exhibits 6.A and 6.B, the Institute for Supply Management (ISM) developed a professional code of ethics that advocates "loyalty to your organization, justice to those with whom you deal, and faith in your profession." The professional code denotes 12 principles and standards "to encourage adherence to an uncompromising level of integrity."[15]

Efforts by professional associations to guide their members toward effective resolution of ethical challenges make one point crystal clear: All areas of business, all people in business, and all levels of authority in business encounter ethics dilemmas from time to time.

[12] "Facebook Study Sparks Soul-Searching and Ethical Questions," *The Wall Street Journal,* June 30, 2014, *www.wsj.com.*

[13] For further discussion of ethics in information technology see Sara Baase, *A Gift of Fire: Social, Legal, and Ethical Issues for Computing and the Internet,* 4th ed. (Upper Saddle River, NJ: Pearson, 2012); and Richard A. Spinello, *Cyberethics: Morality and Law in Cyberspace,* 5th ed. (Burlington, MA: Jones & Bartlett Learning, 2014).

[14] "Mylan Workers Overrode Drug Quality Controls," *Pittsburgh Post-Gazette,* July 26, 2009, *www.post-gazette.com.*

[15] All quotations are from the Institute for Supply Management's Principles and Standards of Ethical Supply Management Conduct, available to members of the association at *www.ism.ws.*

FIGURE 6.2
Percentage of Firms Reporting They Have the Ethical Safeguard

Sources: Center for Business Ethics, "Are Corporations Institutionalizing Ethics?" *Journal of Business Ethics* 5 (1986), pp. 85–91; Center for Business Ethics, "Instilling Ethical Values in Large Corporations," *Journal of Business Ethics* 11 (1992), pp. 863–67; Ethics Resources Center, *Ethics in American Business: Policies, Programs and Perceptions* (Washington, DC, Ethics Resource Center, 1994); Ethics Resource Center, *National Business Ethics Survey: How Employees View Ethics in Their Organizations 1994–2005*, (Washington, DC, Ethics Resource Center, 2005); and James Weber and David Wasieleski, "Corporate Ethics and Compliance Programs: A Report, Analysis and Critique," *Journal of Business Ethics* 112 (2013), pp. 609–26.

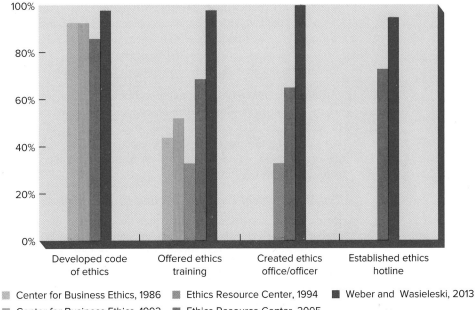

Center for Business Ethics, 1986   Ethics Resource Center, 1994   Weber and Wasieleski, 2013
Center for Business Ethics, 1992   Ethics Resource Center, 2005

Ethics issues are a common thread running through the business world. Specific steps that businesses can take to make ethics work are discussed next.

Making Ethics Work in Corporations

Any business firm can improve the quality of its ethical performance. Doing so requires a company to build ethical safeguards into its everyday routines. This is sometimes called *institutionalizing ethics*. The proportion of the world's largest firms (the *Fortune 500* or *1000* as reported in *Fortune* magazine each year) that have adopted these safeguards since the 1980s is shown in Figure 6.2.

A 2015 Ethics Research Center study found that employees in large organizations with an effective ethics and compliance program were less likely to feel pressure to compromise their ethical standards (3 percent), compared to those without effective programs (23 percent). They were also less likely to observe misconduct (33 percent versus 62 percent) and less likely to experience retaliation (4 percent versus 59 percent). Employees at organizations with an effective ethics program were nearly three times more likely to report observed misconduct at work (87 percent versus 32 percent).[16]

Building Ethical Safeguards into the Company

Managers and employees need guidance on how to handle day-to-day ethical situations; their own personal ethical compass may be working well, but they need to receive directional signals from the company. Several organizational steps can be taken to provide this kind of ethical awareness and direction.

Lynn Sharp Paine, a Harvard Business School professor, has described two distinct approaches to ethics programs: a compliance-based approach and an integrity-based approach. A compliance-based program seeks to avoid legal sanctions. This approach emphasizes the threat of detection and punishment in order to channel employee behavior in a lawful direction. Paine also described an integrity-based

[16] "The State of Ethics in Large Companies," *Ethics Research Center,* 2015, *www.ethics.org.*

approach to ethics programs. Integrity-based ethics programs combine a concern for the law with an emphasis on employee responsibility for ethical conduct. Employees are told to act with integrity and conduct their business dealings in an environment of honesty and fairness. From these values a company will nurture and maintain business relationships and will be profitable.[17]

Researchers found that both approaches lessened unethical conduct, although in somewhat different ways. Compliance-based ethics programs increased employees' willingness to seek ethical advice and sharpened their awareness of ethical issues at work. Integrity-based programs, for their part, increased employees' sense of integrity, commitment to the organization, willingness to deliver bad news to supervisors, and their perception that better decisions were made.[18]

Top Management Commitment and Involvement

Research has consistently shown that the "tone at the top"—the example set by top executives—is critical to fostering ethical behavior. When senior-level managers and directors signal employees, through their own behavior, that they believe ethics should receive high priority in all business decisions, they have taken a giant step toward improving ethical performance throughout the company.

Whether the issue is sexual harassment, honest dealing with suppliers, or the reporting of expenses, the commitments (or lack thereof) by senior management and the employees' immediate supervisor and their involvement in ethics as a daily influence on employee behavior are the most essential safeguards for creating an ethical workplace.

Ethics Policies or Codes

As shown in Figure 6.2, many U.S. businesses, especially large firms, have **ethics policies or codes**. An example of one of the first corporate ethics codes is shown in Exhibit 6.C. The purpose of such policies and codes is to provide guidance to managers and employees when they encounter an ethical dilemma. Research has shown significant differences among countries. In the United States and Latin America, ethics policies were found to be primarily *instrumental*—that is, they provided rules and procedures for employees to follow in order to adhere to company policies or societal laws. In Japan, most policies were a mixture of *legal compliance* and *statements of the company's values and mission. Values and mission* policies were also popular with European and Canadian companies.[19] Despite some differences in orientation, codes of ethics are clearly becoming more common.

Typically, ethics policies cover issues such as developing guidelines for accepting or refusing gifts from suppliers, avoiding conflicts of interest, maintaining the security of proprietary information, and avoiding discriminatory personnel practices. Yet, researchers have found that a written ethics policy, while an important contributor, is insufficient by itself to bring about ethical conduct. Companies must circulate ethics policies frequently and widely among employees and external stakeholder groups (for example, customers, suppliers, or competitors). Many companies use posters, quick reference guides, and brochures to raise awareness and importance of their code. One study reported that 86 percent of all firms made substantial progress toward the deployment of their codes of conduct in 2013.[20]

---

[17] Lynn Sharp Paine, "Managing for Organizational Integrity," *Harvard Business Review,* March–April 1994, pp. 106–17.

[18] Gary R. Weaver and Linda Klebe Trevino, "Compliance and Values Oriented Ethics Programs: Influences on Employees' Attitudes and Behavior," *Business Ethics Quarterly* 9 (1999), pp. 315–35.

[19] Ronald C. Berenbeim, *Global Corporate Ethics Practices: A Developing Consensus* (New York: Conference Board, 1999).

[20] "The 2014 Ethics and Compliance Program Effectiveness Report," *LRN,* 2014, pp. 30–31.

Exhibit 6.C

**United States Steel Corporation's
The Gary Principles**

Drafted by Judge Elbert Gary, the first chairman of United States Steel Corporation, and distributed throughout the company in 1909, The Gary Principles stated the following:

- I believe that when a thing is right, it will ultimately and permanently succeed.
- The highest rewards come from honest and proper practice. Bad results come in the long run from selfish, unfair, and dishonest conduct.
- I believe in competition . . . that the race should be won by the swiftest, and that success should come to him who is most earnest and active and persevering.
- I believe that no industry can permanently succeed that does not treat its employees equitably and humanely.
- I believe thoroughly in publicity. The surest and wisest of all regulation is public opinion.
- If we are to succeed in business, we must do it on principles that are honest, fair, lawful, and just.
- We must put and keep ourselves on a platform so fair, so high, so reasonable, that we will attract the attention and invite and secure the approval of all who know what we are doing.
- We do not advocate combinations or agreements in restraint of trade, nor action of any kind which is opposed to the laws or to the public welfare.
- We must never forget that our rights and interests are and should be subservient to the public welfare, that the rights and interests of the individual must always give way to those of the public.

Reproduced with permission, United States Steel Corporation.

Ethics and Compliance Officers

Ethical lapses in large corporations throughout the 1980s prompted many firms to create a new position: the **ethics and compliance officer** (ECO), or sometimes called the chief compliance officer (CCO) or the chief integrity officer (CIO). A second surge of attention to ethics and the creation of ethics offices came in response to the 1991 U.S. Corporate Sentencing Guidelines, discussed in Chapter 5. Finally, the recent wave of corporate ethics scandals and the passage of the Sarbanes–Oxley Act have again turned businesses' attention toward entrusting ethical compliance and the development and implementation of ethics programs to an ethics or compliance officer. From 2000 to 2004, the number of members in the Ethics Officer Association doubled from 632 to more than 1200 members and continued to grow to approximately 1300 members representing over 400 organizations in over 50 countries by 2015. To reflect the growing number of compliance officers heading companies' ethics programs, this association changed its name to the Ethics and Compliance Officer Association (ECOA). One member of the ECOA is profiled in Exhibit 6.D.

A PricewaterhouseCoopers global survey reported that 41 percent of U.S.- and U.K.-based compliance officers still report to the legal department, but that trend is declining; more CCOs now report formally to the firm's CEO. Although this practice is more common in the United Kingdom, 28 percent of U.S. CCOs in 2013 reported to their CEO, compared to 20 percent in 2012. Another study found that it was more common for the ethics officer to report to the general counsel (chief legal officer) in less effective ethics programs, whereas ethics officers working in more effective ethics programs were more likely to report to the CEO or the board of directors.[21]

[21]"More Compliance Officers Report to CEO—PwC Survey," *Ethikos,* July/August 2013, pp. 9–10; and "2014 LRN Report," *Ibid.,* p. 9.

Ms. Haydee Olinger is McDonald's corporate vice president and chief global compliance officer. After progressing through a series of compliance positions within McDonald's, where Olinger was instrumental in the company's entry into and growth throughout Central and South America, the Caribbean, and Mexico, Olinger was appointed the global compliance officer overseeing the company's global compliance and privacy efforts. She has the responsibility to ensure that McDonald's employees' behaviors are consistent with McDonald's Standards of Business Conduct and that the company meets all legal and regulatory compliance requirements. She reports regularly to the Board of Director's Audit Committee and provides advice and counsel to senior management, general counsels, and presidents throughout the McDonald's global network. She also is entrusted with assessing current and future risks of bribery, kickbacks, fraud, and other forms of criminal activity; developing strategies for the treatment of whistle-blower complaints; and monitors the company's global reporting hotline, in compliance with the U.S. Sarbanes–Oxley Act. Olinger earned a law degree and has a master's of science in leadership and business ethics to support her professional duties as an ethics and compliance officer.

Sources: Information provided by Ms. Haydee Olinger, including her job description and professional biography.

Ethics Reporting Mechanisms

In most companies, when employees are troubled about some ethical issue they seek out their immediate supervisor or someone else in senior management. But what if the employee is reluctant, for whatever reason, to raise the issue with their immediate supervisor? In that case, they can turn to their company's **ethics reporting mechanisms** and call a "helpline" or send an e-mail expressing their concerns, anonymously if they wish. Ethics reporting systems typically have three uses: (1) to provide interpretations of proper ethical behavior involving conflicts of interest and the appropriateness of gift giving, (2) to create an avenue to make known to the proper authorities allegations of unethical conduct, and (3) to give employees and other corporate stakeholders a way to discover general information about a wide range of work-related topics.

A 2014 study found that 87 percent of firms made at least substantial progress on providing employees with a secure and anonymous channel for reporting concerns. Another study found that more than one-third of the firms surveyed reported that the volume of calls to the organization's reporting mechanism increased somewhat or a great deal in the last two years and only 12 percent of firms reported a decline in calls.[22]

While more and more employees are willing to use their companies' ethical reporting mechanisms, a number of challenges remain. Executives tend to use the helpline more often than those farther down the organizational chart. The Ethics Resource Center study found that middle managers were "an area of vulnerability within companies" since they were less likely to use the helpline. The report also discovered that rates of helpline usage were lower in foreign-owned companies than in their U.S. counterparts. Yet, many businesses described greater success when employees use the company's helpline/hotline and were better able to avoid more serious ethical violations. Technology seemed to be the key.

Medtronics' global chief ethics and compliance officer, Tom Schumacher, received hotline reports quicker and more frequently through his handheld device. Employees can report possible violations online. For some firms, 60 to 70 percent of all reports arrived via the Internet. A web-based reporting system can be designed to solicit information from the employee for a more detailed and helpful report.

[22] "2014 LRN Study," *Ibid.,* p. 30; and "Helpline Calls and Incident Reports," *Society of Corporate Compliance,* 2014.

According to Schumacher, "I really like the [enhanced] ability to communicate with an anonymous reporter" since the system is more secure than in the past.[23]

But no matter how advanced the technology used in an ethics and compliance program, the ethics and compliance officer never really knows what to expect when monitoring calls to the helpline, as the following example showed:

> "Oh, boy, this is one of those days," thought the ethics officer at a midsized manufacturing firm when she received a call on the ethics helpline that a toilet in the company's administration building was overflowing. She called maintenance and they found that someone had clogged up the toilet drain. When the same call was received a week later, the ethics officer knew she had to investigate. Through interviews with personnel who worked on that floor, she discovered that the supervisor had refused to allow workers to take bathroom breaks when needed, and an employee had boasted that "he was going to get even with his supervisor and plug up the toilet" to attract attention to unsafe working conditions. The call about the overflowing toilet and subsequent investigation allowed the ethics officer to address the real issue, counsel the supervisor, and repair the deteriorating working conditions at her company.[24]

Ethics Training Programs

Another step companies can take to build in ethical safeguards is to offer **employee ethics training**. This is generally the most expensive and time-consuming element of an ethics program. Studies have shown that only 20 to 40 percent of small businesses formally offer ethics training to their employees, often using less formal ways to communicate ethical values and procedures. Larger businesses, by contrast, usually conduct regular ethics training, as shown in Figure 6.2. An increasing number of companies, nearly 90 percent according to one 2014 study, deployed online learning modules as part or all of their employee ethics training. Some experts argued that the explosion of web-based ethics training may not be as effective as the more traditional but expensive face-to-face training.[25]

Most ethics and compliance training programs focus on making sure employees know what the law requires and the company expects. Few firms, however, systematically measure the effectiveness of this effort or consider the impact of new training approaches. A new approach to employee ethics training emphasizes the importance of varied yet frequent efforts at ethics training, as seen at Raytheon.

> At Raytheon, ethics training tried to guide employees' ethical decision making and communicate important ethics messages throughout the organization. In 2010, 82 percent of employees favorably rated the company's ethics training efforts. The company attributed this high satisfaction rate due to the delivery of ethics training through numerous vehicles. All employees participated in small group sessions to study ethical dilemmas based on real workplace situations, watched videos that presented meaningful and relevant ethical issues in an entertaining way, and studied online learning modules on a wide range of topics. Follow-up assessment of the ethics training program revealed that employees were more likely to report alleged misconduct to the ethics office.[26]

---

[23]For a more detailed description of Medtronics' ethics and compliance program, see Andrew Singer, "Going Beyond Devices: Medtronics Urges Employees to 'Speak Up,'" *Ethikos,* May/June 2011, pp. 1–3, 16.

[24] Based on an interview with an ethics and compliance officer who requested that her firm and her identity remain anonymous.

[25] See "Is Your Ethics and Compliance Training Really Preparing Your Employees?" *Compliance and Ethics Professional,* March–April 2012, *www.corporatecompliance.org.*

[26] "Ethics: Demonstrating Our Values through Our Actions," *Raytheon's 2010 Corporate Responsibility Report,* p. 7.

The effectiveness of the ethics and compliance program is important to executives. Companies used to conduct formal ethics audits to ensure the quality of these programs, but today most firms have turned to a company-wide risk assessment audit to determine the effectiveness of the ethics program along with other risks. Experts believe that integrating various ethics safeguards into a comprehensive program is critically important and minimizes the firm's risk. When all five components discussed in this chapter—top management commitment, ethical policies or codes, compliance officers, reporting mechanisms, and training programs—are used together, they reinforce each other and become more effective.

Corporate Ethics Awards and Certifications

Firms are recognized for their efforts to create an ethical climate and improve ethical performance by various groups and associations.

Ethisphere Magazine honors ethical leadership and business practices worldwide based on an Ethical Quotient (EQ) score. The EQ score considers corporate responsibility performance; governance adherence; innovation that contributes to the public's well-being; exemplary leadership to the industry; executive leadership; the firm's legal, regulatory, and reputation track record; and the internal systems and ethics and compliance program developed at the firm. As seen in Chapter 5, Figure 5.3, Ethisphere's "the world's most ethical companies" financially outperformed the S&P 500 and FTSE 1000 every year since 2005. Figure 6.3 shows the 17 companies that have made the World's Most Ethical Companies list each year since 2007.

The Foundation for Financial Service Professionals sponsored the American Business Ethics Awards (ABEA). Established in 1994, the ABEA "recognizes companies that exemplify high standards of ethical behavior in their everyday business conduct and in response to specific crises or challenges." In the small company category (fewer than 250 employees), Skyline Exhibitor Source of LaVergne, Tennessee, a marketing and design company that specializes in trade show exhibit solutions, received the award in 2014. The company stated on its website that Skyline believes "in taking the time to learn about their clients' business, industry, and audience and to become a trusted partner to satisfy their clients' exhibit needs on time and on budget." The Marvin Companies of Warroad, Minnesota, a family-owned company that provides windows, doors, and allied products, earned the 2014 award in the large company category (more than 2500 employees). The Marvin Companies, according to its website, "was built on an old-fashioned code of honesty, hard work, and service to their neighbors."[27]

These and other award-winning firms provide the foundation for a collection of corporate ethics role models. Their commitment to ethical values and efforts to establish effective ethics programs demonstrate that firms can be financially successful and ethically focused.

FIGURE 6.3
The World's Most Ethical Companies and Their Industries, According to *Ethisphere*

Source: Information is from the *Ethisphere* website at *ethisphere. com/worlds-most-ethical/ wme-honorees.*

These firms were ranked among the highest ethical firms each year from 2007 through 2014.

AFLAC (insurance)	Kao Corporation (consumer products)
Deere and Company (industrial manufacturing)	Milliken & Company (industrial manufacturing)
Eaton Corporation (industrial manufacturing)	PepsiCo (food & beverage)
Ecolab (chemicals)	Salesforce.com (software)
Fluor Corporation (engineering)	Starbucks Coffee Company (restaurants)
The Gap (apparel)	Texas Instrument (computers)
General Electric (diversified)	UPS (transportation)
International Paper (paper products)	Xerox (computers)
Johnson Controls (automotive)	

[27] A full description of the ABEA program can be found at *www.financialpro.org/Foundation/ABEA/currentrecipients.htm;* and the websites for the 2014 winners are *www.esourcetn.com* and *www.marvin.com.*

Ethics in a Global Economy

Doing business in a global context raises a host of complex ethical challenges. One example of unethical activity is **bribery**, a questionable or an unjust payment often to a government official to ensure or facilitate a business transaction. The act of bribery introduces an economic force that is not based on the product or service's quality or other sales characteristics, therefore the element of bribery corrupts the economic exchange.

Bribery is found in nearly every sector of the global marketplace, but is more common in some countries than others.

A Berlin-based watchdog agency, Transparency International, annually publishes a survey that ranks countries by their level of corruption, as perceived by executives and the public. In the 2014 survey, countries where having to pay a bribe was least likely included: Denmark, New Zealand, Finland, Sweden, Norway, and Switzerland. At the other end of the index, North Korea and Somalia were considered the world's most corrupt countries, along with Sudan, Afghanistan, Iraq, Turkmenistan, and Uzbekistan. The United States was tied for 17th on the list of 174 countries, with Canada 10th, Germany and Iceland tied for 12th, the United Kingdom 14th, India 85th, China 100th, and Russia 136th.[28]

In some settings, corruption is so common as to be almost unavoidable. In a Transparency International survey of 114,000 people in 107 countries, 27 percent of respondents admitted they had paid a bribe in 2013. In Liberia and Sierra Leone, more than 75 percent of the respondents reported paying a bribe. More than half of the Russians surveyed thought bribing officials was the best way to solve problems, according to a Reuters poll. In Australia, 9 out of 10 people thought bribery and corruption were wrong but unavoidable. A German newspaper columnist said his business had paid bribes on several occasions, "because there are certain countries where there is no other way to do it."[29]

Bribery has significant economic, as well as ethical, consequences. Mythili Raman, a former senior executive at the Department of Justice explained,

> "Our fight against foreign corruption is critical for so many reasons. The corrosive effects of transnational corruption are felt not just overseas, but also here in the United States. Although we may not experience as acutely, or as personally, some of the consequences of foreign bribery, such as hospitals or roads that go unbuilt because infrastructure funds are siphoned off by a corrupt official, American companies are harmed. They are denied the ability to compete in a fair and transparent marketplace. Instead of being rewarded for their efficiency, innovation and honest business practices, U.S. companies suffer at the hands of corrupt governments and lose out to corrupt competitors."[30]

The following examples further demonstrate the harmful effects of bribery.

- Brazilian state-run oil company Petroleo Brasileiro SA announced that their corruption scandal contributed to their stock shares dropping 6.2 billion reais ($2.1 billion) in value and led to an impairment charge of 44.6 billion reais ($14.8 billion) for 2014 after determining that assets were overvalued on its balance sheet.

---

[28] For a complete list of all countries according to their perceived level of corruption, see *www.transparency.org/cpi2014.*

[29] "Survey Finds 25% of People Paid Bribes in Last Year," *The Wall Street Journal,* July 9, 2013, *blogs.wsj.com;* "Half of Russians Believe Bribery Solves 'Problems'," *Reuters,* May 13, 2010, *www.reuters.com;* "Bribery 'Wrong but Unavoidable' in Oz, Claim Managers," *Sify,* June 20, 2010, *sify.com;* and "Police Raid German Pipeline Contractor Over Kickback Claim," *Earthtimes.org,* August 20, 2010, *www.earthtimes.org.*

[30] "Acting Assistant Attorney General Mythili Raman Speaks At the Global Anti-Corruption Compliance Congress," *Ethikos,* May/June 2014, pp. 1–2.

- Alstom, a French conglomerate, plead guilty and paid $772 million to the United States for bribing Indonesian government officials with more than $4 billion to win power contracts from 2000 to 2011. Since Alstom has U.S. affiliate companies that are headquartered in Connecticut it is governed by United States laws, specifically the Foreign Corrupt Practices Act (the FCPA is introduced later in the chapter).
- The global aluminum manufacturer Alcoa agreed to pay $384 million to resolve one count of federal corruption for using a middleman to bribe members of Bahrain's royal family and other officials to guarantee lucrative contracts with the government-run Aluminum Behrain, one of the largest aluminum smelters in the world.[31]

Efforts to Curtail Unethical Practices

Despite the prevalence of bribery, both companies and countries have taken a strong stand against it.

Huguette Labelle, the chair of Transparency International, stated, "People believe they have the power to stop corruption, and the number of those willing to combat the abuse of power, secret dealings, and bribery is significant." Seventy-one percent of respondents to a Dow Jones Anti-Corruption survey said their companies had delayed or stopped activities with business partners over concerns about breaking anti-corruption regulations.

> In 2012, Walmart was accused of bribing Mexican government officials to expedite the processing of building permits to speed up the firm's expansion into that country. It was alleged that these payments violated the U.S. Foreign Corrupt Practices Act, discussed later in this section. Since these accusations were made, Walmart's chief executive officer, the chief administrative officer in the United States, and its Mexican operations general counsel have all quietly left the company. Walmart reported that it spent nearly $500 million to change its internal operations to prevent any form of bribery in the future. The firm revamped its global compliance program, increasing its staff by more than 30 percent, to 2,000 people. The firm also requires any potential foreign corruption violation to be reported to corporate headquarters and the board of directors—rather than only to the regional operation's managers as in the past—to make it more difficult for senior executives to plead ignorance if these issues arise in the future.[32]

In addition, some businesses and their employees are able to combat bribery through the use of social media technology, as described in Exhibit 6.E.

Numerous efforts are under way to curb unethical business practices throughout the world. The most common control is through government intervention and regulation.

Since 1977, the **U.S. Foreign Corrupt Practices Act** (FCPA) has prohibited executives of U.S.-based companies from paying bribes to foreign government officials, political parties, or political candidates. To achieve this goal, the FCPA requires U.S. companies with foreign operations to adopt accounting practices that ensure full disclosure of the company's transactions. In 2013, the U.S. Department of Justice and the Securities and Exchange Commission combined to collect more than $635 million in civil and criminal penalties from individuals and corporate FCPA investigations. These investigations

---

[31] "Brazil's Petrobras Reports Nearly $17 Billion in Asset and Corruption Charges," *The Wall Street Journal,* April 22, 2015, www.wsj.com; "Alstom to Pay U.S. Record $772 Million in Fine in Bribery Scheme," *The New York Times,* December 22, 2014, www.nytimes.com; and, "Alcoa Agrees to Settlement in Bahrain Bribery Case," *Washington Post,* January 9, 2014, www. washingtonpost.com.

[32] "After Bribery Scandals, a Pattern of Quiet Departures at Walmart," *The New York Times,* June 4, 2014, www.nytimes.com.

The Institute of Business Ethics (IBE), a British nonprofit organization established to encourage high standards of business behavior based on ethical values, created the Say No Toolkit in 2014. The Say No Toolkit seeks to help employees figure out how to respond to a demand for a facilitation payment, or if they should offer a business partner a gift. It also advises organizations on how to develop adequate procedures to combat bribery and corruption. According to IBE director Philippa Foster Back, "Anyone, at any level, in any organization, can be offered a bribe. The Say No Toolkit supports staff by giving them clear and easily accessible guidance about what can and cannot be accepted. Not only will the App provide an adequate procedure to combat bribery, it could help to minimize the risks of corruption taking place." This decision-making tool can be used either as an application on a mobile phone or via a website and the app can be downloaded free at www.saynotoolkit.net.

For more information visit the IBE website at *www.ibe.org.uk.*

covered corporate action in 19 different countries and cut across industries ranging from oil and gas operations to technology and financial services.[33]

The United Kingdom's Bribery Act was passed in 2010. Some believed it was even more stringent than the U.S.'s FCPA. The U.K. Bribery Act differs from the FCPA in that it

- prohibits the bribery of another person and receiving or accepting a bribe, whereas the FCPA only prohibits bribery of non-U.S. government officials. Bribery of a private business executive would be illegal under British, but not U.S., anticorruption law.
- does not require that the improper offer, promise, or payment be made "corruptly," as the FCPA does require evidence of the intent to corrupt.
- does not provide exemptions for "facilitating payments" or the defense that there are reasonable and bona fide contractual or promotional expenses, as the FCPA does.
- contains a strict liability offense for failure to prevent bribery by commercial organizations; the FCPA does not.[34]

Other governments have drafted and passed new legislation to combat corruption and bribery. In 2013, Brazil, one of the world's top 10 largest economies, approved an antibribery law that imposed civil and criminal penalties on firms for acts committed against local and foreign government officials. Fines can be as high as 20 percent of the company's annual gross revenues. India joined Brazil in 2014 by passing its own anticorruption legislation.

While enforcement is often spotty, some countries have enforced their bribery laws aggressively. China imposed a $487 million fine on British pharmaceutical GlaxoSmith-Kline (GSK) for bribery, after Glaxo reportedly used payoffs to persuade hospitals and doctors to administer or sell Glaxo pharmaceuticals to their patients.[35]

While governmental efforts continue to emerge, a business scholar argued that "a legalistic approach, by itself, is unlikely to be effective in curbing bribery," since culture has such a strong influence. Most effective in combating bribery may be an integrative approach of economic development, social investment in education, and business-friendly policies, in addition to anticorruption laws and punishments to combat bribery.[36]

[33] "Foreign Corrupt Practices Act Enforcement Activity: 2013 Year in Review and 2014 Preview," *Ropes & Gray Alert,* March 28, 2014, *ropesgray.com.*

[34] "FCPA vs. the UK Bribery Act," *Ethisphere,* Quarter 3, 2010, pp. 38–41. Also see "Parallels between the UK Bribery Act and the U.S. Foreign Corrupt Practices Act," *Boardmember.com,* July 9, 2010, *www.boardmember.com.*

[35] "Finally, Companies in Brazil Can Be Prosecuted for Corruption," *Transparency International,* July 8, 2013, *blog.transparency.org;* "Indian: New Anti-Corruption Law," *The Law Library of Congress,* January 8, 2014, *www.loc.gov;* and "China Fines GlaxoSmithKline Nearly $500 Million in Bribery Case," *The New York Times,* September 19, 2014, *www.nytimes.com.*

[36] Rajib Sanyal, "Determinants of Bribery in International Business: The Cultural and Economic Factors," *Journal of Business Ethics 59* (2005), pp. 139–45.

Businesses of all sizes and from many diverse industries around the world have attempted to respond to the increasing pressure to create an ethical environment at work. As discussed, the organization's culture and ethical work climate play a central role in promoting ethics at work and encouraging employees to act ethically. Businesses have implemented many ethical safeguards to create effective ethics programs. Challenges remain as organizations expand their operations globally and encounter a complex network of different customs and regulations.

Summary

- A company's culture and ethical climate tend to shape the attitudes and actions of all who work there, sometimes resulting in high levels of ethical behavior and at other times contributing to less desirable ethical performance.
- Not all ethical issues in business are the same, but ethical challenges occur in all major functional areas of business. Professional associations for each functional area often attempt to provide a standard of conduct to guide practice.
- Companies can improve their ethical performance by creating a values-based ethics program that relies on top management leadership and organizational safeguards, such as ethics policies or codes, ethics and compliance offices and officers, ethics reporting mechanisms, and ethics training programs.
- Companies that have a comprehensive, or multifaceted, ethics program often are better able to promote ethical behavior at work and avoid unethical action by employees.
- Ethical issues, such as bribery, are evident throughout the world, and many international agencies and national governments are actively attempting to minimize such unethical behavior through economic sanctions and international codes.

Key Terms

bribery, *127*
corporate culture, *114*
employee ethics training, *125*
ethical climate, *115*

ethics and compliance officer, *122*
ethics policies or codes, *122*

ethics reporting mechanisms, *123*
U.S. Foreign Corrupt Practices Act, *128*

Internet Resources

www.thecro.com	*CR: Corporate Responsibility Magazine*
www.dii.org	Defense Industry Initiative on Business Ethics and Conduct
www.theecoa.org	Ethics & Compliance Officer Association
www.ethicaledge.com	Ethics and Policy Integration Centre
ethisphere.com	Ethisphere Institute
www.ethics.org	Ethics Resource Center
www.globalethics.org	Institute for Global Ethics
www.saiglobal.com	SAI Global
www.business-ethics.org	International Business Ethics Institute
www.corporatecompliance.org	Society of Corporate Compliance and Ethics
www.transparency.org	Transparency International

Discussion Case: *Alcoa's Core Values in Practice*

Alcoa began under the name of the Pittsburgh Reduction Company in 1888, changing its name to the Aluminum Company of America (Alcoa) in 1907. The company was originally founded on a $20,000 investment to capitalize on Charles Martin Hall's invention to smelt bauxite ore into the metal known as aluminum. Within a few years, Alcoa had developed into a model of large-scale vertical integration with control over all the inputs to aluminum production. Now, over 125 years later, Alcoa is a global leader in lightweight metals technology, engineering, and manufacturing, with over 60,000 employees and operations in 30 countries.

Since its inception, Alcoa has had a very strong values-based culture. Employees learn early in their career that every decision they make and everything they do must be aligned with the company's values: Integrity; Environment, Health and Safety; Innovation; Respect; and Excellence.

Since the 1990s Alcoa's leadership has communicated their commitment to the importance of health and safety—one of the company's core values. Alcoa has a stand-alone environmental health and safety (EHS) organization and a dedicated global ethics and compliance (E&C) organization. The Alcoa E&C program incorporates all of the elements specified in the U.S. Federal Sentencing Guidelines and Sarbanes–Oxley Act. The chief ethics and compliance officer makes regular reports to Alcoa's Audit Committee and to the company's Compliance Advisory Council, which includes the CEO, CFO, and chief legal officer. E&C is responsible for global training, the code of conduct, the global anticorruption and trade compliance programs, internal investigations, and the company's global helpline reporting system. The importance of safety, integrity, and "doing the right thing" is regularly reinforced by management and through E&C communications.

In addition to continuous safety training and education programs, the norm at Alcoa is to start all business meetings with a safety message to identify exits, the evacuation plans in the event of an emergency, and other safety procedures. All locations are required to meet the same overall goal: zero work-related injuries and illnesses. Alcoa's management team has made the commitment that no employee should be forced to work in an environment where their safety and the safety of other employees might be jeopardized. Simply stated, no employee should leave work in a worse condition than when they arrived. Through persistent attention over the years, safety at work has become deeply embedded in Alcoa's culture and "the way we do things around here."

In the late 1990s, activists raised allegations at an Alcoa annual shareholders meeting claiming that health and safety conditions at one of Alcoa's Mexican facilities had deteriorated. The individual who spoke at the meeting concluded by saying that the company's behavior in Mexico was "inconsistent with its widely publicized values." The company promptly launched an investigation, and Alcoa's then CEO personally visited the plant. Although the company learned that many of the issues raised at the annual meeting were unfounded, it also discovered that a few injury incidents and the subsequent actions taken by local managers were not reported to corporate headquarters, as required by company policy. Meetings held with local government officials over safety incidents at the facility were also not reported, even though the results of these meetings indicated Alcoa was in compliance with all appropriate laws and regulations.

Following the review, the company concluded that although the business unit management's response to the safety incidents uncovered in the investigation was adequate, there was "a breach of the letter and spirit of our communication practices with respect to major incidents" as well as "a serious lack of understanding when it came to incident classification, reporting, and recordkeeping of occupational illnesses." The lack of reporting these safety incidents to others in the company was viewed as unacceptable—it meant others in the company were denied the opportunity to learn and possibly prevent similar occurrences at other Alcoa facilities.

A change is leadership was made at the facility, despite the manager's stellar record of increased sales and profitability and high marks for quality and customer satisfaction. In an open letter to the entire company, Alcoa's then CEO re-emphasized that full compliance with both the letter—and spirit—of Alcoa's policies was imperative, and anything less unacceptable.

Over time, Alcoa's focus on safety has paid off. In 2013, Alcoa employees and contractors worldwide worked an entire calendar year fatality-free for the first time in over five decades. The 2014 year-end Alcoa lost workday (LWD) incident rate was 0.10. (This number represents the number of injuries and illnesses resulting in one or more days away from work per 100 full-time workers.) That same year:

- 42.7% of Alcoa's locations worldwide had zero recordable injuries
- 80.5% of Alcoa's locations worldwide had zero lost workdays

These numbers reflect the commitment of not only Alcoa leaders but also the employees, who are empowered to take personal responsibility for ensuring their safety and that of their coworkers—even if that means stopping work when they feel unsafe or unsure.

In 2013, in order to further embed and enhance a values-based culture of integrity and compliance, Alcoa formed a global "Integrity Champion Network." This group of high-potential employees was appointed to work within their businesses to raise awareness, promote a "Speak-Up" culture, and provide advice on various ethics and compliance matters.

In 2014, Alcoa released a new Code of Conduct, providing a road map for "Advancing with Integrity." Every employee worldwide received the Code, reinforcing Alcoa's values and the shared responsibility for conducting business in accordance with Alcoa's highest ethical standards and the law. At the same time, Alcoa's 24/7 hotline was rebranded as the "Integrity Line." Alcoa's ethics and compliance program continues to focus on anticorruption, trade compliance, and adherence with all relevant U.S. and national laws and regulations.

Sources: This case was developed with the assistance of Alcoa's Ethics and Compliance Organization.

Discussion Questions

1. How would you classify Alcoa's ethical work climate? Which ethical criterion, as shown in Figure 6.1, was used by the company: egoism (self-centered), benevolence (concern for others), or principles (integrity approach)? Or, using Professor Paine's two distinct ethics approaches, as discussed in this chapter, was Alcoa's approach more compliance or integrity?

2. What role did top management commitment play in developing the ethical work climate and organizational performance seen at Alcoa? What other ethical safeguards are mentioned in the case to support the company's efforts at developing a strong ethical culture?

3. Was Alcoa justified in changing management at the facility for failure to report workplace accidents, even though no serious harm resulted from the workplace incident?

4. Can the focus on safety seen at Alcoa be duplicated into other ethics and compliance areas and how would this be accomplished?

5. Why do you think Alcoa's strong values-based culture failed to prevent corrupt acts by a subsidiary, as described earlier in the chapter? Do you think Alcoa's creation of a new code of conduct in 2014 will help prevent incidents like this in the future?

Business and Public Policy

Business–Government Relations

Governments seek to protect and promote the public good and in these roles establish rules under which business operates in society. Therefore, a government's influence on business through public policy and regulation is a vital concern for managers. Government's relationship with business can be either cooperative or adversarial. Various economic or social assistance policies significantly affect society, in which businesses must operate. Many government regulations also impact business directly. Managers must understand the objectives and effects of government policy and regulation, both at home and abroad, in order to conduct business in an ethical and legal manner.

This Chapter Focuses on These Key Learning Objectives:

LO 7-1   Understanding why sometimes governments and business collaborate and other times work in opposition to each other.

LO 7-2   Defining public policy and the elements of the public policy process.

LO 7-3   Explaining the reasons for regulation.

LO 7-4   Knowing the major types of government regulation of business.

LO 7-5   Identifying the purpose of antitrust laws and the remedies that may be imposed.

LO 7-6   Comparing the costs and benefits of regulation for business and society.

LO 7-7   Examining the conditions that affect the regulation of business in a global context.

Uber, a U.S.-based international transportation network company founded in 2009, developed a mobile app that allowed consumers to submit a trip request, which was then routed to one of its drivers. By 2015, the service was available in 58 countries and 300 cities worldwide. But Uber encountered serious opposition when it attempted to expand into the European Union. Anti-Uber forces claimed that the firm engaged in unfair competition and its drivers did not have professional licenses, required of all taxicab drivers. Under French law, organizing a system that put paying clients in touch with drivers without professional licenses was punishable by 2 years in prison and a €300,000 ($373,540) fine. Uber's general manager for Western Europe responded, "It's up to the courts to ban Uberpop [the French version of Uber]. If we're prosecuted, then we'll respond." The company also filed complaints with European Union regulators against three European Union governments—France, Germany, and Spain—claiming that these governments had blocked their services.

In 2011, Congress passed legislation to prevent the importation of contaminated food into the United States. About 15 percent of the food that Americans ate originated abroad, more than double the amount 10 years earlier, as did nearly two-thirds of all fresh fruits and vegetables. Recent data reported that one in six Americans became ill annually from eating contaminated food; about 130,000 people were hospitalized and 3000 died each year. In 2013, the Food and Drug Administration imposed even more restrictive rules and challenged food companies to better police imported food. American food importers were required to audit foreign facilities, test foods when arriving in the United States, and review records on foreign suppliers. Most major food importers and consumer advocates praised the new rules, but some worried that they might give companies too much discretion about whether to conduct on-site inspections where the food was grown and processed.[1]

What prompted or compelled governments to become more involved in their citizens' transportation options or the assurance of food safety? How do these government's actions affect businesses and what they are permitted to do? How did these actions affect society and its safety? Did government's involvement promote or harm companies or allow other firms to maintain their competitive advantage? Were these efforts by the governments necessary and effective, or can this only be answered in time?

Governments create the conditions that make it possible for businesses to compete in the modern economy. As shown in the opening examples, governments can act in dramatic ways to provide or limit opportunities for businesses and control business activities to better ensure the public's safety. In good times and bad, government's role is to create and enforce the laws that *balance* the relationship between business and society. Governments also hold the power to grant or refuse permission for many types of business activity. Even the largest multinational companies, which operate in dozens of countries, must obey the laws and public policies of national governments.

This chapter considers the ways in which government actions impact business through the powerful twin mechanisms of public policy and regulation. The next chapter addresses the related question of actions business may take to influence the political process.

How Business and Government Relate

The relationship between business and government is dynamic and complex. Understanding the government's authority and its relationship with business is essential for managers in developing their strategies and achieving their organization's goals.

---

[1] "France Blocks Uber 'Ride-Sharing' Service," *The Wall Street Journal*, December 15, 2014, *www.wsj.com;* "Uber Files Complaints Against European Governments Over Bans," *The Wall Street Journal*, April 1/, 2015, *www.wsj.com;* and, "F.D.A. Says Importers Must Audit Food Safety," *The New York Times*, July 26, 2013, *www.nytimes.com.* Files Complaints Against European Governments Over Bans," *The Wall Street Journal*, April 1, 2015, *www.wsj.com;* and, "F.D.A. Says Importers Must Audit Food Safety," *The New York Times*, July 26, 2013, *www.nytimes.com.*

Seeking a Collaborative Partnership

In some situations, government may work closely with business to build a collaborative partnership and seek mutually beneficial goals. They see each other as key partners in the relationship and work openly to achieve common objectives.

The basis for this cooperation may be at the core of the nation's societal values and customs. In some Asian countries, society is viewed as a collective family that includes both government and business. Thus, working together as a family leads these two powers to seek results that benefit both society and business. In Europe, the relationship between government and business often has been collaborative. European culture includes a sense of teamwork and mutual aid. Unions, for example, are often included on administrative boards with managers to lead the organization toward mutual goals through interactive strategies. One example of government–business collaboration is shown next.

> The Export-Import Bank (an agency of the U.S. government that helped finance foreign purchases of American goods) was under pressure from its critics to provide tighter rules for aircraft sales. In response, the bank reached out to Boeing Company, the biggest beneficiary of the bank's assistance, to help write the new rules. What followed was an extraordinary level of cooperation between public officials and corporate executives. The bank and company executives exchanged e-mails, drafted new guidelines, and eventually produced a new set of rules for aircraft financing. The cooperation was mutually beneficial. During the two years after the new rules were developed, all Boeing sales were approved, including the sale of 62 wide-body Boeing aircraft to foreign airlines after the bank guaranteed more than $7 billion in loans. The Export-Import Bank also benefited, as the new rules helped it return to sound financial footing. After they went into effect, the bank was able to provide $20.5 billion in financing for U.S. exports and made $675 million in profit.[2]

The collaborative relationship between the Export–Import Bank and Boeing Corporation served both the U.S. government agency and the U.S.-based firm, but raised some question of a competitive bias against other firms, especially non-U.S. aircraft companies like Airbus.

Working in Opposition to Government

In other situations, government's goals and business's objectives are at odds, and these conflicts result in an adversarial relationship where business and government tend to work in opposition to each other.[3]

> A clash between the U.S. government and the coal industry came to a head in 2013. When the government announced new rules to cut greenhouse gas emissions, coal companies feared that a significant number of coal-burning power plants would be forced to shut down, and they would lose customers. The coal industry teamed up with other business groups to challenge President Obama's climate-change agenda. It coordinated lobbying efforts with manufacturers and other business groups to reach out to members of Congress, especially politicians from coal-producing states and those with coal-burning utilities. The plan was to work with sympathetic congressional representatives to modify or delay White House-supported actions that would limit the use of domestic coal and potentially drive up electricity prices.[4]

Why do businesses sometimes welcome government regulation and involvement in the private sector, and other times oppose it? Companies often prefer to operate without government

---

[2] "Boeing Helped Craft Own Loan Rules," *The Wall Street Journal,* March 12, 2015, *www.wsj.com.*

[3] The "collaborative partnership" and "in opposition" models for business–government relations is discussed in "Managing Regulation in a New Era," *McKinsey Quarterly,* December 2008, *www.mckinseyquarterly.com.*

[4] "Big Coal to Fight Obama Plan," *The Wall Street Journal,* June 26, 2013, *online.wsj.com.*

constraints, which can be costly or restrict innovation. But regulations can also help business, by setting minimum standards that all firms must meet, building public confidence in the safety of a product, creating a fair playing field for competition, or creating barriers to entry to maintain a business's competitive advantage. How a specific company reacts to a specific government policy often depends on their assessment of whether they would be helped or hurt by that rule.

In short, the relationship between government and business can range from one of cooperation to one of conflict, with various stages in between. Moreover, this relationship is constantly changing. A cooperative relationship on one issue does not guarantee cooperation on another issue. The stability of a particular form of government in some countries may be quite shaky, while in other countries the form of government is static but those in power can change unexpectedly or government rulers can change on a regular basis. The business–government relationship is one that requires managers to keep a careful eye trained toward significant forces that might alter this relationship or to promote forces that may encourage a positive business–government relationship.[5]

Legitimacy Issues

When dealing with a global economy, business may encounter governments whose authority or right to be in power is questioned. Political leaders may illegally assume lawmaking or legislative power, which can become economic power over business. Elections can be rigged, or military force can be used to acquire governmental control.

Business managers may be challenged with the dilemma of doing business in such a country where their business dealings would support this illegitimate power. Sometimes, they may choose to become politically active, or refuse to do business in this country until a legitimate government is installed.

Businesses can also influence the ability of a government leader or group of leaders to maintain political power. For example, companies can decide to withdraw operations from a country, as many U.S. firms did from South Africa in the 1970s to protest the practice of apartheid (institutionalized racial segregation). Some believe that the economic isolation of South Africa contributed to the eventual collapse of the apartheid regime. Governments may also order companies not to conduct business in another country because of a war, human rights violations, or lack of a legitimate government. These orders are called *economic sanctions*. As of 2015, the United States had imposed economic sanctions on Iraq, Kuwait, Lebanon, Libya, Qatar, Saudi Arabia, Syria, the United Arab Emirates, and Yemen because of political and human rights concerns.[6]

Government's Public Policy Role

Government performs a vital and important role in modern society. Although vigorous debates occur about the proper size of programs government should undertake, most people agree that a society cannot function properly without some government activities. Citizens look to government to meet important basic needs. Foremost among these are safety and protection provided by homeland security, police, and fire departments. These are collective or public goods, which are most efficiently provided by government for everyone in a community. In today's world, governments are also expected to provide economic security and essential social services, and to deal with the most pressing social problems that require collective action, or public policy.

Public policy is a plan of action undertaken by government officials to achieve some broad purpose affecting a substantial segment of a nation's citizens. Or as the late U.S.

---

[5] See George Lodge, *Comparative Business–Government Relations* (Englewood Cliffs, NJ: Prentice Hall, 1990).

[6] See The Federal Registry, Department of the Treasury at *www.gpo.gov.*

Senator Patrick Moynihan said, "Public policy is what a government chooses to do or not to do." In general, these ideas are consistent. Public policy, while differing in each nation, is the basic set of goals, plans, and actions that each national government follows in achieving its purposes. Governments generally do not choose to act unless a substantial segment of the public is affected and some public purpose is to be achieved. This is the essence of the concept of governments acting in the public interest.

The basic power to make public policy comes from a nation's political system. In democratic societies, citizens elect political leaders who can appoint others to fulfill defined public functions ranging from municipal services (e.g., water supplies, fire protection) to national services, such as public education or homeland security. Democratic nations typically spell out the powers of government in the country's constitution.

Another source of authority is *common law,* or past decisions of the courts, the original basis of the U.S. legal system. In nondemocratic societies, the power of government may derive from a monarchy (e.g., Saudi Arabia), a military dictatorship (e.g., Eritrea or Zimbabwe), or religious authority (e.g., the mullahs in Iran). These sources of power may interact, creating a mixture of civilian and military authority. The political systems in Russia, Libya, Tunisia, and other nations have undergone profound changes in recent times. And democratic nations can also face the pressures of regions that seek to become independent nations exercising the powers of a sovereign state, as does Canada with Quebec.

Elements of Public Policy

The actions of government in any nation can be understood in terms of several basic elements of public policy. These are inputs, goals, tools, and effects. They will be illustrated using the example of distracted driving.

Public policy inputs are external pressures that shape a government's policy decisions and strategies to address problems. Economic and foreign policy concerns, domestic political pressure from constituents and interest groups, technical information, and media attention all play a role in shaping national political decisions. For example, a growing recognition of the dangers of distracted driving has pressured many state and local governments to ban or regulate the use of various electronic devices by drivers. Distracted driving may occur when a driver's attention is diverted by personal grooming tasks, adjusting music or navigation settings, eating, reading, and assorted other activities. It has become an even greater threat to driver and passenger safety as technological advances occur at a rapid pace. More and more drivers are now able to make or receive calls, send text messages, and even browse the Internet—all while driving a car at high speeds, in heavy traffic, or during bad weather conditions.[7]

> According to an annual National Highway Traffic Safety Administration study, more than 3,000 people are killed and nearly a half million injured in distraction-related crashes. A 2014 Insurance Institute for Highway Safety study found that the risk of a crash was 17 percent higher when the driver was distracted by using a cell phone. Teens were particularly vulnerable. Nearly six out of 10 crashes involved teen drivers who were distracted immediately before the accident. In a survey sponsored by Erie Insurance, 30 percent all of drivers admitted to texting while driving and 75 percent reported that they had seen someone else do it—causing researchers to believe that the percentage of texting while driving was much higher than 30 percent. Fifteen percent of drivers admitted they had engaged in "romantic encounters" while behind the wheel and 9 percent said they had changed clothes while driving.[8]

---

[7] "Windshield Devices Bring Distracted Driving Debate to Eye Level," *The New York Times,* May 29, 2015, *www.nytimes.com.*

[8] "Study Asks Just How Distracted Are Motorists?" *Pittsburgh Post-Gazette,* March 30, 2015, *www.post-gazette.com.* For updated information on distracted driving, see *www.distraction.gov* and the *Insurance Institute for Highway Safety's* website at *www.iihs.org.*

The harms associated with distracted driving are alarming. A spokesperson for a major auto insurance company explained, "Distracted driving is becoming a national epidemic and it has to be controlled."[9]

Government bodies—legislatures, town councils, regulatory agencies—need to consider all relevant inputs in deciding whether or not to take action, and if so, what kind of action.

Public policy goals can be broad (e.g., full employment) and high-minded (equal opportunity for all) or narrow and self-serving. National values, such as freedom, democracy, and a fair chance for all citizens to share in economic prosperity, have led to the adoption of civil rights laws and economic assistance programs for those in need. Narrow goals that serve special interests are more apparent when nations decide how tax legislation will allocate the burden of taxes among various interests and income groups, or when public resources, such as oil exploration rights or timber cutting privileges, are given to one group or another. Whether the goals are broad or narrow, for the benefit of some or the benefit of all, most governments should ask, "What public goals are being served by this action?" For example, the rationale for a government policy to regulate distracted driving has to be based on some definition of public interest, such as preventing harm to others, including innocent drivers, passengers, and pedestrians.

> The goal of distracted driving regulation is to prevent deaths and serious injuries resulting from drivers being distracted while driving. However, some members of the public have insisted on their right to use their phones for texting and other activities in their vehicles. Traveling salespersons, for example, depend on their phones as an important tool of the job. Some regulations have addressed this by permitting drivers to use hands-free devices that permit them to keep their hands on the wheel. But some government safety experts have disagreed, saying, "When you are on a call, even if both hands are on the wheel, your head is in the call, and not your driving."

The issue of banning the use of cell phones, hand-held or hands-free, for the sake of making our roads a little safer for all, remains at the forefront, but new technology has created even greater distractions. Devices can project information and data streamed from a smartphone onto the car's windshield. Maps, speed, incoming texts, caller identification, and even social media notifications can be projected just above the dashboard of a car for the driver to read. So, the goals of saving lives, reducing injuries, and eliminating health care costs are increasingly more urgent and the demand for regulation even more critical.

Governments use different *public policy tools* to achieve policy goals. The tools of public policy involve combinations of incentives and penalties that government uses to prompt citizens, including businesses, to act in ways that achieve policy goals. Governmental regulatory powers are broad and constitute one of the most formidable instruments for accomplishing public purposes.

> Federal action limiting cell phone use in the United States stalled, so state and local governments stepped in to ban the use of cell phones by drivers while operating their vehicles. By 2015 14 states had completely banned the use of cell phones while driving without a hands-free device, 37 had banned cell phone use by novice drivers, and 20 had banned school bus drivers from using their cell phones. Forty-six states banned text messaging for all drivers. And this is not just

---

[9] "Texting While Driving Dangerous, Study Confirms: How Dangerous?" *CBS News - Health Pop,* October 6, 2011, *www .cbsnews.com.*

a public policy issue for Americans. More than 45 nations, including Australia, China, France, Germany, India, Israel, Japan, Russia, Spain, Taiwan, and the United Kingdom, ban calling while driving.[10]

Public policy effects are the outcomes arising from government regulation. Some are intended; others are unintended. Because public policies affect many people, organizations, and other interests, it is almost inevitable that such actions will please some and displease others. Regulations may cause businesses to improve the way toxic substances are used in the workplace, thus reducing health risks to employees. Yet other goals may be obstructed as an unintended effect of compliance with such regulations. For example, when health risks to pregnant women were associated with exposure to lead in the workplace, some companies removed women from those jobs. This action was seen as a form of discrimination against women that conflicted with the goal of equal employment opportunity. The unintended effect (discrimination) of one policy action (protecting employees) conflicted head-on with the public policy goal of equal opportunity.

> Different groups disagreed over the possible effects of distracted driving laws. Proponents obviously argued that the ban on cell phone use reduced accidents and saved lives. In fact, from 2012 to 2013, the number of deaths attributed to distracted driving nationwide declined nearly 7 percent, possibly due to the bans enacted by many states. Opponents pointed to numerous other distractions that were not banned, such as drivers reading the newspaper, eating, putting on makeup, or shaving. "People have been driving distracted since cars were invented. Focusing on mobile phones isn't the same as focusing on distracted driving. Distraction is what has always caused car crashes and mobile phones don't appear to be adding to that," said a spokesperson for the Insurance Institute for Highway Safety.[11]

As the distracted driving examples illustrate, managers must try to be aware of the public policy inputs, goals, tools, and effects relevant to regulation affecting their business.

Types of Public Policy

Public policies created by governments are of two major types: economic and social. Sometimes these types of regulation are distinct from each another and at other times they are intertwined.

Economic Policies

One important kind of public policy directly concerns the economy. The term **fiscal policy** refers to patterns of government collecting and spending funds that are intended to stimulate or support the economy. Governments spend money on many different activities. Local governments employ teachers, trash collectors, police, and firefighters. State governments typically spend large amounts of money on roads, social services, and parkland. National governments spend large sums on military defense, international relationships, and hundreds of public works projects such as road building. During the Great Depression of the 1930s, public works projects employed large numbers of people, put money in their hands,

---

[10] For a complete listing of states that have regulated cell phone use while driving see the *Governor's Highway Safety Association* at *www.ghsa.org.*

[11] Statistical information from the *Governor's Highway Safety Association* website at *www.ghsa.org;* and "Study: No Evidence Cell Phone Bans Reduce Crashes," *Fox News,* July 7, 2011, *www.foxnews.com.*

and stimulated consumption of goods and services. Today, fiscal policy remains a basic tool to achieve prosperity, as the following example illustrates.

In 2015, Chinese government leaders and economists were surprised by the country's sharp economic decline and were increasingly worried about the potential risk of job losses throughout the country. The world's second largest economy grew at 7 percent in the first quarter of 2015, the lowest rate since the global financial crisis in 2008–9. The leaders turned to fiscal stimulus to revive the growth of the country. The National Development and Reform Commission, China's top planning agency, infused large amounts of funding in an attempt to speed up investment projects in several key sectors, including water conservation, environmental protection, power grids, and health care. A chief economist explained, "It's hard to boost consumption while external demand is weak, so the only thing they can do is boost investment."[12]

By contrast, the term **monetary policy** refers to policies that affect the supply, demand, and value of a nation's currency. The worth, or worthlessness, of a nation's currency has serious effects on business and society. It affects the buying power of money, the stability and value of savings, and the confidence of citizens and investors about the nation's future. This, in turn, affects the country's ability to borrow money from other nations and to attract private capital. In the United States, the Federal Reserve Bank—known as the Fed—plays the role of other nations' central banks. By raising and lowering the interest rates at which private banks borrow money from the government, the Fed influences the size of the nation's money supply and the value of the dollar. During the Great Recession, the Fed's action to lower interest rates nearly to zero—an example of a monetary policy—was intended to stimulate borrowing and help the economy get moving again.

Other forms of economic policy include *taxation policy* (raising or lowering taxes on business or individuals), *industrial policy* (directing economic resources toward the development of specific industries), and *trade policy* (encouraging or discouraging trade with other countries).

Social Assistance Policies

The last century produced many advances in the well-being of people across the globe. The advanced industrial nations have developed elaborate systems of social services for their citizens. Developing economies have improved key areas of social assistance (such as health care and education) and will continue to do so as their economies grow. International standards and best practices have supported these trends. Many of the **social assistance policies** that affect particular stakeholders are discussed in subsequent chapters of this book.

One area often addressed by social assistance policies is housing. Many governments have programs that subsidize rent payments, guarantee home loans, or provide housing directly for low-income citizens or military veterans. For example, Brazil's *Minha Casa, Minha Vida* ("My House, My Life") program has built one million homes since 2009 for low-income families. Mortgages are provided by a government-affiliated bank and more than $1 trillion in investments had been channeled into this program by 2014. Many of the first units built by the program were intended to house families displaced by development for the World Cup and Olympic Games in Rio de Janeiro.[13]

---

[12] "China Looks to Fiscal Stimulus to Fight Slowdown," *Business Times,* May 7, 2015, *www.businesstimes.com.sg.*

[13] For more information on this program see *myhousemylifebrazil.com.*

One particularly important social assistance policy—health care—has been the focus for concern on the international front and for national and state lawmakers. As discussed later in this chapter, the United States government has wrestled with the need for better health care for its citizens and the challenge of how to pay for this care.

Government Regulation of Business

Societies rely on government to establish rules of conduct for citizens and organizations called *regulations*. **Regulation** is a primary way of accomplishing public policy, as described in the previous section. Because government operates at so many levels (federal, state, local), modern businesses face complex webs of regulations. Companies often require lawyers, public affairs specialists, and experts to monitor and manage the interaction with government. Why do societies turn to more regulation as a way to solve problems? Why not just let the free market allocate resources, set prices, and constrain socially irresponsible behavior by companies? There are a variety of reasons.

Market Failure

One reason is what economists call **market failure**, that is, the marketplace fails to adjust prices for the true costs of a firm's behavior. For example, a company normally has no incentive to spend money on pollution control equipment if customers do not demand it. The market fails to incorporate the cost of environmental harm into the business's economic equation, because the costs are borne by someone else. In this situation, government can use regulation to force all competitors in the industry to adopt a minimum antipollution standard. The companies will then incorporate the extra cost of compliance into the product price. Companies that want to act responsibly often welcome carefully crafted regulations, because they force competitors to bear the same costs.

> The issue of global warming, caused in part by greenhouse gas emissions, is such a big issue that no single firm or industry can afford to take the first step and try to control it in order to minimize the harm to our planet and environment. World leaders have met periodically since 1995—most recently in 2015—under the auspices of the United Nations to negotiate and update a convention (treaty) to limit countries' greenhouse gas emissions. Many hope that this international agreement will create a path for businesses to follow to improve the health of our planet. While people may disagree on how to accomplish this important goal (as the earlier example of the coal industry's opposition to regulation illustrates), the challenge is beyond what the marketplace can tackle and it requires some form of government intervention by many countries.

Negative Externalities

Governments also may act to regulate business to prevent unintended adverse effects on others. **Negative externalities**, or spillover effects, result when the manufacture or distribution of a product gives rise to unplanned or unintended costs (economic, physical, or psychological) borne by workers, consumers, competitors, neighboring communities, or other business stakeholders. To control or reverse these costs, government may step in to regulate business action.

> In 2014 U.S. government regulators announced new rules to fight an increase in black lung disease, caused by breathing coal dust. These new regulations were the first major efforts since the 1969 Coal Mine Health and Safety Act, which

established modern health and safety requirements in mines nationwide. Government health officials attributed increasing rates of the disease to new machinery that generated more dust, longer shifts for younger workers, and an increase in silica dust churned up when thinner coal seams were tapped after many years of mining at the same location.[14]

Natural Monopolies

In some industries, **natural monopolies** occur. The electric utility industry provides an example. Once one company has built a system of poles and wires or laid miles of underground cable to supply local customers with electricity, it would be inefficient for a second company to build another system alongside the first. But once the first company has established its natural monopoly, it can then raise prices as much as it wishes because there is no competition. In such a situation, government often comes in and regulates prices and access. Other industries that sometimes develop natural monopolies include cable TV, broadband Internet service, software, and railroads.

Ethical Arguments

There is often an ethical rationale for regulation as well. As discussed in Chapter 5, for example, there is a utilitarian ethical argument in support of safe working conditions: It is costly to train and educate employees only to lose their services because of preventable accidents. There are also fairness and justice arguments for government to set standards and develop regulations to protect employees, consumers, and other stakeholders. In debates about regulation, advocates for and against regulatory proposals often use both economic and ethical arguments to support their views. Sometimes firms will agree to self-regulate their actions to head off more costly government-imposed regulatory reform, as shown in the following example.

> The National Highway Traffic Safety Administration (NHTSA) decided to launch an investigation after two Tesla Motors cars hit debris on the road, leading to a battery fire in 2013. The first incident occurred when the car struck a metal object on the highway; the second one, when the car hit a tow hitch lying on the road. Immediately after the NHTSA's announcement, Tesla Motors announced that it was conducting its own investigation and would implement certain safety measures aimed at creating more ground clearance in their cars and would extend its warranty policy to cover vehicles damaged by fire.[15]

Whether the actions are self-imposed by a company or forced on businesses by the government, the protection of the public is often the motivation for regulatory action.

Types of Regulation

Government regulations come in different forms. Some are directly imposed; others are more indirect. Some are aimed at a specific industry (e.g., banking); others, such as those dealing with job discrimination or pollution, apply to all industries. Some have been in existence for a long time—for example, the Food and Drug Act was passed in 1906—whereas others, such as the Wall Street Reform and Consumer Protection (or Dodd-Frank) Act of 2010, are of much more recent vintage. Just as public policy can be classified as either economic or social, so regulations can be classified in the same fashion.

---

[14] "Black Lung Disease Spurs New Coal-Mine Rules," *The Wall Street Journal,* April 23, 2014, *online.wsj.com.*

[15] "U.S. Safety Agency Opens Inquiry into Tesla Fires," *The New York Times,* November 19, 2013, *www.nytimes.com.*

Economic Regulations

The oldest form of regulation is primarily economic in nature. **Economic regulations** aim to modify the normal operation of the free market and the forces of supply and demand. Such modification may come about because the free market is distorted by the size or monopoly power of companies, or because the consequences of actions in the marketplace are thought to be undesirable. Economic regulations include those that control prices or wages, allocate public resources, establish service territories, set the number of participants, and ration resources. The decisions by the Federal Trade Commission (FTC) to prevent anticompetitive business practices illustrate one kind of economic regulation. The U.S. Congress responded to the global recession, in part, by passing the **Dodd-Frank Act**, as discussed next.

> The passage of the Dodd-Frank Act in 2011, heralded as the most comprehensive financial regulatory reform measure since the Great Depression, revolutionized many business activities. Among other things, the Dodd-Frank Act affected the oversight and supervision of financial institutions, provided for a new resolution procedure for large financial companies, created a new agency responsible for implementing and enforcing compliance with consumer financial laws, introduced more stringent regulatory capital requirements, effected significant changes in the regulation of over-the-counter derivatives, reformed the regulation of credit rating agencies, implemented changes to corporate governance and executive compensation practices, required registration of advisers to certain private funds, and effected significant changes in the securities markets.[16]

Yet, some businesses generally resisted many of the changes intended by the Dodd-Frank Act and fought back, as discussed in Exhibit 7.A. These efforts caused many to wonder if the Dodd-Frank Act had failed or was much weaker than lawmakers had intended.

Antitrust: A Special Kind of Economic Regulation

One important kind of economic regulation occurs when government acts to preserve competition in the marketplace, thereby protecting consumers. **Antitrust laws** prohibit unfair, anticompetitive practices by business. (The term *antitrust law* is used in the United States; most other countries use the term *competition law.*) For example, if a group of companies agreed among themselves to set prices at a particular level, this would generally be an antitrust violation. In addition, a firm may not engage in **predatory pricing**, the practice of selling below cost to drive rivals out of business. If a company uses its market dominance to restrain commerce, compete unfairly, or hurt consumers, then it may be found guilty of violating antitrust laws.

> For example, in 2015 a federal appeals court upheld a decision that found Apple liable for conspiring with book publishers to raise the price of e-books. The conspiracy, concluded the judge, had unreasonably restrained trade in violation of federal antitrust law. Apple's actions were in response to Amazon's aggressive discounts for e-books and its growing command of the e-book market. Apple entered into an industrywide agreement with five major book publishers to switch to a different pricing model that allowed the publishers rather than retailers to set e-book prices and e-book price began to rise. After the court decision, Apple was expected to have to pay $450 million, mostly to e-book consumers.[17]

---

[16] "The Dodd-Frank Act: A Cheat Sheet," Morrison & Foerster, n.d., *www.mofo.com.* Also see Kelly Richmond Pope and Chin-Chen Lee, "Could the Dodd-Frank Wall Street Reform and Consumer Protection Act of 2010 be Helpful in Reforming Corporate America? *Journal of Business Ethics,* February 2014, pp. 597–607.

[17] "Apple Loses Federal Appeal in E-Books Case," *The Wall Street Journal,* June 30, 2015, *www.wsj.com.*

Exhibit 7.A

Business Pushes Back on the Dodd-Frank Act

Three years after the Dodd-Frank Act was passed, only 40 percent of the regulations had been written. President Obama, an advocate of the act, wanted to know why, so he called in those responsible for writing the act's regulations. Nine different agencies were summoned, reflecting one of the major problems with the act—too many agencies were involved. The U.S. Treasury, the Federal Reserve Board, the Office of the Comptroller of the Currency, the Consumer Financial Protection Bureau, the Federal Housing Finance Agency, the Commodity Futures Trading Commission, the Federal Deposit Insurance Corporation, the National Credit Union Administration, and the Securities and Exchange Commission all had oversight of parts of the law.

In addition, businesses launched a political attack targeting these agencies and Congress. By 2012, more than 3000 lobbyists swarmed Capitol Hill, nearly six for every member of Congress, to influence or delay the full impact of the Dodd-Frank Act. The financial services industry spent more than $1 billion targeting the weakening of the Dodd-Frank Act. As one consumer advocate pointed out, "The lobbyists are just the point of the spear. There are also the regulatory lawyers, the research staffs, the public relations people and all those loyal think tank supporters shilling for the banks."

From 2013 to 2015, Congress voted to roll back major elements of the Dodd-Frank Act, such as repealing the requirement that big banks "push out" some derivatives trading into separate units that are not backed by the government's insurance funds, delaying by two years the mandate that financial firms sell off bundled debt, exempting some private equity firms from registering with the SEC, and allowing some small, publicly traded companies to omit historical financial data from their financial filings.

Sources: "The Red Tape That's Choking Financial Reform," *Bloomberg Businessweek,* August 26–September 1, 2013, p. 14; "How Wall Street Defanged Dodd-Frank," *The Nation,* April 30, 2013, *www.thenation.com;* "House Votes to Repeal Dodd-Frank Provision," *The New York Times,* October 30, 2013, *dealbook.nytimes.com;* and, "House Passes Measure to Ease Some Dodd-Frank Rules," *The New York Times,* January 14, 2015, *www.nytimes.com.*

The two main antitrust enforcement agencies are the Antitrust Division of the U.S. Department of Justice and the Federal Trade Commission. Both agencies may bring suits against companies they believe to be guilty of violating antitrust laws. They also may investigate possible violations, issue guidelines and advisory opinions for firms planning mergers or acquisitions, identify specific practices considered to be illegal, and negotiate informal settlements out of court. Antitrust regulators have been active in prosecuting price fixing, blocking anticompetitive mergers, and dealing with foreign companies that have violated U.S. laws on fair competition. In Europe, the European Commission enforces antitrust regulation, as seen in the Microsoft example that follows.

In 2013 Microsoft was fined €561 million ($732.2 million) by the European Commission (EC) after it broke its voluntary promise to offer more than 15 million Windows users a choice of rival web browsers. The fine was the latest altercation between the EC and Microsoft. A decade earlier, the EC fined Microsoft €1.6 billion ($2.08 billion) for failing to provide rivals with information at fair prices and for tying its media player to its operating system. According to EC's competition chief, "such a breach is of course very serious, irrespective of whether it was intentional or not and it calls for sanctions. I hope this decision makes companies think twice before they ever think of internationally breaching their obligations or even neglecting their duty to ensure strict compliance."[18]

If a company is found guilty of antitrust violations, what are the penalties? The government may levy a fine—sometimes a large one, as the EC did against Microsoft. In another example, Berkshire Hathaway agreed to pay $896,000 to settle U.S. allegations that the

[18] "EU Fines Microsoft $732 Million," *The Wall Street Journal,* March 6, 2013, *online.wsj.com.*

firm violated antitrust laws by failing to report the acquisition of an equity stake in USG Corporation, a gypsum wallboard-maker based in Chicago. "We made a mistake when we overlooked the filing requirement," explained Berkshire's chief executive, Warren Buffet.[19] In the case of private lawsuits, companies may also be required to pay damages to firms or individuals they have harmed. In addition, regulators may impose other, nonmonetary remedies. A *structural remedy* may require the breakup of a monopolistic firm; this occurred when AT&T was broken up by government order in 1984. A *conduct remedy,* more commonly used, involves an agreement that the offending firm will change its conduct, often under government supervision. For example, a company might agree to stop certain anticompetitive practices. Finally, an *intellectual property remedy* is used in some kinds of high-technology businesses; it involves disclosure of information to competitors. All these are part of the regulator's arsenal.

Antitrust regulations cut across industry lines and apply generally to all enterprises. Other economic regulations, such as those governing stock exchanges, may be confined to specific industries and companies.

Social Regulations

Social regulations are aimed at such important social goals as protecting consumers and the environment and providing workers with safe and healthy working conditions. Equal employment opportunity, protection of pension benefits, and health care for citizens are other important areas of social regulation. Unlike the economic regulations mentioned above, social regulations are not limited to one type of business or industry. Laws concerning pollution, safety and health, health care, and job discrimination apply to all businesses; consumer protection laws apply to all relevant businesses producing and selling consumer goods.

An example of a social regulation is federal rules for automobile and truck emissions and mileage standards. Beginning in 2011, the federal government rolled out new standards to be applied to automobiles made between 2011 and 2025. By 2025, all new cars and trucks sold in the United States must have a performance equivalency of 54.5 miles per gallon while reducing greenhouse emission gases to 163 grams per mile. These new requirements could save families an estimated $8,200 in fuel costs over the lifetime of the vehicle, relative to a 2010 standard. In 2015, new standards were proposed to improve fuel efficiency and cut carbon pollution for trucks. The new standards were expected to lower CO^2 emissions by approximately 1 billion metric tons, cut fuel costs by about $170 billion, and reduce oil consumption by up to 1.8 billion barrels over the lifetime of the vehicle. In addition to cost-savings and environmental benefits, this social regulation also would help the country achieve its goal of less dependence on foreign oil.[20]

The most significant social regulation in the United States since the 1960s was the comprehensive reform of health care coverage passed by Congress in 2009. It is described in Exhibit 7.B.

Who regulates? Normally, for both economic and social regulation, specific rules are set by agencies of government and by the executive branch, and may be further interpreted by the courts. Many kinds of business behavior are also regulated at the state level.

---

[19] "Warren Buffet's Berkshire Hathaway to Pay $896,000 Civil Penalty on Antitrust Issue," *The Wall Street Journal,* August 20, 2014, *online.wsj.com.*

[20] "President Obama Announced New Fuel Economy Standards," *The White House Blog,* July 29, 2011, *www.whitehouse.gov/blog;* and, "EPA and DOT Propose Greenhouse Gas and Fuel Efficiency Standards for Heavy-duty Trucks," *National Highway and Traffic Safety Administration,* June 19, 2015, *www.nhtsa.gov.*

In 2010, led by President Obama, Congress passed the Affordable Care Act, often referred to as "Obamacare." The basic purpose of the law was to hold insurance companies accountable for their costs and services to their customers, lower the rising health care costs, provide Americans with greater freedom and control over their health care choices, and ultimately improve the quality of health care in America. Its provisions would be rolled out over 10 years. In 2010, the government began giving subsidies to small businesses that offered health coverage to employees, insurance companies were barred from denying coverage to children with preexisting illnesses, and children were permitted to stay on their parents' insurance policies until age 26.

The health care reform law aroused strong passions on both sides. Proponents of the law argued that the more than 5.1 million people on Medicare would save over $3 billion in prescription drugs costs, 105 million Americans would no longer have lifetime dollar limits on their health care coverage, and approximately 54 million Americans would receive greater preventative medical coverage. Health care fraud would decline by $4.1 billion annually due to new fraud detection measures, and 2.5 million young adults would retain health care coverage under their parents' plan. Most importantly, most Americans would now have health insurance coverage.

But, opponents challenged the new law as filled with myths, untruths, and harmful consequences. Some believed that the act would do nothing to bring down the cost of health care. Business leaders worried that the burden of providing their employees with health care insurance would result in bankruptcy or cause employers to reduce the level of health care coverage for their employees. Many worried that the mandate infringed on individual rights—including the right to go without health insurance if they chose. Several states sued, saying the law violated the constitution.

By 2015, nearly 11.7 million Americans had selected marketplace plans or been automatically enrolled under the act. Twenty-eight states and the District of Columbia had expanded their Medicaid coverage, with more than 10 million more Americans enrolled in Medicaid or the Children's Health Insurance Program. Under the act, millions more Americans received preventive services, such as vaccines, cancer screenings, and annual wellness visits at no out-of-pocket cost, than ever before. In addition, Americans could no longer be denied or dropped from coverage because of pre-existing conditions or because they hit an annual or lifetime cap in benefits.

Sources: "What's in the Bill," *The Wall Street Journal,* March 22, 2010, *online.wsj.com;* "Get the Facts Straight on Health Reform—A More Secure Future," *The White House,* n.d., *www.whitehouse.gov;* and "The Affordable Care Act Is Working," *Department of Health and Human Services, www.hhs.gov.*

Government regulators and the courts have the challenging job of applying the broad mandates of public policy.

Figure 7.1 depicts these two types of regulation—economic and social—along with the major regulatory agencies responsible for enforcing the rules at the federal level in the United States. Only the most prominent federal agencies are included in the chart. Individual states, some cities, and other national governments have their own array of agencies to implement regulatory policy. There is a legitimate need for government regulation in modern economies, but regulation also has problems. Businesses feel these problems first-hand, often because the regulations directly affect the cost of products and the freedom of managers to design their business operations. In the modern economy, the costs and effectiveness of regulation, as well as its unintended consequences, are serious issues that cannot be overlooked. Each is discussed below.

The Effects of Regulation

Regulation affects many societal stakeholders, including business. Sometimes the consequences are known and intended, but at other times unintended or accidental consequences emerge from regulatory actions. In general, government hopes that the benefits arising from regulation outweigh the costs.

FIGURE 7.1 Types of Regulation and Regulatory Agencies

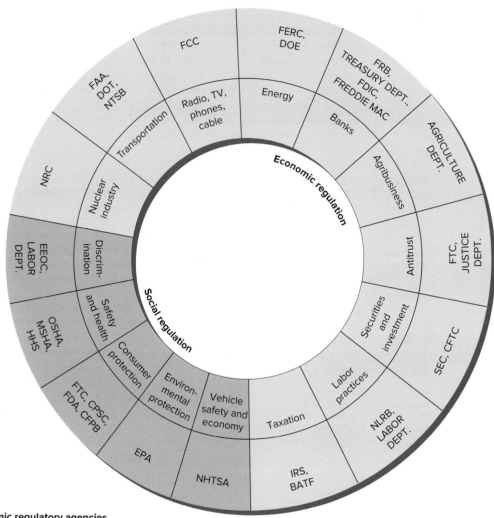

Economic regulatory agencies

NRC	Nuclear Regulatory Commission
FAA	Federal Aviation Administration
FCC	Federal Communications Commission
FERC	Federal Energy Regulatory Commission
FRB	Federal Reserve Board
CFTC	Commodity Futures Trading Commission
FREDDIE MAC	Federal Home Loan Mortgage Corporation
DOT	Department of Transportation

FTC	Federal Trade Commission
SEC	Securities and Exchange Commission
NLRB	National Labor Relations Board
IRS	Internal Revenue Service
BATF	Bureau of Alcohol, Tobacco, Firearms and Explosives
FDIC	Federal Deposit Insurance Corporation
DOE	Department of Energy
NTSB	National Transportation Safety Board

Social regulatory agencies

EEOC	Equal Employment Opportunity Commission
OSHA	Occupational Safety and Health Administration
MSHA	Mine Safety and Health Administration
FTC	Federal Trade Commission
HHS	Department of Health and Human Services

CPSC	Consumer Product Safety Commission
FDA	Food and Drug Administration
EPA	Environmental Protection Agency
NHTSA	National Highway Traffic Safety Administration
CFPB	Consumer Financial Protection Bureau

The Costs and Benefits of Regulation

The call for regulation may seem irresistible to government leaders and officials given the benefits they seek, but there are always costs to regulation. An old economic adage says, "There is no free lunch." Eventually, someone has to pay for the benefits created.

An industrial society such as the United States can afford almost anything, including social regulations, if it is willing to pay the price. Sometimes the benefits are worth the costs; sometimes the costs exceed the benefits. The test of **cost–benefit analysis** helps the public understand what is at stake when new regulation is sought.

Figure 7.2 illustrates the increase in costs of federal regulation in the United States since 1960. Economic regulation has existed for many decades, and its cost has grown more slowly than that of social regulation. Social regulation spending reflects growth in such areas as environmental health, occupational safety, and consumer protection. A rapid growth of social regulation spending occurred in the 1960s and again in the 2000s, but has slowed somewhat recently. The cost of regulation has its critics, especially when the costs to small businesses or manufacturing firms are considered.

> Economists Nicole Crain and Mark Crain reported that complying with federal regulations cost U.S. businesses more than $2 trillion each year. Compliance costs were highest for regulations focusing on the environment and worker safety and fell disproportionately on manufacturers and small businesses. The average manufacturing company paid compliance costs of nearly $20,000 per employee annually, nearly double the average cost paid by all U.S. businesses. "There's no question it's harming our country's economic growth," said the National Association for Manufacturers' president. "This is hidden tax. It's a cost to the economy."[21]

But other economists pointed out that the Crain study, commissioned by the National Association of Manufactures, was flawed since it relied on the opinions of business executives who had a vested interest in overestimating regulatory costs. They also argued that the researchers failed to measure the benefits that regulations provided the country. Some

FIGURE 7.2
Spending on U.S. Regulatory Activities

Source: Susan Dudley and Melinda Warren, "Regulators' Budget Increases Consistent with Growth in Fiscal Budget," Regulatory Studies Center, The George Washington University and Weidenbaum Center, Washington University in Saint Louis, May 2015, *regulatorystudies. columbian.gwu.edu.*

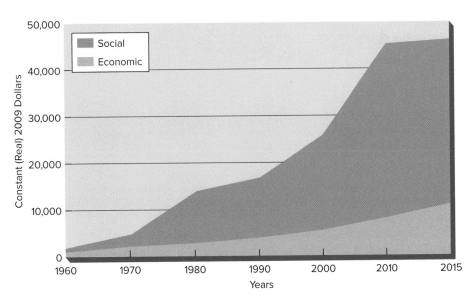

[21] "New Study Places $2T Yearly Price Tag on Federal Regulation," *Pittsburgh Post-Gazette,* September 11, 2014, *www.post-gazette.com.*

felt that the high cost of regulation on business was worth it since the stakes were so high. Controlling environmental pollution and protecting worker and consumer safety, for example, benefits many citizens. How do the costs and benefits of regulation compare? The federal government's Office of Budget and Management reported that the annual benefits of major federal regulations from 2003 to 2013 ranged somewhere from $217 billion to $863 billion, while the estimated annual costs ranged from $57 billion to $84 billion. Although different methodologies produced different estimates, in all scenarios the benefits exceeded the costs.[22]

In addition to paying for regulatory programs, it takes people to administer, monitor, and enforce these regulations. Researchers at two academic research centers have documented staffing regulatory activities in the United States since 1960, as shown in Figure 7.3. In 1960, fewer than 60,000 federal employees monitored and enforced government regulations. Two decades later, in 1980, staffing at federal regulatory agencies had risen to more than 146,000 employees. In the early 1980s, President Reagan led a campaign to cut government regulation. This campaign continued during both of the Bush presidencies and the number of full-time federal employees dedicated to regulatory activities modestly increased through 2000. As noted earlier, with the return to regulatory control and the addition of new funding and new agencies, the number of government employees at regulatory agencies increased to more than 277,000 employees by 2015.

The United States has experimented with different forms of government regulation for more than 200 years, and experts have learned that not all government programs are effective in meeting their intended goals. With new regulations being added each year, redundancy is likely to occur. In 2011, President Obama ordered a massive investigation of overlapping and duplicative regulatory programs. He noted that there were 15 different agencies overseeing food-safety laws, more than 20 separate programs to help the homeless, and 80 programs for economic development. Senator Tom Coburn, who strongly supported this investigation, estimated that between $100 and $200 billion in duplicative

FIGURE 7.3
Staffing of U.S. Regulatory Activities

Source: Dudley and Warren, Ibid.

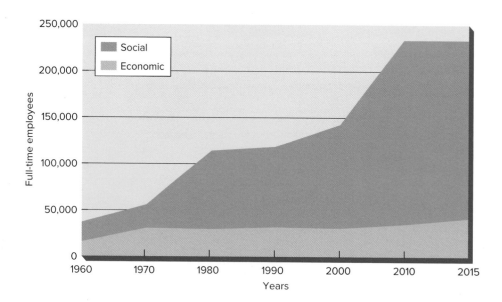

[22] "2014 Draft Report to Congress on the Benefits and Costs of Federal Regulations," *OIRA Report to Congress,* Office of Budget and Management, 2014, *www.whitehouse.gov/omb.*

spending would be uncovered. In only 2 years, regulatory agencies proposed the following cost-savings changes:

- The Department of Health and Human Services finalized new rules to promote tele-medicine to help hospitals and patients in rural areas, saving around $65 million over the next 5 years.
- The Department of Labor coordinated its hazards warning requirements with those of other nations, increasing safety and saving employers over $1.5 billion over the next 5 years.
- The Occupational Safety and Health Administration announced a new rule that removed over 1.9 million annual hours of redundant reporting burdens on employers, saving more than $40 million in annual costs.
- The Department of Agriculture modernized and streamlined poultry inspections rules, saving the private sector over $1 billion over the next 5 years while increasing safety in the process.
- The Federal Communications Commission eliminated over 190 redundant regulations.[23]

Continuous Regulatory Reform

The amount of regulatory activity often is cyclical—historically rising during some periods and declining during others. Businesses in the United States experienced a lessening of regulation in the early 2000s—*deregulation*—only to observe the return of regulatory activity in the late 2000s and early 2010s *reregulation.*

Deregulation is the removal or scaling down of regulatory authority and regulatory activities of government. Deregulation is often a politically popular idea. President Ronald Reagan strongly advocated deregulation in the early 1980s, when he campaigned on the promise to "get government off the back of the people." Major deregulatory laws were enacted beginning in 1975 when Gerald Ford was president and continued through the administrations of Jimmy Carter, Ronald Reagan, and George H.W. Bush, and returned during George W. Bush's administration. During these presidential administrations deregulation occurred in the commercial airlines, interstate trucking, railroads, and financial institutions industries. Some argued that when the 1933 Glass-Steagall Act was repealed in 1999 by the passage of the Financial Modernization Act, the lack of regulatory controls over the banking and securities industries led to the serious financial problems causing the economic recession in the late 2000s.

Deregulation has also occurred in Europe, especially in the arena of social regulation. In the United Kingdom, for example, the Approved Code of Practice (ACoP) governing various employee safety and health issues was downgraded to a "Guidance," a weaker form of regulatory control. In 2015, the U.K. passed the Deregulation Act that relaxed decades of increased regulatory control governing housing accommodations, motor vehicle insurance coverage, energy efficiency, and urban development, with the intention of less governmental influence in the lives of citizens.[24]

Proponents of deregulation often challenge the public's desire to see government solve problems. This generates situations in which government is trying to deregulate in some areas while at the same time creating new regulation in others. **Reregulation** is the increase or expansion of government regulation, especially in areas where the regulatory activities

---

[23] "Regulatory Reform Progress," January 30, 2012, *www.whitehouse.gov.* For an interesting ethical analysis of this regulatory investigation, see "The Obama Administration's Regulatory Review Initiative: A 21st Century Federal Regulatory Initiative?" Thomas Hemphill, *Business and Society Review,* Summer 2012, pp. 185–95.

[24] "Deregulation Act 2015," *Planning Resource,* April 13, 2015, *www.planningresource.co.uk.*

had previously been reduced. The scandals that rocked corporate America in the 2000s—and the failure or near-failure of a number of big commercial and investment banks in the late 2000s—brought cries from many stakeholder groups for reregulation of the securities and financial services industries. As a result, the United States has seen much reregulation in the 2010s with the passage of laws and rules governing the financial services and health care industries, as discussed earlier. As in the United States, many governments around the world reasserted their regulatory authority over the banking industry in the aftermath of the global recession. The economic think tank McKinsey & Company described the worldwide return to regulation, or *reregulation,* in these words:

> Since the financial crisis of 2008, governments have assumed a dramatically expanded role in financial markets. Policy makers have gone to great lengths to stabilize them, to support individual companies whose failure might pose systemic risks, and to prevent a deep economic downturn. . . . In short, governments will have their hand in industry to an extent few imagined possible only recently.[25]

Regulation in a Global Context

International commerce unites people and businesses in new and complicated ways, as described in Chapter 4. U.S. consumers routinely buy food, automobiles, and clothing from companies located in Europe, Canada, Latin America, Australia, Africa, and Asia. Citizens of other nations do the same. As these patterns of international commerce grow more complicated, governments recognize the need to establish rules that protect the interests of their own citizens. No nation wants to accept dangerous products manufactured elsewhere that will injure its citizens, and no government wants to see its economy damaged by unfair competition from foreign competitors. These concerns provide the rationale for international regulatory agreements and cooperation.

In cases where businesses operate in multiple countries, regulations imposed in one jurisdiction can affect companies operating out of others. But imposing regulatory controls on businesses from other countries can be difficult.

> For example, in 2012, the European Union imposed a carbon emissions fee on all airlines flying in and out of EU airspace in an effort to limit greenhouse gas emissions, a serious environmental problem discussed in Chapter 9. Within one month after the new rule went into effect, more than two dozen countries expressed their opposition to the EU's carbon emissions fee. The Chinese Air Transport Association, which includes China's four largest airlines, issued a prohibition on its airline members from paying the EU emissions fee. A few months later, India joined the group of nations protesting the fee, which had grown to 26 nation members, including airlines from the United States, Russia, and Japan. Despite these objections, the EU reported that "more than 99 percent of all major global airlines have complied with the first step" of Europe's carbon emission fee. But, six months later, the EU announced it was putting the fee "on hold" to allow the United Nations' International Civil Aviation Organization time to reach a global agreement on aviation emissions.[26]

[25] "Leading through Uncertainty," *McKinsey Quarterly,* December 2008, *www.mckinseyquarterly.com.*

[26] "China Bans Its Airlines from Paying EU Emissions Fee," *The Wall Street Journal,* February 6, 2012, *online.wsj.com;* "EU Hails Airline Emission Tax Success," *The Guardian,* May 15, 2012, *www.theguardian.com;* and "EU Halts Carbon Emission Fees for Airlines," *The Hill,* November 12, 2012, *www.thehill.com.*

At other times, the issues themselves cut across national borders, so international regulation is needed. Sometimes, nations negotiate agreements directly with one another, and at other times they do so under the auspices of the United Nations or regional alliances. For example, the United Nations monitors international uses of nuclear power due to the great potential for harm to those living near nuclear power plants and based on the threat of converting this technology into nuclear weapons.

In 2012, the United Nations was called to Iran to investigate and determine if this country was developing enriched uranium that could be used for nuclear weaponry. Some enriched uranium was discovered, but it was unclear if Iran was developing nuclear weapons. Three years later, the world's major economic powers—the United States, the United Kingdom, France, Germany, Russia, and China—reached an accord with Iran that would require Iran to dismantle its nuclear program in exchange for the lifting of some economic sanctions by the United Nations and the major economic powers.[27]

Whether at the local, state, federal or international levels, governments exert their control seeking to protect society through regulation. The significant challenge involves balancing the costs of this form of governance against the benefits received or the prevention of the harms that might occur if the regulation is not in place and enforced. Businesses have long understood that managing and, if possible, cooperating with the government regarding regulation generally leads to a more productive economic environment and financial health of the firm.

Summary

- Government's relationship with business ranges from collaborative to working at arm's length. This relationship often is tenuous, and managers must be vigilant to anticipate any change that may affect business and its operations.
- A public policy is an action undertaken by government to achieve a broad public purpose. The public policy process involves inputs, goals, tools or instruments, and effects.
- Regulation is needed to correct for market failure, overcome natural monopoly, and protect stakeholders who might otherwise be hurt by the unrestricted actions of business.
- Regulation can take the form of laws affecting an organization's economic operations (e.g., trade and labor practices, allocation of scarce resources, price controls) or focus on social good (e.g., consumer protection, employee health and safety, environmental protection).
- Antitrust laws seek to preserve competition in the marketplace, thereby protecting consumers. Remedies may involve imposing a fine, breaking up a firm, changing the firm's conduct, or requiring the disclosure of information to competitors.
- Although regulations are often very costly, many believe that these costs are worth the benefits they bring. The ongoing debate over the need for and effectiveness of regulation leads to alternating periods of deregulation and reregulation.
- The global regulation of business often occurs when commerce crosses national borders or the consequences of unregulated business activity by a national government are so large that global regulation is necessary.

[27]"Iran, World Powers Reach Nuclear Deal," *The Wall Street Journal*, July 14, 2015, *www.wsj.com*.

Key Terms	antitrust laws, *144*	market failure, *142*	regulation, *142*
	cost–benefit analysis, *149*	monetary policy, *141*	reregulation, *151*
	deregulation, *151*	natural monopoly, *143*	social assistance policies,
	Dodd-Frank Act, *144*	negative externalities, *142*	*141*
	economic regulation, *144*	predatory pricing, *144*	social regulation, *146*
	fiscal policy, *140*	public policy, *137*	

Internet Resources

www.cato.org	Cato Institute
www.consumerfinance.gov	U.S. Consumer Financial Protection Bureau
www.economywatch.com	Economy Watch
www.federalreserve.gov	Board of Governors of the Federal Reserve System
www.ftc.gov	U.S. Federal Trade Commission
mercatus.org	Mercatus Center, George Mason University
www.ncpa.org	National Center for Policy Analysis
www.reginfo.gov	U.S. Office of Information and Regulatory Affairs
www.regulations.gov	Regulations.gov
www.un.org/en/law	International Law, United Nations
www.usa.gov	Government Made Easy

Discussion Case: *Should E-Cigarettes Be Regulated?*

The tobacco industry and government regulators worldwide spent decades battling over whether tobacco cigarettes should be regulated. By the mid-2010s, almost all governments had passed legislation to control the ingredients in cigarettes, how this product could be advertised, and limited their sale to individuals of a certain age, typically 18 years and older. But a new, related issue was just emerging: whether or not governments should regulate e-cigarettes.

Electronic cigarettes, or e-cigarettes, are products designed to deliver nicotine or other substances to a user in the form of a vapor. Typically, they are composed of a rechargeable, battery-operated heating element, a replaceable cartridge that may contain nicotine or other chemicals, and an atomizer that, when heated, converts the contents of the cartridge into a vapor. This vapor can then be inhaled by the user. These products are often made to look like cigarettes, cigars, or pipes. They are also sometimes made to look like everyday items such as pens and USB memory sticks, for people who wish to use the product without others noticing.

Introduced to the global marketplace in 2004, e-cigarettes have become increasingly popular around the world. By 2015, 466 brands of e-cigarettes were available globally, generating $3 billion in sales. Most e-cigarette sales initially occurred on the Internet, making the product easily accessible to both adults and teens, and at specialty vape shops. More recently, e-cigarette manufacturers have packaged their products and sold them at higher prices in convenience and grocery stores.

Advocates of e-cigarettes argued that they did not have the same harmful effects as tobacco cigarettes, claiming that they did not produce harmful secondhand smoke affecting nonsmokers. They also touted the product as a possible smoking cessation aid. Early

research on the effects of e-cigarettes showed that the nicotine in e-cigarettes was addictive, just as it was in tobacco cigarettes, but because e-cigarettes did not produce smoke they were less harmful to a user's lungs than tobacco. However, much remained unknown. As one medical school professor explained, "E-cigarettes may be less harmful than cigarettes, but we still don't know enough about their long-term risks or the effects of second-hand exposure."

A few countries took up the issue of e-cigarette regulation. In 2013, Singapore banned importing and selling e-cigarettes. This move surprised many, as most Asian countries have a high tolerance for smoking and Singapore did not restrict the importation or sale of tobacco cigarettes. In 2014, the European Parliament approved rules governing e-cigarettes. Beginning in mid-2016, e-cigarette advertising was banned in the 28 nations of the European Union, as it already was for ordinary tobacco products. E-cigarette packages were required to carry a graphic health warning and be childproof. The amount of nicotine was limited to 20 milliliters per milliliter, similar to ordinary cigarettes. But the issue of regulating e-cigarettes soon moved to the global stage.

Despite the inconclusive evidence of harms caused by e-cigarette smoking, the World Health Organization (WHO) urged governments to restrict its use. The WHO report recommended that governments "ban the use of electronic cigarettes indoors and in public places and outlaw tactics to lure young users." It argued that the ban on indoor use was necessary "until exhaled vapor is proven to be not harmful to bystanders." It also called for regulation to ensure the products contained a standard dose of nicotine (since the dose varied widely among manufacturers), ban sales to minors, and prohibit the manufacture of fruity, candy–type e-cigarette flavorings.

Initially, most of the e-cigarette regulatory activity in the United States occurred at the state and local levels. By 2015, three states—North Dakota, New Jersey, and Utah—had banned e-cigarettes in public places such as restaurants and bars, and 18 states had passed some limitations on the use or sale of e-cigarettes. Nearly 400 cities or countries had restrictions on e-cigarettes. Yet, actions taken by the U. S. Food and Drug Administration in 2009, when it aggressively attacked the manufacturing, sale, and use of tobacco cigarettes by enforcing the Family Smoking Prevention and Tobacco Control Act, set the stage of more regulation targeting e-cigarettes.

In 2014 the U.S. Food and Drug Administration took a limited regulatory approach when it announced new rules that prohibited sales of battery-powered nicotine delivery devices to anyone under 18 years of age and required manufacturers to submit their products for FDA approval, in addition to disclosing ingredients and warning consumers that nicotine was addictive. But, the new FDA rules stopped short of attempting to ban advertising of e-cigarettes, Internet sales, or candy or fruit flavors, as recommended by the WHO. Makers of e-cigarettes breathed a big sigh of relief when they heard these limited restrictions. "I'm pleased the FDA has created a structure to treat these products differently than traditional combustible cigarettes," said Miguel Martin, president of Logic Technology Development, a leading e-cigarette maker.

Perhaps U.S. tobacco manufacturers had learned an important lesson from the severe regulatory controls imposed on the marketing of cigarettes, because they took initiative in effect to regulate themselves. Many placed the strongest health warnings ever on e-cigarettes, going even further than the warnings mandated on tobacco cigarette packages. Altria, the maker of Marlboro cigarettes, stated on its packages of MarkTen, its e-cigarette line, "People with heart disease, high blood pressure and diabetes should not use this product. Neither should children. Nicotine can cause dizziness, nausea and stomach pains, and may worsen asthma. Nicotine is addictive and habit forming, and is very toxic by inhalation, in contact with the skin, or if swallowed." Similarly, Reynolds American, makers of Camel cigarettes

and Vuse, an e-cigarette product, printed on their e-cigarette packages the following warning, "This product is not intended for persons who have an unstable heart condition, high blood pressure, or diabetes; or persons who are at risk for heart disease or are taking medicine for depression or asthma." These warnings were entirely voluntary. Yet, some critics saw them as ploys to reduce potential legal liability or the threat that governments would ban this product altogether. A professor at Stanford's School of Medicine said, "When I saw [the warning labels on e-cigarettes], I nearly fell off my chair. Is this part of a noble effort for the betterment of public health, or a cynical business strategy? I suspect the latter."

The battle over the regulatory control on e-cigarettes will likely continue. After the FDA announced its rules in 2014, Senator Durbin of Illinois said, "Shame on the FDA. Parents across America lost their best ally in protecting their kids from this insidious product." The director of the FDA's Center for Tobacco Products told reporters it was continuing its investigation into the effects of e-smoking. "It's sort of like, walk before you run," indicating that more severe regulations could be forthcoming. Whether controls will come from Congress or the FDA, the issue of regulating e-cigarettes appears to be far from over.

Sources: "E-Cigarettes: Questions and Answers," *Food and Drug Administration* website, January 21, 2015, *www.fda.gov;* "E-Cigarettes: Health and Safety Issues," *WebMD,* accessed June 2015, *www.webmd.com;* "States and Municipalities with Laws Regulating Use of Electronic Cigarettes" *American Nonsmokers' Rights Foundation,* June 2015, *www.no-smoke.org;* "European Parliament Approves Tough Rules on Electronic Cigarettes," *The New York Times,* February 26, 2014, *www.nytimes.com;* "World Health Organization Urges Stronger Regulation of Electronic Cigarettes," *The New York Times,* August 26, 2014, *www.nytimes.com;* "E-Cig Makers Breathe Easier after FDA Proposes Rules," *The Wall Street Journal,* April 24, 2014, *online.wsj.com;* and "Dire Warnings by Big Tobacco on E-Smoking," *The New York Times,* September 28, 2014, *www.nytimes.com.*

Discussion Questions

1. Should the U.S. and other national governments ban or more severely regulate the manufacture, sale, and use of e-cigarettes? Why or why not?

2. Which stakeholders are most affected by the sale and regulation of e-cigarettes?

3. Is the tobacco industry demonstrating a strategy of working in a collaborative partnership with the FDA by its voluntary warning labels on e-cigarettes?

4. Using the elements of public policy presented earlier in this chapter, identify the inputs, goals, tools, and effects of the FDA's effort to regulate e-cigarettes.

5. What reasons, discussed earlier in this chapter, could the FDA or other national regulatory agencies use to justify greater regulatory control of e-cigarettes?

Influencing the Political Environment

Businesses face complicated issues in managing their relationships with politicians and government regulators. Managers must understand the political environment and be active and effective participants in the public policy process. They need to ensure that their company is seen as a relevant stakeholder when government officials make public policy decisions and must be familiar with the many ways that business can influence these decisions. The opportunities afforded businesses to participate in the public policy process differ from nation to nation. Sound business strategies depend on an understanding of these differences, enabling businesses to manage worldwide business–government relations effectively.

This Chapter Focuses on These Key Learning Objectives:

LO 8-1 Understanding the arguments for and against business participation in the political process.

LO 8-2 Knowing the types of corporate political strategies and the influences on an organization's development of a particular strategy.

LO 8-3 Assessing the tactics businesses can use to be involved in the political process.

LO 8-4 Examining the role of the public affairs department and its staff.

LO 8-5 Recognizing the challenges business faces in managing business–government relations in different countries.

In 2015, Arkansas state legislators voted in favor of a controversial "religious freedom" law to allow people to freely exercise their religious beliefs without intervention or limitation by government. (The Indiana legislature passed a similar bill at the same time.) Although the new bill did not explicitly mention discrimination against homosexuals, many believed that this effort would protect conservative Christian individuals and businesses if they withheld services to anyone, such as same-sex couples, based on their beliefs. Not surprisingly, organizations representing gays and lesbians were outraged and publicly protested the new bill before it was signed by the governor and became law.

What surprised some people was the opposition from businesses, including Walmart, General Electric, Gap, Levi Strauss, Nike, and Apple. These companies made public announcements, as well as orchestrated private lobbying efforts, against the new bill. Walmart's chief executive, Doug McMillon, speaking from the company's headquarters in Bentonville, Arkansas, said on Twitter, "The bill threatens to undermine the spirit of inclusion present through the state of Arkansas and does not reflect the values we proudly uphold." McMillon called on the Arkansas governor to veto that state's bill. Other companies aligned with community groups opposed to this law, citing the growing acceptance of gay marriages in many states and understanding how this law could impact the firms' employees and customers.

Arkansas Governor Hutchinson did sign the bill into law, but only after demanding that the state's legislators amend it to mirror current federal legislation that prohibited denying services to anyone, including gay men and lesbians."[1]

As the example above demonstrates, many businesses are active participants in the political process to promote organizational goals, such as some did in this instance when they confronted the state legislature and governor. While not always successful, corporate political actions can alter legislation and protect stakeholders, as seen in Arkansas. In general, business recognizes the necessity of understanding the political environment and of addressing political issues as they arise. This is a constant challenge for business and managers entrusted with managing the political environment, because what issues warrant intervention is often controversial.

This chapter focuses on managing business–government relations and political issues. Businesses do not have an absolute right to exist and pursue profits. The right to conduct commerce depends on compliance with appropriate laws and public policy. As discussed in Chapter 7, public policies and government regulations are shaped by many actors, including business, special interest groups, and government officials. The emergence of public issues often encourages companies to monitor public concerns, respond to government proposals, and participate in the political process. This chapter discusses how managers can ethically and practically meet the challenge of managing the business–government relationship.

Participants in the Political Environment

In many countries the political environment features numerous participants. These participants may have differing objectives and goals, varying access to political tools, and disparate levels of power or influence. The outcomes sought by businesses may be consistent, or at odds, with the results desired by interest groups. Participants may argue that their needs are greater than the needs of other political actors, or that one group or another group does not have the right to be involved in the public policy process. To better understand the dynamic nature of the political environment, it is important to explore who participates in the political process and their claims of legitimacy.

[1] "US Corporate Backlash Hits Religious Freedom Bills," *Financial Times,* April 1, 2015, *www.ft.com;* "Arkansas Moves to Revise Legislation as Concerns of Religion and Gay Rights Intensify," *The New York Times,* April 1, 2015, *www.nytimes.com;* "In Va. Politics, Renewable Energy Dwarfed by Big Utility," *The Virginian Pilot,* March 1, 2014, *hamptonroads.com.*

Business as a Political Participant

There is a serious debate between those who favor and those who oppose business involvement in governmental affairs. This debate involves the question of whether, and to what extent, business should legitimately participate in the political process. As shown in Figure 8.1, some people believe business should stay out of politics, while others argue that business has a right to be involved.

Proponents of business involvement in the political process often argue that since other affected groups (such as special interest groups) are permitted to be involved, it is only fair that business should be, too. This justice and fairness argument becomes even stronger when one considers the significant financial consequences that government actions may have on business.

> An Irishman walks into a bar. This may sound like the opening line of a joke but it actually is the beginning of a television advertisement about responsible drinking, developed by British beverage maker Diageo. The company-sponsored ads promoting moderation in drinking, the first of their kind in the United Kingdom, were aired during prime time to maximize their impact. A Diageo spokesperson admitted that while the company wanted to discourage binge drinking by young people, a growing concern, it also hoped its campaign would help Diageo avoid possible governmental regulation of their product and its advertisements.[2]

Businesses see themselves as countervailing forces in the political arena and believe that their progress, and possibly survival, depends on influencing government policy and regulations. But others are not as confident that the presence of business enhances the political process. In this view, business has disproportionate influence, based on its great power and financial resources.

> Recent annual Harris polls consistently show that a large majority of Americans believed that big companies had too much political power (88 percent). Political action committees, a favorite political instrument for businesses, were seen as too powerful by 87 percent of the public, as were political lobbyists (by 84 percent). What is the group perceived as having the least amount of power in politics? The answer is small businesses; only 5 percent of those surveyed felt that they had too much political power. In the nearly two decades that the Harris Poll has been asking these questions, people have become increasingly concerned about big companies, lobbyists, and labor unions having too much political power.[3]

Although the debate over whether businesses should be involved in the political environment rages on, the facts are that in many countries businesses are permitted to engage in political discussions, influence political races, and introduce or contribute to the drafting of laws and regulations, as discussed later in this chapter. But businesses do not act alone in these activities. One significant opposition to businesses in the political arena comes from labor unions.

FIGURE 8.1
The Arguments for and against Political Involvement by Business

Why Business Should Be Involved	Why Business Should Not Be Involved
A pluralistic system invites many participants.	Managers are not qualified to engage in political debate.
Economic stakes are high for firms.	Business is too big, too powerful—an elephant dancing among chickens.
Business counterbalances other social interests.	Business is too selfish to care about the common good.
Business is a vital stakeholder of government.	Business risks its credibility by engaging in partisan politics.

[2] "Promoting Moderation," *Ethical Performance Best Practices,* Winter 2007/2008, p. 8.

[3] "Big Companies, PACs, Banks, Financial Institutions and Lobbyists Seen by Strong Majorities as Having Too Much Power and Influence in DC," June 1, 2011, *www.harrisinteractive.com.*

Labor unions have been involved in U.S. politics for decades. Labor union federal political action committees distributed nearly $13 million to candidates in 2013, with 87 percent going to Democrats. Some of the top labor union PAC donors included the Engineers Political Education Committee, the AFL-CIO's Committee on Political Education, the International Brotherhood of Electrical Workers PAC, the Carpenters Legislative Improvement Committee, and the American Federation of State County & Municipal Employees. The top unions donating to Super PACs, a source for campaign funds explained later in chapter, was the United Brotherhood of Carpenters and Joiners, which gave nearly $2 million in 2013, the AFL-CIO, and the American Federation of State, County & Municipal Employees, who each contributed $1.5 million in 2013. (Some of these organizations are mentioned later in Figure 8.4.)[4]

Influencing the Business–Government Relationship

Most scholars and businesspeople agree: Business must participate in politics. Why? Quite simply, the stakes are too high for business not to be involved. Government must and will act upon many issues, and these issues affect the basic operations of business and its pursuit of economic stability and growth. Therefore, businesses must develop a corporate political strategy.[5]

Corporate Political Strategy

A **corporate political strategy** involves the "activities taken by organizations to acquire, develop, and use power to obtain an advantage."[6] These strategies might be used to further a firm's economic survival or growth. Alternatively, a corporate political strategy might target limiting a competitor's progress or ability to compete. Strategies also may be developed to simply exercise the business's right to a voice in government affairs, such as some companies' protest against the Arkansas "religious freedom" bill discussed at the beginning of this chapter. Organizations differ in how actively they are involved in politics on an ongoing basis. Some companies essentially wait for a public policy issue to emerge before building a strategy to address that issue. This is likely when they believe the threat posed by unexpected public issues is relatively small.

On the other hand, other companies develop an ongoing political strategy, so that they are ready when various public issues arise. Firms are most likely to have a long-term political strategy if they believe the risks of harm from unexpected public issues are great, or when the firm is a frequent target of public attention. For example, firms in the chemical industry, which must contend with frequently changing environmental regulations and the risk of dangerous accidents, usually have a sophisticated political strategy. The same may be true for firms in the entertainment industry, which must often contend with policy issues such as intellectual property rights, public standards of decency, and licensing rights to new technologies.

Political actions by businesses often take the form of one of the following three strategic types, also shown in Figure 8.2:

- *Information strategy* (where businesses seek to provide government policymakers with information to influence their actions, such as lobbying).

- *Financial-incentives strategy* (where businesses provide incentives to influence government policymakers to act in a certain way, such as making a contribution to a political action committee that supports the policymaker).

---

[4] "Labor Union PACs Give $12.6 Million in Political Contributions in 2013," *Rollcall.com,* September 2, 2013, *blogs.rollcall.com.*

[5] For a contrarian view, see Miguel Alzola, "Corporate Dystopia: The Ethics of Corporate Political Spending," *Business & Society,* 52 (2013), pp. 388–426.

[6] The quotation is from John F. Mahon and Richard McGowan, *Industry as a Player in the Political and Social Arena* (Westport, CT: Quorum Press, 1996), p. 29. Also see Jean-Philippe Bonardi, Amy J. Hillman, and Gerald D. Keim, "The Attractiveness of Political Markets: Implications for Firm Strategy" *Academy of Management Review* 30 (2005), pp. 397–413, for a thorough discussion of this concept.

FIGURE 8.2
Business Strategies for Influencing Government

Source: Adapted from Amy J. Hillman and Michael A. Hitt, "Corporate Political Strategy Formulation: A Model of Approach, Participation, and Strategy Decisions" *Academy of Management Review* 24 (1999), Table 1, p. 835. Used by permission.

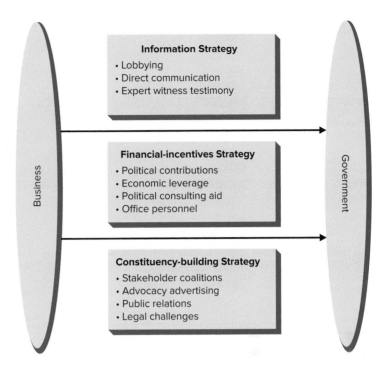

- *Constituency-building strategy* (where businesses seek to gain support from other affected organizations to better influence government policymakers to act in a way that helps them).

The various tactics used by businesses when adopting each of these political strategies are discussed next in this chapter.

Political Action Tactics

The tactics or tools used by business to influence the public policy process are often similar to those available to other political participants. Sometimes business may have an advantage since it might have greater financial resources, but often it is how tactics are used—not the amount of money spent—that determines their effectiveness. This section will discuss tactics used by business in the three strategic areas of information, financial incentives, and constituency building.

Promoting an Information Strategy

As shown in Figure 8.2, some firms pursue a political strategy that tries to provide government policymakers with information to influence their actions. Lobbying is the political action tool most often used by businesses when pursuing this type of political strategy, but some firms also use various forms of direct communication with policymakers. These various information-strategy approaches are discussed next.

Lobbying

An important tool of business involvement in politics is **lobbying**. Many companies hire full-time representatives in Washington, DC, state capitals, or local cities (or the national capital in other countries where they operate) to keep abreast of developments that may affect the company and, when necessary, to communicate with government officials. These individuals are called lobbyists. Their job is to represent the business before the people and agencies

FIGURE 8.3
Total Federal Lobbying Spending and Number of Lobbyists, 1998–2014, by U.S. Business

Source: Center for Responsive Politics at www.opensecrets .org. Used by permission.

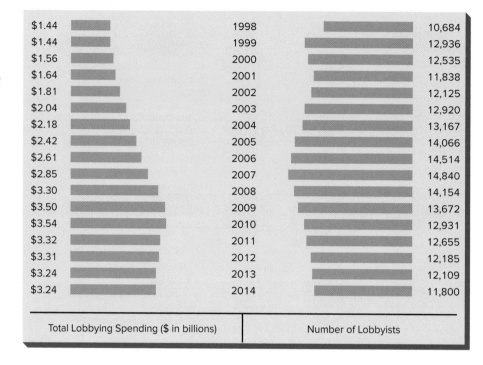

Total Lobbying Spending ($ in billions)	Year	Number of Lobbyists
$1.44	1998	10,684
$1.44	1999	12,936
$1.56	2000	12,535
$1.64	2001	11,838
$1.81	2002	12,125
$2.04	2003	12,920
$2.18	2004	13,167
$2.42	2005	14,066
$2.61	2006	14,514
$2.85	2007	14,840
$3.30	2008	14,154
$3.50	2009	13,672
$3.54	2010	12,931
$3.32	2011	12,655
$3.31	2012	12,185
$3.24	2013	12,109
$3.24	2014	11,800

involved in determining legislative and regulatory outcomes. Lobbying involves direct contact with a government official to influence the thinking or actions of that person on an issue or a public policy. Lobbyists communicate with and try to persuade others to support an organization's interest or stake as they consider a particular law, policy, or regulation.

Businesses, trade associations, and other groups spend a great deal on lobbying. Figure 8.3 shows the total number of lobbyists and the amount spent on lobbying activity from 1998 to 2014. As illustrated, the number of lobbyists peaked in 2008 and 2009 but declined recently. The amount spent on lobbying rose to $3 billion each year by 2008 and has shown little decline since that time. The organizations spending the most on lobbying since 2000 were the U.S. Chamber of Commerce, the American Medical Association, General Electric, the Pharmaceutical Research and Manufacturers of America, the American Hospital Association, and the AARP (formerly the American Association of Retired People).[7]

Under U.S. law and EU directive (and in other nations as well), lobbying activities are severely limited and must be disclosed publicly.[8] Lobbying firms and organizations employing in-house lobbyists must register with the government. They must also file regular reports on their earnings (lobbyists) or expenses (organizations), and indicate the issues and legislation that were the focus of their efforts. These rules are supposed to guarantee that politicians are free from undue influence and represent the public interest. However, they are not always effective, as the following examples show.

A senior politician in the British House of Lords was accused in 2013 of arranging to pay undercover reporters to pose as lobbyists and bribe other Lords to ask questions and influence debates during Parliamentary sessions. For a fee of £2,000

[7] For a complete listing of lobbyists and their expenses by organization and by industry, see *www.opensecrets.org/lobby.*

[8] For a detailed account of lobbying regulations in the United States, see Lobbying Disclosure Act Guidance at *lobbyingdisclosure.house.gov,* and for a description of the EU directive, see "New EU Lobbying Rules to Cover National Embassies," *EurActiv,* October 29, 2009, *www.euractiv.com.*

(nearly $3,000) a month, these "lobbyists" would intervene for the senior politician and offer other politicians cash or trips to Fiji. The intention was to show widespread support for the senior politician's views in the House. The House of Lords rules state that Lords are not allowed to "accept any financial inducements as an incentive or reward for exercising parliamentary influence" and should act in the public interest at all times. The British lobbying scandal escalated two years later when two former British foreign secretaries were exposed for using their governmental positions to favor foreign investors. One of the accused boasted that he operated under the radar to use his influence to change European Union rules on behalf of a foreign commodity firm, paying him £60,000 (nearly $100,000) a year.[9]

Businesses sometimes hire former government officials as lobbyists and political advisors. These individuals bring with them their personal connections and detailed knowledge of the public policy process. This circulation of individuals between business and government is often referred to as the **revolving door**. Some examples of this revolving door phenomena are shown in Exhibit 8.A.

While it is perfectly legal for government officials to seek employment in industry, and vice versa, the revolving door carries potential for abuse. Although it may be praised as an act of public service when a business executive leaves a corporate position to work for a regulatory agency, that executive may be inclined to act favorably toward his or her former employer. Such favoritism would not be fair to other firms also regulated by the agency. Businesses can also seek to influence public policy by offering jobs to regulators in exchange for favors, a practice that is considered highly unethical. "Is it any wonder that the public holds such a low esteem for Congress?" said Joel Hefley, who served as chairman of the House ethics committee before he retired from Congress. "You can dance around these rules in so many ways it really does not accomplish much of anything."[10]

Despite the public's strong concerns, lobbying—as well as hiring former government officials for positions in the corporate world—is normally legal, but great care must be exercised to act ethically.

Direct Communications

Businesses can also promote an information strategy through direct communication with policymakers, another kind of information strategy.

Democracy requires citizen access and communication with political leaders. Businesses often invite government officials to visit local plant facilities, give speeches to employees, attend awards ceremonies, and participate in activities that will improve the officials' understanding of management and employee concerns. These activities help to humanize the distant relationship that can otherwise develop between government officials and the public.

One of the most effective organizations promoting direct communications between business and policymakers is **The Business Roundtable**. Founded in 1972, the Roundtable is an organization of chief executive officers (CEOs) of leading corporations representing $7.2 trillion in annual revenues and more than 16 million employees. The organization studies various public policy issues and advocates for laws that it believes "foster vigorous economic growth and a dynamic global economy." Some issues the Roundtable has taken a position on in recent years include corporate governance, job creation and training, sustainability, health care, international trade, immigration, and cybersecurity.[11]

[9] "Peer Drawn into Lobbying Sandal Resigns from Party," *The Telegraph,* June 2, 2013, *www.telegraph.co.uk;* and "A UK Lobbying Scandal," *Kiwiblog,* February 24, 2015, *www.wikiblog.co.nz.*

[10] "Law Doesn't End Revolving Door on Capitol Hill," *The New York Times,* February 1, 2014, *dealbook.nytimes.com.*

[11] More information about the Business Roundtable is available at *www.businessroundtable.org.*

Exhibit 8.A

The Revolving Door of Political Influence

What job opportunities are available for politicians after they decide to retire from Congress or lose a recent reelection campaign? Lucrative positions await many of them just months after leaving Congress.

- Rep. Howard Berman, the former chairman of the foreign affairs committee and after 20 years of service in the House, was employed by Covington & Burling, a Washington law firm, as its lobbyist on foreign relations.
- Rep. Norm Dicks, the former chair of the House subcommittee that oversaw the Environmental Protection Agency's budget and served as a Congressman for 36 years, was employed by Van Ness Feldman, an environmental law firm.
- Rep. Charlie Gonzalez, 14-year Congressman, was hired by Via Metropolitan Transit, a public transit company that received $35 million in federal funds with Gonzalez's help when he was in Congress.
- Dennis Hastert, the longest serving Republican Speaker of the House of Representatives, joined the law and lobbying firm Dickstein Shapiro six months after leaving Congress in 2007. Over the next few years, he earned millions of dollars lobbying his former colleagues on behalf of foreign governments and various businesses, including tobacco and coal companies
- Sen. Kay Bailey Hutchison, after 10 years in the Senate and serving as the top Republican on the Commerce Committee, became a lobbyist for Yamaha Motors on consumer product safety issues.

Federal ethics rules, revised in 2007 after a lobbying scandal, were supposed to prohibit former senior officials from lobbying for at least one year after they left their government positions. Yet, more than 1,650 congressional aides registered as lobbyists within one year after leaving Capitol Hill, accounting for 44 percent of all registered lobbyists. They had apparently taken advantage of loopholes in the ethics rules, such as agreeing to a salary just below the cutoff point established in the lobbying restrictions or were previously paid by an individual lawmaker or leadership office, so they were allowed to lobby other House committee members they had worked closely with as a House aide.

Sources: "Lobbying From Capitol to K Street in a Hot Second," *Bloomberg Businessweek,* May 27–June 2, 2013, p. 37; and "Law Doesn't End Revolving Door on Capitol Hill," *The New York Times,* February 1, 2014, *dealbook.nytimes.com.* See also "Glenn R. Parker, Suzanne L. Parker, and Matthew S. Dabros, "The Labor Market for Politicians: Why Ex-Legislators Gravitate to Lobbying," *Business & Society* 52 (2013), pp. 427–50.

Expert Witness Testimony

A common method of providing information to legislators is for CEOs and other executives to give testimony in various public forums. Businesses may want to provide facts, anecdotes, or data to educate and influence government leaders. One way that government officials collect information in the United States is through public congressional hearings, where business leaders may be invited to speak. These hearings may influence whether legislation is introduced in Congress, or change the language or funding of a proposed piece of legislation, or shape how regulation is implemented. In some cases, the very future of the firm or industry may be at stake.

General Motors' CEO Mary Barra appeared before Congress multiple times in 2014 to address policymakers' concerns about faulty ignition switches in GM automobiles, which had resulted in as many as 100 deaths and leading to nearly 2.6 million recalled automobiles. (This story is detailed in the case, "General Motors and the Ignition Switch Recalls," at the end of the book.) In one appearance, Barra commented on the recently published report by former U.S. Attorney Anton Valukas, which was critical of GM's culture. Barra called the report "brutally tough and deeply troubling," but also highlighted the personnel changes made by the automaker, including firing 15 employees and adding 35 safety investigators. She also

reiterated the point she made in her town hall address to employees two weeks earlier: "I also told them that while I want to solve the problems as quickly as possible, I never want anyone associated with GM to forget what happened. I want this terrible experience permanently etched in our collective memories," Barra said. "This isn't just another business challenge. This is a tragic problem that never should have happened. And it must never happen again."[12]

Promoting a Financial-Incentive Strategy

A major method businesses use to influence government policymakers is to provide financial incentives. They can do this by contributing to a politician's election campaign, in order to persuade him or her—once in office—to support certain policies or to vote in a manner favorable to the firms' interests. In recent years, a series of Supreme Court and lower court decisions have dramatically expanded the ability of corporations to make campaign contributions. This section will describe the various mechanisms businesses can now use to influence the outcome of elections, including political action committees, Super PACs, tax-exempt organizations, and direct contributions by both corporations and their executives and employees.

Political Action Committees

One of the oldest political action tools used by business is to form and support **political action committees (PACs)**, independently incorporated organizations that can solicit contributions and then channel those funds to candidates seeking public office. Since the mid-1970s, companies have been permitted to spend company funds to organize and administer political action committees. (They cannot give directly to PACs, however.) PAC contributions to political campaigns are limited to certain amounts per candidate and per election. In 2014, large PACs (with 50 contributors or more) could give up to $5000 per candidate per election and $15,000 per national party per calendar year; for small PACs, these limits were $2600 and $32,400, respectively. The amounts that could be donated *to* a PAC were also limited.

PACs are particularly active in industries that are highly regulated or are the target of proposed regulations, such as the financial services and health care industries. Figure 8.4 lists the top political action committees by contribution, comparing data from two periods. It shows that the labor unions and trade associations that dominated the top 10 PAC list in 2001–02 (with 7 of the top 10 spots) have been replaced by a growing number of business organizations (Honeywell International, Lockheed Martin, and AT&T) and business trade groups (National Association of Realtors, National Beer Wholesalers Association, National Auto Dealers Association, and American Bankers Association).

Business PACs have been somewhat balanced in their support of Democrat and Republican candidates. For example, the following companies, through political action committee contributions, have generally supported both Democrat and Republican candidates: Honeywell International (43%–57%), Comcast (53%–47%), Goldman Sachs (46%–54%), Blue Cross/Blue Shield (39%–61%), AT&T (35%–65%), Lockheed Martin, (40%–60%), General Electric (40%–60%), and Google (71%–29%).[13]

Although companies have continued to operate PACs, this mechanism has some disadvantages, from a business perspective. Contributions are capped at fairly low levels, and

---

[12] "GM's CEO Tells Congress: 'I Will Not Rest Until These Problems Are Resolved'," *Fortune,* June 18, 2014, *fortune.com.*

[13] For a more comprehensive listing of business contributions by political party, see *www.opensecrets.org/pacs.*

FIGURE 8.4 **Political Action Committee Activity**

Sources: "Top PACs" for 2001–02, 2007–08, and 2013–14, Center for Responsive Politics, *www.opensecrets.org.*

	PAC Name	2001–02	PAC Name	2007–2008	PAC Name	2013–14
1.	National Association of Realtors	$3,648,526	National Association of Realtors	$4,020,900	National Association of Realtors	$3,822,955
2.	Laborers Union	$2,814,200	International Brotherhood of Electrical Workers	$3,344,650	National Beer Wholesalers Association	$3,213,000
3.	Association of Trial Lawyers of America	$2,813,753	AT&T, Inc.	$3,108,200	Honeywell International	$3,002,603
4.	National Auto Dealers Association	$2,578,750	American Bankers Association	$2,918,143	National Auto Dealers Association	$2,805,350
5.	American Medical Association	$2,480,972	National Beer Wholesalers Association	$2,869,000	Lockheed Martin	$2,629,750
6.	American Federation of State/County/Municipal Employees	$2,423,500	National Auto Dealers Association	$2,864,000	American Bankers Association	$2,537,375
7.	Teamsters Union	$2,390,003	International Association of Fire Fighters	$2,734,900	AT&T Inc.	$2,507,250
8.	United Auto Workers	$2,339,000	Operating Engineers Union	$2,704,067	Operating Engineers Union	$2,488,462
9.	International Brotherhood of Electrical Workers	$2,249,300	American Association for Justice	$2,700,500	Credit Union National Association	$2,470,650
10.	Carpenters & Joiners Union	$2,243,000	Laborers Union	$2,555,850	International Brotherhood of Electrical Workers	$2,440,214

companies cannot give money directly to their affiliated PACs. For these reasons, companies have turned increasingly to other mechanisms of political influence that have recently become available, as described next.

Super PACs

In 2010, a federal district court ruling in a lawsuit filed by *SpeechNow.org* opened the door for the creation of another mechanism of political influence. The court ruled that as long as PACs did not contribute directly to candidates, parties, or other PACs, they could accept *unlimited* contributions from individuals, unions, or corporations. This decision led the rise of **super PACs**, technically known as independent expenditure-only committees. Because contribution limits had been removed by the court, these organizations were able to raise and spend vast amounts of money, so long as they were not actually affiliated with any campaigns.

By 2015, 1360 groups had organized as Super PACs. They reported total contributions of nearly $700 million and spent more than $345 million in the 2014 election cycle. Although super PACs were technically independent, they often worked to support particular

candidates or parties, such as the two largest super PACs, the Senate Majority PAC and the House Majority PAC (both allied with the Democrat Party). But many super PACs represented a group of potential voters or a political stance, such as the Women Speak Out PAC, the Southern Conservatives Fund, or the Montanans for Limited Government.

While some companies were eager to take advantage of the new opportunity to support Super PACs, others found that doing so could be risky.

> As campaign financing laws began to change, Target welcomed the opportunity to get more involved in politics. The Minnesota retailer donated $150,000 to a super PAC called Minnesota Forward, which supported pro-business candidates throughout the state. Minnesota Forward backed a conservative candidate running for governor who, in addition to being pro-business, was against same-sex marriage. Hundreds of gay rights supporters demonstrated outside Target stores across the nation, and more than 240,000 people signed a petition promising a boycott. A note was placed on the retailer's Facebook page that read, "Boycott Target until they cease funding anti-gay politics."
>
> Target chief executive Gregg Steinhafel later apologized in a letter to his employees, saying, "The intent of our political contribution to [Minnesota] Forward was to support economic growth and job creation. While I firmly believe that a business climate conducive to growth is critical to our future, I realize our decision affected many of you in a way I did not anticipate, and for that I am genuinely sorry." Target declined to comment on the suggestion that the firm withdraw its donation.[14]

Tax-Exempt Organizations

A third mechanism businesses can use to direct money to election campaigns is tax-exempt organizations, such as 527, 501(c)4, or 501(c)6 organizations, each named after the relevant section of the tax code. These organizations are political campaign groups officially unaffiliated with individual parties or candidates, and therefore not liable for campaign spending restrictions. They gained prominence after the passage of the Bipartisan Campaign Reform Act (BCRA) of 2002, which prohibited **soft money**—unlimited contributions to the national political parties by individuals or organizations for party-building activities. As a way to get around these restrictions, some companies turned to tax-exempt organizations as vehicles for their political contributions. In the 2014 election cycle, 527 organizations raised more than $715 million.

> One of the most active 527 organizations leading up to the 2016 elections was Next-Gen Climate Action. This political fund was founded in 2013 by Tom Steyer, an investor and philanthropist. Steyer explained, "We act politically to prevent climate disaster and preserve American prosperity. Working at every level, we are committed to supporting candidates, elected officials and policymakers across the country that will take bold action on climate change—and to exposing those who deny reality and cater to special interests." In 2014, NextGen Climate Action had collected nearly $24 million in contributions and allocated more than $22 million. Other examples of large 527 organizations are ActBlue, a fund that enabled individuals to raise money for the Democratic candidates of their choosing using the Internet, and EMILY's List, a fund that supported pro-choice, Democrat female candidates.[15]

---

[14] "Target Discovers Downside to Political Contributions," *The Wall Street Journal,* August 7, 2010, *online.wsj.com.*

[15] See *www.opensecrets.org, secure.actblue.com,* and *emilyslist.org.*

The term **dark money** was used to describe contributions made to these tax-exempt organizations since the donors' names and amount of their contributions were not reported to the Federal Election Commission. Contributions to these organizations are often used for various advocacy tactics, such as telephone calls, television or radio announcements, and social media messages to bring attention to a political issue. These types of organizations have no contribution or spending limits.

The Conservative Solutions Project, a 501(c)4 tax-exempt organization formed by allies of Senator Marco Rubio, a Florida Congressman, announced that it was preparing to spend more than $20 million on issue advertising (a political tactic discussed later in this chapter) during the 2016 presidential campaign. The organization said it had already raised $15.8 million from donors, whose names were not required to be disclosed. By July 2015, the organization had spent $3.3 million on television and radio advertising primarily focusing on Rubio's attacks on the Obama administration's proposed nuclear deal with Iran. The Conservative Solutions Project represented a new form of political support, assuming activities normally carried out by a candidate's campaign but operating under greater anonymity.[16]

These tax-exempt organizations were intended to promote what the Internal Revenue Service called "social welfare," rather than be used as a political tactic to support politicians running for office. The IRS reportedly is preparing rules to define more clearly what social welfare groups can spend on politics but these rules were not expected until after the 2016 elections.

Direct Contributions by Corporations

Until 2010 corporations were not permitted by law to make direct contributions to political candidates for national and most state offices. As noted above, companies could organize PACs and contribute to super PACs or tax-exempt organizations, but they could not simply write a check from their own corporate treasuries to support a candidate, say, for president. But that all changed with the 2010 Supreme Court ruling in *Citizens United v. the Federal Election Commission.* As further explained in Exhibit 8.B, this decision allowed companies for the first time to contribute directly to political campaigns.

In 2012, the first full election cycle after the *Citizen United* decision, outside spending for all political campaigns tripled from the previous four-year cycle to more than $1 billion. Super PACs accounted for more than $600 million of that spending. The Brennan Center for Justice reported that nearly 60 percent of all super PAC money came from 195 individuals and their spouses. In 2014, the Supreme Court, in a separate case called *McCutcheon v. Federal Election Commission,* abolished all limits on election spending by corporations, as well as other organizations such as unions. Combined with the *Citizens United* decision, this opened the floodgates to corporate political spending. In an analysis of the 2014 Senate races, outside spending more than doubled since 2010 to nearly $500 million, accounting for 47 percent of all campaign funds.

Executive and Employee Personal Contributions

A final way that companies can influence elections is by encouraging their executives or employees to make personal contributions to the campaigns of candidates whose views they feel are aligned with their interests. The *McCutcheon v. Federal Election Commission*

---

[16] "Nonprofit Group Tied to Marco Rubio Raises Millions While Shielding Donors," *The New York Times,* July 6, 2015, *www.nytimes.com.*

In a 5-to-4 decision in 2010 the U.S. Supreme Court upheld the argument made by Citizens United, a conservative nonprofit political organization, that its First Amendment right to free speech was violated by the Federal Election Commission's restrictions on campaign contributions. Justice Anthony Kennedy wrote for the majority opinion, "if the First Amendment has any force, it prohibits Congress from fining or jailing citizens, or associations of citizens, for simply engaging in political speech." Republican campaign consultant Ed Rollins stated that the decision added transparency to the election process and would make it more competitive.

The *Citizens United* decision sent shock waves through the world of campaign financing since it allowed corporations, and also labor unions, for the first time in the history of the United States to directly contribute to candidates for public office. Critics said it would "corrupt democracy" by allowing corporate funds to flow directly into campaigns. At the time of the decision, 80 percent of Americans surveyed opposed the *Citizens United* ruling, and 65 percent strongly opposed it. Nearly three out of four Americans supported an effort by Congress to reinstate limits on corporate and union spending on election campaigns.

On the five-year anniversary of the *Citizens United* decision President Barack Obama spoke out on the Supreme Court ruling. "Our democracy works best when everyone's voice is heard, and no one's voice is drowned out. But five years ago, a Supreme Court ruling allowed big companies—including foreign corporations—to spend unlimited amounts of money to influence our elections," Mr. Obama said. "The *Citizens United* decision was wrong, and it has caused real harm to our democracy."

Sources: "Summary *Citizens United v. Federal Election Commission* (Docket No. 08-205)," Cornell University School of Law, n.d., *topics.law.cornell.edu/supct/cert/08-205;* "Money Grubbers: The Supreme Court Kills Campaign Finance Reform," *Slate,* January 21, 2010, *www.slate.com;* "Justices, 5–4, Reject Corporate Spending Limit," *The New York Times,* January 21, 2010, *www.nytimes.com;* "*Citizens United v. Federal Election Commission,*" IIT Chicago—Kent College of Law, June 1, 2012, *www.oyez.org;* "Supreme Court Strikes Down Overall Political Donation Cap," *The New York Times,* April 2, 2014, *www.nytimes.com;* and, "Obama: *Citizens United* Caused 'Real Harm' to U.S. Democracy," *The Wall Street Journal,* January 21, 2015, *blogs.wsj.com.* Also see David Silver, "Business Ethics after *Citizens United:* A Contractualist Analysis," *Journal of Business Ethics* 127 (2015), pp. 385–97.

decision, mentioned earlier, also struck down the cap on the total amount any individual can contribute to federal candidates in a two-year election cycle. In 2014, just 31,976 donors—about 1 percent of 1 percent of the U.S. population—provided $1.18 billion in federal political contributions.

Given the multiple mechanisms for campaign financing and the lack of caps on the amount contributed, individuals are able to significantly influence the political process if they have enough money. One example of the potential for political power through contributions is described next.

In 2015, a political network overseen by conservative billionaires Charles G. and David H. Koch was ready to spend close to $900 million on the 2016 campaign. This represented an unparalleled effort by coordinated outside groups to influence the U.S. presidential election that already was to be the most expensive in history. The political network coordinated contributions from the Koch brothers, as well as 300 other donors recruited over the years. This amount of political campaign financing was on the same scale as what was predicted to be spent by either of the Democrat or Republican parties' presidential candidates. Since most of the Koch brothers' causes and ideology were conservative, experts argued that nearly all of their political influence would support the Republican Party and its candidates and aim to unseat Democratic members of Congress, governors, and members of state legislatures.[17]

Generally, any contribution by an individual of more than $200 needs to be reported to the FEC by the candidate or administrators of the political action fund to the Federal

[17] "Koch Brothers' Budget of $889 Million for 2016 Is on Par with Both Parties' Spending," *The New York Times,* January 26, 2015, *www.nytimes.com.*

Election Commission. These data are periodically published by the Federal Election Commission. Individuals can also make such contributions electronically.

> In 2012 the Federal Election Commission (FEC) ruled that individuals could make modest contributions to the politician of their choice via mobile messaging. By acquiring the correct six-digit "short code," unique to each political candidate running for an office, individuals could text that number with the amount of their donation and the contribution would appear on their cell phone bill. Those running the political campaign did not see the name of the contributor, only the telephone number, so contributions were limited to $50 a month per cell phone number since any larger amount would have to be filed with the FEC and a donor's name would be required. Donors had to attest that they were U.S. citizens, at least 18-years-old, and were using their own funds (not those of a relative or employer).[18]

In short, recent court decisions have expanded the mechanisms available to corporations (as well as unions and other organizations) to use their resources to influence politics. To some, these developments represent a confirmation of business free speech rights. To others, they represent a distortion of the political process in favor of organizations and individuals with money to spend.

Economic Leverage

Another political action tool often used by businesses when pursuing a financial incentive strategy is to use their economic leverage to influence public policymakers. **Economic leverage** occurs when a business uses its economic power to threaten to leave a city, state, or country unless a desired political action is taken. Economic leverage also can be used to persuade a government body to act in a certain way that would favor the business, as seen in the following story.

> When the state of Pennsylvania was considering legalizing slot machines at racetracks, the owners of a National Hockey League team located in the state, the Pittsburgh Penguins, were lobbying for a new ice hockey arena to be built with public funds. Government leaders were hesitant to use public funds for a new arena unless substantial private funds were also available. Ted Arneault, owner of the Mountaineer Racetrack and Gaming Resort and part owner of the Pittsburgh Penguins, offered a deal. He said his company would contribute $60 million to build the new ice hockey arena if the state would approve the use of slot machines at Pennsylvania racetracks, including his proposed racetrack facility near Pittsburgh. Legislators agreed.[19]

In this example, the business owner successfully used economic leverage. By committing his own private money to help support the construction of a new ice hockey arena, he was able to persuade politicians to vote in favor of legislation to approve the use of slot machines at racetracks in the state.

Promoting a Constituency-Building Strategy

The final strategy used by business to influence the political environment is to seek support from organizations or people who are also affected by the public policy or who are sympathetic to business's political position. This approach is sometimes called a *grassroots strategy*, because its objective is to shape policy by mobilizing the broad public in

---

[18] "Please Text $$$ To My Campaign ☺," *Bloomberg BusinessWeek,* June 18–24, 2012, p. 28.

[19] "Penguins, Arneault Make $107 Million Private Funding Proposal for New Arena Project," *Pittsburgh Post-Gazette,* June 24, 2003, p. A1.

support of a business organization's position, or a *grasstops strategy,* because its objective is to influence local opinion leaders. Firms use several methods to build support among constituents. These include advocacy advertising, public relations, and building coalitions with other affected stakeholders. With the increase in the availability of technology, firms have turned to social media as a grassroots tool as the following example shows.

> Social media has dramatically changed how the public connects to the political environment. The day before the Iowa caucuses formally began the U.S. 2012 presidential campaign, Google launched a new election website, called Google Politics and Elections. The site allowed users to compare candidates' rankings in searches, news stories, blogs, and YouTube videos and provided a "politics and election toolkit" and a 2012 political calendar to track the whereabouts of the candidates. Google expanded this website by providing information on political candidates, emerging political issues, and elections results from around the world, as well as state and local elections in the United States. "Our goal is to bring people closer to politics by making relevant information and resources easier to find and interact with. This page will focus on impartial data and digital trends surrounding the political process. We are non-partisan and don't support or endorse any political candidates."[20]

Stakeholder Coalitions

Businesses may try to influence politics by mobilizing various organizational stakeholders— employees, stockholders, customers, and the local community—to support their political agenda. If a political issue can negatively affect a business, it is likely that it also will negatively affect that business's stakeholders. If pending regulation will impose substantial costs on the business, these costs may result in employee layoffs, or a drop in the firm's stock value, or higher prices for the firm's customers. Often, businesses organize programs to get organizational stakeholders, acting as lobbyists or voters, to influence government officials to vote or act in a favorable way.

> In 2012, politicians and businesspeople from the region wanted to convince Shell Oil Company to build its new petrochemical plant in southwestern Pennsylvania. Shell was looking for a convenient location for a plant to process the growing supply of natural gas extracted from the region by hydraulic fracturing (also called *fracking* and further discussed in Chapter 10). The southwestern Pennsylvania area had many attractive elements—access to railroad and water transportation systems, business-friendly politicians, a trained and available workforce, and plenty of natural gas. Pennsylvania governor Tom Corbett spent months hosting meetings where Shell's executives could meet with various political and business leaders. Then he learned that many of the Shell Oil executives were big Pittsburgh Steeler fans, the local professional football team. Corbett arranged for the Shell executives to tour Heinz Field, home of the Steelers, including a glimpse into the team's locker room, and to meet with Steelers executives. Soon after, Shell announced that it would build its new plant in Monaca, just 25 miles northwest of Pittsburgh. Shell Oil's spokesperson declined to confirm that the Heinz Field outing and meeting with Steeler officials had "clinched the deal," but he did say that "the governor is an excellent ambassador and salesman for his state and hometown of Pittsburgh, and he is a huge Steelers fan."[21]

---

[20] "Google Launches New Election Site," *Pittsburgh Business Times,* January 3, 2012, *www.bizjournals.com.* Also see *plus.google.com/+GooglePolitics.*

[21] "Corbett Made Pass to Oil Execs with Steelers," *Pittsburgh Post-Gazette,* March 16, 2012, *www.post-gazette.com.*

Advocacy Advertising and Public Relations

A common method of influencing constituents is **advocacy advertising**. Advocacy ads focus not on a particular product or service, like most ads, but rather on an organization's or a company's views on controversial political issues. Advocacy ads, also called *issue advertisements,* can appear in newspapers, on television, or in other media outlets. They have been legal in the United States since 1978, but greater involvement by businesses and other nonprofit (advocacy) organizations in the political process resulted in their use to dramatically increase after the *Citizens United v. FEC* U.S. Supreme Court decision, discussed earlier. A media expert reported that since the *Citizens United* decision, television and radio stations received more than $2.5 million in revenue each year from issue advertisements, compared with less than $1 million each year previously. (Examples of advocacy advertisements are provided in Chapter 19.)

Another constituency-building tactic is the use of public relations firms to promote the company's message to various stakeholders. The American Petroleum Institute, which represents numerous oil and gas companies, spent more than $7 million lobbying federal officials in 2012, but $85.5 million to four public relations and advertising firms to educate the American public. From 2008 through 2012, the American Petroleum Institute paid one global public relations firm $327.4 million for advertising and public relations services. Another example of political activity through public relations is described next.

> Locust Street Group, one of the top 10 public relations and advertising firms, was paid $23.6 million from 2008 through 2012, almost all of which came from America's Health Insurance Plans. As stated on the Locust Street Group website, "DC may have K Street with tons of lobbyists, but small towns all over America have a Locust Street." Businesses have turned to firms like the Locust Street Group to take their message to the American public, in addition to lobbying directly on Capitol Hill and politicians.[22]

Trade Associations

Many businesses work through **trade associations**—coalitions of companies in the same or related industries—to coordinate their grassroots mobilization campaigns, such as the National Realtors Association (real estate brokers), National Federation of Independent Businesses (small businesses), the National Association of Manufacturers (manufacturers only), or the U.S. Chamber of Commerce (broad, diverse membership).[23]

> The U.S. Chamber of Commerce represents more than 3 million businesses of all sizes, sectors, and regions. The chamber has a multimillion-dollar budget, publishes a widely circulated magazine, and operates a satellite television network to broadcast its political messages. Its agenda includes expanding trade, producing more domestic energy, improving infrastructure, modernizing the regulatory process, making essential changes to entitlements, fixing the flaws in Obamacare, curbing lawsuit abuse, and advancing American innovation by protecting intellectual property. The agenda also focuses on revitalizing capital markets, passing immigration reform, and improving education and training, which will expand opportunity, address inequality, and create jobs.[24]

[22] "Who Needs Lobbyists? See What Big Business Spends to Win American Minds," *Moyers & Company,* January 28, 2015, *billmoyers.com.*

[23] The classic discussion of corporate political action can be found in Edwin Epstein, *The Corporation in American Politics* (Englewood Cliffs, NJ: Prentice Hall, 1969). A more recent handbook of current strategies in American political activity is in Kenneth A. Gross, Lawrence M. Noble, Ki P. Hong, and Patricia M. Zweibel, *Corporate Political Activities Deskbook* (New York: Practicing Law Institute, 2014).

[24] See the U.S. Chamber of Commerce website, *www.uschamber.com.*

Businesses focus on various trade associations for promoting their political activities. The Center for Public Integrity reported that trade associations spent more than $1 million on lobbying in 2012. According to an IRS report, of the $3.4 billion in contracts reported by the 144 trade groups from 2008 through 2012, more than $1.2 billion, or 37 percent, went toward advertising, public relations, and marketing services; more than any other category. The second-highest total, $682.2 million, or 20 percent of the total, was directed toward legal, lobbying, and government affairs.[25]

Activities of trade associations may include letters, telephone calls, tweets, blogs, e-mails, and other Internet communications to register approval or disapproval of a government official's position on an important issue.

Legal Challenges

A political tactic available to businesses (and other political participants) is the use of legal challenges. In this approach, business seeks to overturn a law or portions of a law after it has passed or threatens to challenge the legal legitimacy of the new regulation in the courts. Such an approach is shown in the following example:

> A few years after Congress passed the Affordable Care Act, many organizations began to legally challenge the provision that required employers to provide employees with contraceptive coverage in their health plans. Many of those filing lawsuits were churches and religious-affiliated businesses, like Hobby Lobby and its owners David and Barbara Green. The Greens argued that the contraceptive requirement directly challenged their faith, which was the foundation of their business. Based on strong, traditional Christian values, Hobby Lobby stores were not open on Sunday, and the owners and employees supported various Christian charities with their time and financial contributions. Hobby Lobby's owners also were strongly opposed to any form of birth control based on their religious convictions. According to CEO David Green, "Our family is now being forced to choose between following the laws of the land that we love or maintaining the religious beliefs that have made our business successful and have supported our family and thousands of our employees and their families." In 2014, the U.S. Supreme Court ruled, in a 5 to 4 decision, in favor of Hobby Lobby, exempting the company from the Affordable Care Act requirements and citing the legal principle that one can maintain their religious beliefs even when acting as a business owner.[26]

Levels of Political Involvement

Business executives must decide on the appropriate level of political involvement for their company. As shown in Figure 8.5, there are multiple levels of involvement and many ways to participate. To be successful, a business must think strategically about objectives and how specific political issues and opportunities relate to those objectives.

Organizations often begin at the lowest level of political participation, *limited organizational involvement.* Here managers of the organization are not ready or willing to become politically involved by giving their own time or getting their stakeholders involved, but they want to do something to influence the political environment. Organizations at this level may show their political interest, for example, by writing out a check to a trade association to support an industry-backed political action, such as hiring a lobbyist on a specific issue.

[25] For more information, see Center for Public Integrity, *www.publicintegrity.org.*

[26] "Businesses Sue Government over Birth Control Mandate," *National Public Radio,* January 11, 2013, *www.npr.org;* and for a detailed timeline and analysis of the lawsuit see *www.hobbylobbycase.com.*

FIGURE 8.5
Levels of Business
Political Involvement

Level 3   Aggressive Organizational Involvement—direct and personal

- Executive participation
- Involvement with industry working groups and task forces
- Public policy development

Level 2   Moderate Organizational Involvement—indirect yet personal

- Organizational lobbyist
- Employee grassroots involvement
- Stockholders and customers encouraged to become involved

Level 1   Limited Organizational Involvement—indirect and impersonal

- Contribution to political action committee
- Support of a trade association or industry activities

When the organization is ready for *moderate political involvement,* managers might directly employ a lobbyist to represent the company's political strategy in Washington or the state capital to push the firm's political agenda. This is a more active form of political involvement since the lobbyist is an employee of the organization. Getting the organization's stakeholders involved is another way a firm can increase its political involvement. Employees can write letters or send e-mails or tweets to their congressperson or become involved in a political campaign. Senior executives might communicate with stockholders or customers on particular issues that might affect the firm and its stakeholders and encourage them to write letters, blog, or otherwise voice their concerns. Some firms have sent letters to their stockholders soliciting their political contributions for a particular candidate or group of candidates but have asked that the contributions be sent to the company. Then the company takes all of the contributions to the candidate or candidates, clearly indicating that the contributions are from the firm's stockholders. This technique is called **bundling**.

The most direct and personal involvement in the political environment is achieved at the third level—*aggressive organizational involvement*—where managers become personally involved in developing public policy. Some executives are asked to sit on important task forces charged with writing legislation that will affect the firm or the firm's industry. When state legislatures were writing laws limiting the opportunities for corporate raiders to acquire unwilling companies in their states, the legislators turned to corporate general counsels, the company attorneys, to help draft the laws. Another example of aggressive organizational involvement is provided by The Business Roundtable, described earlier in this chapter.

Managing the Political Environment

In many organizations, the task of managing political activity falls to the department of public affairs or government relations. The role of the **public affairs department** is to manage the firm's interactions with governments at all levels and to promote the firm's interests in the political process. (*Public relations,* discussed in Chapter 19, is a different business function.) The creation of public affairs units is a global trend, with many companies in Canada, Australia, and Europe developing sophisticated public affairs operations.[27]

[27] The global patterns of public affairs practice are documented in *Journal of Public Affairs,* published by Henry Stewart Publishing beginning in 2001. For an excellent review of public affairs development around the world, see Craig S. Fleisher and Natasha Blair, "Surveying the Field: Status and Trends Affecting Public Affairs across Australia, Canada, the EU, and the U.S.," in *Assessing, Managing and Maximizing Public Affairs Performance,* Management Handbook series, ed. Craig S. Fleisher (Washington, DC: Public Affairs Council, 1997).

Activities Conducted within the Public Affairs Department	Percent of Companies, 2005	Percent of Companies, 2014
Federal government relations	95%	96
State government relations	85	92
Issues management	82	85
Local government relations	79	81
Business/trade association oversight	75	92
Political action committee	83	80
Coalitions	71	90
Grassroots/grasstops	75	79

Source: Foundation for Public Affairs, *The State of Corporate Public Affairs, 2014–15* (2014), based on a survey of 110 companies. Used by permission.

As shown in Exhibit 8.C, nearly all of the most frequently performed activities by public affairs officers or departments involve a political action tactic and attention has remained relatively stable for most of these political activities since 2005.

Most companies have a senior manager or executive to lead the public affairs department. This manager is often a member of the company's senior management committee, providing expertise about the company's major strategy and policy decisions. The size of the department and the support staff varies widely among companies, but more than half reported an increase in budget and staffing since 2011. Many companies assign employees from other parts of the business to work on public affairs issues and to help plan, coordinate, and execute public affairs activities. In this way, the formulation and implementation of the policies and programs developed by a company's public affairs unit are closely linked to the primary business activities of the firm.

Over one-third of the heads of public affairs departments report directly to the CEO, while others report to the firm's general counsel. Most work out of company headquarters; most of the rest—particularly those whose work focuses on government relations—work in Washington, DC. The typical public affairs executive spends most of the day direct lobbying with federal or state politicians, hosting visits by politicians to the company's locations, attending funding raising activities, or participating in coalition building. Over 70 percent of the public affairs officers reported that funding for international public affairs activities increased over the past 3 years.[28]

Business Political Action: A Global Challenge

Most of the discussion so far in the chapter has focused on business political activity in the United States. As more companies conduct business abroad, it is critical that managers be aware of the opportunities for and restrictions on business involvement in the political processes in other countries. Other societies and governments also struggle with issues

[28] Foundation for Public Affairs, *The State of Corporate Public Affairs, 2014–2015* (Washington, DC: Foundation for Public Affairs, 2014).

of participation in the political environment, campaign financing, and maintaining a fair ethical climate throughout the public policy process. The following example focuses on lobbying and constituency-building tactics:

> In 2015, Google was embroiled in an escalating EU antitrust case and the Right To Be Forgotten controversy (the subject of a case study at the end of this book and also discussed in Chapter 12). The firm doubled its direct lobbying expenditures in Europe in 2013 to nearly €4 million (about $4.3 million). By comparison, Google spent $16.8 million lobbying in the United States. Other U.S. technology firms increased their political activities in Europe. Microsoft belonged to 33 European trade associations. By comparison, Deutsche Telekom, a German telecommunications company, maintained 13 trade association memberships, while Axel Springer, the leading digital publisher in Europe, belonged to only four.
>
> StandWithUs, a pro-Israeli American advocacy group closely tied to the Israeli government, opened up an office in China in 2015. Announcing that China was "a country in which we can make a difference," StandWithUs set about correcting what it characterized as "misinformation in the Chinese media about Israel." Their approach was focused on "utilizing social media, university programs, and networking events" to better connect with the next generation of Chinese political leadership and the Chinese media.[29]

In Japan, a more pluralistic political environment than China's characterizes the public policy process. The major actors are members of big business, agriculture, and labor. These special interest groups are quite powerful and influential. Some of the largest interest groups support more than a few hundred candidates in each important election and provide them with large financial contributions. The *Kiedanren,* or federation of economic organizations, is mostly concerned with Japanese big business, but other interest groups promote the concerns of small and medium-sized businesses, such as barbers, cosmeticians, dry cleaners, innkeepers, and theater owners. Some political influence is in the hands of smaller groups such as the teachers union (*Nikkyoso*), Japan Medical Association, employers association (*Nikkeiren*), and a labor union (*Rengo*).[30]

Although political alliances and favoritism appears around the world, in varying degrees, there have been efforts to promote fairness in the electoral process, control the rapid rise in the costs of campaigning, enhance the role of political parties in elections, and encourage grassroots participation by various societal groups.

> Since 1999, the Global Electoral Organization (GEO) has brought together more than 300 of the world's top election officials and democracy advocates to celebrate "transparency in the election process." In 2011, the GEO met in Botswana, Africa, where delegates from western and eastern Europe, central Asia, the Middle East, North America, and Africa discussed the most critical issues in election administration, including how to resolve election disputes, the role of the media in elections, electoral reform, engaging electoral stakeholders, and tracking money in political campaigns. One conference delegate explained, "I think standards are changing and politicians will have to recognize this—that as we are now in the 21st century, public opinion is applying different standards to politics, to politicians, to political

---

[29] "U.S. Tech Firms Increase EU Lobbying Efforts," *The Wall Street Journal,* April 29, 2015, *www.wsj.com;* and "An Israeli Lobby in China?" *The Diplomat,* April 30, 2015, *thediplomat.com.*

[30] Ryan Beaupre and Patricia Malone, "Interest Groups and Politics in Japan," *alpha.fdu.edu/~woolley/JAPANpolitics/Beaupre.htm.*

parties. They're not allowed to do things they were doing in the 19th and 20th centuries. People have high expectations, high demands, and they will keep politicians accountable."[31]

Political action by business—whether to influence government policy or the outcome of an election—is natural in a democratic, pluralistic society. In the United States, business has a legitimate right to participate in the political process, just as consumers, labor unions, environmentalists, and others do. One danger arising from corporate political activity is that corporations may wield too much power. As businesses operate in different communities and countries, it is important that ethical norms and standards guide managers as they deal with political issues. If corporate power tips the scales against other interests in society, both business and society may lose. Whether it is in the media-rich arena of electoral politics or the corridors of Congress where more traditional lobbying prevails, business leaders must address the issues of how to manage relationships with government and special interests in society in ethically sound ways. Ultimately, business has an important long-term stake in a healthy, honest political system.

Summary

- Some believe that businesses should be involved in politics because their economic stake in government decisions is great and they have a right to participate, just as do other stakeholders in a pluralistic political system. But others believe that businesses are too big, powerful, and selfish, and that they wield too much influence in the political arena.

- There are three political strategies: information, financial incentives, and constituency-building. Some firms implement strategies as needed, on an issue-by-issue basis, while other firms have a long-term, ongoing political strategy approach.

- Some of the political action tactics available for business include lobbying, direct communications, expert witness testimony, political action committee contributions, economic leverage, advocacy advertising and public relations, trade association involvement, legal challenges, and encouraging the involvement of other stakeholders.

- Businesses manage their government interactions through a public affairs department. Most public affairs officers report to the CEO or some high-level official, although how these departments are structured is widely varied.

- The differing national rules and practices governing political activity make business's political involvement complex in the global environment. Many governments, like the United States, are trying to restrict lobbying or political contributions or are trying to make the political process more transparent.

[31] "Credible Elections for Democracy," *Institute for Democracy and Electoral Assistance, www.idea.int.*

Key Terms

advocacy advertising, *172*
bundling, *174*
Citizens United decision, *169*
corporate political strategy, *160*
dark money, *168*

economic leverage, *170*
lobbying, *161*
political action committees (PACs), *165*
public affairs departments, *174*
revolving door, *163*

soft money, *167*
super PACs, *166*
The Business Roundtable, *163*
trade associations, *172*

Internet Resources

www.businessroundtable.org	The Business Roundtable
www.commoncause.org	Common Cause
explore.data.gov/ethics	Ethics.data.gov—government data center
lobbyingdisclosure.house.gov	Lobbying Disclosure, U.S. House of Representatives
www.ncpa.org	National Center for Policy Analysis
www.nfib.com	National Federation of Independent Businesses
www.opensecrets.org	Opensecrets.org
www.politicsonline.com	PoliticsOnline: News, Tools & Strategies
pac.org	Public Affairs Council
www.pdc.wa.gov	Public Disclosure Commission
www.fec.gov	U.S. Federal Election Commission

Discussion Case: *Stop Online Piracy Act—A Political Battle between Old and New Media*

The Stop Online Piracy Act (SOPA) was introduced in the U.S. House of Representatives in 2011, along with a companion bill in the U.S. Senate, the Protect Intellectual Property Act (PIPA). If passed, SOPA would give the owners of film, music, or other intellectual property new tools to protect themselves from online piracy or theft. They could sue to force Internet service providers, search engines, payment processors, and advertisement networks to block or stop doing business with websites linked to online piracy. Business was split on the proposed law. The Motion Picture Association of America, the Recording Industry Association of America, and the U.S. Chamber of Commerce—considered "old media"—supported SOPA. But online companies, such as AOL, Twitter, Google, Facebook, Yahoo!, eBay, and others—the "new media"—opposed it. As one blogger remarked, this could become "the biggest controversy in 2012."

Old media proponents argued that the SOPA legislation was needed since rogue websites steal America's innovative and creative products by attracting more than 53 million visits per year, leading to unauthorized downloads of music, films, and books and threatening more than 19 million American jobs in creative industries. More than 400 businesses and organizations, many from the entertainment or publishing industries, collectively contributed $91 million to congressional lobbying efforts in support of SOPA. This was the most the entertainment industry had ever spent on a lobbying effort. Other supporters turned to social media and sent out tweets advocating the necessity of SOPA.

Opponents of SOPA, by contrast, argued that "the bill, as drafted, would expose law-abiding U.S. Internet and technology companies to new uncertain liabilities, private rights of action, and technology mandates that would require monitoring of Web sites," according to a letter sent to members of the House and Senate Judiciary Committees by Goggle, Facebook, Yahoo!, and eBay. Several Internet companies proposed an alternative bill that would punish foreign websites that engaged in copyright infringement through international trade law. "We have a chance to reset the legislative table to find out what kind of legislation is needed," said Markham Erickson, executive director of NetCoalition, a trade group comprised mostly of Internet companies. "We have an opportunity to step back, recalibrate and understand what the problem is." Google's director of public policy added, "Like others, we

believe Congress wants to get this right, and we know there are targeted and smart ways to shut down foreign rogue Web sites without asking U.S. companies to censor the Internet."

The new media organizations introduced novel political strategies to combat the act. Critics created a "Censorship US" day and its website encouraged political protest using social media tactics. In January 2012, Reddit.com, a social news site, was joined by other Internet sites, including the politically oriented MoveOn.org, the popular technology and culture blog BoingBoing, and the Internet humor site Cheezburger Network, for a day-long, sitewide blackout to protest SOPA. Wikipedia, the world's free online encyclopedia, was dark for a day except for a short paragraph urging users to protest SOPA on the ground it could "fatally damage the free and open Internet." (Google, Facebook, and Twitter declined to participate in the blackout, despite their public opposition to SOPA. Some criticized the companies, accusing them of being unwilling to sacrifice a day's worth of revenue.)

The critics of SOPA also undertook more traditional political efforts, such as a letter writing campaign, sending of e-mails, and making telephone calls to various influential members of Congress. Facebook hired former a White House press secretary, Joe Lockhart, to push the company's opposition in Congress. Goggle reportedly spent $5 million in the first quarter of 2012 to combat SOPA (a 240 percent increase from Google's lobbying spending in the first quarter of 2011), with Microsoft spending $1.8 million, and Amazon and Apple $500,000 each during the same period.

The Stop Online Piracy Act "awakened the entire world," said a Harvard law professor. "They are realizing just how big this fight was becoming." In response, many in Congress reversed their initial position in support of SOPA. "Thanks for all the calls, e-mails and tweets. I will be opposing #SOPA and #PIPA," tweeted Senator Jeff Merkley. Later, Senator Grassley, a senior Republican on the Senate Judiciary Committee, withdrew his support for a bill he helped write.

Political analysts commented that the new media's protests seemed to have worked. Initially 81 members of Congress supported the bill, compared with only 25 legislators opposed (the rest were undecided), but crumbling support may have contributed to Senator Harry Reid's announcement in January 2012 that the Senate's vote on the SOPA counterpart, PIPA, would be delayed. The House quickly followed, announcing that the House Judiciary Committee would postpone consideration of the legislation "until there is wider agreement on a solution." The committee's chair, Lamar Smith, commented, "I have heard from the critics and I take seriously their concerns regarding proposed legislation to address the problem on online piracy." Three years later, no new legislation had been introduced in either the House or Senate.

Sources: "Google, Facebook Warn against New US Piracy Legislation," *BBC News: Technology,* November 16, 2011, *www.bbc.com/news/technology;* "Bills to Stop Web Piracy Invite a Protracted Battle," *The New York Times,* January 15, 2012, *www.nytimes.com;* "Stop Online Piracy Act (SOPA): 2012's Biggest Controversy-to-be?" *Toonari Post,* January 16, 2012, *www.toonaripost.com;* "In Fight over Piracy Bills, New Economy Rises against Old," *The New York Times,* January 18, 2012, *www.nytimes.com;* "Wikipedia Dark, Google Lobbies in Protest of Anti-piracy Bill," *Canada.com,* January 18, 2012, *www.canada.com;* "PIPA Vote and SOPA Hearing Pushed Off as Copyright Bills' Congressional Support Collapses," *Forbes,* January 20, 2012, *www.forbes.com;* and "Under Scrutiny, Google Spends Record Amount on Lobbying," *The New York Times—Bits,* April 23, 2102, *bits.blogs.nytimes.com.*

Discussion Questions

1. Which of the political tactics discussed in this chapter are evident in this case?
2. Why were the political tactics used by the "new media" so effective in this case?
3. Would the effectiveness of these tactics vary, depending on the political issue at stake?
4. What can traditional companies learn from the new forms of political activity described in this case?

Business and the Natural Environment

CHAPTER NINE

Sustainable Development and Global Business

The world community faces unprecedented ecological challenges in the 21st century, including climate change, resource scarcity, and threats to biodiversity. Many political and business leaders have embraced the idea of sustainable development, calling for economic development without depleting the natural capital on which future generations depend. A critical task in coming decades for government policymakers, civil society organizations, corporate leaders, and entrepreneurial innovators will be to find ways to meet simultaneously both economic and environmental goals.

This Chapter Focuses on These Key Learning Objectives:

LO 9-1   Understanding how business and society interact within the natural environment.

LO 9-2   Defining sustainable development.

LO 9-3   Recognizing the ways in which population growth, inequality, and economic development interact with the world's ecological crisis.

LO 9-4   Examining common environmental issues that are shared by all nations and businesses.

LO 9-5   Analyzing the steps both large and small businesses can take globally to reduce ecological damage and promote sustainable development.

LO 9-6   Describing the leading global codes of environmental conduct.

On the 20th anniversary of the first World Summit on Sustainable Development, representatives of the world's nations gathered in Rio de Janeiro, Brazil. Their goal was to take a hard look at how far the world had come in the previous two decades and what needed to be done, moving forward, to address the urgent need for sustainable development. Their 2012 report, *The Future We Want,* affirmed a commitment to lifting the world's people out of poverty without hurting the ability of future generations to meet their own needs. To do so, the report reasoned, would require progress on many fronts, including promoting sustainable patterns of production and consumption and tackling the daunting challenges of accelerating climate change, loss of biodiversity, deforestation, and water scarcity.[1]

Of the many changes that have occurred since the first Earth Summit, one of the most striking has been the involvement of businesses, both large and small, from all over the globe, in the pursuit of sustainability. In 1992, a few visionary business organizations had met alongside world leaders to consider the implications, for them, of the conference proceedings. Now, nearly a quarter century later, companies of all types have embraced the challenges of operating within the limits of the Earth's natural systems. Many have recognized the cost savings associated with operating more efficiently, the opportunities to serve consumer markets in emerging economies, the benefits of reducing regulatory risk, and the competitive advantages of innovation in sustainable technology. Consider the following examples:

- In 2015, Nike reported on its website that its remarkable new athletic shoe, the Flyknit, was made with 80 percent less waste than conventional designs. Constructed from synthetic yarn and fashioned by a high-tech knitting machine, the Flyknit's upper was made in a single continuous piece, rather than by stitching together dozens of odd-shaped cloth and leather pieces as in a typical shoe. The shoe offered many advantages to athletes, including its light weight and superior comfort. But an important added benefit was that the product was much more sustainable. Nike's vice president of footwear innovation called the Flyknit a "trifecta of performance and style and sustainability benefits."[2]

- Taylor Guitars makes high-end acoustic and electric guitars, played by such well-known musicians as Taylor Swift, Jason Mraz, and Dave Matthews. To assure its supply of ebony, a hardwood that grows in tropical rain forests and is used to make fret boards, the company bought a saw mill in Cameroon, West Africa. Taylor Guitars quickly ended the wasteful practice of cutting down 10 ebony trees to find one with solid black wood, which had stressed the forest and endangered remaining supplies. "Our vision was to transform the way that ebony is harvested, processed, and sold," said Bob Taylor, the president of the company, in 2014. "To accomplish this, we assumed the role of guardian of the forest, and we operate with the philosophy to use what the forest gives us."[3]

- In 2014, Hertz, the rental car company, introduced an innovative method of car washing at 3,700 locations in Europe and the United States that used no water at all. Instead of hosing down each vehicle, employees sprayed it with eight ounces of a concentrated, biodegradable cleaning solution and wiped it down with a microfiber towel. The process saved 130 million gallons of water a year, as well as the energy needed to heat it. "Managing one of the largest car rental fleets in the world requires a significant amount

[1] "Report of the United Nations Conference on Sustainable Development," Rio de Janeiro, Brazil, June 20–22, 2012, at *www.uncsd2012.org.*

[2] "The Extraordinary Future of Shoes," July 22, 2014, *www.citylab.com;* and "Flyknit: More Haste, Less Waste," *www.nikeresponsibility.com/innovations.*

[3] "The Crelicam Mill in Cameroon," *www.taylorguitars.com/about/sustainable-ebony;* and Bob Taylor, "Remarks at the Remarks at the 15th Annual Awards for Corporate Excellence," *www.state.gov/secretary/remarks/2014/01/220756.htm.*

of car washing," said Hertz's CEO. "Moving to a waterless car wash system is [an] innovative way Hertz is addressing both its sustainability and business needs."[4]

These examples suggest some of the tremendous creativity that businesses were bringing to the ecological challenges of the 21st century. Could businesses, governments, and society, working together, put the global economy on a more sustainable course? This chapter will describe the major sustainability challenges facing society and both the risks and opportunities these challenges present to businesses globally. The following chapter will focus on specific areas of government regulation and the ways in which businesses, in the United States and other countries, have sought to manage for sustainability.

Business and Society in the Natural Environment

Business, society, and the environment are deeply interrelated. Business and society operate within, and depend on, the natural environment. The extraordinary planet on which we live provides the abundant resources humans use to thrive, but it also imposes constraints. We have only one Earth, and its resources are finite. **Natural capital** refers to the world's stocks of natural assets, including its geology, soil, air, water, and all living things.[5] These assets make human life possible. For human society to survive over time it must operate *sustainably,* in a way that does not destroy or deplete these natural resources for future generations. This fundamental truth confers on business leaders both great challenges and great opportunities.

Chapter 1 introduced the idea of systems theory and explained how businesses cannot be understood in isolation, but only in relationship to the broader society in which they operate. This idea can be extended to the relationship between business and society, on one hand, and the natural environment, on the other. In this view, business and society can be most fully understood in relationship to the broader *natural environment* in which they are embedded and with which they interact. This relationship is illustrated in Figure 9.1. The well-known image of the Earth as seen from space—a blue-and-green globe, girdled

FIGURE 9.1
Business, Society, and the Natural Environment: An Interactive System

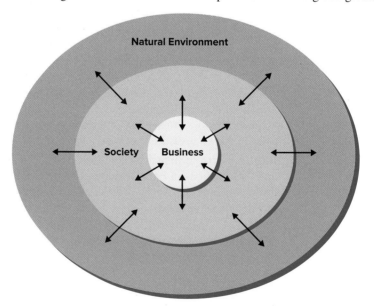

---

[4] "Hertz Goes Green with Waterless Car Washing," January 20, 2014, *www.examiner.com.*

[5] "What is Natural Capital," *www.naturalcapitalforum.com.* See also Paul Hawken, Amory Lovins, and L. Hunter Lovins, *Natural Capitalism: Creating the Next Industrial Revolution* (Boston: Little, Brown, 1999).

by white clouds, floating in blackness—dramatically shows us that we share a single, unified natural system, or **ecosystem**. Preserving our common ecosystem and assuring its continued use is an urgent imperative for governments, business, and society. As KPMG International stated in its report, *Expect the Unexpected,* "The central challenge of our age must be to decouple human progress from resource use and environmental deterioration."[6]

Sustainable Development

The need for balance between economic progress and environmental protection is captured in the concept of **sustainable development**. This term refers to development that "meets the needs of the present without compromising the ability of future generations to meet their own needs" or, more simply, "ensuring a better quality of life for everyone, now and for generations to come."[7] The concept includes two core ideas:

- Protecting the environment will require economic development. Poverty is an underlying cause of environmental degradation. People who lack food, shelter, and basic amenities misuse resources just to survive. For this reason, environmental protection will require providing a decent standard of living for all the world's citizens.
- But economic development must be accomplished sustainably, that is, in a way that conserves and regenerates the Earth's resources for future generations. It cannot occur at the expense of degrading the forests, farmland, water, and air that must continue to support life on this planet. We must leave the Earth in as good shape—or better shape—than we found it.

Meeting the goal of sustainability is like trying to solve an extraordinarily complex puzzle, in which businesses, governments, civil society, and individuals must work together to achieve common goals.

At its core, sustainable development is about fairness—a central tenet of ethics, as explained in Chapter 5. Fairness requires that the benefits and burdens of an action be distributed equitably, according to an accepted rule. Sustainable development requires an equitable distribution of the benefits gained from the use of natural resources for both current generations (the developing world countries should receive its fair share along with the countries in the developed world) and across generations (the present generation should not gain at the expense of future generations). This can only occur if governments and business leaders work to promote economic development that does not further degrade the environment. The very nature of consumption itself will need to change as people come to emphasize the quality of their lives over the quantity of goods they own, and innovation in a dynamic market economy will need to find new ways to meet human aspirations in a more resource-efficient manner.

What would a sustainable society look like? Of course, there are many paths to sustainability, and there is no way to know for sure what the future will hold. But, one vision of what might be possible is provided by Masdar, a new city in the Persian Gulf that is being designed from the ground up as a completely sustainable community. Masdar is described in Exhibit 9.A.

Threats to the Earth's Ecosystem

Humanity has entered a new geological era, called the *Anthropocene* (the period in which human activity has been the dominant influence on climate and the environment). Since the Industrial Revolution, humans have become a powerful force, altering the face of the planet and rivaling the forces of nature herself—glaciers, volcanoes, asteroids, and

---

[6] *"Expect the Unexpected: Building Business Value in a Changing World,"* KPMG International, 2012.

[7] World Commission on Environment and Development, *Our Common Future* (Oxford: Oxford University Press, 1987), p. 8; "Sustainable Development: The UK Government's Approach," *http://sd.defra.gov.uk.*

Exhibit 9.A
Masdar: A Completely Sustainable Community

Masdar City is a planned development within the boundaries of Abu Dhabi, the capital of the Persian Gulf nation United Arab Emirates (UAE) and, by *Fortune Magazine*'s estimate, the wealthiest city in the world. Separated from the rest of Abu Dhabi by a perimeter wall, Masdar has been conceived as the world's first completely sustainable community—and a preview of what a "greener" society might look like. In this futuristic city, no regular cars will be allowed. Rather, people will travel from place to place in a state-of-the-art light rail transit system or in personal rapid transit pods that will zip through underground tunnels. Buildings will be constructed of sustainably harvested wood and other environmentally friendly materials. The city's all-renewable energy will come from a solar power plant and a wind farm outside the perimeter walls. Eighty percent of the city's water, which will come from a desalinization plant, will be recycled; and waste will be incinerated or turned into fertilizer. The city will house both people and clean-tech enterprises, along with the postgraduate Masdar Institute for Science and Technology. The entire project, which will cost the government and other investors around $20 billion, is slated for completion by 2025.

Why would a nation that is home to one of the largest oil companies in the world want to develop an urban model of clean technology and innovation? Recognizing that its oil reserves will eventually run out, the UAE has decided to position itself as a global leader in the transition to a non–carbon-based economy.

Source: *www.masdar.ae.*

earthquakes—in impact. Human beings have literally rerouted rivers, moved mountains, and burned vast forests. By the early part of the 21st century, human society had transformed about half of the Earth's ice-free surface and made a major impact on most of the rest. In many areas, as much land was used by transportation systems as by agriculture. The climate itself had been profoundly altered by emissions of global warming gases. Although significant natural resources—fresh water, fertile land, and forest—remained, exploding populations and rapid economic development had reached the point where, by most measures, the demands of human society had already exceeded the carrying capacity of the Earth's ecosystem.

These rapid changes pose severe threats to many businesses. They face limited supplies of critical resources, unpredictable weather changes, and increased political risk, among many other challenges. Yet the environmental problems faced by society also present business with great opportunities. Established firms and innovative entrepreneurs who can figure out, for example, how to build offices and houses that are more energy-efficient, produce energy without irreversibly altering the climate, or devise systems to recycle and reuse obsolete electronics, can both help society and enjoy great commercial success.

Forces of Change

Pressure on the Earth's resource base is becoming increasingly severe. Three critical factors have combined to accelerate the ecological crisis facing the world community and to make sustainable development more difficult: population growth, world income inequality, and the rapid industrialization of many developing nations.

The Population Explosion

A major driver of environmental degradation is the exponential growth of the world's population. A population that doubled every 50 years, for example, would be said to be growing exponentially. Many more people would be added during the second 50 years than during the first, even though the rate of growth would stay the same. Just 10,000 years ago, the Earth was home to no more than 10 million humans, scattered in small settlements. For many thousands of years, population growth was gradual. Around 1950, the world population reached 2.5 billion. World population crossed the 6 billion mark in 1999 and the 7 billion mark in late 2011. The United Nations estimates that the population will reach almost 11 billion by 2100. To gain some perspective on these figures, consider that a person born in 1950 who lives to be 75 years old will have seen the world's population increase by more than 5 billion people.

Population growth in the coming decades will not be distributed equally. In the industrialized countries, especially in Europe, population growth has already slowed. Almost all of the world's population growth over the next century is predicted to be in less developed countries, especially in Africa, as shown in Figure 9.2.

The world's burgeoning population will put increasing strain on the Earth's resources. Each additional person uses raw materials and adds pollutants to the land, air, and water. The world's total industrial production would have to quintuple over the next 40 years just to maintain the same standard of living that people have now, if technology remains unchanged. Protecting the environment in the face of rapid population growth is very difficult. For example, in some parts of western Africa, population growth has put great pressure on available farmland, which is not allowed to lie fallow. Because much of the available firewood has already been cut, people use livestock dung for fuel instead of fertilizer. The result has been a deepening cycle of poverty, as more and more people try to live off less and less productive land.

World Income Inequality and Economic Development

A second important cause of environmental degradation is the inequality between rich and poor. Although economic development has raised living standards for many, large numbers of the world's people continue to live in severe poverty. As explained in Chapter 4, inequality can be measured in two ways, by wealth and income. According to the most recent estimates, around 2.2 billion people (slightly under a third of the world's population) had incomes below the international "moderate" poverty line of $2 a day. These people, most of them in sub-Saharan Africa, South Asia, East Asia, and the Pacific, lived very near the margin of subsistence. They had only a tiny fraction of the goods and services enjoyed by those in the industrialized nations.[8]

FIGURE 9.2
Population of the World and Major Areas, 1950–2100

Source: United Nations Population Division, "World Population Prospects: The 2012 Revision: Key Findings and Advance Tables," 2013. The projections represent the medium-range scenario. Other estimates are higher and lower. All estimates are available at *www.un.org/esa/population*.

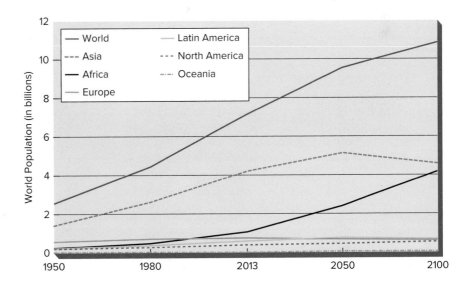

[8] Current data may be found at *www.worldbank.org*.

Some of the most extreme poverty is found on the outskirts of rapidly growing cities in developing countries. In many parts of the world, people have moved to urban areas in search of work. Often, they must live in slums, in makeshift dwellings without sanitation or running water. In Manila in the Philippines, a sprawling metropolitan area of 12 million people, more than a third of the inhabitants live in such shantytowns. Hundreds died when a garbage dump nearby shifted, burying scores of people. Today, more than half of all humans live in cities—many recent migrants to so-called megacities of 10 million or more, such as Lagos, Jakarta, and Mumbai—that lack adequate housing or infrastructure to support them.[9]

The world's income is not distributed equally. The gap between people in the richest and poorest countries is large and getting larger. In 2015, the income of the average American, for example, was 31 times the income of the average Vietnamese and 85 times that of the average Tanzanian. Figure 9.3 illustrates the distribution of private consumption among the world's people, one measure of inequality. The 20 percent of people in the highest-income countries consumed 77 percent of world's good and services, while the 20 percent in the poorest countries consumed just 1.5 percent. The 60 percent in the middle-income countries consumed 22 percent.

Inequality is an environmental problem because countries (and people) at either extreme of income tend to behave in more environmentally destructive ways than those in the middle. People in the richest countries consume far more fossil fuels, wood, and meat, for example. People in the poorest countries, for their part, often misuse natural resources just to survive; for example, cutting down trees for fuel to cook food and keep warm.

A final source of pressure on the Earth's resource base is the rapid industrialization of many countries. Many parts of Africa, Asia, and Latin America are developing at a

FIGURE 9.3
Share of the World's Private Consumption by Income Fifths

Source: "Consumption and Consumerism," *www.globalissues.org,* based on data from *World Bank Development Indicators 2008.*

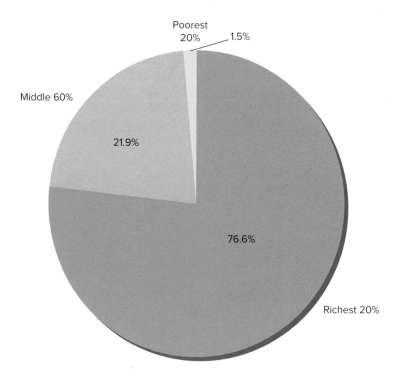

[9] Data on urban population trends are available at *www.unpa.org.*

rapid pace. This is positive because it is reducing poverty and slowing population growth. But economic development has also contributed to the growing ecological crisis. Industry requires energy, much of which comes from burning fossil fuels, releasing pollutants, and disrupting the climate. The agricultural "green" revolution, although greatly increasing crop yields in many parts of the world, has caused contamination by pesticides, herbicides, and chemical fertilizers. Development is often accompanied by rising incomes, bringing higher rates of both consumption and waste. In many instances, environmental regulations have lagged the pace of development.

> China dramatically illustrates the tight connection between rapid economic development and environmental risk. China is one of the fastest-growing economies in the world, expanding at a rate approaching 10 percent annually on average over the past 30 years (although its economy has recently slowed somewhat). The evidence of industrialization is everywhere, from skyscrapers under construction, to cars crowding the streets, to factories operating 24/7 to produce goods for export. Yet a major consequence has been increased pollution. Ninety percent of China's cities fail to meet national air quality standards, according to a recent report; in Beijing, residents can rarely see nearby mountains because of bad air. In 2015, a documentary film decrying the problem, called "Under the Dome," drew more than 150 million online viewers before the Chinese authorities abruptly censored it. Nonetheless, government leaders said they were "determined to tackle environmental pollution" and moved forward on efforts to strengthen regulations and promote wind and solar power. China and other fast-growing developing nations challenge business and society to "leapfrog" stages and move directly to cleaner technologies and methods of production.[10]

The Earth's Carrying Capacity

The Earth's rapid population growth, people's rising expectations, and the industrialization of developing countries are on a collision course with a fixed barrier: the limited **carrying capacity** of the Earth's ecosystem. The world's resource base, the air, water, soil, minerals, and so forth, is essentially finite, or bounded. We have only one Earth; the ecosystem itself is not growing. If human societies use up resources faster than they can be replenished, and create waste faster than it can be dispersed, environmental devastation will be the inevitable result.[11] Human society is already overshooting the carrying capacity of the Earth's ecosystem. Just as it is possible to eat or drink too much before your body sends you a signal to stop, so too are people and businesses using up resources and emitting pollution at an unsustainable rate. But because of delays in feedback, society may not understand the consequences of its actions until the damage has been done.

One method of measuring the Earth's carrying capacity, and how far human society has overshot it, is called the **ecological footprint**. This term refers to the amount of land and water a human population needs to produce the resources it consumes and to absorb its wastes, given prevailing technology. According to the Global Footprint Network, which maintains a public data set that is updated as new information becomes available, for each living human being, the Earth contains 4.5 acres of biologically productive area—farmland,

---

[10] "Hundreds of Chinese Cities Not Meeting Air Quality Standards," *The New York Times,* April 21, 2015; and "This Documentary Went Viral in China. Then It Was Censored. It Won't Be Forgotten," *The Washington Post,* March 16, 2015.

[11] James Gustave Speth, *The Bridge at the Edge of the World* (New Haven: Yale University Press, 2008); and Herman E. Daly, *Beyond Growth: The Economics of Sustainable Development* (Boston: Beacon Press, 1996).

forest, fresh water, and so forth. At the same time, each person has, on average, an ecological footprint of 6.7 acres. What that means is that human society is using resources and producing waste at a rate about one-and-a-half times above what the Earth's ecosystem can sustainably support. (Overshooting the Earth's carrying capacity is possible in the short run because people can consume resources without allowing them to regenerate, and generate waste at a rate higher than can be absorbed or recycled.) Historical data show that human society first exceeded world ecological capacity in the 1970s, and the gap between the two has been widening steadily since then.

Not surprisingly, some nations and individuals have bigger ecological footprints than others. For example, in the United States the average citizen has an ecological footprint of 17 acres, about four times his or her share of the world's resources. By comparison, in Panama the average citizen's ecological footprint is 6 acres, and in Bangladesh it is less than 2 acres.[12] These differences reflect the higher levels of consumption and less efficient use of resources in some countries, relative to others.

Acting together, how can human society bring the Earth's carrying capacity—and the demands placed on it—back into balance? This is without a doubt one of the great challenges now facing the world's people. Any solution will require change on many fronts.

- *Technological innovation.* One approach is to develop new technologies to produce energy, food, and other necessities of human life more efficiently and with less waste. Vast solar arrays in the desert, offshore wind turbines, or state-of-the-art utility plants that pump carbon dioxide deep under the ground could power homes and businesses. Genetic engineering could create more nutritious and productive crops. (Some concerns about genetic engineering are explored in Chapter 11.) Energy-efficient homes and commercial buildings could allow people to go about their lives while using fewer of the Earth's resources.

- *Changing patterns of consumption.* Individuals and organizations concerned about environmental impact could decide to consume less or choose less harmful products and services, or to buy from companies committed to sustainability in their own operations. Mobile applications, such as those developed by goodguide.com, now allow individuals to scan a product's barcode in a store with their smartphones and receive instant information on its environmental impact. They can modify their purchasing decisions, based on this knowledge. In a consumer society, when many people decide to reduce their personal footprints, society's overall footprint becomes smaller. For example, homes, workplaces, and places of entertainment could be built closer to each other and to public transit, so people could get where they needed to go with less wasted energy.[13]

- *"Getting the prices right."* Some economists have called for public policies that impose taxes on environmentally harmful products or activities. For example, when an individual bought gasoline—or a utility burned coal to make electricity—they would be charged an added carbon tax. Because prices would reflect true environmental costs, individuals and firms would have an incentive to make less harmful choices. Along these lines, *New York Times* columnist Thomas Friedman has argued for "a fixed, durable, long-term price signal that raises the price of dirty fuels and thereby creates sustained consumer demand for, and sustained private sector investment in, renewables."[14]

---

[12] The most recent data are available from the Global Footprint Network, *www.footprintnetwork.org.* Individuals can estimate their own ecological footprint by taking a quiz available at the "personal footprint" link at this website.

[13] A discussion of sustainable urban planning and design may be found in Jonathan Barnett et al., *Smart Growth in a Changing World* (Washington DC: American Planning Association, 2007).

[14] "Is It Weird Enough Yet?" *The New York Times,* September 13, 2011.

Some contemporary thinkers have gone even further and suggested that what is needed is nothing less than a completely new set of values about what is truly important. In this view, society needs a new "sustainability consciousness" that views the quality of life—not the quantity of things—as the most worthy goal of human aspiration. David Korten has stated this view eloquently in his book, *The Great Turning:*

> The Great Turning begins with a cultural and spiritual awakening—a turning in cultural values from money and material excess to life and spiritual fulfillment, from a belief in our limitations to a belief in our possibilities, and from fearing our differences to rejoicing in our diversity. . . . The values shift of the cultural turning leads us to redefine wealth—to measure it by the health of our families, communities, and natural environment.[15]

Technological innovation, smart consumption, and accurate accounting all hold the promise of helping human society realize this vision of the future.

 Global Environmental Issues

A **commons** is a shared resource, such as land, air, or water that a group of people use collectively. The *paradox of the commons* is that if all individuals attempt to maximize their own private advantage in the short term, the commons may be destroyed, and all users, present and future, lose. The only solution is restraint, either voluntary or through mutual agreement.[16] The *tragedy of the commons*—that freedom in a commons brings ruin to all—is illustrated by the following parable.

> There was once a village on the shore of a great ocean. Its people made a good living from the rich fishing grounds that lay offshore, the bounty of which seemed inexhaustible. Some of the cleverest fishermen began to experiment with new ways to catch more fish, borrowing money to buy bigger and better equipped boats. Since it was hard to argue with success, others copied their new techniques. Soon fish began to be harder to find, and their average size began to decline. Eventually, the fishery collapsed, bringing economic calamity to the village. A wise elder commented, "You see, the fish were not free after all. It was our folly to act as if they were."[17]

In a sense, we live today in a global commons, in which many natural resources, like the fishing grounds in this parable, are used collectively. Some environmental problems are inherently global in scope and require international cooperation. Typically these are issues pertaining to the *global commons,* that is, resources shared by all nations. Five global problems that will have major consequences for business and society are climate change, ozone depletion, resource scarcity, decline of biodiversity, and threats to the world's oceans.

Climate Change

A critically important challenge facing the world community is **climate change**. This term refers to changes in the Earth's climate caused by increasing concentrations of carbon dioxide and other pollutants produced by human activity. These have caused the average surface temperature of the Earth to rise over time, a phenomenon known as **global warming**.

---

[15] David Korten, *The Great Turning* (San Francisco: Berrett Kohler, 2006).

[16] Garrett Hardin, "Tragedy of the Commons," *Science* 162 (December 1968), pp. 1243–48.

[17] Abridgment of "The Story of a Fishing Village," from *1994 Information Please Environmental Almanac.* Copyright © 1993 by World Resources Institute. Reprinted by permission of Houghton Mifflin Co. All rights reserved.

FIGURE 9.4
Global Warming

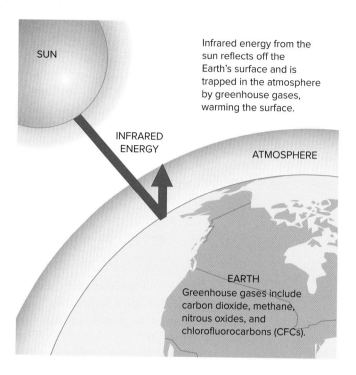

Infrared energy from the sun reflects off the Earth's surface and is trapped in the atmosphere by greenhouse gases, warming the surface.

SUN

INFRARED ENERGY

ATMOSPHERE

EARTH
Greenhouse gases include carbon dioxide, methane, nitrous oxides, and chlorofluorocarbons (CFCs).

But because these gases also have a variety of other complex effects on the climate, scientists often prefer the more general term *climate change.*

The Earth's atmosphere contains carbon dioxide and other trace gases that, like the glass panels in a greenhouse, prevent some of the heat reflected from the Earth's surface from escaping into space, as illustrated in Figure 9.4. Without this so-called greenhouse effect, the Earth would be too cold to support life. Since the Industrial Revolution, the concentration of carbon dioxide in the atmosphere has increased by more than 40 percent, largely due to the burning of fossil fuels such as oil, natural gas, and coal. According to the 2014 report of the Intergovernmental Panel on Climate Change (IPCC), a group of the world's leading atmospheric scientists, since 1880 the Earth has warmed by between 0.7 and 1.1 degrees Celsius. (One degree Celsius equals 1.8 degrees Fahrenheit, the unit commonly used in the United States.) Each of the past three decades has been the warmest of any in the last century and a half. The IPCC found that climatic warming was "unequivocal" and "extremely likely" due to human-generated greenhouse gases, which were at their highest atmospheric levels in at least 800,000 years.[18]

The possible causes of global warming are numerous. The burning of fossil fuels, which releases carbon dioxide, is the leading contributor. Increased emissions of nitrous oxides, resulting in part from the manufacture and use of synthetic fertilizers, also contributes. But consider the following additional causes.

- *Black carbon.* Recent scientific research has shown that black carbon—the sooty smoke that is created by the incomplete combustion of diesel engines, wildfires, and cookstoves fueled by dung, wood, and charcoal—is the second largest contributor to climate change,

---

[18] Intergovernmental Panel on Climate Change, "Climate Change 2014: Synthesis Report—Summary for Policymakers," 2014. A complete set of materials may be found at IPCC's website, *www.ipcc.ch.*

responsible for as much as 18 percent of global warming. Black carbon, which can travel thousands of miles in the atmosphere, absorbs heat and settles on glaciers, speeding up melting. A global alliance to reduce black carbon and simultaneously reduce global warming and advance economic development by promoting the use of clean cookstoves in developing nations is described in the discussion case at the end of this chapter.

- *Deforestation.* Trees and other plants absorb carbon dioxide, removing it from the atmosphere. Deforestation—cutting down and not replacing trees—thus contributes to higher levels of carbon dioxide. Scientists have estimated that about half of all original forests have already been cut. Burning forests to clear land for grazing or agriculture also releases carbon directly into the atmosphere as a component of smoke. And when trees are removed, their leaves do not shade the ground, leading to still more warming. Large-scale deforestation thus contributes in several ways to climate change.

- *Beef production.* Cattle ranching contributes to global warming in several ways. Methane, a potent greenhouse gas, is produced as a by-product of the digestion of ruminants, and feed production and manure processing have additional climate impacts. According to the Food and Agriculture Organization of the United Nations, livestock are responsible for 15 percent of greenhouse gas emissions, measured in carbon equivalents; beef and dairy production account for three-fifths of this amount. As the world's economies develop, people tend to eat more meat; the world's beef consumption is projected to nearly double by 2050.[19]

If global warming continues, the world may experience extreme heat waves, air pollution crises, violent storms, and damaging wildfires in the 21st century. The polar ice caps may partially melt, raising sea levels and causing flooding in low-lying coastal areas such as Florida, Bangladesh, and the Netherlands. It may become as difficult to grow wheat in Iowa as it is now in arid Utah. Such climate change could harm peoples' health, leading to breathing problems, epidemics of tropical diseases, and injuries from extreme weather events. It could devastate many of the world's economies and destroy the habitats of many species.[20]

The most important international treaty on global warming is the **Convention on Climate Change**, first negotiated in 1992. The United Nations hosts an annual Conference of the Parties, where representatives of virtually all the world's nations meet to hammer out agreements to cut the fossil fuel emissions that cause global warming. The first major breakthrough occurred in 1997, when the *Kyoto Protocol* (named after the city in Japan where representatives met) set limits aimed at stabilizing the concentration of greenhouse gases in the atmosphere at a level that would prevent dangerous interference with the climate system. At the 2014 conference, for the first time, all participating nations agreed to enact domestic laws to reduce carbon emissions.[21] The next annual conference was scheduled for late 2015 in Paris, France.

Many companies—whether or not required by treaty to do so—have taken action to reduce their impact on climate change.

> CSX, a railroad, has worked aggressively to reduce its carbon emissions, investing more than $1.5 billion to lower its use of fuel. The company has adopted new technology to provide auxiliary power to its locomotives, allowing their diesel engines to shut down while idling. It has also trained its engineers to use the most

---

[19] *Tackling Climate Change Through Livestock: A Global Assessment of Emissions and Mitigation Opportunities* (Rome: United Nations Food and Agriculture Organization, 2013); and *Creating a Sustainable Food Future* (World Resources Institute, 2013).

[20] Photographs of observable evidence of global warming may be found on the website of *National Geographic, http://environment.nationalgeographic.com/environment/global-warming.*

[21] "A Climate Accord Based on Global Peer Pressure," *The New York Times,* December 14, 2014.

fuel-efficient throttle settings and lubricated its rails to reduce friction. These steps, among others, now allow CSX to move a ton of freight 500 miles on just one gallon of diesel fuel. Commented the Carbon Disclosure Project's CEO, "Business must continue to forge ahead, innovate and seek out opportunities by doing more with less. The decisions that perpetuate a legitimate, low carbon and high growth economy will bring considerable value to those that have the foresight to make them."[22]

Ozone Depletion

Another global environmental challenge is ozone depletion. **Ozone** is a bluish gas, composed of three bonded oxygen atoms, that floats in a thin layer in the stratosphere between 9 and 28 miles above the planet. Although poisonous to humans in the lower atmosphere, ozone in the stratosphere is critical to life on Earth by absorbing dangerous ultraviolet light from the sun. Too much ultraviolet light can cause skin cancer and damage the eyes and immune systems of humans and other species.

Since the mid-1970s, scientists have understood that chlorofluorocarbons (CFCs), manufactured chemicals formerly widely used as refrigerants, insulation, solvents, and propellants in spray cans, could react with and destroy ozone in the upper atmosphere. This has caused a thin spot, or hole, in the Earth's ozone layer, particularly over Antarctica and in the northern latitudes over Europe and North America during the summer, when the sun's ultraviolet rays are the strongest and pose the greatest danger. In addition to destroying the ozone, CFCs are also greenhouse gases.

In 1987, world leaders negotiated the *Montreal Protocol,* agreeing to cut CFC production; the agreement was later amended to ban CFCs, along with several other ozone-depleting chemicals. Participating countries will have until 2030 to phase out chlorofluorohydrocarbons (HCFCs), related chemicals also damaging to the ozone layer. As of 2015, 197 countries, all but a tiny handful, had signed the protocol. Scientists believe that if the agreement is honored, the ozone layer will recover by 2050.[23]

An ongoing problem is that HCFCs, often used as substitutes for CFCs, are themselves powerful greenhouse gases. (In fact, one pound of some HCFCs released into the atmosphere has more than 2,000 times the warming impact as the same amount of carbon dioxide.)

The Coca-Cola Company, PepsiCo, and Red Bull, normally fierce competitors, have collaborated to find a substitute for fluorinated gases, including HCFCs, in refrigeration units such as vending machines and convenience-store coolers. Working in a partnership called Refrigerants Naturally!, the beverage firms have experimented with a variety of natural refrigerants, energy-efficient fans, intelligent controllers, and insulated glass. "Competitors working together to help address environmental issues is definitely a strong message to the industry," said a representative of Coca-Cola.[24]

Resource Scarcity: Water and Land

The Earth also faces serious challenges of resource scarcity involving both fresh water and arable land.

[22] Carbon Disclosure Project, *CDP Global 500 Report 2011: Accelerating Low Carbon Growth,* available online at *www.cdproject.net.*

[23] The text of the Montreal Protocol and its various amendments and a list of signatories may be found at *http://ozone.unep.org.*

[24] "Why Rivals Like PepsiCo, Coca Cola, Unilever and P&G Are Joining Forces," *The Guardian,* October 23, 2014.

Fresh Water Resources

Only 2.5 percent of the water on the Earth is fresh, and most of this is underground or locked up in ice and snow. Only about one-tenth of 1 percent of the Earth's water is in lakes, rivers, and accessible underground supplies, and thus available for human use. Water is, of course, renewable: Moisture evaporates from the oceans and returns to the Earth as freshwater precipitation, replenishing used stocks. But in many areas, humans are using up or polluting water faster than it can be replaced or naturally purified, threatening people and businesses that depend on it. This has been especially true in developing countries.

> The Ganges River supports more than 400 million Indians, providing water for drinking, irrigation, fishing, transportation, and trade along its 1,500 mile course from high in the Himalayan mountains to the coastal city of Kolkata (Calcutta). Hindus believe the river to be holy, and it is the site of many religious observances. But the Ganges is increasingly polluted, choked with raw sewage, industrial waste, animal carcasses, and even human remains. "The [river] is the silken thread which binds this country together. What will happen if it breaks?" asked one Indian.

All four of the world's leading irrigators—China, India, Pakistan, and the United States—are using groundwater faster than it is being replenished on crop-producing land.[25] By one estimate, if society were able to eliminate all pollution, capture all available fresh water, and distribute it equitably—all of which are unlikely—demand would exceed the supply within a hundred years. By the early 2010s, water shortages had already caused the decline of local economies and in some cases had contributed to regional conflicts. In Africa, for example, water disputes had flared among Egypt, Ethiopia, and Sudan, the three countries traversed by the world's longest river, the Nile. In the Middle East, disagreement over access to water from the River Jordan had exacerbated conflict between Israel and Palestine. By 2030, an estimated 3.9 billion people will be living under conditions of water scarcity.[26]

Arable Land

Arable (fertile) land is necessary to grow crops to feed the world's people. Land, if properly cared for, is a renewable resource. Although the productivity of land increased through much of the 20th century, by the 2010s much of the world's arable land was threatened with decline from soil erosion, loss of nutrients, and water scarcity. Worldwide, one-fifth of irrigated land required reclamation because of salinization (excess salt) or poor drainage.[27] In many areas, overly intensive farming practices and climate change have caused previously arable land to turn into desert (this process is called *desertification*). In 2001, a massive dust storm caused by overgrazed grasslands in China blew all the way across the Pacific, darkening skies over North America. The United Nations has estimated that 12 million hectares of arable land are lost every year to desertification (one hectare equals about two-and-a-half acres).[28] This will prompt migration and the potential for civil unrest.

> In 2013, Syngenta, a Swiss company that sells seeds and agricultural chemicals, committed to a specific goal of improving the fertility of 10 million hectares of farmland (about the size of Iceland) on the brink of degradation. The firm partnered

[25] Sandra Postel, "Sustaining Freshwater and its Dependents," in WorldWatch Institute, *State of the World, 2013: Is Sustainability Still Possible.*

[26] "Increasing Water Stress," in World Economic Forum, *Outlook on the Global Agenda 2015.*

[27] The most recent statistics may be found at the website of the United Nations Environmental Program, *www.unep.org.*

[28] The most recent statistics may be found at the website of the United Nations Convention to Combat Desertification, *www.unccd.int/en.*

with the United Nations to launch the Soil Leadership Academy. Together with local nongovernment organizations (NGOs), it trained growers of potatoes in Colombia, wine grapes in Hungary, and maize in Vietnam, among others, to reduce soil erosion by planting cover crops and limiting tillage. In 2015, the company reported on its website that its efforts had had a positive impact on 800,000 hectares of land, preventing and reversing degradation. "I think sustainability, over time, will be the driving force for everybody's business," said Syngenta's CEO.[29]

Decline of Biodiversity

Biodiversity refers to the number and variety of species and the range of their genetic makeup. To date, approximately 1.7 million species of plants and animals have been named and described. Many scientists believe these are but a fraction of the total. According to recent research, the total number may be closer to 9 million, but no one knows for sure. Scientists estimate that species extinction is now occurring at 100 to 1,000 times the normal, background rate, mainly because of pollution and the destruction of habitat by human society. A 2014 study by the World Wildlife Fund found that populations of vertebrate species (mammals, birds, reptiles, amphibians, and fish) were about half of what they were just 40 years earlier.[30] Biological diversity is now at its lowest level since the disappearance of the dinosaurs some 65 million years ago. Genetic diversity is vital to each species' ability to adapt and survive and has many benefits for human society as well. By destroying this biological diversity, we are actually undermining our survivability as a species.

A major reason for the decline in the Earth's biodiversity is the destruction of rain forests, particularly in the tropics. Rain forests are woodlands that receive at least 100 inches of rain a year. They are the planet's richest areas in terms of biological diversity. Rain forests cover only about 7 percent of the Earth's surface but account for somewhere between 40 and 75 percent of the Earth's species. At the rate that the original tropical rain forests are currently being cut, all will be gone or severely depleted within 30 years. The reasons for destruction of rain forests include commercial logging, cattle ranching, and conversion of forest to plantations to produce cash crops such as palm oil and soybeans for export. Overpopulation also plays a part, as landless people clear forest to grow crops, raise livestock, and cut trees for firewood.

The destruction is ironic because rain forests may have more economic value standing than cut. Rain forests are the source of many valuable products, including foods, medicines, and fibers. The pharmaceutical industry, for example, each year develops new medicines based on newly discovered plants from tropical areas. The U.S. National Cancer Institute has identified 1,400 tropical forest plants with cancer-fighting properties. Moreover, rain forests absorb carbon dioxide from the atmosphere, so their destruction worsens climate change.

Some businesses have taken important steps to conserve tropical rain forests. Members of the Consumer Products Forum, an alliance of 400 leading companies including Coca-Cola, Unilever, and Walmart, have adopted a goal of "zero net deforestation" by 2020 and agreed not to buy any raw materials—such as beef, soybeans, palm oil, timber, and paper—whose production requires the destruction of forest. In another initiative, in 2015 Archer Daniels Midland (ADM), a major trader of agricultural commodities, partnered with the Forest Trust to assure it purchased no soybeans from threatened ecosystems. This was important because much of the

---

[29] "Growing More With Less," *Swiss Style,* January 17, 2014. Syngenta's commitments and progress toward meeting them may be reviewed at *www.syngenta.com/global/corporate/en/goodgrowthplan.*

[30] World Wildlife Fund, *Living Planet: Species, Spaces, People and Places* (2014).

world's soybean crop came from Brazil, where Amazonian rain forests were being cleared for farming. "We're at a critical juncture now to break the link between agriculture, especially for soy production, and deforestation in Latin America," said a representative of the activist group Forest Heroes. "ADM's announcement is a major step forward for the soy industry."[31]

The Convention on Biological Diversity, an international treaty first negotiated in 1992, addresses many of these issues. By 2015 it had been ratified by 195 countries. (The United States was not among them; it declined to ratify, citing concerns with provisions on intellectual property rights and financial assistance to developing countries.) The treaty commits these countries to draw up national strategies for conservation, to protect ecosystems and individual species, and to take steps to restore degraded areas. It also allows countries to share in the profits from sales of products derived from their biological resources.

Threats to Marine Ecosystems

A final issue of concern is threats to the world's **marine ecosystems**. This term refers broadly to oceans and the salt marshes, lagoons, and tidal zones that border them, as well as the diverse communities of life that they support. Salt water covers 70 percent of the Earth's surface and is home to a great variety of species, from tiny plankton to the giant blue whale, from kelp beds to mangrove forests. Marine ecosystems are important to human society in many ways. Fish, marine mammals, and sea plants provide food and other useful products such as fertilizer, animal feed, cooking and heating oil, medicines, clothing, and jewelry. Healthy coastal zones protect coastlines from erosion and filter runoff from the land. Many communities have survived for centuries off the bounty of the sea.

Today, the health of these ecosystems is increasingly threatened. Some of the key issues include the following:

Fish populations. Oceans provide 90 percent of the world's fish catch. The United Nations has estimated that of the world's marine fisheries, 90 percent are fully exploited or overexploited, and some fisheries—such as those for cod off the Grand Banks (eastern United States and Canada) and for anchovies off Peru—have probably been permanently destroyed by overfishing.[32] Active management, such as limiting the number of fishing boats, establishing fish quotas, or banning fishing for periods of time, has allowed fish to regenerate in some areas.

Coral reefs. Coral reefs are limestone structures that develop from the skeletons of aquatic life and are host to great biological diversity. Today, however, they are in decline from pollution, oceanic warming, damage from ships, and cyanide and dynamite fishing. The Nature Conservancy estimates that at their current rate of decline, 70 percent of coral reefs will be gone by 2050.

Coastal development. Much of the world's population growth is now concentrated in coastal areas, often in ecologically fragile areas. In the United States, for example, 50 percent of the population lives in counties bordering the ocean—which comprise just 17 percent of the land. Inappropriate development can put pressure on ecologically fragile areas.[33]

---

[31] "Agribusiness Giant Adopts Historic No-Deforestation Policy," *Climate Progress,* April 1, 2015. The commitments of the Consumer Goods Forum are reported at *www.theconsumergoodsforum.com.*

[32] "The State of World Fisheries and Accquaculture, 2014," *www.fao.org.*

[33] Pew Charitable Trusts, "Coastal Sprawl: The Effects of Urban Development on Aquatic Ecosystems in the United States," *www.pewtrusts.org.*

Ocean acidity. One effect of increased concentrations of greenhouse gases in the atmosphere has been gradual acidification of the oceans, as seawater has absorbed excess carbon dioxide (which becomes carbonic acid). The result has been the destruction of aquatic life, which is often highly sensitive to acidity.[34]

One group of businesses whose actions directly affect the health of the oceans is the cruise ship industry. A case describing the efforts of one company, Holland America Line, to reduce its adverse effects on the oceans appears at the end of this book.

Response of the International Business Community

Since so many ecological challenges cross national boundaries, the international business community has a critical role to play in addressing them. This section describes some of the important voluntary initiatives undertaken by companies around the world to put the principle of sustainable development into practice. Other actions by business to address environmental challenges will be explored in Chapter 10.

Life-cycle analysis (LCA), also called *life-cycle assessment,* involves collecting information on the lifelong environmental impact of a product, all the way from extraction of raw material to design, manufacturing, distribution, use, and ultimate disposal. The aim of life-cycle analysis is to minimize the adverse impact of a particular product at all stages, from *cradle to grave.* Having this information can permit companies to make informed choices about how to reduce a product's footprint. For example, a Procter & Gamble life-cycle analysis of its Tide detergent brand found that its greatest environmental impact occurred in the home—when customers washed their clothes in hot water. The company subsequently introduced Tide Coldwater as a more environmentally friendly alternative. Walmart, Dell, Aloca, and other companies work through the Sustainability Consortium to advance LCA for thousands of products.[35]

Industrial ecology refers to designing factories and distribution systems as if they were self-contained ecosystems. For example, businesses can save materials through closed-loop recycling, use wastes from one process as raw material for others, and make use of energy generated as a by-product of production.

An example of industrial ecology may be found in the town of Kalundborg, Denmark, where several companies have formed a cooperative relationship that produces both economic and environmental benefits. The local utility company sells excess process steam, which had previously been released into a local fjord (waterway), to a local pharmaceutical plant and oil refinery. Excess fly ash (fine particles produced when coal is burned) is sold to nearby businesses for use in cement making and road building. Meanwhile, the oil refinery removes sulfur in the natural gas it produces to make it cleaner burning and sells the sulfur to a sulfuric acid plant. Calcium sulfate, produced as a residue of a process to cut smoke emissions, is sold to a gypsum manufacturer for making wallboard. The entire cycle both saves money and reduces pollution.[36]

Extended product responsibility refers to the idea that companies have a continuing responsibility for the environmental impact of their products or services, even after they are sold. This implies, for example, that firms pay close attention to the energy efficiency

[34] "How Will Ocean Acidification Impact Marine Life?" *Science Daily,* February 3, 2015.

[35] For more information on the Sustainability Consortium, see *www.sustainabilityconsortium.org.*

[36] "Life Cycle Analysis and Green Business Development," October 20, 2011, *www.claritycommunicationsconsulting.com.*

Exhibit 9.B

HP's Moonshot: Reducing Carbon Impact through Extended Product Responsibility

In an analysis of its carbon impact, HP learned that more than three-fifths of the company's greenhouse gas emissions were caused by its product portfolio—that is, by its products in use once they were in the customers' hands. Reducing the climate impacts of its own operations, manufacturing, and transportation could only fix part of the problem, the company reasoned. So, in 2014, HP announced a new goal of reducing the emissions intensity in use of all of its high-volume products, including printers, computers, and mobile devices, by 40 percent overall by 2020, compared with 10 years earlier.

A major part of this effort was the creation of a new generation of energy-efficient servers—the powerful computers that store, share, and route data on behalf of customers in enormous data centers. Astonishingly, humans today produce more data in 12 hours than they did in all of history up to 2003. Handling and storing this volume of data requires more energy than the entire nation of Japan, and the additional space required to hold new servers needed in the next three years will require more land mass than Manhattan. HP's answer was the Moonshot, an innovative new high-volume server that uses up to 90 percent less energy than current servers and 80 percent less space. "We need to think differently about the technology that powers our life and work—creating solutions that go beyond incremental efficiency improvements," said the company's CEO, Meg Whitman.

Sources: CDP, *Climate Action and Profitability: CDP S&P 500 Climate Change Report 2014, www.cpd.net;* "HP Announces Goal to Reduce Greenhouse Gas Emissions of Product Portfolio," HP press release, September 24, 2014; and "Living Progress: A Holistic Approach to Creating A Better Future," October 14, 2014, *www.triplepundit.com.*

of their products when used by the consumer. It also implies that companies design products for disassembly, that is, so that at the end of their useful life they can be disassembled and recycled. At Volkswagen, the German carmaker, engineers design cars for eventual disassembly and reuse. At the company's specialized auto recycling plant in Leer, old cars can be taken apart in just three minutes. Steel, precious metals, oil, acid, and glass are separated and processed. A new process enables even shredder residue—formerly unusable bits of plastic and upholstery fabric—to be diverted from landfill and reused.[37] This is sometimes called *cradle to cradle,* because materials that are used to create one product are later reused to create another. The efforts of one company, HP, to reduce its carbon impact through extended product responsibility is profiled in Exhibit 9.B.

Carbon neutrality is when an organization or individual produces net zero emissions of greenhouse gases. Since virtually all activity produces some atmospheric warming, this is usually accomplished by a combination of energy efficiencies (to reduce their own emissions) and carbon offsets (to reduce others' emissions). **Carbon offsets** (sometimes called *carbon credits*) are investments in projects that remove carbon dioxide (or its equivalent in other climate-warming pollutants, such as black carbon) from the atmosphere. This can be done, for example, by paying others to plant trees, produce clean energy, or sequester (bury underground) earth-warming gases. A number of organizations now broker carbon offsets to businesses and individuals wishing to reduce their climate impact.

In 2014, the British retailer Marks & Spencer announced its Plan A 2020 (so-called because, as their chief executive explained "there is no Plan B"), setting out to become the "world's most sustainable retailer. The company had already met a prior commitment to become carbon neutral. To achieve this ambitious goal, the company had built an experimental "learning store" in the United Kingdom as well as an "eco-factory" in partnership with a supplier in Sri Lanka, to try out

[37] More information about this technology is available at *www.sicontechnology.com.*

new approaches that could be diffused through its system. It had installed solar panels and radically cut energy use at its stores and warehouses, improved the fuel efficiency of its delivery fleet, and reduced the number of business flights taken by employees. It also introduced new products, such as the "first ever carbon neutral bra," part of its Autumn Leaves lingerie collection. Marks & Spencer offset the remainder of its carbon emission by investing in carbon reduction projects. (Mark's & Spencer's partnership to promote less polluting cook stoves— mitigating their climate impacts—is described in the discussion case at the end of this chapter.)[38]

Other companies that have achieved—or pledged to achieve—carbon neutrality include salesforce.com, Nike, News Corporation, Timberland, and Van City.[39]

Sustainable development will also require **technology cooperation** through long-term partnerships between companies in developed and developing countries to transfer environmental technologies, as shown in the following example.

In Vietnam, Schneider Electric, a global energy company based in France, entered into a partnership with an affiliated local company and a French NGO to provide electricity to villagers in the rural province of Quang Binh, which was not connected to the Vietnamese national power grid. The partnership built a small solar power plant to supply power to homes, schools, and government offices. Local residents, who paid for the electricity with interest-free microcredit, received training in the operation of the system—generating jobs and transferring technical knowledge to an isolated region. Gaining experience in renewable power generation was critical in Vietnam, where energy demand was expected to increase 15-fold by mid-century.[40]

The idea of sustainable development is not only widely accepted in the business community, many firms are increasingly viewing it as a core business issue. A 2014 global survey of more than 3,000 business leaders, for example, reported that 43 percent said their companies sought "to align sustainability with their overall business goals, mission, or values," up from 30 percent in 2012. The following chapter explores in more detail the steps companies are taking to do so.[41]

Codes of Environmental Conduct

Earlier chapters of this text have discussed the emergence of standards and codes of conduct in the areas of ethics and global corporate citizenship. Similarly, a number of national and international organizations have developed *standards and codes of environmental conduct.* Some are designed to be universally applicable, while others are tailored to particular industries. All, however, share the characteristic that they are private and voluntary: Corporations choose to comply with these codes to show customers, investors, regulators, and others that they have met certain environmental standards in their operations.

---

[38] Marks & Spencer, *Plan A Report 2014,* http://planareport.marksandspencer.com.

[39] A list of companies that have pledged or achieved carbon neutrality may be found in "Who's Going 'Carbon Neutral,'" at *www.bsr.org.*

[40] "Vietnam [Moves] Towards Using Green Energy," September 22, 2014, *www.vietmaz.com;* and World Business Council for Sustainable Development, "Schneider Electric: Business Enabling Access to Energy," [case study], *www.wbcsd.org.*

[41] "Sustainability's Strategic Worth: McKinsey Global Survey Results," July 2014, *www.mckinsey.com.*

Some of the leading universal codes and standards include the following:

- The International Chamber of Commerce has developed the *Business Charter for Sustainable Development,* 16 principles that identify key elements of environmental leadership and call on companies to recognize environmental management as among their highest corporate priorities.[42]

- The *CERES Principles,* 10 voluntary principles developed by the Coalition for Environmentally Responsible Economies (CERES) and later updated as the *CERES Roadmap,* commit signatory firms to protection of the biosphere, sustainable use of natural resources, energy conservation, risk reduction, and other environmental goals.[43]

- *ISO 14000* is a series of voluntary standards developed by the ISO, an international group based in Geneva, Switzerland, that permit companies to be certified as meeting global environmental performance standards.[44]

- The *Greenhouse Gas Protocol* is a tool developed by the World Resources Institute and the World Business Council for Sustainable Development to help businesses measure and manage their greenhouse gas emissions.[45]

Codes of environmental conduct have also been developed by and for specific industries.

A prominent example is the Equator Principles, a set of environmental standards for the financial services industry. Their focus is specific to banking: they commit signatories to determine, assess, and manage environmental risk in project financing. In other words, when a bank considers whether or not to lend money, for example, for the construction of an oil pipeline, it must examine the environmental impact of the project and whether or not its sponsors have systems in place to mitigate adverse impacts. If borrowers are unable to comply, the bank will not loan them money. The Equator Principles, launched in 2003 and most recently reviewed in 2013, have spread widely in the financial industry. By 2015, 80 financial institutions around the world had signed on, ranging from huge institutions such as Citigroup to regional banks such as Egypt's Arab African International Bank, China's Industrial Bank Company, and Uruguay's Banco de la Republica Oriental.[46]

Other industry-specific standards include the Forest Stewardship Council Principles in the forest products industry, the Marine Stewardship Council in the fishing industry, and the Leadership in Energy and Environmental Design (LEED) standards in the commercial and residential construction industry.

Protecting the environment and the well-being of future generations is not only a necessity, but also an opportunity for business. Companies operate in a resource-constrained world, where climate change and scarcity of fresh water, arable land, and healthy forests pose pressing challenges. Environmental regulations are getting tougher, consumers want cleaner products, and employees want to work for environmentally responsible companies. Finding ways to reduce or recycle waste saves money. Many executives are championing the idea that corporations have moral obligations to future generations. The most successful global businesses in coming years may be those, like the ones profiled in this chapter, that recognize the imperative for sustainable development as an opportunity both for competitive advantage and ethical action.

---

[42] *www.iisd.org.*

[43] "The Road to 2020: Corporate Progress on the Roadmap for Sustainability," *www.ceres.org.*

[44] *www.iso.org.*

[45] *www.ghgprotocol.org.*

[46] The website of the Equator Principles is *www.equator-principles.com.*

Summary

- Business and society operate within a finite natural environment. This reality confers constraints but also provides opportunities.

- Many world leaders have supported the idea of sustainable development, that is, development that meets the needs of the present without hurting the ability of future generations to meet their own needs. Governments, businesses, and civil sector organizations are engaged in a range of innovations in an effort to reach this goal.

- Population growth, income inequality, and rapid economic development in many parts of the world have contributed to these ecological problems. Human society is now using resources and producing waste at a rate well above what the Earth's ecosystem can sustainably support.

- Five environmental issues—climate change, ozone depletion, resource scarcity, declining biodiversity, and threats to the marine ecosystem—are shared by all nations. International agreements are addressing some of these issues, although more remains to be done.

- Global businesses have begun to put the principles of sustainable development into action through such innovative actions as life-cycle analysis, extended product responsibility, carbon neutrality, and technology cooperation.

- Nationally and internationally, businesses and nongovernmental organizations have worked together to develop voluntary codes of environmental conduct to promote sustainability.

Key Terms

biodiversity, *196*
carrying capacity, *189*
carbon neutrality, *199*
carbon offsets, *199*
climate change, *191*
commons, *191*
Convention on Climate Change, *193*

ecological footprint, *189*
ecosystem, *185*
extended product responsibility, *198*
global warming, *191*
industrial ecology, *198*
life-cycle analysis, *198*
marine ecosystems, *197*

natural capital, *184*
ozone, *194*
sustainable development, *185*
technology cooperation, *200*

Internet Resources

www.ipcc.ch	Intergovernmental Panel on Climate Change
www.unep.org	United Nations Environmental Program
newsroom.unfccc.int	United Nations Framework Convention on Climate Change
www.wbcsd.ch	World Business Council on Sustainable Development
www.iclei.org	Local Governments for Sustainability
www.triplepundit.com	New media company that covers sustainable business practices
www.worldwatch.org	The Worldwatch Institute
www.wri.org	World Resources Institute

Discussion Case: *Clean Cooking*

In a small village in rural Kenya, a woman bent over an open fire pit in the center of her hut cooking the evening meal. That morning, she had spent two hours collecting wood, animal dung, and scrap paper to use as fuel. Now, as she stirred the pot, the cook fire gave off a steady stream of sooty, acrid smoke, which filled the room despite a ventilation hole in the roof. The woman's young son played dangerously close to the open flame, while her daughter, coughing from the smoke, tried to read by the weak light of the fire.

In 2015, according to the World Bank, a similar scene was repeated in households with 2.8 billion people every day across the developing world, with devastating effects on human health, the environment, and economic development.

Indoor air pollution from open cookstoves is a killer. The World Health Organization has estimated that soot, particles, and smoke from cooking is the fifth worst risk factor for health in developing countries, causing two million premature deaths a year from lung and heart disease—more than malaria and tuberculosis combined. Open cookstoves also lead to disfiguring burns, asthma, eye damage, and pregnancy complications. The effects are greatest on women and young children, who spend the most time near the hearth.

Women and girls also suffer from head and back injuries, animal attacks, and sexual violence while searching for and carrying heavy loads of fuel, often far from home. Time spent collecting fuel is time not spent attending school, working at a paid job, or running a small business.

Primitive cooking methods also harm the environment. Cutting trees to produce wood or charcoal leads to deforestation, loss of biodiversity, and watershed degradation. Moreover, the combustion of biomass in cooking produces more than a quarter of the world's black carbon, or soot. Scientists now believe that soot is second only to carbon dioxide in its overall contribution to global warming. Policymakers have been intrigued by the fact that while carbon dioxide stays in the atmosphere for decades, black carbon washes out within days or weeks. Reducing soot in the atmosphere would thus have a much more immediate effect on global warming than cutting carbon emissions.

In 2010, the United Nations Foundation, in collaboration with several governments (including the United States), launched the Global Alliance for Clean Cookstoves, with the ambitious goal of "100 by 20"—that 100 million households worldwide adopt clean and efficient cookstoves and fuels by 2020. The alliance recognized that reaching this goal would require more than money; it would require technical innovation in fuels and stove design, new mechanisms of financing, and on-the-ground campaigns to engage users from a wide range of cultures and cooking traditions. It would also require the support of businesses—large and small.

Many companies saw an opportunity in the Global Alliance for Clean Cookstoves. CEMEX, a global building products company based in Mexico, developed and contributed $2 million worth of clean-burning concrete cookstoves. Marks & Spencer, the British retailer, joined the Alliance in 2014 and committed to helping employees of its suppliers of products such as coffee and textiles to cook more efficiently; and it had already partnered with UNICEF (the United Nations Children's Fund) to install 40,000 clean cookstoves in Bangladesh. Dow Corning, a Midland, Michigan-based maker of silicon-based materials, donated both money and expertise in manufacturing and material science to the Alliance.

At the same time, motivated by greater attention to the issue, social entrepreneurs across the globe began generating innovative ideas about how to design, manufacture, and

finance more efficient and cleaner cookstoves—potentially a "win–win" for the environment and human health and well-being. (Social entrepreneurs are individuals who are driven by a core mission to create and sustain social and environmental value, in addition to economic value.)

For example, in the west African country of Ghana, Suraj Wahab founded a small business, Toyola Energy Ltd., to produce a cookstove he invented called the *gyapa* ("good fire"). His company constructed the stove from locally sourced materials—scrap metal from construction sites and fired clay liners. Because it was designed to burn charcoal, a fuel used by 30 percent of Ghanaian households, twice as efficiently as in an open fire, each stove over the course of its life would prevent the release of global-warming emissions equivalent to the amount generated by a Honda Civic driven for one year.

Wahab had difficulty obtaining needed capital until he partnered with E+Co, a clean energy nonprofit that invested $270,000. E+Co helped Toyola calculate the carbon offset value of its cookstoves, which was then monetized and sold to the investment banking firm Goldman Sachs. Within a short period, Toyola employed 150 people and had sold more than 150,000 cookstoves to eager Ghanaians, who welcomed the cost savings and health benefits they provided. More than a quarter of the company's revenue came from the sale of carbon offsets, helping keep the price to consumers as low as $7.

Similar stories of creative partnerships were occurring around the globe. The nonprofit Trees, Water, & People, based in Fort Collins, Colorado, built and distributed almost 50,000 cookstoves in Guatemala. Their stove was an insulated metal box topped by a removable cooking surface adapted to cooking tortillas and a chimney pipe to vent smoke through a roof hole. Increased fuel efficiency saved families about ten dollars a month, in a society in which 80 percent of the population lived on two dollars a day or less. Other organizations, such as Solar Cookers International, experimented with ways to harness the power of the sun—a completely renewable, clean, and free source of energy—to boil water and cook food.

Contributions like these moved the Alliance closer to its ambitious goal. "As we build a cookstoves market to the scale necessary to combat and defeat this silent killer," said its executive director, "the strong support and unique expertise of our partners and champions will be invaluable."

Sources: "Push for Cleaner Cook Stoves in Poor Countries to Cut Pollution," *Associated Press,* April 8, 2015; "Clean Stoves Bring a Better Life," May 7, 2014, *www.worldbank.org;* "How Marks & Spencer is Cooking Its Way to a Cleaner Future," March 30, 2015, *www.greenbiz.com;* "Forest Saving Stoves Program," *www.treeswaterpeople.org;* "Case Study: Toyola Energy Limited, Ghana," *www.cleancookstoves.org;* and "Clean Cookstoves: Dow Corning's Path to Public-Private Partnership," *http://dowcorningcitizenservicecorps.wordpress.com,* February 28, 2012. The website of the Global Alliance for Clean Cookstoves is at *www.cleancookstoves.org.*

Discussion Questions

1. In what ways would the widespread adoption of clean cookstoves address the global environmental issues discussed in this chapter?

2. In what ways would the widespread adoption of clean cookstoves address the issues of economic development and poverty discussed in this chapter?

3. Which sectors (e.g., government, business, civil society) would need to be involved in a successful campaign to promote clean cookstoves in the developing world, and what would be the contributions of each?

4. What would be the benefit to multinational corporations, such as CEMEX, Marks and Spencer, and Dow Corning, of participating in this effort? What distinctive contributions can social entrepreneurs make to promoting clean cookstoves?

CHAPTER TEN

Managing for Sustainability

Growing public concern about sustainability has prompted political, corporate, and civil society leaders to become increasingly responsive to environmental issues. In the United States and other nations, government policymakers have moved toward greater reliance on economic incentives, rather than command and control regulations, to achieve environmental goals. At the same time, many businesses have become increasingly proactive and have pioneered new approaches to effective sustainability management, sometimes in partnership with advocacy organizations. These actions have often given firms a competitive advantage by cutting costs, gaining public support, and spurring innovation.

This Chapter Focuses on These Key Learning Objectives:

LO 10-1 Knowing the main features of environmental laws in the United States and other nations.

LO 10-2 Understanding the advantages and disadvantages of different regulatory approaches.

LO 10-3 Assessing the costs and benefits of environmental regulation.

LO 10-4 Defining an ecologically sustainable organization and the stages through which firms progress as they become more sustainable.

LO 10-5 Understanding how businesses can best manage for sustainability.

LO 10-6 Analyzing how effective sustainability management makes firms more competitive and improves their financial performance.

In 2015, Levi Strauss & Company reported that $500 million worth of garments it sold the prior year were "sustainably enhanced," up from none just five years earlier. The maker of the iconic Levi's jeans had worked with cotton farmers to reduce their use of water and pesticides, integrated recycled plastic from soda bottles into their fabric, and worked with the World Bank to provide low-cost loans to suppliers that met sustainability goals. The company encouraged its customers to wash their jeans less often and to keep them longer. The company aimed for a day when all Levi's apparel would be recycled in a closed loop, worn for many years and then returned to be made into new garments. "People buy Levi's because of the style, quality, and fit," said the company's vice president for social and environmental sustainability. "But we do believe that, all things being equal, if we can surprise and delight them with what we are doing around sustainability, it's additive."[1]

In the months leading up to United Nations–sponsored climate change talks in Paris, France, in late 2015, the European Union struggled to fix its cap-and-trade regulations. For a decade, the continent had been experimenting with a market-based system that allowed companies that cut their emissions of greenhouse gases to sell permits to others that had exceeded their quota, providing an incentive to reduce their pollution. But the system had not worked well, partly because the price of permits had fallen so low that they did little to change companies' behavior. In response, the European parliament agreed to reduce the number of permits issued (forcing up their price) and committed to invest the resulting revenue in clean energy and other climate initiatives. But, as the secretary-general of the United Nations pointed out, even the most sophisticated public policies by themselves would be insufficient to address climate change. "It is not only government," he said at the 2015 World Economic Forum. "Government cannot do it alone."[2]

The Environmental Defense Fund (EDF), a leading environmental advocacy organization, has formed partnerships with a number of companies, including McDonald's, DuPont, Starbucks, and FedEx, to improve environmental performance and gather information. In its most recent effort, EDF partnered with Google Earth Outreach to find, measure, and map natural gas leaks in a number of cities across the United States. Specially equipped Street View cars, which Google uses to photograph streetscapes for use with its map application, gathered data on even small gas leaks. Escaping gas—mostly from aging pipes—was a problem because it cost customers money, heightened the risks of explosion, and worsened climate change. In 2014, EDF and Google released interactive maps of several cities, including Boston, Syracuse, Indianapolis, and Burlington, showing the results. Some utilities welcomed the effort, saying it helped them identify pipes that needed repair. "This project puts information in the hands of people who can make a difference," said the program manager for Google Earth Outreach.[3]

In the early years of the 21st century, many businesses, governments, and environmental advocacy organizations became increasingly concerned that old strategies for promoting environmental protection were failing and new approaches were necessary. Government

[1] "Levi's Wants to Convert Social Ambition to Cash," *San Francisco Chronicle.* March 13, 2015; "Stop Washing Your Jeans: LS&Co. CEO Chip Bergh at Brainstorm Green," May 20, 2014, *www.levistrauss.com/unzipped-blog;* "Levi's Offers WasteLess Denim," October 20, 2012, *www.sfgate.com.*

[2] "Europe Reforms Cap-and-Trade, Lays Out Climate Vision," February 25, 2015, *www.climatecentral.com/news;* "Europe's Evolving Climate Position," March 7, 2015, *http://roadtoparis.info;* and "24 Quotes on Climate Change from Davos 2015," January 23, 2015, *http://agenda.weforum.org.*

[3] "EDF Partners with Google Earth Outreach to Map Natural Gas Leaks Under U.S. City Streets," July 16, 2014, *www.edf.org;* and "Google Teams Up with Environmentalists to Track Natural Gas Leaks," *Boston Magazine,* July 16, 2014, *www.boston-magazine.com.* The methane maps are available at *http://edf.org/methanemaps.* More information about EDF's corporate partnerships is available at *www.edf.org/approach/partnerships/corporate.*

policymakers moved toward greater reliance on economic incentives to achieve environmental goals. Environmentalists engaged in greater dialogue and cooperation with industry leaders. Many businesses pioneered new approaches to sustainability, such as developing products with fewer adverse environmental impacts.

The challenge facing government, industry, and environmental advocates alike, as they tried out new approaches and improved on old ones, was how to promote ecologically sound business practices in an increasingly integrated world economy.

Role of Government

In many nations, government is actively involved in regulating business activities in order to protect the environment. Business firms have few incentives to minimize pollution if their competitors do not. A single firm acting on its own to reduce discharges into a river, for example, would incur extra costs. If its competitors did not do the same, the firm might not be able to compete effectively and could go out of business. Government, by setting a common standard for all firms, can take the cost of pollution control out of competition. It can also provide economic incentives to encourage businesses, communities, and regions to reduce pollution, and offer legal and administrative systems for resolving disputes. Government cannot accomplish environmental goals by itself; its role, rather, is to make a critical contribution to a collective effort, together with business and civil society, to move toward sustainability.

In the United States, government has been involved in environmental regulation since the late 19th century, when the first federal laws were passed protecting navigable waterways. The government's role began to increase dramatically, however, around 1970, when Congress passed the National Environmental Policy Act (NEPA), which created the **Environmental Protection Agency (EPA)**, the nation's main environmental regulatory agency. Figure 10.1 summarizes the major federal environmental laws enacted by the U.S. Congress since the passage of NEPA. It is organized into four categories: air; water; land, species, and habitat; and cross-media (referring to the regulation of forms of pollution that have multiple impacts on air, water, and land).

Various regional, state, and local agencies also have jurisdiction over some environmental issues in their respective areas. Figure 10.1 shows no recent legislation. Since 2000, most changes in federal regulatory oversight have come through agency rulemaking and executive action rather than legislation. For example, new regulations in 2013 that limited carbon dioxide emissions from power plants came not from Congress, but from the EPA.[4]

Major Areas of Environmental Regulation

In the United States, the federal government regulates in three major areas of environmental protection: air pollution, water pollution, and land pollution (solid and hazardous waste). This section will review the major ecological issues and the U.S. laws pertaining to each, with comparative references to similar initiatives in other nations.

Air Pollution

Air pollution occurs when more pollutants are emitted into the atmosphere than can be safely absorbed and diluted by natural processes. Some pollution occurs naturally, such as smoke and ash from volcanoes and forest fires. But most air pollution today results from human activity, especially industrial processes and motor vehicle emissions. Air pollution degrades buildings,

---

[4] "Administration Presses Ahead with Limits on Emissions from Power Plants," *The New York Times,* September 19, 2013.

FIGURE 10.1
Leading U.S.
Environmental
Protection Laws

AIR

- CLEAN AIR ACT (1970) Established national air quality standards and timetables.
- CLEAN AIR ACT AMENDMENTS (1977) Revised air standards.
- CLEAN AIR ACT AMENDMENTS (1990) Required cuts in urban smog, acid rain, and greenhouse gas emissions; promoted alternative fuels.

WATER

- WATER POLLUTION CONTROL ACT (1972) Established national goals and timetables for clean waterways.
- SAFE DRINKING WATER ACT (1974 and 1996) Authorized national standards for drinking water.
- CLEAN WATER ACT AMENDMENTS (1987) Authorized funds for sewage treatment plants and waterways cleanup.

LAND, SPECIES, AND HABITAT

- ENDANGERED SPECIES ACT (1973) Conserved species of animals and plants whose survival was threatened or endangered.
- HAZARDOUS MATERIALS TRANSPORT ACT (1974) Regulated shipment of hazardous materials.
- RESOURCE CONSERVATION AND RECOVERY ACT (1976) Regulated hazardous materials from production to disposal.
- TOXIC SUBSTANCES CONTROL ACT (1976) Established national policy to regulate, restrict, and, if necessary, ban toxic chemicals.
- COMPREHENSIVE ENVIRONMENTAL RESPONSE COMPENSATION AND LIABILITY ACT (SUPERFUND) (1980) Established Superfund and procedures to clean up hazardous waste sites.
- SUPERFUND AMENDMENTS AND REAUTHORIZATION ACT (SARA) (1986) Established toxics release inventory.

CROSS-MEDIA POLLUTION

- PESTICIDE CONTROL ACT (1972) Required registration of and restrictions on pesticide use.
- POLLUTION PREVENTION ACT (1990) Provided guidelines, training, and incentives to prevent or reduce pollution at the source.
- OIL POLLUTION ACT (1990) Strengthened EPA's ability to prevent and respond to catastrophic oil spills.
- CHEMICAL SAFETY INFORMATION, SITE SECURITY, AND FUELS REGULATORY RELIEF ACT (1999) Set standards for the storage of flammable chemicals and fuels.

reduces crop yields, mars the beauty of natural landscapes, and harms people's health. The American Lung Association (ALA) estimated in 2014 that 148 million Americans, almost half of the population, were breathing unsafe air for at least part of each year. Fully 70 percent of the cancer risk from air pollution is due to diesel exhaust from trucks, farm and construction equipment, marine vessels, and electric generators. People living near busy highways and workers in occupations that use diesel equipment are particularly at risk.[5]

[5] American Lung Association, "State of the Air: 2014," *www.lungusa.org;* and "Health Effects of Diesel Exhaust," *http://ochha .ca.gov.*

One approach to reducing diesel pollution is a service called IdleAir, operated by Convoy Solutions of Knoxville, Tennessee. IdleAir provides an alternative for long-haul truck drivers who idle their engines at truck stops in order to provide power to the cab during rest breaks. An inexpensive window-mounted adapter allows drivers to hook up to a service module, so they can continue to enjoy heating, cooling, cable TV, and Internet access with their engines off. The solution is less expensive for truckers because it uses one-tenth the energy of idling, and reduces pollution by completely eliminating diesel emissions during rest breaks.[6]

The EPA has identified six criteria pollutants, relatively common harmful substances that serve as indicators of overall levels of air pollution. These are lead, carbon monoxide, particulate matter, sulfur dioxide, nitrogen dioxide, and ozone. (Ozone at ground level is a particularly unhealthy component of smog.) In addition, the agency also has identified a list of toxic air pollutants that are considered hazardous even in relatively small concentrations. These include asbestos, benzene (found in gasoline), dioxin, perchloroethylene (used in some dry-cleaning processes), methylene chloride (used in some paint strippers), and radioactive materials. Emissions of toxic pollutants are strictly controlled. In 2014, the Supreme Court ruled that the EPA could regulate emissions of carbon dioxide (one of the main contributors to global warming) at facilities it already regulated for other pollutants.[7]

A special problem of air pollution is **acid rain**. Acid rain is formed when emissions of sulfur dioxide and nitrogen oxides, by-products of the burning of fossil fuels by utilities, manufacturers, and motor vehicles, combine with natural water vapor in the air and fall to earth as rain or snow that is more acidic than normal. Acid rain can damage the ecosystems of lakes and rivers, reduce crop yields, and degrade forests. Structures, such as buildings and monuments, are also harmed. Within North America, acid rain is most prevalent in New England and eastern Canada, regions that are downwind of coal-burning utilities in the Midwestern states.[8] The major law governing air pollution is the Clean Air Act, passed in 1970 and amended in 1990. The 1990 Clean Air Act toughened standards in a number of areas, including stricter restrictions on emissions of acid rain–causing chemicals.

The efforts of the U.S. government to reduce acid rain illustrate some of the difficult trade-offs involved in environmental policy. These are described in Exhibit 10.A.

Water Pollution

Water pollution, like air pollution, occurs when more wastes are dumped into waterways, lakes, or oceans than can be naturally diluted and carried away. Water can be polluted by organic wastes (untreated sewage or manure), by chemicals from industrial processes, and by the disposal of nonbiodegradable products (which do not naturally decay). Heavy metals and toxic chemicals, including some used as pesticides and herbicides, can be particularly persistent. Like poor air, poor water quality can harm ecosystems, decrease crop yields, threaten human health, and degrade the quality of life. Failure to comply with clean water laws can be very expensive for business, as the following example shows.

In 2010, a wellhead blowout at a deepwater drilling platform operated on behalf of BP (formerly British Petroleum) in the Gulf of Mexico caused the largest marine oil spill in U.S. history. For three months, as crews struggled to cap the well, as much as 5 million barrels of oil gushed into the waters of the Gulf of Mexico, causing

---

[6] The company's website is *www.idleair.com.*

[7] PBS Newshour, "Supreme Court Limits EPS's Authority to Regulate Carbon Dioxide Emissions," June 23, 2014, *www.pbs.org/newshour.*

[8] More information about acid rain may be found at *www.epa.gov/acidrain.*

Exhibit 10.A

Moving Mountains to Fight Acid Rain

As part of its efforts to control acid rain, the U.S. government in 1990 initiated stricter new restrictions on the emission of sulfur dioxide by utilities. Many electric companies complied with the law by switching from high-sulfur coal, which produces more sulfur dioxide when burned, to low-sulfur coal, which produces less. This action had the beneficial effect of reducing acid rain.

But the law had some environmentally destructive results that had been unintended by regulators. Much of the highest-quality low-sulfur coal in the United States lies in horizontal layers near the tops of rugged mountains in Appalachia, including parts of West Virginia, Kentucky, Tennessee, and Virginia. Some coal companies discovered that the cheapest way to extract this coal was through what came to be known as mountaintop removal. Explosives were used to blast away up to 500 feet of mountaintop. Massive machines called draglines, 20 stories tall and costing $100 million each, were then used to remove the debris to get at buried seams of coal. A 2009 study using satellite images estimated that 1.2 million acres had been ravaged in this manner by surface mining. Although coal operators were required to reclaim the land afterward—by filling in adjacent valleys with debris and planting grass and shrubs—many environmentalists believed the damage caused by mountaintop removal was severe. Many rivers and creeks were contaminated and habitat destroyed. Aquifers dried up, and the entire region became vulnerable to devastating floods. Many felt it was deeply ironic that a law that was designed to benefit the environment in one way had indirectly harmed it in another.

Since 2008, coal production at mountaintop removal mines has declined. Partly, this reflected an overall shift from coal to natural gas during this period. But, it also reflected decisions by major banks, including PNC, Bank of America, and Citigroup, to stop funding these environmentally destructive practices.

Sources: "A New Tack in the War on Mining Mountains," *The New York Times,* March 9, 2015; "Coal Production Using Mountaintop Removal Mining Decreases 62% Since 2008," July 9, 2015, *www.theenergycollective.com;* and "The High Cost of Cheap Coal: When Mountains Move," *National Geographic,* March 2006, pp. 105–23. Aerial maps showing the location and extent of surface mines may be found at *www.skytruth.org.* Studies on the extent of mountaintop removal mining and reclamation efforts are available at *http://ilovemountains.org.*

extensive damage to marine life and devastating the coastal economies of adjacent states. Subsequent government investigations found that BP's relentless cost cutting and inadequate safety systems had contributed to the spill. In 2015, BP agreed to pay $18.7 billion to settle claims by federal, state, and local governments arising from the spill, the largest environmental settlement in U.S. history. BP estimated that the *total* cost of the spill—including the actual cleanup, payments to individuals and shareholders, criminal fines, and other costs not included in the settlement—would be nearly $54 billion.[9]

In the United States, regulations address both the pollution of rivers, lakes, and other surface bodies of water and the quality of the drinking water. The main U.S. law governing water pollution is the Water Pollution Control Act, also known as the Clean Water Act. This law aims to restore or maintain the integrity of all surface water in the United States. It requires permits for most *point* sources of pollution, such as industrial emissions, and mandates that local and state governments develop plans for *nonpoint* sources, such as agricultural runoff or urban storm water. The Pesticide Control Act specifically restricts the use of dangerous pesticides, which can pollute groundwater. The quality of drinking water is regulated by another law, the Safe Drinking Water Act of 1974, amended in 1996. This law sets minimum standards for various contaminants in both public water systems and aquifers that supply drinking water wells.

[9] "BP to Pay $18/7 Billion for Deepwater Horizon Oil Spill," *The New York Times,* July 2, 2015. For an account of the environmental impact of the spill, see *Four Years Into the Gulf Oil Disaster: Still Waiting for Restoration* (National Wildlife Federation, April 8, 2014), *www.nwf.org.*

The impacts of hydraulic fracturing, a method for extracting natural gas from underground shale formations, on the quality of drinking water—and how these impacts should be regulated—is explored in the discussion case at the end of this chapter.

Land Pollution

The third major focus of environmental regulation is the contamination of land by both solid and hazardous waste. The United States produces an astonishing amount of solid waste, adding up to more than four pounds per person per day. Of this, 46 percent is recycled, composted, or incinerated, and the rest ends up in municipal landfills.[10] Many businesses and communities have tried to reduce the solid waste stream by establishing recycling programs.

> Sweden is one of the world's leaders in reducing solid waste. Astonishingly, less than 1 percent of the country's household waste ends up in landfills. Swedes sort their trash, separating paper, plastics, metal, glass, food waste, light bulbs, and batteries. All residential areas have convenient recycling stations, and special trucks pick up electronics and other hazardous waste. About half of these materials are recycled and reused in some way, and the other half are burned to generate energy. Sweden's waste incineration plants have become so efficient that the country routinely imports waste from its neighbors. Swedish companies have joined the effort, too; the retailer H&M, for example, accepts used clothing from customers in exchange for coupons. "Zero waste, that's our slogan," said the CEO of the Swedish Waste Management and Recycling Association.[11]
>
> The safe disposal of hazardous waste is a special concern. Several U.S. laws address the problem of land contamination by hazardous waste. The Resource Conservation and Recovery Act of 1976 (amended in 1984) regulates hazardous materials from "cradle to grave." The Toxic Substances Control Act (TSCA) of 1976 requires the EPA to inventory the thousands of chemicals in commercial use, identify which are most dangerous, and, if necessary, ban them or restrict their use. In 2014, an aging and rusty storage tank holding toxic chemicals used to wash coal leaked, spilling 7,500 gallons into the nearby Elk River near Charleston, West Virginia. Three hundred thousand people who relied on the river for their water supply were told not to drink or bathe with it for several weeks afterwards. (The owner of the tank, Freedom Industries, shortly afterwards declared bankruptcy and shut down.) This frightening incident led to calls to update the almost 40-year-old TSCA, but reform efforts failed in Congress. Several states, however, including West Virginia, passed new laws requiring the inspection of chemical storage tanks.[12]

As this example illustrates, states are able to pass regulations that are stricter than federal rules. (They can also regulate industries that do not engage in interstate commerce.)

Some studies have suggested that hazardous waste sites are most often located near economically disadvantaged African American, Hispanic, and Native American communities. Since 1994, the EPA has investigated whether state permits for hazardous waste sites violate civil rights laws and has blocked permits that appear to discriminate against minorities. The effort to prevent inequitable exposure to risk, such as from hazardous

---

[10] Environmental Protection Agency, "Municipal Solid Waste Generation, Recycling, and Disposal in the United States: Facts and Figures for 2012," *www.epa.gov/solidwaste.*

[11] "The Swedish Recycling Revolution," November 28, 2014, *https://sweden.se/nature/the-swedish-recycling-revolution/.*

[12] "A Year after West Virginia Chemical Spill, Some Signs of Safer Water," *National Geographic,* January 10, 2015; and "Chemical Spill Muddies Picture in a State Wary of Regulations," *The New York Times,* January 18, 2014.

waste, is sometimes referred to as the movement for **environmental justice**.[13] For example, Native American tribes in Utah, Nevada, and New Mexico have organized to block the construction of nuclear waste disposal facilities on their land, saying the facilities would threaten their health, culture, and economic viability.[14]

The major U.S. law governing the cleanup of existing hazardous waste sites is the Comprehensive Environmental Response, Compensation, and Liability Act, or **CERCLA**, popularly known as **Superfund**, passed in 1980. This law established a fund, supported primarily by a tax on petroleum and chemical companies that were presumed to have created a disproportionate share of toxic wastes. The EPA was charged with establishing a National Priority List of the most dangerous toxic sites; around 1,700 sites were eventually designated as Superfund sites. Where the original polluters could be identified, they would be required to pay for the cleanup; where they could not be identified or had gone out of business, the Superfund would pay.

> One of the largest hazardous waste sites on the Superfund list is an almost 200-mile long stretch of the Hudson River, extending from Hudson Falls, New York, to Manhattan. Over a period of three decades until the late 1970s, General Electric (GE) factories discharged an estimated 1.3 million pounds of PCBs, cancer-causing chemicals formerly used in electrical equipment, into the river. Since the company was responsible, it was required to supervise and pay for the cleanup. GE was set to complete dredging the riverbed to remove PCB-contaminated sediment, removing and treating the water it contained, and trucking the residue to a permitted landfill in 2015, but still had more work to do investigating possible contamination farther upriver. The cost to the company was expected eventually to reach around $2 billion.[15]

Remarkably, nearly one in six U.S. residents now lives within three miles of a Superfund site. But the government has been making progress; cleanup has been completed at 380 sites and is underway at 1,160 others.[16]

Alternative Policy Approaches

Governments can use a variety of policy approaches to control air, water, and land pollution. The most widely used method of regulation historically has been to impose environmental standards. Increasingly, however, government policymakers have relied more on market-based and voluntary approaches, rather than command and control regulations, to achieve environmental goals. These different approaches are discussed next.

Environmental Standards

The traditional method of pollution control is through **environmental standards**. Standard allowable levels of various pollutants are established by legislation or regulatory action and applied by administrative agencies and courts. This approach is also called **command and control regulation**, because the government commands business firms to comply with certain standards and often directly controls their choice of technology.

---

[13] Robert D. Bullard, "Environmental Justice in the 21st Century," Environmental Justice Resource Center, available at *www.ejrc.cau.edu/ejinthe21century.htm;* and Christopher H. Foreman, Jr., *The Promise and Perils of Environmental Justice* (Washington, DC: Brookings Institution, 2000).

[14] Nuclear Information and Resource Service, "Environmental Racism, Tribal Sovereignty, and Nuclear Waste," at *www.nirs.org.*

[15] "EPA Announces Agreement with GE to Further Investigate Upper Hudson River Floodplain," October 10, 2014, *http://yosemite.epa;* and "GE Says Completion of Hudson River Dredging Will Resolve Liabilities," *The Wall Street Journal,* December 27, 2013. The EPA posts regular reports on the progress of the cleanup at *www.epa.gov/hudson.*

[16] "Wasteland," *National Geographic,* December 2014.

One type of standard is an *environmental-quality standard.* In this approach a given geographical area is permitted to have no more than a certain amount or proportion of a pollutant in the air. Polluters, such as utilities and factories, are required to control their emissions to maintain the area's standard of air quality. For example, in 2014, the EPA issued new, more stringent standards for air concentrations of ground-level ozone, which the agency called the "most pervasive and widespread pollutant in the country."[17] A second type is an *emission standard.* For example, the law might specify that manufacturers could release into the air no more than 1 percent of the ash (a pollutant) they generated. Sometimes, the EPA mandates that companies use the *best available technology,* meaning a particular process that the agency determines is the best economically achievable way to reduce negative impacts on the environment.

Market-Based Mechanisms

In recent years, regulators have begun to move away from command and control regulation, favoring increased use of **market-based mechanisms**. This approach is based on the idea that the market is a better control than extensive standards that specify precisely what companies must do.

One approach that has become more widely used is to allow businesses to buy and sell the right to pollute, in a process known as **cap-and-trade**. The European Union's *tradable permit* program for carbon emissions, described in one of the opening examples of this chapter, illustrates this approach. The U.S. Clean Air Act of 1990 also incorporated the concept of tradable permits as part of its approach to pollution reduction. The law established emission levels (called "caps") and permitted companies with emissions *below* the cap to sell ("trade") their rights to the remaining permissible amount to firms that faced penalties because their emissions were above the cap. Over time, the government would reduce the cap, thus gradually reducing overall emissions, even though individual companies might continue to pollute above the cap. Companies could choose whether to reduce their emissions—for example, by installing pollution abatement equipment—or to buy allowances from others. One study showed that the tradable permit program for acid rain may have saved companies as much as $3 billion per year, by allowing them the flexibility to choose the most cost-effective methods of complying with the law.[18]

Another market-based type of pollution control is establishment of *emissions charges* or *fees.* Each business is charged for the undesirable waste that it emits, with the fee varying according to the amount of waste released. The result is, "The more you pollute, the more you pay." In this approach, polluting is not illegal, but it is expensive, creating an incentive for companies to clean up. In recent years, governments have experimented with a variety of so-called *green taxes* or *eco-taxes* that levy a fee on various kinds of environmentally destructive behavior. In addition to taxing bad behavior, governments may also offer various types of positive incentives to firms that improve their environmental performance. For example, it may decide to purchase only from those firms that meet a certain pollution standard, or offer aid to those that install pollution control equipment. Tax incentives, such as faster depreciation for pollution control equipment, also may be used. Governments may also levy eco-taxes on individuals.

Since 2008, for instance, auto registration fees in Ireland have been based on greenhouse gas emissions, with owners paying €104 to €2,100, depending how polluting their vehicle is. The eco-tax was designed to encourage people to buy cleaner cars. Other countries with similar programs include the Netherlands, Portugal,

---

[17] "E.P.A. Ozone Rules Divide Industry and Government," *The New York Times,* November 26, 2014.

[18] For more on the tradable permit system for acid rain, see *www.epa.gov/acidrain.*

Canada, Spain, and Finland. Germany has enacted eco-taxes on gasoline and electricity, with the intention of promoting energy efficiency.[19]

In short, the trend has been for governments to use more flexible, market-oriented approaches—tradable allowances, pollution fees and taxes, and incentives—to achieve environmental objectives where possible.

Information Disclosure

Another approach to reducing pollution is popularly known as *regulation by publicity,* or *regulation by embarrassment.* The government encourages companies to pollute less by publishing information about the amount of pollutants individual companies emit each year. In many cases, companies voluntarily reduce their emissions to avoid public embarrassment.

The major experiment in regulation by publicity has occurred in the area of toxic emissions to the air and water. The 1986 amendments to the Superfund law, called SARA, included a provision called the Community Right-to-Know Law, which required manufacturing firms to report, for a list of specified toxic chemicals, the amount on site, the number of pounds released, and how (if at all) these chemicals were treated or disposed of. The EPA makes this information available to the public in the *Toxics Release Inventory,* or *TRI,* published annually. Evidence shows that at least initially, reporting manufacturers in the United States cut their releases and disposal of these chemicals to the air, water, and land, apparently fearing negative publicity. Recently, however, the TRI numbers have begun to trend up—mostly reflecting toxic emissions from the metal mining industry.[20]

The advantages and disadvantages of alternative policy approaches to reducing pollution are summarized in Figure 10.2.

Civil and Criminal Enforcement

Companies that violate environmental laws are subject to stiff civil penalties and fines, and their managers can face prison if they knowingly or negligently endanger people or the environment. Proponents of this approach argue that the threat of fines and even imprisonment can be an effective deterrent to corporate outlaws who would otherwise degrade the air, water, or land. In 2014, the EPA brought criminal charges against 187 defendants. For example, in 2014 the environmental control manager of Tonawanda Coke was convicted of violations of environmental law and sentenced to one year in prison after he was found to have concealed the illegal release of gases containing dangerous benzene directly from coke ovens into the air.[21] Companies can also be charged, as the following example shows.

> In 2014, Anadarko Petroleum, an oil and gas exploration company, paid more than $5 billion to settle charges of widespread environmental contamination and to pay for cleanup. Anadarko had purchased Kerr-McGee, a company responsible for dumping radioactive uranium, rocket fuel, wood creosote, and other contaminants at 2,000 sites in 11 states over an 85-year period. Kerr-McGee had tried to spin off its environmental liabilities before selling its remaining assets to Anadarko, but the court had rejected that argument. "Today's settlement is a just resolution of an historic injustice to the American people and our environment," said one of the prosecutors.[22]

[19] Ireland's auto registration system is explained at *www.motortax.ie.*

[20] TRI data are available at *www2.epa.gov/toxics-release-inventory-tri-program.* Maps showing the geographical distribution of chemical releases reported under TRI are available at *http://toxmap.nlm.nih.gov.*

[21] "Enforcement Annual Results for FY 2014" and "Tonawanda Coke Gets One of the Largest Air Pollution Fines Levied at a Federal Criminal Trial," *www2.epa.gov/enforcement.*

[22] "United States Announces $5.15 Billion Settlement of Litigation Against Subsidiaries of Anadarko Petroleum Corp.," press release, U.S. Department of Justice, April 3, 2014.

FIGURE 10.2
Advantages and Disadvantages of Alternative Policy Approaches to Reducing Pollution

Policy Approach	Advantages	Disadvantages
Environmental standards	• Enforceable in the courts • Compliance mandatory	• Across-the-board standards not equally relevant to all businesses • Requires large regulatory apparatus • Older, less-efficient plants may be forced to close • Can retard innovation • Fines may be cheaper than compliance • Does not improve compliance once compliance is achieved
Market-based mechanisms		
Cap-and-trade systems	• Gives businesses more flexibility • Achieves goals at lower overall cost • Saves jobs by allowing some less-efficient plants to stay open • Permits the government and private organizations to buy allowances to take them off the market • Encourages continued improvement	• Gives business a license to pollute • Permit levels are hard to set • May cause regional imbalances in pollution levels • Enforcement is difficult.
Emissions fees and taxes	• Taxes bad behavior (pollution) rather than good behavior (profits)	• Fees are hard to set • Taxes may be too low to curb pollution
Government incentives	• Rewards environmentally responsible behavior • Encourages companies to exceed minimum standards	• Incentives may not be strong enough to curb pollution
Information disclosure	• Government spends little on enforcement • Companies able to reduce pollution in the most cost-effective way	• Does not motivate all companies
Civil and criminal enforcement	• May deter wrongdoing by firms and individuals	• May not deter wrongdoing if penalties and enforcement efforts are perceived as weak

European regulators and prosecutors have also actively pursued corporate environmental criminals. For example, the EU standardized its laws against marine pollution and raised maximum penalties after a series of oil tanker wrecks fouled the coasts of France, Spain, and Portugal. Europe is the world's largest importer of oil, and 90 percent is transported to the continent by seagoing ships.[23]

The U.S. Sentencing Commission, a government agency responsible for setting uniform penalties for violations of federal law, has established guidelines for sentencing environmental wrongdoers. Under these rules, penalties would reflect not only the severity of

[23] "The Community Framework for Cooperation in the Field of Accidental or Deliberate Marine Pollution," at *http://ec.europa.eu/echo/civil_protection/civil/marin/mp01_en_introduction.htm.*

the offense but also a company's demonstrated environmental commitment. Businesses that have an active compliance program, cooperate with government investigators, and promptly assist any victims would receive lighter sentences than others with no environmental programs or that knowingly violate the law. These guidelines provide an incentive for businesses to develop active compliance programs to protect themselves and their officers from high fines or even prison if a violation should occur.

Costs and Benefits of Environmental Regulation

One central issue of environmental protection is how costs are balanced by benefits. In the four decades or so since the modern environmental era began, the nation has spent a great deal to clean up the environment and keep it clean. Some have questioned the value choices underlying these expenditures, suggesting that the costs—lost jobs, reduced capital investment, and lowered productivity—exceeded the benefits. Others, in contrast, point to significant gains in the quality of life and to the economic payoff of a cleaner environment.

Businesses in the United States have invested heavily in environmental protection. According to the U.S. Census Bureau, in 2005, for example, manufacturing firms spent about $6 billion in capital expenditures (e.g., installing pollution controls) and about $21 billion in operating costs (e.g., paying for wages and supplies) to comply with environmental regulations. The industries that spent the most were chemicals, oil, and coal.[24] Business spending to comply with environmental regulation has diverted funds that might otherwise have been invested in new plants and equipment or in research and development, and strict rules have sometimes led to plant shutdowns and loss of jobs. Some regions and industries, in particular, have been hard hit by environmental regulation, especially those with high abatement costs, such as paper and wood products, chemicals, petroleum and coal, and primary metals. Inevitably, many of these costs are passed on to customers. On the other hand, emissions of nearly all pollutants have dropped significantly since the beginning of the modern environmental era. These improvements have benefited human health and the environment.

> For any particular regulation, weighing the costs and benefits—called a *regulatory impact analysis*—is mandated by law. For example, the EPA estimated that its recent regulations on ozone, mentioned earlier in this chapter, would cost businesses $15 billion in 2025, when the rule would be fully implemented (based on the middle of three possible scenarios). However, the estimated benefits were even bigger: $19 to $38 billion, the valuation the EPA calculated for fewer premature deaths, heart attacks, asthma attacks, and other adverse impacts on human health. Not surprisingly, reactions differed among stakeholders. "We're facing a series of regulations, and the cumulative cost of compliance . . . is significant," said the president of the American Chemistry Council, which had vigorously opposed the new rules. But the American Lung Association praised them, saying, "The science is clear. A more protective standard is needed to protect the health of millions of Americans breathing polluted air every day."[25]

[24] U.S. Census Bureau, "Pollution Abatement Costs and Expenditures: 2005." This survey, formerly conducted annually, has not been reissued since 2005.

[25] EPA, "Regulatory Impact Analysis of the Proposed Revisions to the National Ambient Air Quality Standards for Ground-Level Ozone," November 2014, *www.epa.gov;* "Health Professionals across the Nation Urge EPA to Finalize Most Protective Ozone Air Quality Standard," March 17, 2015, *www.lung.org;* and "EPA Ozone Rules Divide Industry and Environmentalists," *The New York Times,* November 26, 2014.

FIGURE 10.3
Costs and Benefits of Environmental Regulations

Costs	Benefits
• Manufacturers, mining companies, and utilities spend billions of dollars annually to comply with environmental regulations. • Some jobs are lost in particularly polluting industries. • Competitiveness of some capital-intensive, "dirty" industries is impaired.	• Emissions of pollutants drop. • Air and water quality improves; toxic-waste sites are cleaned up; and natural beauty is preserved or enhanced. • People live longer and healthier lives in less polluted environments.
• Consumers pay more when companies pass along increased costs of regulations.	• Jobs are created in the clean economy sector, such as environmental products and services, alternative energy, and tourism.

As this example illustrates, whether a particular regulation is worthwhile depends on the stakeholder's point of view, since its costs and benefits often accrue to different parties.

More broadly, environmental regulations stimulate some sectors of the economy. While jobs are lost in industries such as forest products and high-sulfur coal mining, others are created in areas like recycling, environmental consulting, wind turbine and solar panel production and installation, waste management equipment, and air pollution control. For example, operators of coal-fired power plants predicted that big required cuts in mercury emissions, adopted in 2012, would cost thousands of jobs. But trade groups said that the regulations could add 300,000 jobs a year through 2017 in companies that make equipment to reduce emissions.[26] Jobs are saved or created in industries such as fishing and tourism when natural areas are protected or restored. Moreover, environmental regulations can stimulate the economy by compelling businesses to become more efficient by conserving energy, and less money is spent on treating health problems caused by pollution.

Sectors of the economy that produce goods and services with an environmental benefit are known as the **clean economy**. In 2012, the U.S. government for the first time estimated the size of the clean economy, reporting that 3.1 million people (2.4 percent of the total number employed) were employed there. Three-quarters of these jobs were in the private sector. A similar study conducted by the Brookings Institution found that most "green jobs" were in mature industries, such as wastewater treatment and mass transit. But the fastest-growing segment of the clean economy was in the newer alternative energy industries such as wind energy, solar power, and the so-called smart grid (which used technology to deliver electricity more efficiently).[27]

Because of the complexity of these issues, economists differ on the net costs and benefits of environmental regulation. In some respects, government controls hurt the economy, and in other ways they help, as summarized in Figure 10.3. What is clear is that choices in the area of environmental regulation reflect underlying values, expressed in a democratic society through an open political process. Just how much a society is prepared to pay and how "clean" it wants to be are political choices, reflecting the give and take of diverse interests in a pluralistic society.

[26] "Regulations Create Jobs, Too," *Bloomberg Businessweek,* February 9, 2012.

[27] "A Tally of Green Jobs," *New York Times,* March 22, 2012; "Measuring Green Jobs," *www.bls.gov/green;* and "Sizing the Clean Economy: A National and Regional Green Jobs Assessment," July 13, 2011, *www.brookings.edu.*

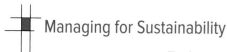

Managing for Sustainability

Environmental regulations, such as the laws governing clean air, water, and land described in this chapter, establish minimum legal standards that businesses must meet. Most companies try to comply with these regulations, if only to avoid litigation, fines, and, in the most extreme cases, criminal penalties. But many firms are now voluntarily moving beyond compliance to improve environmental performance in all areas of their operations and to manage proactively for sustainability. This section describes the stages of corporate environmental responsibility and discusses the organizational approaches companies have used to manage environmental issues effectively. The following section explains why managing for sustainability can improve a company's strategic competitiveness.

Stages of Corporate Environmental Responsibility

Although environmental issues are forcing all businesses to manage in new ways, not all companies are equally proactive in their response. One widely used model identifies three main stages of corporate environmental responsibility.

According to this model, companies pass through three distinct stages in sustainability management.[28] The first stage is *pollution prevention,* which focuses on "minimizing or eliminating waste before it is created." The second stage is *product stewardship.* In this stage, managers focus on "all environmental impacts associated with the full life cycle of a product," from the design of a product to its eventual use and disposal. HP, for example, has designed its laser printer ink cartridges so they can be refurbished and reused, and provides a mailing label for customers to return them free of charge. Finally, the third and most advanced stage is *clean technology,* in which businesses develop innovative new technologies that support sustainability—that actually provide environmental benefits, rather than simply prevent harm.

> General Electric, a company long associated with pollution, from building coal-fired power plants to dumping toxic chemicals in the Hudson River, took a dramatic turn in 2005. Jeffrey Immelt, the company's new CEO, announced a new strategy he dubbed "ecomagination." He pledged to double GE's investment in developing renewable energy, fuel cells, efficient lighting, water filtration systems, and cleaner jet engines. Immelt's reason was that clean technologies represented a huge commercial opportunity. "Increasingly for business," he said, "green is green." In 2013, the company reported that it had invested $12 billion in clean tech research and development and had earned $160 billion in revenues from its ecomagination portfolio of products and services; the following year, it committed to another $10 billion investment.[29]

Evidence suggests that many companies are now moving quickly toward the final stage in this model. Surveys of senior executives by McKinsey Global document a notable shift from 2012, when the main reason cited for addressing sustainability was to "improve operational efficiency and cut costs," to 2014, when the main reason cited was to "align with [the] company's business goals, mission, or values." The more recent report concluded that "sustainability is becoming a more strategic and integral part of their businesses."[30]

---

[28] Stuart Hart, "Beyond Greening: Strategies for a Sustainable World," *Harvard Business Review,* January–February 1997. All quotes in this paragraph are taken from this article. An alternative stage model may be found in Dexter Dunphy, Suzanne Benn, and Andrew Griffiths, *Organisational Change for Corporate Sustainability* (New York: Routledge, 2003).

[29] "GE 2013 Global Impact Report," *www.ge.com;* and "Natural Gas at Heart of GE's $10B Ecomagination Boost," February 24, 2014, *greentechmedia.com.*

[30] McKinsey Global, "Sustainability's Strategic Worth," July 2014.

The Ecologically Sustainable Organization

An **ecologically sustainable organization (ESO)** is a business that operates in a way that is consistent with the principle of sustainable development, as presented in Chapter 9. In other words, an ESO could continue its activities indefinitely, without altering the carrying capacity of the Earth's ecosystem. Such businesses would not use up natural resources any faster than they could be replenished or substitutes found. They would make and transport products efficiently, with minimal use of energy. They would design products that would last a long time and that, when worn out, could be disassembled and recycled. They would not produce waste any faster than natural systems could absorb and disperse it. They would work with other businesses, governments, and organizations to meet these goals.[31]

Of course, no existing business completely fits the definition of an ecologically sustainable organization. The concept is what social scientists call an ideal type; that is, a kind of absolute standard against which real organizations can be measured. A few visionary businesses, however, have embraced the concept and begun to try to live up to this ideal.

> One such business is Interface, a $1 billion company based in Atlanta, Georgia, that makes 40 percent of the world's commercial carpet tiles. In 1994, CEO Ray C. Anderson announced, to many people's surprise, that Interface would seek to become "the first sustainable corporation in the world." Anderson and his managers undertook hundreds of initiatives. For example, the company started a program by which customers could *lease,* rather than *purchase,* carpet tile. When tile wore out in high-traffic areas, Interface technicians would replace just the worn units, reducing waste. Old tiles would be recycled, creating a closed loop. The company later adopted a goal of "Mission Zero"—no negative impact on the environment—by 2020. Another initiative was to tag all products with a special label called an *environmental product declaration (EPD).* Similar to a nutrition label on packaged food, the third-party verified EPD listed the raw materials, energy use, emissions, and waste generation associated with each product, allowing Interface customers to make environmentally informed decisions. The company charted its sustainability progress on its website on a graphic superimposed on an image of Mount Everest.[32]

No companies, including Interface, have yet become truly sustainable businesses, and it will probably be impossible for any single firm to become an ESO in the absence of supportive government policies and a widespread movement among many businesses and other social institutions. However, many companies are demonstrating leadership in responding to environmental challenges. The next section will describe actions leading companies are taking now to operate their businesses as sustainably as possible.

Sustainability Management in Practice

Companies that have begun to move toward sustainability have learned that new structures, processes, and incentives are often needed.

An emerging role at many leading firms is the **chief sustainability officer (CSO).** The first such officer was appointed in 2004 at DuPont; a 2014 survey found 36 such officers at large U.S. firms. Most of these CSOs reported directly to the CEO or to an individual who did. They often supervised staffs of specialists and coordinated the work of managers across

---

[31] Mark Starik and Gordon P. Rands, "Weaving an Integrated Web: Multilevel and Multisystem Perspectives of Ecologically Sustainable Organizations," *Academy of Management Review,* October 1995.

[32] Interface's sustainability initiatives are described at *www.interfaceglobal.com/sustainability.* Ray Anderson's story is told in Ray C. Anderson with Robin White, *Business Lessons From a Radical Industrialist* (New York: St. Martin's Press, 2011).

many functional areas, including research and development, marketing, facilities, and supply chain management, whose work was related to the firm's sustainability mission.[33]

> An example is Rhonda Clark, appointed vice president of environmental affairs and chief sustainability officer at UPS in 2014. Clark, an engineer who had formerly managed the UPS Airlines facilities in Louisville, was put in charge of a cross-functional team responsible for a range of sustainability initiatives. Among other projects, they tested alternative-fuel and advanced technology vehicles and implemented software that enabled drivers to cover their routes more efficiently—and with lower carbon emissions. "It is just good common sense," Clark commented. "Once individuals as well as businesses understand the value proposition, sustainability will become a way of life."[34]

Sustainability managers reported that when they first took the job, they thought that the most important determinant of success would be their subject-matter expertise—how much they knew about pollutants, energy efficiency, regulations, and the like. But after serving in the position, these managers changed their minds, saying that interpersonal skills—being able to work effectively with people across the organization—were the most critical. "I think of myself and my team as chameleons," said AT&T's vice president of sustainability. "Being able to think and communicate in the same fashion as the business unit we're working with is, for me, the most important skill set needed to be successful."[35]

Chief sustainability officers may be based in departments with a variety of names, such as sustainability, citizenship, and corporate affairs. But wherever they are located, recent research shows that effective sustainability management shares a number of common characteristics:[36]

> *Top management commitment.* The most environmentally proactive companies almost all have CEOs and other top leaders with a strong espoused commitment to sustainability. Paul Polman, the CEO of Unilever, who was named sustainable business leader of the year in 2014, told an interviewer that a different executive team could come into the company, shut down all sustainability initiatives, wring out costs, and drive the share price up—at least in the short term. But he favored the long-term view. "I would like to be remembered for leaving the place a little bit better than I found it," he said. In 2014, more than a third of CEOs named sustainability as one of their top three strategic priorities.[37] Boards of directors have also become involved, setting environmental policies and taking responsibility for their implementation. For example, Prudential Financial, a financial services company that sells insurance as well as other products, now requires candidates for the board to have sustainability expertise.

> *Clear goals and metrics.* Another characteristic of leading companies is that they set measurable sustainability goals and regularly assess and report their performance. About a fifth of companies in a global survey recently reported doing so.[38] By setting specific goals, these firms hold themselves accountable (and allow their stakeholders to do so). A particularly dramatic example is the German sportswear firm Puma, one

[33] *CSO Back Story II: The Evolution of the Chief Sustainability Officer* (Weinreb Group, 2014).

[34] "Rhonda Clark: Chief Sustainability Officer and Vice President of Environmental Affairs," UPS press release, *www.pressroom.ups.com*, and "UPS Exec: Sustainability is All about Efficiency," *The Guardian*, October 23, 2014.

[35] "Making the Pitch: Selling Sustainability From *Inside* Corporate America," VOX Global, Weinreb Group, and NetImpact, 2012.

[36] Data in this section are drawn from "Gaining Ground: Corporate Progress on the CERES Roadmap for Sustainability 2014," *www.ceres.org*, unless otherwise noted. The CERES study was based on a survey of executives of 613 companies, representing 80 percent of the total market capitalization of all publicly traded companies in the United States.

[37] McKinsey and Co., "Sustainability's Strategic Worth," July 2014.

[38] The Economist Intelligence Unit, "New Business Models: Shared Value in the 21st Century," October, 2014.

of the first firms to release an environmental profit-and-loss statement, covering all significant environmental impacts from the production of raw materials to the final sale. After the company learned that most adverse impacts occurred during the production of raw materials, it introduced new products made from recycled content or that could themselves be recycled.[39]

Employee engagement. Sustainability leaders have found they are most effective when they involve line managers and employees from across the organization in the process of change. The CSO of the software firm CA Technologies commented in a blog post, "Finding ways to engage employees in the process of improving corporate sustainability was a must or meaningful change would be limited. Our internal sustainability motto quickly became 'Driven from the top down, energized from the bottom up.'" The company gives "green star" awards to individuals and teams that go "above and beyond" to meet sustainability goals.[40] In 2014, 40 percent of U.S. companies had programs in place to engage employees on sustainability issues.[41]

Alignment of rewards and incentives. Businesspeople are most likely to consider the environmental impacts of their actions when their organizations acknowledge and reward this behavior. The most sustainable organizations tie the compensation of their managers, including line managers, to environmental achievement and take steps to recognize these achievements publicly. In 2014, 24 percent of U.S. companies linked executive compensation to sustainability metrics, up from 15 percent just two years earlier. (Only three percent of companies, however, linked pay to meeting goals that went beyond legal and regulatory requirements.) For example, at Xcel Energy, a utility that is a leading supplier of wind power, a portion of the CEO's bonus was linked to meeting specific sustainability goals set annually by the board, including reductions in energy use by customers.

Environmental Auditing and Reporting

As noted earlier, leading companies not only organize themselves to achieve sustainability goals; they also closely track their progress toward meeting them. Chapter 3 introduced the concept of corporate social reporting and presented evidence on what proportion of companies report results to their stakeholders. In the 1990s, in a parallel development, many companies began to audit their environmental performance. More recently, many firms have moved to integrate their social and environmental reporting into a single **sustainability report**. In 2013, as reported in Chapter 3, 93 percent of the world's largest companies issued a corporate responsibility report; most of these covered both social and environmental issues. A much smaller proportion, however—only about 10 percent—integrated social, environmental, *and* financial data in a single document. This is called **triple bottom line** reporting. Bottom line refers, of course, to the figure at the end of a company's financial statement that summarizes its earnings, after expenses. Triple bottom line reporting occurs when companies report to stakeholders not just their financial results—as in the traditional annual report to shareholders—but also their environmental and social impacts.[42]

An example of a company that has undertaken a fully audited, integrated report is Novozymes, a Danish biotechnology firm. The company produced its first

[39] For information about Puma's Environmental Profit & Loss Account and other sustainability initiatives, see *www.puma.com.*

[40] "Sustainability and Employee Engagement: A Win–Win for Business" [blog], March 15, 2012, at *http://community.ca.com/blogs.*

[41] John Davies, "Sustainability and Employee Engagement: The State of the Art," September 2014, at *www.greenbiz.com.*

[42] *KPMG International Survey of Corporate Responsibility Reporting 2013,* at *www.kpmg.com.*

environmental report in 1993 and its first combined social and environmental report six years later. Since 2002, it has produced a single report to stakeholders that integrates its financial, social, and environmental results. The company acknowledges the challenge of preparing a single report "in accordance with more than one set of rules and guidelines," but says that the process improves transparency and accurately reflects its commitment to sustainability.[43]

As discussed earlier in Chapter 3, the movement to audit and report on social and environmental performance—and to integrate these efforts with financial auditing and reporting—has gained momentum in recent years in many regions of the world.

Environmental Partnerships

Many businesses that are seeking to become more sustainable have formed voluntary, collaborative partnerships with environmental organizations and regulators to achieve specific objectives, as illustrated by the Google Earth Outreach example at the beginning of this chapter. These collaborations, called **environmental partnerships**, draw on the unique strengths of the different partners to improve environmental quality or conserve resources.[44]

> Starbucks Corporation is the largest coffeehouse company in the world, with almost 22,000 stores in 66 countries. For more than 15 years, the company has partnered with Conservation International (CI) to promote coffee farming methods that protect biodiversity, mitigate climate change, and reduce harm from pesticides and fertilizers. For example, in Chiapas, Mexico, and Sumatra, Indonesia, the partners have worked with local farmers to develop coffee varieties that thrive in the shade of native trees, conserving habitat and sequestering carbon. The company has also worked with CI to develop a set of purchasing guidelines based on sustainability and has committed to paying a premium price to suppliers who meet the standards. Conservation International noted that it viewed Starbucks "as a natural partner to our work because of shared geographies: most of the world's key coffee-growing regions are the same areas where biological diversity is richest and most threatened."[45]

Sustainability Management as a Competitive Advantage

Some researchers believe that by moving toward sustainability, business firms gain a competitive advantage. That is, relative to other firms in the same industry, companies that proactively manage environmental issues will tend to be more successful than those that do not. Effective sustainability management confers a competitive advantage in five different ways, as follows.[46]

[43] Novozymes' website and integrated reports are at *http://novozymes.com/en*. For a full discussion of the movement toward triple bottom line reporting, see Robert G. Eccles and Michael P. Krzus, *The Integrated Reporting Movement: Meaning, Momentum, Motives, and Materiality* (Hoboken, NJ: John Wiley & Sons, 2014).

[44] Dennis A. Rondinelli and Ted London, "How Corporations and Environmental Groups Cooperate," *Academy of Management Executive* 17, no. 1 (2003).

[45] The partnership's progress can be followed at *www.conservation.org/partners/Pages/starbucks* and *www.starbucks.com/responsibility/sourcing/coffee*.

[46] Daniel C. Esty and Andrew S. Winston, *Green to Gold: How Smart Companies Use Environmental Strategy to Innovate, Create Value, and Build Competitive Advantage* (New Haven, CT: Yale University Press, 2006); and Sanjay Sharma and J. Alberto Aragon-Correa, eds., *Corporate Environmental Strategy and Competitive Advantage* (Northampton, MA: Edgar Elgar Academic Publishing, 2005).

Exhibit 10.B

Greening the Built Environment

For most companies, their buildings—the offices, factories, stores, and warehouses where their employees work—account for a huge share of their overall environmental impact. The U.S. Energy Information Administration has estimated that commercial buildings and industrial facilities together account for almost half of the nation's energy consumption (the rest comes from transportation and residential use). Many companies have realized that improving operating efficiencies in their real estate holdings can yield tremendous savings, as well as reduce their environmental footprint.

One approach is to design buildings from the ground up to conserve resources both in their construction and use. The U.S. Green Building Council has developed a certification process called LEED (Leadership in Energy and Environmental Design) for both new and retrofitted buildings. Adopting these standards has brought companies many benefits. For example, Adobe, the maker of digital authoring tools, owns five LEED-certified buildings, including its corporate headquarters in San Jose, California, which was completely retrofitted. Adobe introduced scores of improvements—from motion sensors that turned off lights when people left their offices to landscape irrigation linked to weather satellites, so sprinklers did not operate when it was raining. The improvements cost a total of $1.4 million, but saved Adobe $1.2 million per year. "I was one of the naysayers saying, no, green costs money, it doesn't save money. [But] once I started seeing the cost savings, [I jumped] right up on that bandwagon . . . because it works," said the company's director of global facilities services.

Sources: Rocky Mountain Institute, "Adobe Systems Corporate Headquarters" [case study], at *http://bet.rmi.org/files/case-studies/adobe/adobe_systems.pdf;* "Green Building for a Profitable Future," *http://bet.rmi.org/rmi-news/green-building-for-a-profitable-future.html;* and U.S. Energy Information Administration, "Annual Energy Outlook 2012," at *www.eia.gov.* The website of the U.S. Green Building Council is *www.usgbc.org.*

Cost Savings

Companies that reduce pollution and hazardous waste, reuse or recycle materials, and operate with greater efficiency can reap significant cost savings. An example is Subaru's automobile assembly plant in Lafayette, Indiana, which has gone to great lengths to reduce waste, saving a great deal of money in the process.

> Subaru's Indiana factory has achieved its goal of "zero waste": it sends no waste at all to landfills. The company returns packaging materials—including the styrofoam used to protect engines in transit—to suppliers, to be used again. Cafeteria scraps go to a nearby waste-to-energy power plant. The company processes and reuses solvent and oil. Dried paint sludge is shipped to other companies that use it to make railroad ties, parking lot bumpers, and bicycle helmets. Leftover metal slag goes to a company that extracts the copper it contains. These initiatives not only reduce the plant's environmental impact, they also save the company more than $2 million a year.[47]

Many companies have found they are able to obtain significant cost savings by more efficiently managing their real estate portfolios. How some companies have managed the built environment to save money and improve their environmental performance is described in Exhibit 10.B. One company that has benefited from this trend is Autodesk, a maker of software for architects and other designers. The company has developed specialized software that enables architects to calculate the energy and water usage of proposed designs, and to make the most efficient use of daylight and shadows. "I think [sustainability] is one of single biggest problems we face as a civilization," said Autodesk CEO Carl Bass. "We are trying to give people better tools to make better decisions."[48]

[47] "Inside Subaru's Zero Waste Factory," December 30, 2013, at *www.takepart.com.* The website of Subaru Industries of America is at *www.subaru-sia.com.*

[48] "Carl Bass: Environmentalist, Craftsman, CEO," February 9, 2012, at *www.greenbiz.com.* Autodesk's sustainable building design software is described at *http://usa.autodesk.com/ecotect-analysis.*

Brand Differentiation

Companies that develop a reputation for environmental excellence distinguish their brand and attract like-minded customers. Sustainable products and services can attract environmentally aware customers. For example, shoppers might select cell phones with power-saving features, such as "unplug charger" reminders, or cleaning products formulated with ingredients that are not environmentally harmful. Services can also be marketed based on their environmental attributes, as the following example illustrates.

> One company that has benefited from its repuation for sustainability is Intrepid Travel. Founded in Australia in 1989, the tour operator now offers itineraries for adventurous travelers on seven continents. Early on, Intrepid Travel embraced the principle of sustainable development and committed to reducing its environmental footprint, so its travel destinations could be enjoyed for many generations to come. The company employed local guides, used public transit, offset the carbon emissions of its air travel, and gave back to local communities through its foundation. In the past 10 years, the company has grown at an annual compound rate of 25 percent. Said one of the company's founders: "We became known as a responsible company, and responsible travel became a selling feature for Intrepid."[49]

In general, promoting particular products or services based on their environmental attributes, a practice sometimes known as *green marketing,* has not been particularly effective. Evidence shows that most consumers select products and services based on price, convenience, and quality—not "greenness." No specific eco-labeled product has captured more than 2 percent of its market. However, what consumers *do* respond to is a company's overall reputation for environmental responsibility and the credibility of its communications with stakeholders. Joel Makower, an expert on environmental marketing, concluded that "It's at the company or brand level that this [environmental marketing] makes sense: Why offer a few good, eco-labeled products if the organization behind them is headed in the wrong direction?" In his view, consumers generally do not seek out "green" products, but they do buy from companies they perceive as responsible.[50]

Technological Innovation

Environmentally proactive companies are often technological leaders, as they seek imaginative new methods for reducing pollution and increasing efficiency. In many cases, they produce innovations that can win new customers, penetrate new markets, or even be marketed to other firms as new regulations spur their adoption.

> IBM's semiconductor chip-making plant in Burlington, Vermont, uses vast quantities of ultrapure water to clean its products. The water bill for this single facility has been as high as $10,000 *a day.* To reduce costs, IBM managers devised an elaborate system of electronic sensors to track the movement of water at every point and used the data to drive greater efficiencies—nearly doubling the "water productivity" of the plant over 10 years. "We did fifty different things," reported the plant's operation manager. "Angles of usage, treatment, energy capture, using less pump capacity, capturing internal pressure that comes with the water in the line—fifty different things." In the process, IBM had the startling revelation that it had done more than

---

[49] Geoff Manchester, "Why We Must Act Now on Sustainability," May 1, 2014 [blog post], at *www.travelweekly.com.au.* For Intrepid Travel's reports on its progress on sustainability, see *www.intrepidtravel.com/rb-our-progress-sustainability-policy.*

[50] Joel Makower, "Five Reasons Green Marketing is Going Nowhere," March 12, 2013, *www.linkedin.com.*

save money on water; it had created an entirely new business of consulting with other firms on how to do the same thing. The head of IBM's "Big Green Innovations" project told a reporter, "We think there is a big business opportunity around managing water."[51]

Reduction of Regulatory and Liability Risk

Another benefit for companies that are proactive with respect to their environmental impacts is that they are often better positioned than their competitors to respond to new government mandates. For example, when new rules went into effect in Europe in 2006 that banned all electronics products that included six toxic substances, including lead, cadmium, and mercury, companies that had learned how to make their products free of these substances prior to the ban suddenly had a big advantage in winning European accounts. More recently, when the United Kingdom announced that all large British companies would be required to report annually on their greenhouse gas emissions, the companies that had taken earlier steps to measure and report on carbon voluntarily were better prepared for compliance.[52] Similarly, proactively managing for sustainability can avoid expensive fines and lawsuits, such as those experienced by Anadarko, in the example mentioned earlier in this chapter.[53]

Strategic Planning

Companies that cultivate a vision of sustainability must adopt sophisticated strategic planning techniques to allow their top managers to assess the full range of the firm's effects on the environment. The complex auditing and forecasting techniques used by these firms help them anticipate a wide range of external influences on the firm, not just ecological influences. Wide-angle planning helps these companies foresee trends—new markets, materials, technologies, and products. For example, Toyota, well known for its ability to anticipate market trends, was among the first to produce a commercially successful hybrid vehicle, the Prius. As U.S. car makers struggled—and some went into bankruptcy—in the deep recession of the late 2000s, Toyota fared relatively well. The same sophisticated planning that enabled Toyota to weather the recession had also contributed to its ability to meet the public's increased interest in less-polluting, more-efficient transportation.[54] The McKinsey survey mentioned earlier in this chapter found that 57 percent of executives said that their companies had integrated sustainability into their strategic planning process.[55]

Figure 10.4 lists the companies viewed by a panel of experts as the world's leaders in integrating sustainability into their business strategy.

If managing for sustainability confers a competitive advantage, it follows that it should have a measurable impact on financial performance. Scholars have begun to study this relationship. A comprehensive examination of almost two decades of data on U.S. companies by Robert Eccles and colleagues at the Harvard Business School concluded that "high-sustainability firms" significantly outperformed others, as measured by both financial and

[51] Charles Fishman, *The Big Thirst: The Secret Life and Turbulent Future of Water* (New York: Free Press, 2011), Chapter 5, "Money in the Pipes."

[52] "A Consensus on Carbon Reporting," *The Guardian (U.K.),* September 26, 2013.

[53] "U.K. to Mandate CO_2 Reporting for Largest Corporations," June 20, 2012, *www.greenbiz.com.*

[54] Information on Toyota's sustainability initiatives is at *www.toyota.co.jp/en/environment.*

[55] The Business of Sustainability: McKinsey Global Survey Results," October 2011, at *www.mckinsey.com/insights.quarterly.com.*

FIGURE 10.4   Corporate Leaders in Integrating Sustainability into Their Business Strategy

Question: *What specific companies do you think are leaders in integrating sustainability into their business strategy?*

Source: Globe Scan/SustainAbility, *The 2015 Sustainability Leaders,* p. 13. Based on a survey of 816 qualified sustainability experts from government, NGOs, academia, corporations, and the media from 82 countries. Respondents were asked to list a maximum of three companies. The numbers shown are the percentage of respondents who named that particular company. Used by permission.

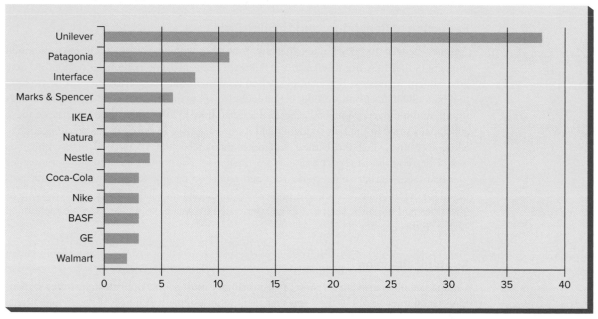

stock market returns.[56] The most recent work on this topic has focused on **material sustainability issues**. To explain, the term *material* in financial reporting refers to issues that are relevant to evaluating a firm's financial condition; the law requires that firms report to investors and the public not *all* information, but *material* information. In the same way, material sustainability issues refer to those that are particularly relevant to an evaluation of a particular company or industry's sustainability management. For example, greenhouse gas emissions are highly material in the transportation industry, but of lower materiality in the financial services industry. Building on this concept, recent research shows that firms with good performance on material sustainability issues significantly outperform firms with poor performance on these issues.[57]

A theme of this chapter is that achieving a sustainable economy and society will require a collaborative effort among government, business, and civil society. The U.S. government, like that of many other countries, has adopted many environmental laws and regulations constraining business behavior. These are critically important, as they assure that minimum standards are met by all. But many proactive companies are moving beyond compliance, recognizing that operating sustainably will help them become more competitive in the global marketplace by cutting costs, attracting environmentally aware customers, spurring innovation, reducing regulatory and liability risk, and encouraging long-range strategic planning. Recent research shows that managing for sustainability pays off for companies in the long run.

[56] Robert G. Eccles, Ioannis Ioannou, and George Serafeim, "The Impact of a Corporate Sustainability on Organizational Processes and Performance," *Management Science* 60(11), 2014.

[57] Mozaffar Khan, George Serafeim, and Aaron Yoon, "Corporate Sustainability: First Evidence on Materiality," Harvard Business School Working Paper, 2015.

Summary

- Government environmental laws and regulations focus on protecting the ecological health of the air, water, and land, and limiting the amount of pollution that companies may emit.

- Environmental laws have traditionally been of the command and control type, specifying standards and results. New laws, in both the United States and Europe, have added market incentives to induce environmentally sound behavior.

- Environmental laws have brought many benefits. Air, water, and land pollution levels are in many cases lower than in 1970. A continuing challenge is to find ways to promote a clean environment and sustainable business practices without impairing the competitiveness of the U.S. economy.

- Companies pass through three distinct stages in the development of green management practices. Many businesses are now moving from lower to higher stages. An ecologically sustainable organization is one that operates in a way that is consistent with the principle of sustainable development.

- Effective environmental management requires an integrated approach that involves all parts of the business organization, including top leadership, sustainability managers, and employees in many functional areas, as well as strong partnerships with stakeholders and effective auditing.

- Many companies have found that proactive environmental management can confer a competitive advantage by saving money, attracting customers, promoting innovation, reducing regulatory risk, and developing skills in strategic planning. Emerging evidence shows a positive relationship between sustainability practices and stock market and financial performance.

Key Terms

acid rain, *209*
cap-and-trade, *213*
chief sustainability officer (CSO), *219*
clean economy, *217*
command and control regulation, *212*
ecologically sustainable organization (ESO), *219*

environmental justice, *212*
environmental partnerships, *222*
Environmental Protection Agency (EPA), *207*
environmental standards, *212*
market-based mechanisms, *213*

material sustainability issues *226*
Superfund (CERCLA), *212*
sustainability report, *221*
triple bottom line, *221*

Internet Resources

www.epa.gov	Environmental Protection Agency
www.envirolink.org	Environmental organizations and news
www.GreenBiz.com	Green Business Network
www.sustainablebusiness.com	Network of sustainable small businesses
www.environmentalleader.com	Briefing for executives
www.sustainability.com	SustainAbility (consultancy)
www.sustainablog.org	Blogs on green and sustainable businesses
www.theguardian.com/us/sustainable-business	*The Guardian* [newspaper] coverage of sustainable business

Discussion Case: *Hydraulic Fracturing—Can the Environmental Impacts Be Reduced?*

Hydraulic fracturing—or *fracking,* as it is sometimes known—has been called the gold rush of the 21st century because so many companies and people are rushing to make their fortunes by extracting oil and natural gas from underground shale formations. What are the environmental impacts of fracking, and what can business, government, and society do to reduce them?

In recent years, technology has evolved to make possible the economic extraction of crude oil and natural gas from vast underground shale formations. In hydraulic fracturing, a vertical well is drilled as deep as 7,000 feet before turning horizontally into the oil- or gas-bearing layer. Operators then pump in vast quantities of water, sand, and chemicals under high pressure to break up the shale and release hydrocarbons, which are then brought back up the drill hole. By rotating the horizontal turns in successive passes, a single well can reach a large area underground.

The growth of hydraulic fracturing in the United States in recent years has been astonishing. In 2014, more than 1 million oil and gas wells were operating in 36 states. The biggest fracking booms were underway in several shale formations: the Baaken (North Dakota), Marcellus (Pennsylvania, West Virginia, New York, Ohio, and Maryland), and Barnett (Texas).

Hydraulic fracking has a number of benefits. In 2012, the United States became the leading natural gas producer in the world, overtaking Russia, and is predicted to become the leading oil producer, overtaking Saudi Arabia, within the next few years. At current rates of growth, the United States will be energy self-sufficient by 2030. The fracking boom has created jobs, tax revenue, and royalties to property owners who lease their mineral rights. Natural gas burns cleaner than either coal or oil, providing a possible bridge to a future economy based on renewable energy.

But fracking also carries serious environmental risks. Trucks and heavy equipment cause noise and air pollution in and around drilling sites. The process uses vast quantities of water—at least 250 billion gallons since 2005, according to some estimates—depleting supplies available for drinking and irrigation. Chemicals injected underground include a host of toxins. Fluid that returns to the surface—called *flowback*—is often further contaminated by radioactive substances, heavy metals, and volatile organic compounds from deep in the earth. Improper disposal of this wastewater can contaminate land, wells, and rivers—and even cause earthquakes. Methane can be released at multiple stages in the fracking process, powerfully contributing to climate change. Wildlife habitat is destroyed as forests and fields give way to industrial drilling sites.

In 2015, the Department of the Interior issued new regulations governing hydraulic fracturing on public and tribal lands. The new regulations required companies to disclose the chemicals they used and set stricter rules for the storage and disposal of wastewater, among other provisions. States, which had jurisdiction over fracking on private and state-owned land, had taken a wide range of approaches. At one extreme, two states—Vermont and New York—had banned fracking outright. In announcing the decision, the health commissioner of New York said, "The potential risks are too great. In fact, they are not even known." At the other extreme, government oversight in North Dakota—site of a huge oil boom—was considered highly permissive; in fact, the state's top environmental regulator described himself on a radio show as "not a regulations guy." Some states had charted a middle course; California, for example, implemented regulations in 2015 that allowed fracking but required strict monitoring of groundwater and air quality near wells.

As the practice of hydraulic fracturing spread, some companies experimented with new technologies to extract oil and gas with less environmental damage. Halliburton developed solar-powered storage silos and natural gas–fueled pumps, reducing on-site emissions. Southwestern Energy installed infrared cameras to detect fugitive methane emissions, so leaks could be plugged. General Electric tested a system that enabled water to be treated and reused on site, and GasFrac, a Canadian company, introduced a fracking method that used no water at all.

Said a professor who studied these trends, "[It is] the same as with any industry—if you come out with a game-changing technology, you can get in the market first and ride that."

Sources: "New Federal Rules are Set for Fracking," *The New York Times,* March 20, 2015; "Citing Health Risks, Cuomo Bans Fracking in New York State," *The New York Times,* December 17, 2014; "The Downside of the Boom," [series of articles], *The New York Times,* various dates starting November 22, 2014; "American Power and the Fracking Boom," October 1, 2014, *www.aljazeera.com;* "Fracking the USA: New Map Shows 1 Million Oil, Gas Wells," March 27, 2014, *www.climatecentral.org;* "Green Fracking? 5 Technologies for Cleaner Shale Energy," *National Geographic,* March 21, 2014; Environment America Research and Policy Center, "Fracking by the Numbers: Key Impacts of Dirty Drilling at the State and National Level," October 2013. Maps showing the distribution of fracking wells in the United States are available online at *www.fractracker.org/map.*

Discussion Questions

1. What is hydraulic fracturing, or fracking, and what are its costs and benefits?
2. Using the classification system presented in this chapter, what type(s) of pollution is (are) generated by fracking?
3. Using the classification system presented in this chapter, what type(s) of government regulation has (have) been used to address the concerns you identified in question 1, and which do you think would be most effective?
4. What are the benefits to companies of moving beyond compliance and developing more sustainable methods of fracking?
5. What factors might influence a company to use more or less environmentally responsible methods of fracking?

PART FIVE

Business and Technology

CHAPTER ELEVEN

The Role of Technology

Technology is an unmistakable economic and social force in both business and the world where we live. Global and local communications, business exchanges, the science that affects the quality of our lives, and the simple tasks that make up our daily lives are all significantly influenced by technology. Whether we are at home, in school, or in the workplace, emerging technological innovations have dramatically changed how we live, play, learn, work, and interact with others, raising important social and ethical questions for business.

This Chapter Focuses on These Key Learning Objectives:

LO 11-1   Defining technology and its characteristics.

LO 11-2   Recognizing how technology has evolved throughout history and what fuels technological innovation today.

LO 11-3   Analyzing and assessing how technology impacts organizations and individuals in society.

LO 11-4   Recognizing the benefits, as well as the ethical and social challenges, that arise from technological breakthroughs in science and medicine.

LO 11-5   Examining how technological innovations change the way organizations operate.

LO 11-6   Evaluating the emerging ethical challenges raised by the increased presence of technology in our lives.

In 2014, flooding devastated the Kashmir region in South Asia. Thousands of residents were presumed hurt and in need to medical treatment, and even more were stranded and required assistance. Rescue efforts were hampered since floodwaters inundated ground-floor equipment rooms for most of the region's telecommunication service providers, crashing cellular telephone networks across the state. Local officials had no way to contact the federal government, or one another, or the military troops in charge of rescue operations. Though the army had satellite phones, they were of little help without knowing where people were waiting for rescue. There was only one place where information was flowing—and that was on social media. The relief forces turned to Twitter and other social media networks and began to screen the tens of thousands of messages being posted to identify where people most urgently needed emergency assistance. In a near communications vacuum, 3G Internet connections remained usable and enabled more than 130,000 people to be rescued from the flood zone.[1]

Even a few years earlier, these dramatic rescues would have been impossible. But mobile phones and the cellular networks that supported them had spread rapidly across South Asia, even into remote rural areas, connecting people as never before. In the past two or three decades, the rate of technology change has been extraordinary, encompassing the wireless revolution, the ability to process enormous amounts of data, and smart manufacturing. Today, processing power and data storage are virtually free in the cloud, and a simple handheld iPhone has the same computing power as the room-sized IBM mainframe computer of the 1970s. Utilizing new materials—such as metal alloys, graphene (instead of silicon) transistors, and meta-metals that possess properties not found in nature—will enable engineers to design and build from the molecular level, radically improving quality and reducing waste. The wireless revolution enables billions of people to communicate, socialize, and trade in real time. How we embrace and use technology is also changing dramatically.

Technology is a major factor in our lives, helping us communicate with others around the world and across town, providing new opportunities for business to promote its activities, and improving the quality of our lives. But what are the consequences of the extraordinarily rapid pace of technological change? Has technology replaced human contact and, if so, what are the consequences of this change in how we relate to others? Who decides what technology should emerge and dramatically affect our lives? Should businesses be allowed to use technology freely or should there be some constraints on its use by business? Who should determine what these constraints are?

Technology Defined

Technology is a broad term referring to the practical applications of science and knowledge to commercial and organizational activities. The dominant feature of technology is *change and then more change.* As discussed at the beginning of this chapter, new technological breakthroughs are again changing our lives. Sometimes the pace of change is so fast and furious that it approaches the limits of human tolerance, and people lose their ability to cope with it successfully. Although technology is not the only cause of change in society, it is a primary cause. It is either directly or indirectly involved in most changes that occur in society, as noted in a recent article in *Foreign Affairs:*

---

[1] "Embrace of Social Media Aids Flood Victims in Kashmir," *The New York Times,* September 12, 2014, *www.nytimes.com.*

"Technology has spcd globalization forward, dramatically lowering communication and transaction costs and moving the world much closer to a single, large global market for labor, capital, and other inputs to production. Even though labor is not fully mobile, the other factors increasingly are. As a result, the various components of global supply chains can move to labor's location with little friction or cost."[2]

Another feature of technology is that *its effects are widespread,* reaching far beyond the immediate point of technological impact in unpredictable ways. Technology ripples through society until every community is affected by it.

A final feature of technology is that it is *self-reinforcing.* As stated by Alvin Toffler, "Technology feeds on itself. Technology makes more technology possible."[3] This self-reinforcing feature means that technology acts as a multiplier to encourage its own faster development. It acts with other parts of society so that an invention in one place leads to a sequence of inventions in other places. Thus, invention of the microprocessor led rather quickly to successful generations of the modern computer, which led to new banking methods, electronic mail, bar-code systems, global tracking systems, and so on.

Phases of Technology in Society

Six broad phases of technology have developed, as shown in Figure 11.1. Societies have tended to move sequentially through each phase, beginning with the lowest technology and moving higher with each step, so the six phases roughly represent the progress of civilization throughout history. The first phase was the nomadic-agrarian, in which people hunted wild animals for meat and gathered wild plants for food. The second was the agrarian, corresponding with the domestication of animals and plants. The first two used manual labor exclusively. The third was the industrial, characterized by the development of powered machinery, first in the textile industry and later in many other forms of manufacturing. The fourth was the service phase, marked by the rise of service industries and intellectual labor. The fifth was the **information phase**. This phase emphasized the use and transfer of knowledge and information rather than manual skill. Businesses of all sizes, including the smallest firms, explored the benefits of the information age through the availability of nanotechnology and similar inventions. These inventions catapulted societies into **cyberspace**, where information is stored, ideas are described, and communication takes place in and through an electronic network of linked systems. The technology developed in this age provided the mechanisms for more information to be produced in a decade than in the previous 1,000 years.

The **semantic phase**, which began around 2000, saw the development of processes and systems to enable organizations and people to navigate through the expanding amount of links and information available on the Internet. Search engines, such as Google, employed massive clusters of computers to analyze the *metadata* or descriptive information embedded within web pages, documents, and files. A Google search for a specific airline flight, for example, might return links to a flight tracking website, an estimated time of departure or arrival for that day's flight, weather forecasts, and airport maps. Social interaction is an important part of the semantic phase. Services such as Facebook, Twitter and, LinkedIn analyzed the transactions and metadata from each user's activity to suggest new contacts, entertainment, and links.[4]

---

[2] Erik Brynjolfsson, Andrew McAfee, and Michael Spence, "New World Order: Labor, Capital, and Ideas in the Power Law Economy," *Foreign Affairs,* July/August 2014, *www.foreignaffairs.com.*

[3] Alvin Toffler, *Future Shock* (New York: Bantam, 1971), p. 26.

[4] Tim Berners-Lee, James Hendler, and Ora Lassila, "The Semantic Web," *Scientific American,* May 2001, *www.scientificamerican.com.*

FIGURE 11.1   **Phases in the Development of Technology**

Technology Level	Phases in the Development of Technology	Approximate Period	Activity	Primary Skill Used
1	Nomadic-agrarian	Until 1650	Harvesting	Manual
2	Agrarian	1650–1900	Planting and harvesting	Manual
3	Industrial	1900–1960	Building material goods	Manual and machine
4	Service	1960–1975	Providing services	Manual and intellectual
5	Information	1975–2000	Thinking and designing	Intellectual and electronic
6	Semantic	2000–today	Relevance and context	Intellectual and networking

Where will technology head next? Some observers have suggested that society is now at the beginning of a new phase dominated by *biotechnology*. **Biotechnology** is a technological application that uses biological systems or living organisms to make or modify products or processes for specific use. Its applications are common in agriculture, food science, and medicine. This emerging phase of technology extends beyond the design and analysis of information to the manipulation of organisms that produce fabricated products or act as components within a computer network.

Fueling Technological Growth

As Figure 11.1 demonstrates, in recent decades the pace of technological change has accelerated, and the time lapse between phases has dramatically shortened. Various government and corporate programs are fueling these developments.

Government: Government investment has helped launch many new technologies, including the Internet, and these trends continue.

In 2012, President Obama unveiled the Big Data R&D Initiative and committed more than $200 million in new funding to "improve our ability to extract knowledge and insights from large and complex collections of digital data." Numerous government agencies were involved in this project, including the White House Office of Science and Technology, National Science Foundation, National Institute of Health, Department of Defense, and many others. The initiative's goals were to advance state-of-the-art core technologies needed to collect, store, preserve, manage, analyze, and share huge quantities of data, to harness these technologies to accelerate the pace of discovery in science and engineering, to strengthen the country's national security, and to expand the workforce needed to develop and use Big Data technologies.[5]

Business investment. Business firms have also invested directly in technology through their research and development (R&D) operations. Some firms have seen these investments are directly benefiting their business, as well as producing innovations that have moved their industries forward.

IBM announced a change in its strategic initiatives for 2015 and committed $4 billion to projects focusing on cloud computing, data analytics, and mobile, social, and

---

[5] "Obama Administration Unveils $200M Big Data R&D Initiative," *The Computing Community Consortium Blog,* March 29, 2012, *www.cccblog.org/2012/03/29.* For an update on this initiative see *www.nitrd.gov.*

security technologies. IBM set a financial target of $40 billion in annual revenues by 2018, more than 40 percent of the company's expected total revenues. This new and aggressive focus on technology was a response to IBM's total revenue decline from operations of 6 percent in 2014 and stagnant total revenue projected for 2015. IBM saw a need to transform its operational focus from a lagging semiconductor manufacturing business and declining technology services and software provider to new technologies and products to boost IBM's revenues.[6]

The combination of government and business investment in technology has continued to drive innovation forward. But ultimately, technology continues to evolve because of people's insatiable desire for it. They forever seek to expand the use of technology in their lives, probably because of the excitement in having new things and their belief that these new things may help them better adapt to their environment. As Bill Joy, Sun Microsystems' chief scientist, prophetically explained in 2000,

> By 2030, we are likely to be able to build machines, in quantity, a million times as powerful as the personal computer of today. As this enormous computing power is combined with the manipulative advances of the physical sciences and the new, deep understanding in genetics, enormous transformative power is being unleashed. These combinations open up the opportunity to completely redesign the world, for better or worse: The replicating and evolving processes that have been confined to the natural world are about to become realms of human endeavor.[7]

The Role of Technology in Society

Technology and society have been intertwined since the Industrial Revolution. The connection between the two became even stronger in the information and semantic phases. Today, technology has the potential to influence every aspect of every individual's global activity—driving innovation, affecting collaborative partnerships, and changing business–stakeholder relationships. It has created great opportunities for people—but also serious ethical and social challenges. This section will explore some ways in which four technologies—the Internet, the digital divide, mobile telephones, and social media—have presented both opportunities and challenges for people and profoundly affected society.

The Internet

More people have more access to technology than ever before. Residents of developing countries increasingly enjoy energy-powered appliances, entertainment devices, and communications equipment. Individuals in developed countries in North America, Europe, portions of Asia, and the Middle East more than ever are dependent on electronic communication devices for access to information and for interactions with others and businesses. In today's environment, nearly every individual in a developed country has a desktop or laptop computer, tablet, mobile phone, and a host of other electronic devices to connect them with others in their family, neighborhood, country, or world. These technology devices have become common.

[6] "IBM Pumps $4 Billion into Cloud and Mobile Initiatives," *The Wall Street Journal*, February 26, 2015, *www.wsj.com.*

[7] Bill Joy, "Why the Future Doesn't Need Us," *Wired*, April 2000, *www.wired.com/wired/archive/8.04/joy.*

The Emergence of the Internet

One of the most visible and widely used technological innovations over the past decade has been the Internet. Springing to life in 1994, this conduit of information revolutionized how business was conducted, students learned, and households operated.

Any estimate of the number of Internet users is quickly out of date but some important trends have emerged. In 2008, China surpassed the United States with the most Internet users by country. Just four years later China had more than 500 million Internet users, compared to the United States' 245 million. The top 20 countries by Internet usage by 2014 are shown in Figure 11.2. Since 2012, India and Brazil surpassed Japan as the third and fourth largest number of Internet users by country. Russia jumped from #9 in 2012 to #6 in 2014

FIGURE 11.2

Top 20 Internet Use by Country, 2014, and Growth in World Internet Usage by Region, 2012–2014

Sources: "Top Ten Languages Used in the Web" and "World Internet Usage and Population Statistics—June 2014," Internet World Statistics, *www.internetworldstats.com*.

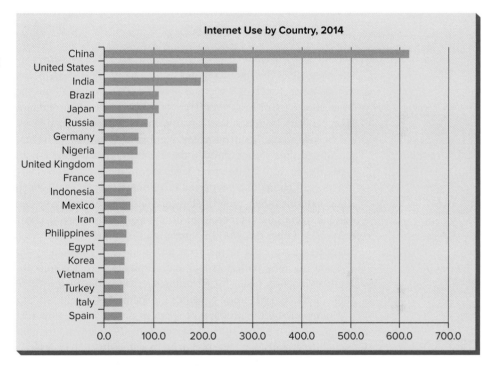

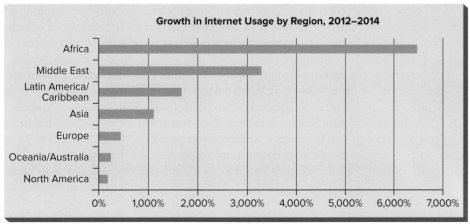

and Nigeria went from #11 in 2012 to #8 by 2014. Figure 11.2 also shows the new emerging markets for Internet usage: Africa, the Middle East, and Latin America/Caribbean. The developing countries, especially in the Southern Hemisphere, are catching up to the integration of Internet usage into the lives of managers and citizens in developed countries.

New ways of connecting online are contributing to the growing use of the Internet. Digital music players and game consoles from Apple, Microsoft, Sony, and Ninetendo include web browsers, e-mail and messaging capability, and wireless Internet access. Smartphones include Wi-Fi connectivity to provide users with faster data transfer speeds than mobile phone carriers can provide. Manufacturers added new features, such as digital cameras, video recording, and GPS, to enable these portable devices to become even more useful tools for collecting and distributing information. Smartwatches hit the marketplace in 2014, allowing individuals to connect with the Internet (and others) with greater easy and convenience.

Thousands of new Internet users each day demonstrate the power of this technology as a force in our lives. The Internet is increasingly being used as a place for shopping and businesses are quick to create new opportunities for e-commerce, as described later.

Unwanted Internet Threats

The presence of the Internet in our lives is a welcomed benefit, but also opened the door to various threats, such as *spam* and *phishing*. **Spam** refers to unsolicited commercial e-mails (also called *UCE* or *junk e-mail*) sent in bulk to valid e-mail and mobile accounts. These messages can vary from harmless advertisements for commercial products to offensive material and finance scams. Spam has created problems for users as it has caused extra network traffic and wasted time sorting through the irrelevant or unwanted e-mails to access desired messages. By the early 2010s, spam began to infiltrate e-mail accounts on mobile or cell phones.

U.S. cell phone users reported receiving nearly 4.5 million spam e-mails annually by 2012, but since then reports of receiving spam e-mail have declined. The main reason was the overall heightened level of antispam protection, according to a spokesperson at Kaspersky Labs, the world's largest antivirus and Internet security software company. Spam filters are now in place on just about every e-mail system, reducing the amount of spam reaching both personal and corporate user accounts to a bare minimum. Also, aggressive action taken by governments, especially in the United Kingdom and United States, have created strong penalties for spammers caught sending out malicious e-mails.

Compounding the problem of spam or unsolicited commercial e-mail is **phishing**, the practice of stealing consumers' personal identity data and financial account credentials by using fake e-mails that appeared to be from legitimate businesses to trick users into divulging identifying personal data such as usernames and passwords, or to open attachments that installed viruses or malware (malicious software). According to a 2015 report from the Anti-Phishing Working Group (APWG), a U.S. industry association, reports of new phishing sites was on the decline but the number of malware attacks was on the rise. The malware samples consisted of three groups: crimeware (data-stealing malicious code designed specifically to be used to victimize financial institutions' customers and to co-opt those institutions' identities); data stealing and generic trojans (code designed to send information from the infected machine, control it, and open backdoors on it); and other (the remainder of malicious code commonly encountered in the field such as auto-replicating worms, dialers for telephone charge-back scams, etc.).[8]

Although Internet users were more aware of potential problems that might be encountered when using their e-mail and smartphones, and were taking precautions to prevent unwanted spam or phishing, threats remained and users needed to remain vigilant.

[8] "Phishing Activities Trends Report," Anti-Phishing Working Group, published March 2015, *www.antiphishing.org/reports.*

The Digital Divide in the United States and Worldwide

The gap between those who have access to the Internet through technology and those who do not is called the **digital divide**.[9] Some people have Internet access through computers, cell phones, and other devices; others do not. People in developing countries often have less Internet access than people in developed countries; and within developed countries, persons of color and the less affluent often have less access. The presence of a digital divide is a problem because less advantaged individuals and societies may not enjoy the same benefits of technology as others.

In the United States, the government has acted to break down the digital divide.

> The U.S. government launched a $7 billion effort to expand access, chiefly thorough grants to build wired and wireless systems in the most technologically neglected areas of the country. This government effort subsidized Internet upgrades for schools and libraries and provided digital textbooks in poor and rural areas. The falling prices of laptops and the newest generation of cell phones and Internet-enabled handheld devices enabled Internet access to be more affordable to many. The government also provided free cell phones and up to 250 free minutes for individuals who qualified, such as people seeking housing or job opportunities.[10]

By 2013, nearly 98 percent of American homes were able to access the Internet on some sort of high-speed broadband network, either at home or work.[11]

Some experts argued that the most important issue going forward was not access, but educating Americans on how the Internet could be a valuable aid for job hunting, acquiring health insurance, and accessing government services and other benefits. Yet, some pointed out that Internet access was still be too expensive for a majority of families in the poorest U.S. cities. The U.S. Census Bureau data reported that less than 50 percent of households (about 31 million) in the most economically depressed cities in the United States had access to broadband service.[12]

Globally, progress in narrowing the digital divide was slower, but there appeared to be reasons for optimism. Many businesses saw providing Internet access at the bottom of the pyramid as a lucrative business opportunity.

> Smartphone maker BlackBerry unveiled a new model exclusively targeting mobile phone users in Indonesia in 2014. Its low-cost touch-screen model retailed for 2.2 million rupiah, or about $190, and contained a number of special applications for Indonesian users, including local banking and travel services and a directory of halal food outlets, critical in the world's largest Muslim-majority country. Google, Facebook, and other companies joined forces to fund the Alliance for Affordable Internet, a global coalition seeking to bring down the cost of getting online for individuals in developing countries. Intel partnered with African phone manufacturers to bring down the price of smartphones running on Intel processors.[13]

The African marketplace, with only 16 percent of its population connected to the Internet, was a very attractive market for technology companies and corporate initiatives, such

[9] For a different viewpoint, see Walter Block, "The 'Digital Divide' Is Not a Problem in Need of Rectifying," *Journal of Business Ethics* (2004), pp. 393–406.

[10] "F.C.C. Chief Aims to Bolster Internet for Schools," *The New York Times*, November 17, 2014, *www.nytimes.com*.

[11] "Most of U.S. Is Wired, but Millions Aren't Plugged In," *The New York Times*, August 18, 2013, *www.nytimes.com*.

[12] "Digital Divide Exacerbates US Inequality," *Financial Times*, October 28, 2014, *www.ft.com*.

[13] "Blackberry Unveils Low-Cost Smartphone with Indonesia in Mind," *The New York Times*, May 13, 2014, *www.nytimes.com;* and "Using Free Wi-Fi to Connect Africa's Unconnected," *The Wall Street Journal*, April 13, 2014, *online.wsj.com*.

as those described above. Christopher Vollmer, executive at Booz & Company, explained the vital importance of bridging the digital divide globally: "We found that economically, the more countries are able to move up the digitization index, it actually improves GDP [gross domestic product] performance, it's associated with positive job growth and it's very critical for innovation."[14] Yet, more work was needed; some countries, such as Sweden, Singapore, Finland, Denmark, Switzerland, Netherlands, Norway, United States, Canada, and Britain, were at the high end of the digitization index, while poorer countries, such as Nepal, Syria, East Timor, and Haiti, were at the low end.

Mobile Telephones

Mobile telephones, or cell phones, use radio technology to enable users to place calls from a mobile device, with transmission over a service area divided into small "cells," each with its own low-power radio transmitter. The first generation of cell phones, introduced in the 1980s, were clumsy analog devices; today's digital smartphones provide a range of applications, including e-mail and Internet access, voice communications, video recording, and many more.

In North America, mobile phones were initially used mainly as a communications tool. But American cell phone users have recently joined many Europeans and Asians to embrace using their mobile phones for commerce. **M-commerce,** commerce conducted via mobile or cell phones, allows consumers to use their mobile phones as an electronic wallet. People can trade stocks or make consumer purchases of everything from hot dogs to washing machines. France Telecom marketed a mobile phone with a built-in credit card slot for easy wireless payments.

> In 2014, Apple hoped to change how shopping was done with the introduction of Apple Pay, a mobile payment and digital wallet service that lets users make payments using Apple devices, phones, tablets, and watches. Credit cards and banks, including American Express, Mastercard, Visa, Citi, Bank of America, and PNC, supported the system. Among retailers on board at the launch of Apple Pay were Macy's, Bloomingdales, Walgreens, Duane Reade, Whole Foods, Disney stores, and Staples. Restaurants supporting Apple Pay included Subway and Panera Bread. Apple touted its proprietary system as safe and secure because it created one-time payment numbers for purchases, rather than transmitting credit card numbers and security codes. "It's easy, it's secure and yes, it's a private way to pay for things," said Apple CEO Tim Cook.[15]

Mobile devices can be used for more than making calls or shopping. These devices can run apps and GPS systems, access the Internet, send text messages and photos, and stream music and videos. Mobile data usage was predicted to significantly increase by 2018, an 11-fold increase in traffic, according to technology experts at Cisco Systems. "Global mobile network will increase three times as fast as global fixed traffic, helped primarily by the increase in the number of mobile device users worldwide, which will rise to 4.9 billion by 2018," according to Cisco's Visual Networking Index Forecast.[16]

But with the potential for greater mobile device activity worldwide, some stakeholder groups warned that accompanying the increased usage would be increased frustration. Critics predicted more unwanted and unsolicited mobile text messages and incidents of malware and spyware. Some other undesirable consequences of mobile technology are described in Exhibit 11.A.

---

[14] "Digital Divide Splits Developed and Developing Nations," *Dawn.com,* April 5, 2012, *dawn.com.*

[15] "Apple Pay to Launch Monday," *USA Today,* October 16, 2014, *www.usatoday.com.*

[16] "Mobile Data Usage to Increase 11-fold by 2018 – Cisco," *TechWeek Europe,* February 6, 2014, *www.techweekeurope.co.uk.*

Exhibit 11.A

Too Much of a Good Thing? Wireless Dependency

Robert Bornstein, a psychologist at Adelphia University, says, "The superconnected may develop a dual-dependency. They're not only counting on other people too much, they're also hooked on the devices themselves, sometimes to the point where they feel utterly disconnected, isolated and detached without them." Exactly how bad is the dependency on technology, specifically wireless devices? Some experts have warned that handheld e-mailing devices are so addictive that soon compulsive users will need to be weaned off them using treatment programs like the ones used by drug addicts. This overreliance upon technology can also cause physical problems, such as:

- BlackBerry thumb—a pain or numbness in the thumbs caused by constant e-mailing, messaging, or Internet surfing on handheld devices,

- Cell phone elbow—arthritic pain and swelling in the elbow from constantly holding a cell phone to the ear, which in some severe cases may cause nerve damage.

- PDA (personal data assistant) hunch—neck pain caused by looking straight down at your PDA minimonitor.

Or, psychological dependency problems:

It is common in the technological world for someone to view multiple screens, listen to music on an iPod, and send an e-mail or tweet all at the same time and for hours on end. The extensive interaction with many technological devices can be hazardous for the user. The term *web junkie* has been applied to individuals who become hooked on video games, playing for dozens of hours at a time often without breaks to eat, sleep, or even use the bathroom. Many come to view the real world as fake. Loren Frank, a researcher at the University of California, San Francisco, concluded, "Almost certainly, downtime lets the brain go over experiences it's had, solidify them and turn them into permanent long-term memories." When the brain is constantly stimulated, this learning process is prevented. "Instead of having long relaxing breaks [allowing time for the brain to process the information], like taking two hours for lunch, we have a lot of micro-moments," explained Marc Berman, a University of Michigan neuroscientist.

Sources: "Wireless Dependency," *New York Times,* February 17, 2007, *www.nytimes.com;* "Digital Devices Deprive Brain of Needed Downtime," *The New York Times,* August 24, 2010, *www.nytimes.com;* and "Screen Addiction Is Taknig a Toll on Children," *The New York Times,* July 6, 2015, *well.blogs.nytimes.com.*

Social Networking

Social networking, a system using technology to enable people to connect, explore interests, and share activities around the world, exploded onto the technology scene in the 2000s, altering many social and human interactions. One positive example of social networking and how it saved lives was presented at the beginning of this chapter.

Similar to estimating the number of Internet users, any estimate on the number of people using social media is quickly outdated the moment the calculations are completed. In 2011, 1.2 billion people worldwide used social networking sites at least once per month; by 2015, that number was estimated to be more than 2 billion. Facebook was the most frequently used social network, with nearly 1.5 billion users by 2015, with QZone (a social networking site popular in China), Google, LinkedIn, Instagram, Twitter, and Tumblr also among the top seven social network sites with more than 250 million users each by 2015. The most engaged countries for social networking in 2015 were Israel (where users spent an average of 11.1 hours per month on social networking), Argentina (10.7 hours), Russia (10.4 hours), Turkey (10.2 hours), and Chile (9.8 hours). In the United States, social network users spend 7.6 hours per month on networking sites.[17]

[17] "Social Networking Reaches Nearly One in Four Around the World," *eMarketer,* June 18, 2013, *www.emarketer.com;* and "Social Networking Statistics," *Statistic Brain Research Institute,* accessed May 3, 2015, *www.statisticbrain.com.*

Clearly the dramatic rise in social networking has taken the world by storm and has become a central aspect of individuals' lives. With these news ways to interact with others comes additional responsibilities to ensure that the interactions are ethical and socially beneficial.

The Impact of Scientific Breakthroughs

Dramatic advances in the biological sciences also have propelled the impact of technology on our lives. Recent unprecedented applications of biological science have made possible new, improved methods of agricultural food production as well as medical care, but they have also posed numerous ethical challenges regarding safety and the quality of life. Three of the most profound impacts on our lives come from the scientific breakthroughs in genetically modified (GM) or engineered foods; the sequencing of the human genome and the use of genetic information; and the advent of biotechnology and the resulting stem cell research. These topics are discussed in this section.

> As Bill Joy of Sun Microsystems warns, speaking of biotechnology as well as other innovative applications of science, "21st century technologies . . . are so powerful that they can spawn whole new classes of accidents and abuses. Most dangerously, for the first time, these accidents and abuses are widely within the reach of individuals or small groups. They will not require large facilities or rare raw materials. Knowledge alone will enable the use of them."[18]

Genetically Engineered Foods

The biotechnological revolution resulted in applications for use by the agricultural industry and brought promises of larger than ever crop production through advances in genetic engineering of food. *Genetic engineering* involves altering the natural makeup of a living organism and allows scientists to insert virtually any gene into a plant and create a new crop or a new species. **Genetically modified foods**, or GM foods, are foods that are processed from genetically modified crops. The explosion of GM foods into our food chain in just a few decades was remarkable. In 1982 the first tomato plant was genetically engineered. Corn became genetically modified and developed a resistance to insects that allowed corn crop yields to double to 26 bushels per acre from 2001 to 2010. Commercial planting of an herbicide-tolerant sugar beet began in the United States in 2008. And, more than 90 percent of all soybeans grown in the United States annually are genetically engineered.[19]

Despite a lack of scientific evidence that GM foods are harmful to humans, social advocates in Europe led the charge against genetically modified foods, calling GM foods "Frankenstein foods."

> In the late 2000s, both France and Germany passed national bans on the use of various kinds of GM seeds. Despite French and German farmers' protests that the ban would inflict great economic harm on them and their countries' economies, the German agriculture minister said, "The decision is not a political decision, it's a decision based on the facts." He affirmed the government's commitment to protect

---

[18] Bill Joy, "Why the Future Doesn't Need Us," *Wired,* April 2000, *www.wried.com.*

[19] "GMOs Are Everywhere," *Bloomberg Businessweek,* July 31, 2014, *www.bloomberg.com.*

the safety of consumers and the environment. Austria and Hungary also passed their own national bans on growing GM crops. While Europe continued to allow each nation to decide whether to allow the planting or sale of GM foods, the European Union passed a GM food labeling law so that all European consumers can also make their own decisions to purchase this type of food or not.[20]

By contrast with Europe, GM foods became quite common in grocery stores in the United States. Although most GM corn grown in the United States was made into animal feed or ethanol, it was also processed into food industry staples such as corn syrup or tortilla chips. But problems with using GM seed surfaced in the early 2010s.

In 2011 Monsanto reported that some of its GM seed, grown to resist attacks by bugs that could ruin crops, was losing its bug resistance possibly due to the way that farmers were using biotech crops. This could cause some farmers to switch to a different strain of GM seed produced by one of Monsanto's competitors. The problem continued to grow when it was reported that other seed makers, including DuPont and Dow Chemical, also began to experience problems. The Environmental Protection Agency considered proposing limits on some genetically engineered corn to combat a greedy pest that evolved and was resistant to the bug-killing crops.[21]

It appears that the tide against GMO food in the United States was gaining momentum by the 2010s. In 2013, Ben & Jerry's Homemade initiated a plan to eliminate GM ingredients from its ice cream. A year later, General Mills started selling its original flavored Cheerios without GMOs. Post Holdings took the GMOs out of Grape-Nuts. In 2015, Chipotle Mexican Grille was the first major restaurant chain to serve only food free of genetically engineered ingredients. Whole Foods stores were on track to be free of all GMO products by 2018 and Walmart vastly expanded its selection of organic foods, free from genetic alternation.[22]

Yet, growing GMO crops appears to be flourishing globally. In some economically developed countries and most developing countries around the world GM food was welcomed as a way to increase crop yields. According to a report from the International Service for the Acquisition of Agri-biotech Applications (ISAAA), of the 28 countries that planted biotech crops in 2012, 20 were developing and 8 were industrial countries. As shown in Figure 11.3, the top nine each grew more than 2 million hectares, meaning more than half the world's population, 60 percent or nearly 4 billion people, live in the 28 countries planting biotech crops.[23]

Some activists have supported a movement to label food products that include GM ingredients. Vermont became the first state in the United States, in April 2014, to require food makers to label products that included GMOs. The law, which takes effect in 2016, was hailed as a victory by activists who argued that consumers have the right to

[20] "French Court Says Ban on Gene-Altered Corn Seed Will Remain, Pending Study," *New York Times*, March 20, 2008, *www.nytimes.com;* "Germany Bars Genetically Modified Corn," *New York Times*, April 15, 2009, *www.nytimes.com;* "Europe to Allow Two Bans on Genetically Altered Crops," *New York Times*, March 3, 2009, *www.nytimes.com;* and "Europe Has GM Food Label Law," *Health Impact News Daily*, May 22, 2012, *healthimpactnews.com.*

[21] "Monsanto Corn Plant Losing Bug Resistance," *The Wall Street Journal*, August 29, 2011, *online.wsj.com;* and "Limits Sought on GMO Corn as Pest Resistance Grows," *The Wall Street Journal*, March 5, 2015, *www.wsj.com.*

[22] "The GMO Fight Ripples Down the Food Chain," *The Wall Street Journal*, August 7, 2014, *online.wsj.com;* and "Chipotle to Stop Serving Genetically Altered Food," *The New York Times*, April 26, 2015, *www.nytimes.com.*

[23] See the ISAAA Brief 44–2012: Executive Summary, *ISAAA*, 2012, *www.isaaa.org.*

FIGURE 11.3   **Biocrop Production by Country and Type of Crops Grown, 2012 (in thousands of hectares)**

Source: ISAAA Brief 44-2012: Executive Summary, *ISAAA*, 2012, *www.isaaa.org.*

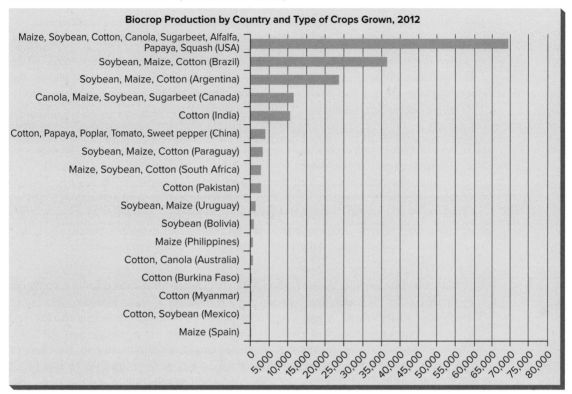

transparency. It was opposed by food and agricultural industry groups, saying that the Vermont law was backed by faulty science and would harm consumers. Nonetheless, consumers in poll after poll have overwhelmingly said they want labels on food that contain GM ingredients, often as many as 66 percent of those surveyed.[24]

But the GMO labeling movement took a step back in November 2014 when GMO labeling measures in Oregon and Colorado were defeated. In Oregon, the food and agricultural industries, led by Kraft Food, Pepsi, and Monsanto, outspent advocates for the bill by $20.5 million to $8.2 million; whereas, in Colorado the ratio was $16.7 million for anti-labeling forces to less than $1 million for proponents. These results followed the pattern seen earlier, before the labeling victory in Vermont, when voters in 2013 in California and Washington voted against a labeling bill. In these two states, opponents of the law spent more than $100 million during the campaign and outspent the advocates of the bill four to one.[25]

Sequencing of the Human Genome

When Celera Genomics Group announced that it had finished the first sequencing of a **human genome**, the achievement was hailed as the most significant scientific breakthrough since landing a man on the moon. Strands of human deoxyribonucleic acid, or DNA, are arrayed across 23 chromosomes in the nucleus of every human cell, forming

[24] "Vermont to Enact GMO Food-Labeling Law," *The Wall Street Journal,* April 23, 2014, *online.wsj.com.*

[25] "Food Industry Wins Round in GMO-Labeling Fight," *The Wall Street Journal,* November 5, 2014, *online.wsj.com.*

a unique pattern for every human. These strands are composed of four chemical units, or letters, used over and over in varying sequences. These replicated letters total 3 billion and form the words, or genes—our unique human signature—that instruct cells to manufacture the proteins that carry out all of the functions of human life.[26] The identification of human genes is critical to the early diagnosis of life-threatening diseases, the invention of new ways to prevent illnesses, and the development of drug therapies to treat a person's unique genetic profile.

By 2014, the Human Genome Project had fueled the discovery of more than 1,800 disease genes and more than 2,000 genetic tests for human conditions were ongoing. These tests enabled a countless number of patients to learn their genetic risks for disease and also helped healthcare professionals to diagnose disease. One major step forward was taken in 2005 with the creation of the HapMap,[27] which catalogs common genetic variation, or haplotypes, in the human genome. By 2010, the third phase of the HapMap project was published, with data from 11 global populations, the largest survey of human genetic variation performed to date.

However, in addition to the remarkable advances in understanding DNA, touted as one of humanity's greatest achievements, numerous ethical challenges emerged in private and public research focusing on genetics.

> One family, afflicted by a rare genetic heart disease called Brugada syndrome, wondered how others might react if they learned of the family's medical condition. Would employers want to hire someone who might die prematurely or require an expensive implantable defibrillator? Would they be eligible for individual health care coverage or be able to afford life insurance if their condition were known? The underlying fear for this family and others with genetic conditions was whether they would be treated fairly if their genetic fingerprints became public.

The debate over whether advances in human genome sequencing and genetic research outweigh the risks or harms will continue for years. What is clear is that our scientific understanding of the human body and its makeup has changed, and significant technological innovations are on the horizon. What is not clear is who, if anyone, can manage these changes to better ensure the improvement of the quality of our lives and society.

Biotechnology and Stem Cell Research

Complementing the discovery of DNA sequencing were numerous medical breakthroughs in the area of regenerative medicine. **Tissue engineering**, the growth of tissue in a laboratory dish for experimental research, and **stem cell research**, research on nonspecialized cells that have the capacity to self-renew and to differentiate into more mature cells, were two such breakthroughs. Both offered the promise that failing human organs and aging cells could be rejuvenated or replaced with healthy cells or tissues grown anew. While the promise of immortality may be overstated, regenerative medicine provided a revolutionary technological breakthrough for the field of medicine.

Stem cell research spilled over from the laboratories into the public arena as citizens weighed in on the issue, often with strong religious opinions affecting their viewpoints. As shown in Figure 11.4, public approval of stem cell research increased in the United States since 2002 and in 2014 was at its highest approval rating—65 percent believed stem cell research is morally acceptable; whereas only 27 percent, the lowest since 2002, believed it is morally wrong.

---

[26] "Genetic Secrets of Malaria Bug Cracked at Last" *The Wall Street Journal,* January 18, 2002, pp. B1, B6.

[27] For more information, see *hapmap.ncbi.nlm.nih.gov.*

FIGURE 11.4
Number of Americans Morally in Favor of Stem Cell Research versus Opposed, from 2002 to 2014

Source: "Stem Cell Research: Gallup Historical Trends," *Gallup Research Group,* May 2014, *www.gallup.com.*

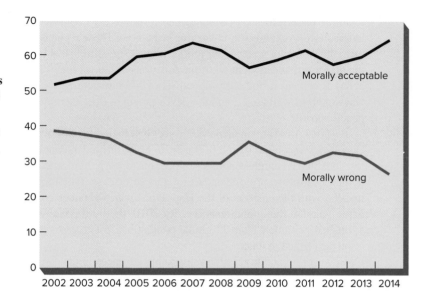

Supported by private and government funding, hundreds of biotechnology companies and university laboratories were actively pursuing new approaches to replace or regenerate failed body parts. New discoveries were occurring quickly. Some promising breakthroughs included the following: researchers were able to insert bone-growth factors or stem cells into a porous material cut to a specific shape, creating new jaws or limbs; genetically engineered proteins were successfully used to regrow blood vessels that might repair or replace heart valves, arteries, and veins; and the process to regrow cartilage was used to grow a new chest for a boy, and a human ear was grown on a mouse.

By 2012, stem cell research continued to make significant progress. A notable breakthrough occurred when Chinese scientists developed a safe and easy way to produce stem cells, raising hopes for treating a range of diseases. By using a mixture of very small molecules to chemically reprogram the adult stem cells, scientists said they could become as versatile as embryonic stem cells, which was controversial since they were taken from human embryos.[28]

The controversies that emerge over scientific breakthroughs from advancements in technology—GM food production, the sequencing of the human genome, and stem cell research—raise serious ethical and social issues. How to maximize the benefits to individuals and society yet minimize or eliminate the negative consequences regarding these technological developments must continue to be addressed, as new innovations appear on the horizon.

The Role of Technology in Business

Not only is technology intertwined in our personal lives but has also infiltrated how business is done. Today, every aspect of business is influenced by technology—the distribution and sale of products; how businesses are created, formed, and sustained; the business–employee

---

[28] "Scientists Develop Safe and Easy Way to Make Stem Cells," *Medical News Today,* July 19, 2013, *www.medicalnewstoday.com.*

FIGURE 11.5
Global E-Business Sales Growing

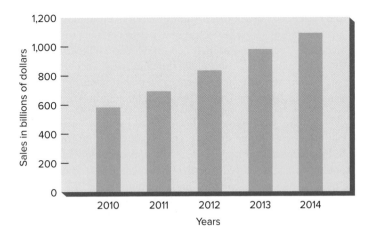

relationship, whether human or mechanical employees; and other business elements. It has created great opportunities for businesses, but serious ethical and social challenges also have emerged. This section will explore some ways in which emerging technologies have presented both opportunities and challenges for business, and ultimately society. We will discuss three specific topics at the intersection of business, technology, and society: e-business, the transformation of business models, and the use of robotics.

E-Business

During the information and semantic phase of technological development, shown in Figure 11.1, electronic business exchanges between businesses and between businesses and their customers emerged. These electronic exchanges, generally referred to as **e-business**, consist of buying and selling goods and services between businesses, organizations, and individuals electronically; that is, via Internet-based systems. During the past decade, e-business revenue increased at a fast pace, as shown in Figure 11.5, and more than that of traditional, or nonelectronic, business. E-business revenues were predicted to continue to rise significantly through 2018, fueled by consumers in emerging markets.

In the United States, online sales topped $300 billion in 2014 and were projected to rise through 2017 to nearly $450 billion. Sales made through mobile devices rose from nearly $25 billion in 2012 to more than $60 billion in 2014, with mobile sales projected to be more than $114 trillion by 2017.[29] E-business has become a way of life, from large companies and smaller start-up businesses to individuals interested in shopping online. As technology became more affordable and easier to use, small and medium-sized businesses committed investment dollars to e-business and technology systems.

Transforming Prevailing Business Models

Businesses, especially small-sized companies, discovered that adopting new technology could save them money in the long run and give them a competitive edge over rivals by enabling them to add new services and operate more efficiently, as the following example shows.

> When a computer programmer offered to create a custom package for Top Dog Daycare, owners Joelle and Tom Hilfers were shocked but agreed to take the plunge, on a payment plan. Three years and nearly $30,000 in technology investments later,

[29] Data from "E-Commerce / Online Sales Statistics," *Statistic Brain Research Institute,* October 9, 2014, *www.statisticbrain.com;* and, "Quarterly Retail E-Commerce Sales, 4th Quarter 2014," *U.S. Census Bureau News,* February 17, 2015, *census.gov.*

the Hilfers do not know how they ever survived without the company's K-9 Connect software, which allows dog owners to book appointments online, view their accounts, post photos of their pets, and look in on them during the day through a live web cam. K-9 Connect also stores the pets' vaccination records, meal plans, and special requirements and has pages on e-commerce, dog training, and dog grooming. Business at Top Dog Daycare tripled after adopting the computerized system.[30]

The Hilfers' experience has been shared by other businesses as they switch from traditional brick-and-mortar stores to online sales. During the 2013 holiday shopping season, U.S. brick-and-mortar retailers received approximately half of the holiday foot traffic they experienced just three years earlier. As consumers lead busier and more active lives, they are more frequently researching and shopping online.

Amazon, the world's leader in online shopping, had its best season to date in 2013, with more than 36.8 million items ordered worldwide on Cyber Monday alone (three days after the traditional Black Friday shopping day—the day after Thanksgiving in the United States). Alibaba, China's online retail leader, sold more than 30 billion renminbi, or about $5 billion, worth of goods on Singles' Day. This "shopper's holiday" is celebrated on November 11 (since this day has four 1's, or singles) and targets young Chinese men and women who are single and lamenting or toasting their unmarried status. Online shopping is obviously big business and the dramatic growth of online purchases reflects on how shoppers' actions have changed causing businesses to change as well.[31]

Seventy-one percent of shoppers expect to view in-store inventory online and 50 percent want to be able to buy online and pick up their purchases at a brick-and-mortar store. Smartphones are also changing how businesses must accommodate consumers. According to a Forrester Research survey, 38 percent of consumers used their mobile devices to check inventory availability while on their way to a store and 34 percent used a mobile device to research products while in a store.

These new trends gave rise to the notion of **omnichannel**, the idea that every distribution channel must work together to deliver a unified and consistent customer experience. Businesses are adjusting and attempting to serve the multiple needs of their consumers.

> Amazon is building dozens of "fulfillment centers," brick-and-mortar stores located in major cities to have high-demand products close enough to consumers for same-day or next-day delivery. Brick-and-mortar stores, such as those operated by Apple or Verizon, understand that customers can find out about inventory on their phones before coming to the store. Retailers are focusing more on providing technical assistance for their customers in the stores, equipping employees with tablets or mobile technology to check inventory at other stores, locate complimentary accessories, or enable faster payment of items ordered.[32]

As technology changes the shopping experiences for customers, businesses, too, must understand how they need to change to accommodate and better serve their customers.

The Use of Robotics at Work

Another area where technology has made a significant impact on business is the development of robotic engineering and the increased availability of robots. Initially, robots were used in

---

[30] See the company's website at *topdogdaycare.net.*

[31] "Retail in Crisis: These Are the Changes Brick-and-Mortar Stores Must Make," *Forbes,* February 12, 2014, *www.forbes.com;* and "Online Shopping Marathon Zooms off the Blocks in China," *The New York Times,* November 11, 2013, *www.nytimes.com.*

[32] "Retail in Crisis: These Are the Changes Brick-and-Mortar Stores Must Make," *Forbes,* February 12, 2014, *www.forbes.com.*

high-risk situations, such as bomb detection or handling toxic chemicals, but as they have become more affordable and smarter, they have generated new opportunities for businesses.

A new breed of machines, called *collaborative machines,* were designed to work alongside people in close settings and changed how many small manufactures did business. Priced as low as $20,000, manufacturers, toy makers, and other businesses are using these machines to increase overall productivity and lower labor costs.

> Panek Precision, founded in 1945 as a small, precision machine shop in Northbrook, Illinois, uses robots to place metal pieces into cutting machines and remove the parts after the cutting is completed. A job difficult for a human employee because of its tediousness, robots can accomplish the tasks quickly, effectively, and less expensively than machine operators paid $16.50 per hour. The robot doubled the output of a human worker "because robots work overnight and don't take a lunch break and they just keep going," said Panek Precision's president.[33]

Robots have found their way into other types of work. They can replace workers who could be injured from doing the work previously assigned to humans. "It's gotten easier to substitute machines for many kinds of labor. We should be able to have a lot more wealth with less labor," explained economist Erik Brynjolfsson.[34]

Another technological breakthrough is in the use of driverless cars. Google announced that a specially equipped fleet of driverless Toyota Prius cars had safely traveled more than 1,000 miles in the United States. Rio Tinto, a global mining company, used self-driving trucks and drills that need no human operators at its iron ore mines. Automated trains carried the ore to a port 300 miles away.

However, the spread of robots in the workplace posed a clear threat to workers' employment. Gartner, Inc., a technology research firm, predicted that one-third of all jobs would be lost to automation within a decade. Within two decades, economists at Oxford University forecast, nearly half of the current jobs would be performed by machine technology. In the United Kingdom, economists predicted that 10 million jobs would be taken over by computers and robots over the next 20 years. They said that people earning less than £30,000, or about $46,000, a year were most likely to see their jobs eliminated.

In the crosshairs are middle-class workers such as clerks and bookkeepers. Today's computers can conduct legal research, write stock reports and news stories, and translate conversations. At banks, machines can produce government-required documents to flag potential money laundering—all work done by humans a short time ago. Banks using automated teller machines (ATMs) spread quickly throughout the United States from the 1980s to today. In 1985, there were 484,000 bank tellers in the United States; by 2014, this number had fallen to 361,000, a drop of more than 25 percent.[35]

Others argue that robots and advanced technology might actually increase labor demand, especially for low-skilled laborers. The presence of technology might allow low-skilled workers to perform tasks previously assigned only to high-skilled employees. "Employees gain much critical knowledge about new technologies through experience on the job and such learning often does not require a high degree of education," according to scholar James Bessen. Whether technology creates more or fewer jobs remains to be seen, but the impact of technology through robotics is undeniably profound.

[33] "Robots Work Their Way into Small Factories," *The Wall Street Journal,* September 17, 2014, *online.wsj.com.*

[34] "What Clever Robots Mean for Jobs," *The Wall Street Journal,* February 24, 2015, *www.wsj.com.*

[35] *The Wall Street Journal,* February 24, 2015, *Ibid;* "High Tech and Robots Can Create More Low Skilled Jobs, Not Just Destroy Them," *Forbes,* March 23, 2014, *www.forbes.com;* and "Ten Million Jobs at Risk from Advancing Technology," *The Telegraph,* November 10, 2014, *www.telegraph.co.uk.*

Ethical Challenges Involving Technology

With each new technological innovation comes the important ethical question: *Should* we develop and offer the new application? At present, many inventors, computer programmers, and business managers appear only to be asking: *Can* we develop and offer the new application? Both questions are paramount as technology continues to influence individuals, businesses, and society interactions in the world in which we live. Some of the most profound ethical issues involve privacy and free speech.

The Loss of Privacy

Jeffrey Hancock, a Cornell University professor, warned of the increased potential for privacy invasion due to technology: "This is a new era. I liken it a little to when chemistry got the microscope."[36] Individuals are indeed under a technology microscope with vast amounts of data collected each minute and available to be analyzed in great detail, sometimes by people with the individuals' interests in mind, such as marketers, job recruiters, and loan grantors, but also by others who have criminal motives. Others warn that individuals, especially the newest generation, are willing to give up this expectation of privacy. According to Richard Clarke, former senior White House cybersecurity adviser:

> "Over time there will be few people who recall pre-Information Age privacy, more people who will have grown up with few expectations of privacy. While a backlash against the erosion of privacy is possible, it is more likely that people acting on their fear of big government and big corporate data will be a minority."[37]

Invasions of individual privacy come from many different directions. Automobiles are becoming smarter, with global positioning systems, Internet connections, data recorders, and high-definition cameras. While automakers say they are only responding to consumer demands for more technology, the new technologies increase the number of people with access to this data. In 2014 a law was introduced in the United States that would require car owners to control the data collected on the in-car device called the *event data recorder,* commonly known as a black box. The legislation was spurred by the clash over the use of personal data by law enforcement agencies and insurance companies, seeking to use the information against the car owners.

Smartphones are another common device that can capture vast amounts of information. Who should have access to this information? In 2014, Apple and Google announced that they were creating a new operating system for smartphones that would prevent law enforcement agencies from retrieving the data stored on a locked phone, such as photos, videos, and contacts. Apple acknowledged that it could still be required to hand over such data to law enforcement agencies if their users had backed it up on the company's iCloud servers. In addition, the police can access some iPhone data without Apple's help, because phone companies keep call logs, and Apple does not control data collected by third-party apps. But, can this information be accessed to better serve people?[38]

> Fan Zhang, the owner of Happy Child, a trendy Asian restaurant in downtown Toronto, knows that 170 of his customers went clubbing last month, 250 went to the

---

[36] "As Data Overflows Online, Researchers Grapple with Ethics," *The New York Times,* August 12, 2014, *www.nytimes.com.*

[37] "Will Privacy Be a Thing of the Past?" *The Wall Street Journal,* July 8, 2014, *blogs.wsj.com.*

[38] "The Next Data Privacy Battle May Be Wages inside Your Car," *The New York Times,* January 10, 2014, *www.nytimes.com;* and "New Level of Smartphone Encryption Alarms Law Enforcement," *The Wall Street Journal,* September 22, 2014, *online .wsj.com.*

gym, and 216 came into town from nearby Yorkville, an upscale neighborhood. He accessed this information without his customers' knowledge or permission. As a client of Turnstyle Solutions, a Toronto company that has placed sensors in about 200 businesses within a one-mile radius of downtown Toronto, Zhang can track individuals as they move about in the city. These sensors can track individuals anywhere as long as their Wi-Fi is turned on. Zhang said that he wants the information to better serve his customers, with special promotions or changes in his restaurant's menu.[39]

Ethical challenges on how this information is collected and analyzed are becoming increasingly salient.

Free Speech Issues

Another important ethical issue arising through the advances in technology involves free speech. As discussed in Chapter 5, individuals have certain ethical rights, including the right to free speech. However, this right is not absolute and must be weighed against its consequences for the community. For example, an individual is not permitted to yell "fire" in a crowded movie theater, even though some might see this as an expression of free speech, since the potential harms caused by panicked moviegoers outweighs the right of free expression. The issue of free speech was at the core of *Elonis v. United States,* a case scheduled to be heard by the U.S. Supreme Court in 2015.

> Anthony Elonis was accused of threatening his estranged wife based on a series of Facebook posts. Elonis likened the posts to Eminem's Grammy-winning songs "Kim" and "Kill You," which included threats of violence. He argued that he was only venting frustration after a run of personal setbacks, including the collapse of his marriage and loss of his job. He thought, like the artist Eminem, that he was just expressing his thoughts to a crowd, those accessing his Facebook page, as the singer had to his concert audience. The Justice Department argued that Elonis's posts indicated a "clearly sinister meaning of a threat" and were meant as expressions of his intent to harm his wife. The Supreme Court overturned Elonis' earlier conviction arguing that criminal threats cannot be based solely on whether a reasonable person would regard communications posted on social media or elsewhere as threatening.[40]

Other free speech issues have appeared recently, such as the *Yelp, Inc. v. Hadeed Carpet Cleaning, Inc.* case. Joe Hadeed, owner of a carpet cleaning company, argued that his business dropped 30 percent after two negative posts appeared on Yelp, a social media site where individuals can post reviews about businesses or read reviews posted by others. According to the Federal Trade Commission, they received more than 2,000 complaints about Yelp from 2008 through 2014. Most of the complaints were from small businesses, like Hadeed's, that claimed to have received unfair or fraudulent reviews. Others argued that Yelp had attempted to intimidate owners. "I was contacted by a Yelp salesperson to advertise, which I declined, and since have only had negative posts in their site," said a business owner from New Jersey.[41] These issues raised the ethical and legal question whether anyone can post anything they want on a social media site, even if untrue or unsubstantiated and negative consequences occur due to the posting. In some cases it appears acceptable, but not in other situations.

---

[39] "What Secrets Your Phone Is Sharing about You," *The Wall Street Journal,* January 13, 2014, *online.wsj.com.*

[40] "In Social-Media Era, When Is Free Speech Illegal?" *The Wall Street Journal,* November 23, 2014, *online.wsj.com;* and "Supreme Court Overturns Conviction for Threats on Facebook," *The Wall Street Journal,* June 1, 2015, *www.wsj.com.* Also see *Elonis v. United States* at *www.scotusblog.com/case-files/cases/elonis-v-united-states.*

[41] "Yelp Reviews Brew a Fight over Free Speech vs. Fairness," *The Wall Street Journal,* April 2, 2014, *online.wsj.com.*

Summary

- Technology is the practical application of science and knowledge that is rapidly changing and spreading across societies.
- Technology has exponentially increased our ability to communicate with others around the world through the Internet, e-mail, mobile phones, and social networking.
- Technology has changed how businesses offer, sell, and account for their goods and services in the global marketplace through e-business, transforming traditional business practices, and the use of robotics.
- The use of technology often raises important ethical questions, such as the protection of an individual's privacy or the proper use of the right to free speech.
- Genetically modified foods, sequencing the human genome, biotechnology, and stem cell research carry great promise for individuals in society, but have also raised serious concerns.

Key Terms

biotechnology, *235*
cyberspace, *234*
digital divide, *239*
e-business, *247*
genetically modified foods, *242*
human genome, *244*

information phase, *234*
m-commerce, *240*
mobile telephones, *240*
omnichannel, *248*
phishing, *238*
semantic phase, *234*
social networking, *241*

spam, *238*
stem cell research, *245*
technology, *233*
tissue engineering, *245*

Internet Resources

www.antiphishing.org	Anti-Phishing Working Group
www.improveagriculture.com	A Place to Learn about Sustainable Agriculture
www.bio.org	Biotechnology Industry Organization
www.digitaldividenetwork.org	Digital Divide Network
www.ecommercetimes.com	E-Commerce Times
www.eff.org	Electronic Frontier Foundation
genomics.energy.gov	Genome Projects of the U.S. Department of Energy, Office of Science
isscr.org	International Society for Stem Cell Research
www.internetsociety.org	Internet Society
socialmediatoday.com	Social Media Today
www.whatissocialnetworking.com	Social Networking
www.statisticbrain.com	Statistic Brain Research Institute

Discussion Case: *How Safe Is Your Personal Information?*

Technological advances have resulted in profound changes in society. One of the greatest transformations is the collection, storage, and use of personal information. Access to personal information originates from many different sources, often without the individual being fully aware of it. Businesses may endeavor to use this information to recruit strong

employee applicants, offer more attractive products or services to prospective consumers, package desirable investment options to potential investors, and so on.

But, the risk that this information will fall into the wrong hands or be used for criminal purposes is ever present. In August 2014, the Department of Homeland Security announced that breaches of company safeguards meant to protect personal information had occurred at more than 1,000 American businesses already that year. This situation was so dire that some security analysts said that it had become the exception if businesses' information systems had *not* been compromised.

Criminals had become astonishingly adept at breaking into company records. They had learned how to scan corporate information systems for remote access opportunities—a vendor with remote access to a company's system, for example, or employees with the ability to work remotely—and then deploy computers to guess their usernames and passwords until they found a working combination. They used these footholds to virtually crawl through corporate networks until they gained access to in-store cash register systems. From there, they collected payment card data and sent it back to their servers, often outside the United States. Millions of American consumers' payment card details were allegedly sold on the black market to criminals all over the world. Some of the more significant break-ins are described below.

- At Home Depot, the nation's largest home improvement retailer, 56 million credit card accounts were compromised and 53 million e-mail addresses were exposed. Cybercriminals targeted the firm's 7,500 self-checkout lanes, since these terminals were clearly referenced in their computer systems as payment terminals. Analysts believed that the intruders went undetected as they moved around Home Depot's systems during regular daytime business hours and designed their malware to collect data, transmit it to an outside system, and then erase its tracks before the company's detection systems could discover the attack.

- At Target, a global retailer with revenues approaching $100 billion annually, an estimated 40 million shoppers' information was exposed. More than 17 million new credit cards had to be reissued following the attack, at an estimated cost of more than $200 million to the financial institutions involved.

- Anthem, one of the nation's largest health insurers, had up to 80 million records accessed by cybercriminals; these included Social Security numbers, birthdays, physical and e-mail addresses, employment information and income data for customers and employees, including the company's own chief executive. Anthem officials became aware of the breach when one of their senior administrators noticed that someone was using his identity to request information from the company's database. "This is one of the worst breaches I have ever seen," said Paul Stephens, director of Privacy Rights Clearinghouse.

- A cyberattack at Japan Airlines, one of the Japan's two largest airlines, exposed the personal information of more than 750,000 members of their frequent-flier program. The stolen data included names, genders, birth dates, addresses, e-mail addresses, and places of work. The company noticed that their customer information systems were running slowly for a few days; it later estimated that 190,000 customers' data were stolen during this time.

- Twitter, the online social networking service, announced that data for 250,000 of its users were vulnerable after it detected unusual access patterns and discovered their systems had been compromised. Accessed were usernames, e-mail addresses, and encrypted passwords. Some believed that the company's systems were entered through a well-publicized vulnerability in Oracle's Java software, a system installed on more than 3 billion devices.

As these examples show, various weaknesses in companies' software systems can leave customers' information vulnerable to theft (although most credit card companies have fraud protection programs that eliminate any liability for their customers when their cards are fraudulently used). Many companies were deeply worried about the growing risks of cyberattack, and major financial institutions wanted to minimize their potential liability from the fraudulent use of customer data.

How could these companies better protect themselves and their customers? Some firms realized they needed to upgrade security measures within their computer systems to limit access by vendors at remote sites and to require employees working off-site to better secure their computers or other devices with more complex and more difficult-to-detect passwords.

Another possible protection afforded to customers was to upgrade credit and debit cards, using technology first developed and adopted in Europe. So-called EMV cards (for Europay-MasterCard-Visa, the companies that first backed this new technology), easily recognized by their gold, square symbols, were designed to be inserted into a card payment terminal, where they stayed until the transaction was completed. EMVs were more secure, since they were embedded with a special chip that made it harder to access information than from the magnetic strip used on most cards in the United States. EMV cards also created a unique code for each transaction, making them more difficult to counterfeit than striped cards.

Credit card networks embraced the new technology and established October 2015 as the deadline for most U.S. retailers to upgrade their payment systems to accommodate EMV cards. Merchant Warehouse, which processed credit and debit card transactions for 80,000 U.S. merchants, reported however that only 60 percent of its clients' locations would be able to meet that deadline. A major reason for the delay was cost, estimated to be between $500 and $1,000 per payment terminal.

Some big retailers, including Walmart, Kroger, and Target, were aggressive in their upgrades and expected to meet the deadline. "We saw the fact that it was being implemented in the U.K. and many other countries around the globe; we saw the fraud decrease once this solution was implemented," said a Walmart financial executive. By 2015, all of the 4,838 Walmart stores, including Sam's Clubs, had the chip-based hardware in place and nearly 1,000 had turned it on.

Another concern was the cost of creating and distributing these new cards. By 2014 about 1 billion credit and debit cards were in use in the United States, but just 20 million chip cards had been issued, according to Smart Card Alliance. The new cards could cost up to $2 each, compared to pennies for the magnetic-strip cards. With some financial institutions issuing millions of cards, the investment was in the tens of millions of dollars.

The increasing costs for security raised an important issue: Who should pay for protection against cyberattacks? Should it be the retailers or the banks? Predictably, banks said retailers should pay to reissue the new and safer cards after a security breach in which the retailer had been at fault. Retailers countered by saying that banks should take steps to keep cards secure so they cannot be corrupted. This debate made its way to the U.S. Congress, where lawmakers began to examine the issue at a Senate banking committee hearing on data security issues.

Sources: "U.S. Finds 'Backoff' Hacker Tool Is Widespread," *The New York Times,* August 22, 2014, *bits.blogs.nytimes.com;* "Home Depot Hackers Exposed 53 Million Email Addresses," *The Wall Street Journal,* November 6, 2014, *online.wsj.com;* "What Did the Target Hack Really Cost? The Numbers Trickle In," *The Wall Street Journal,* February 18, 2014, *blogs.wsj.com;* "Anthem Hacking Points to Security Vulnerability of Health Care Industry," *The New York Times,* February 5, 2015, *www. nytimes.com;* "J.P. Morgan Says About 76 Million Households Affected by Cyber Breach," *The Wall Street Journal,* October 2, 2014, *online.wsj.com;* "Japan Airlines Reports Hacker Attacks," *The Wall Street Journal,* September 30, 2014, *online.wsj. com;* "PF Chang Hack Hit 33 Restaurants for 8 Months," *PCWorld,* August 4, 2014, *www.pcworld.com;* "Twitter Hacked: Data for 250,000 Users May Be Stolen," *The New York Times,* February 4, 2013, *bits.blogs.nytimes.com;* "In a Cyber Breach, Who Pays, Banks or Retailers?" *The Wall Street Journal,* January 12, 2014, *online.wsj.com;* and "Why U.S. Retailers Are Still Vulnerable to Card Fraud," *Bloomberg Businessweek,* April 10, 2014, *www.businessweek.com.*

Discussion Questions

1. What are the benefits and risks to consumers of using paperless, electronic systems to pay for products and services both online and in stores? Do the benefits to consumers justify the risks, or not?

2. Do you think technology will be able to stay ahead of sophisticated cybercriminals, or not? Why do you think so?

3. Who do you think should be responsible for the costs of switching to the more secure EMV card? Retailers? Banks? Consumers? How would different stakeholders answer this question?

4. Why did it take so long for American companies to better protect their customers' personal information by turning to the more secure technology that existed and was used in Europe and Asia for many years? Should the government have stepped in and mandated this technology?

5. If you were managing a retail store or chain, what steps would you take to protect your customers from others accessing their confidential information? If customer information theft had occurred, what steps would you take to win back your customers' trust and loyalty?

CHAPTER TWELVE

Regulating and Managing Information Technology

The rapid advances in information technology in just the past few decades mean that more information than ever before—about individuals, organizations, and governments—is located in servers or in "the cloud." This extraordinary development raises difficult challenges for governments and businesses related to information privacy, security, and ownership. What are the challenges facing governments and businesses in the management of information? What roles have governments and businesses played, and what are the ethical implications of their actions?

This Chapter Focuses on These Key Learning Objectives:

LO 12-1   Understanding why the management and regulation of information technology is a challenge for governments and businesses.

LO 12-2   Identifying the various information technology interventions undertaken by governments.

LO 12-3   Examining challenges businesses face in managing information about key stakeholders, including employees and customers.

LO 12-4   Knowing the causes and partial remedies to the problem of cybercrime.

LO 12-5   Assessing the emerging role and responsibilities of the organization's chief information officer and other organizational functions that are responsible to ensure information security and privacy.

LO 12-6   Identifying international and national governments' efforts to combat cybercrime.

The rapid evolution of information technology raises serious challenges for businesses engaged in global operations. Differences in national customs and regulations and the necessity of ensuring security and privacy of personal information are daily challenges for technology-based companies, as well as any business using technology, as shown by the following examples.

Using Apple's iCloud service became a major concern for its users in China after the service was hit by a cyberattack that could allow the perpetrators to intercept and see usernames, passwords, and other personal data. The attack, in 2014, occurred during a period of tense relations between the U.S. and Chinese governments over accusations of cyberespionage and hacking attacks. The online censorship watchdog GreatFire.org claimed that Chinese authorities were behind the attack, though other experts said that the source of the attacks could not be determined. A spokeswoman for China's Foreign Ministry said she was unaware of the matter and reiterated Beijing's position that it was opposed to cyberattacks. Nonetheless, Apple advised its users to not sign into iCloud.com if they received a warning from their browser that it was not a trusted site.

In another incident, the Federal Communications Commission announced in 2015 that AT&T was fined $25 million for failing to protect their customers' personal information, including Social Security numbers. Employees at A&T call centers were accused of stealing the names and Social Security numbers of about 300,000 of the wireless carrier's customers in the United States. The customer service employees at call centers in Mexico, Colombia, and the Philippines reportedly sold the information to third parties. The fine was the largest for data security and privacy violations that the FCC had ever issued. "The commission cannot—and will not—stand idly by when a carrier's lax data security practices expose the personal information of hundreds of thousands," said Tom Wheeler, chairman of the FCC.[1]

Who should protect people from attacks to their privacy by hackers or theft of their data, as shown in these examples? How can technology users guard against the inappropriate use of personal information? What role do governments or businesses need to play to protecting individuals' privacy and security?

Bill Joy, Sun Microsystems' chief scientist, warned of the dangers of rapid advances in technology:

The experiences of the atomic scientists clearly show the need to take personal responsibility, the danger that things will move too fast, and the way in which a process can take on a life of its own. We can, as they did, create insurmountable problems in almost no time flat. We must do more thinking up front if we are not to be similarly surprised and shocked by the consequences of our inventions.[2]

As this quotation implies, technology and innovation can be used for both good and evil. The development of nuclear science made possible both the atomic bomb and tremendous advances in modern medicine, for example. By the same token, the explosion of information that technology makes possible carries both promise and risk for business, government, and society.

---

[1] "Apple iCloud Service Is under Attack in Mainland China," *USA Today,* October 21, 2014, *www.usatoday.com;* and "F.C.C. Fined AT&T $25 Million for Privacy Breach," *The New York Times,* April 8, 2015, *bits.blogs.nytimes.com.*

[2] Bill Joy, "Why the Future Doesn't Need Us," *Wired,* April 2000, *www.wired.com/wired/archive/8.04/joy.*

Information Technology Challenges for Governments and Businesses

As discussed in Chapter 11, the dominant feature about technology is change. It is quick, widespread, and self-reinforcing. Like individuals, businesses and government also experience these features of technology. While scientists and technicians keep technology moving quickly, governments must try to keep pace, ensuring that the public is protected. Consider the invention of Google Glass.

> Google Glass is a computerized device that allows users to display access to the Internet right before their own eyes. It is a wearable technology that allows the user to capture and share the world they see straight from their eyewear. With smartphone integration and natural-language voice commands, Google Glass aims to transform the way people use technology to access information. State governments, however, are trying to enact legislation restricting the use of Google Glass and other similar technologies, especially when it could pose a safety hazard. West Virginia, for example, amended its legislation to include "wearable computer with a head-mounted display" among those actions prohibited while driving. Forty-one states by 2014 had used similar language to lump Google Glass and like devices with the use of text messaging while driving. But when Cecilia Abadie was cited for this violation while driving in California, she successfully fought the charges, since there was no evidence that she had Google Glass activated during her drive.[3]

The challenges become even greater when they occur outside state or national jurisdictions and therefore necessitate international cooperation. The negative impact on society from international crime continues to grow as criminals exploit the globalization of trade and finance and rapid changes in information technology. These developments have helped create new mechanisms for stealing data, trafficking contraband, conducting illicit trade, laundering money, and engaging in large-scale economic crimes. As this sort of criminal activity increases, the need for international cooperation among governments and businesses is essential. But, as discussed later in this chapter, that cooperation is often of limited effectiveness.

One of the major obstacles to achieving the right balance between enjoying the benefits of information technology and controlling its potential threats is that government and business often do not understand each other very well.

> Jason Chaffetz, a Republican member of the House of Representatives, argued that fewer than a dozen members of Congress can explain how Wi-Fi works and fewer than five can explain what the Domain Name System is. But, others also note that technicians located in the Silicon Valley do not understand how Congress works either. "In the startup community, they're on an emotional high from having killed SOPA [Stop Online Piracy Act] and PIPA [Protect Intellectual Property Act]," says Garrett Johnson, a staffer for the Senate Foreign Relations Committee, referring to legislation that would have tightened controls against digital piracy. "One thing they don't understand is that it's relatively easy to kill legislation. It's harder to pass a bill."[4]

Getting governments and businesses to work together will be a challenge. But, cooperation will be necessary if society is to reap the full benefits of technology without threat to people's security and safety.

---

[3] "Is Technology Advancing Too Fast for Legislative Comfort?" *Syracuse Journal of Science and Technology Law,* April 1, 2014, jost.syr.edu.

[4] "Silicon Valley Purists Are Clueless about How Washington Works, Too." *Bloomberg Businessweek,* February 20, 2013, www.bloomberg.com.

Government Interventions of Information and Ideas

Governments play various and sometimes conflicting roles with respect to information and ideas. In some countries, particularly in nondemocratic regimes, governments censor and restrict citizen access to information. In democratic countries, the role of government is more likely to look out for the public good and protect intellectual property; that is, the private ownership of certain kinds of information. What is the appropriate role of government in protecting individuals' personal information and the intellectual ideas owned by individuals and companies? What level of protection is necessary and desired by citizens or by businesses? Does the government overstep its authority, for example, when imposing censorship on social media sites? These various government approaches to information technology are addressed next.

Government Internet Censorship and Control

In a number of nondemocratic or authoritarian societies, governments have attempted to limit their citizens' access to information found on the Internet based on political, security, and religious grounds. These efforts have become increasingly more common and more sophisticated in recent years.

- *China.* As mentioned in the example at the beginning of this chapter, the Chinese government operates one of the most sophisticated systems of **Internet censorship** in the world. It requires all China-based websites and blogs to register with the government and blocks access to many kinds of information, including material critical of the government. Recently, China passed new rules requiring Internet users to provide their real names to service providers and required all Chinese video-streaming sites to receive approval from China's top broadcasting regulator or have the content banned. Google found its popular Gmail service unavailable in China. Users in China could not browse their photo-sharing websites, like Flickr or Facebook. In 2015, Chinese Internet companies deleted tens of thousands of user accounts based on new rules that increased government control over online disclosure. According to the Chinese government, many of these deletions were based on misleading or harmful usernames, including users who were masquerading as government departments or used usernames such as "Come Shoot Guns" and spread terrorist information or sported erotic avatars.[5]

- *Pakistan.* In 2010, the Pakistani government, with the support of conservative Islamic groups, broadened an existing ban on social networking sites to include YouTube, some Flickr and Wikipedia sites, and about 450 individual web pages, because of what it described as "growing sacrilegious content." (The ban followed one day after a Pakistani court ruled that access to the Facebook site should be temporarily suspended for 12 days, citing offensive drawings of the Prophet Muhammad.) Despite the objections of many Pakistani citizens, who included nearly 25 million Internet users, the Pakistan Telecommunications Authority said in a statement that the ban was "in line with the Constitution of Pakistan, the wishes of the people of Pakistan." After YouTube removed offensive material, the ban on this site was lifted.[6]

---

[5] For additional information on China's censorship of the Internet, see "Chinese Web Firms Delete More Than 60,000 Accounts as New Rules Loom," *The Wall Street Journal*, February 27, 2015, *www.wsj.com;* "China Is Said to Use Powerful New Weapon to Censor Internet," *The New York Times*, April 10, 2015, *www.nytimes.com;* and "China's Internet Regulators Put Explicit New Censorship Rules in Place," *The Wall Street Journal*, April 28, 2015, *www.wsj.com.*

[6] "Pakistan Widens Online Ban to Include YouTube," *The New York Times*, May 20, 2012, *www.nytimes.com;* and "Here Are Countries That Block Facebook, Twitter, and YouTube," *Mother Jones*, March 28, 2014, *www.motherjones.com.*

Just 10 days before a local election in Turkey, government authorities blocked user access to Twitter. Turkey was one of Twitter's top 10 markets with more than 12 million users. A week later individuals were prevented from accessing YouTube, Google's video-sharing website. This move came a few hours after a leaked recording appeared on YouTube showing a conversation between a Turkish foreign minister, the nation's spy chief, and a top general discussing scenarios that could lead to an attack against Jihadist militants in Syria. Other pirated videos connected the country's prime minister to an investigation of corruption that implicated a dozen of his closest allies.

A week later the Turkish government's Telecommunications Board unblocked Twitter accounts, a day after the country's highest court ruled that the two-week ban on social media violated freedom of expression. This action came a few days after Prime Minister Erdogan's Islamist-rooted Justice and Development Party had won a resounding victory in the local elections.

Turkey's president, Abdullah Gul, posted to Twitter this statement, "Shutting down social media platforms cannot be approved," adding that "it is not technically possible to fully block access to globally active platforms like Twitter, anyway." President Gul was likely referring to the thousands of Turks who protested the ban on using Twitter by using Twitter accounts after disguising the location of their computers or by using text messaging services. Others denounced the actions as a digital coup more befitting China or North Korea, claiming that Turkey was a model of democracy. Yet, even after the court ordered the Turkish government to unblock the video-sharing website, the government ignored the court ruling and access to YouTube remained unavailable to Turkish residents.

Sources: "In Turkey, Twitter Roars After Effort to Block It," *The New York Times,* March 21, 2014, *www.nytimes.com;* "Turkey Blocks YouTube," *The Wall Street Journal,* March 27, 2014, *online.wsj.com;* "Turkey Lifts Block on Twitter After Top Court Ruling," *The Wall Street Journal,* April 3, 2014, *online.wsj.com;* and "YouTube Remains Blocked in Turkey, Despite Court Order," *Mashable,* April 10, 2014, *mashable.com.*

- *Iran.* Since 2009, after contentious presidential elections that pitted various religious groups against each other, the elected Iranian government banned Facebook, Twitter, YouTube, and later Instagram. Based on the ruling party's religious-political stance and the country's official philosophy: "the media should be used as a forum for healthy encounter of different ideas, but they must strictly refrain from diffusion and propagation of destructive and anti-Islamic practices." The political hard-liners in that country argued that the country's president had not done enough to "stop the spread of the decadent Western culture."[7]

- *North Korea.* North Korea is one of the world's most recognized censors of the Internet. But its government made an unprecedented move in 2013 when it allowed Internet searches on mobile devices and laptops by foreigners—but not by its citizens. Based on the efforts by Google's chairman, Eric E. Schmidt, North Korean officials allowed Koryolink, a state-owned telecommunications company, to give foreigners access to 3G mobile Internet services, but retained the ban applied to the country's citizens. (North Korea took a more restrictive stance toward free expression in 2014, as presented in the discussion case at the end of this chapter on the hacking of Sony Pictures.)[8]

One particular government censorship of social media and the Internet occurred around a local election, calling into question the political motivations behind these actions, as shown in Exhibit 12.A.

[7] For the arguments leading to Iran's ban of social media, see "Iran," *Open Net Initiative, openet.net* and "Instagram Joins Facebook, Twitter as Banned Social Media in Iran," *CBC News,* May 23, 2014, *www.cbc.ca.*

[8] "North Korea Widens Internet Access, but Just for Visitors," *The New York Times—Global Edition,* February 22, 2013, *rendezvous.blogs.nytimes.com.*

Exhibit 12.B

PRISM was a clandestine surveillance program, launched in 2007, under which the U.S. National Security Agency (NSA) collected certain online communications from major U.S. Internet companies. Its existence was first revealed by whistle-blower Edward Snowden. The technology companies subject to the PRISM program included Google, Facebook, Apple, and Microsoft. When asked by the government, these companies were required to turn over to the government communications (such as e-mails or posts) containing certain court-approved search terms. The purpose of the program was to track terrorist activity and protect the United States against attack. But critics of the program called it an unwarranted intrusion by Big Brother (the government) into the lives of citizens and a violation of peoples' privacy rights. How did the companies involved respond to the government's demands? Although most of the companies complied with legally mandated sharing of information, they asked the National Security Agency if they could make public government requests for information about their subscribers and users. The companies wanted their customers to know the extent and scope of the government's inquiries. Six months later the federal government agreed to allow the technology companies to make more information public about how often the government monitored Internet usage. However, the data released by the companies, the government said, had to be in broad ranges, and the agreement did not grant the companies any new ways to block government demands for information that the companies viewed as intrusive.

Yahoo! chose to challenge the NSA orders, refusing to provide information and claiming that the government was spying on certain foreign users of their site without a warrant. In what was described as a "secret court in Washington, D.C.," the judges disagreed with Yahoo! and ordered them to hand over the data or be accused of breaking the law. While handing over of the data was private, it was presumed that Yahoo! complied with the judges' decision since no criminal charges were filed against the company.

Sources: "U.S. Official Releases Details of Prism Program," *The Wall Street Journal,* June 8, 2013, *online.wsj.com;* "3 Tech Giants Want to Reveal Data Requests," *The New York Times,* June 11, 2013, *www.nytimes.com;* "Government Reaches Deal with Tech Firms on Data Requests," *The Wall Street Journal,* January 27, 2014, *online.wsj.com;* and "Secret Court Ruling Put Tech Companies in Data Bind," *The New York Times,* June 13, 2013, *www.nytimes.com.*

In all of these instances, governments intervened to restrict their citizens' access to information and various Internet and social media sites, generally to suppress political dissent or to impose particular religious or ideological views. In most democratic, Western nations, such interventions would not be tolerated. Yet, how Western countries intervene when it comes to information technology has varied. Sometimes a government accesses information for the public good and limits individual rights; while at other times, governments support individuals' control over their personal information or protect the individual's intellectual property.

Government Acquisition of Information to Protect the Public Good

The U.S. government was faced with a difficult trade-off when attempting to combat increasing threats of terrorism. Does the government protect individuals' right to personal information or does the government acquire massive amounts of personal information, often held by technology or social media companies, to protect the public? The government appeared to weigh the importance of acquiring information to better protect the public from terrorism and other threats more heavily than respecting individuals' rights to privacy when it comes to personal information. One such example—the U.S. PRISM program—is profiled in Exhibit 12.B.

In 2015, the French Parliament faced a similar challenge—protect the citizens of the country or respect individuals' right to personal information. The government leaders passed legislation that allowed authorities to conduct some of the most intrusive spying activities ever, with almost no judicial oversight. Following the public outcry after the terrorist attacks in and around Paris in early 2015, in which 17 people affiliated with the satirical magazine *Charlie Hebdo* were killed, the French government wanted greater access to private, personal information. The new law allowed government intelligence services to tap cellphones, read e-mails, and force Internet companies to comply with requests to allow the government to sift through virtually all of their subscribers' communications. These actions were designed to protect the public, but they were criticized by individuals who felt that government intrusion into their personal lives had gone too far.

Government Protecting Individuals' Rights and Property

Governments also have stepped in to protect individuals and their personal information. In an important case in 2014, the European high court ruled against Google in a dispute with an individual user, a Spanish attorney. The attorney had sued, asking that Google remove from its search results some personal information about him that he believed was damaging. His right to request such removal came to be known as the **right to be forgotten**. The court agreed with the attorney and ordered Google to set up a system to respond to requests from European customers. This case and its ramifications are further explored in a case at the end of this book.

Governments also have protected individuals and companies' ideas—their intellectual property. With advances in technology, protecting the ownership of *intellectual property* has become more challenging than ever. The ideas, concepts, and other symbolic creations of the human mind are often referred to as **intellectual property**. In the United States, intellectual property is protected through a number of special laws and public policies, including copyrights, patents, and trademark laws. Not all nations have policies similar to those in the United States.

The illegal copying of copyrighted software, or **software piracy**, is a global problem. According to the Business Software Alliance (BSA), in a survey of nearly 22,000 consumers and PC users, 43 percent of the software installed on personal computers around the world in 2013 was not properly licensed, up slightly from 42 percent two years earlier. Wide variations in the use of unlicensed software usage occurred worldwide, as shown in Figure 12.1.

FIGURE 12.1

Top 10 Countries by Percentage of Users Using Unlicensed Software, 2013

Source: "The Compliance Gap: BSA Global Software Survey," *Business Software Alliance,* June 2014, *www.bsa.org.*

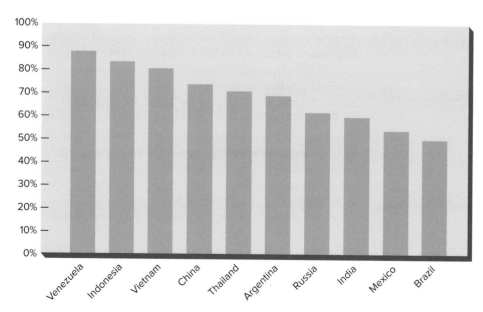

Use of unlicensed software appears greatest in select Asia and South American countries. The data in Figure 12.1 mirrors additional discoveries by the BSA in its global study. The greatest rise in the commercial value of unlicensed software use was in the Asia-Pacific region, with a price tag of $21 billion. Worldwide the use of unlicensed software costs software manufacturers and retailers more than $62 billion annually.[9]

In 1998, the United States passed the **Digital Millennium Copyright Act**, making it a crime to circumvent antipiracy measures built into most commercial software agreements between the manufacturers and their users. In China, the government announced that computer makers must ship all their product with licensed operating systems preinstalled and inspected all government computer systems for licensed software. In 2009, China sent 11 people to prison for manufacturing and distributing pirated Microsoft software throughout the world. Microsoft called the group part of "the biggest software counterfeiting organization we have ever seen, by far" and estimated its global sales at more than $2 billion.[10] Laws attempting to stem software piracy and reinforce intellectual property rights exist in many other countries, including Saudi Arabia, the United Arab Emirates, Vietnam, and India.[11] As expected, some laws are more rigorously enforced and are successful in stemming the use of pirated software than others.

Governments have, at times, taken various steps to ensure that an individual's information and intellectual property are protected; yet, governments have also placed the public good ahead of individuals' rights or placed their own protection of power ahead of their citizenry. Next the focus shifts to business organizations and their collection of confidential information and the potential for invasions of privacy or lack of security measures. How much information about the company's stakeholders should be acquired or shared? How much protection is necessary to safeguard individual and corporate confidential information?

Business Access to and Use of Confidential Information

In the course of conducting ordinary business, many companies acquire large amounts of personal information from various stakeholders and are then faced with the challenge of using it appropriately. Technology gives businesses access to a great deal of information—sometimes called **big data**. Managers often find that their strong attraction to using big data can be at odds with the protection of individuals' rights to their own information.

Access to Stakeholders' Personal Information

Two major market stakeholders targeted by business organizations for the collection of information are employees and consumers. One example of a company's use of information about their customers—involving AT&T—was profiled at the beginning of this chapter.

Most state governments ruled that businesses have the right to monitor their employees at work. Businesses need to ensure that the time employees spend on the job is productive, since wasting time can result in significant economic losses.

Dennis Gray, general manager of Accurid Pest Solutions, a Virginia pest-control company, suspected that his workers were spending too much time on personal issues during the workday. He quietly installed a piece of GPS tracking software on

[9] For additional information on the use of unlicensed software, see "The Compliance Gap: BSA Global Software Survey," *Business Software Alliance,* June 2014, *www.bsa.org.*

[10] "Chinese Court Jails 11 in Microsoft Piracy Ring," *New York Times,* January 1, 2009, *www.nytimes.com.*

[11] For a description of India's 2010 Copyright Amendment Bill, see "India to Align Copyright Norms with Global Standards," *The Economic Times,* October 15, 2010, *economictimes.indiatimes.com.*

the company-issued smartphones given to his drivers. The software allowed Gray to log into his computer to see a map displaying the location and movement of his drivers. One employee, he discovered, was visiting the same address a few times a week for a few hours during the workday. Gray confronted his driver and told him that he was being tracked. The driver confessed that he was meeting a woman during work hours. A second driver, when Gray told him he was bring tracked, admitted that he was "blowing off work." Both drivers were fired. "We were certainly impressed with the [GPS tracking] software," said Gray.[12]

Was Accurid's use of tracking software to identify where the company's drivers were during work hours an appropriate use of technology? Due to advances in technology, companies today can know where their workers are, eavesdrop on their telephone calls, tell if a driver is wearing a seat belt in the company's vehicle, and even if he is tailgating another vehicle while driving. Employees, likewise, know that every keystroke on the company computer or laptop can be monitored. But, when is surveillance too much and an invasion of an employees' privacy? While high-tech monitoring may feel like a violation of privacy to some workers, others argue that it is necessary to ensure and improve workplace safety and productivity. Technology can also reduce employee theft, protect the company's intellectual property and secrets, and be used to investigate claims of harassment or discrimination at work. (These issues are further explored in Chapter 15.)

No federal statutes in the United States restrict the use of GPS or similar tracking devices to monitor employees. Only two states, Delaware and Connecticut, require employers to tell workers that their electronic communications—anything from e-mails to instant message to texts—are being monitored. "It is not a question of whether companies should monitor," said Lewis Maltby, founder of the National Workrights Institute, which promotes employee privacy. "It's a question of how."[13]

Consumers' shopping habits are also a rich source of data for businesses. While individuals may believe they are just an anonymous or nameless shopper among a pool of millions of shoppers, companies tracking big data, sometimes called metadata, can pick out specific details about an individual's shopping habits, preferences, or tendencies. Researchers at MIT analyzed credit card transactions by 1.1 million shoppers and claimed they needed only four bits of secondary information, such as location or time, to identify the unique individual purchasing patterns of 90 percent of the people involved in their study. Even when the data was cleaned of names, account numbers, and other obvious identifiers, the shoppers' identity could be found.[14]

Cybersecurity experts warned Verizon in 2015 that the company was putting the privacy of its customers at risk by using computer codes, called unique ID headers, to tag and follow its mobile subscribers around the web. These codes created databases that could make the consumers more vulnerable to covert tracking and profiling. Johnathan Mayer, a lawyer and computer science graduate student at Stanford University, reported in *Turn*, the name of Mayer's blog, that the cybersecurity experts' fears were valid. He used computer code to track individuals even after they tried to delete their digital footprints. "Verizon is not in a position to control how others use its [ID] headers," said Mayer. "There is no doubt that this particular approach does introduce new privacy problems."[15]

---

[12] "Memo to Workers: The Boss Is Watching," *The Wall Street Journal*, October 22, 2013, *www.wsj.com*. Also see "Unblinking Eyes Track Employees: Workplace Surveillance Sees Good and Bad," *The New York Times*, June 21, 2014, *www.nytimes.com*.

[13] Maltby's quote is from "Memo to Workers: The Boss Is Watching," *The Wall Street Journal*, October 22, 2013, *www.wsj.com*.

[14] "Metadata Can Expose Person's Identity Even without Name," *The Wall Street Journal*, January 2, 2015, *www.wsj.com*.

[15] "Verizon's Mobile 'Supercookies' Seen as Threat to Privacy," *The New York Times*, January 25, 2015, *www.nytimes.com*.

Exhibit 12.C

Does the Electronic Collection of a Patient's Medical Records Improve Medical Care?

The use of electronic medical records was central to the U.S. government's aim to overhaul and stream-line the health care system as part of the Affordable Care Act. Advocates contended that electronic record systems would improve patient care and lower costs through better coordination of medical services. The Obama Administration supported this view and spent billions of dollars to encourage doctors and hospitals to switch to electronic records to track patient care. Critics countered that electronic record keeping was filled with flaws. Primarily, the new technology failed to provide adequate safeguards to ensure that information being provided by hospitals and doctors about their patients was accurate.

Scot Silverstein's 84-year-old mother, Betty, was allegedly one of the casualties of improper medical records. After Betty began to mix-up her words, her son, a doctor, worried that she was having a stroke. He rushed Betty to the local hospital and saw in his mother's medical records that Sotalol, which controls rapid heartbeats, was correctly listed as one of her medications.

Days later, when Betty's heart condition flared up, Scot was stunned to see that the drug, Sotalol, was no longer listed in his mother's medical records. After complications, Betty died, and Scot blamed her death on problems with the hospital's electronic medical records, claiming that the disappearance of Sotalol from his mother's records led to the prescription of other medications that interacted dangerously with this drug. "If paper records had been in place, unless someone had been using disappearing ink, this would not have happened," said Silverstein.

Supporters of electronic medical records argue that digital records have dramatically reduced common medical errors. More than 17 million medication mistakes were avoided in the United States annually because hospitals used computerized prescription-ordering systems, according to a study published in the *Journal of the American Medical Informatics Association.* In such systems, sloppy handwriting is irrelevant and doctors receive pop-up alerts when attempting to prescribe dangerous drug combinations.

Sources: "Medicare Is Faulted on Shift to Electronic Records," *The New York Times,* November 29, 2012, *www.nytimes.com;* and "Digital Health Records' Risk Emerge as Deaths Blamed on Systems," *Bloomberg,* June 25, 2013, *www.bloomberg.com.*

The collection of consumer information raises important ethical issues of privacy and security. (These issues are further explored in Chapter 14.) Another important consumer issue involving the ethical use of information technology includes the collection and use of patients' medical records, as presented in Exhibit 12.C.

The questions of how much information companies should collect about their stakeholders and if the collection of stakeholders' information benefits these stakeholders or not remain controversial. Whether businesses have adequately built protections against unwanted invasions of stakeholder privacy and breaches of information security remain to be seen.

Special Issue: Cybercrime—A Threat to Organizations and the Public

Another important issue regarding the effect of information technology on both govern-ments and business organizations is the growing presence of cybercrime in the global community. **Cybercrime** is criminal activity done using computers and the Internet. This includes anything from downloading illegal music files to stealing millions of dollars from online bank accounts. Cybercrime also includes nonmonetary offenses, such as creating and distributing viruses on other computers or posting confidential business information on the Internet.

Cybercrime is often committed by individuals or groups gaining unauthorized access to a business organization through its computer system. They are called hackers. **Hackers** are indi-viduals, acting alone or in groups often with advanced technology training, who, for thrill or profit, breach a business's information security system. Hackers may be individuals employed by the business organization, or formerly employed, or are strangers and completely unknown to the business. Some violations are simply careless actions, while others are intentional.

A new threat emerged on the scene in the 2010s for security experts to confront—**hacktivists**. Hacktivists are individuals or groups who hack into government or corporate computer networks and then release information to try to embarrass the organizations or gain leverage against the organizations. This invasion of government and business computer networks became so well known that there was a film dedicated to activities by hacktivists, called *We Are Legion: The Story of the Hacktivists,* released in 2012.

The most publicized group of hacktivists is called Anonymous, a loosely associated international network of hacktivists easily distinguished by the type of masks they wore (a stylized face with an over-sized smile and red cheeks, a wide moustache upturned at both ends, and a thin vertical pointed beard). Criminal actions attributed to this group included targeting government agencies in the United States, Israel, Tunisia, Uganda, and others; child pornography sites; copyright protection agencies; and corporations, such as PayPal, MasterCard, Visa, and Sony. This group also publicly supported WikiLeaks during the time when classified U.S. government documents were leaked to the media; it also supported the Occupy movement, which launched protests against Wall Street and other global financial institutions to bring light to social and economic injustices.[16]

The following section discusses the costs of cybercrime and then investigates who these malicious hackers are. Efforts taken by governments and businesses to combat these violations will be discussed in the following sections.

Costs of Cybercrime

According to a study by the Ponemon Institute, the cost of cybercrime per U.S. business organization was $12.7 million in 2014, a 9.3 percent increase from the prior year. What accounted for these rising costs? The study noted that a majority of the costs occurred when detecting the intrusion and efforts taken to recover from the hacking. The study further found that it took an average of 31 days for a business to resolve or recover from the cyberattack. In addition, the firm encountered significant costs due to disruption of the business organization's computer systems. And the forecast was even bleaker. The study concluded by noting that the volume of cyberattacks was increasing, with 138 attacks during a single week in 2014. This was up from an average of 50 attacks per week in 2010.[17]

Worldwide, a similar picture emerges. Global estimates of the costs of cybercrime range between $300 billion to $1 trillion in annual global losses, according to a study conducted by the Center for Strategic and International Studies (CSIS). The CSIS study considered criminal activity focusing on intellectual property loss; the loss of sensitive business in formation; opportunity costs associated the service disruptions and reduced trust toward online activity with that business organization; the additional costs of securing networks, acquiring additional insurance, and developing recovery plans to recuperate from cyberattacks; and reputational damage to the hacked company—all considered in the cost of cybercrime.[18] Banks and other financial institutions are especially vulnerable to cyberattacks, as the following incident shows.

[16] For additional information, see "The History of Anonymous," *InfoSec Institute* at *resources.infosecinstitute.com/a-history-of-anonymous.*

[17] "Cyber-Crime Costs Rise at U.S., Worldwide Companies," *eWeek,* October 16, 2014, *www.eweek.com.*

[18] "Survey Reveals True Global Cost of Cyber Attacks," *ComputerWeekly.com,* July 23, 2013, *www.computerweekly.com.*

FIGURE 12.2
Why Do Hackers Hack?

> While hackers may have any number of reasons underlying the motivations for their actions, three of the more common motivations appear to be:
>
> - Hackers hack to profit from their actions—*the financial-incentive motive.*
> - Hackers hack in retaliation against action or inaction by a company or government—*the retaliation motive.*
> - Hackers hack to gain media attention for their political or social viewpoint or to boost their own ego—*the seeking media attention motive.*

From 2013 into 2015, a gang of computer criminals allegedly stole millions of dollars from banks in Russia, Eastern Europe, and the United States, according to a Kaspersky Lab ZAO report, a Russian computer-security firm. According to the report, the thieves captured video of what was happening on bank computer screens to learn how to mimic the way bank employees accessed their systems. They hacked into computers that controlled automated teller machines (ATMs) so that they would dispense cash when criminals walked by. They also were able to move cash from one account to another, seemingly without being noticed. The report said that one bank lost $7.3 million to ATM fraud to the group and another lost $10 million to hackers exploiting its online banking platform. Cumulatively, the losses could be as high as $1 billion, according to the report.[19]

Research conducted by the McKinsey & Company in partnership with the World Economic Forum suggested that companies were struggling with their capabilities to keep up with criminals when it came to cyber-risk management. As more and more highly visible breaches occurred with growing regularity, most technology executives believed that they were losing ground to cyberattackers. Current strategies were ineffective and many managers admitted that they have difficulty quantifying the true impact of risks and mitigation plans. Moreover, much of the economic harm incurred by business organizations came from an inadequate response to the breach rather than the breach itself.[20]

Exploring Why Hackers Hack

Hacking into businesses and other organizations is undoubtedly a powerful and destructive force. Why do hackers do it? The many reasons seem to be to make money, to retaliate against a company or government, or to gain media attention for an issue or the hackers themselves, as shown in Figure 12.2. This section explores these selected motivations for hacking.

A new website, called Hacker's List, seeks to match hackers with people looking to gain access to e-mail accounts, take down unflattering photos from a website, or gain access to a company's database. In its first three months of operation, over 800 hacking jobs were posted for bid, asking hackers—obviously using anonymous names—to bid on performing the task. The website's operator, identified as Charles Tendell, calls himself an "ethical hacker" who helps companies and individuals fight back against the bad guys operating online. Tendell admitted that he began Hacker's List as an "off-the-cuff idea," and it grew far faster than he anticipated. He collects the fee for each assignment, holding the fee until the task is complete

---

[19] "New Report Says Computer Criminals Stole Millions from Banks," *The Wall Street Journal,* February 15, 2015, *www.wsj.com.*

[20] "The Rising Strategic Risks of Cyberattacks," *McKinsey & Company,* May 2014, *www.mckinsey.com.*

and payment is agreed to by the person posting the job. Some requests may clearly be illegal, yet others, such as breaking into another person's e-mail account are not. A man in Sweden posted that he would pay $2,000 to anyone who could break into his landlord's website. A California woman agreed to pay $500 for someone to hack into her boyfriend's Facebook and Gmail accounts to see if he is cheating on her. And the list continues and grows each day.[21]

At the core of this business arrangement is the hacker's motivation to profit from her or his computer skills and willingness to break the law for payment. The Hacker's List website received a favorable review on *hackerforhirereview.com,* which specializes in assessing the legitimacy of such services. The owner of the site gave his top rating to Hacker's List because "it's a really cool concept" that limits the ability of customers and hackers to take advantage of one another.[22]

Other hackers are more politically motivated. The ongoing political tensions between the United States and China in the mid-2010s were said to provoke some remarkable hacking efforts. Chinese hackers allegedly targeted U.S. media companies to penetrate inside their newsgathering systems. Accessing reporters' computers provided the opportunity for Chinese government officials to identify sources in articles and information about pending stories. The Chinese government historically has penalized Chinese nationals who passed information to foreign reporters. Mainstream business organizations also were targeted for cyberattacks, allegedly attributed to Chinese hackers.

In 2014, the U.S. government indicted five members of the Chinese army, accusing them of online attacks on U.S. businesses. The hacking was intended to steal trade and military secrets from foreign victims. Major U.S. corporations were the targets of these attacks, including Alcoa, Westinghouse Electric, and the United States Steel Corporation. A few weeks later, new accusations arose, again targeting Chinese army members. This round of cyberattacks named a specific group, Unit 61486, just one of more than a dozen Chinese hacking groups with strong ties to the Chinese People's Liberation Army. A U.S. National Security Agency report claimed that Unit 61486 shared computer resources and communicated with members of another Chinese Army group, Unit 61398, whose members were the focus of the first set of indictments. The Chinese government, as expected, denounced the indictments, denied the charges, and cited recent revelations that the United States had engaged in its own cyberespionage. The Chinese government vowed retaliatory measures, including new inspections procedures for American technologies, which could lead to an escalating trade war.[23]

The discussion case at the end of this chapter, describing a hacking effort led by individuals associated with North Korea's government, is another example of a cyberattack motivated by retaliation.

Another reason for hacking is to gain media attention—a factor that was also involved in the North Korean cyberattack on Sony. Hackers also may have a political agenda and use their skills to seek attention toward a social injustice or government action. As profiled earlier, the Anonymous group assumes this motivation for their hacking efforts.

---

[21] "Owner of Anonymous Hackers-for-Hire Site Steps Forward," *The New York Times,* May 12, 2015, *www.nytimes.com.*

[22] "Need Some Espionage Done? Hackers Are for Hire Online," *The New York Times,* January 15, 2015, *dealbook.nytimes.com.*

[23] "Chinese Hackers Hit U.S. Media," *The Wall Street Journal,* January 31, 2013, *online.wsj.com;* and "2nd China Army Unit Implicated in Online Spying," *The New York Times,* June 9, 2014, *www.nytimes.com.*

In 2015, Anonymous announced that it would target the online activities of ISIS, a radical organization whose goal was establishing an Islamic state in Syria, Iraq, and other countries, by taking down and exposing the organization's websites. ISIS was known for numerous murders, often carrying out public executions, crucifixions, and other barbaric acts. Anonymous took a political stance against this form of terrorism by vowing to use their hacking skills to disrupt and expose this organization and its operations. Anonymous pledged, "no place is safe for you online . . . You will be treated like a virus, and we are the cure . . . We own the Internet . . . We are Anonymous. . . ." Only a few months after their announcement, Anonymous reported that it had taken down at least 100 Twitter and several Facebook accounts they believed were linked to ISIS and used "to expand their influence and recruit new members."[24]

Other cyberattacks aimed at raising public awareness were less radical than Anonymous but nonetheless could be damaging to business organizations by disrupting their operations and exposing personal information of their customers or employees to the public. Some hackers are just trying to prove a point—your system is vulnerable and subject to attack. Some of these efforts are welcomed by businesses; others are not. **White hatters** are individuals employed by businesses or governments to hack their systems deliberately to discover possible vulnerabilities of their own systems; typically the discovered weaknesses are used to strengthen these systems' defenses. **Grey hatters** are hackers working on their own, often seeking media attention, but inclined to share their hacking exploits with the businesses they hacked in the expectation that the firm will pay them for the information. The grey hatters are less welcomed by businesses since they might expose the company's security weaknesses publicly to bring greater attention to the need for more aggressive security measures.[25]

Whether the motivation is for personal profit, retaliation against a company or government, or to gain public attention, the instances of hacking are numerous and the potential for damage profound. Governments and businesses are challenged to create systems that thwart cyberattacks to ensure public safety and secure business assets. Some of these efforts are discussed in the next sections of this chapter.

Business Responses to Invasions of Information Security

Faced with the serious threat of cybercrime, many businesses have gone to great lengths to build strong defenses to protect information and ensure stakeholder privacy. These defenses must be comprehensive, cut across all organizational functions, and receive the support of the organization's executive leadership.

Cybersecurity experts point out that most business organizations only protect their digital perimeters with intrusion detection devices. Yet, any strong-minded hacktivist or organized criminal syndicate can find a way to penetrate a business's information system. Experts encourage companies to develop an *incident-response plan for cyberattacks*. These plans complement the effort to prevent access to information but also focuses on what to do when a breach occurs.

According to McKinsey & Company, a leading business consulting firm, an incident-response plan's primary objective is to manage a cybersecurity event or

[24] "Anonymous Hackers: ISIS 'Like a Virus, and We Are the Cure'," *Newsmax*, February 9, 2015, *www.newsmax.com;* and "Anonymous: Hacktivists Taking Action against ISIS," *I Love Philosophy*, February 10, 2015, *www.ilovephilosophy.com.*

[25] "Hacking—A New Classification System," *Truth, Lies, Deception, and Coverups*, www.truthliesdeceptioncoverups.info.

incident in a way that limits damage, increases the confidence of external stakeholders, and reduces recovery time and costs. The benefits in having such a plan include improved decision making enabling a quicker response; internal coordination throughout the organization in response to an attack; external coordination with third parties, such as law enforcement agencies and forensic experts; clear, established roles and responsibilities across the organization; and limiting the damage incurred after the attack.[26]

Most businesses have recognized the likelihood and damaging impact of a cyberattack. After its own bank's cybersecurity was breached in 2014, JPMorgan Chase CEO James Dixon announced that his firm would double its spending on cybersecurity over the next five years, totaling more than $500 million annually. eBay asked its 145 million users to change their passwords after a cyberattack in 2014. Facebook offered a privacy checkup to every one of its 1.28 billion users. Facebook CEO Mark Zuckerberg said the company is more sensitive to privacy and it also is good for business to be more vigilant. According to Pam Dixon, executive director of the World Privacy Forum, "They [tech companies] have gotten enough black eyes at this point that I tend to believe that they realized they have to take care of consumers a lot better."

> Apple's new iPhones and smartwatch, introduced in 2014, handled information differently from its rivals, a fact the company used in its marketing pitches. "We don't build a profile based on your email content or web browsing habits to sell to advertisers," explained Apple's CEO Tim Cook. "We don't 'monetize' the information you store on your iPhone or in iCloud. And we don't read your email or your messages to get information to market to you."[27] Clearly how businesses conduct their business and relate to their customers is changing, and greater protection of information has become a priority.

Organizations' leaders also stepped up and took on the fight against cyberattacks. The issue of computer hacking was on the agenda for most corporate boards when they met in the mid-2010s. In 2012, Kellogg Company's board created a dedicated security group and hired the company's first chief information-security officer. Tyson Foods' directors adopted a policy of being briefed annually on cybersecurity, as well as on an as-needed basis. Delta Air Lines added a board member because of his "substantial expertise in the information technology and security industry."[28]

Another method some businesses use is to reduce criminal intrusion of their sites by paying hackers, often called white hatters and discussed earlier in this chapter. Businesses use the white hatters' computer skills to identify weaknesses in the company's information systems.

> An ethical hacking contest was held at a Swiss security conference in Geneva. So-called bug bounty programs became popular in Silicon Valley's high-tech sector. PayPal paid about 1,000 hackers for confidentially reporting on big security holes found in their systems. "If you care about the product [and] care about your customers, you care about your customers' security—this is what you have to do,"

---

[26] For a more thorough description, see "How Good Is Your Cyberincident-Response Plan?" *McKinsey & Company,* December 2013, *www.mckinsey.com.*

[27] "eBay Asks Users to Change Passwords after Cyberattack," *The Wall Street Journal,* May 21, 2014, *online.wsj.com;* "Facebook Offers Privacy Checkup to All 1.28 Billion Users," *The New York Times,* May 22, 2014, *www.nytimes.com;* and "Apple's New iPhone Pitch: Privacy," *The Wall Street Journal,* September 23, 2014, *online.wsj.com.*

[28] "Corporate Boards Race to Shore up Cybersecurity," *The Wall Street Journal,* June 29, 2014, *online.wsj.com.*

said the director of security intelligence at PayPal. As Yahoo!s chief security officer also explained, "There are thousands of people out there with the skill sets that could help us find these bugs and get them fixed faster. And there's nothing lost by bringing them into the fold and giving them the opportunity to participate."[29]

Many companies have institutionalized their attention toward protecting information by hiring managers trained in this field and able to implement strong safeguards within the company and its system. These managers are profiled next.

The Chief Information, Security, Technology Officer

Businesses often entrust the responsibility for managing information technology and its many privacy and security issues to the **chief information officer (CIO)** or individuals with other similar titles such as *chief security officer* or *chief technology officer.* Many firms have elevated the role of their data processing managers by giving them the title of chief information officer. In a study of CIOs from around the world, McKinsey & Company found that most CIOs reported to their chief executive officer rather than to the chief financial officer or chief operating officer. Recently this role has expanded even more to include broader responsibilities and greater influences on corporate policies and practices. By 2015, given the increase in costly cyberattacks, experts were pointing out that the business organizations' demand for qualified cybersecurity experts was far greater than the supply.[30] In today's technology-driven world, the CIO plays a critical role.

> According to one security expert, "The CIO is a 'General.' Generals are not concerned with how the weapons function or how the rank-and-file are performing. This is the job of the lieutenants. The General focuses on the strategic application of resources on the battlefield. It is his/her duty to bring the plans of the sovereign (e.g., the CEO, the Board of Directors) to fruition."[31]

Along with reporting to the highest levels within the business came additional responsibilities. The CIO's role was changing dramatically, becoming more integrated into the overall strategic direction of the firm. "CIOs themselves are in the midst of a make-or-break personal change-management project: CIOs who can only take orders, who can't speak the language of the business, who can't step out of the proverbial back-office and into the front lines of customer service, social media or supply chain management will soon go the way of the ancient tech gear," warned Thomas Wailgum of *CIO Magazine.* Wayne Shurts, CIO of the grocery chain SuperValu concurred, "You're part of the strategic leadership team; you're on the inside of all the issues to help the company win today, tomorrow, and the next decade."[32] As shown in Figure 12.3, the duties assigned to a CIO are quite diverse.

Whether businesses have adequately built protections against unwanted invasions of cyberattacks on their stakeholders' privacy remains to be seen. Clearly efforts are being made given the increasing costs of cyberattacks and the growing amount of information being collected and used by business organizations.

[29]"Banks Reluctant to Use 'White Hat' Hackers to Spot Security Flaws," *National Public Radio,* November 5, 2014, *www.npr.org.*

[30]"More CISOs Needed to Battle Cybersecurity Threats in 2015," *The Wall Street Journal,* December 18, 2014, *blogs.wsj.com.*

[31]Steven Fox, "The Art of CIO Success," *CSO Security and Risk,* June 29, 2009, *blogs.csoonline.com.*

[32]"The New CIO Role: Big Changes Ahead," *CIO.com,* August 20, 2010, *www.cio.com.*

FIGURE 12.3

The Roles and Responsibilities of the Chief Information Officer (CIO)

Sources: The Meta Group study of the role of the CIO can be found at "New Roles, New Responsibilities: Today's CIO," *www.cioupdate.com.* Additional information for this figure is from "What Are the Duties of a CIO?" *eHow, www.ehow.com;* and "The Duties of a CIO," *Ezine Articles, ezinearticles. com.*

In a study conducted by the Meta Group entitled *The CIO as Enterprise Change Agent,* almost half (47%) of the CIOs surveyed reported that they have broadened their responsibilities beyond the traditional CIO-only role. Some of these emerging responsibilities include:

- Establishing an innovative language to enable everyone throughout the organization to be clear of the objectives, processes, and timetables for any project that involves technology or information.
- Providing structure to welcome inventive thinking and creating protocols for testing and reviewing these novel ideas.
- Educating others in the organization to help open the eyes of organizational members to what is possible or what is not regarding technological initiatives or information.
- Applying marketing knowledge to ensure that innovative ideas reach the proper stakeholders inside and outside of the organization and have a meaningful impact.
- Acting as the lead security officer to protect information and data integrity by overseeing all functions of information technology in the organization.
- Participating in organizationwide committees and projects to maintain a clear emphasis on the value of information, as well as protect against threats to information.

In the past decade, since the creation of the CIO position within most business organizations, the CIO role has evolved from primarily being focused only on the collection and protection of information to a senior executive role essential to all business functions and operations.

Government Efforts to Combat Cybercrime

In general, the Internet is plagued by a lack of a well-integrated system to protect the enormous amount of private, medical, and financial data and to coordinate the nation's computerized critical infrastructure—oil pipelines, railroad tracks, water treatment facilities, and the power grid. Leon Panetta, former U.S. secretary of defense, predicted in 2012 that it would take a "cyber-Pearl Harbor," referring to the devastating attack on the U.S. military base in Hawaii that catapulted the United States into World War II against the Japanese, to wake up the nation to the vulnerabilities in its computer systems. While no such attack has occurred—yet—the question remains: What have governments done to slow down, if not stop, the wave of cyberattacks?

Given the global nature of the problem, some believe international governmental coordination is necessary. Since 2007, representatives from the United States and dozens of European countries have gathered annually for what is known as Data Privacy Day, held annually on January 28. This event, which brings together privacy professionals, government leaders, academics, students, and business executives, was designed to raise awareness and empower people to protect their privacy, control their digital footprint, and escalate the protection of privacy and data as everyone's priority. Led by the National Cyber Security Alliance, a nonprofit, public–private partnership, people can signup for free security checks, check their privacy settings, and access various resources for parents, educators, and businesses.

More dramatic and legal measures were taken at the multinational level in 2014 when leaders of the North Atlantic Treaty Organization (NATO) ratified a change in the organization's mission of collective defense. For the first time, a cyberattack on any of the 28 NATO nations could be declared an attack on all of them, much like a ground invasion or an airborne bombing. The most obvious target of the new policy was Russia, which was believed to be behind computer attacks that disrupted financial and telecommunication systems in Estonia in 2007 and Georgia in 2008. NATO officials also pointed to increased cyberactivity by China and Iran—calling them "patriotic hackers"—and the need for the organization to keep up with increasingly sophisticated modern warfare.

Under the direction of President Obama, the United States took a number of measures to establish a system of voluntary cybersecurity standards. In 2013, a federal government–led group partnered with the private sector to improve information sharing and bolster existing cybersecurity regulations. "American must face the rapidly growing threat from cyberattacks," said Obama. "We know foreign countries and companies swipe our corporate secrets. Now our enemies are also seeking the ability to sabotage our power grid, our financial institutions, and our air-traffic control systems." In 2015, the U.S. federal government opened a new center to more quickly assess and deter cyberattacks on the United States. This action came on the heels of the cyberattack on Sony Pictures, discussed at the end of this chapter, and after weaknesses were exposed in the government's ability to determine how the attack originated and how to best respond. All of these government actions were an effort to better cut across boundaries so that information was made available and protection against and responses to cyberattacks were better coordinated and more effective.

Additional coordinated efforts by international governmental agencies are needed to better ensure that the threat of cyberattacks on the infrastructure of a country or the invasion of citizens' information are thwarted. These efforts must be in harmony with businesses' anti-cybercrime efforts.

Summary

- The management and regulation of information technology poses challenges for businesses and governments since technology changes so quickly, is global in its impact, and requires the coordinated efforts of businesses and government to ensure privacy and security.

- Some countries have imposed censorship on online information, based on political, security, and religious grounds. But, in many democratic nations, most people believe that information should be accessible. These governments have taken steps to acquire personal data to better protect the public from terrorism and other threats. These governments have also attempted to better ensure protection of intellectual property.

- Two major market stakeholders targeted by business organizations for the collection of information are employees and consumers, raising numerous ethical issues. The access to big data can be at odds with the protection of individuals' rights to their own information.

- Cybercrime is criminal activity committed by individuals or groups, called hackers, which gain unauthorized access to a business organization through its computer system. It imposes substantial costs on businesses that are hacked. Hackers appear motivated by financial incentives, government or business retaliation, or media attention for an issue or the hackers themselves.

- Many businesses have gone to great lengths to build strong defenses to protect information and ensure stakeholder privacy. These defenses must be comprehensive, companywide, and be supported by the organization's executive leadership. Businesses have increasingly entrusted the management of technology to their chief information officer. These managers often report to the company's CEO and are being entrusted with greater strategic responsibilities within the company.

- International and national government groups have attacked cybercrime through voluntary efforts. Additional coordinated efforts are needed and must be in harmony with businesses' anti-cybercrime efforts.

Key Terms	big data, *263*	grey hatters, *269*	right to be
	chief information officer	hackers, *265*	forgotten, *262*
	(CIO), *271*	hacktivists, *266*	software piracy, *262*
	cybercrime, *265*	intellectual	white hatters, *269*
	Digital Millennium	property, *262*	
	Copyright Act, *263*	Internet censorship, *259*	

Internet Resources	www.ama-assn.org	American Medical Association
	www.ftc.gov/infosecurity	Bureau of Consumer Protection, Data Security
	www.bsa.org	Business Software Alliance
	www.cio.com	Chief Information Officer professional website
	www.cybersecurity.org	Cybersecurity Association
	www.foresight.org	Foresight Institute
	www.issa.org	Information Systems Security Association
	www.opensecurityfoundation.org	Open Security Foundation
	www.robotics.org	Robotics Industries Association

Discussion Case: *Sony Pictures and North Korean Hackers*

In November 2014, just in time to capitalize on the rush of moviegoers during the Thanksgiving and Christmas holiday seasons, Sony Pictures was set to release a new comedy *The Interview.* Executives at Sony already knew that *The Interview* would be controversial. The plot involved a television tabloid show host and producer who discovered that the North Korean dictator, Kim Jong-un, was a big fan of their show. When they set up a trip to visit Kim Jong-un, they were recruited by the CIA to turn their trip to Pyongyang, Korea, into an assassination mission. Not surprisingly, the real Korean government leaders were displeased with the plot of the movie, and they apparently took drastic measures to convince Sony Pictures' executives not to release the movie to theaters.

During a one-week period hackers, going by the name *Guardians of Peace* and allegedly with ties to North Korea, stole 100 terabytes of sensitive company data from computers belonging to Sony Pictures Entertainment (to put that into perspective, 10 terabytes can hold the entire printed collection of the Library of Congress). The first sign of a digital break-in appeared when the image of a stylized skull with long skeletal fingers flashed on every Sony employee's computer screen at the same time, accompanied by a threatening message warning that "This is just the beginning." The message continued, "We've obtained all your internal data," and then warned that if Sony did not comply with their demands, the hackers would release the company's top secrets. Hackers slowly posted the information online or circulated information over file-sharing networks. North Korea formally denied any involvement in the hacking incident, but did praise the actions as a "righteous deed."

The leaked information revealed highly sensitive information, like passwords and executives' salaries, secret details about other upcoming films, and passport and visa information for Sony actors. Other leaked information contained the medical records of dozens of Sony employees and listed conditions including cancers, cirrhosis of the liver, and premature births. The hackers went as far as to threaten Sony employees and their families. The hackers also made threats of violence toward anyone who went to see the movie, with references to the terrorist's attacks in the United States on September 11, 2001. These threats prompted the nation's largest theatre chains to announce that they would not show the film.

Sony executives considered releasing the film only via video-on-demand or on television. Comcast, the nation's largest cable provider, declined the opportunity to show the film through their cable network due to its politically sensitive material. Eventually Sony decided to cancel the distribution of the film. The hackers responded to Sony's decision by saying "pulling *The Interview* was a 'very wise decision'." "We are deeply saddened at this brazen effort to suppress the distribution of a movie, and in the process do damage to our company, our employees, and the American public," said Sony's press release. "We stand by our filmmakers and their right to free expression and are extremely disappointed by this outcome." The implications of these decisions extended beyond the moviemaking industry. "This is now a case study that is signaling to attackers that you can get all that you want and even more," said a cybersecurity strategist.

President Obama criticized Sony for pulling the movie, saying it set a bad precedent and could encourage further censorship. While he was sympathetic to the problem Sony faced, the president said, "Yes, I think they made a mistake." He also pledged that the United States would hit back at North Korea for their role in this incident. "They caused a lot of damage and we will respond. We will respond proportionately and we will respond in a place and time and manner we choose." (One month later, President Obama, in an executive order, imposed sanctions on three North Korean organizations and 10 individuals, allegedly in response to the hacking of Sony Pictures.) Obama continued, "We cannot have a society in which some dictator someplace can start imposing censorship here in the United States, because if somebody is able to intimidate folks out of releasing a satirical movie, imagine what they start doing when they see a documentary they don't like, or news reports they don't like." Companies in the United States, according to the president, needed to come to terms with the possibility of having their computer systems penetrated, but added that "we can't start changing our patterns of behavior." To do so, he said, would be like cancelling the Boston Marathon because bombs were detonated there.

Sony's CEO Michael Lynton responded to the president's remarks. "We did not cave. We did not back down. The decision not to move forward with the December 25 theatrical release of *The Interview* was made as a result of the majority of the nation's theater owners choosing not to screen the film. This was their decision. Let us be clear—the only decision that we have made with respect to release of the film was not to release it on Christmas Day in theaters, after the theater owners declined to show it. Without theaters, we could not release it in the theaters on Christmas Day. We had no choice."

On December 23, Sony did an about-face and announced it would release *The Interview* on Christmas Day after all, saying that the film would be released to any theaters that wanted to screen it. The film was also released simultaneously in homes on video-on-demand. "We have never given up on releasing *The Interview* and we're excited our movie will be in a number of theaters on Christmas Day," said Lynton. "At the same time, we are continuing our efforts to secure more platforms and more theaters so that this movie reaches the largest possible audience." President Obama praised Sony's decision to release the film. The number of independent movie theaters that eventually showed *The Interview* grew to nearly 600. No incidents of violence against the moviegoers were reported. Initially, Sony made *The Interview* available for rent online for $5.99 via YouTube Movies,

Google Play, and Microsoft's Xbox Video. Later, Sony expanded its distribution of the film to DirecTV, most of the major video-on-demand services through cable carriers, and other outlets.

Sources: "Sony Pictures Hack: The Whole Story," *Engadget,* December 10, 2014, *www.engadget.com;* "Sony Pulls Korea Film 'The Interview;' U.S. Blames Pyongyang for Hack," *The Wall Street Journal,* December 17, 2014, *www.wsj.com;* "Obama Says Sony 'Made a Mistake' Cancelling Film," *The Wall Street Journal,* December 19, 2014, *www.wsj.com;* "Sony Hack: A Timeline," *Deadline,* December 22, 2014, *deadline.com;* "Sony to Release 'The Interview' in Theaters," *The Wall Street Journal,* December 23, 2014, *www.wsj.com;* and "Sony Hack," *NBC News,* December 31, 2014, *www.nbcnews.com.*

Discussion Questions

1. Did Sony Pictures' executives, eventually, make the right decision by releasing the film? What were the risks and benefits to Sony and to its customers (both movie theater operators and movie viewers) of doing so?

2. What actions, if any, could Sony employees take to protect themselves from the theft and release of their data on their employer's servers?

3. What role should the U.S. government play in protecting the privacy and security of individual citizens, such as Sony employees in this case? What specific actions could the government take?

4. What actions should the U.S. government have taken against North Korea? Should the U.S. government have reacted sooner than it did?

5. Using tools presented in this chapter, what additional measures could Sony take to better protect its company's information from attack by hackers?

Business and Its Stakeholders

Shareholder Rights and Corporate Governance

Shareholders occupy a position of central importance in the corporation because they own shares of the company's stock. As owners, they pursue both financial and nonfinancial goals. How can shareholders' rights best be protected? What are the appropriate roles of top managers and boards of directors in the governance of the corporation? How can their incentives be aligned with the purposes of the firm, including the interests of the company's shareholders? And how can government regulators best protect the rights of investors and promote good corporate governance?

This Chapter Focuses on These Key Learning Objectives:

LO 13-1 Identifying different kinds of shareholders and understanding their objectives and legal rights.

LO 13-2 Knowing how corporations are governed and explaining the role of the board of directors in protecting the interests of investors and other stakeholders.

LO 13-3 Analyzing the function of executive compensation and debating if top managers are paid too much.

LO 13-4 Evaluating various ways shareholders can promote their economic and social objectives.

LO 13-5 Understanding how the government protects against stock market abuses, such as fraudulent accounting and insider trading.

AIG International was one of the largest insurance companies in the world—an organization that for decades had insured individuals and organizations against all manner of hazards. In late 2008, investors—and those holding its policies—were shocked to learn that the firm was on the verge of collapse. It turned out that the company had written large numbers of insurance contracts (called "credit default swaps") on complex financial instruments, including mortgage-backed securities. For a time, these contracts had been big moneymakers for AIG. But as housing prices fell and the value of securities backed by their mortgages plunged, the insurance company was forced to put up collateral—money it did not have. Alarmed at the effect AIG's collapse might have on the financial system, the U.S. government stepped in with a $182 *billion* bailout—the largest of a private firm in history—becoming, in the process, AIG's majority shareholder. Eventually, the company paid back the government in full—along with $23 billion in interest. Oddly, Hank Greenberg—the ousted former CEO and still a major shareholder—then brought a suit against the government, saying he and other investors had been shortchanged by the high interest rates charged by the government.[1]

The near-collapse of AIG was, without a doubt, a disaster for the company's shareholders; in a single year, the stock price fell from around $50 to mere pennies. Why did the board of directors and top executives fail to manage the apparently excessive risk taken on by the firm? Why didn't government regulators do a better job of protecting shareholders' interests? What role did compensation and reward systems play in the firm's behavior? Why didn't investors themselves figure out what was going on and sell their shares before it was too late? And did the government harm them once more by charging the company onerous interest rates on its bailout loans?

As owners, shareholders have many rights. But as the debacle at AIG so vividly illustrates, these rights are not always protected. In the late 2000s and early 2010s, in the wake of major losses by investors at AIG and other firms, many groups took steps to improve the overall system of corporate governance. This chapter will address the important legal rights of shareholders and how corporate boards, government regulators, managers, and activist investors can protect them. It will also discuss changes in corporate practice and government oversight designed to better guard shareholder interests, in both the United States and other nations, and how legislation enacted in the wake of the financial crisis has strengthened regulation of the stock market.

Shareholders around the World

Shareholders (or investors or stockholders, as they also are called) are an important market stakeholder of the firm, as explained in Chapter 1. By purchasing shares of a company's stock, they become owners. For this reason, they have a stake in how well the company performs.[2]

Stock ownership today is increasingly global. In 2012, the total value of stocks in the world was $53 trillion, down from $64 trillion before the stock market collapse of 2008–09. The market capitalization (total value) of stocks in the United States is by far larger than

---

[1] "Five Questions AIG Bailout Judge Wants Answered," *Bloomberg Business,* April 21, 2015; and "Maurice Greenberg Puts U.S. Handling of AIG Bailout on Trial," *Los Angeles Times,* November 9, 2014.

[2] The following discussion refers to publicly held corporations; that is, ones whose shares of stock are owned by the public and traded on the various stock exchanges. U.S. laws permit a number of other ownership forms, including sole proprietorships, partnerships, and mutual companies. (A *privately held* company, by contrast, is one whose shares are not publicly traded.)

FIGURE 13.1
**Stock Market
Capitalization as
a Percentage of
Gross Domestic
Product, for Selected
Countries, 2012**

Source: "Stocks Traded, Total
Value (% of GDP), 2012," at
http://data.worldbank.org.

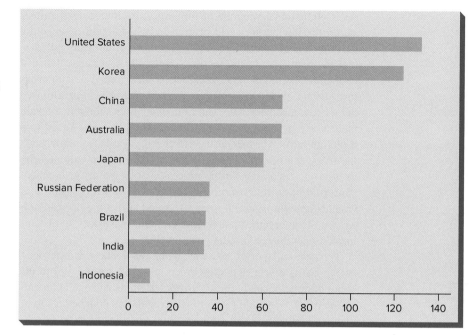

that of any other country, but stock ownership has grown in many other parts of the world.[3] One way to compare the extent of stock ownership among countries is to examine their market capitalization as a percentage of their GDP (gross domestic product, a measure of the size of their economies). By this yardstick, the United States leads, but many other countries are not far behind, as shown in Figure 13.1. This figure shows value at a particular point in time. Another way to look at this is in terms of growth over time. By this measure, some of the fastest growing national stock markets in 2014 were in India (up 32 percent in the previous four years), Egypt (up 26 percent), and Indonesia (up 21 percent), according to World Bank data. (Some of the worst declines, by contrast, were in southern and eastern Europe.) Not only are domestic stock markets growing in many nations, but investors are crossing borders in their search for well-diversified portfolios. Extensive cross-border investing has occurred among the United States, Europe, and Japan—and increasingly among these regions and the emerging markets of China, Latin America, central and eastern Europe, and other parts of Asia.

Who Are Shareholders?

Whether in the United States or other countries, two main types of investors own shares of stock in corporations: individual and institutional.

- *Individual shareholders* are people who directly own shares of stock issued by companies. These shares are usually purchased through a stockbroker and are held in brokerage accounts. For example, a person might buy 100 shares of Apple or Sony Corporation for his or her portfolio, and hold these in an account at a firm such as Edward Jones, Fidelity, or Charles Schwab. Such shareholders are sometimes called "Main Street" investors, because they come from all walks of life.

[3] Comprehensive data on stock market capitalization by countries is available in "Market Capitalization of Listed Companies," at *http://data.worldbank.org.*

FIGURE 13.2
Household versus Institutional Ownership in the United States, 1965–2010, by Market Value

Source: U.S. Census Bureau, *Statistical Abstract of the United States, 2012,* Table 1201; and Securities Industry Association, *Securities Industry Fact Book* (New York: Securities Industry Association, 2008). Household sector includes nonprofit organizations. Based on Federal Reserve Flow of Funds Accounts (revised). Used by permission.

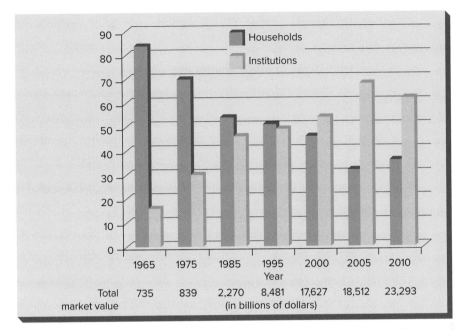

Total market value	735	839	2,270	8,481	17,627	18,512	23,293

(in billions of dollars)

- *Institutions,* such as pensions, mutual funds, insurance companies, and university endowments, also own stock. For example, mutual funds such as Vanguard Wellington and pensions such as the California Public Employees Retirement System (CalPERS) buy stock on behalf of their investors or members. These institutions are sometimes called "Wall Street" investors. For obvious reasons, institutions usually have more money to invest and buy more shares than individual investors.

Since the 1960s, growth in the numbers of such **institutional investors** has been phenomenal. In 2010, institutions accounted for 63 percent of the value of all equities (stocks) owned in the United States, worth a total of about $15 *trillion*—about eight times the value of institutional holdings two decades earlier.[4]

In 2013, slightly over half of all U.S. households (52 percent) owned stocks, either directly or indirectly through holdings in mutual funds or retirement accounts, according to a Gallup survey. This proportion had fallen significantly since just before the stock market collapse of 2008 (when 65 percent owned stocks), possibly reflecting investors' lower confidence. Although people of every age, race, and socioeconomic status own stocks, ownership tended to be higher among some groups than others. For example, whites (55 percent) were more likely to own stocks than African Americans (28 percent), and the college educated (77 percent) were more likely than those with a high school education or less (25 percent). The affluent (with household incomes of $75,000 or more) (80 percent) owned stocks as a higher rate than lower-income people (with household incomes of less than $30,000) (15 percent). Age also made a difference: 57 percent of people between 50 and 64 years old owned stocks, compared with just 24 percent of young adults under 30.[5]

Figure 13.2 shows the relative stock holdings of individual and institutional investors from the 1960s through 2010 in the United States. It shows the growing influence of the

---

[4] U.S. Census Bureau, *Statistical Abstract of the United States 2012,* "Equities, Corporate Bonds, and Treasury Securities—Holdings and Net Purchases by Type of Investor: 2000 to 2012," Table 1201. These data are based on the Federal Reserve Bank's flow of funds accounts.

[5] "The Stock Market Is at an All-Time High—Here's Why So Many Americans Don't Care," *Business Insider,* December 1, 2013. Data are based on Gallup's annual economics and personal finance survey.

institutional sector of the market over the past four decades, with an apparent reversal of the overall trend following the financial crisis.

Objectives of Stock Ownership

Individuals and institutions own corporate stock for a number of reasons. Foremost among them is to make money. People buy stocks because they believe stocks will produce a return greater than they could receive from alternative investments. Shareholders make money when the price of the stock rises (this is called *capital appreciation*) and when they receive their share of the company's earnings (called *dividends*). Most companies pay dividends, but some—particularly new companies with good prospects for rapid growth—do not. In this case, investors buy the stock with the goal of capital appreciation only.

Stock prices rise and fall over time, affected by both the performance of the company and by the overall movement of the stock market. For example, in 2008 and early 2009 share values declined sharply—for example, the Dow Jones Industrial Average, a widely tracked index, lost almost half its value in just a year and a half—as the global economy fell into a severe recession. This is called a *bear market.* This was followed by a period in which markets rose again in a *bull market,* which produced gains for many investors. Typically, bull and bear markets alternate, driven by the health of the economy, interest rates, world events, and other factors that are often difficult to predict. Although stock prices are sometimes volatile, stocks historically have produced a higher return over the long run than investments in bonds, bank certificates of deposit, or money markets.

Shareholders are not a uniform group. Some seek long-term appreciation, while others seek short-term returns. Some are looking for capital gains, while others are looking for dividend income. Although the primary motivation of most shareholders is to make money from their investments, some have other motivations as well. Some investors use stock ownership to achieve social or ethical objectives, a trend that is discussed later in this chapter. Investors may also buy stock in order to take control of a company in a hostile takeover bid. Some investors have mixed objectives; for example, they wish to make a reasonable return on their investment but also to advance social or ethical goals.

Shareholders' Legal Rights and Safeguards

As explained in Chapter 1, managers have a duty to all stakeholders, not just to those who own shares in their company. Nevertheless, in the United States and most other countries, shareholders have extensive legal rights. They have the right to share in the profits of the enterprise if directors declare dividends. They have the right to receive annual reports of company earnings and company activities and to inspect the corporate books, provided they have a legitimate business purpose for doing so and that it will not be disruptive of business operations. They have the right to elect members of the board of directors, usually on a "one share equals one vote" basis. They have the right to hold the directors and officers of the corporation responsible for their actions, by lawsuit if they want to go that far. Furthermore, they usually have the right to vote on mergers, some acquisitions, and changes in the charter and bylaws, and to bring other business-related proposals before the shareholders. And finally, they have the right to sell their stock.

Figure 13.3 summarizes the major legal rights of shareholders.

Many of these rights are exercised at the annual shareholders' meeting, where directors and managers present an annual report and shareholders have an opportunity to approve or disapprove management's plans. Typically only a small portion of shareholders vote in person, however. Those not attending are given an opportunity to vote by absentee ballot, called a **proxy**. Most shareholders do not vote their proxies, either, however; currently, just 30 percent

FIGURE 13.3
Major Legal Rights
of Shareholders

- To receive dividends, if declared

- To vote on
    Members of board of directors
    Major mergers and acquisitions
    Charter and bylaw changes
    Proposals by stockholders

- To receive annual reports on the company's financial condition

- To bring shareholder suits against the company and officers

- To sell their own shares of stock to others

of all shareholders—and just 13 percent of individual shareholders—cast their ballots. The use of proxy elections by activists to influence corporate policy is discussed later in this chapter.

Who protects these rights? Within a publicly held company, the board of directors bears a major share of the responsibility for making sure that the firm is run with the interests of shareholders, as well as those of other stakeholders, in mind. We turn next, therefore, to a consideration of the role of the board in the system of corporate governance.

Corporate Governance

The term **corporate governance** refers to the process by which a company is controlled, or governed. Just as nations have governments that respond to the needs of citizens and establish policy, so do corporations have systems of internal governance that determine overall strategic direction and balance sometimes divergent interests.

The Board of Directors

The **board of directors** plays a central role in corporate governance. The board of directors is an elected group of individuals who have a legal duty to establish corporate objectives, develop broad policies, and select top-level personnel to carry out these objectives and policies. The board also reviews management's performance to be sure the company is well run and all stakeholders' interests are protected, including those of shareholders. Like any group, it also has its own interests, which it seeks to protect. Boards typically meet in full session around six times a year.

Corporate boards vary in size, composition, and structure to best serve the interests of the corporation and its shareholders. A number of patterns do exist, however. According to one survey of governance practices in 100 market-leading firms, corporate boards average 12 members. Typically, 10 or 11 of these are *outside* directors (not managers of the company, who are known as *inside* directors when they serve on the board). (The New York Stock Exchange requires listed companies to have boards with a majority of outsiders.) Board members may include chief executives of other companies, major shareholders, bankers, former government officials, academics, representatives of the community, or retired executives from other firms. Women now make up 19 percent of U.S. corporate boards; African Americans, 7 percent; Latinos, 3 percent; and Asian Americans, 2 percent. (The representation of women on boards of directors and new laws mandating quotas for women on boards in some European countries are further discussed in Chapter 16.)[6]

[6] "Women Still Hold Only 19 Percent of U.S. Board Seats," *The Washington Post,* January 13, 2015; and Richard L. Zweigenhaft, "Diversity Among CEOs and Corporate Directors: Has the Heyday Come and Gone?" presentation at the annual meeting of the American Sociological Association, August 12, 2013.

Board structure in Europe is quite different from its counterpart in the United States. Many European boards use what is called a *two-tier system.* This means that instead of one board, as is common in the United States, these companies have two boards. One, which is called the *executive board,* is made up of the CEO and other insiders. The other, which is called the *supervisory board,* is made up of outsiders—sometimes including labor representatives—and has an independent chairperson. These boards operate autonomously, but of course also coordinate their work. This system is used in all firms in Germany and Austria and in many firms in Denmark, Finland, the Netherlands, Norway, Poland, and Switzerland. Other European nations often use a hybrid system, which has elements of both the unitary and two-tiered systems.[7]

Corporate directors are typically well paid. Compensation for board members is composed of a complex mix of retainer fees, meeting fees, grants of stock and stock options, pensions, and various perks. In 2013, median compensation for directors at the largest U.S. corporations was nearly $240,000, an increase of 6 percent from the prior year. (Of this compensation, 44 percent was paid in cash and 56 percent in stock or stock options.)[8] Directors spent, on average, 278 hours annually (about five hours a week) on their board-related duties, so their pay works out to more than $850 an hour.[9] Some critics believe that board compensation is excessive, and that high pay contributes to complacency by some directors who do not want to jeopardize their positions by challenging the policies of management. (Compensation of executives is discussed later in this chapter.)

Most corporate boards perform their work through committees as well as in general sessions. The compensation committee (required by U.S. law and staffed exclusively by outside directors) administers and approves salaries and other benefits of high-level managers in the company. The nominating committee is responsible for finding and recommending candidates for officers and directors, especially those to be elected at the annual shareholders' meeting. The executive committee works closely with top managers on important business matters. A significant minority of corporations now has a special committee devoted to issues of corporate responsibility. Often, this committee works closely with the firm's department of corporate citizenship, as discussed in Chapter 3.

One of the most important committees of the board is the audit committee. Present in virtually all boards, the audit committee is required by U.S. law to be composed entirely of outside directors and to be "financially literate." It reviews the company's financial reports, recommends the appointment of outside auditors (accountants), and oversees the integrity of internal financial controls. Their role is often critical; at Enron, for example, lax oversight by the audit committee was a major contributor to the firm's collapse in 2001. (This failure helped spur passage of the Sarbanes–Oxley Act, which was discussed in Chapter 6.) Directors who fail to detect and stop accounting fraud, as occurred at Enron, may be liable for damages. At WorldCom—a leading telecommunications company that collapsed in 2002 in the wake of a major accounting fraud—investors successfully sued former members of the board of directors for $55 million.

How are directors selected? Board members are elected by shareholders at the annual meeting, where absent owners may vote by proxy, as explained earlier. Thus, the system is formally democratic. However, as a practical matter, shareholders often have little choice. Typically, the nominating committee, working with the CEO and chairman, develops a

---

[7] Information about corporate governance in Europe is available in Heidrick & Struggles, "Towards Dynamic Governance 2014: European Corporate Governance Report," at *www.heidrick.com.*

[8] "Compensation for U.S. Corporate Directors Increased 6%, Towers Watson 2014 Analysis Finds," at *www.towerswatson.com.*

[9] "Results of Public Company Governance Survey," *NACD Directorship,* March/April 2015.

list of possible candidates and presents these to the board for consideration. When a final selection is made, the names of these individuals are placed on the proxy ballot. Shareholders may vote to approve or disapprove the nominees, but because alternative candidates are rarely presented, the vote has little significance. The selection process therefore tends to produce a kind of self-perpetuating system. This has begun to change, however, as shareholders have increasingly demanded the right to nominate their own candidates, in a move for greater **proxy access**. The discussion case at the end of the chapter describes such efforts at Whole Foods, the natural foods grocery chain.

Because boards typically meet behind closed doors, scholars know less about the kinds of *processes* that lead to effective decision making by directors than they do about board composition and structure.

> In their book *Back to the Drawing Board,* Colin Carter and Jay Lorsch observe, based on their extensive consulting experience, that boards develop their own norms that define what is—and is not—appropriate behavior. For example, *pilot boards* see their role as actively guiding the company's strategic direction. *Watchdog* boards, by contrast, see their role as assuring compliance with the law—and intervening in management decisions only if something is clearly wrong. These norms are often powerfully influenced by the chairman. Boards that share a consensus on behavioral norms tend to function more effectively as a group than those that do not.[10]

Principles of Good Governance

In the wake of the corporate scandals of the early 2000s and the financial crisis later in the decade, many sought to define the core principles of good corporate governance. What kinds of boards were most effective? By the 2010s, a broad consensus had emerged among public agencies, investor groups, and stock exchanges about some key features of effective boards. These included the following:

- *Select outside directors to fill most positions.* Normally, no more than two or three members of the board should be current managers. Moreover, the outside members should be truly independent; that is, should have no connection to the corporation other than serving as a director. This would exclude, for example, directors who themselves performed consulting services for the company on whose board they served, or who were officers of other firms that had a business relationship with it. The audit, compensation, and nominating committees should be comprised *solely* of outsiders. By the late 2010s, virtually all major companies were following these practices.

- *Hold more open elections for members of the board.* In recent years, dissident shareholders have organized to put their own candidates for the board on the proxy ballot, creating elections with genuine choice. (This trend is further explored in the discussion case at the end of this chapter.) Some have argued that candidates should have to get at least 50 percent of votes to be elected (most companies required only a plurality; that is, more votes than other candidates, but not necessarily a majority of votes cast). Some thought that directors should stand for election every year (a practice called *board declassification),* allowing more opportunities to unseat underperforming directors.

- *Appoint an independent lead director (also called a nonexecutive chairman of the board)* Many experts in corporate governance believed that boards should separate the

---

[10] Colin B. Carter and Jay W. Lorsch, *Back to the Drawing Boards: Designing Corporate Boards for a Complex World* (Boston: Harvard Business School Press, 2003).

duties of the chief executive and the board chairman, rather than combining the two in one person as done in many corporations, especially in the United States. The independent lead director can hold meetings without management present, improving the board's chances of having completely candid discussions about a company's affairs. For example, Arthur Levinson was named nonexecutive chairman at Apple after the death of Steve Jobs and continued in this position after Tim Cook assumed the role of chief executive. One study found that separating the positions of CEO and chairman was most likely in companies that had experienced shareholder activism and had recently appointed a new chief executive. In 2015, slightly more than half of all boards in the United States had independent lead directors.[11]

- *Align director compensation with corporate performance.* Some thought that directors should be paid based, at least in part, on how well the company does. For example, Intel Corporation compensates its directors largely through performance-based shares, which are increased or reduced based on how well the company does relative to its peers. Coca-Cola has a similar system.[12] In Japan, directors' compensation has traditionally been seniority-based, but in recent years some companies have introduced performance-based pay.[13] In 2014, directors in the United States received more than half their pay in company stock.[14]

- *Evaluate the board's own performance on a regular basis.* Directors themselves should be assessed on how competent they were and how diligently they performed their duties. Normally, this would be the responsibility of the governance committee of the board. In the wake of the corporate scandals of the early 2000s, many companies made dramatic improvements in this area, and almost all companies now evaluate director performance. For example, the board of directors of Becton, Dickinson, a medical technology company, sponsors an annual evaluation of its own performance and effectiveness, examining its role, organization, and meetings. In Europe, three-quarters of public companies now conduct regular board evaluations.[15]

The movement to improve corporate governance has been active in other nations and regions, as well as the United States, as some of these examples show. The Organization for Economic Cooperation and Development (OECD), representing 34 nations, has issued a set of principles for corporate governance to serve as a benchmark for companies and policymakers worldwide. In 2009, OECD issued a report that concluded that the financial crisis affecting many of its member states had been caused, to an important extent, by failures of corporate governance, and in 2015 it issued a revised set of corporate governance principles.[16] For its part, the European Union has worked hard to modernize corporate governance practices and harmonize them across its member states. Corporate governance reforms have also taken hold in South Africa, India, and many other nations.

---

[11] Korn Ferry Institute (in partnership with the National Association of Corporate Directors), *Annual Survey of Board Leadership, 2014 Edition,* www.kornferryinstitute.com. Data based on boards of directors at the 500 U.S.-based firms that made up the S&P Large Cap Index and the 400 firms that made up the Mid-Cap Index, as of December 31, 2012; and "Results of Public Company Governance Survey," op. cit.

[12] "Results of Public Company Governance Survey," op. cit.

[13] ISS, "Increase in Director Compensation Ceiling Proposals," *www.issgovernance.com.*

[14] "Total Board Compensation Up Among Early Proxy Filers," *NACD Directorship,* April 28, 2015.

[15] Heidrick & Struggles, *European Corporate Governance Report 2011: Challenging Board Performance,* www.heidrick.com.

[16] Grant Kirkpatrick, "The Corporate Governance Lessons from the Financial Crisis," OECD, February 2009. For the revised principles, see *www.oecd.org.* Information about recent changes in corporate governance practices in Europe is available at the website of the European Corporate Governance Institute, *www.ecgi.org.*

In short, by the late 2010s the movement to make boards more responsive to shareholders was an international one.

Special Issue: Executive Compensation

Setting **executive compensation** is one of the most important functions of the board of directors. The emergence of the modern, publicly held corporation in the late 1800s effectively separated ownership and control. That is, owners of the firm no longer managed it on a day-to-day basis; this task fell to hired professionals. This development gave rise to what theorists call the *agency problem*. If managers are merely hired agents, what will guarantee that they act in the interests of shareholders rather than simply helping themselves? The problem is a serious one, because shareholders are often geographically dispersed, and government rules make it difficult for them to contact one another and to organize on behalf of their collective interests. Boards meet just a few times a year. Who, then, is watching the managers?

An important mechanism for aligning the interests of the corporation and its shareholders with those of its top managers is executive compensation. But recent events suggest that the system is not always doing its job.

> In the period leading up to the financial crisis, a number of top executives made out handsomely, even as their companies were spiraling toward collapse. At Merrill Lynch, Stanley O'Neal earned $70 million in compensation over his four years as CEO—and then an additional $161 million in severance pay when the board fired him in 2007. Just a year later, Merrill went under. Angelo Mozilo, the CEO of the disgraced subprime mortgage lender Countrywide, was paid $125 million in the year before his company collapsed and was taken over by the Bank of America. In response to these and other similar cases, some called for "clawback"—a process by which executives of failed firms would have to pay back some of their earnings. The 2010 Dodd-Frank Act required top executives to repay excess incentive compensation received as a result of improper accounting, but as of 2015 the SEC had not yet implemented this provision.[17]

Many critics feel that executive pay has become excessive—not just at companies accused of fraud but in fact at most companies—reflecting aggressive self-dealing by managers without regard for the interests of others.

Executive compensation in the United States, by international standards, is very high. In 2014, the median total compensation of chief executives of the largest corporations in the United States was $17.6 million, including salaries, bonuses, and the present value of retirement benefits, incentive plans, and stock options, according to the compensation firm Equilar. This amount was the largest since Equilar started collecting these data in 2006. The highest paid executive in 2014 was David M. Zaslav, CEO of Discovery Communications (whose brands included the Discovery Channel, TLC, and Animal Planet), who took home an eye-popping $156 million.[18] Because the Equilar survey included only public companies, it did not capture the often outsized pay of hedge fund and private equity firm executives. In many cases, these individuals earned much more than their public company counterparts:

---

[17] "A Blank Page in the S.E.C. Rule Book, Four Years Later," *The New York Times,* November 9, 2014. Updates on SEC rulemaking are available at *www.sec.gov.*

[18] "For the Highest Paid CEOs, the Party Goes On," *The New York Times,* May 17, 2015; and "Discovery Communications CEO Gets 2014 Compensation of $156.1 Million," *The Wall Street Journal,* April 4, 2015.

FIGURE 13.4

Relative Executive Compensation in the United States and Selected Developed Nations, in Millions of Dollars

Source: "CEO-to-Worker Pay Ratios around the World," at *www.afl-co.org*. U.S. data are from the Bureau of Labor Statistics; all other data are from the OECD. Data are for 2012 or the nearest available year.

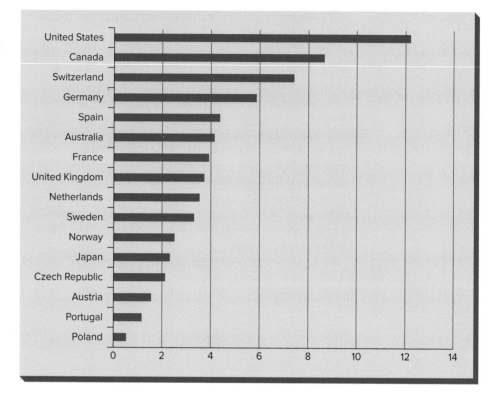

Kenneth C. Griffin, CEO of the hedge fund Citadel, for example, earned an astonishing $1.3 *billion* in 2014.[19] (Hedge funds and private equity firms are further discussed later in this chapter.)

Many companies, like Discovery Communications, compensate their senior executives in part with grants of stock or **stock options**. The latter represent the right (but not obligation) to buy a company's stock at a set price (called the strike price) for a certain period. The option becomes valuable when, and if, the stock price rises above this amount. Grants of stock and stock options are often seen as a way to align executives' interests with those of shareholders. The idea behind such *pay-for-performance* approaches is that executives will work hard to improve the company's results, because this will increase the stock price and therefore the value of their compensation. In 2014, more than half (54 percent) of executive pay was performance-based.[20] But critics have highlighted a danger of equity-based compensation: that unscrupulous executives may become so fixated on their performance pay that they will do anything to increase the stock price, even if this involves unethical accounting practices or actions that would hurt employees, customers, or other stakeholders.

By contrast, top managers in other countries earn much less. Although the pay of top executives elsewhere is catching up, it is still generally well below what comparable managers in the United States earn. Figure 13.4 represents graphically the large gap between executive pay in the United States and that of other developed nations.

---

[19] "Top 5 Hedge Fund Earners," *The New York Times,* May 5, 2015.

[20] "CEOs Awarded More Cash Pay," *The Wall Street Journal,* April 20, 2015.

FIGURE 13.5   **Ratio of Average CEO Pay to Average Production Worker Pay, 1990–2014**

Sources: Data for 2013 and 2014 are from the AFL-CIO Corporate Watch website at *www.aflcio.org/Corporate-Watch* © AFL-CIO, used by permission. Data for earlier years are drawn from the Institute for Policy Studies' Executive Excess annual surveys conducted by the Institute for Policy Studies and United for a Fair Economy, available at *www.ips-dc.org* and *www.faireconomy.org*. Used by permission.

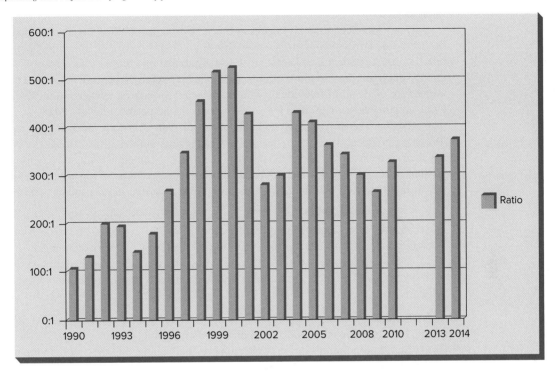

These disparities have caused friction in some global firms.

A case in point is Carlos Ghosn, the Brazilian-born chief executive of the Renault–Nissan Alliance, a strategic partnership of automakers that also includes companies in Germany, China, and Russia. In 2014, Ghosn received $8.7 million for his services as CEO of the French partner Renault. Although his compensation was above average for CEO pay in France, it did not seem excessive for a leader that *Forbes* magazine called an "exceptional manager and visionary." But in Japan, where he earned a separate $9.8 million as CEO of Nissan, his compensation seemed out of line to many; it was four times greater than that earned by Toyota Motor Corporation president Akio Toyoda, whose company made five times the profit. "I understand the sensitivity of the issue," said Ghosn, who regularly commuted between homes in Paris and Tokyo. "[But] being in Japan should not be a handicap to attract talent."[21]

Another way to look at executive compensation is to compare the pay of top managers with that of average employees. In the United States, CEOs in 2014 made 373 times what the average worker did. Figure 13.5 shows that since 1990 the ratio of average executive to average worker pay has increased markedly during periods of economic expansion, but fallen back during periods of economic contraction, such as the Great Recession of 2008–09. The ratio, which has started to rise again, is now more than three times greater than it was in 1990.

[21] "Nissan's $10 Million CEO Set to Top Japan Pay Rankings," *Bloomberg Business,* June 23, 2014; and "Is Carlos Ghosn Worth $15 Million to Renault and Nissan?" *Forbes,* March 24, 2015.

A provision of the 2010 Dodd-Frank Act (introduced in Chapter 7) required major U.S. firms for the first time to disclose the ratio of their CEO's compensation to the median compensation of all their employees. But business groups lobbied intensely to repeal or weaken this rule, calling it unnecessarily burdensome, and in 2015 it had still not been implemented.[22]

Why are American executives paid so much? Corporate politics play an important role. In their book, *Pay without Performance: The Unfulfilled Promise of Executive Compensation,* Lucian A. Bebchuk and Jesse M. Fried argue that one reason salaries are so high is that top managers have so much influence over the pay-setting process. Compensation committees are made up of individuals who are selected for board membership in part by the CEO, and they are often linked by ties of friendship and personal loyalty. Many are CEOs themselves and sensitive to the indirect impact of their decisions on their own salaries. Moreover, compensation committees rely on surveys of similar firms and usually want to pay their own executives above the industry average, over time ratcheting up pay for all.[23]

Some observers say that the comparatively high compensation of top executives is justified. In this view, well-paid managers are simply being rewarded for outstanding performance.

> For example, Leslie Wexner, the CEO of L Brands (which includes Victoria's Secret, PINK, and Bath & Body Works), earned $24 million in 2014, up more than 50 percent from the previous year. But the company had been stunningly successful: in 2014, the total return to shareholders (change in the share price plus dividends paid) jumped 66 percent. To at least some investors, his generous compensation was clearly worth it.[24]

Supporters also argue that high salaries provide an incentive for innovation and risk taking. In an era of intense global competition, restructuring, and financial crisis, the job of CEO of large corporations has never been more challenging, and the tenure in the top job has become shorter. Another argument for high compensation is a shortage of labor. In this view, not many individuals are capable of running today's large, complex organizations, so the few that have the necessary skills and experience can command a premium. Today's high salaries are necessary for companies to attract or retain top talent. Why shouldn't the most successful business executives make as much as top athletes and entertainers?

On the other hand, critics argue that inflated executive pay hurts the ability of U.S. firms to compete with foreign rivals. High executive compensation diverts financial resources that could be used to invest in the business, increase shareholder dividends, or pay average workers more. Multimillion-dollar salaries cause resentment and sap the commitment—and sometimes lead to the exodus of—hard-working lower- and mid-level employees who feel they are not receiving their fair share. As for the performance issue, most empirical evidence finds little relationship overall between executive pay and company success. A study of 500 large U.S. companies by the nonprofit organization As You Sow, published in 2015, found no statistically significant relationship between total shareholder return (capital gains and dividends) and top executive compensation averaged over the preceding five-year period. In other words, higher-paid executives did not necessarily produce higher returns for shareholders.[25]

[22] "SEC Has Yet to Set Rule on Tricky Ratio of C.E.O.'s Pay to Workers'," *The New York Times,* January 26, 2015.

[23] Lucian A. Bebchuk and Jesse M. Fried, *Pay without Performance: The Unfulfilled Promise of Executive Compensation* (Cambridge, MA: Harvard University Press, 2004).

[24] Equilar data, private correspondence.

[25] As You Sow, "The 100 Most Overpaid CEOs: Executive Compensation at S&P 500 Companies," February 2015, and private correspondence. Calculations were contributed by HIP Investor, a partner of As You Sow. The organization's work on executive compensation is available at *www.asyousow.org/our-work/power-of-the-proxy/executive-compensation/.*

Executive compensation has also been the subject of government regulations. Under U.S. government rules, companies must clearly disclose what their five top executives are paid, and lay out a rationale for their compensation. Companies must also report the value of various perks, from the personal use of corporate aircraft to free tickets to sporting events, which had previously escaped investor scrutiny. Under the so-called **say-on-pay** provisions of the Dodd-Frank Act, which went into effect in 2011, public companies must hold shareholder votes on executive compensation at least once every three years. Many voluntarily now do so annually. Although such say-on-pay referendums are not binding on management, they provide a mechanism for shareholders to voice displeasure over excessive compensation—and boards often take notice. For example, in 2012 the board of Citigroup asked for the resignation of CEO Vikram Pandit shortly after a majority of shareholders voted against his proposed executive compensation package in a say-on-pay referendum.[26] The governments of the United Kingdom, Norway, and Australia require such votes. A study found that in Australia, executive compensation had fallen relative to average workers' pay after these rules went into effect—a "testament to investor vigilance," the study concluded.[27]

Some unusual companies have voluntarily set caps on executive pay or pay differentials, and some executives have taken pay cuts. In 2015, the CEO of Gravity Payments, a Seattle credit card processor, slashed his own pay and set the minimum salary of workers at $70,000, saying that he thought that "CEO pay is way out of whack."[28] (This story is the subject of the discussion case in Chapter 3.) Whole Foods Market—as explored in the discussion case at the end of this chapter—set a rule that no executive's salary could be more than 19 times what the average worker makes. "We have a philosophy of shared fate, that we're in this together," said John Mackey, the company's cofounder and CEO.

> Legal scholar Michael Dorff recently recommended in his book *Indispensable and Other Myths* that performance pay be eliminated, or at least restructured. Citing evidence that performance pay does not actually improve company performance—and, in fact, may simply "focus executives on their chances of winning the pay lottery rather than on running the company"—Dorff proposed that executives be paid mostly in cash. Base pay could be supplemented by carefully constructed bonuses based on meeting performance targets that are easy to measure, hard to manipulate, and actually within the executives' control.[29] Some evidence suggests that boards are beginning to agree: in 2014, the proportion of executive pay comprised of cash was the highest it had been since 2010.[30]

How to structure executive compensation to best align managers' interests with those of shareholders and other stakeholders will remain a core challenge of corporate governance.

Shareholder Activism

Shareholders do not have to rely exclusively on the board of directors. Some owners, both individual and institutional, have also taken action directly to protect their own interests, as they define them. This section will describe the increased activism of three shareholder groups: large institutions (including hedge funds and private equity firms), social investors, and owners seeking redress through the courts.

---

[26] "Pandit, Citigroup's Chief, Resigns His Post in Surprise Step," *The New York Times,* October 16, 2012.

[27] Australian Council of Superannuation Investors, "Boards Respond to Investors on CEO Pay," *press release,* September 19, 2013.

[28] "CEO Cuts His Pay by Almost $1 Million to Give His Employees Big Raises," *Los Angeles Times,* April 15, 2015.

[29] Michael B. Dorff, *Indispensable and Other Myths: Why the CEO Experiment Failed and How to Fix It* (Berkeley: University of California Press, 2014).

[30] "CEOs Awarded More Cash Pay," *The Wall Street Journal,* April 20, 2015.

The Rise of Institutional Investors

As shown earlier, institutional investors—pensions, mutual funds, endowment funds, and the like—have enlarged their stockholdings significantly over the past two decades and have become more assertive in promoting the interests of their members.

One reason institutions have become more active is that it is more difficult for them to sell their holdings if they become dissatisfied with management performance. Large institutions have less flexibility than individual shareholders, because selling a large block of stock could seriously depress its price, and therefore the value of the institution's holdings. Accordingly, institutional investors have a strong incentive to hold their shares and organize to change management policy.

The Council of Institutional Investors (CII) is an organization that represents institutions and pension funds with investments collectively exceeding $3 trillion. The council has developed a Shareholder Bill of Rights and has urged its members to view their proxies as assets, voting them on behalf of shareholders rather than automatically with management. Two organizations, ISS (formerly Institutional Shareholder Services) and Glass Lewis, analyze shareholder resolutions and advise institutions how to vote. The activism of institutional shareholders has often improved company performance. One study showed that in the five years before and after a major pension fund became actively involved in the governance of companies whose shares it owned, stock performance improved dramatically, relative to the overall market.[31]

The activism of institutional investors has begun to spread to other countries. In many cases, U.S.-based pension and mutual funds that have acquired large stakes in foreign companies have spearheaded these efforts. As of late 2013, U.S. stock mutual fund investors had allocated more than a quarter of their portfolios to foreign securities.[32] To protect their globalized investments, fund managers have become active in proxy battles in Japan, Britain, Hong Kong, and many other countries. In addition, sovereign wealth funds operated by the governments of Singapore, Abu Dhabi, and China have recently become more active as institutional investors.

Another important group of activist investors is made up of private equity and hedge funds. **Private equity firms** are managed pools of money invested by very wealthy individuals and institutions (they are not usually open to ordinary individuals). **Hedge funds** are also pools of private capital; they are so-called because of the aggressive strategies they use to earn high returns for their investors. Collectively, they manage about $120 billion. Both types of funds often invest in public companies with the intention of intervening to dramatically improve their shareholder returns.

> For example, in 2014 an activist hedge fund called Starboard Value purchased a 9 percent stake in Darden Restaurants, the operator of Red Lobster, Olive Garden, LongHorn Steakhouse, and other well-known eateries. (This story is also mentioned in Chapter 1.) The hedge fund lambasted management for "its blatant disregard for shareholder concerns" and joined with other institutional shareholders to call a special meeting and elect an entirely new board of directors. Said Starboard's CEO, "It's amazing how many people reached out to me in the days following [the board's ouster] to say that they had a conversation with a CEO who said, 'The world has just changed.'"[33]

[31] "The 'CalPERS Effect' on Targeted Company Share Price," July 31, 2009, at *www.calpers-governance.org.*

[32] Christopher B. Philips, "Global Equities: Balancing Home Bias and Diversification," Vanguard Group, February 2014.

[33] "Activist Hedge Fund Starboard Succeeds in Replacing Darden Board," *The New York Times,* October 10, 2014; and "Starboard Value's Jeff Smith: The Investor CEOs Fear Most," *Fortune,* December 3, 2014.

Although some individual investors no doubt welcomed the intervention of activist shareholders like Starboard, others sounded an alarm. Commented Jeffrey Sonnenfeld, a professor at the Yale School of Management, "Too often activists pressure companies to cut costs, add debt, sell divisions and increase share repurchases, rather than invest in jobs, R&D, and growth. They do all this in the name of creating shareholder value. But that value is often short-lived."[34]

Social Investment

Another movement of growing importance among a very different kind of activist shareholder is **social investment**, sometimes also called *socially responsible investment* or *sustainable, responsible, and impact investment* (both of which terms use the acronym SRI). Social investment refers to the use of stock ownership as a strategy for promoting social, environmental, and governance objectives. This can be done in two ways: through selecting stocks according to various social criteria, and by using the corporate governance process to raise issues of concern.

Stock Screening

Shareholders wishing to choose stocks based on social, environmental, or governance criteria often turn to screened funds. A growing number of mutual funds and pension funds use *social screens* to select companies in which to invest, weeding out ones that pollute the environment, overpay their executives, discriminate against employees, make dangerous products like tobacco or weapons, or do business in countries with poor human rights records. In 2014, according to the Global Sustainable Investment Alliance, $6.6 trillion in the United States was invested in mutual funds or pensions using social responsibility as an investment criterion, accounting for more than one in every six investment dollars, a 76 percent increase from just two years earlier. In recent years, socially responsible investing has also grown rapidly in Europe and beyond. In Europe, $13.6 trillion—59 percent of all managed assets—were invested using social criteria.[35] Growth has been driven, in part, by government rules requiring pension funds to disclose the extent to which they use social, environmental, or ethical criteria in selecting investments. It has also been influenced by growing demand by investors who want to align their investment choices with their values. Most evidence shows that socially screened portfolios provide returns that are competitive with the broad market.[36]

Social criteria may also be used when selling stocks. For example, some have at various times called for *divestment* (sale of stock) from companies that had operations in China, where some products were made by forced labor, and in Nigeria, Myanmar (Burma), and Sudan, where repressive regimes had been accused of human rights abuses. More recently, activists have called for divestment from companies that mine, extract, and market fossil fuels, because of their impact on climate change.

Social Responsibility Shareholder Resolutions

Another important way in which shareholders have been active is by sponsoring **social responsibility shareholder resolutions**. This is a resolution on an issue of corporate social responsibility placed before shareholders for a vote at the company's annual meeting.

---

[34] "Activist Shareholders, Sluggish Performance," *The Wall Street Journal* [commentary], April 1, 2015.

[35] Global Sustainable Investment Alliance, "2014 Global Sustainable Investment Review," at *www.gsi-alliance.org*. Data are as of early 2014.

[36] A review of studies on the performance of socially responsible investments, relative to the broader market, may be found in Lloyd Kurtz, *Looking Forward, Looking Back: A Hitchhiker's Guide to Research on Social and Sustainable Investment* (Tilburg University, Netherlands: 2013).

The Securities and Exchange Commission (SEC), a government regulatory agency that is further described later in this chapter, allows shareholders to place resolutions concerning appropriate social issues, such as environmental responsibility or alcohol and tobacco advertising, in proxy statements sent out by companies. The SEC has tried to minimize harassment by requiring a resolution to receive minimum support to be resubmitted—3 percent of votes cast the first time, 6 percent the second time, and 10 percent the third time it is submitted within a five-year period. Resolutions cannot deal with a company's ordinary business, such as employee wages or the content of advertising, since that would constitute unjustified interference with management's decisions.[37]

In 2015, shareholder activists sponsored more than 400 resolutions dealing with major social issues. Backers included faith-based institutions, individual shareholders, unions, environmental groups, socially responsible asset managers, universities, and public pension funds. In the 2015 proxy season, some of the issues most commonly raised in these resolutions included climate change, corporate political activity, antibias policies, and governance practices such as board composition and executive compensation.[38]

When a social responsibility shareholder resolution is filed, several outcomes are possible. In some cases, managers enter into a dialogue with shareholder activists and resolve an issue before the election. For example, activists withdrew a shareholder proposal at Verizon Communications after the company met their key request to disclose details of customer information it shared with law enforcement.[39] In 2014, half of all companies engaged with shareholder activists, and more than half of these engagements resulted in some company action, as it did at Verizon.[40] If no resolution is reached, the proposal will generally be submitted for a vote by shareholders. In 2014, such resolutions garnered, on average, around a fifth of all votes cast; executive compensation and corporate governance proposals were supported by more than a third of voters, a threshold at which many boards pay serious attention.[41]

> Moreover, social responsibility shareholder resolutions do not necessarily have to win a majority of votes in order to have an impact. For example, the New York State Common Retirement Fund, a huge public pension fund, filed resolutions at more than 50 companies over a several-year period, calling on them to fully disclose their political spending. "Without disclosure, shareholders have no way of knowing whether a company's political spending best serves the company's own bottom line and long-term value," said the New York State Controller. Although only one of these resolutions won majority support from voting shareholders, more than half the companies—including such major firms as U.S. Steel, Safeway, Southwest Airlines, and PepsiCo—voluntarily agreed to the pension fund's demands.[42]

Shareholder Lawsuits

Another way in which shareholders can seek to advance their interests is by suing the company. If owners think that they or their company have been damaged by actions of company officers or directors, they have the right to bring lawsuits in the courts, either on

---

[37] Current SEC rules on shareholder proposals may be found at *www.sec.gov/rules/final*.

[38] As You Sow, *"Proxy Preview 2015: Helping Shareholders Vote Their Values,"* Oakland, Calif.: 2015.

[39] "Shareholders End Push for Verizon Data-Sharing Details," *The New York Times,* January 28, 2014.

[40] EY Center for Board Matters, *"Let's Talk Governance: 2014 Proxy Season Review,"* Ernst & Young, July 2014. This and additional information about shareholder resolutions are available at *www.ey.com/US/en/Issues/Governance-and-reporting*.

[41] The Conference Board, *"Director Notes: Shareholder Proposals on Social and Environmental Issues,"* December, 2014.

[42] "DiNapoli: Five Major Companies Adopt Pension Fund's Call for Transparency on Political Contributions," Office of the New York State Comptroller, press release, February 4, 2015; and "Transparent Win for Political Disclosures," *Bloomberg View,* March 23, 2015.

behalf of themselves or on behalf of the company (the latter is called a *derivative* lawsuit). **Shareholder lawsuits** may be initiated to check many abuses, including insider trading, an inadequate price obtained for the company's stock in a buyout (or a good price rejected), or failure to disclose material information in a timely manner. The outcome can be very expensive for companies, as illustrated by the following example.

> Several institutional shareholders sued Bank of America, saying that the bank and its top executives had failed to disclose what they knew about billions of dollars in losses suffered by Merrill Lynch in the weeks leading up to its acquisition by the bank in early 2009. Shareholders had voted to approve the buyout, only to learn of Merrill's huge losses two weeks later. When the news broke, Bank of America's stock promptly fell by 60 percent. The shareholder suit demanded $50 billion—the approximate market losses experienced by investors at that time. The lawsuit was finally settled in 2012 for $2.43 billion, far short of what shareholders had demanded but still the largest settlement to date in lawsuits arising from the financial crisis.[43]

In many ways—whether through their collective organization, the selection of stocks, the shareholder resolution process, or the courts—shareholder activists can and do protect their economic and social rights.

Government Protection of Shareholder Interests

The government also plays an important role in protecting shareholder interests. This role has expanded, as legislators have responded to the corporate scandals of the early 2000s and the financial crisis later in the decade.

Securities and Exchange Commission

The major government agency protecting shareholders' interests is the **Securities and Exchange Commission (SEC)**. Established in 1934 in the wake of the stock market crash and the Great Depression, its mission is to protect shareholders' rights by making sure that stock markets are run fairly and that investment information is fully disclosed. The agency, unlike most in government, generates revenue to pay for its own operations. (The revenue comes from fees paid by companies listed on the major stock exchanges.)

Government regulation is needed because shareholders can be damaged by abusive practices. Two areas calling for regulatory attention are protecting shareholders from fraudulent financial accounting and from unfair trading by insiders.

Information Transparency and Disclosure

Giving shareholders more and better company information is one of the best ways to safeguard their interests, and this is a primary mission of the SEC. By law, shareholders have a right to know about the affairs of the corporations in which they hold ownership shares. Those who attend annual meetings learn about past performance and future goals through speeches made by corporate officers and documents such as the company's annual report. Those who do not attend meetings must depend primarily on annual reports issued by the company and the opinions of independent financial analysts.

---

[43] "Recent Trends in Securities Class Action Litigation," NERA Economic Consulting, January 20, 2015; and "Bank of America Settles Suit over Merrill for $2.43 Billion," *The New York Times,* September 28, 2012.

In recent years, management has tended to disclose more information than ever before to shareholders and other interested people. Prompted by the SEC, professional accounting groups, and individual investors, companies now disclose a great deal about their financial affairs, with much information readily available on investor relations sections of company web pages. Shareholders can learn about sales and earnings, assets, capital expenditures and depreciation by line of business, details of foreign operations, and many other financial matters. Corporations also are required to disclose detailed information about directors and top executives and their compensation. In addition, many companies have begun reporting detailed information about social and environmental, as well as financial, performance, as discussed in Chapters 3, 10, and 17.

Although the overall trend has been toward greater transparency, some observers felt that a lack of disclosure about complex financial instruments, such as mortgage-backed securities, that became common in the mid-2000s, may have led investors to underestimate their risk. The Dodd-Frank Act has tightened regulation on issuers of complex securities, such as those backed by subprime mortgages. The role of credit rating agencies in evaluating risk is explored in the case, "Moody's Credit Ratings and the Subprime Mortgage Meltdown," at the end of this book.

Insider Trading

Another area the SEC regulates is stock trading by insiders. **Insider trading** occurs when a person gains access to confidential information about a company's financial condition and then uses that information, before it becomes public knowledge, to buy or sell the company's stock. Since others do not know what an inside trader does, the insider has an unfair advantage.

> In 2011, Raj Rajaratnam, founder and former manager of the prominent hedge fund Galleon Group, was sentenced to 11 years in prison for 14 counts of illegal insider trading, the longest-ever sentence for this crime. He was also ordered to pay $157 million in fines and forfeitures. Federal prosecutors built their case from wiretap evidence. Over several months, they listened as Rajaratnam—as *The New York Times* put it—"brazenly and matter-of-factly swapped inside stock tips with corporate insiders and fellow traders." In one particularly shocking example, a member of the board of directors of Goldman Sachs called Rajaratnam seconds after a board meeting to share earnings information. The government said that Galleon Group had made $63 million in all from illegal trades. "The defendant knew the rules, but he did not care," said one of the government prosecutors. "Cheating became part of his business model."[44]

Insider trading is illegal under the Securities and Exchange Act of 1934, which outlaws "any manipulative or deceptive device." The courts have generally interpreted this to mean that it is against the law to trade stock (or stock options) based on material, nonpublic information. This includes company officials, of course, who may have inside information based on their work. But it also includes also other individuals who obtain such information through a "breach of trust," that is, a tip from someone who has an obligation to keep the information confidential. The tipper can also be guilty, if he or she benefits from the exchange. It is not, however, illegal to trade based on information developed from publicly available sources. Unfortunately, drawing these distinctions in practice has

---

[44] "Hedge Fund Billionaire Is Guilty of Insider Trading" and "A Circle of Tipsters Who Shared Illegal Secrets," *The New York Times,* May 11, 2011; and "Rajaratnam Ordered to Pay $92.8 Million Penalty," *The New York Times,* November 8, 2011.

been challenging, and the courts and Congress have gone back and forth trying to pin down exactly what constitutes a consequential benefit to the tipper, and what information can be said to come from inside versus public sources.[45] Insider trading is also illegal in most other countries; in Australia, for example, a former government statistician and an employer of a large bank were sentenced to multiyear prison terms in 2015 after they were found guilty in what the judge called "the worst case of insider trading" ever brought before an Australian court.[46]

> Insider traders are not necessarily high-placed executives, wealthy individuals, or household names. In 2015, a circle of friends and family members were convicted in an insider trading scheme. John Femenia, who at the time of the crime was employed at Wells Fargo in Charlotte, North Carolina, passed along information about upcoming deals involving the bank's clients to a high-school buddy, Shawn Hegedus. Hegedus and his wife then passed the information along a phone tree of family and friends, trading for their own accounts and rewarding Femenia with cash and gold bars. All told, participants made $11 million on the scheme, much of which was laundered through Las Vegas casinos. Eventually, nine people were convicted and received various sentences ranging up to 10 years in prison.[47]

The best-known kind of insider trading—as in this case—occurs when people improperly acquire confidential information about forthcoming mergers and acquisitions before these are announced to the public. A startling new study conducted by professors at New York University and McGill University, which examined stock trades between 1996 and 2012, found that insider trading had probably occurred in no less than a quarter of all such deals.[48] In another kind of insider trading, called *front-running,* traders place buy and sell orders for stock in advance of the moves of big institutional investors. They also track big trades in real time and act on them quickly; with today's high-speed trading, even a few milliseconds of advance notice of news about to hit the market can be enough to execute valuable insider trades.

Insider trading is contrary to the logic underlying the stock markets: All stock buyers and sellers ought to have access to the same information. In the Galleon Group case described above, Rajaratnam had insider information that ordinary investors did not—information that he used to give his fund and its investors an unfair advantage over others. If ordinary investors think that insiders can use what they know for personal gain, the system of stock trading could break down from lack of trust. Insider trading laws are important in order for investors to have full confidence in the fundamental fairness of the markets.

Another responsibility of the SEC is to protect investors against fraud. One situation where they apparently failed to guard against a massive scheme to cheat investors was the fraud perpetrated by Bernard Madoff.

> The victims of Madoff's fraud—including prominent universities, charities, and cultural institutions, as well as individual investors—lost as much as $65 *billion.* Where were the government regulators in all of this? In congressional hearings, SEC chairman Christopher Cox admitted that his agency had missed repeated warnings, dating back to 1999, that things might be amiss at Madoff's firm. "I

[45] "U.S. Weighs Whether to Act or Wait on Insider Trading," *The New York Times,* April 6, 2015.

[46] "Two Sentenced in Australia Insider-Trading Case," *The Wall Street Journal,* March 17, 2015.

[47] "Ex-Wells Fargo Banker, Others Jailed for $11M Insider Plot," February 13, 2015, *www.law360.com;* and "Insider Case Highlights Ties of Friends, Family," *The Wall Street Journal,* August 11, 2013.

[48] "Study Asserts Startling Numbers of Insider Trading Rogues," *The Wall Street Journal,* June 16, 2014.

am gravely concerned by the apparent multiple failures over at least a decade to thoroughly investigate these allegations or at any point to seek formal authority to pursue them," said Cox. *The New York Times* wrote in a harsh editorial that the agency's failure to uncover the Madoff fraud "exemplifies its lackadaisical approach to enforcing the law on Wall Street."[49]

An analysis by *Bloomberg Businessweek* showed that the SEC has become much more assertive in pursuing fraud since 2009, when Madoff was sentenced, because of the greater regulatory authority granted to the agency under the Dodd-Frank Act.[50]

Shareholders and the Corporation

Shareholders have become an increasingly powerful and vocal stakeholder group in corporations. Boards of directors, under intense scrutiny after the recent wave of corporate scandals and business failures, are giving close attention to their duty to protect owners' interests. Reforms in the corporate governance process are under way that will make it easier for them to do so. Owners themselves, especially institutional investors, are pressing directors and management more forcefully to serve shareholder interests. The government, through the Securities and Exchange Commission, has taken important new steps to protect investors and promote fairness and transparency in the financial marketplace.

Clearly, shareholders are a critically important stakeholder group. By providing capital, monitoring corporate performance, assuring the effective operation of stock markets, and bringing new issues to the attention of management, shareholders play a very important role in making the business system work. A major theme of this book is that the relationship between the modern corporation and *all* stakeholders is changing. Corporate leaders have an obligation to manage their companies in ways that attempt to align investors' interests with those of employees, customers, communities, and others. Balancing these various interests is a prime requirement of modern management. While shareholders are no longer considered the only important stakeholder group, their interests and needs remain central to the successful operation of corporate business.

Summary

- Individuals and institutions own shares of corporations primarily to earn dividends and receive capital gains, although some have social objectives as well. Shareholders are entitled to vote, receive information, select directors, and attempt to shape corporate policies and action.

- In the modern system of corporate governance, boards of directors are responsible for setting overall objectives, selecting and supervising top management, and assuring the integrity of financial accounting. The job of corporate boards has become increasingly difficult and challenging, as directors seek to balance the interests of shareholders, managers, and other stakeholders. Reforms have been proposed to make boards more responsive to shareholders and more independent of management.

- Some observers argue that the compensation of top U.S. executives is justified by performance, and that high salaries provide a necessary incentive for innovation and risk

---

[49] "Standing Accused: A Pillar of Finance and Charity," *The New York Times,* December 13, 2008; "SEC Issues Mea Culpa on Madoff," *The New York Times,* December 17, 2008; "SEC Knew Him as a Friend and Foe," *The New York Times,* December 18, 2008; and "You Mean That Bernie Madoff?" *The New York Times* [editorial], December 19, 2008.

[50] "Outmanned, Outgunned, and on a Roll," *Bloomberg Businessweek,* April 23–April 29, 2012.

taking in a demanding position. Critics, however, believe that it is too high. In this view, high pay hurts firm competitiveness and undermines employee commitment.

- Shareholders have influenced corporate actions by forming organizations to promote their interests, intervening in board elections, and by filing lawsuits when they feel they have been wronged. They have also organized under the banner of social investment. These efforts have included screening stocks according to social and ethical criteria, and using the voting process to promote shareholder proposals focused on issues of social responsibility.

- Recent enforcement efforts by the Securities and Exchange Commission have focused on improving the accuracy and transparency of financial information provided to investors. They have also focused on curbing insider trading, which undermines fairness in the marketplace by benefiting those with illicitly acquired information at the expense of those who do not have it.

Key Terms

board of directors, *283*
corporate governance, *283*
executive
compensation, *287*
hedge fund, *292*
insider trading, *296*
institutional investors, *281*

private equity firm, *292*
proxy, *282*
proxy access, *285*
say-on-pay, *291*
Securities and Exchange
Commission
(SEC), *295*

shareholders, *279*
shareholder lawsuits, *295*
social investment, *293*
social responsibility
shareholder
resolutions, *293*
stock option, *288*

Internet Resources

www.nyse.com — New York Stock Exchange
www.cii.org — Council of Institutional Investors
www.ussif.org/ — Forum for Sustainable and Responsible Investment
www.socialfunds.com — Site for socially responsible individual investors
www.ecgi.org — European Corporate Governance Institute
www.issgovernance.com — ISS (formerly Institutional Shareholder Services)
www.calpers-governance.org — California Public Employees Retirement System
www.sec.gov — U.S. Securities and Exchange Commission

Discussion Case: *Whole Foods Adopts Egalitarian Compensation Policies—But Fights Back on Board Elections*

In 2015, Whole Foods Markets surprised many by abruptly canceling its annual shareholders' meeting, saying it needed time to respond to new rules on proxy access. This rather odd term referred to a simple concept: the right of shareholders to nominate their own candidates for the board of directors. The upscale grocer, widely known for its socially and environmentally responsible practices, apparently opposed moves by its own shareholders to expand their democratic rights. The corporate governance director for CalPERS, California's public pension fund, called the company's action "a not-so-wholesome move."

In 2015, Whole Foods was the leading retailer of natural and organic foods in the United States and a perennial member of the "100 best companies to work for" list. The grocer operated around 400 stores, with more than $600 billion in sales annually. It referred to itself as a "mission-driven company" and stated that its purpose was "not only to generate profits but to create value for all of our major stakeholders." Whole Foods promoted healthy eating and was committed to local sourcing, sustainable farming and fishing, animal welfare, and community volunteerism. It operated several foundations that gave generously to support better health and nutrition in underserved communities.

Whole Food's compensation policies, by the standards of most U.S. firms, were radically egalitarian. The average annual salary at the company for full-time employees was around $40,000. The company had a policy of internal pay equity, committing to paying no one more than 19 times the average annual wage of its full-time employees (in 2014, the salary cap was a bit under $760,000). (Some top executives earned more—up to $3 million or so—when stock awards were included.) The company refused to benchmark its top managers' pay, saying that this "had been a factor in the exponential growth in executive compensation that is common at other companies." Executive officers received the same health benefits as other full-time employees.

John Mackey, the company's cofounder and, in 2015, its co-CEO (a position he shared with Walter Robb), drew an annual salary of exactly $1. "I have reached a place in my life where I no longer want to work for money, but simply for the joy of the work itself and to better answer the call to service that I feel so clearly in my own heart," the founder told employees in a 2006 letter. The company also made compensation data available to all employees. "If you're trying to create a high-trust organization, an organization where people are all-for-one and one-for-all, you can't have secrets," Mackey said.

The issue that Whole Foods confronted in 2015—proxy access—was one that had burst on the corporate governance scene in the 2010s. In the United States, for many years the nominating committee of the board had nominated candidates for director; their names were then placed on the proxy ballot for a vote by shareholders. Normally, dissident shareholders did not have the right to nominate their own candidates, so boards tended to fill vacancies with other like-minded individuals. This changed after 2011, when activist shareholders began filing shareholder resolutions demanding greater proxy access. In 2014, 17 such proposals were considered, garnering on average about a third of the vote.

James McRitchie, a shareholder activist and publisher of a corporate governance website, submitted such a proposal for a vote at Whole Food's 2015 shareholder meeting. Known as a "three-and-three," McRitchie's proposal would allow a group of shareholders owning at least 3 percent of the company for at least three years to nominate candidates for the board. (Of course, these individuals would have to receive a majority of shareholder votes to be elected, just like any nominee.) Whole Foods reacted by offering its *own* proposal—that would give proxy access to a *single* shareholder who had owned *9* percent of the company's stock for at least *five* years—and asked the SEC to block McRitchie's proposal on the grounds that it directly conflicted with the company's proposal. (The company later changed its proposal, saying that the shareholder would need to own just 5 percent of the company's stock.) The SEC initially agreed, but reversed itself after pressure from institutional shareholders, saying it needed to further study the issue.

In the meantime, many other companies simply loosened their own proxy access provisions without waiting for a fight with activist shareholders or a ruling from the SEC. Bank of America, General Electric, CF Industries, Yum Brands, and Prudential Insurance all voluntarily adopted three-and-three rules—a development that a representative of CalPERS called a "sea change." Others in the business community objected, however. The Chamber of Commerce and the Business Roundtable, for example, warned that greater proxy access could give unions and other "outside groups" too much power.

Why did Whole Foods take such a strong stand against proxy access? The company declined to explain its position against greater shareholder rights, simply saying that it had a policy of "not commenting on proxy-related matters." Some thought that the company's actions were inconsistent with its commitment to broad responsiveness to stakeholders. But others thought that Whole Foods was simply trying to protect its distinctive corporate culture from investors who might be single-mindedly focused on raising the company's share price.

Sources: "Bank of America Joins Shareholder 'Proxy Access' Push," *Investor's Business Daily,* March 20, 2015; "SEC Shift on 'Conflicting' Shareholder Proposals Sparked by Abuse Concerns," *The Wall Street Journal,* March 19, 2015; "CalPERS, Activist Shareholder Battle Whole Foods," *http://calpensions.com;* "At Whole Foods, Chipotle, and Others, Shareholders Prepare for Battle," *Fortune,* February 3, 2015; "Whole Foods Dispute Prompts SEC Review of Corporate Ballots," *The Wall Street Journal,* January 19, 2015; Whole Foods, Forms 10-K and 10-KA [2014 Annual Report to Stakeholders], *www.wholefoodsmarket.com;* "Here's Why Whole Foods Lets Employees Look Up Each Other's Salaries," *Business Insider,* March 3, 2014; "Food Fighter: Does Whole Foods' C.E.O. Know What's Best for You?" *The New Yorker,* January 4, 2010; and "I No Longer Wish to Work for Money," [John Mackey's Letter to Team Members], in *Fast Company,* February 2007.

Discussion Questions

1. If you owned shares of stock in Whole Foods, would you support McRitchie's 3-and-3 proposal or the company's 5-and-5 proposal ? Why?

2. How do Whole Foods' executive compensation practices compare with those of other firms, as described in this chapter? Do you think Whole Foods' approach is better or worse than that of most other companies, and why?

3. Some companies described in the case have voluntarily supported greater proxy access for shareholders. What do you think has motivated them to do so?

4. Several business support groups mentioned in the case have opposed greater proxy access for shareholders. What do you think has motivated them to do so?

5. Do you believe Whole Foods' opposition to expanded proxy access is consistent or inconsistent with other aspects of the company's culture and policies?

CHAPTER FOURTEEN

Consumer Protection

Safeguarding consumers while continuing to supply them with the goods and services they want, at the prices they want, is a prime social responsibility of business. Many companies recognize that providing customers with excellent service and product quality is an effective, as well as ethical, business strategy. Consumers, through their organizations, have advocated for their rights to safety, to be informed, to choose, to be heard, and to privacy. Government agencies serve as watchdogs for consumers, supplementing the actions taken by consumers to protect themselves through self-advocacy and use of the courts and by the actions of socially responsible corporations.

This Chapter Focuses on These Key Learning Objectives:

LO 14-1   Knowing the five major rights of consumers.

LO 14-2   Analyzing the reasons for consumer advocacy and the methods consumer organizations use to advance their interests.

LO 14-3   Assessing the ways in which government regulatory agencies protect consumers and what kinds of products are most likely to be regulated.

LO 14-4   Determining how consumer privacy online can best be protected.

LO 14-5   Examining how the courts protect consumers and efforts by businesses to change product liability laws.

LO 14-6   Evaluating how socially responsible corporations can proactively respond to consumer needs.

In May 2015, the Japanese company Takata admitted that air bags it had supplied to many carmakers were defective. The air bags—which were intended to protect people in a crash—had a tendency to explode violently, sending shrapnel-like shards of metal flying into the passenger compartment. More than 100 injuries and six deaths had been linked to the defect. At the same time, Takata doubled the number of recalled vehicles to 34 million—about one in every seven cars on the road—making the automotive recall the largest in U.S. history. Analysts estimated that the cost of the recall could run as high as $5 billion, approaching Takata's total revenue in 2014. In addition, the company faced liability lawsuits from victims that could eventually cost billions more. "It is fair to say that this is probably the most complex consumer safety recall in U.S. history," said the secretary of transportation.[1]

When Corinthian Colleges, a group of for-profit vocational schools, declared bankruptcy in 2015, it created a big problem for their half-a-million current and former students. Many of these students had taken out loans to attend Corinthian's various colleges, including Heald, Everest, and WyoTech. Now, their programs had been terminated and their degrees devalued, but they still owed an estimated $1.2 billion. At the time of the shutdown, the Department of Education had charged Corinthian with deceptive recruitment practices, enticing prospective students—many of them low-income—with false job-placement and graduation figures. "The rep I talked to told me how great it would be, how they'd help me find a job when I graduated, how their grads were highly sought after," said one Texas student, who had unsuccessfully sought a career as a detective after attending Everest College and still owed more than $80,000 on her student loans. Shortly after the bankruptcy, the Department of Education announced it had set up a process for former Corinthian students to apply to have their government educational debt forgiven. Many students welcomed the move, but other observers criticized it, saying that taxpayers should not have to pay for Corinthian's fraud.[2]

What would happen if businesses could literally read your mind to determine why you choose to buy some products or services, but not others? A new field, called *neuromarketing,* does just that. Scientists working for one of some 150 neuromarketing firms worldwide scan the brains of volunteers, using functional magnetic resonance imaging (fMRI) machines, while asking questions, showing them images and videos, and allowing them to examine products. As the volunteers respond, the fMRI records how the parts of their brains associated with pleasurable feelings, memory, and comprehension react. One such study showed, for example, that people responded more positively to perfume ads showing the source of the fragrance—say, roses—than ones showing a couple in a passionate embrace. Another study showed that fMRI results predicted actual behavior better than simply asking people what they planned to do. Many leading companies—including Facebook, McDonald's, Disney, Citigroup, and Unilever—already use this technology to understand better how to boost the effectiveness of advertising. But some consumer activists sounded a warning. "It's having an effect on individuals that individuals are not informed about," said the director of the Center for Digital Democracy.[3]

---

[1] "Airbag Recall Widens to 34 Million Cars as Takata Admits Defects," *The New York Times,* May 19, 2015; "Takata Air-Bag Recalls Expand to 34 Million Cars in the U.S.," *The Wall Street Journal,* May 19, 2015; and "Takata's Future Clipped by Steep Recall Costs, *The Wall Street Journal,* May 20, 2015.

[2] "Obama Administration Opens Door for More Student-Debt Forgiveness," *The Wall Street Journal,* June 8, 2015; and "For-Profit Colleges Face a Loan Revolt by Thousands Claiming Trickery," *The New York Times,* May 3, 2015.

[3] "Neuromarketing: Pseudoscience No More," *Forbes,* February 24, 2015; "How the Ad Man Can Get Inside Your Head," *The Observer* (United Kingdom), January 15, 2012; "Marketing on the Brain," *Marketing,* November 2, 2011; and "Making Ads That Whisper to the Brain," *The New York Times,* November 13, 2010.

These three examples demonstrate some of the complexities of serving consumers today. They show how important it is for businesses to ensure their customers' safety, promote their services honestly, and be transparent in their advertising. Companies face challenging—and often conflicting—demands to produce a safe and high-quality product or service, keep prices down, protect privacy, prevent fraud and manipulation, and meet the changing expectations of diverse customers around the world. This chapter examines these issues and the various ways that consumers and their advocates, government regulators, the courts, and proactive business firms have dealt with them.

The Rights of Consumers

Over time, consumers and their advocates have defined five core rights to which they are entitled in their relationships with business. (Consumer advocacy is further described in the following section.) These five rights are as follows:

1. *The right to be informed:* to be protected against fraudulent, deceitful, or grossly misleading information, advertising, and labeling, and to be given the facts to make an informed purchasing decision.
2. *The right to safety:* to be protected against the marketing of goods that are hazardous to health or life.
3. *The right to choose:* to be assured, wherever possible, access to a variety of products and services at competitive prices; and in those industries in which competition is not workable and government regulation is substituted, to be assured satisfactory quality and service at fair prices.
4. *The right to be heard:* to be assured that consumer interests will receive full and sympathetic consideration in the formulation of government policy and fair and expeditious treatment in the courts.
5. *The right to privacy:* to be assured that information disclosed in the course of a commercial transaction, such as health conditions, financial status, or identity, is not shared with others unless authorized.

Figure 14.1 shows the four main ways that these core rights of consumers can be protected. Consumers and their advocates can act to protect their own interests in their interactions with business. The government can protect consumers through the regulation of product safety, quality, and fair dealing. People can use the courts to seek compensation when they have been injured by unsafe products or unfair practices and to compel businesses to pay greater attention to consumer rights. And finally, companies can proactively protect their own customers through careful attention to safety and quality and by taking swift action when something goes wrong. This chapter will take up each of these methods in turn, beginning with consumer self-organization and advocacy.

Self-Advocacy for Consumer Interests

As long as business has existed—since the ancient beginnings of commerce and trade—consumers have tried to protect their interests when they buy goods and services. They have haggled over prices, taken a careful look at the goods they were buying, compared the quality and prices of products offered by other sellers, and complained loudly when they felt cheated by shoddy products. So, consumer self-reliance—best summed up by the Latin phrase *caveat emptor,* meaning "let the buyer beware"—has always been one form of consumer protection and is still practiced today.

FIGURE 14.1
Four Methods
of Protecting
Consumers

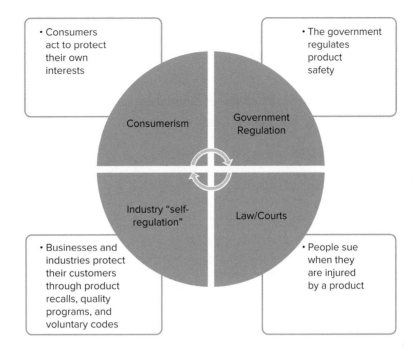

- Consumers act to protect their own interests

- The government regulates product safety

Consumerism

Government Regulation

Industry "self-regulation"

Law/Courts

- Businesses and industries protect their customers through product recalls, quality programs, and voluntary codes

- People sue when they are injured by a product

However, the increasing complexity of economic life has led to organized, collective efforts by consumers to safeguard their own rights in many nations. These organized activities are usually called *consumerism* or the **consumer movement**.

Today, many organized groups actively promote and speak for the interests of millions of consumers.

Consumers International (CI) is an international nongovernmental organization that represents more than 250 consumer groups in 120 nations. Headquartered in London, it has offices in Asia, Latin America, and Africa. Its growth since 1960 has paralleled the expansion of global trade and the integration of many developing nations into the world economy, as discussed in Chapter 4. In 2015, CI adopted a new strategy, calling for partnering with member organizations to deliver coordinated, multi-national campaigns to address common problems faced by consumers in the global marketplace. For example, the group launched an online campaign to pressure the World Health Organization to develop a global treaty to support consumers' rights to healthy food, pointing out that unhealthy diets contributed to more than 11 million deaths a year.

In the United States, one organization alone, the Consumer Federation of America, brings together more than 250 nonprofit groups to espouse the consumer viewpoint. Other active U.S. consumer advocacy organizations include Public Citizen, the National Consumers League, the Public Interest Research Group (PIRG), and the consumer protection unit of the American Association for Retired People (AARP). Consumer Reports (CR, formerly called Consumers Union) conducts extensive tests on selected consumer products and services and publishes the results of its tests, with ratings on a brand-name basis, online at *www.consumerreports.org*. In addition, the organization's extensive website provides a great deal of free information. Consumers Union also hosts online chats on a range of consumer rights topics and sponsors a site called *HearUsNow.org* to aggregate consumer appeals to companies. A recent petition on the site, for example, called on Facebook to strengthen users' privacy controls, saying, "Let me see all my data and control it!" CR also offers RSS feeds on various topics and a service that alerts supporters by e-mail so they can make their voices heard electronically on various legislative issues relevant to consumer rights.[4]

Reasons for the Consumer Movement

The consumer movement exists because consumers want to be treated fairly and honestly in the marketplace. Some business practices do not meet this standard. Consumers may be harmed by abuses such as unfairly high prices, unreliable and unsafe products, excessive or deceptive advertising claims, violations of privacy, and the sale of products that may be harmful to human health.

Additional reasons for the existence of the consumer movement are the following:

- *Complex products have enormously complicated the choices consumers need to make when they shop.* For this reason, consumers today are more dependent on business for product quality than ever before. Because many products, from smartphones to hybrid automobiles, are so complex, most consumers have no way to judge at the time of purchase whether their quality is satisfactory. In these circumstances, unscrupulous business firms can take advantage of customers.

- *Services, as well as products, have become more specialized and difficult to judge.* When choosing health plans, Internet service providers, credit cards, or colleges (like Corinthian, mentioned in one of the opening examples of this chapter), most consumers do not have adequate guides for evaluating whether they are good or bad. They can rely on word-of-mouth experiences of others, but this information may not be entirely reliable. Or the consumer may not be told that service will be expensive or hard to obtain.

- *When businesses try to sell either products or services through advertising, claims may be inflated or they may appeal to emotions.* For example, Samsung's print and video ads for its SF notebook computer showed a naked woman, with her long hair strategically covering her breasts, under the slogan "true beauty is curved." One blogger, a woman, found the ad "distasteful"; she commented that a computer and the female form were "certainly two things that I thought would never have anything in common."[5] In the process, consumers do not always receive reliable and relevant information about products and services.

- *Technology has permitted businesses to learn more than ever about their customers—potentially violating their privacy.* As more and more people go online to browse, compare products and services, and purchase items, companies are able to learn a great deal about their preferences, desires, and habits. New businesses, such as Acxiom, described later in this chapter, have emerged that track and aggregate consumer data for others. Such tracking poses threats to individual privacy. And, new technologies like neuromarketing, mentioned in one of the opening examples of this chapter, also present opportunities for abuse.

- *Some businesses have ignored product safety.* Business has not always given sufficient attention to product safety. Certain products, such as automobiles, pharmaceutical drugs, medical devices, processed foods, and children's toys, may be particularly susceptible to causing harm. The case of Takata's defective air bags, mentioned in the opening example of this chapter, is just one of the latest incidents of unsafe products.

---

[4] See *www.consumersunion.org* and *http://hearusnow.org.*

[5] *http://christine-gazette.blogspot.com.*

FIGURE 14.2
Major Consumer Protections Specified by Consumer Laws

Information protections

Hazardous home appliances must carry a warning label.

Home products must carry a label detailing contents.

Automobiles must carry a label showing detailed breakdown of price and all related costs.

Lenders must provide timely and understandable information about mortgages and other consumer loans.

Tobacco advertisements and products must carry a health warning label.

Alcoholic beverages must carry a health warning label.

All costs related to real estate transactions must be disclosed.

Warranties must specify the terms of the guarantee and the buyer's rights.

False and deceptive advertising are prohibited.

Food and beverage labels must show complete nutritional information.

Food advertising must not make false claims about nutrition.

Direct hazard protections

Hazardous toys and games for children are banned from sale.

Safety standards for motor vehicles are required.

National and state speed limits are specified.

Hazardous, defective, and ineffective products can be recalled under pressure from the EPA, CPSC, NHTSA, and FDA.

Pesticide residue in food is allowed only if it poses a negligible risk.

Pricing protections

Unfair pricing, monopolistic practices, and noncompetitive acts are regulated by the FTC and Justice Department and by states.

Liability protections

When injured by a product, consumers can seek legal redress.

Privacy protections

Limited collection of information online from and about children is allowed.

Other protections

No discrimination in the extension of credit is allowed.

How Government Protects Consumers

The role of government in protecting consumers is extensive in many nations. This section will describe legal protections afforded to consumers in the United States and offer some comparisons with other countries.

Goals of Consumer Laws

Figure 14.2 lists some of the safeguards provided by U.S. **consumer protection laws**. Taken together, these safeguards reflect the goals of government policymakers and regulators in the context of the five rights of consumers outlined above. Many of these safeguards are also embedded in the laws of other nations.

First, some laws are intended to provide consumers with better information when making purchases. Consumers can make more rational choices when they have accurate information about the product. For example, the laws requiring health warnings on cigarettes and alcoholic beverages broaden the information consumers have about these items. Manufacturers, retailers, and importers must spell out warranties (a guarantee or assurance by the seller) in clear language and give consumers the right to sue if they are not honored. The Truth in Lending Act requires lenders to inform borrowers of the annual rate of interest to be charged, plus related fees and service charges. For example, Countrywide—the largest mortgage lender in the United States until its collapse in 2008—later paid over $8 billion to settle charges that it had used unfair, deceptive, or fraudulent practices in dealing with its customers.[6]

Deceptive advertising is illegal in most countries. Manufacturers may not make false or misleading claims about their own product or a competitor's product, withhold relevant information, or create unreasonable expectations. In the United States, the Federal Trade Commission (FTC) enforces the laws prohibiting deceptive advertising, and the U.S. Justice Department enforces related laws prohibiting false claims.

> For example, in 2014 the global pharmaceutical company Shire paid almost $57 million to settle charges brought by the U.S. Justice Department. The government said that Shire had deceptively marketed its attention-deficit disorder drug Adderall XR, making false claims that the medicine could prevent poor academic performance, job loss, criminal behavior, traffic accidents, and even sexually transmitted diseases. It had also promoted other medicines for unapproved uses, the government alleged. "Our agency will continue to hold drug companies responsible for seeking to boost profits using false and misleading claims about products, such as the powerful medications prescribed to children," said a representative of the U.S. Department of Health and Human Services.[7]

U.S. law also requires food manufacturers to adopt a uniform nutrition label, specifying the amount of calories, fat, salt, and other nutrients contained in packaged, canned, and bottled foods. Labels must list the amount of trans fat—partially hydrogenated vegetable oils believed to contribute to heart disease—in cakes, cookies, and snack foods. Nutritional information about fresh fruits and vegetables, as well as fish, must be posted in supermarkets. Strict rules also define what can properly be labeled "organic." An emerging issue is the use of the "organic" label on personal care products, such as shampoos, toothpaste, and skin lotions, for which labeling rules are much weaker. "The [personal care products] industry is still rife with unsubstantiated organic claims," said the executive director of the Center of Environmental Health, which brought a suit against 26 companies under a California state labeling law.[8]

A second aim of consumer legislation is to protect consumers against possible hazards. As the opening example about defective air bags showed, consumers can be injured—and even killed—by dangerous products. U.S. laws seek to safeguard consumers in many ways, such as requiring warnings about possible side effects of pharmaceutical drugs, placing limits on flammable fabrics, restricting pesticide residues in fresh and processed foods,

---

[6] Countrywide Settles Fraud Cases for $8.4 Billion," *Bloomberg.com,* October 6, 2008; and "Bank of America in Settlement Worth over $8 Billion: Up to 390,000 Borrowers Covered in Deal with State Attorneys General over Risky Loans Originated by Countrywide Financial," *The Wall Street Journal,* October 6, 2008.

[7] "Shire Pharmaceuticals LLC to Pay $56.5 Million to Resolve False Claims Act Allegations Relating to Drug Marketing and Promotion Practices," U.S. Justice Department press release, September 24, 2014; and "A $56.5 Million Settlement for Adderall False Claims," *The New York Times,* September 25, 2014.

[8] "Environmental Group Sues 26 Companies for False Organic Labeling of Personal Care Products," June 22, 2011, *www.naturalnews.com.*

banning lead-based paints, and requiring regular inspections to eliminate contaminated meats. In 2008, following a major recall of toys contaminated with lead paint, Congress passed the Consumer Product Safety Improvement Act, which required that toys and infant products be tested before sale and gave regulators more resources to work with. The law was viewed as controversial, because it impacted many small businesses that were not implicated in the toy recall.

The third and fourth goals of consumer laws are to promote competitive pricing and consumer choice. When competitors secretly agree to divide up markets among themselves, or when a single company dominates a market, this artificially raises prices and limits consumer choice. Both federal and state antitrust laws forbid these practices, as discussed in Chapter 7. Competitive pricing also was promoted by the deregulation of the railroad, airline, trucking, telecommunications, banking, and other industries in the 1970s and 1980s and of the telecommunications, ocean shipping, and parts of the financial services industries in the late 1990s. Before deregulation, government agencies frequently held prices artificially high and, by limiting the number of new competitors, shielded existing businesses from competition.

A fifth and final goal of consumer laws is to protect privacy. This issue has recently received heightened regulatory attention, as discussed later in this chapter. The Children's Online Privacy Protection Act, which took effect in 2000, limits the collection of information online from and about children under the age of 13. The Federal Trade Commission has established a "do not call" list to protect individuals from unwanted telemarketing calls at home, and some have called for similar "do not track" rules to protect Internet users. Unwanted calls to a person's mobile phone are also illegal. Other threats to privacy caused by the emergence of new technologies are discussed later in this chapter and in Chapters 11 and 12.

Major Consumer Protection Agencies

Figure 14.3 depicts the principal consumer protection agencies that operate at the federal level of the U.S. government, along with their major areas of responsibility.

In addition to the eight agencies listed in Figure 14.3, several others are also involved in consumer protection. The Civil Rights Division of the Department of Justice enforces the provisions of the Civil Rights Act that prohibit discrimination against consumers. For example, in 2015 the department brought a complaint against Provident Funding Associates, a mortgage lender, for charging higher fees to African American and Hispanic borrowers.[9]

The National Highway Traffic Safety Administration (NHTSA), which is part of the Department of Transportation, affects many consumers directly through its authority over automobile safety. For example, the agency develops regulations for car air bags, devices that inflate rapidly during a collision, preventing the occupant from striking the steering wheel, dashboard, or side window. Another issue the NHTSA is involved in is distracted driving.[10]

> According to the Centers for Disease Control, more than 3,000 people die and nearly half a million are injured every year in the United States in crashes caused by drivers who are distracted by another activity, such as texting, talking on a handheld phone, or eating and drinking. More than a two-thirds of American drivers aged 18 to 64 reported talking on a cell phone and nearly one-third said they had read

[9] "CFPB and Department of Justice Take Action Against Provident Funding Associates for Discriminatory Mortgage Pricing," Consumer Financial Protection Bureau press release, May 28, 2014.

[10] The most recent rules concerning air bags are available at *www.nhtsa.dot.gov.*

FIGURE 14.3
Major Federal Consumer Protection Agencies and Their Main Responsibilities

Federal Trade Commission	Competitive pricing Deceptive trade practices Packaging and labeling Consumer credit disclosure and reporting Online privacy
Food and Drug Administration	Safety, effectiveness, and labeling of drugs, foods, food additives, cosmetics, and medical devices Standards for radiation exposure Toxic chemicals research
Consumer Product Safety Commission	Safety standards for consumer products Flammable fabrics, hazardous substances, poison prevention packaging
National Highway Traffic Safety Administration (Transportation Department)	Motor vehicle safety standards Automobile fuel economy standards National uniform speed limit Consumer safeguards for altered odometers
Department of Justice	Fair competition Consumer civil rights
National Transportation Safety Board	Airline safety
Consumer Financial Protection Bureau	Fairness and transparency in consumer financial products and services
Department of Agriculture	Safety of meat and poultry

or sent a text or e-mail while driving in the past 30 days. In response, several states have passed laws banning drivers' use of handheld devices. In 2013, the NHTSA issued guidelines for carmakers, to encourage them to design vehicles that allowed drivers to interact safely with communications, navigation, entertainment, and other tools. "Distracted driving is a deadly epidemic that has devastating consequences on our nation's roadways," said the U.S. transportation secretary.[11]

One consumer protection agency with particularly significant impact on the business community is the Food and Drug Administration (FDA). The FDA's mission is to assure the safety and effectiveness of a wide range of consumer products, including pharmaceutical drugs, medical devices, foods, and cosmetics. The agency has authority over *$1 trillion* of products, about a quarter of all consumer dollars spent each year.

One of the FDA's main jobs is to review many new products prior to their introduction. This job requires regulators to walk a thin line as they attempt to protect consumers. On one hand, the agency must not approve products that are ineffective or harmful. On the other hand, the agency must also not delay beneficial new products unnecessarily. The FDA can also pull existing products off the market or put restrictions on their use, if they are found to harm consumers. Historically, the FDA has had a reputation as a cautious agency that has advocated tough and thorough review before approval. This policy has stood in contrast to those of its counterparts in Europe and some other nations, which have tended to favor quick approval followed by careful field monitoring to spot problems.

> One group of products that is *not* fully regulated by the FDA is dietary supplements, such as the vitamins, minerals, and herbal remedies often sold at health food stores. In 1994, the supplement industry successfully lobbied Congress for a law that exempted their products from most government regulation. As a result, unlike pharmaceutical drugs, supplements do not have to be approved by the FDA before being sold, although the manufacturer itself is supposed to ensure that the product is safe—and the government can take action after a supplement is on the market. For example, the FDA banned ephedra, an herbal stimulant, after several users, including a professional athlete, died, and it warned the makers of body-building supplements containing a substance known as DMAA, sold under names like Napalm, Code Red, and Jack3D, that they had not shown them to be safe.[12]

In 2010, Congress established, as part of the Dodd-Frank Act (also discussed in Chapters 7 and 13), a new consumer regulatory body, called the Consumer Financial Protection Bureau. The purposes and actions of this agency are described in Exhibit 14.A. The debate over whether government should become involved in protecting consumer privacy is discussed in the next section of this chapter.

All eight government regulatory agencies shown in Figure 14.3 are authorized by law to intervene directly into the very center of free market activities, if that is considered necessary to protect consumers. In other words, consumer protection laws and agencies substitute government-mandated standards and the decisions of government officials for decision making by private buyers and sellers.

---

[11] "U.S. DOT Releases Guidelines to Minimize In-Vehicle Distractions," press release, April 23, 2013, *www.nhtsa.gov.*

[12] "FDA Challenges Marketing of DMAA Products for Lack of Safety Evidence," press release, April 27, 2012, *www.fda.gov/ NewsEvents.* Information on the FDA's regulation of dietary supplements is at *www.fda.gov/food/dietarysupplements.*

Exhibit 14.A

The Consumer Financial Protection Bureau

In 2010, as part of the Dodd-Frank Act, Congress created a new agency called the Consumer Financial Protection Bureau (CFPB). Its purpose was "to make markets for consumer financial products and services work in a fair, transparent, and competitive manner." The CFPB consolidated under one roof various consumer financial protection activities, which had previously been spread across seven different federal agencies. Among its mandates were to ensure that consumers had timely and understandable information about loans, to protect them from unfair and deceptive practices and discrimination, and to promote healthy innovation in the financial services industry.

One of the bureau's initiatives was "Know Before You Owe," a campaign to help consumers clearly understand the costs and risks of various financial products, such as student loans. In 2014, the amount owed on student loans—estimated at $1.2 trillion—was second only to mortgages as a portion of household debt. But students and their families had difficulty comparing aid packages, because colleges often failed to distinguish clearly between loans and scholarships or to disclose the total debt a student would accumulate during their education. The bureau worked with the Department of Education to develop a standardized disclosure form that would allow students to make side-by-side comparisons of financial aid offers from several colleges; for example, by seeing how much their monthly payments would be after graduation.

The law also allowed the CFPB to oversee previously unregulated nonbank financial institutions, such as so-called payday lenders, which regularly provided short-term, emergency loans at high interest rates to the working poor. In 2015, the bureau released new rules for this $46 billion industry, requiring lenders to provide affordable payment options and to make sure borrowers were able to make them. "Too many short-term and longer-term loans are made based on a lender's ability to collect and not on a borrower's ability to repay," said the CFPB's director.

Sources: "Payday Loan Rules Proposed by Consumer Protection Agency," *The New York Times,* March 26, 2015; and "CFPB Moves Closer to Tougher Payday-Lending Rules," *The Wall Street Journal,* March 26, 2015. The CFPB's website is at *www.consumerfinance.gov.*

Special Issue: Consumer Privacy in the Digital Age

Rapidly evolving information technologies have given new urgency to the broad issue of **consumer privacy**. Shoppers have always been concerned that information they reveal in the course of a sales transaction—for example, their credit card or driver's license numbers—might be misused. But in recent years, fast-changing technologies have increasingly enabled businesses to collect, buy, sell, and use vast amounts of personal data about their customers and potential customers. The danger is not only that this information might rarely be used fraudulently, but also that its collection represents a violation of privacy and might lead to unanticipated harms.

Individuals are often unaware of how much information about themselves they reveal to others as they shop, interact with friends, play games, or look for information online. A variety of technologies make this possible. Many websites place *cookies*—or more powerful *Flash cookies*—on a computer hard drive, to identify the user during each subsequent visit and to build profiles of their behavior over time. *Web beacons* embedded in e-mails and websites retrieve information about the viewer. In *deep packet inspection,* third parties access and analyze digital packets of information sent over the Internet, such as pieces of e-mails or Skype calls, to infer characteristics of the sender. Not just retailers, but also Internet and mobile phone service providers such as AT&T, search engine operators such as Google, and informational services such as Dictionary.com, also track their users. So-called *data aggregators* purchase and combine data about individuals collected from various sources and compile them into highly detailed portraits to be sold to retailers, service providers, and advertisers.[13]

[13] This discussion of the use of technology to collect information about customers draws on Lori Andrews, *I Know Who You Are and I Saw What You Did: Social Networks and the Death of Privacy* (New York: Free Press, 2012), Chapter 2.

An example of a data aggregator is Acxiom Corporation, based in Conway, Arkansas. Acxiom, called the "quiet giant" of the industry, has built the largest consumer database in the world, with as many as 3,000 data points on each of 700 million consumers. It not only collects information from multiple sources, but also analyzes it, placing individuals into categories such as "urban scramble," "frugal families," and "rural everlasting." Acxiom's customers include many of the Fortune 1,000 companies, which pay for "360-degree views" of customers and prospective customers.[14]

In 2014, the Federal Trade Commission issued a report on the data aggregation industry and recommended legislation to give consumers greater control over information collected about them.[15] Perhaps anticipating this push for regulation, Acxiom introduced the website *aboutthedata.com* where individuals could look up some of the information the company had collected about them—and even change it if inaccurate.[16]

The main reason for all this tracking is to tailor commercial messages to individuals. The term **behavioral advertising** refers to advertising that is targeted to particular customers, based on their observed online behavior. For example, a shopper might view a dress while browsing online for an outfit for an upcoming event, and then later when checking a news site might see an advertisement for the same dress pop up on her screen. According to AudienceScience, a digital marketing technology company, behavioral advertising was used by 85 percent of ad agencies. The reason most often cited by survey respondents was that targeted ads were simply "more effective."[17]

Advertisements tailored to a user's interests and preferences have many advantages for both buyer and seller. The buyer is more likely to receive messages that are relevant, and the seller is more likely to reach prospective customers. For example, Amazon tracks its customers' preferences, so on subsequent visits to the website it can recommend books, electronics, and other products that a person might like—a potential benefit to shoppers. But the vast collection of information that makes behavioral advertising possible also carries risks. For example, in a practice called *weblining,* individuals may be denied opportunities, such as credit, based on their online profiles. A 2015 Pew Research Center survey found that only a quarter (26 percent) of adults were "very" or "somewhat" confident that the companies and retailers they did business with would keep their information "private and secure."[18]

The dilemma of how best to protect consumer privacy in the digital age, while still fostering legitimate commerce, has generated a wide-ranging debate. Three major solutions have been proposed: consumer self-help, industry self-regulation, and privacy legislation.

- *Consumer self-help.* In this view, the best solution is for users to employ technologies that enable them to protect their own privacy. For example, special software can help manage cookies, encryption can protect e-mail messages, and surfing through intermediary sites can provide user anonymity. Individuals can learn about and use privacy settings on websites they access. Specialized services, such as one called Privacy-Choice, score various sites on how they handle personal data, offering consumers tools

---

[14] Acxiom Corporation, *Annual Report 2014;* and Bruce Schneider, *Data and Goliath: The Hidden Battles to Collect Your Data and Control Your World* (New York: W.W. Norton, 2015).

[15] "FTC Recommends Congress Require Data Broker Industry to be More Transparent and Give Consumers Greater Control over their Personal Information," Federal Trade Commission press release, May 27, 2014.

[16] "A Data Broker Offers a Peek Behind the Curtain," *The New York Times,* August 31, 2013.

[17] "Audience Targeting—Key Indicator of Online Advertising Success," press release, May 5, 2011, *www.audiencescience.com.*

[18] "Americans' Attitudes about Privacy, Security, and Surveillance," May 20, 2015, *www.pewinternet.org.*

for choosing which to do business with. "We have to develop mechanisms that allow consumers to control information about themselves," commented a representative of the Center for Democracy and Technology, a civil liberties group.[19] Critics of this approach argue that many unsophisticated web surfers are unaware of these mechanisms, or even of the need for them. A recent survey of Facebook users, for example, estimated that 28 percent of them shared all or almost all of their "wall" posts with the general public—not just their "friends."[20]

- *Industry self-regulation.* Many Internet-related businesses have argued that they should be allowed to regulate themselves. In their view, the best approach would be for companies to adopt voluntary policies for protecting individual privacy. For example, the Digital Advertising Alliance, a marketing trade group, developed an icon—a turquoise triangle placed in the upper right-hand corner of some online ads—that users could click to shield their behavior from tracking; and in 2015 it introduced two apps that allow consumers to set preferences for data collection and advertising on their mobile phones.[21] One advantage of this approach is that companies, presumably sophisticated about their own technology, might do the best job of defining technical standards. Critics, however, feel that self-regulation would inevitably be too weak. After all, companies often made money from selling personal information to advertisers, giving them a disincentive to protect it.

- *Privacy legislation.* Some favor new government regulations protecting consumer privacy online. In 2012, the Federal Trade Commission issued a comprehensive report on protecting consumer privacy. The commission recommended that businesses adopt a number of best practices, including greater disclosure of how they collected and used consumers' information, simple "opt out" tools, improved security, and time limits on the retention of data. The FTC also recommended that Congress enact new legislation addressing these issues; as of 2015, however, it had not done so.[22] Consumer privacy protections are generally stronger in the European Union than in the United States. Under European data protection laws, people must be notified when information is collected about them and be given a chance to review and correct it if necessary. A European court recently ruled on the right of individuals to remove information about themselves from Google searches; this development is explored in a case at the end of this book, "Google and the Right to Be Forgotten," as well as in Chapter 12.

Any approach to online privacy would face the challenge of how best to balance the legitimate interests of consumers—to protect their privacy—and of business—to deliver increasingly customized products and services in the digital age.

---

[19] "A New Tool in Protecting Online Privacy," *The New York Times,* February 12, 2012. More information about privacy protection for consumers is available at *www.cdt.org* (Center for Democracy and Technology), *www.epic.org/privacy* (Electronic Privacy Information Center), and *www.privacyrights.org* (Privacy Rights Clearinghouse).

[20] "Facebook and Your Privacy," *Consumer Reports,* June 2012.

[21] "Digital Advertising Alliance Announces Mobile Friendly Privacy Enforcement to Begin September 1," press release, May 7, 2015, *www.digitaladvertisingalliance.org.*

[22] "FTC and White House Push for Online Privacy Laws," *The New York Times,* May 9, 2012; "FTC Issues Final Commission Report on Protecting Consumer Privacy," press release, March 26, 2012, *www.ftc.gov/opa;* and Federal Trade Commission, *Protecting Consumer Privacy in an Era of Rapid Change* (2012). More information about these legislative approaches is available in Bruce Schneider, *Data and Goliath: The Hidden Battles to Collect Your Data and Control Your World* (New York: W. W. Norton, 2015), Chapter 14: and Helen Nissenbaum, "Respect for Context: Fulfilling the Promise of the White House Report," in Marc Rotenberg, ed., *Privacy in the Modern Age* (New York: New Press, 2015).

Using the Courts and Product Liability Laws

Who is at fault when a consumer is harmed by a product or service? This is a complex legal and ethical issue. The term **product liability** refers to the legal responsibility of a firm for injuries caused by something it made or sold. Under laws in the United States and some other countries, consumers have the right to sue and to collect damages if harmed by an unsafe product. Consumer advocates and trial attorneys have generally supported these legal protections, saying they are necessary both to compensate injured victims and to deter irresponsible behavior by companies in the first place. Some in the business community, by contrast, have argued that courts and juries have unfairly favored plaintiffs, and they have called for reforms of product liability laws. This section describes this debate and recent changes in relevant U.S. law. The liability of a retailer, Lumber Liquidators, for selling vinyl flooring containing dangerous chemicals is explored in the discussion case at the end of this chapter.

Strict Liability

In the United States, the legal system has generally looked favorably on consumer claims. Under the doctrine of **strict liability**, courts have held that manufacturers are responsible for injuries resulting from use of their products, whether or not the manufacturers were negligent or breached a warranty. That is, they may be found to be liable, whether or not they knowingly did anything wrong. Consumers can also prevail in court even if they were partly at fault for their injuries.

Some product liability cases have led to large settlements, as the following example illustrates.

> In 2015, a jury in Delaware awarded $100 million to a former 51-year-old former bank teller for injuries she had suffered from vaginal mesh inserts made by Boston Scientific. The woman had testified that the inserts—intended to treat organ prolapse and urinary incontinence—had eroded, leaving her in constant pain and unable to have sex. The jury also found that the inserts had been defectively designed, and the company had failed to warn patients about possible risks. Its verdict included $25 million in *compensatory* damages (to compensate the woman for her injuries) and $75 million in *punitive* damages (to punish the company for wrongdoing). "The jury spoke loudly and clearly that Boston Scientific's defective devices injured [my client] and many other women, and they should step up and take responsibility for causing that harm," said the woman's lawyer. But the company declared that product safety was "of the utmost importance" and said it would appeal.[23]

Huge product liability settlements, like the Boston Scientific case, are often well publicized, but they remain the exception. According to the U.S. Department of Justice, one in five noncriminal cases was a tort (liability) case, and plaintiffs (the people suing companies) won 34 percent of product liability cases filed. The average settlement in all tort cases was $201,000, although a few settlements were much higher.[24]

The product liability systems of other nations differ significantly from that of the United States. In Europe, for example, judges, not juries, hear cases. Awards are usually smaller,

---

[23] "Boston Scientific Ordered to Pay $100 Million Over Mesh," *BloombergBusiness,* May 28, 2015; "$100 Million Verdict Rocks Boston Scientific," *Boston Herald,* May 29, 2015; and "Boston Scientific Ordered to Pay $100 Million in Transvaginal Mesh Trial," *Reuters,* May 28, 2015.

[24] U.S. Department of Justice, Office of Justice Programs, Bureau of Justice Statistics, "Federal Tort Trials and Verdicts, 2002–03," August 2005, *www.ojp.gov/bjs.*

Should the food industry—such as fast-food restaurants and snack-makers—be held liable for their customers' obesity?

Although some evidence shows that rates of obesity are stabilizing, they remain remarkably high: 69 percent of adults and 32 percent of children in the United States are either obese or overweight, by the most recent measures. Obesity is a major cause of breathing problems, type 2 diabetes, heart disease, arthritis, infertility, and some kinds of cancer. According to the Institute of Medicine, an independent group that advises the government, the annual cost of treating obesity-related chronic disease and disability is now around $190 billion annually. "Left unchecked," the institute concluded, "obesity's effects on health, health care costs, and our productivity as a nation could become catastrophic."

Some observers felt that the food industry was at least partly at fault—and possibly even legally liable for the epidemic of obesity. Fast food had become a big part of Americans' diets. In 1970, they spent $6 billion a year on it; four decades later, they spent nearly $140 billion. This trend seemed to parallel the rise in obesity rates. The problem was not just the relatively high fat and sugar content of fast foods, but the super-sizing of portions. When fast-food restaurants increasingly began to compete on the basis of value—more for less—customers simply ate more.

For their part, food companies had concentrated on developing processed products, such as candy, gum, snacks, and bakery goods, which carried high profit margins along with excessive calories. They had introduced many more new products in these categories than entrées, fruits, and vegetables since the early 1980s, data showed. Moreover, both restaurants and food processors, in their critics' view, had failed to communicate adequately the health risks of some foods and had inappropriately marketed their products to children.

By contrast, others felt that individuals should be held responsible for their own weight—or in the case of children, the parents should be held responsible. Americans consume, on average, more than 2,500 calories a day, well above the healthy amount for most people. Only 3 percent of Americans meet the government's dietary recommendations, and less than one-fifth exercise enough. Unlike cigarettes, food products are not normally addictive. Moreover, obesity has many causes, and the exact role of particular companies is unclear. How could one know whether a person's obesity was caused by eating particular foods, overeating generally, a sedentary lifestyle, or genetic predisposition?

Sources: The Institute of Medicine, "Accelerating Progress in Obesity Prevention: Solving the Weight of the Nation," (2012) at *www.iom.edu.* Overweight and obesity statistics are available from the Center for Disease Control's National Center for Health Statistics (*www.cdc.gov/nchs*) and the office of the U.S. Surgeon General (*www.surgeongeneral.gov*). Data on fast-food industry sales are from *www.fastfoodmarketing.org.*

---

partly because the medical expenses of victims are already covered under national health insurance, and partly because punitive damages are not allowed.

Historically, product liability cases have been exceedingly rare in China. But that began to change in 2009, in the wake of China's tainted-milk scandal. The previous year, almost 300,000 children became ill—and at least six died—after drinking baby formula contaminated by the industrial chemical melamine. Milk producers had apparently knowingly added the hazardous chemical to boost the formula's protein content. More than 200 families brought suit against the formula companies, even though the government sought to keep the case out of the courts. Eventually, two people were executed for their roles in the scandal, and the company most responsible was fined and declared bankruptcy.[25]

The controversial issue of food industry liability for obesity is explored in Exhibit 14.B.

[25] "China Milk Scandal: First Court Agrees to Hear Case," May 25, 2011, *www.huffingtonpost.com;* "Two Executed in China over Tainted Milk," *CNN World, http://articles.cnn.com;* "Tainted-Milk Victims File Lawsuit in China's Highest Court," *The Wall Street Journal,* January 20, 2009; and "Chinese Parents File Milk Lawsuit," *The Wall Street Journal,* October 1, 2008.

Product Liability Reform and Alternative Dispute Resolution

Many businesses have argued that the evolution of strict liability has unfairly burdened them with excess costs. Liability insurance rates have gone up significantly, especially for small businesses, as have the costs of defending against liability lawsuits and paying large settlements to injured parties. Moreover, businesses argue that it is unfair to hold them financially responsible in situations where they were not negligent.

Businesses have also argued that concerns about liability exposure sometimes slow research and innovation. For example, many pharmaceutical companies halted work on new contraceptive methods because of the risk of being sued. Despite the need for new contraceptives that would be more effective and also provide protection against viral diseases, such as herpes and AIDS, research had virtually come to a halt by the late 1990s, according to some public health groups.

In 2005, Congress passed the Class Action Fairness Act, the first significant reform of product liability laws in many years. The two key elements of this legislation were as follows:

- *Most large class-action lawsuits were moved from state to federal courts.* This provision applied to cases involving $5 million or more and that included plaintiffs from more than one state. Supporters of the law said this would prevent lawyers from shopping for friendly local venues in which to try interstate cases.

- *Attorneys in some kinds of cases were paid based on how much plaintiffs actually received, or on how much time the attorney spent on the case.* Under the old system, attorneys were often paid a percentage of the settlement amount. This sometimes led to excessive compensation for the lawyers.

Although most businesses welcomed these changes, some called for further reforms, such as shifting the burden of proof to consumers and limiting punitive damages.

Product liability reforms such as those included in the Class Action Fairness Act have faced vigorous opposition from consumers' organizations and from the American Trial Lawyers Association, representing plaintiffs' attorneys. These groups have defended the existing product liability system, saying it puts needed pressure on companies to make and keep products safe.

> Plaintiffs scored a legal victory in 2009 when the U.S. Supreme Court decided an important case called *Wyeth v. Levine*. Diana Levine, a musician, was injected with an antinausea drug made by Wyeth after complaining of migraines. The drug's label said that "extreme care" should be used to avoid hitting an artery, which could lead to "gangrene requiring amputation." Unfortunately, this happened to the musician, whose right arm had to be amputated. In the ensuing lawsuit, Wyeth defended itself on the grounds that because the FDA had approved the warning label, the company was shielded from the lawsuit. The Supreme Court disagreed and said the suit could go forward—federal regulatory approval had not preempted the company's liability under state laws.[26]

One approach to settling disagreements between companies and consumers, other than going to court, is **alternative dispute resolution** (ADR). ADR can take the form of *mediation,* a voluntary process to settle disputes using a neutral third party, or *arbitration,* the use of an impartial individual to hear and decide a case outside of the judicial system. The American Arbitration Association (AAA), for example, offers mediation of mortgage foreclosure claims and disputes over insurance claims arising from natural disasters. AAA

[26] "High Court Eases Way to Liability Lawsuits," *The Wall Street Journal,* March 5, 2009.

also offers due process guidelines for companies that want to utilize arbitration to resolve disputes over products or services. Proponents of ADR argue that it is a faster and less expensive way to resolve company–consumer disputes and does not tie up the judicial system with minor issues.

A controversial aspect of consumer ADR is the use of mandatory arbitration clauses. These are clauses in a purchase agreement—for example, for cell phone service, a credit card, or moving services—that require customers to agree to take any future disputes to arbitration rather than to court. A 2015 study by the Consumer Financial Protection Bureau found that mandatory arbitration clauses were in place in 44 percent of checking accounts, 53 percent of credit cards, 99 percent of payday loans, and almost 100 percent of mobile wireless service contracts.[27] Companies often favor such clauses, because they enable them to avoid sometimes-expensive lawsuits and, they contend, charge customers less. Consumer rights organizations, on the other hand, have tried to restrict the use of mandatory arbitration on the grounds that it limits consumers' rights to file suit when they have been harmed. In general, these provisions have been upheld by the courts.

Positive Business Responses to Consumerism

The consumer movement has demonstrated that business is expected to perform at high levels of efficiency, reliability, and fairness in order to satisfy the consuming public. Because business has not always responded quickly or fully enough, consumer advocates have turned to government for protection. On the other hand, much effort has been devoted by individual business firms and by entire industries to encourage voluntary responses to consumer demands. Some of the more prominent positive responses are discussed next.

Managing for Quality

One way that many businesses address consumer interests is to manage quality in a highly proactive way. Quality has been defined by the International Organization for Standardization (ISO) as "a composite of all the characteristics, including performance, of an item, product, or service that bear on its ability to satisfy stated or implied needs." **Quality management,** by extension, refers to "all the measures an organization takes to assure quality." These might include, for example, defining the customer's needs, monitoring whether or not a product or service consistently meets these needs, analyzing the quality of finished products to assure they are free of defects, and continually improving processes to eliminate quality problems. Taking steps at all stages of the production process to ensure consistently high quality has many benefits. Responsible businesses know that building products right the first time reduces the risk of liability lawsuits and builds brand loyalty.

> Chrysler Corporation, the U.S. car company, worked hard to boost its products' quality as it emerged from bankruptcy in the early 2010s. Understanding the crucial role of mechanical reliability and consistent fit-and-finish, the company invested $20 million in upgrading the Illinois factory where it planned to build its Dart, Jeep Compass, and Jeep Patriot models, and trained workers to audit vehicles randomly for problems. Chrysler's CEO empowered its quality chief to shut down production or delay a model launch if he needed to—as he did when inspectors found that the rear taillight on the new Chrysler 300 was not completely flush with the body.

[27] Consumer Financial Protection Bureau, *Arbitration Study: Report to Congress Pursuant to Dodd-Frank Wall Street Reform and Consumer Protection Act,* March, 2015. The percentage figure refers to the percentage of the relevant market, not the percentage of contracts.

What should a company do when customers use a legitimate product for an illegal or unethical purpose? This problem confronted General Electric (GE), the diversified global technology firm, in Asia. Among GE's many health care products was a line of lightweight, portable ultrasound scanners used for diagnostic imaging. These devices were less expensive and easier to transport than earlier models, making their use in developing nations and rural areas more practical—and popular. For example, by the mid-2000s, sales of ultrasound devices in India, where GE was the market leader, had reached $77 million annually.

But GE's portable ultrasound machines were, in some settings, used in a shocking and unexpected way: to identify the gender of female fetuses, which were then aborted. In some cultures, including parts of India and China, many families had a strong preference for sons over daughters. Sometimes, this preference reflected a belief that sons were responsible for caring for their parents in old age, or for carrying on the family name or traditions. At other times, poor families felt they could not afford the high cost of a dowry when a daughter got married. Whatever the reason, some unscrupulous medical practitioners used GE's ultrasound devices to facilitate the selective abortion of female fetuses. In 2011, the ratio of boys to girls in India was 112 to 100; in China it was 121 to 100. (In nature, the ratio is 105 to 100). Millions of girls were simply never born.

As it became aware of the scope of the problem, General Electric moved proactively to prevent the unethical use of its products. In both India and China, laws prohibited the use of ultrasound for sex selection. GE worked closely with regulators responsible for enforcing these laws to assure that its products were only sold to (and serviced for) properly licensed practitioners, and it trained its sales representatives not to deal with anyone suspected of participating in selective abortions. It followed up with audits. The company also promoted positive images of women, for example, by sponsoring female athletes. GE wrote in a blog posted to its website that its experience had shown that "a manufacturer can take [steps] to reduce the risk that its products will be misused in ways that violate human rights."

Sources: Mara Hvistendahl, *Unnatural Selection: Choosing Boys over Girls and the Consequences of a World Full of Men* (New York: PublicAffairs, 2011); "The War Against Girls," *The Wall Street Journal*, June 24, 2011; "Medical Quandary: India's Skewed Sex Ratio Puts GE Sales in Spotlight," *The Wall Street Journal*, April 18, 2007; and "Promoting Ethical Product Use," at *http://citizenship.geblogs.com*.

"Chrysler has made good strides in the products that are in the showrooms now, but it will take time," said the director of *Consumer Reports'* automotive test center.[28]

Managing for product and service quality is an attempt by business to address its customers' needs. It is an example of the interactive strategy discussed in Chapter 2, where companies try to anticipate and respond to emerging stakeholder expectations.

The Malcolm Baldrige National Quality Award, named for a former U.S. Secretary of Commerce, is given annually to organizations that demonstrate quality and performance excellence. A 2014 recipient was Hill Country Memorial, a nonprofit community hospital system in Texas. The hospital was cited for its high patient satisfaction scores (it ranked first in the nation). Said CEO Jayne Pope, "It's my job as a leader to serve the people who serve the people."[29]

The challenging issue of business's responsibility for products that are safe and of high quality—but used by others in illegal or dangerous ways—is profiled in Exhibit 14.C.

[28] "New Chrysler Battling Old Defects," *The Wall Street Journal*, May 10, 2012; and "Chrysler Invests to Boost Quality," *The Wall Street Journal*, April 3, 2012.

[29] "Baldrige Awards Are Just the Icing on the Cake for 2014 Winners," *Hospitals & Health Networks Magazine*, November 19, 2014; and "Insights from Leaders of the 2014 Baldrige Award Recipients," April 23, 2015, *www.nist.gov/baldrige*.

Voluntary Industry Codes of Conduct

In another positive response, businesses in some industries have banded together to agree on voluntary codes of conduct, spelling out how they will treat their customers. This action may be taken to forestall even stricter regulation by the government. One such voluntary code is described in the following example.

> The Western Growers Association, a trade association of farmers, adopted voluntary guidelines for growers and handlers of leafy green vegetables. The move followed an outbreak of *E. coli* poisoning, in which three people died and hundreds were sickened. Public health investigators traced the rash of illnesses to spinach grown on a California farm that had become contaminated with infected wild pig feces. Over 100 farm companies subsequently signed on to the new standards in an effort to alleviate customer concerns—and to reduce pressure for mandatory government rules. Voluntary standards have also been developed to assure the safety of other kinds of fresh produce, including melons and tomatoes.[30]

Consumer Affairs Departments

Many large corporations operate consumer affairs departments, often placing a vice president in charge. The **consumer affairs officer** typically manages a complex network of contacts with customers. The contact infrastructure usually includes a website with a self-service component; many sites are interactive, allowing customers to post comments or questions that are answered electronically by customer relations staff. Most companies also host a call center, using an interactive voice response system that leads callers to an appropriately trained customer service representative. Increasingly, they use sophisticated software that pulls customer feedback from multiple channels, including surveys, social media, and unsolicited feedback, to analyze and respond to issues in real time.[31]

Cutting-edge consumer affairs offices also proactively monitor customer reactions to their products and advertising, using a wide range of social media. Doing so can help companies avoid costly gaffes.

> Johnson & Johnson posted a promotion for its pain reliever, Motrin, on its website. The ad showed a mother who was suffering from back and neck pain from wearing a baby carrier, and referred to mothers who "wear their babies." Many mothers who saw the ad were annoyed, and they started messaging, blogging, and twittering. "A baby will never be a fashion statement," said one. Fortunately, Johnson & Johnson actively monitored its brand in the social media, and within 24 hours had taken down the ads and issued an apology to its customers. What could have been a public relations nightmare was quickly averted.[32]

Experienced companies are aware that consumer complaints and concerns can be handled more quickly, at lower cost, and with less risk of losing goodwill by a consumer affairs department than if customers take a legal route or if their complaints receive widespread publicity.

Product Recalls

Companies also deal with consumer dissatisfaction by recalling faulty products. A **product recall** occurs when a company, either voluntarily or under an agreement with a

---

[30] "Current Issues in Product Safety: The Packinghouse," *Food Safety News,* February 25, 2015.

[31] "Listening to the Voice of the Customer," *Customer Relationship Management,* July 1, 2012.

[32] "Strategy and Social Media: Everything's Social Now," *Customer Relationship Management,* June 2009.

government agency, takes back all items found to be dangerously defective. Sometimes these products are in the hands of consumers; at other times they may be in the factory, in wholesale warehouses, or on the shelves of retail stores. Wherever they are in the chain of distribution or use, the manufacturer tries to notify consumers or potential users about the defect. For example, in 2015 Cycling Sports Group voluntarily recalled its GT Fury mountain bicycles because it learned that the front wheel hub could break and cause the disc brakes to fail, posing a hazard to the user, even though no injuries had been reported. The company offered to replace the front wheels free of charge.[33] The case "General Motors and the Ignition Switch Recalls," which appears at the end of this book, describes a series of recalls carried out by General Motors to correct defects in the ignition switches of some of its models, which caused the cars to stall while moving.

One problem with recalls is that the public may not be aware of them, so dangerous products continue to be used. For example, several babies were killed when Playskool Travel-Lite portable cribs unexpectedly collapsed, strangling them. Although the Consumer Product Safety Commission (CPSC) ordered an immediate recall, not all parents and child care providers heard about it, and additional deaths occurred.[34] Some consumer organizations advocated a system that would require manufacturers of certain products—such as cribs—to include purchaser identification cards so users could be quickly traced in the event of a recall.[35]

The four major government agencies responsible for most mandatory recalls are the Food and Drug Administration, the National Highway Traffic Safety Administration, the Environmental Protection Agency (which can recall polluting motor vehicles), and the Consumer Product Safety Commission.

Consumerism's Achievements

The leaders of the consumer movement can point to important gains in both the United States and other nations. Consumers today are better informed about the goods and services they purchase, are more aware of their rights when something goes wrong, and are better protected against inflated advertising claims, hazardous or ineffective products, and unfair pricing. Several consumer organizations serve as watchdogs of buyers' interests, and a network of government regulatory agencies act for the consuming public.

Some businesses, too, have heard the consumer message and have reacted positively. They have learned to assign high priority to the things consumers expect: high-quality goods and services, reliable and effective products, safety in the items they buy, fair prices, and marketing practices that do not threaten important human and social values.

All of these achievements, in spite of negative episodes that occasionally occur, bring the consuming public closer to realizing the key consumer rights: to be safe, to be informed, to have choices, and to be heard—as well as the newer right to privacy.

[33] "Cycling Sports Group Recalls GT Fury Mountain Bicycles Due to Crash, Injury Hazards," press release, May 28, 2015, *www.cpsc.gov.*

[34] David Zivan, "The Playskool Travel-Lite Crib (A), (B), and (C)," Center for Decision Research, University of Chicago, November 5, 2002.

[35] For information on initiatives to protect children from dangerous products, see *www.kidsindanger.org.*

Summary

- The five key consumer rights are the rights to safety, to be informed, to choose, to be heard, and to privacy.

- The consumer movement represents an attempt to promote the interests of consumers by balancing the amount of market power held by sellers and buyers.

- Consumer protection laws and regulatory agencies attempt to assure that consumers are treated fairly, receive adequate information, are protected against potential hazards, have free choices in the market, and have legal recourse when problems develop.

- Rapidly evolving information technologies have given new urgency to the issue of consumer privacy. Three approaches to safeguarding online privacy are consumer self-help, industry self-regulation, and protective legislation.

- Business has complained about the number of product liability lawsuits and the high cost of insuring against them. Although consumer groups and trial attorneys have opposed efforts to change product liability laws, modest tort reforms have been legislated.

- Socially responsible companies have responded to the consumer movement by giving serious consideration to consumer problems, increasing channels of communication with customers, instituting arbitration procedures to resolve complaints, and recalling defective products. They have also pursued voluntary codes of conduct and quality management in an effort to meet, and even anticipate, consumers' needs.

Key Terms

alternative dispute resolution, *317*
behavioral advertising, *313*
consumer affairs officer, *320*

consumer movement, *305*
consumer privacy, *312*
consumer protection laws, *307*
deceptive advertising, *308*
product liability, *315*

product recalls, *320*
quality management, *318*
strict liability, *315*

Internet Resources

www.consumersinternational.org	Consumers International
www.cpsc.gov	U.S. Consumer Product Safety Commission
www.ftc.gov	U.S. Federal Trade Commission
www.bbb.org	Better Business Bureau
www.consumerfed.org	Consumer Federation of America
www.consumeraffairs.com	Consumer news and resource center
www.beuc.eu	The European Consumer Organization
www.consumerreports.org	Consumer Reports

Discussion Case: *Lumber Liquidators' Laminate Flooring*

People shopping for new flooring for their homes usually focus on appearance and price, not safety. But this changed abruptly in 2015 when the CBS News program, *60 Minutes,* aired a segment alleging that wood laminate flooring sold by Lumber Liquidators contained dangerous levels of formaldehyde, leading to a wave of consumer concern about the safety of products they walked on every day.

Lumber Liquidators was a leading retailer of hardwood flooring, selling to both home-owners and contractors in around 350 stores in the United States and Canada. It carried a range of products, including solid hardwood; laminate flooring; and bamboo, cork, and vinyl planks. Under the slogan "Hardwood Floors for Less!" the company pursued a low-cost strategy, telling its customers on its website that it negotiated "directly with the mills, eliminating the middleman and passing the savings on to customers." This strategy had proven successful, and the company had grown steadily since its founding in 1996, earning revenues of over a billion dollars in 2013. Its share price had risen dramatically from $13 in 2011 to $119 in 2013.

Formaldehyde was a strong-smelling chemical used in some building materials and household products because of its properties as a preservative, fungicide, germicide, and disinfectant. In laminate flooring (a cheaper alternative to solid wood), formaldehyde was sometimes used in glues that adhered composites that were then topped with a thin layer of real wood. These products could release formaldehyde into the air, in a process called *off-gassing*. At relatively low levels, airborne formaldehyde could cause short-term eye, throat, and skin irritation. The chemical's long-term effects were not fully understood. Some studies showed that formaldehyde caused cancer in rats, and in 1987 the Environmental Protection Agency (EPA) classified it as a human carcinogen (cancer-causing agent) under conditions of high or prolonged exposure.

In 2015, regulation of formaldehyde in consumer products was, however, spotty. The EPA had drafted national emission standards, but had not finalized them. The Consumer Product Safety Commission had no rules for formaldehyde. Congress had passed a Formaldehyde Standards Act, but it had not yet gone into effect. One state—California—had adopted its own standards; in 2008 the California Air Resources Board, known as CARB, had established limits for formaldehyde emissions for composite wood products sold in that state, known as the CARB 2 standards.

In the *60 Minutes* segment, which first aired on March 1, 2015, the executive director of the activist organization Global Community Monitor told CBS that his group, working with an environmental attorney, had purchased 150 boxes of laminate flooring from stores in California and sent them to independent labs for testing. Products purchased at Home Depot and Lowe's—other home improvement stores—met the CARB 2 standards, but every sample of Lumber Liquidators' products, which were made in China, failed. In some cases, their formaldehyde levels were six to seven times over the standard.

"You're in a chamber so you're living with it," the activist said on the *60 Minutes* episode, speaking of consumers with the products installed in their homes. "You're sleeping in there. And you're constantly exposed. That's the threat. The constant exposure to a potent carcinogen over a long period of time."

60 Minutes followed up by sending investigators to several mills in China that manufactured laminate wood flooring for Lumber Liquidators, posing as buyers and using hidden cameras. In one scene, a Chinese manager said that flooring made with formaldehyde was 10 to 15 percent cheaper and admitted that his mill fraudulently labeled the product. Here was the exchange, as the investigator pointed to laminate flooring the manager had described as a "bestseller for Lumber Liquidators:

Investigator: "Is this CARB 2?"

Manager: "No, no, no. . . . I have to be honest with you. It's not CARB 2."

Investigator: "Can I get CARB 2?"

Manager: "Yes, you can. It's just the price issue. We can make CARB 2 but it would be very expensive."

Interviewed on the *60 Minutes* segment, company founder Tom Sullivan stated, "Our goal is to sell a good product at a good price. We get the price by low overhead, huge volume, and being very efficient at what we do. And we're never going to sell something unsafe." In response to footage showing the apparently fraudulently labeled product, Sullivan said, "I will guarantee we'll be in that mill tomorrow and test it. And that is not anything we can condone in any way, to save a cent."

In the wake of the *60 Minutes* episode, Lumber Liquidators voluntarily offered free indoor air quality screening to customers who had purchased Chinese-made laminate flooring, suspended all sales of laminate products made in China, and hired an outside organization headed by former FBI director Louis Freeh to review the company's compliance programs. For their part, advocacy organizations and attorneys pursued several class action product liability lawsuits against Lumber Liquidators, accusing them of endangering consumers and breaking California law. The government also took action; the Consumer Product Safety Commission launched an investigation of Lumber Liquidators in collaboration with several other federal agencies. "We are committed to move as fast as possible to get answers for consumers," said the CPSC director, "especially for the parents of young children."

Sources: "Lumber Liquidators Faces U.S. Safety Inquiry," *The New York Times,* March 25, 2015; "Lumber Liquidators Under Investigation by Consumer Agency," *BloombergBusiness,* March 25, 2015; "Lumber Liquidators Provides Update on Laminate Flooring Sourced from China," press release, May 7, 2015; and National Cancer Institute, "Formaldehyde and Cancer Risk," *www.cancer.gov.* Lumber Liquidators' website is at *www.lumberliquidators.com.* The *60 Minutes* segment is available at *www.cbsnews.com/news/lumber-liquidators-linked-to-health-and-safety-violations.*

Discussion Questions

1. If you were a manager at Lumber Liquidators, what if anything would you do now, beyond what the company has already done?

2. If you were a consumer who had installed Lumber Liquidators laminate flooring in your home or business, what would you do now?

3. Do you think the government acted appropriately to protect consumers? What more can or should it have done?

4. Do you believe that lawsuits filed by consumer activists will help solve the problem of unsafe flooring?

5. In your opinion, who was most responsible for the fact that consumers were exposed to formaldehyde at levels that exceeded the safety limits established by California regulations?

6. Who *should be* responsible for assuring the safety of flooring products: the retailer, the supplier, the customer, lawyers, or government regulators? Why do you think so?

CHAPTER FIFTEEN

Employees and the Corporation

Employees and employers are engaged in a critical relationship affecting the corporation's performance. There is a basic economic aspect to their association: Employees provide labor for the firm, and employers compensate workers for their contributions of skill and productivity. Yet, also present in the employee–employer exchange are numerous social, ethical, legal, and public policy issues. Attention to the rights and duties of both parties in this relationship can benefit the firm, its workers, and society.

This Chapter Focuses on These Key Learning Objectives:

LO 15-1   Understanding workers' rights to organize unions and bargain collectively.

LO 15-2   Knowing how government regulations assure occupational safety and health and what business must do to protect workers.

LO 15-3   Evaluating the limits of employers' duty to provide job security to their workers.

LO 15-4   Analyzing employer obligations to pay workers fairly and how pay policies can contribute to income inequality.

LO 15-5   Appraising the extent of employees' right to privacy, when businesses monitor employee communications, police romance in the office, test for drugs or alcohol, or subject employees to honesty tests.

LO 15-6   Debating if employees have a duty to blow the whistle on corporate misconduct, or if employees should always be loyal to their employer.

In 2015, Target announced that it would raise its workers' pay to at least $9 an hour. The discount retailer, which employed almost 350,000 people in 1,800 stores, did not disclose what it was currently paying, but at the time the federal minimum wage was $7.25. The announced raise came against a backdrop of a tightening labor market for low-paid workers as the economy recovered. "Our goal has always been to be competitive with the marketplace," said a Target spokesperson. But, the raise also came in the wake of efforts by the United Food and Commercial Workers union to organize Target workers, and by management to counter the union's appeal with a video in which narrators "Dawn" and "Ricardo" told viewers that if a union came in, "chances are they would change our fast, fun, and friendly culture."[1]

What is a fair pay level for workers? Who or what should determine wages—the free market, the employer acting unilaterally, collective bargaining negotiations between employers and unions, or government mandates such as minimum wage laws?

In 2014, Starbucks announced it would make changes to its scheduling practices to provide more "stability and consistency" for its 130,000 baristas. According to the new rules, the company said it would post hours at least a week in advance, end the practice of "clopening" (requiring a worker to close a store and then reopen it the next morning, just a few hours later), and allow local managers more say in overriding scheduling software. More than 27 million Americans, like most Starbucks baristas, worked part-time, and many found their family and schooling commitments in constant turmoil as employers kept them "on call" and made last minute changes to their hours. "Encouraging managers not to rely entirely on the automated software is the best thing they could do," said one Starbucks barista. "But I'm doubtful how many managers will actually do it."[2]

What is the best way to balance the employer's need for flexibility and efficiency in scheduling part-time workers' hours with the employee's need for predictability in organizing their lives and finances? Should scheduling be subject to government regulation, or be left to employers and employees to work out?

Applying for a position as a correctional officer, a man was startled when the interviewer asked him for his Facebook login information, saying it was needed to check for possible gang affiliations. The man did as he was asked but later complained, calling the demand "invasive" and a "violation of [my] personal privacy." Increasingly, employers are conducting background checks on prospective hires by reviewing their social media history, and some use specialized services that "scrape" the web for anything applicants might have done or said online. By 2014, legislation prohibiting employers from asking for access to applicants' social media accounts had been adopted in 11 states and was under consideration in several others.[3]

Should employers, like the correctional services department in this example, have a right to review job applicants' social media pages? What if the job was not in the correction services field but in some other line of work, would the employer have the right to review an applicant's Facebook page then? Who should be responsible for protecting applicant and employee privacy?

All of these difficult questions will be addressed later in this chapter. As the situations giving rise to them suggest, the rights and duties of employers and employees in the modern workplace are incredibly complex.

[1] "Target to Increase Wages to at Least $9/Hour for All Workers in April," *The Wall Street Journal,* March 19, 2015; "Target Plans to Raise Pay to at Least $9 an Hour," *The New York Times,* March 18, 2015; "Exclusive: Target's Cheesy Anti-Union Propaganda Gets a Modern Makeover," *Salon,* March 19, 2014.

[2] "Starbucks to Revise Policies to End Irregular Schedules for Its 130,000 Baristas," *The New York Times,* August 14, 2014; and "A Push to Give Steadier Shifts to Part-Timers," *The New York Times,* July 15, 2014.

[3] "Will Employers Still Ask for Facebook Passwords in 2014?" *USA Today,* January 10, 2014; and "Some U.S. Employers Asking for Applicants' Facebook Login Info," *Associated Press,* March 21, 2012. The current status of state legislation may be found on the website of the National Conference of State Legislatures, at *www.ncsl.org.*

FIGURE 15.1
Rights and Duties of Employees and Employers

Employee Rights/Employer Duties	Employee Duties/Employer Rights
• Right to organize and bargain • Right to a safe and healthy workplace • Right to privacy • Duty to discipline fairly and justly • Right to blow the whistle • Right to equal employment opportunity • Right to be treated with respect for fundamental human rights • Right to fair and decent wages	• No drug or alcohol abuse • No actions that would endanger others • Treat others with respect and without harassment of any kind • Honesty; appropriate disclosure • Loyalty and commitment • Respect for employer's property and intellectual capital

The Employment Relationship

As noted in Chapter 1, employees are a market stakeholder of business—and a critically important one. Businesses cannot operate without employees to make products, provide services, market to customers, run the organization internally, and plan for the future. At the same time, employees are dependent on their employers for their livelihood—and often much more, including friendship networks, recreational opportunities, health care, retirement savings, even their very sense of self. Because of the importance of the relationship to both parties, it must be carefully managed, with consideration for both legal and ethical obligations.

The employment relationship confers rights and duties on both sides. (As further explained in Chapter 5, a *right* means someone is entitled to be treated a certain way; rights often confer *duties* on others.) Some of these responsibilities are legal or contractual; others are social or ethical in nature. For their part, employers have an obligation to provide some measure of job security, a safe and healthy workplace, and equal opportunity for all. They must pay a fair and decent wage and respect workers' rights to organize and bargain collectively, as guaranteed by U.S. law (and the laws of many other nations). Employers are also obliged to respect employees' rights to privacy and—to some extent at least—their rights to free speech and to do what they want outside the workplace.

But employees also have a duty to behave in acceptable ways. For example, most would agree that employees should not abuse drugs or alcohol in a way that impairs their work performance, use company e-mail to send offensive messages, or take the employer's property for their own personal use. Employees should deal with customers and coworkers in an honest, fair, and nondiscriminatory way. They should not reveal proprietary information to others outside the company, unless there is compelling reason to do so—such as an imminent threat to the public's safety. Some main rights and duties of employers and employees are summarized in Figure 15.1. How to balance these sometimes conflicting obligations poses an ongoing, and frequently perplexing, challenge to business.

This chapter considers the rights and duties—both legal and ethical—of both parties in the employment relationship. The following chapter explores the related issue of workforce diversity and discusses the specific legal and ethical obligations of employers with respect to equal employment opportunity.

Workplace Rights

Employees in the United States enjoy several important legal guarantees. They have the right to *organize and bargain collectively,* to have a *safe and healthy workplace* and, to some degree, to have *job security.* This section will explore these three rights, emphasizing U.S. laws and regulation, but with comparative references to policies in other nations.

FIGURE 15.2
**Unionization
Rates in Selected
Industrialized
Countries**

Source: Organization for
Economic Cooperation and
Development, at *https://stats
.oecd.org.* Figures have been
rounded to the nearest integer.
All data are for 2013.

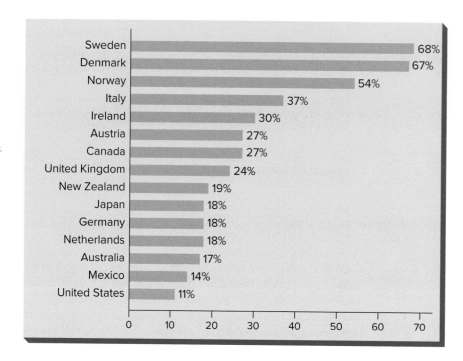

The Right to Organize and Bargain Collectively

In the United States, and in most other nations, employees have a fundamental legal right
to organize **labor unions** and to bargain collectively with their employers. The exceptions
are some communist countries (such as China, Vietnam, Cuba, and the People's Democratic Republic of Korea) and some military dictatorships (such as Eritrea), where workers
are not permitted to form independent unions. Labor unions are organizations, such as the
Service Employees International Union or the Teamsters, that represent workers on the
job. Under U.S. laws, most private and public workers have the right to hold an election
to choose what union they want to represent them, if any. Unions negotiate with employers over wages, working conditions, and other terms of employment. Employers are not
required by law to agree to the union's demands, but they are required to bargain in good
faith. Sometimes, if the two sides cannot reach agreement, a strike occurs, or employees
apply pressure in other ways, such as appealing to politicians or refusing to work overtime.

Workers are more highly unionized in some countries than in others. Figure 15.2 shows
the percentage of employees who are represented by unions in selected industrialized
nations. It shows that unionization rates are very high in the Scandinavian countries; of all
countries shown, the unionization rate is the lowest in the United States.

The influence of labor unions in the United States has waxed and waned over the years.
During the New Deal period in the 1930s, many workers, particularly in manufacturing industries such as automobiles and steel, joined unions, and the ranks of organized labor grew rapidly. Unions negotiated with employers for better wages, benefits such as pensions and health
insurance, and improved job safety—significantly improving the lot of many workers. In
2014, the median weekly pay of full-time workers who were members of unions ($970) was
27 percent higher than that of nonunion workers ($763). (All workers, whether or not they are
members of unions, are protected by wage and hour laws that require employers to pay at least
a minimum wage and extra pay for certain kinds of overtime work.) Since the mid-1950s,

the proportion of American workers represented by unions has declined. In 2014, only about 11 percent of all employees were union members. The percentage was higher—36 percent—in government employment than in the private sector, where just 7 percent were unionized.[4]

In the wake of the Great Recession, elected officials in several states sought to weaken unions by limiting the rights of public sector workers. For example, the Wisconsin legislature passed a law that took away the right of public sector unions (except those representing public safety officers) to bargain over pensions and health care benefits. In 2015, Wisconsin joined 24 other states in adopting a so-called *right-to-work* law, which barred unions from requiring all workers they represented to pay dues or fees.[5]

Although unions overall remained weak, some groups of workers continued to organize.

In 2015, for example, the Teamsters union successfully organized the drivers of what were widely known as the "Google buses." Many high-tech companies, including Google, contracted with local transportation firms to shuttle employees from their neighborhoods to their jobs and back. The gleaming white buses with darkened windows, lined up curbside in San Francisco, became a symbol of inequality between well-paid tech workers and other residents—and the bus drivers themselves, who often worked exhausting split shifts at low pay. After drivers for Facebook, Apple, eBay, Genentech, Yahoo!, and Zynga joined the Teamsters, they won big wage increases, a split-shift premium, and access to break rooms. "[The companies] should welcome this," said the president of the local union. "These [union contracts] allow the drivers who drive around a very valuable commodity—their workers—to have a decent life."[6]

Other significant recent union organizing wins occurred at IKEA's furniture factory in Virginia; Smithfield Pork in North Carolina, the world's largest pork slaughterhouse; Delta Pride, a catfish processor in Mississippi; and even Gawker Media, the publisher of the Gawker and Jezebel websites.[7]

Labor unions sought to exercise influence in other ways, as well. Unions organized in the political arena, using political action committees (PACs) and other methods (discussed in Chapter 8), and voted shares of stock in which their pension funds were invested (discussed in Chapter 13) to pursue their institutional objectives. A major legislative goal of unions was labor law reform; they sought legislation that would make it easier for workers to organize, for example, by shortening the time before an election and stiffening penalties for employers who intervened unfairly in the process.

One issue that unions and others have been concerned with is job safety and health. It is discussed next.

The Right to a Safe and Healthy Workplace

Many jobs are potentially hazardous and a threat to worker health and safety. In some industries, the use of high-speed and noisy machinery, high-voltage electricity, extreme temperatures, or hazardous gases or chemicals poses risks. Careful precautions, extensive training, strict regulations, and tough enforcement are necessary to avoid accidents, injuries, illnesses, and even deaths on the job.

---

[4] U.S. Bureau of Labor Statistics, "Union Members 2014," January 23, 2015, *www.bls.gov.*

[5] "Unions Suffer Latest Defeat in Midwest with Signing of Wisconsin Measure," *The New York Times,* March 9, 2015.

[6] "Bus Drivers for Apple, Yahoo, eBay, Zynga, Genentech Vote for Union Representation," *Forbes,* February 27, 2015, *www.forbes.com;* "Longtime Union Activist Helps Organize Facebook's Shuttle Drivers," *San Jose Mercury News,* April 17, 2015.

[7] "Gawker Media Employees Vote to Form a Union, and the Bosses Approve," *The New York Times,* June 4, 2015.

A 31-year-old technician, on the job for only a month, was electrocuted while testing equipment at Ferro Magnetics, a manufacturer of high-frequency battery chargers in Bridgeton, Missouri, in 2014. Government investigators later found that his death could have been prevented if the company had provided appropriate protective equipment and trained him properly. "[A] company that operates with high-voltage electricity must train its workers to recognize hazards and use proper procedures to prevent electrical shock. No one should die on the job," said the regional OSHA director.[8]

Over the past few decades, new categories of accidents or illnesses have emerged, including the fast-growing job safety problem of repetitive motion disorders, such as the wrist pain sometimes experienced by supermarket checkers, meat cutters, or keyboard operators. Some workers have even complained of "BlackBerry thumb," hand strain caused by using their thumbs to tap out messages on the small keyboards of their smartphones when working away from the office. In response, many businesses have given greater attention to **ergonomics**, adapting the job to the worker, rather than forcing the worker to adapt to the job. For example, ergonomically designed office chairs that conform to the shape of the worker's spine may help prevent low productivity and lost time due to back injuries.

Annually, slightly more than three million workers in private industry are injured or become ill while on the job, according to the U.S. Department of Labor. This amounts to more than three hurt or sick workers out of every hundred. Some of the most dangerous jobs are in protective services (police, fire fighters, and prison guards); transportation and material moving; farming; and buildings and grounds maintenance and cleaning. In general, manufacturing and construction jobs are riskier than service jobs—although workers in nursing homes and hospitals suffer relatively high rates of injury.[9] More than 4,000 workers die on the job annually. The reasons range from vehicle accidents, to contact with dangerous equipment, to explosion and fire. For example, a massive explosion at the Upper Big Branch coal mine in West Virginia in 2010 killed 29 workers in the worst coal mining disaster in the United States in 40 years. The causes of this disaster are explored in a case study at the end of this book.

Workplace violence—a particular threat to employee safety—is profiled in Exhibit 15.A.

In the United States, the Occupational Safety and Health Act, passed in 1970 during the great wave of social legislation discussed in Chapter 7, gives workers the right to a job "free from recognized hazards that are causing or likely to cause death or serious physical harm." This law is administered by the **Occupational Safety and Health Administration (OSHA)**. Congress gave OSHA important powers to set and enforce safety and health standards. Employers found in violation can be fined and, in the case of willful violation causing the death of an employee, jailed as well. In 2009, for example, OSHA fined BP $87 million—on top of $21 million the company had already paid—for safety violations linked to an explosion of a refinery in Texas that killed 15 workers and injured 170, the largest fine ever levied by the agency.[10]

OSHA has had considerable success in improving worker safety and health. Although workers—such as the victims of the Upper Big Branch coal mine and BP refinery explosions—continue to die on the job, since OSHA's creation in 1970 the number of workplace deaths has fallen by more than two-thirds, even as the workforce has almost doubled. Very serious occupational illnesses, such as brown lung (caused when textile workers inhale cotton dust) and black lung (caused when coal miners inhale coal dust), have been

---

[8]"Lack of Safety Equipment and Training Cost Electrical Technician His Life," *OSHA Regional News Release,* May 18, 2015.

[9] U.S. Bureau of Labor Statistics data, *www.bls.gov.* These data are for 2013.

[10]"U.S. Department of Labor's OSHA Issues Record Breaking Fines to BP," press release, October 30, 2009, at *www.osha.gov.*

Exhibit 15.A

Violence in the Workplace

Stories of angry or distraught employees, ex-employees, or associates of employees attacking workers, coworkers, or superiors at work are disturbingly common. In some cases, workers who have lost their jobs—or who face some other financial threat—seek vengeance, often in calculated and cold-blooded fashion. In other cases, seemingly trivial events can provoke an assault. In one recent incident, a worker at a sign company in Minneapolis, Minnesota, was fired for chronic lateness and poor performance. He went out to his car, got a semiautomatic pistol and returned to the building, shooting and killing five people and wounding three others before turning the gun on himself.[11]

Homicide is the fourth leading cause of death on the job (only vehicle accidents, contact with objects or equipment, and falls kill more). Every year, around 400 workers are murdered, and as many as 2 million are assaulted at work in the United States. Police officers, prison guards, taxi drivers, and people who handle money are most at risk. Although workplace violence is often considered an American problem, a survey by the International Labor Organization found that workplace assaults were actually more common in several other industrial nations, including France, England, and Argentina, than in the United States. Four percent of workers in the European Union said they had been subjected to physical violence in the past year.

OSHA has developed recommendations to help employers reduce the risk of violence. Employers should try to reduce high-risk situations, for example, by installing alarm systems, convex mirrors, and pass-through windows. They should train employees in what to do in an emergency situation. Unfortunately, many companies are poorly prepared to deal with these situations. Only 24 percent of employers offer any type of formal training to their employees in coping with workplace violence.

Sources: "Fatal Occupational Injuries by Industry and Selected Event or Exposure, 2013," at *www.bls.org;* and International Labor Organization, *Violence at Work,* 3rd ed., 2006. Current statistics are available at *www.cdc.gov/niosh/topics/violence.*

significantly reduced. The rate of lead poisoning suffered by workers in smelters and battery plants, among other workplaces, has also fallen dramatically.

Although many businesses have credited OSHA with helping reduce lost workdays and worker compensation costs, others have criticized the agency's rules as being too costly to implement and administer. For example, OSHA withdrew a proposed noise exposure standard, intended to prevent hearing loss, after employers complained it would be too expensive.[12] Some studies showed that the burdens of complying with regulations fell hardest on small businesses.[13] In part in response to employer criticisms, OSHA has entered into cooperative partnerships with employers, aimed at improving occupational safety and health for the benefit of both companies and their workers.

Although problems remain, four decades of occupational safety and health regulation in the United States and efforts by businesses and unions have significantly lowered deaths and injuries on the job. In many developing nations, however, conditions remain brutally dangerous. In Bangladesh, for example, a fast-growing garment and textile industry—mostly sourcing apparel to Western companies—has been the site of numerous tragedies, including a terrible building collapse at the Rana Plaza garment factory complex in 2013 that killed more than 1,100 workers. This incident—and the involvement of Western retailers whose products were manufactured there—is profiled in a case at the end of this book.

[11] "Minneapolis Workplace Shooting: Gunman Was Fired, Then the Rampage Began," October 1, 2012, at *www.twincities.com.*

[12] "OSHA Withdraws Proposed Interpretation Involving Occupational Noise Exposure Standard," *Washington DC Employment Law Update,* January 19, 2011, at *www.dcemploymentlawupdate.com.*

[13] U.S. House of Representatives Committee on Oversight and Government Reform, *Assessing Regulatory Impediments to Job Creation,* February 9, 2011, at *http://oversight.house.gov.*

The Right to a Secure Job

Do employers have an obligation to provide their workers with job security? Once someone is hired, under what circumstances is it legal—or fair—to let him or her go? In recent years, the expectations underlying this most basic aspect of the employment relationship have changed, both in the United States and in other countries around the globe.

In the United States, since the late 1800s, the legal basis for the employment relationship has been **employment-at-will**. Employment-at-will is a legal doctrine that means that employees are hired and retain their jobs "at the will of"—that is, at the sole discretion of—the employer. However, over time, laws and court decisions have changed this. Today, employers' freedom to terminate workers has been dramatically curtailed. Some of the restrictions include the following:

- An employer may not fire a worker because of race, gender, religion, national origin, age, or disability. The equal employment and other laws that prevent such discriminatory terminations are further described in Chapter 16.

- An employer may not fire a worker if this would constitute a violation of public policy, as determined by the courts. For example, if a company fired an employee just because he or she cooperated with authorities in the investigation of a crime, this would be illegal.

- An employer may not fire a worker if, in doing so, it would violate the Worker Adjustment Retraining Notification Act (WARN). This law, passed in 1988, requires most big employers to provide 60 days' advance notice whenever they lay off a third or more (or 500 or more, whichever is less) of their workers at a work site. If they do not, they must pay workers for any days of advance notice that were missed.

- An employer may not fire a worker simply because the individual was involved in a union organizing drive or other union activity.

- An employer may not fire a worker if this would violate an implied contract, such as a verbal promise, or basic rules of "fair dealing." For example, an employer could not legally fire a salesperson just because he or she had earned a bigger bonus under an incentive program than the employer wanted to pay.

Of course, if workers are covered by a collective bargaining agreement, it may impose additional restrictions on an employer's right to terminate. Many union contracts say employees can be fired only "for just cause," and workers have a right to appeal the employer's decision through the union grievance procedure. Many European countries and Japan have laws that extend "just cause" protections to all workers, whether or not they are covered by a union contract.

The commitments that employers and employees make to each other go beyond mere legal obligations, however. Cultural values, traditions, and norms of behavior also play important roles. Some have used the term **social contract** to refer to the *implied understanding* (not a legal contract, but rather a set of shared expectations) between an organization and its stakeholders. This concept includes, perhaps most significantly, the understanding between businesses and their employees.

Research suggests that the social contract governing the employment relationship has varied across cultures, and also across time. For example, in Europe, employers have historically given workers and their unions a greater role in determining company policy than do most U.S. employers. Employee representatives are often included on boards of directors, in a practice sometimes called *codetermination*. For many years, big Japanese companies offered a core group of senior workers lifelong employment; in exchange, these workers felt great loyalty to the company. This practice has declined in recent years, however.

When the global recession hit Japan in 2008–2009, many employees found themselves without job security or a social safety net. By then, more than a third of the nation's workers were so-called nonregulars, hired on short-term contracts with fewer benefits and no protections against layoffs. In Japan, where workers must be employed for at least a year to get jobless benefits, many nonregulars who lost their jobs in the recession had nothing to fall back on. One worker who had been laid off from a Canon digital camera factory said, "We did our best, so Canon should have taken care of us. That is the Japanese way. But this isn't Japan anymore." As the economy recovered, unemployment dropped to a very low 3.6 percent—but not the use of nonregulars, who surged to 38 percent of the workforce.[14]

In the former Soviet Union, many enterprises felt an obligation to provide social benefits, such as housing and child care, to their workers. These benefits declined with the advent of privatization in these formerly state-run economies.

Fierce global competition and greater attention to improving the bottom line have resulted in significant corporate restructuring and downsizing (termination) of employees in many countries. This trend has led some researchers to describe a *new social contract.* Increasingly, bonds between employers and employees have weakened. Companies aim to attract and retain employees not by offering long-term job security, but rather by emphasizing interesting and challenging work, performance-based compensation, and ongoing professional training. For their part, employees are expected to contribute by making a strong commitment to the job task and work team and to assume a share of responsibility for the company's success. But they cannot count on a guaranteed job.[15]

An important aspect of the weakening of the social contract between employers and workers has been the elimination of defined benefit pensions (which provide a fixed payout based on age at retirement, years of service, and average pay). In the 1980s, about 60 percent of private sector employers in the United States offered such a pension. By 2015, this had dropped to around 10 percent, as employers such as IBM, Verizon, Lockheed Martin, and General Motors replaced them with 401(k) or similar plans where workers contributed to tax-deferred savings accounts, sometimes matched by employer contributions. In 2013, employees contributed $30 billion to their own retirement accounts. These so-called defined contribution plans gave workers more control over their investments and enabled them to carry their retirement savings with them when they changed jobs, but were also much less secure. "People just have to deal with a lot more risk in their lives, because all of these things that used to be more or less assured—a job, health care, a pension—are now variable," said one expert.[16]

Should companies have strong or weak bonds with their employees? When businesses invest in their employees by providing a well-structured career, job security, and benefits including pensions, they reap the rewards of enhanced loyalty, productivity, and commitment. But such investments are expensive, and long-term commitments make it hard for companies to adjust to the ups and downs of the business cycle. Some firms resolve this

[14] "Japan Has Plenty of Jobs, but Worker Still Struggle," *The Wall Street Journal,* March 12, 2015; and "In Japan, New Jobless May Lack Safety Net," *The New York Times,* February 8, 2009.

[15] James E. Post, "The New Social Contract," in Oliver Williams and John Houck, eds., *The Global Challenge to Corporate Social Responsibility* (New York: Oxford University Press, 1995).

[16] Towers Watson, "Defined Contribution Plans of Fortune 100 Companies in 2013," February, 2015, at *www.towerswatson .com;* and "Just How Common Are Defined Benefit Plans," at *http://money.cnn.com.* The quotation is from "IBM to Freeze Pension Plans to Trim Costs," *The New York Times,* January 6, 2006.

Exhibit 15.B

Workers in the Sharing Economy

In 2015, the California Labor Commission (a state government agency that enforces labor laws) ruled that a particular driver for Uber, the ride-hailing service, should be considered an *employee*, not an *independent contractor*, and awarded her about $4,000 in expense reimbursements. It was a small amount of money for Uber, but a decision with potentially far-reaching implications for that company and others in the so-called sharing or on-demand economy.

On-demand companies like Uber, Lyft, and Sidecar (rides), Instacart (grocery delivery), and TaskRabbit (household errands and skilled tasks) were growing rapidly. Their business model was to deploy technology to match customers (for example, a person needing a ride) with someone willing to do the work (a driver with a car), and then take a portion of the payment. Such companies had attracted more than $9 billion in venture capital funding since 2010. A consulting firm, MBO Partners, estimated that 17.7 million Americans were working at least part-time as "independent contributors," but no one knew exactly how many of these were working in the sharing economy.

The Internal Revenue Service distinguished between employees, whose wages were reported on a W-2 form, and independent contractors, whose compensation was reported on a Form 1099. In 2015, the Labor Department issued further clarification, saying that workers who were "economically dependent" on an employer should be classified as employees, as contrasted with independent contractors, who were in business for him or herself. The distinction was important, because employers were required to comply with various labor laws governing employees, such as minimum wage and overtime rules; to pay various benefits such as workers' compensation and unemployment insurance; and to reimburse expenses, such as gasoline. They were not required to provide such benefits for independent contractors. Not surprisingly, most companies in the sharing economy insisted that they were not employers, but technology companies that simply brokered transactions.

Workers in the sharing economy were themselves split on the issue. Some felt they should have the rights of employees, like the driver who brought the case against Uber, who said, "I don't like being ripped off. . . . People who drive for Uber and Lyft [should] at least get minimum wages and get their expenses paid and [be] paid for overtime." But others appreciated the freedom to work whenever and wherever they wished, without being subject to an employer's dictates. And, classifying on-demand workers as employees could retard innovation in the new economy, some believed. "Many new platforms and other businesses that might have used on-demand labor may not emerge because of the risk they will be considered employers," said a New York University professor.

Sources: "Employee or Contractor? Labor Seeks to Clarify Rules," *The New York Times,* July 15, 2015; "Uber Driver an Employee, California Labor Commission Rules," *San Francisco Chronicle,* June 17, 2015; "California Says Uber Driver is Employee, Not a Contractor," *The New York Times,* June 17, 2015; "In the Sharing Economy, Workers Find Both Freedom and Uncertainty," *The New York Times,* August 16, 2014; and "The On-Demand Mobile Industry in 9 Charts," May 28, 2015, at *www.CBInsights.com.*

dilemma by employing two classes of employees: permanent workers, who enjoy stable employment and full benefits, and temporary workers and independent contractors, who do not. The tax preparation software company Intuit has estimated that as high as 40 percent of the U.S. workforce could have at least some income from freelancing or work as independent contractors or temporary workers by 2020.[17] This temporary work sector is sometimes referred to as the "gig economy." The rise of the gig economy has allowed companies to become more cost-efficient, but it has also shifted risk to workers, sowed anxiety, and in many cases driven down incomes. And although some workers preferred the flexibility of jobs in the gig economy, many ended up there simply because they could not find stable, permanent employment.[18]

Some of the particular challenges facing workers in the so-called sharing economy, in which they function as independent contractors rather than employees, are further explored in Exhibit 15.B.

[17] "40 Percent of Americans Will Be Freelancers by 2020," *Business Insider,* March 21, 2015.

[18] "Growth in the 'Gig Economy' Fuels Work Force Anxieties," *The New York Times,* July 12, 2015.

Special Issue: Wages and Income Inequality

An important duty of employers, as noted in Figure 15.1, is to pay a fair and decent wage. Yet, how wages should be determined, and what exactly is fair or decent, remains contentious. This issue has taken on greater prominence in recent years, as public attention has turned to growing income inequality in the United States and other developed nations. What is the relationship between inequality and wages, and what responsibility if any does business bear for the sharp differences in life circumstances between those at the top and bottom of society?

Figure 15.3 shows changes in the level of income inequality in the United States over the past century, as measured by the share of all income going to the top 10 percent of households. (As explained in Chapter 4, inequality can be expressed for both wealth and income; this figure shows inequality of income.) The figure shows that income inequality fell dramatically during World War II and stayed low during the postwar years until around 1980, and since then has increased dramatically.

The rise in income inequality, as illustrated by Figure 15.3, has many causes, and some have little directly to do with business practices. These include federal and state minimum wage laws, taxation policy, economic growth, unionization rates, and other factors. But corporate policy plays an important role. When businesses decide to pay very high executive compensation (as discussed in Chapter 13) and to keep wages as low as possible for ordinary employees, they are contributing to inequality in the broader society. In the four decades between 1973 and 2013, hourly wages went up just 9.2 percent, adjusted for inflation (productivity went up 74.4 percent during this period). The situation was particularly dire for the lowest wage workers, whose compensation actually fell.[19]

FIGURE 15.3 Income Inequality in the United States, 1910–2010

Source: Thomas Piketty and Emmanuel Saez, "Income Inequality in the United States, 1913–1998," *Quarterly Journal of Economics,* 118(1), 2003, updated at *http://emlab .berkeley.edu/users/saez.* Used by permission.

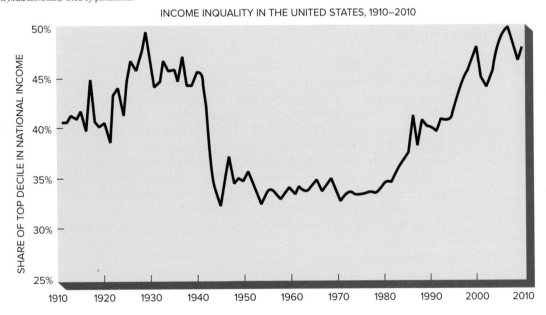

[19] Economic Policy Institute, "Wage Stagnation in Nine Charts," January 6, 2015, *www.epi.org.*

What can companies do to address income inequality? The simple answer is to increase wages—and to reduce pay differentials within their organizations. When Target raised its minimum wage to $9, as mentioned in one of the opening examples of this chapter, it was making a small but important contribution to raising compensation at the bottom of the employment pyramid. Other employers of low-paid workers, including Walmart and McDonald's, have also recently raised their workers' pay. Aetna announced in 2015 it would pay all its employees, including part-timers, at least $16 an hour, a raise of as much as 33 percent for some of them. A few companies—such as Gravity Payments, discussed in Chapter 3—have taken even more dramatic actions to improve compensation for their employees.

One approach, taken by a small minority of companies, has been to commit to paying all employees what is called a **living wage**. This has been defined by the Ethical Trading Initiative as a wage "that enables workers, for their labor during a standard work week, to support half the basic needs of an average-sized family, based on local prices near the workplace."[20] Of course, figuring out what exactly this would mean can be challenging. For example, when Novartis, a major multinational pharmaceutical firm, committed to paying a living wage to all its employees around the world, it had to bring in an outside consultant to help estimate a "basic needs basket" of goods and services in the many nations where it operated.[21] U.S. companies that pay well above minimum wage for entry-level work (although they have not necessarily committed to the living wage concept) include Costco, Trader Joe's, In-N-Out Burger, Gap, REI, QuikTrip, and IKEA.[22]

Recent evidence suggests that companies that adopt such a "good jobs" strategy reap benefits from doing so. Of course, paying workers well costs more, and in that way can detract from the bottom line. But a study of four retail chains that paid above-average wages by MIT professor Zeynep Ton found that these firms had achieved healthy growth and excellent shareholder returns. They had done so because they had "invest[ed] in their employees with the expectation that they [would] get even more back in terms of labor productivity, customer service, cost-cutting, innovation, and flexibility during difficult times," the researcher concluded.[23] In short, a high-road strategy had paid off for these socially responsible companies.

Privacy in the Workplace

An important right in the workplace, as elsewhere, is privacy. Privacy can be most simply understood as the right to be left alone. In the business context, **privacy rights** refer primarily to protecting an individual's personal life from unwarranted intrusion by the employer. Many people believe, for example, that their religious and political views, their health conditions, their credit history, and what they do and say off the job are private matters and should be safe from snooping by the boss. Exceptions are permissible only when the employer's interests are clearly affected. For example, it may be appropriate for the boss to know that an employee is discussing with a competitor, through e-mail messages, the specifications of a newly developed product not yet on the market.

But other areas are not so clear-cut. For example, should a job applicant who is experiencing severe financial problems be denied employment out of fear that he may be more

[20] Ethical Trading Initiative, at *www.ethicaltrade.org/in-action/issues/living-wage/standards*.

[21] "Novartis: Implementing a Living Wage Globally," World Business Council for Sustainable Development, 2007, at *oldwww.wbcsd.org*.

[22] "IKEA, Gap, and 8 More Companies That Pay More Than Minimum Wage," *The Christian Science Monitor*, June 26, 2014.

[23] "Why Companies That Pay Above the Minimum Wage Come Out Ahead," July 1, 2014, at *www.forbes.com*; and Zeynep Ton, *The Good Jobs Strategy* (Boston: Houghton Mifflin, 2014).

inclined to steal from the company? Should an employee be terminated after the firm discovers that she has a serious medical problem, although it does not affect her job performance, since the company's health insurance premiums may dramatically increase? At what point do company interests weigh more heavily than an employee's right to privacy? This section will address several key workplace issues where these privacy dilemmas often emerge: electronic monitoring, office romance, drug and alcohol abuse (including medical marijuana), and honesty testing.

Electronic Monitoring

As discussed in Chapters 11 and 12, changing technologies have brought many ethical issues to the forefront. One such issue is employee **electronic monitoring**. A wide range of technologies—e-mail and messaging, social media sites, cell phones, location tracking, Internet browsing, and digitally stored video—enable companies to gather, monitor, and analyze information about employees' activities. For example, a company called Sociometric Solutions makes sensor-rich badges that can be worn by employees. They are equipped with microphones, a location sensor, and an accelerometer (similar to those used in fitness trackers). The company uses "big data" technology to analyze the resulting information and provides a summary in aggregated form to the employer. Another company, Volometrix, mines data from online calendars, e-mail, and messaging logs to analyze patterns of employee interaction with each other and with customers. Such data analytics can help companies make more productive use of their employees' time.[24]

A company's need for information, particularly about its workers, may be at odds with an employee's right to privacy, however.

> A police officer in Ontario, California, sued his employer, saying his Fourth Amendment rights against unreasonable search and seizure had been violated. The police department had reviewed transcripts of text messages the officer had sent on an employer-issued device, including highly personal ones sent to his wife and mistress. But the Supreme Court disagreed, saying that as a government employee, the officer should not have expected that messages sent using government equipment would be private.[25]

Management justifies the increase in employee monitoring for a number of reasons. Employers have an interest in efficiency. When employees log on to the Internet at work to trade stocks, plan their vacations, chat with friends—or text-message their wives or mistresses, as in the Ontario example—this is not a productive use of their time. Employers also fear lawsuits if employees act in inappropriate ways. An employee who views pornographic pictures on a computer at work, for example, might leave the company open to a charge of sexual harassment—if other workers observed this behavior and were offended by it. (Sexual harassment is further discussed in the following chapter.) The employer also needs to make sure that employees do not disclose confidential information to competitors or make statements that would publicly embarrass the company or its officers. And monitoring is often used for training and quality control purposes.

Is electronic monitoring by employers legal? For the most part, yes. The Electronic Communications Privacy Act (1986) exempts employers. In general, the courts have found that privacy rights apply to personal, but not business, information, and that employers have a right to monitor job-related communication. The courts have generally ruled that

---

[24] "The Office is Watching You," May 22, 2015, at *www.fastcompany.com;* and "Unblinking Eyes Track Employees," *The New York Times,* June 21, 2014.

[25] "Privacy in the Cellular Age," *The New York Times,* June 18, 2010.

employers may monitor employee e-mail, messages, and texts. An evolving area of the law involves GPS tracking. A recent example involved a woman in California who worked as a regional sales representative. Her employer had required her to install a phone app so it could track her movements as she drove around her territory making sales calls. But she was offended that her employer could also track her movements while she was not working, so she deleted the app—and was promptly fired. The woman sued. The courts' response to cases like this is still evolving.[26] (Employee monitoring is further discussed in Chapter 12.)

In seeking to balance their employees' concerns about privacy with their own concerns about productivity, liability, and security, businesses face a difficult challenge. One approach is to monitor employee communication only when there is a specific reason to do so, such as poor productivity or suspicion of theft. For example, the chipmaker Intel Corporation chose not to check its employees' e-mail routinely, feeling this would undermine trust. Most management experts recommend that employers, at the very least, clearly define their monitoring policies, let employees know what behavior is expected, and apply any sanctions in a fair and evenhanded way.

Romance in the Workplace

Another issue that requires careful balancing between legitimate employer concerns and employee privacy is romance in the workplace. People have always dated others at work. In fact, a 2013 survey showed that 38 percent of workers said they had dated a coworker at least once during their careers, and of these relationships almost a third had led to marriage.[27] In fact, workplace dating has probably become more common as the average age of marriage has risen. (For women, that age is now around 27; for men, around 29.) Said one human resources director, "It's a reality that work is where people meet these days. When you don't meet at college, that's a pool of people that's taken away from you." Yet office romance poses problems for employers. If the relationship goes sour, one of the people may sue, charging sexual harassment—that is, that he or she was coerced into the relationship. When one person in a relationship is in a position of authority, he or she may be biased in an evaluation of the other's work, or others may perceive it to be so.

For many years, most businesses had a strict policy of forbidding relationships in the workplace outright. They assumed that if romance blossomed, one person—usually the subordinate—would have to find another job. Today, however, companies are more likely to draw distinctions, permitting some kinds of office relationships, and not others. A 2013 survey by the Society for Human Resource Professionals found that 42 percent of companies had either a written or verbal policy on workplace romance. Almost all of these policies (99 percent) banned relationships within a direct chain of command (such as between a supervisor and subordinate). Forty-five percent banned romances between employees of significantly different rank. But less than a third banned relationships between workers of the same rank who reported to the same supervisor, and only 12 percent banned relationships between workers in different departments. A small proportion of companies (about 5 percent) require their managers to sign a document, sometimes called a *consensual relationship agreement*, stipulating that an office relationship is welcome and voluntary—to protect against possible harassment lawsuits if the people involved later break up.[28]

[26] "Woman Fired After Disabling GPS on Work Phone," *CNN Money*, May 13, 2015. A summary of the law with respect to employee monitoring may be found in "Fact Sheet 7: Workplace Privacy and Employee Monitoring," at the website of the Privacy Rights Clearinghouse at *www.privacyrights.org.*

[27] "Thirty-Eight Percent of Workers Have Dated a Co-Worker, Find CareerBuilder Survey," press release, February 12, 2014, at *www.careerbuilder.com.*

[28] "Forbidden Love: Workplace-Romance Policies Now Stricter," September 24, 2013, at *www.shrm.org.*

Employee Drug Use and Testing

Abuse of drugs, both illegal drugs such as heroin and methamphetamine and legal drugs such as Oxycontin or Xanax when used inappropriately, can be a serious problem for employers. Only a small fraction of employees abuse illegal or prescription drugs. But those who do can cause serious harm. They are much more likely than others to produce poor-quality work, have accidents that hurt themselves and others, and steal from their employers. Some break the law by selling drugs at work to support their habits. Drug abuse costs U.S. industry and taxpayers an estimated $193 billion a year. This figure includes the cost of lost productivity, medical claims, rehabilitation services, and crime and accidents caused by drugs.[29]

One way business has protected itself from these risks is through **drug testing**. About two-thirds of companies test employees or job applicants for illegal substances, according to a 2015 study.[30] Significant drug testing first began in the United States following passage of the Drug-Free Workplace Act of 1988, which required federal contractors to establish and maintain a workplace free of drugs. At that time, many companies and public agencies initiated drug testing to comply with government rules. The use of drug tests has fallen somewhat in the past decade, as fewer people have tested positive. (The one class of drugs whose use has recently risen is prescription opiates—medicines such as hydrocodone that are used to treat pain.)

Typically, drug testing is used on three different occasions.

- *Preemployment screening.* Some companies test all job applicants or selected applicants before hiring, usually as part of a physical examination, often informing the applicant ahead of time that there will be a drug screening.

- *Random testing of employees.* This type of screening may occur at various times throughout the year. In many companies, workers in particular job categories (e.g., operators of heavy machinery) or levels (e.g., supervisors) are eligible for screening at any time.

- *Testing for cause.* This test occurs when an employee is believed to be impaired by drugs and unfit for work. It is commonly used after an accident or some observable change in behavior.

An emerging issue is whether or not employers may terminate workers for testing positive for marijuana in states that permit its medical use. In 2015, the Colorado Supreme Court upheld the decision of Dish Network, a satellite television company, to fire an employee who had failed a random drug test. The employee, a customer service representative, had used marijuana off the job to treat painful spasms caused by a serious car accident. Colorado was one of 23 states that permitted medical marijuana (and one of only four that permitted recreational use by adults). Even though Colorado law said that an employee could not be fired for "any lawful activity" outside of work, because marijuana was still illegal under federal law the court said the firing was justified.[31]

Employee drug testing is controversial. Although businesses have an interest in not hiring, or getting rid of, people who abuse drugs, many job applicants and employees who have never used drugs feel that testing is unnecessary and violates their privacy and due process rights. The debate over employee drug testing is summarized in Figure 15.4. In

---

[29] "Consequences of Illicit Drug Use in America," April 2014, at *www.whitehouse.gov.*

[30] "HireRight Annual Employment Screening Benchmark Report, 2015 Edition" at *http://hireright.com/benchmarking.*

[31] "Workers Can Be Fired for Marijuana Use, Colorado Court Rules," *The New York Times,* June 15, 2015.

FIGURE 15.4
Pros and Cons of Employee Drug Testing

Arguments Favoring Employee Drug Testing	Arguments Opposing Employee Drug Testing
• Supports U.S. policy to reduce illegal drug use and availability	• Invades an employee's privacy
• Improves employee productivity	• Violates an employee's right to due process
• Promotes safety in the workplace	• May be unrelated to job performance
• Decreases employee theft and absenteeism	• May be used as a method of employee discrimination
• Reduces health and insurance costs	• Lowers employee morale
	• Conflicts with company values of honesty and trust
	• May yield unreliable test results
	• Ignores effects of prescription drugs, alcohol, and over-the-counter drugs
	• Drug use an insignificant problem for some companies

general, proponents of testing emphasize the need to reduce potential harm to other people and the cost to business and society of drug use on the job. Opponents challenge the benefits of drug testing and emphasize its intrusion on individual privacy.

Alcohol Abuse at Work

Another form of employee substance abuse—which causes twice the problems of all illegal drugs combined—is alcohol use and addiction. About 9 percent of full-time employees are heavy drinkers—that is, they had five or more drinks on five or more occasions in the past month. Like drug abusers, they can be dangerous to themselves and others. Studies show that up to 40 percent of all industrial fatalities and 47 percent of industrial injuries are linked to alcohol. The problem is not just hard-core alcoholics, however. Most alcohol-related problems in the workplace, one study found, were caused by people who occasionally drank too much after work and came in the next day with a hangover, or who went out for a drink on their lunch break. U.S. businesses lose an estimated $88 billion per year in reduced productivity directly related to alcohol abuse.[32]

Company programs for drug abusers and alcohol abusers are often combined. Many firms recognize that they have a role to play in helping alcoholic employees. As with drug rehabilitation programs, most alcoholism programs work through **employee assistance programs (EAPs)** that offer counseling and follow-up. Almost all U.S. companies employing 1,000 or more workers provide EAPs for alcohol and drug abusers. Even small companies (employing 50 to 99) are involved; almost three-quarters now offer assistance, often by contracting with outside vendors.[33]

[32] The statistics reported in this paragraph are from the U.S. Substance Abuse and Mental Health Services Administration (SAMHSA) at *www.samhsa.gov;* 10th Annual Report to the U.S. Congress on Alcohol and Health, at *http://pubs.niaaa.nih.gov/publications/10report/intro.pdf;* and the website of the National Drug-Free Workplace Alliance at *www.ndwa.org.*

[33] Kenneth Matos and Ellen Galinsky, "2014 National Study of Employers," at *http://familiesandwork.org.*

Employee Theft and Honesty Testing

Employees can irresponsibly damage themselves, their coworkers, and their employer by stealing from the company. Employee theft has emerged as a significant economic, social, and ethical problem in the workplace. A 2015 survey of large retail stores in the United States showed that almost 35 percent of all inventory losses were due to employee theft (shoplifting, administrative error, and vendor fraud accounted for most of the rest). The retail value of goods stolen by employees was more than $15 billion.[34]

> Employee theft is also a problem in other parts of the world, as well. According to the 2013–14 Global Retail Theft Barometer, so-called retail crime costs European, North American, and Asian-Pacific businesses around $129 billion annually, or about 1.3 percent of sales. Of this, 28 percent was due to employee theft (shoplifting, administrative error, and vendor fraud accounted for the rest). The items most commonly stolen were clothing, accessories, power tools, wines, and make-up.[35]

Many companies in the past used polygraph testing (lie detectors) as a preemployment screening procedure or on discovery of employee theft. In 1988, the Employee Polygraph Protection Act became law. This law severely limited polygraph testing by employers and prohibited approximately 85 percent of all such tests previously administered in the United States. In response to the federal ban on polygraphs, many corporations have switched to written psychological tests that seek to predict employee honesty on the job by asking questions designed to identify desirable or undesirable qualities. When a British chain of home improvement centers used such tests to screen more than 4,000 applicants, theft dropped from 4 percent to 2.5 percent, and actual losses from theft were reduced from £3.75 million to £2.62 million.

The use of **honesty tests**, however, like polygraphs, is controversial. The American Psychological Association noted there is a significant potential for these tests to generate false positives, indicating the employee probably would or did steal from the company even though this is not true. Critics also argue that the tests intrude on a person's privacy and discriminate disproportionately against minorities.

In all these areas—monitoring employees electronically, policing office romance, testing for drugs, and conducting psychological tests—businesses must balance their needs to operate safely, ethically, and efficiently with their employees' right to privacy.

 ## Whistle-Blowing and Free Speech in the Workplace

Another area where employer and employee rights and duties frequently conflict involves free speech. Do employees have the right to openly express their opinions about their company and its actions? If so, under what conditions do they have this right?

The U.S. Constitution protects the right to free speech. This means the government cannot take away this right. For example, the legislature cannot shut down a newspaper that editorializes against its actions or those of its members. However, the Constitution does not explicitly protect freedom of expression in the workplace. Generally, employees are

---

[34] Richard C. Hollinger and the National Retail Federation, *2015 National Retail Security Survey* (University of Florida and the National Retail Federation, 2015).

[35] These data are for the 12-month period ending December 2013. The Global Retail Theft Barometer is available at *www.globalretailtheftbarometer.com.*

not free to speak out against their employers, since companies have a legitimate interest in operating without harassment from insiders. Company information is generally considered to be proprietary and private. If employees, based on their personal points of view, were freely allowed to expose issues to the public and allege misconduct, a company might be thrown into turmoil and be unable to operate effectively.

On the other hand, there may be situations in which society's interests override those of the company, so an employee may feel an obligation to speak out. When an employee believes his or her employer has done something that is wrong or harmful to the public, and he or she reports alleged organizational misconduct to the media, government, or high-level company officials, **whistle-blowing** has occurred.

An example of a whistle-blower was Michael Winston, a former executive at Countrywide Financial Corporation with responsibility for leadership development. Countrywide, which was later acquired by Bank of America, was a leading subprime lender during the housing boom of the mid-2000s. Winston had complained vigorously to the chief production officer about the company's strategy of funding almost all loans, whether or not the borrower was qualified. "I told him that you need to focus on customer satisfaction, on the quality of the loan portfolio, and on building leaders who would focus their people on that," Winston recalled. "I wrote him a very comprehensive memo." Soon afterward, Winston's budget was cut, he was excluded from meetings, and his office was relocated. Eventually, he was fired. In 2011, he won a lawsuit against his former employer. "It [was] the littlest of Davids beating the biggest of Goliaths," said Winston.[36]

Speaking out against an employer can be risky; many whistle-blowers find their charges ignored—or worse, find themselves ostracized, demoted, or even fired for daring to go public with their criticisms. Whistle-blowers in the United States have some legal protection against retaliation by their employers, though. As noted earlier in this chapter, most workers are employed *at will,* meaning they can be fired for any reason. However, most states now recognize a public policy exception to this rule. Employees who are discharged in retaliation for blowing the whistle, in a situation that affects public welfare, may sue for reinstatement and in some cases may even be entitled to punitive damages. The federal Sarbanes-Oxley Act, passed in 2002 (and described more fully in Chapters 5 and 13), makes it illegal for employers to retaliate in any way against whistle-blowers who report information that could have an impact on the value of a company's shares. More recently, the Dodd-Frank Act of 2010 (described more fully in Chapters 7 and 14) requires the government to pay a reward to whistle-blowers who voluntarily provide information that leads to successful prosecutions for violations of federal securities laws. Dodd-Frank also prohibits retaliation against employees who do so.[37]

Moreover, whistle-blowers sometimes benefit from their actions. The U.S. False Claims Act (also known as the Lincoln Law), as amended in 1986, allows individuals who sue federal contractors for fraud to receive up to 30 percent of any amount recovered by the government. In the past decade, the number of whistle-blower lawsuits—perhaps spurred by this incentive—increased significantly, exposing fraud in the country's defense, health care, municipal bond, and pharmaceutical industries.

[36] "How a Whistle-Blower Conquered Countrywide," *The New York Times,* February 19, 2011.

[37] "SEC Approves New Rewards for Whistleblowers," *Washington Post,* May 25, 2011; and Securities and Exchange Commission, "Implementation of the Whistleblower Provisions of Section 21F of the Securities Exchange Act of 1934," August 12, 2011, at *www.sec.gov.*

For example, several whistle-blowers at Johnson & Johnson, the pharmaceutical company, shared a $112 million reward in 2013 after they helped the government bring a successful case against their employer for illegally marketing the anti-psychotic drug Risperdal (which had been approved to treat schizophrenia and bipolar disorder). The government said the company had promoted the drug for unapproved uses, such as for elders with dementia, children with attention deficit hyperactivity disorder, and people with developmental disabilities, in spite of known health risks for these groups. Johnson & Johnson eventually paid $2.2 billion in criminal and civil fines to settle the charges. The government was able to build a successful case against Johnson & Johnson because several employee whistle-blowers came forward. Said one of the whistle-blowers' lawyers, "She quit without a job. They were asking her to market the drug for the elderly. She knew that was dangerous."[38]

Whistle-blowing has both defenders and detractors. Defenders point to the successful detection of fraudulent activities and prosecution of wrongdoers. Under the False Claims Act, through 2012 $55 billion had been recovered by the federal and state governments that would otherwise have been lost to fraud.[39] Situations dangerous to the public or the environment have been exposed and corrected because insiders have spoken out. Yet opponents cite hundreds of unsubstantiated cases, often involving disgruntled workers seeking to blackmail or discredit their employers.

When is an employee morally justified in blowing the whistle on his or her employer? According to one expert, four main conditions must be satisfied to justify informing the media or government officials about a corporation's actions. These are

- The organization is doing (or will do) something that seriously harms others.
- The employee has tried and failed to resolve the problem internally.
- Reporting the problem publicly will probably stop or prevent the harm.
- The harm is serious enough to justify the probable costs of disclosure to the whistle-blower and others.[40]

Only after each of these conditions has been met should the whistle-blower go public.

Employees as Corporate Stakeholders

The issues discussed in this chapter illustrate forcefully that today's business corporation is open to a wide range of social forces. Its borders are very porous, letting in a constant flow of external influences. Many are brought inside by employees, whose personal values, lifestyles, and social attitudes become a vital part of the workplace.

Managers and other business professionals need to be aware of these employee-imported features of today's workforce. The employment relationship is central both to getting a corporation's work done and to helping satisfy the aspirations of those who contribute their skills and talents to the company.

---

[38] "How Risperdal Whistle-Blowers Made Millions From J&J," *BloombergBusiness,* December 9, 2013; and "J&J to Pay $2.2 Billion in Risperdal Settlement," *The New York Times,* November 4, 2013.

[39] U.S. Department of Justice statistics, summarized at the website of Taxpayers against Fraud, *www.taf.org.*

[40] Manuel G. Velasquez, *Business Ethics: Concepts and Cases,* 7th ed. (Upper Saddle River, NJ: 2012), p. 430.

Summary

- U.S. labor laws give most workers the right to organize unions and to bargain collectively with their employers. Although unions have weakened over time, they continue to represent workers in some parts of the economy, particularly in the public sector.

- Job safety and health concerns have increased as a result of rapidly changing technology in the workplace. U.S. employers must comply with expanding OSHA regulations and respond to the threat of violence at work.

- Employers' right to discharge "at will" has been limited, and employees now have a number of bases for suing for wrongful discharge. The expectations of both sides in the employment relationship have been altered over time by globalization, business cycles, and other factors.

- Corporate wage policies contribute to growing income inequality. Pursuing a high-wage "good jobs" strategy can benefit a company through high productivity, strong customer service, and innovation.

- Employees' privacy rights are frequently challenged by employers' needs to have information about their health, their work activities, and even their off-the-job lifestyles. When these issues arise, management has a responsibility to act ethically toward employees while continuing to work for a high level of economic performance.

- Blowing the whistle on one's employer is often a last resort to protest company actions considered harmful to others. In recent years, U.S. legislation has extended new protections to whistle-blowers.

Key Terms

drug testing, *339*
electronic monitoring, *337*
employee assistance programs (EAPs), *340*
employment-at-will, *332*
ergonomics, *330*

honesty tests, *341*
labor union, *328*
living wage, *336*
Occupational Safety and Health Administration (OSHA), *330*

privacy rights, *336*
social contract, *332*
whistle-blowing, *342*

Internet Resources

www.drugfreeworkplace.org	Institute for a Drug-Free Workplace
www.osha.gov	Occupational Safety and Health Administration
www.whistleblowers.org	National Whistleblowers Center
www.aclu.org	American Civil Liberties Union
www.afl-cio.org	American Federation of Labor-Congress of Industrial Organizations
www.workrights.org	National Workrights Institute
www.business.com/human-resources	Business.com (human resources topics)
www.ethicaltrade.org	Ethical Trading Initiative

Discussion Case: *The Ugly Side of Beautiful Nails*

For many people, going to a nail salon for a manicure or pedicure is a small, affordable luxury and a pleasant way to relax. For workers in these salons, however, the story is often

less glamorous: low pay, abusive working conditions, and constant exposure to dangerous chemicals that threaten to ruin their health.

In 2015, nail care was riding a wave of popularity. Women (and some men) spent more than $8 billion a year on nail care at around 200,000 nail salons across the nation. The publisher of the magazine *Nails* explained the phenomenon this way: "Nail care isn't just about grooming anymore; it's self-expression. Just as tattoos have become mainstream, nail art has too." Technical innovations such as gel polishes, which lasted longer and were easier to remove, also drove the trend. For most customers, the price of the service—averaging less than $20 for a manicure—was easy to fit into their budgets.

Who were the manicurists and pedicurists laboring over all these hands and feet? According to *Nails*, 380,000 people worked in nail salons in the United States in 2014. Ninety-four percent were women. Over half were Vietnamese, although ethnicity varied by location; in New York City, for example, Koreans dominated the industry. Many workers had limited English proficiency, and a significant proportion were undocumented immigrants.

Wages were very low. According to government data, the median annual wage for a manicurist was $19,620. Only a quarter of the 100 workers interviewed by a reporter for *The New York Times* said they had been paid the equivalent of the state minimum wage. The *Times'* exposé also reported that sometimes workers were not paid at all; many new workers were required to pay a so-called training fee and to work without wages during an apprenticeship period. Overtime pay was "almost unheard-of," the newspaper found, even though long work days and weeks were commonplace. *Nails* magazine reported that more than a fifth of nail salon workers' income came from tips, which relied entirely on the goodwill of customers.

Most salons were small. Barriers to entry were low: an operator could set up business by renting a storefront and investing a few thousand dollars in furnishings, equipment, and supplies. Eighty-one percent of manicurists and pedicurists worked in a shop with three or fewer technicians. The industry was highly competitive, and salons went in and out of business frequently.

Nail technicians worked with polishes, solvents, hardeners, and glues that caused respiratory and skin ailments, reproductive harm, and even cancer. Although occupational health in nail salons had not been fully studied, the three most dangerous chemicals used there were believed to be toluene (which made polish glide on smoothly), dibutyl phthalate (which made it pliable), and formaldehyde (which hardened it). Workers also inhaled acrylic dust; acquired fungal infections from customers' hands and feet; and injured their backs, necks, and shoulders from constant repetitive motion. *Nails* reported that more than half of nail technicians said they suffered from a work-related ailment.

The Occupational Safety and Health Administration set standards for workplace exposure to many of the chemicals used in nail salons, and urged workers to wear protective gear like gloves and masks and to properly ventilate their salons. States also set safety and health rules. But as a practical matter these rules were routinely ignored, and inspections were conducted only in response to specific complaints.

In New York, in the wake of the exposé published by *The New York Times,* officials rushed to assemble a task force to address conditions in the industry and said they would post a manicurist's "bill of rights" in 10 languages in every salon, describing minimum wage laws and required safety measures. "We will not stand idly by as workers are deprived of their hard-earned wages and robbed of their most basic rights," said the governor of New York. But it was unclear how much impact these measures would have. One official observed that manicurists were particularly reluctant to cooperate with investigators, saying, "They are totally running scared in this industry."

Sources: "The Price of Nice Nails," *The New York Times,* May 7, 2015; "Perfect Nails, Poisoned Workers," *The New York Times,* May 8, 2015; "Cuomo Orders Emergency Measures to Protect Workers at Nail Salons," *The New York Times,* May 11, 2015; "New York Salons Now Required to Post Workers' Bill of Rights," *The New York Times,* May 29, 2015; California Health Nail Salon Collaborative, *Overexposed and Underinformed: Dismantling Barriers to Health and Safety in California Nail Salons* (April 2009); and *2014–2015 Nails Big Book,* at *http://files.nailsmag.com/site/NAILS-Magazine-Big-Book-2014.pdf.* Wage data are from the Bureau of Labor Statistics at *www.bls.gov.*

Discussion Questions

1. This section describes several "workplace rights." Which of these rights are violated in the nail salon industry, and what evidence do you have of this?
2. To what degree do you think managers in the nail salon industry would be able to improve conditions voluntarily if they wished to do so, and why do you think so?
3. What factors make it particularly difficult for workers in the nail industry to organize to improve their own conditions, and how could these factors be overcome?
4. What factors make it particularly difficult for government policy makers and regulators to make rules for the nail industry and enforce them? How could these factors be overcome?
5. What do you think is the best way to improve conditions for workers in the nail industry?

Managing a Diverse Workforce

The workforce in the United States is more diverse than it has ever been, reflecting the entry of women into the workforce, immigration from other countries, the aging of the population, and shifting patterns of work and retirement. Equal opportunity laws and changing societal expectations have challenged corporations to manage workforce diversity effectively. Full workplace parity for women and persons of color has not yet been reached. However, businesses have made great strides in reforming policies and practices in order to draw on the skills and contributions of their increasingly varied employees.

This Chapter Focuses on These Key Learning Objectives:

LO 16-1 Knowing in what ways the workforce of the United States is diverse and evaluating how it might change in the future.

LO 16-2 Understanding where women and persons of color work, how much they are paid, and the roles they play as managers and business owners.

LO 16-3 Identifying the role government plays in securing equal employment opportunity for historically disadvantaged groups and debating whether or not affirmative action is an effective strategy for promoting equal opportunity.

LO 16-4 Assessing the ways diversity confers a competitive advantage.

LO 16-5 Formulating how companies can best manage workforce diversity, making the workplace welcoming, fair, and accommodating to all employees.

LO 16-6 Understanding what corporate policies and practices are most effective in helping today's employees manage the complex, multiple demands of work and family obligations.

Marriott International, the global hospitality chain, employs 360,000 workers in 79 countries, doing jobs ranging from managing vacation resorts, to flipping burgers, to cleaning bathrooms and changing sheets. Their employees speak more than 50 different languages and represent dozens of distinct cultures. Many of Marriott's employees in the United States are immigrants, some are in welfare-to-work programs, and many are single parents. In an effort to address its employees' needs, Marriott established a Committee for Excellence—an external board of experts—to set diversity objectives and monitor progress. Among other initiatives, the company provided consultations on a wide range of personal issues, offered child care services, and operated *Sed de Saber* (thirst for knowledge) to teach life skills to Spanish-speaking employees. It recently initiated a goal to double the number of hotels in the chain owned by women and minorities. Marriott credited its innovative diversity programs with helping it attract and retain committed employees from many backgrounds. "We strive to create an inclusive environment," said senior diversity executive David Rodriguez. "When our associates feel respected and valued, we know that they'll make our guests, suppliers, owners, and franchisees feel the same way too."[1]

The example of Marriott Corporation demonstrates both the promise and the perils of a workforce that encompasses tremendous diversity on every imaginable dimension. Having many different kinds of workers can be a great benefit to businesses, as it gives them a wider pool from which to recruit talent, many points of view and experiences, and an ability to reach out effectively to a diverse, global customer base. Yet, it also poses great challenges, as businesses must meet the mandates of equal employment laws and help people who differ greatly in their backgrounds, values, and expectations get along—and succeed—in the workplace.

The Changing Face of the Workforce

Human beings differ from each other in many ways. Each person is unique, as is each employee within an organization. Individuals are also similar in many ways, some of which are more readily visible than others. The term **diversity** refers to variation in the important human characteristics that distinguish people from one another. The *primary* dimensions of diversity are age, ethnicity, gender, mental or physical abilities, race, and sexual orientation. The *secondary* dimensions of diversity are many; they include such characteristics as communication style, ways of thinking and interacting, family status, and first language. Individuals' distinguishing characteristics clearly impact their values, opportunities, and perceptions of themselves and others at work. **Workforce diversity**—diversity among employees—thus represents both a challenge and an opportunity for businesses.

Today, the U.S. workforce is as diverse as it has ever been, and it is becoming even more so. Consider the following major trends:[2]

- *Immigration has profoundly reshaped the workplace.* Between 2000 and 2010, nearly 14 million immigrants entered the United States, making it the highest decade of immigration in U.S. history; by 2023, more than one in seven residents are expected to be foreign-born. The leading countries of origin are now Mexico, China (including Hong Kong and Taiwan), India, the Philippines, Vietnam, El Salvador, Cuba, and Korea.

---

[1] "Marriott Doubles Down on Diversity Commitment," *Washington Business Journal,* October 2, 2014. More information about Marriott's diversity programs is available at *www.marriott.com/diversity.*

[2] Except as noted, the figures in the following paragraphs are drawn from "Labor Force Projections to 2020: A More Slowly Growing Workforce," *Monthly Labor Review,* January 2012, and *Statistical Abstract of the United States 2012* (Washington, DC: U.S. Census Bureau).

In a recent shift, Asians have surpassed Hispanics as the largest group of immigrants overall. Immigrants now make up almost 17 percent of U.S. workers, increasing linguistic and cultural diversity in many workplaces. Although immigrants live in all states, they are concentrated in the West and the South.[3] The discussion case at the end of this chapter focuses on how businesses and government have addressed the special issue of **undocumented immigrant workers** (noncitizens working without the legally required documents)—who now make up 5 percent of the U.S. workforce.

- *Ethnic and racial diversity is increasing.* Hispanics (defined by the Census as persons of Spanish or Latin American ancestry), now about 16 percent of U.S. workers, are expected to comprise more than 19 percent by 2022. Although less numerous than Hispanics overall (6 percent of workers), Asians are now the fastest-growing segment of the labor force. The proportion of African Americans is expected to hold steady at around 12 percent. By 2022, the U.S. workforce is projected to be about 39 percent nonwhite (this category includes persons of Hispanic origin). In some states, such as California, these trends will be much more pronounced.[4]

- *The workforce will continue to get older.* As the baby boom generation matures, birth rates drop, and people live longer and healthier lives, the population will age. Many of these older people will continue to work, whether out of choice or necessity. After the Great Recession, many older workers postponed retirement—or even re-entered the workforce—to recoup losses in their savings and home values. Said one 67-year-old utility company employee, "I felt that I was in a good position to retire until the market kept going down and down . . . [But] there's no point in retiring in this time of uncertainty until I have a better feel for where the economy is going." Between 2006 and 2016, the number of persons aged 65 to 74 who are still working is expected to jump 84 percent. Employers will have to find new ways to accommodate older workers.[5]

- *Millennials are entering the workforce.* Even as many baby boomers extend their working years, so-called *millennials*—young people born in the 1980s and 1990s and reaching adulthood around the turn of the century—are entering the workforce in large numbers, bringing fresh perspectives and practices. In 2015, millennials became the largest generation in the U.S. workforce, and more than a quarter say they are already in management positions. A survey of hiring managers reported they thought millennials were quick learners and more technologically adept than their seniors. But they also found millennials to be narcissistic (self-centered) and said it was hard to retain them. More than half of millennials themselves said they expected to stay in their jobs fewer than 3 years. "I believe that younger generations . . . will [have] less long-term commitment to organizations," said one Japanese millennial.[6]

Workforce diversity creates many new employee issues and problems. This chapter will consider the changing face of today's workplace, and its implications for management.

---

[3] "Center for Immigration Studies, "Immigrant Population to Hit Highest Percentage Ever in 8 Years," Center for Immigration Studies, April 2015; "Facts About Immigration Today," October 23, 2014, at *www.americanprogress.org;* "In a Shift, Biggest Wave of Migrants is Now Asian," *The New York Times,* June 18, 2012; "A Record-Setting Decade of Immigration: 2000–2010," Center for Immigration Studies, October 2011, *www.cis.org;* and U.S. Bureau of Labor Statistics, "Labor Force Characteristics of Foreign-Born Workers Summary," May 21, 2015, at *www.bls.gov.*

[4] U.S. Bureau of Labor Statistics, *Monthly Labor Review,* "Labor Force Projections to 2022," December 2013.

[5] "39 Ways the American Workforce is Dramatically Changing in 2015," *Business Insider,* June 4, 2015; and Towers Watson, "Workers Still Uneasy About Financial Security and Retirement," March 2014.

[6] "Hiring Managers Say Millennials Surpass Prior Generations in Several Key Business Skills, New Study Reveals," October 29, 2014, at *www.upwork.com;* and Pricewaterhouse Cooper, "Millennials at Work: Reshaping the Workplace," 2011.

Laws and regulations clearly require that businesses provide equal opportunity, and avoid discrimination and harassment. How to meet—and exceed—these mandates presents an ongoing challenge to businesses seeking to reap the benefits of a well-integrated, yet culturally diverse work population. We turn first to two important dimensions of workforce diversity: gender and race.

Gender and Race in the Workplace

Gender and race are both important primary dimensions of workforce diversity. Women and persons of color have always worked, contributing both paid and unpaid labor to the economy. Yet, the nature of their participation in the labor force has changed, posing new challenges to business.

Women and Minorities at Work

One of the most significant changes in the past six decades has been the growing labor force participation of women. During the period following World War II, the proportion of women working outside the home rose dramatically. In 1950, about a third of adult women were employed. This proportion rose steadily for several decades; it peaked at 59 percent in 1999, stabilized for a few years, and then fell slightly to 57 percent in 2013. Analysts of recent pullbacks in women's labor force participation have pointed to a lack of family-friendly policies, which have made it far more difficult for mothers to work.[7] (These policies will be discussed later in this chapter.) Men's participation rates declined during this period; between 1950 and 2013, the proportion of adult men who worked fell from 86 percent to slightly less than 70 percent—with a particularly sharp drop as a result of the recession of 2008–09, from which many men have not recovered. Figure 16.1 shows the convergence of the labor force participation rates for men and women over the past six decades.

Labor force participation rates for minorities, unlike those of women, have always been high. For example, in 1970 about 62 percent of all African Americans (men and women combined) worked; the proportion is almost the same today. Participation rates have also been consistently high for most other minority groups; for Asians, it is 65 percent; for Hispanics, 66 percent. The key change here has been the move of persons of color, in recent decades, into a wider range of jobs as barriers of discrimination and segregation have fallen; minorities have become better represented in the ranks of managers, professionals, and the skilled trades. These trends will be further discussed later in this chapter.

The face of success in the United States is diverse, just as the workforce is. Consider Indra Nooyi, chairman and CEO of PepsiCo. Nooyi was born in Madras, India, and was educated at the Indian Institute of Management in Calcutta. In India, she held management positions in the pharmaceutical and textile industries before immigrating to the United States to attend the Yale School of Management. She joined PepsiCo in 1994, where she moved up quickly and became president and CEO in 2001. *Fortune Magazine* named Nooyi the third most powerful woman in business in 2014 (behind Ginni Rometty of IBM and Mary Barra, the CEO of General Motors). Speaking of the talents women bring to the executive suite, Nooyi joked in an interview, "If the Three Wise Men had happened to be women, they

---

[7] "Why U.S. Women Are Leaving Jobs Behind," *The New York Times,* December 12, 2014.

FIGURE 16.1
Proportion of Women and Men in the Labor Force, 1950–2013

Source: U.S. Bureau of Labor Statistics, *Women in the Labor Force: A Databook* (December 2014).

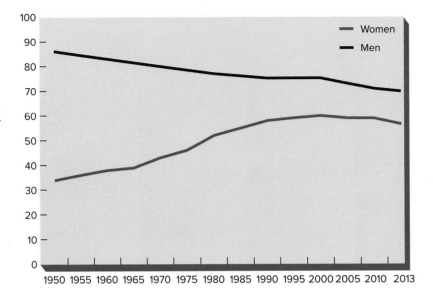

would have stopped and asked for directions, arrived at the stable on time, helped deliver the baby, cleaned up the stable after, made a casserole, brought practical gifts and there would have been peace on Earth."[8]

The Gender and Racial Pay Gap

One persistent feature of the working world is that women and persons of color on average receive lower pay than white men do. This disparity, called the **pay gap**, narrowed over the past quarter century, as Figure 16.2 shows. But in 2013 black men still earned only slightly more than three-quarters of white men's pay; black women earned about 69 percent, and white women 82 percent. (These data are based on full-time workers only.) The pay gap for both Hispanic women and men declined by about 5 percent since 2000. The one group that tops white men in median weekly earnings is Asian American men; they make about 20 percent more, on average. (Asian American women make 93 percent of what white men earn.) An important reason is education; almost half of Asian American adults hold a bachelor's degree or above, far more schooling than any other ethnic or racial group.[9]

Experts disagree about the cause of the pay gap between women and men. Some believe the continuing gender disparity in pay is evidence of sex discrimination by employers; others believe the gap reflects women's choices to pursue lower-paying jobs or slower advancement because of time off for family responsibilities. Many observers agree, however, that the pay gap persists, in part, because of what is called **occupational segregation**. This term refers to the inequitable concentration of a group, such a minorities or women, in particular job categories. The large pay gap for Hispanic workers, for example, partly reflects their concentration in several low-paid occupations. Fifty-five percent of drywall installers, 45 percent of grounds maintenance workers, 50 percent of agricultural workers, and 44 percent of private household cleaners are of Hispanic origin, according to government

[8] "Most Powerful Women 2014," at *www.fortune.com;* and "Indra Nooyi on How to Find Your Voice," *Good Housekeeping* (2011), *www.goodhousekeeping.com.*

[9] Pew Research Center, "The Rise of Asian Americans," April 4, 2013.

FIGURE 16.2 The Gender and Race Pay Gap, 1990–2013 (median weekly earnings of full-time workers, as a percentage of those of white men)

Source: U.S. Bureau of Labor Statistics, *Labor Force Characteristics by Race and Ethnicity, 2013,* August 2014, Table 16; U.S. Census Bureau, *Statistical Abstract of the United States 2009,* Table 626; and *Statistical Abstract of the United States 2000,* Table 696.

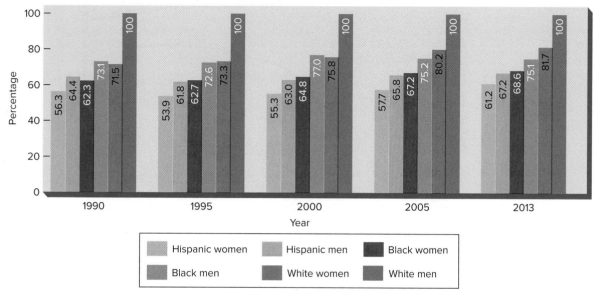

data, although Hispanics make up only 16 percent of the workforce as a whole. Although women, for their part, have made great strides in entering occupations where they were formerly underrepresented, many remain concentrated in a few sex-typed jobs that some have called the "pink-collar ghetto." Women still make up 98 percent of preschool and kindergarten teachers, 95 percent of hairdressers, and 98 percent of dental hygienists, for example. Eliminating the pay gap will require, therefore, business programs and government policies that create opportunity for women and people of color to move out of more segregated jobs into ones where the pay and chances for upward mobility are greater.[10]

Occupational segregation is common in other societies, as well. In the United Kingdom, the government's Equality and Human Rights Commission found continuing high levels of labor market segmentation. In its triennial report, "How Fair Is Britain?" the Commission reported that a quarter of all Pakistani men in Britain worked as taxi drivers, and women made up 77 percent of secretaries but just 6 percent of engineers. Persons of Indian and Chinese descent were twice as likely to work as professionals as whites in Britain, the study found.[11]

One study found that even after taking into consideration differences in education, experience, race, industry, and occupation, women still earned 5 to 7 percent less than they otherwise would have—presumably the remaining effect of outright gender discrimination.[12]

---

[10] The data in this paragraph are drawn from two reports by the U.S. Bureau of Labor Statistics, *Labor Force Characteristics by Race and Ethnicity, 2013* (August 2014)*; and Women in the Labor Force: A Databook* (December 2014).

[11] U.K. Equality and Human Rights Commission, "How Fair Is Britain? The First Triennial Review 2010," *www.equality humanrights.com.*

[12] "Shortchanged: Why Women Get Paid Less Than Men," *Bloomberg Businessweek,* June 21, 2012. Data are from "An Analysis of Reasons for the Disparity in Wages Between Men and Women," prepared for the U.S. Department of Labor by CONSAD Research Corp., January 12, 2009.

Exhibit 16.A

The Dearth of Diversity in High-Tech Firms

One of the sectors of the economy where women and minorities are grossly underrepresented is the fast-moving world of high-tech—despite a few high-profile exceptions such as Marissa Mayer of Yahoo! and Sheryl Sandberg of Facebook. After years of pressure from journalists and activists, some high-technology firms began releasing workforce statistics and they revealed a striking dearth of diversity. At Facebook, 55 percent of employees were white and 36 percent Asian; only 4 percent were Hispanic and 2 percent African American. Men made up 68 percent of all employees (and 84 percent in technical positions). The story was similar at Google (91 percent white or Asian; 70 percent male) and Twitter (88 percent white or Asian; 70 percent male). Pinterest had a similar racial and ethnic profile, but employed a higher proportion of women (40 percent), perhaps reflecting the fact that its user base was mostly female. A number of these companies pointed to a lack of diversity in the pipeline of qualified women and minorities in technology-related fields, and they cited their efforts to support computer science education and broaden their recruitment networks. But others said they had not gone far enough. "Facebook and other tech companies must go beyond aspiring to do better and set measurable goals, targets and timetables to move the needle in diversity and inclusion," said the Reverend Jesse Jackson, president of the Rainbow/PUSH Coalition.

Sources: "Behind Silicon Valley's Self-Critical Tone on Diversity, A Lack of Progress," *The New York Times,* June 28, 2015; "Driving Diversity at Facebook," press release, June 25, 2015; "Getting to Work on Diversity at Google," May 28, 2014, at *http:// googleblog.blogspot.com;* "Building a Twitter We Can Be Proud Of," July 23, 2014, at *http://blog.twitter.com;* and "Diversity and Inclusion at Pinterest," July 24, 2014, at *http://engineering.pinterest.com.*

One area of the economy where racial and gender discrimination seems stubbornly persistent is high technology. The challenges faced by minorities and women in the world of high tech is profiled in Exhibit 16.A.

The most prestigious and highest-paying jobs in a corporation are in top management. Because most corporations are organized hierarchically, management jobs—particularly those at the top—are few. For that reason, only a small fraction of workers, of whatever gender or race, can hope to reach the upper levels in the business world. White men have traditionally filled most of these desirable spots. Business's mandate now is to broaden these high-level leadership opportunities for women and persons of color, a topic to which we turn next.

Where Women and Persons of Color Manage

Slightly more than 9 million U.S. women were working as managers by the mid-2010s. As Figure 16.3 reveals, in 2013 more than 4 out of 10 managers—and a majority of managers in some categories—were women. Clearly, women have broken into management ranks. Women are more likely to be managers, though, in occupational areas where women are more numerous at lower levels, such as health care and education. Grouped by industry, women tend to be concentrated in service industries and in finance, insurance, real estate, and retail businesses. Women managers have also made gains in newer industries, such as biotechnology, where growth has created opportunity.

Where do persons of color manage? As is shown in Figure 16.3, African Americans and Hispanics are underrepresented in management ranks in the United States, making up just 8.5 and 8.3 percent of managers, respectively. But they have approached or exceeded parity in a few areas. Blacks make up 13.4 percent of educational administrators (more than their 11.2 percent of the workforce), for example. Hispanics are best represented in food service management. By contrast, Asians are somewhat overrepresented in management ranks, particularly in the field of information systems. Figure 16.3 shows the patterns of diversity by gender, race, and ethnicity in various management categories.

FIGURE 16.3
Extent of Diversity in Selected Management Occupations

Sources: U.S. Bureau of Labor Statistics, *Women in the Labor Force: A Databook,* December 2014; and *Labor Force Characteristics by Race and Ethnicity 2013,* August 2014.

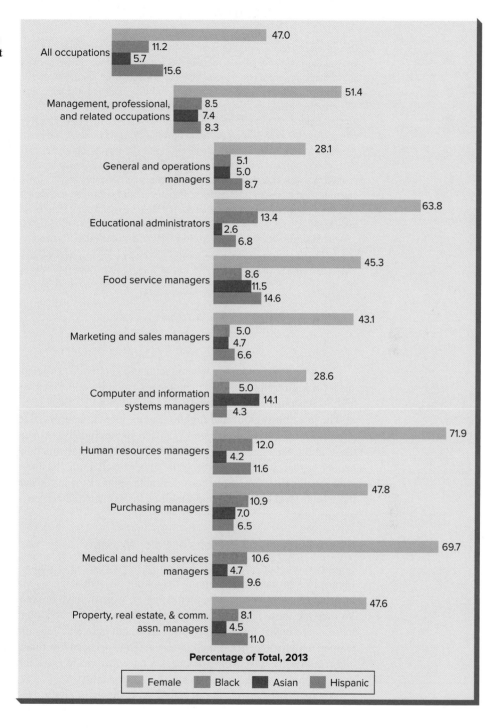

Breaking the Glass Ceiling

A few exceptional women and persons of color—and some women of color—have reached the pinnacles of power in corporate America.

In 2015, the chairman and CEO of Xerox Corporation was Ursula Burns, the first African American woman to lead a major U.S. company. (She was also the first

woman CEO to succeed another woman, Anne Mulcahy, who stepped down to become the chairman of the board in 2009.) Burns, who had been raised in a New York City housing project by a single mother, had gone on to earn a graduate degree in mechanical engineering at Columbia. She was recognized early in her career for extraordinary potential, and had worked her way up at Xerox through a series of increasingly responsible positions. When appointed CEO, Burns commented, "I'm in this job because I believe I earned it through hard work and high performance."[13]

High achievers such as Ursula Burns and Indra Nooyi remain unusual, however. Although women and minorities are as competent as white men in managing people and organizations, they rarely attain the highest positions in corporations. Their ascent seems to be blocked by an invisible barrier, sometimes called a **glass ceiling**. According to Catalyst, an advocacy organization for female executives, in 2015 women held 23 (slightly under 5 percent) of CEO positions at S&P 500 companies.[14] That same year, persons of color held 25 (25 percent) of CEO positions at *Fortune 500* companies. The latter group included Kenneth Chenault of American Express, George Paz of Express Scripts, and Ajaypal Banga of MasterCard.[15] (The *S&P 500* and *Fortune 500* are both lists of large companies and have considerable overlap, but the latter includes private as well as public companies.) In Europe, diversity in top executive ranks is also rare.

Another key measure of diversity is the representation of women on corporate boards. Worldwide, women held 17 percent of directorships in 2014, according to a global survey by MSCI.[16] This number, however, obscures significant variations among nations, as shown in Figure 16.4.

What explains the sharp differences in board diversity shown in Figure 16.4? A key factor is that several nations in Europe have passed laws that set quotas for women's representation on boards of directors. Most recently, in 2015 Germany required companies to give 30 percent of board seats to women, joining Norway, Spain, France, Iceland (with 40 percent quotas), Italy (one-third), and Belgium (30 percent). "The proof is in the pudding: regulatory pressure works," said the European Union's justice commissioner, a leader in the campaign for gender parity.[17] In the United States and the United Kingdom, where similar legislation was unlikely, some institutional investors had started pressuring companies to appoint more women and minorities to directorships.[18]

Although research on the effects of board diversity on performance has yielded mixed results, a 2014 study by MSCI, an investment research firm, found that companies with a higher proportion of women on their boards were less likely to be involved in corruption and earned higher scores for management of carbon emissions, toxic releases, water, labor, and health and safety issues than other firms.[19] Another recent study found that adding even a single woman to a board of directors improved corporate governance practices, with a particularly strong effect in traditionally male-dominated industries like mining and energy.[20] Why would adding women to boards improve performance? A recent literature

---

[13] "An Historic Succession at Xerox," *BusinessWeek,* June 8, 2009.

[14] "Women CEOs of the S&P 500," April 3, 2015, at *www.catalyst.org.*

[15] "Why Top 50 Companies Beat *Fortune* 500 in Diversity Recruiting, Promotions," *DiversityINC,* posted April 23, 2015.

[16] MSCI Inc., *Governance Issue Report: 2014 Survey of Women on Boards,* November 2014, *www.msci.com.*

[17] "Germany Sets Gender Quota in Boardrooms," *The New York Times,* March 6, 2015 and "Push for Gender Balance on Boards Gains Steam," *The New York Times,* January 24, 2013.

[18] "Women Still Hold Only 19 Percent of U.S. Board Seats. What Could Change That?" *The Washington Post,* January 13, 2015.

[19] MSCI, "Governance Issue Report: 2014 Survey of Women on Boards," November 2014.

[20] Judith Zaichkowsky, "Women in the Board Room: One Can Make a Difference," *International Journal of Business Governance and Ethics,* 9(1): 2014.

FIGURE 16.4
Women as a Percentage of Members of Boards of Directors, Selected Countries, 2014

Source: *2014 Catalyst Census: Women Board Directors.* Data are as of October 2014. Used by permission.

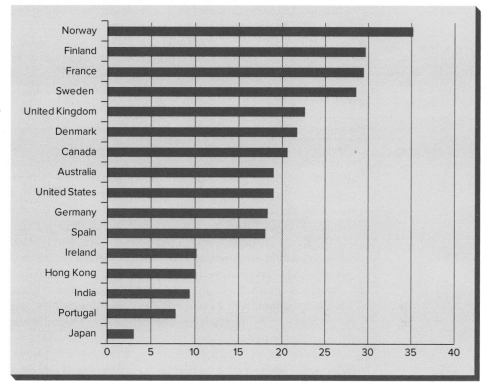

Women's Percentage Share of Board Seats, Selected Countries

review found that more gender-diverse boards were more likely to avoid a rush to consensus and realistically consider alternative courses of action. Women brought different life experiences to the table and were more likely to raise multiple stakeholder concerns. Having more diverse boards also signaled to the public a company's commitment to diversity and inclusion.[21]

What continues to hold women and minorities back—in the executive suite and on boards of directors? A study in the *Harvard Business Review* reported that one primary obstacle is **glass walls**: fewer opportunities to move sideways into jobs that lead to the top. Female and minority managers are often found in staff positions, such as public relations or human resources, rather than in line positions in such core areas as marketing, sales, or production where they can acquire the broad management skills necessary for promotion.[22] Another problem is that in filling top positions, recruiters rely on word-of-mouth—the old boys' network from which women and persons of color are often excluded. Sometimes women voluntarily choose to step off the career track to care for children or elderly relatives. Other causes include a company's lack of commitment to diversity and too little accountability at the top management level for equal employment opportunity. However, recent advances by both women and minorities in the executive suite suggest that the glass ceiling may finally be cracking.

[21] The Conference Board, "Diversity on Corporate Boards: How Much Difference Does Difference Make?" February 2015.
[22] "What's Holding Women Back?" *Harvard Business Review,* June 1, 2003. The reports of the Glass Ceiling Commission of the U.S. Department of Labor may be accessed at *www.dol.gov/oasam/programs/history/reich/reports/ceiling.pdf.*

Women and Minority Business Ownership

Some women and minorities have evaded the glass ceiling and risen to the top by founding or taking over their own businesses. By the mid-2010s, of the 28 million small businesses in the United States, 36 percent were owned by women, and 15 percent were owned by minorities, according to the Small Business Administration.[23]

> An example of a successful female entrepreneur of color is Tina Wells, who founded the Buzz Marketing Group in 1996 when she was still a teenager to help companies market successfully to young people. Today, the company uses social media and trend-spotting on behalf of many companies, including Nike, Steve Madden, SonyBMG, Procter & Gamble, and American Eagle Outfitters. Wells, who is black, is also the author of several children's books and *Chasing Youth Culture and Getting It Right* and blogs for the Huffington Post. She told an interviewer that technology had been critical to the success of her business. "I have the world at the touch of my smartphone," Wells explained. "I can talk to thousands of millennials in our buzzSpotter network where they are the most: online!"[24]

Among minority-owned firms active in the mid-2010s, Hispanic-owned businesses were the most numerous, followed by African American and Asian-owned businesses.[25] Immigrants were responsible for a good share of the entrepreneurial spirit in the minority community. Immigrants are more likely to start a business than are nonimmigrants; over the past two decades, they have been responsible for 30 percent of small business growth.[26]

Government's Role in Securing Equal Employment Opportunity

Eliminating workplace discrimination and ensuring equal job opportunity has been a major goal of public policy in the United States for four decades. This section reviews the major laws that govern business practices with respect to equal opportunity, affirmative action, and sexual and racial harassment.

Equal Employment Opportunity

Beginning on a major scale in the 1960s, U.S. presidents issued executive orders and Congress enacted laws intended to promote equal treatment of employees—that is, **equal employment opportunity**. These government rules apply to most businesses in the following ways:

- Discrimination based on race, color, religion, sex, national origin, physical or mental disability, or age is prohibited in all employment practices. This includes hiring, promotion, job classification and assignment, compensation, and other conditions of work. (Discrimination based on sexual orientation and gender identity is not prohibited by federal law, although it is prohibited by some state laws.)
- Government contractors must have written affirmative action plans detailing how they are working positively to overcome past and present effects of discrimination in their

---

[23] U.S. Small Business Administration, "Frequently Asked Questions About Small Businesses," March 2014.

[24] "25 Inspiring Black Women Entrepreneurs," *Essence,* March 5, 2012; and "Tina Wells, Founder & CEO, Buzz Marketing Group: Technology Enables Me to Keep in Touch with Thousands of Teens Across the Globe," *The Next Women Business Magazine,* January 5, 2012. A profile of Tina Wells may be found at *www.huffingtonpost.com/tina-wells.*

[25] U.S. Census Bureau, "Survey of Business Owners: Company Summary: 2007," *www.census.gov.*

[26] Fiscal Policy Institute, "Immigrant Small Business Owners: A Significant and Growing Part of the Economy," June 2012.

FIGURE 16.5
Major Federal Laws and One Executive Order Prohibiting Job Discrimination

Equal Pay Act (1963)—Mandates equal pay for substantially equal work by men and women.

Civil Rights Act (1964; amended 1972, 1991, 2009)—Prohibits discrimination in employment based on race, color, religion, sex, or national origin.

Executive Order 11246 (1965)—Mandates affirmative action for all federal contractors and subcontractors.

Age Discrimination in Employment Act (1967)—Protects individuals who are 40 years of age or older.

Equal Employment Opportunity Act (1972)—Increases power of the Equal Employment Opportunity Commission to combat discrimination.

Pregnancy Discrimination Act (1978)—Forbids employers to discharge, fail to hire, or otherwise discriminate against pregnant women.

Americans with Disabilities Act (1990)—Prohibits discrimination against individuals with disabilities.

Family and Medical Leave Act (1993)—Requires companies with 50 or more employees to provide up to 12 weeks unpaid leave for illness, care of a sick family member, or the birth or adoption of a child.

Genetic Information Nondiscrimination Act (2008)—Prohibits the use of genetic information in employment decisions.

Lilly Ledbetter Fair Pay Act (2009)—Eliminates certain time restrictions for filling pay discrimination lawsuits.

workforce. However, affirmative action plans must be temporary and flexible, designed to correct past discrimination, and cannot result in reverse discrimination against whites or men.

- Women and men must receive equal pay for performing equal work, and employers may not discriminate on the basis of pregnancy.

Figure 16.5 outlines the major laws and one executive order that are intended to promote equal opportunity in the workplace. The major agency charged with enforcing equal employment opportunity laws and executive orders in the United States is the **Equal Employment Opportunity Commission (EEOC)**. The EEOC was created in 1964 and given added enforcement powers in 1972 and 1990.

Companies that fail to follow the laws shown in Figure 16.5 often find themselves facing expensive lawsuits. One that threatened an enormous payout was dismissed by the nation's high court in 2011.

> The Supreme Court ruled in a 5–4 vote against the plaintiffs in a huge class action sex discrimination lawsuit against Walmart—the largest ever brought in the United States. The women who brought the suit claimed that female employees at Walmart were paid less than men in comparable positions, in spite of having greater seniority and equal or better qualifications. They also charged that women received fewer promotions to store management positions and waited longer to move up than men did. The court did not decide whether or not Walmart had discriminated against the specific plaintiffs. Rather, it ruled that the case could not move forward as a class action, because Walmart had not "operated under a general policy of discrimination." If the class action suit had prevailed, Walmart could have been required to pay hundreds of millions of dollars to current and past female employees.[27]

Potentially costly lawsuits can involve other forms of discrimination as well, such as those based on age, race, or disability.

[27] "Justices Rule for Wal-Mart in Class-Action Bias Case," *The New York Times,* June 20, 2011.

Affirmative Action

One way to promote equal opportunity and remedy past discrimination is through **affirmative action**. Since the mid-1960s, major government contractors have been required by presidential executive order to adopt written affirmative action plans specifying goals, actions, and timetables for promoting greater on-the-job equality. Their purpose is to reduce job discrimination by encouraging companies to take positive (that is, affirmative) steps to overcome past employment practices and traditions that may have been discriminatory.

Affirmative action has long been controversial. Some states have passed laws banning or limiting affirmative action programs in public hiring and university admissions, and the issue has been debated in Congress and in the courts. In 2015, the U.S. Supreme court agreed to hear a case involving racial preferences at the University of Texas, brought by a white student who had been denied admission.[28] Backers of affirmative action argued that these programs provided an important tool for achieving equal opportunity. In this view, women and minorities continued to face discriminatory barriers and affirmative action was necessary to level the playing field. Some large corporations backed affirmative action programs, finding them helpful in monitoring their progress in providing equal job opportunity. General Electric, AT&T, and IBM, for example, have said that they would continue to use affirmative action goals and timetables even if they were not required by law.

Critics, however, argued that affirmative action was inconsistent with the principles of fairness and equality. In some cases, one group could be unintentionally discriminated against in an effort to help another group. For example, if a more qualified white man were passed over for a job as a police officer in favor of a less qualified Hispanic man to remedy past discrimination in a police department, this might be unfair to the white candidate.

> In 2009, the Supreme Court heard a case brought by Frank Ricci, a white firefighter in New Haven, Connecticut. Earlier, Ricci had taken an exam for promotion to lieutenant and had scored sixth among 77 candidates. But the city decided to discard the results, because none of the 19 African Americans who took the test qualified for promotion. Ricci and 19 other firefighters (one of whom was Hispanic) then sued the city, saying they had been the victims of bias. The city defended its action, saying the test was flawed. The Supreme Court ruled in favor of the firefighter plaintiffs, saying they had been subjected to race discrimination "solely because the higher-scoring candidates were white."[29]

Critics of affirmative action also argued that these programs could actually stigmatize or demoralize the very groups they were designed to help. For example, if a company hired a woman for a top management post, other people might think she got the job just because of affirmative action preferences, even if she were truly the best qualified. This might undermine her effectiveness on the job or even cause her to question her own abilities. For this reason, some women and persons of color called for *less* emphasis on affirmative action, preferring to achieve personal success without preferential treatment.[30]

Sexual and Racial Harassment

Government regulations ban both sexual and racial harassment. Of the two kinds, sexual harassment cases are more prevalent, and the law covering them is better defined. But racial harassment cases are a growing concern to employers.

---

[28] "Supreme Court to Weigh Race in College Admissions," *The New York Times,* June 29, 2015.

[29] "Justices to Hear White Firefighters Bias Claims," *The New York Times,* April 10, 2009; and "Supreme Court Finds Bias against White Firefighters," *The New York Times,* June 30, 2009.

[30] See, for example, Ward Connerly, *Creating Equal: My Fight Against Race Preferences* (San Francisco: Encounter Books, 2000).

Sexual harassment at work occurs when any employee, woman or man, experiences repeated, unwanted sexual attention or when on-the-job conditions are hostile or threatening in a sexual way. It includes both physical conduct—for example, suggestive touching— as well as verbal harassment, such as sexual innuendoes, jokes, or propositions. Sexual harassment is not limited to overt acts of individual coworkers or supervisors; it can also occur if a company's work climate is blatantly and offensively sexual or intimidating to employees. Women are the targets of most sexual harassment. Sexual harassment is illegal, and the EEOC is empowered to sue on behalf of victims. Such suits can be very costly to employers who tolerate a hostile work environment, as the following example shows.

> In 2012, a jury awarded a woman $168 million, believed to be the largest settlement ever for an individual in a sexual harassment suit. The plaintiff, a physician's assistant who had graduated from the Yale School of Medicine, was employed by Mercy General Hospital in Sacramento, California. She testified that the cardiac surgery center where she worked was a "raunchy, vile, toxic workplace" where surgeons and other medical staff called her "a stupid chick" and told her she performed surgical tasks "like a girl." One surgeon greeted her each morning by slapping her on the rear and proclaiming, "I'm horny." When the physician's assistant complained repeatedly about the behavior in the operating room, the hospital fired her. "The bullying and intimidation and retaliation—I have never seen an environment so hostile and pervasive," said the woman.[31]

Increasingly, sexual harassment cases are settled in arbitration hearings, so the amounts paid are not made public.[32]

Women employees regularly report that sexual harassment is common. From 40 to 70 percent of working women (and from 10 to 20 percent of working men) have told researchers they have been sexually harassed on the job. In almost two-thirds of the cases, the individual who was the target did not report the incident.[33] This kind of conduct is most likely to occur where jobs and occupations are (or have been) sex-segregated and where most supervisors and managers are men. It is also common where women workers have low power relative to their supervisors. One study found, for example, that female farmworkers were commonly sexually harassed and assaulted. About 60 percent were illegal immigrants, the study found, and many were afraid of deportation if they complained. "It's easiest for abusers to get away with sexual harassment where there's an imbalance of power, and the imbalance of power is particularly stark on farms," said the study's author.[34]

> Although the European Union has recognized sexual harassment as a form of gender discrimination, these behaviors remain all too common. A 2014 study found that 45 to 55 percent of women in the 28 EU nations had experienced sexual harassment. It was most frequent in Denmark, Sweden, the Netherlands, France, and Belgium (where 30 percent or more of survey respondents reported being harassed in the past year). Young women were more likely to be harassed than older women; they also were more likely to experience online victimization, such as unwanted sexually explicit e-mails or text messages. "This is no minor issue. We're talking about mothers, sisters, daughters across the EU," said the director of the European Agency for Fundamental Rights, which had conducted the survey.[35]

[31] "California Physician Assistant Wins $168 Million in Harassment Suit," *Los Angeles Times,* March 2, 2012.

[32] "The Silencing of Sexual Harassment," *Bloomberg Businessweek,* November 12, 2011.

[33] "Sexual Harassment Statistics in the Workplace," *www.sexualharassmenlawfirms.com.*

[34] "Report: Sexual Abuse of Female Farmworkers Common," *Washington Post,* May 16, 2012.

[35] European Agency for Fundamental Rights, "Violence Against Women: An EU-Wide Survey," 2014.

Harassment can occur whether or not the targeted employee cooperates. It need not result in the victim's firing, or cause severe psychological distress; the presence of a hostile or abusive workplace can itself be the basis for a successful suit. Moreover, a company can be found guilty as a result of actions by a supervisor, even if the incident is never reported to top management.

Racial harassment is also illegal, under Title VII of the Civil Rights Act. Under EEOC guidelines, ethnic slurs, derogatory comments, or other verbal or physical harassment based on race are against the law, if they create an intimidating, hostile, or offensive working environment or interfere with an individual's work performance. Although fewer racial than sexual harassment charges are filed, their numbers have more than doubled since the early 1990s (to about 9,000 a year in 2011), and employers have been liable for expensive settlements. For example, YRC/Roadway Express, the nation's largest less-than-truckload freight hauling company, had to pay $10 million to settle charges of racial harassment at two Illinois facilities. African American workers there charged that they had been subjected to multiple incidents of racist graffiti, comments, and cartoons—and even a hangman's noose, long a symbol of violence against blacks. Despite their complaints, the company had failed to take corrective action.[36]

What can companies do to combat sexual and racial harassment—and protect themselves from expensive lawsuits? The Supreme Court has ruled that companies can deflect lawsuits by taking two steps. First, they should develop a zero-tolerance policy on harassment and communicate it clearly to employees. Then they should establish a complaint procedure—including ways to report incidents without retaliation—and act quickly to resolve any problems. Companies that take such steps, the court said, would be protected from suits by employees who claim harassment but have failed to use the complaint procedure.

Developing mechanisms for preventing sexual and racial harassment is just one important action companies can take. Others positive steps by business are discussed in the following section.

What Business Can Do: Diversity and Inclusion Policies and Practices

All businesses, of course, are required to obey the laws mandating equal employment opportunity and prohibiting sexual and racial harassment; those that fail to do so risk expensive lawsuits and public disapproval. But it is not enough simply to follow the law. The best-managed companies go beyond compliance; they not only assemble diverse teams but implement a range of policies and practices to include all employees in a workplace that is welcoming, fair, and accommodating. A recent study by Deloitte Consulting explained that "promoting diversity is an expected commitment; it's now a ticket to play." The next essential step, the study concluded, was to "create a work environment that promotes inclusion in all its variations." In this context, **inclusion** means policies and practices that tap into the diverse perspectives, life experiences, and approaches that every individual brings to the workplace. As Deloitte put it, "diversity is the measure; inclusion is the mechanism."[37]

Companies that manage diversity and promote inclusion effectively take a number of related actions, in addition to obeying all relevant laws. Research shows that these actions include the following.

[36] Equal Employment Opportunity Commission, "$10 Million Consent Decree Ends Racial Harassment Case Against YRC/Roadway Express," press release, September 15, 2010, at *www.eeoc.gov*. Information on the latest government policies on racial and sexual harassment may be found at the EEOC website at *http://www.eeoc.gov/eeoc/statistics/enforcement/race_harassment.cfm*.

[37] Deloitte Consulting LLP, *Global Human Capital Trends 2014: Engaging the 21st Century Workforce.*

Articulate clear diversity goals, set quantitative objectives, and hold managers accountable. An important trend in diversity management is metrics—setting specific goals and offering incentives for meeting them.

An example of a company that has done this is the German carmaker BMW. Historically, BMW has had difficulty attracting and retaining female executives, even though women make up a large share of its customers. Believing that "what gets measured is what gets done," the company set numerical goals for the proportion of women at all levels—including doubling the number of women managers by 2020. To assure that the job got done, BMW included specific targets in the annual performance reviews of its top executives. Their success in meeting them would impact their annual bonuses. These targets were cascaded down to lower management levels as well. "You need to hold people accountable," declared the company's human resource and industrial relations director.[38]

Spread a wide net in recruitment, to find the most diverse possible pool of qualified candidates. Those in charge of both hiring and promotion need to seek all workers who may be qualified—both inside and outside the company. This often involves moving beyond word-of-mouth networks, which may produce a pool of applicants who are similar to people already working for the company or in particular jobs. One company's efforts to promote diversity in its hiring using a range of techniques that are described in the following example.

The accounting firm KPMG works hard to build a diverse workforce. The firm actively recruits at historically black colleges and universities and is a member of INROADS, a program that places minorities in internships with the company. It sponsors the PhD Project, which supports persons of color in doctoral programs that lead to faculty positions in colleges of business—where they can serve as role models for many students. KPMG has embraced the use of technology to cast a wider net in hiring, holding "virtual" recruiting fairs where registrants from around the world can interact with company recruiters online. "We know that our ability to successfully sustain a high-performance culture also requires that our people be as diverse as the clients we serve, and the communities in which we live and work," said the company website.[39]

Identify promising women and persons of color, and provide them with mentors and other kinds of support. What techniques work to shatter the glass ceiling? Some companies have promoted inclusion by assigning mentors—more senior counselors—to promising women and minority managers and providing them with opportunities for wide-ranging line experience. For example, Chevron Corporation, the energy company, has adopted a wide range of programs to foster inclusion, including employee networks that operate an extensive mentoring program. Adriana Sandoval, as information management supervisor, explained the importance of such mentorship in her career. She recalled that her father had asked her why she has chosen to work for an oil company. "You're a Latina; you're going to get lost," her father had told her. But her first day on the job, "a woman who was a Latina was there, and she was a representative of SOMOS, the Hispanic employees' network. . . . There's a lot of attention to making sure that folks have the opportunity to grow and learn within the company."[40]

---

[38] "Hard-Wiring Diversity into Your Business," *Boston Consulting Group Perspectives,* June 8, 2011, at *www.bcgperspectives.com.*

[39] Information on KPMG's diversity initiatives is available at *www.kpmg.com/us/en/about/csr/diversity-inclusion.*

[40] "The Chevron Way: Engineering Opportunities for Women," [video transcript], March 2015, at *www.chevron.com;* and "Chevron Corporation—The Chevron Way: Engineering Opportunities for women," 2015 Catalyst Award Winner," at *www. catalyst.org.*

Set up diversity councils to monitor the company's goals and progress toward them. A **diversity council** is a group of managers and employees responsible for developing and implementing specific action plans to meet an organization's diversity goals. Sometimes, a diversity council will be established for a corporation as a whole; sometimes, it will be established within particular business units.

> An example of a company that has used diversity councils effectively is Novartis Pharmaceuticals, the U.S. affiliate of the Swiss multinational Novartis AG, which in 2015 ranked number one (for the second year in a row) on *DiversityInc*'s Top 50 list. The company has an executive diversity and inclusion council, which is cochaired by country head Christi Shaw and vice president for diversity and inclusion Rhonda Chrichlow and includes representatives of all functional areas. This body is supported by self-organized groups of employees who take responsibility for promoting inclusion within their particular units.[41]

Businesses that manage diversity and inclusion effectively enjoy a strategic advantage. While fundamental ethical principles, discussed in Chapters 5 and 6, dictate that all employees should be treated fairly and with respect for their basic human rights, there are also bottom-line benefits to doing so.

- Having a widely diverse workforce boosts innovation, many executives believe. In a study by *Forbes,* 85 percent of executives of large global enterprises agreed with the proposition that "a diverse and inclusive workforce is crucial to encouraging different perspectives and ideas that drive innovation." "We have a vast amount of diversity [within the company] that comes into work every day to build technology that plays out around the world. You can't be successful on a global stage without it," commented the director of global diversity and inclusion at Intel.[42] Businesses with employees from varied backgrounds can often more effectively serve customers who are themselves diverse and can provide valuable insights into changing tastes and preferences. Explained the vice president of human resources, worldwide operations, for the toy maker Mattel, "Our Employee Resource Groups (ERGs) . . . help us define products that work for their regions or demographics. We have to make sure we are culturally sensitive. There have been some big near misses that we might not have avoided without the ERGs."[43]

- The global marketplace demands a workforce with language skills, cultural sensitivity, and awareness of national and other differences across markets. For example, Dr. Sally Saba, vice president for operations performance and compliance [and] diversity and inclusion for the Kaiser Foundation Health Plan, was born into a Muslim family in Egypt and later came to the United States, where she successfully ran a small business. Her own experiences as a minority business owner have given her deep insight into the challenges of promoting diversity and inclusion. "All of my life experiences contribute to the complexity of how I view the world and how I view people," Dr. Saba explained.[44]

Finally, companies with effective diversity programs can avoid costly lawsuits and damage to their corporate reputations from charges of discrimination or cultural insensitivity.

---

[41] "No. 1: Novartis Pharmaceuticals Corporation," at *www.diversityinc.com.*

[42] "Global Diversity and Inclusion: Fostering Innovation through a Diverse Workforce," *Forbes Insights,* July 2011, at *www.forbes.com.*

[43] Ibid.

[44] "Diversity Management at Kaiser Permanente: This Female Muslim Entrepreneur Brings Sensitivity to Suppliers," May 25, 2012, at *http://diversity.inc.com.*

Another important step businesses can take to manage diversity effectively is to accommodate the wide range of family and other obligations employees have in their lives outside work. This subject is discussed in the next section.

Balancing Work and Life

The nature of families and family life has changed, both in the United States and in many other countries. The primary groups in which people live are just as diverse as the workforce itself. One of the most prominent of these changes is that dual-income families have become much more common. According to the latest U.S. government data, in three-fifths of married couples with children at home (60 percent), both parents worked at least part-time. This was up from just a third of such families in 1976. (To round out the picture, in 31 percent of married couples with children, just the father worked; in 6 percent, just the mother worked. In the remainder, both parents were unemployed.)[45] Families have adopted a wide range of strategies for combining full- and part-time work with the care of children, elderly relatives, and other dependents. How to help employees trying to balance the complex, multiple demands of work and family life has become a major challenge for business.

Child Care and Elder Care

One critical issue for business is supporting workers with responsibilities for children and elderly relatives.

The demand for **child care** is enormous. Millions of children need daily care, especially the more than half of preschool-aged children whose mothers hold jobs. A major source of workplace stress for working parents is concern about their children; and problems with child care are a leading reason why employees fail to show up for work.

Business has found that child care programs, in addition to reducing absenteeism and tardiness, also improve productivity and aid recruiting by improving the company's image and helping to retain talented employees. Most large U.S. companies provide some type of child care assistance, including dependent care accounts (77 percent) and referral services (61 percent). About one in five large companies subsidizes on-site or near-site child care services.[46] An example is S.C. Johnson, a consumer products firm that cares for 500 children in a state-of-the-art center at its Racine, Wisconsin, headquarters. "This isn't a benefit," explained a company spokesperson. "It's a good business decision because we want to attract the best."[47]

In addition to caring for children, many of today's families have responsibilities for **elder care**. Employees' responsibilities for aging parents and other older relatives will become increasingly important to businesses in the coming decade as baby boomers pass through their forties and fifties, the prime years for caring for elderly family members. Forty-two million adults in the United States now care for an older person. More than half (58 percent) of family caregivers are currently employed. Fifteen percent of U.S. workers either are currently or have in the past cared for a person with Alzheimer's or other form of dementia. This is a concern for employers because caregivers often have to go to work late or leave early to attend to these duties, or are distracted or stressed at work by their

---

[45] U.S. Bureau of Labor Statistics, "Families with Own Children: Employment Status of Parents by Age of Youngest Child and Family Type." Data are for 2014.

[46] Families and Work Institute, "2014 National Study of Employers," at *www.familiesandwork.org.* An open-source website for research on work and family is the Work and Family Researchers Network at *https://workfamily.sas.upenn.edu.*

[47] Information about S.C. Johnson's child care center is available at *www.scjohnson.com.*

responsibilities.[48] Some have recognized the demand for family caregiving—of both children and elders—as a business opportunity, as the following example illustrates.

Entrepreneur Sheila Lirio Marcelo, a Filipina American, founded Care.com to use an online platform to connect people looking for caregivers with others looking to provide these services. She got the idea for the company when her father, then 54, had a heart attack and fell down the stairs while carrying her infant son. (Fortunately, the boy was not hurt, but Marcelo realized she needed to hire a caregiver right away— for her son *and* her father.) The company now has 13 million users and is adding thousands more every day. A number of companies, including Facebook and LinkedIn, offer Care.com services as a benefit for their employees. "Caregiving is among the fastest growing job categories in the country, and there's a need there," said a scholar at the Pew Research Center. "It's the most important work families do."[49]

Many firms offer referral services, dependent care accounts, long-term care insurance, and time off to deal with the often unpredictable crises that occur in families caring for children and elders.

When a mother or father is granted time off when children are born or adopted and during the important early months of a child's development, this is called a **parental leave**; when the care of elderly relatives is involved, this is called a **family leave**. Under the Family and Medical Leave Act (FMLA), passed in 1993, companies that employ 50 or more people must grant unpaid, job-protected leaves of up to 12 weeks to employees faced with serious family needs, including the birth or adoption of a baby. Smaller companies, not covered by the FMLA, usually do less for expectant and new parents and for those with ill family members.

Work Flexibility

Companies have also accommodated the changing roles of women and men by offering workers more flexibility through such options as flextime, part-time employment, job sharing, and working from home (sometimes called telecommuting because the employee keeps in touch with coworkers, customers, and others by phone or over the Internet). Abbott Laboratories, a global health care company that was named one of the "best companies" in 2014 by *Working Mother* magazine, demonstrates the benefits of the many kinds of work flexibility for both business and employees.

Many of Abbott's employees, men and women, work flextime schedules, beginning and quitting at different times of the day. Others share jobs, with each working half a week. Many jobs are held on a part-time basis, leaving the worker time to be at home with children or elderly parents. Other Abbott employees telecommute from their homes. "After my son got sick, I needed to . . . drop down to part-time and work from home a few days a week," said one manager. "Abbott gave me the flexibility I needed to take care of my family." The company, whose work/life programs have been widely honored, says that its employees return the investment through their increased productivity, innovative thinking, and loyalty.[50]

Abbott is not the only corporation using these practices. A 2014 study found that many companies offered some kind of flexible work schedules, such as allowing employees to

[48] "Just How Valuable Is Family Caregiving?" July 19, 2013, at *http://blog.aarp.org;* AARP Public Policy Institute, "Valuing the Invaluable: The Economic Value of Family Caregiving," 2011, *www.aarp.org;* and "How Alzheimer's Will Change Your Workplace," *U.S. News and World Report,* March 14, 2013.

[49] "Who Profits? Care.com Finds Sitters for Baby or Dad," December 8, 2014, at *www.bloomberg.com.*

[50] "Abbott Included in Top 10 Best Companies By *Working Mother* Magazine," press release, September 16, 2014. The quote is from a press release dated September 23, 2008. Both are available at *www.abbott.com.*

change starting or quitting times periodically (81 percent), work from home at least occasionally (67 percent), or compress workweeks into fewer days (43 percent).[51] These arrangements can benefit employers by attracting and retaining valuable employees, reducing absences, and improving job satisfaction. "Organizations are realizing the value in giving employees more autonomy to produce their best work," commented a representative of the Society for Human Resource Management, which participated in the study. "At the same time," she noted, "organizations still struggling in a recovering economy are dependent on their workforce and less able to provide employees extended time away from work."[52]

However, many observers believe that most careers are still structured for people who are prepared to put in 40 hours a week at the office—or 50 or 60—giving their full and undivided commitment to the organization. Many women and men have been reluctant to take advantage of various flexible work options, fearing that this would put them on a slower track, sometimes disparagingly called the *Mommy track* or *Daddy track*. In this view, businesses will need to undergo a cultural shift, to value the contributions of people who are prepared to make a serious, but less than full-time, commitment to their careers.

What would such a cultural shift look like? Some have used the term **family-friendly corporation** to describe firms that would fully support both men and women in their efforts to balance work and family responsibilities. Job advantages would not be granted or denied on the basis of gender. People would be hired, paid, evaluated, promoted, and extended benefits on the basis of their qualifications and ability to do the tasks assigned. The route to the top, or to satisfaction in any occupational category, would be open to anyone with the talent to take it. The company's stakeholders, regardless of their gender, would be treated in a bias-free manner. All laws forbidding sex discrimination would be fully obeyed. Programs to provide leaves or financial support for child care, elder care, and other family responsibilities would support both men and women employees and help promote an equitable division of domestic work. And persons could seek, and achieve, career advancement without committing to a full-time schedule, year after year.[53] An example of a family-friendly corporation is General Mills, long admired for its support of working parents. Forty-four percent of managers and executives are women, and half of the company's employees use a flextime schedule. The company has a special program to allow women to ramp up their hours gradually when they return to work after the birth or adoption of a child.[54]

An important step businesses can take is to support their lesbian, gay, bisexual, and transgender employees. This issue is further explored in Exhibit 16.B.

No other area of business illustrates the basic theme of this book better than the close connection between work and life. Our basic theme is that business and society are closely and unavoidably intertwined, so that what affects one also has an impact on the other. As the workforce has become more diverse, business has been challenged to accommodate their employees' differences and to include their multiple perspectives. When people go to work, they do not shed their identities at the office or factory door. When employees come from families where there are young children at home, or where elderly parents require care, companies must learn to support these roles. Businesses that help their employees achieve a balance between work and life and meet their obligations to their families and communities often reap rewards in greater productivity, loyalty, and commitment.

---

[51] Families and Work Institute, "2012 National Study of Employers," at *www.familiesandwork.org.*

[52] "2012 National Study of Employers Reveals Increased Workplace Flexibility," Society for Human Resource Management, press release, April 30, 2012, at *www.shrm.org.*

[53] *Working Mother* magazine publishes an annual list of the "100 Best Companies for Working Mothers." The current year's list may be viewed at *www.workingmother.com.*

[54] "2014 *Working Mother* Best Companies," at *www.workingmother.com.*

When the U.S. Supreme Court legalized same-sex marriage in 2015, it in effect codified actions that many corporations had already taken toward full inclusion of their lesbian, gay, bisexual, and transgender (LGBT) employees. A 2015 report by the Human Rights Campaign Foundation found that 89 percent of the *Fortune* 500 companies included sexual orientation in their nondiscrimination policy, and two-thirds included gender identity. One of the top-ranking companies in the survey was Walmart, which had publicly asked the governor of its home state of Arkansas to reject legislation that would permit discrimination against gays and lesbians. Ironically, one effect of the Supreme Court ruling was to jeopardize domestic partner benefits, which had spread widely in the corporate world as a way to extend insurance benefits to couples who could not legally marry. Even before the Supreme Court decision, companies such as Delta Airlines and Verizon had begun phasing out these benefits in states where same-sex marriage was legal. Said one Delta employee, who supported his employer's actions: "Marriage is something we as gays and lesbians have fought for, for years, and Delta is acting as our ring bearer."

Sources: Human Rights Campaign Foundation, *Corporate Equality Index 2015: Rating American Workplaces on Lesbian, Gay, Bisexual, and Transgender Equality* at *www.hrc.org;* and "Walmart Emerges as Unlikely Social Force," *The New York Times,* April 1, 2015; and "Firms Tell Gay Couples: Wed or Lose Your Benefits," *The Wall Street Journal,* May 12, 2015.

Summary

- The U.S. workforce is as diverse as it has ever been and is becoming more so. More women are working than ever before, many immigrants have entered the labor force, ethnic and racial diversity is increasing, the workforce is aging, and millennials are entering the workplace.

- Women and persons of color have made great strides in entering all occupations, but they continue to be underrepresented in many business management roles, especially at top levels. Both groups face a continuing pay gap. The number of women-owned businesses has increased sharply, and many minorities, especially immigrants, also own their own businesses.

- Under U.S. law, businesses are required to provide equal opportunity to all, without regard to race, color, religion, sex, national origin, disability, or age. Sexual and racial harassment are illegal. Affirmative action plans remain legal, but only if they are temporary and flexible, designed to correct past discrimination, and do not result in reverse discrimination.

- Companies that manage diversity effectively have a strategic advantage because they are able to foster innovation, serve a diverse customer base, and avoid expensive lawsuits and public embarrassment.

- Successful diversity and inclusion management includes articulating goals and measuring progress, recruiting widely, mentoring promising women and persons of color, and establishing mechanisms for assessing progress.

- Many businesses have helped employees balance the complex demands of work and family obligations by providing support programs such as child and elder care, flexible work schedules, domestic partner benefits, and telecommuting options.

Key Terms

affirmative action, *359*
child care, *364*
diversity, *348*
diversity council, *363*
elder care, *364*
equal employment
opportunity, *357*
Equal Employment
Opportunity Commission
(EEOC), *358*

family-friendly
corporation, *366*
family leave, *365*
glass ceiling, *355*
glass walls, *356*
inclusion, *361*
occupational
segregation, *351*
parental leave, *365*
pay gap, *351*

racial
harassment, *361*
sexual
harassment, *360*
undocumented immigrant
worker, *349*
workforce
diversity, *348*

Internet Resources

www.eeoc.gov	U.S. Equal Employment Opportunity Commission
www.familiesandwork.org	Families and Work Institute
www.abcdependentcare.com	American Business Collaboration for Quality Dependent Care
www..sba.gov	U.S. Small Business Administration
www.catalyst.org	Catalyst—"expanding opportunities for women and business"
www.multiculturaladvantage.com	Resources for diversity officers and professionals of diverse backgrounds
www.diversityinc.com	*Diversity Inc.* magazine and other resources
www.workingmother.com	*Working Mother* magazine and other resources

Discussion Case: *Unauthorized Immigrant Workers at Chipotle Mexican Grill Restaurants*

In 2015, Chipotle Mexican Grill acknowledged that it was still under investigation by the Securities and Exchange Commission and the U.S. attorney for the District of Columbia for possible failure to comply with laws on employee work eligibility. "It is not possible to know at this time," the company stated in its annual report to shareholders, "whether the company will incur, or to reasonably estimate the amount of, any fines, penalties or further liabilities in connection with these matters."

Chipotle's troubles with immigration had begun four years earlier, when federal agents had descended on dozens of Chipotle Mexican Grill restaurants around the country, from Los Angeles to Atlanta, interviewing employees and managers. Their purpose was to determine whether—and to what extent—the fast-food chain was hiring unauthorized immigrant workers in violation of U.S. law.

Chipotle was a fast-growing chain of restaurants specializing in burritos, tacos, and salads made on premises from fresh ingredients. Founded in Colorado in 1993 by chef Steve Ells, at the time of the immigration raids the company owned more than 1,200 restaurants in 41 states, Ontario, London, and Paris. Chipotle employed 31,000 people, 92 percent of whom were hourly employees. Operating under the slogan "Food with Integrity," the chain reported $2.27 billion in revenue and 11 percent sales growth in 2011, despite the struggling economy. Some analysts believed that one of the reasons for Chipotle's strong performance was, as the news service Reuters put it, its "uncanny ability to hold down labor costs."

Under government rules, foreign-born individuals are permitted to work legally in the United States under some conditions. They can obtain a green card, a work permit issued to permanent residents (most of whom are close relatives of U.S. citizens). Highly skilled workers in short supply can apply for an H-1 visa. Low-skilled workers can apply for an H-2 visa for temporary, seasonal work; however, these are available to only about 1 percent of the unauthorized population. When hiring, employers are required to fill out and keep on file an I-9 form, documenting a person's eligibility to work, and present it to government investigators if asked.

About half a million undocumented immigrants entered the United States every year during the past decade, two-thirds by crossing the Mexican–U.S. border and the rest by overstaying temporary visas. The Pew Research Center estimates there are 8.1 undocumented immigrants in the U.S. workforce, about 5 percent of the total. Three-quarters of them are Hispanic, mostly from Mexico but also from Central and South America. The main reason they immigrate is for economic opportunity; studies show, for example, that a Mexican man with a high school education can make two and a half times as much in the United States as in his home country, even after taking into account differences in the cost of living.

Most take low-skilled jobs in a small number of occupations and industries. Fully a quarter of farmworkers in the United States—and about a fifth of building and grounds maintenance workers—are undocumented immigrants. In the restaurant industry, they make up 12 percent of food-preparation workers and servers nationally—and much more in some regions, such as southern California. A study by the Food Chain Workers' Alliance found that undocumented workers earned a median hourly wage of $7.60 (compared with about $10 for other workers in the food industry) and were more than twice as likely to experience some kind of wage theft, such as unpaid hours. Forty-four percent of undocumented workers in the food industry were actually earning less than minimum wage.

Over the past decade, government policy toward people working in the United States illegally has undergone a sharp about-face. Under President George W. Bush, Immigration and Customs Enforcement (ICE), a division of the Department of Homeland Security, conducted a series of high-profile raids of factories, targeting foreign workers who were unable to produce authentic work papers. For example, in 2008, ICE agents arrested and deported hundreds of workers at a meatpacking plant in Iowa.

The Obama administration took a different approach, focusing its enforcement efforts on employers. ICE began conducting I-9 audits, checking businesses to make sure their employees' papers were in order. The Social Security Administration also began investigating situations where Social Security numbers provided by employees did not match their records (in the case of illegal workers, these numbers were often fictitious). If the agents found evidence of problems, they ordered that employers comply with the law—and in some cases imposed fines or even brought criminal charges against managers.

Chipotle was not the only employer targeted by these investigations. For example, American Apparel, a garment company based in Los Angeles, terminated 1,800 undocumented workers after an ICE audit found widespread irregularities. At L.E. Cooke Company, a family-owned nursery in California's Central Valley, the owner was forced to fire 26 of his 99 employees who had entered the country illegally. Many had worked for the nursery for many years and had specialized skills. "Telling them was probably the worst day of my life," the owner said. "I don't just sit at a desk here, I'm actually out in the fields harvesting with them."

As it awaited resolution of the government investigations, Chipotle's management took steps to tighten up its employment procedures. In addition to terminating workers it found to be undocumented, Chipotle ordered all its restaurants to use the federal E-Verify system, even in states where this was not required. (E-Verify is an online system that compares information from a new employee's Form I-9 to social security and homeland security data to confirm work eligibility.) It also adopted an electronic Form I-9 to reduce errors. But the company's CEO acknowledged that its systems were not foolproof. "Whatever systems you have for anything really, there are always going to be people who try to game the system," he said. "But I think that we are going above and beyond . . . to ensure that we are complying with the immigration [laws]."

Sources: Food Chain Workers' Alliance, *The Hands That Feed Us: Challenges and Opportunities For Workers Along the Food Chain,* June 6, 2012, at *www.foodchainworkers.org;* Restaurant Opportunities Centers United (ROC), *Behind the Kitchen Door: A Multi-Site Study of the Restaurant Industry,* February 14, 2011, at *http://rocunited.org;* "Chipotle's Undocumented Worker Problem Resurges," *Bloomberg Businessweek,* May 24, 2012; "Chipotle Under Investigation for Immigration Law Violations," May 23, 2012, at *www.marketplace.org;* Gordon H. Hanson, "The Economics and Policy of Illegal Immigration in the United States," Migration Policy Institute, December 2009; Pew Research Center, "5 Facts About Illegal Immigration in the U.S.," November 18, 2014; Chipotle Mexican Grill annual reports at *www.chipotle.com;* and news reports appearing in *The Wall Street Journal, The New York Times,* and *reuters.com.*

Discussion Questions

1. Do you consider being an unauthorized immigrant a form of workplace diversity? How is it similar to and different from other kinds of workplace diversity discussed in this chapter?

2. What are the benefits and risks to employers, such as Chipotle and others mentioned in this case, of hiring unauthorized immigrants—whether or not they do so knowingly?

3. Other than employers, which stakeholders are helped and which are hurt when a business hires unauthorized immigrants?

4. Do you agree with the public policies and enforcement strategies described in this case? If not, what changes in both would you recommend?

5. Do you agree with Chipotle's response to the government's enforcement effort? What else should Chipotle's managers do now, and why?

CHAPTER SEVENTEEN

Business and Its Suppliers

Corporations have complex relationships with their *suppliers,* other firms that provide them with goods and services and in some cases manufacture their products. In today's interconnected world, many firms are embedded in complex, global supply chain networks. Increasingly, managers are responsible for social, ethical, and environmental issues that arise in supplier firms. A failure to manage these issues proactively can lead to reputational and financial losses; conversely, success in doing so can yield benefits. Many companies have adopted supplier codes of conduct, carried out audits, and remediated failures. A growing trend is for lead firms to work collaboratively with their suppliers to build capabilities and create shared value.

This Chapter Focuses on These Key Learning Objectives:

LO 17-1 Understand what suppliers are, the nature of suppliers' interests and power, and the scope of the global supply chain.

LO 17-2 Examine the social, ethical, and environmental issues that arise in global supply chains and how they can affect a company's reputation and bottom line.

LO 17-3 Describe contemporary trends in the private regulation of supply chain practices and analyze the reasons for the emergence of company and industrywide codes of conduct.

LO 17-4 Understand the various methods businesses and nonprofit organizations use to audit global supply chains for compliance with codes of conduct and other standards.

LO 17-5 Analyze the reasons for and benefits of engaging collaboratively with suppliers to build capability and create shared value and the conditions under which such initiatives are likely to succeed.

In 2014, the apparel maker Gap announced plans to produce some of its garments in two independently owned factories in Burma. The company was the first major retailer to return to the Southeast Asian nation, also known as Myanmar, after the U.S. government lifted trade sanctions following democratic reforms. Gap executives wanted to return to Burma because of its legacy of garment production, but also realized they faced supply chain risks in a country that had long been ruled by a repressive military regime and isolated from the world economy. Gap consulted with a wide range of stakeholders, including the International Labor Organization, U.S. government agencies, and civil society organizations, and worked closely with its Burma-based suppliers to assure that they could comply fully with the company's policies on human rights. Wilma Wallace, a Gap vice president, commented, "By entering Myanmar, we hope to . . . build on our track record of improving working conditions and building local capacity in garment factories around the world."[1]

Also in 2014, a massive explosion at a metal parts factory in eastern China, apparently caused when polishing dust ignited, killed 75 workers and injured more than 180 others. The plant was part of a vast, far-flung network of suppliers to General Motors: it made parts for an aluminum car-wheel manufacturer, which in turn supplied the automaker. At the time, the company operated 17 assembly plants in China in partnership with local firms and sold more cars there than in the United States. China Labor Watch, an activist organization, immediately charged that GM "shares responsibility for this deadly explosion." But GM's president disputed this, saying that the factory where the tragedy occurred "was a supplier to a supplier, as opposed to us, so we are a couple of steps removed." In the company's view, so-called tier-1 suppliers—not General Motors—were responsible for assuring that tier-2 suppliers met safety standards.[2]

Patagonia is an outdoor apparel company with a long-standing commitment to the environment. The firm recently initiated "The Footprint Chronicles," a blog intended to "use transparency about our supply chain to help us reduce our adverse social and environmental impacts—and on an industrial scale." One of the projects the company reported was a partnership with The Nature Conservancy and Ovis 21, an Argentine organization that promoted sustainable ranching. In 2013, Patagonia committed to purchasing all of its merino wool—a key component of its outerwear and socks—from ranches in Argentina's Patagonia region (after which the company had been named) that practiced rotational sheep grazing and other methods aimed not only at conserving, but actually restoring, environmentally degraded grasslands. The company's order gave a big boost to the conservation effort. "We have often sought to be sustainable," said Patagonia's director of environmental strategy. "But this is the first time we have actually been able to improve an environment by placing business there."[3]

These three examples capture some of the extraordinary complexity of the relationship between businesses and their suppliers. To what lengths should a company go to assure that the rights of workers in supplier factories halfway around the world are protected? Who should bear responsibility when something goes wrong in a multi-tiered supply chain several steps removed from the company that sells the final product? Should a company concern

---

[1] "Gap Plans to Start Producing Apparel in Myanmar," *The Wall Street Journal,* June 9, 2014; "Gap: First U.S. Retailer to Enter Burma," *USA Today,* June 7, 2014; and "Responsible Sourcing in Myanmar," Gap Inc., August 25, 2014.

[2] "GM Doesn't Plan to Alter Standards for Suppliers," *The Wall Street Journal,* August 6, 2014; "GM's China Bet Mirrors Toyota's Bet on U.S. Last Century," *Bloomberg.com,* April 29, 2013; "Zhongrong Metal Parts Factory Explosion: How Does It Affect General Motors in China?" *International Business Times,* August 4, 2014.

[3] "Responsibly Sourced Merino Wool," *www.patagonia.com/us/footprint;* "Wool from Sustainably Raised Sheep Play Surprising Role in Patagonia's Grasslands Restoration," January 23, 2013, press release issued by The Nature Conservancy, Patagonia, and Ovis 21; "Can Sheep Restore Patagonia's Grasslands?" *Guardian Sustainable Business,* December 23, 2013.

itself with the environmental impact of suppliers of raw materials, or even collaborate with them to promote conservation? This chapter will explore the social and ethical responsibilities of firms toward their suppliers and people working for them, as well as the impacts of the global supply chain on surrounding communities and the natural environment.

Suppliers

In business, the term **supplier** refers to an organization that provides goods or services to another organization. Suppliers are also known as *vendors* or *contractors*. They are an important market stakeholder of businesses, since they provide critical inputs and often manufacture entire products that companies then sell to customers under their own brand.

Major transnational firms can have an enormous number of suppliers. Intel, for example, has 16,000 suppliers in 100 countries. The exact number of suppliers in the world is uncountable: new ones emerge, and others go out of business, every day. One study by the consultancy CVM Solutions estimated that *Fortune* 1000 companies (the thousand largest U.S. companies, ranked by revenue) had 4.9 million unique suppliers (meaning that suppliers that served multiple companies were counted only once). However, the number of widely used suppliers was much smaller: only 6 percent (about 300,000) supplied two or more companies.[4] Some evidence suggests that in the wake of the global financial crisis, the number of suppliers has dropped. A study by the World Bank found that the crisis had accelerated lead firms' preference for larger, more capable suppliers with whom they had ongoing strategic relationships.[5] (Because a business and its supplier are both companies, this chapter will sometimes use the term *lead firm* to distinguish a company from its supplier.)

Suppliers are a diverse group. They range from tiny—a farmer growing vegetables on a small plot for a local restaurant, for example—to enormous, such as Foxconn, the world's largest electronics manufacturer, which makes iPads and iPhones for Apple, Kindles for Amazon, and PlayStations for Sony, among other products. Foxconn, with over a million employees and $132 billion in revenue in 2013, is itself a major transnational corporation. (Foxconn is further profiled in the discussion case at the end of this chapter.) Lead firms often categorize their suppliers according to *tier,* or level. **Tier-1 suppliers** (sometimes called *contractors*) are hired to manufacture products and provide them directly to the company. These may in turn work with **tier-2 suppliers** (sometimes called *subcontractors*), who may in turn work with even more distant suppliers. In the automobile industry, for example, there may be six to ten levels of suppliers between the automaker and the source of raw materials, and a company may not even be aware of some of the parties that contribute at some point to the finished product. The term **supply chain** refers to the multiple steps involved in the movement of a product or service from the most distant supplier to the customer. Because of the complexity of these systems, firms sometimes refer to their *supply webs* or *networks,* rather than use the term *supply chain,* which implies a simple, linear relationship.

Although several steps removed, distant suppliers can still have a big impact on a company's reputation and bottom line.

The toy company Mattel learned this the hard way, when it discovered that toxic lead paint had been applied to several of its toys, including Sarge vehicles and Dora the Explorer characters. In its investigation, the company found that a tier-1 supplier, a Chinese firm called Early Light Industrial, had subcontracted painting to

[4] "How Many Suppliers are in the Global Supply Chain?" *Industry Market Trends,* August 25, 2010.

[5] Olivier Cattaneo, Gary Geriffi, and Cornelia Staritz, eds., *Global Values Chains in a Postcrisis World* (Herndon, VA: World Bank Publications, 2010), Chapters 1 and 2.

another firm, which had violated Mattel's specifications and substituted cheaper lead paint. "Early Light . . . is every [bit as] much the victim as Mattel is," the CEO later commented. Mattel ended up spending $110 million dollars to recall the tainted toys and communicate with the public, all because of unapproved actions by a tier-2 supplier.[6]

As this example illustrates, companies need to understand and monitor actions by all participants throughout their supply networks, not just those with whom they have direct relationships.

Chapter 1 introduced the concepts of stakeholder *interest,* that is, what a stakeholder wants from its relationship with a firm, and *power,* a stakeholder's ability to secure a desired outcome. What are the interests—and sources of power—of suppliers? Despite their tremendous diversity, most suppliers share an interest in obtaining orders that will enable them to make money, use their productive capacity efficiently, and build long-term, stable relationships with business customers.[7] Naturally, suppliers' power, relative to lead firms, varies. Suppliers may have both economic and informational power. A supplier that is a sole source for a key component or natural resource naturally has more leverage, relative to its lead firms, than one that is not. Similarly, suppliers that control critical worker skills, technical know-how, or relevant manufacturing infrastructure have more leverage than others. When Apple wanted to launch the iPad, for example, only one supplier—Foxconn—had the immediate capability to do the job competently and at scale, giving the Taiwanese company strong bargaining power. Proximity to major markets, long-standing relationships with other contractors, and a reputation for quality, speed, and low cost also enhance supplier power.

As was further discussed in Chapter 4, the world's economy has become increasingly globalized. Although much manufacturing still occurs in the developed economies of the United States, Japan, and Germany, the developing nations of Brazil, India, and Mexico also have significant shares. Particularly striking has been the emergence of what has been called "Factory Asia." In 2010, China passed the United States as the nation with the largest share of global manufacturing, and in 2012 made more than one-fifth—22 percent—of the world's products. Almost half of all manufacturing production now takes place in Asia; and in some industries, such as footwear and apparel, the shift has been almost total.[8] As the world's economy has globalized, so has its supply chain. Richard M. Locke, a scholar who has extensively studied business–supplier relationships, has described the process this way:

> Globalization, with its volatile mix of economic opportunity and social disruption, is redefining the boundaries of the firm; changing dynamics among consumers, global corporations, and their suppliers; and shaping the working conditions of the millions of individuals employed in today's global supply chains. The world of global supply chains links thousands of firms, large and small, across multiple cultural and political boundaries.[9]

---

[6] Pricewaterhouse Coopers (PwC) and EcoVadis in collaboration with the INSEAD Social Innovation Centre, "Value of Sustainable Procurement Practices," 2010.

[7] Richard M. Locke, *The Promise and Limits of Private Power: Promoting Labor Standards in a Global Economy* (Cambridge University Press, 2013), p. 13.

[8] "The Future of Factory Asia," *The Economist,* March 14, 2015; "China Has Dominant Share of World Manufacturing," *Manufacturer's Alliance for Productivity and Innovation,* January 4, 2014; and data reported by Global Production, Inc., at *www.global-production.com.*

[9] Richard M. Locke, p. 3.

In such a network, even seemingly simple products can have a truly worldwide footprint. Consider just one familiar, everyday product: a cotton T-shirt. In her book, *The Travels of a T-Shirt in the Global Economy,* economist Pietra Rivoli described the probable history of a cotton T-shirt emblazoned with a colorful design that she had purchased at a Walgreen's drugstore in Fort Lauderdale, Florida. This is what she surmised from her research:

> Cotton for the T-shirt had been grown on a large, mechanized cotton farm near Lubbock, Texas, and processed, graded, and baled at a nearby mill. From there, a truck carried it to the port of Long Beach, California, where it was loaded onto a freighter for shipment across the Pacific. In Shanghai, China, a mill spun the raw cotton into yarn and knitted it into fabric. Nearby, garment workers cut and sewed the fabric into plain, white T-shirts. The T-shirts were returned to the port, put back on another freighter, and shipped through the Panama Canal to Miami. There, they were purchased by a Florida maker of novelty clothing, who screened the shirts with tourist-friendly images and sold them to Walgreen's—where the economist bought her T-shirt and took it back home to Washington D.C.[10]

Figure 17.1 shows a **supply chain map** that graphically depicts the travels of this T-shirt. A supply chain map is a visual representation of the multiple links between a lead firm (in this case, the novelty clothing maker), its suppliers, and eventually its customers. It shows the movement of a particular product from the beginning of the supply chain to the end, superimposed on a geographical map.

FIGURE 17.1 A Supply Chain Map for a Cotton T-Shirt

Source: Graphic design by The Sketchy Pixel. © 2015. All rights reserved. Used by permission.

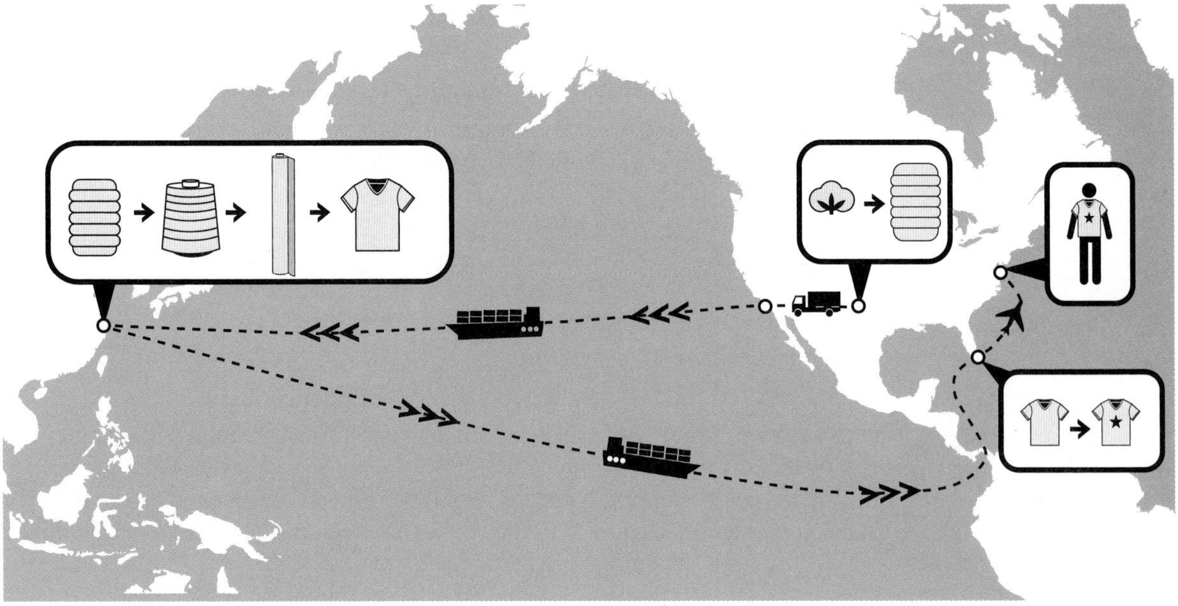

[10] Pietra Rivoli, *The Travels of a T-Shirt in the Global Economy,* 2nd edition (Hoboken, NJ: John Wiley & Sons, 2015).

Social, Ethical, and Environmental Issues in Global Supply Chains

As supply chains have globalized, their social, ethical, and environmental impacts have become increasingly complex, and their potential risks to corporate reputation heightened. This section will describe these three kinds of issues and provide examples of companies that are actively considering social, ethical, and environmental risks in their sourcing decisions. It will also show some of the risks of failing to manage these issues proactively, as well as the benefits associated with doing this well.

Social Issues

Global supply chains have many social impacts. Prominent among them are the wages, working conditions, and health and safety of employees in supplier factories.

Wages in overseas supplier factories are generally much lower than they would be in the United States, Europe, or the developed Asian economies of Japan and Korea. In the garment industry, to cite one example, a survey by the Worker Rights Consortium found monthly wages ranging from $755 in Mexico, to $359 in Honduras, to just $91 in Bangladesh—all far below the minimum wage a U.S. employer would be required to pay.[11] Low wages are, of course, one of the main reasons that brands contract with suppliers in developing countries; they reduce overall costs and enable brands to price their products more competitively. Low wages are not necessarily unethical. People in developing countries need jobs and are often willing to work at pay below what would be considered acceptable in developed nations. Employment in export-oriented factories often offer workers—particularly young women— their first point of entry into the wage economy and an alternative to domestic and farm labor. On the other hand, if a company's customers believe that its products are made in **sweatshops**—a derogatory term referring to factories where workers toil long hours, at low wages, and under unsafe conditions—its reputation can be harmed. Workers who believe they are treated unfairly can quit, go on strike, or produce poor quality work.

The challenge for businesses, then, is to assure that their suppliers pay wages that are perceived as fair and that permit workers and their families to achieve a decent standard of living. (The related concept of a *living wage* is discussed in Chapter 15.) Minimum wages established by law may not be sufficient.

> In 2013, the fashion retailer H&M announced a plan to eliminate the gap between its suppliers' wages and a fair living wage that covered families' basic needs. "Textile workers should be able to live on their wage," said the company's global head of sustainability. "Wage revisions from the government are taking too long." H&M rolled out its plan for a fair living wage first in several model factories, with the aim of extending it to 750 factories, making 60 percent of its products, by 2018. The company saw a benefit in doing so. "Strikes and disruptions to production are costly to us," said the sustainability officer. "The increase in productivity will be profitable to us in the long term."[12]

In this situation, H&M saw benefits in working proactively to require that suppliers pay wages above legally mandated minimums.

Just as what constitutes a fair wage varies across cultures and economies, so do other terms and conditions of work. For example, in some countries, unions are legal and the

---

[11] Worker Rights Consortium, *Global Wage Trends for Apparel Workers, 2001–2011*, July 2011.

[12] "H&M's Goal on Pay—Retailer Wants Garment Workers to Earn a Living Wage," *The Wall Street Journal*, November 26, 2013; and "A Fair Living Wage to Garment Workers," at *http://about.hm.com/en/About/sustainability/commitments/ responsible-partners/fair-living-wage*.

right to organize is protected; in others, unions are illegal or actively discouraged. Excessive overtime (usually defined as more than 60 hours or six days a week) is not permitted in most developed countries. Yet, in some settings, workers are eager to work as many hours as they can, to save for marriage, for example, or to remit earnings to family members. Finding the right balance can be a challenge.

A special concern for many brands is **child labor**. Child labor has been defined by the International Labor Organization (ILO) as "work that deprives children of their childhood, their potential and their dignity, and that is harmful to physical and mental development." As the ILO points out, whether or not work can be considered child labor depends on a number of factors, including the child's age, the type and hours of work performed, and the conditions under which it is performed, and may vary among cultures and countries.[13] In 2012, despite progress, child labor remained a persistent problem; 168 million children continued to work, more than half of them in hazardous jobs. Many observers trace the modern antisweatshop movement to a famous photograph that appeared in *Life* magazine in 1996, showing a 12-year-old Pakistani boy, crouched on a dirt floor hand-stitching the hexagonal pieces of a Nike-branded soccer ball. Within days, activists were standing in front of Nike stores, holding up the photograph and demanding an elimination of child labor in the supply chain. Although virtually all lead companies require their suppliers, at the least, to comply with relevant national laws regarding child labor, the possibility that children continue to be employed somewhere in the supply chain poses a risk.

An issue of emerging importance is worker health and safety in supplier factories. As illustrated by one of the examples that opened this chapter, combustible dust can cause explosions and fires. Workers can be exposed to dangerous chemicals in poorly ventilated spaces. Malfunctioning or improperly guarded mechanical equipment or tools can maim and kill. In some developing countries, structurally unsound buildings have been repurposed for use as factories, with horrifying results.

> In April 2013, an eight-story building in Bangladesh collapsed catastrophically, killing 1,134 workers, most of them young women, who had been working in six separate garment factories on different floors. More than 2,500 others were injured, many severely. It was the worst industrial disaster in the history of the garment industry. The building, known as Rana Plaza, was partially situated on a drained swamp, and additional floors had been illegally added. The structure was carrying almost six times the weight it was designed to bear. Although workers had earlier reported large cracks in the walls, managers dismissed the problem and threatened workers if they did not report for duty. At the time Rana Plaza collapsed, dozens of well-known North American and European brands were sourcing products from factories in the building. Photos of the carnage, which were widely reported around the world, showed scattered garments—some showing their brand labels—lying alongside workers' corpses.

This incident shocked the conscience of many customers and precipitated a reputational crisis for some brands. The collapse of Rana Plaza and the challenge it posed to Western manufacturers sourcing from Bangladesh are further profiled in a case at the end of this book.

Ethical Issues

Violations of human rights by suppliers are a serious risk, particularly for companies that use suppliers in agriculture and natural resources-based industries, such as mining.

Human trafficking (also called *forced labor*) is modern-day slavery—the illegal recruitment and movement of people against their will, usually to exploit them for economic gain.

---

[13] "What is Child Labor?" International Labor Organization, at *www.ilo.org/ipec/facts.*

Of the estimated 2.5 million victims of human trafficking in the world, about 80 percent are women and girls forced into prostitution. Most of the rest are coerced into working on farms and in factories in many industries, including food processing, construction, textiles, and hospitality, often for low pay or even no pay at all. Six out of ten trafficking victims are moved across national borders, but human trafficking also occurs close to the victims' homes.[14]

Few major companies, of course, knowingly tolerate human trafficking in their organizations or those of their suppliers. But in today's complex supply networks, the presence of such forced labor can pose a serious reputational and legal risk.

> In 2014, a federal court in California ruled that Nestlé and other companies that sourced chocolate from cocoa farms in the Ivory Coast (in West Africa) could be sued for child slavery practiced by their suppliers. The plaintiffs in the lawsuit were three former workers, between 12 and 20 years old at the time, who said they had been forced to work up to 14 hours a day without pay, six days a week, and were beaten and whipped by overseers. Nestlé reacted sharply, saying that it did not tolerate illegal labor practices in its supply chain. Indeed, the company had already adopted a code of conduct, commissioned a study of its cocoa supply chain, and worked to train farmers. But with most cocoa still grown on small land holdings deep in the tropical forest, child labor had remained stubbornly intractable in the Ivory Coast—and Nestlé vulnerable to charges of exploiting underage workers.[15]

Companies that set up operations in countries with antidemocratic, repressive regimes can be caught up in violations of human rights. Some governments require foreign firms to partner with state-owned companies in order to do business there, adding another level of risk. For example, when the energy companies Unocal and Total undertook to build a gas pipeline across Burma to link a natural gas field in the Andaman Sea to a power plant in Thailand, they were required to partner with the government, a notorious abuser of human rights. Activists later charged that the Burmese government had used brute military force to clear the pipeline area, relocating entire villages and terrorizing the civilian population. Many civilians, including women, children, and the elderly, had been forcibly conscripted to clear land and build roads, barracks, and helipads. Although Unocal and Total had not engaged in these acts directly, the companies' critics felt that as the government's business partners, they shared responsibility.

A specific human rights challenge in global supply chains is sourcing minerals and other valuable commodities from conflict zones. For example, much of the world's *coltan,* a metallic ore used to make tantalum (which regulates electricity in portable consumer electronics) is sourced from mines in the Democratic Republic of the Congo. As further described in the discussion case at the end of Chapter 4, warring groups there have traded coltan to fund horrific civil conflict—and the electronics industry has been accused of indirectly contributing to the murder of civilians, sexual assault, and labor abuses. A coalition of electronics firms recently committed to buying tantalum only from certified processors, and in 2014, Intel announced the production of the world's first semiconductor chip completely free of any conflict minerals.[16] Other metals and minerals coming from war zones in Africa and elsewhere include tin, tungsten, and gold.

[14] United Nations Office on Drugs and Crime, *Global Report on Trafficking in Persons 2014,* November 2014; and Verité, "Strengthening Protections against Trafficking in Persons in Federal and Corporate Supply Chains," 2015.

[15] "U.S. Court Rules OK to Sue Chocolate Firms Over Slave Labor," *San Francisco Chronicle,* September 5, 2014; "Nestlé, ADM, and Cargill Can't Escape Liability for Cocoa Child Slavery, Rules Court," *www.confectionerynews.com,* September 8, 2014,; and Fair Labor Association, *Sustainable Management of Nestlé's Cocoa Supply chain in the Ivory Coast—Focus on Labor Standards,* June 2012.

[16] "Intel's Conflict Mineral Stand Should Kick Start a Trend," *Manufacturing Digital,* January 8, 2014.

Transnational companies that depend on resources that are farmed, extracted, or mined—such as the cocoa, natural gas, metals, and minerals mentioned in this section—are particularly at risk for human rights abuses by their suppliers. Often, their choices of where and from whom to source their supplies are limited. Under these conditions, these companies must take special precautions to avoid complicity in ethical violations in their supply chains.

Environmental Issues

When a supplier of raw materials, parts, or finished goods contributes to climate change, dumps toxic chemicals, emits air pollution, or reduces biodiversity, it can threaten the reputation of companies at the top of the supply chain.

> Activist stakeholders, including environmentalists and public pension funds, criticized ConAgra for the practices of its suppliers of palm oil, an ingredient in many processed foods. The U.S. food company sourced much of its palm oil from Indonesia and Malaysia, where tropical rainforests had been cleared to make way for commercial plantations. This destroyed the habitat of endangered species like the Sumatran orangutan, released pollutants into waterways, and destroyed peat bogs that sequestered carbon. Facing shareholder resolutions demanding change, ConAgra announced that it would buy only sustainably sourced palm oil, beginning in 2015. "The rampant deforestation for palm oil has captured public attention, creating real reputational risks for companies that use the ingredient in their branded products," said a manager of socially responsible mutual funds.[17]

Another issue of concern to supply chain managers is the environmental impact of transporting products long distances from where they are made, grown, or extracted to where they are further processed or sold to consumers. Much of the coffee, fruit, and fish from Latin America; toys, electronics, and garments from Asia; and wine, meat, and wool from Australia, for example, is shipped to Europe and North America on enormous container ships, which now carry more than half of global seaborne trade.[18] These ships, which burn dirty bunker fuel, emit about three percent of all greenhouse gas emissions.[19] Some companies have responded to environmental concerns by adopting a policy of **local sourcing**, seeking to source from nearby suppliers where practical. Others have taken steps to improve efficiency in their supply chains. For example, when Patagonia, the outerwear company, made the simple decision to switch its port of entry for products coming from Asia from Long Beach to Oakland, California, it reduced the distance the goods traveled by truck to its Reno, Nevada, distribution center—reducing its carbon emissions on the route by 31 percent.[20] In 2015, Walmart reported it had improved its fleet efficiency in the United States by 87 percent since 2005 by replacing its trucks with more fuel-efficient models and improving route and delivery efficiencies.[21] This move had both reduced emissions and saved money.

---

[17] "ConAgra's Palm Oil Commitment: Saving Forests and Reducing Greenhouse Gases," *The Guardian Sustainable Business,* August 22, 2014; and "ConAgra Joins Movement to Eliminate Deforestation," *Sustainability Investment News,* August 16, 2014. For more information about efforts to improve the sustainability of the palm oil supply chain, see the Roundtable on Sustainable Palm Oil, at *www.rspo.org.* ConAgra's 2014 citizenship report is online at *www.conagrafoodscitizenship.com.*

[18] Review of Marine Transport 2013, at *www.unctad.org.*

[19] International Maritime Organization, *Third IMO Greenhouse Gas Study 2014* (Suffolk, UK: Micropress, 2015), Table 1.

[20] "Changing Ports Pays Dividends," at *www.patagonia.com.*

[21] *Walmart 2015 Global Responsibility Report, www.walmart.com.*

FIGURE 17.2
Social and Environmental Issues Ranked in Importance by Supply Chain Managers
"Which of the following SER (social and environmental responsibility) issues are the most important in your supply chains?"

Source: "The Chief Supply Chain Officer Report 2013: Pulse of the Profession," *SCM World,* September 2013. Used by permission.

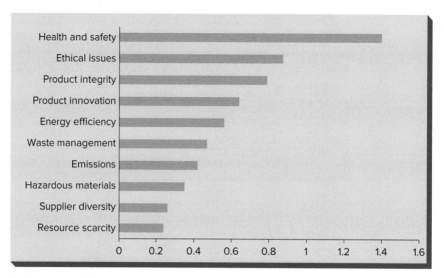

Based on a survey of 746 senior supply chain executives; weighted average where 0 was the lowest score and 3 was the highest score.

Supply Chain Risk

In short, supply chain managers face a number of significant social, ethical, and environmental issues. How do they rank these issues in order of importance? Figure 17.2 shows how a sample of senior supply chain managers ranked social and environmental issues in a 2013 survey. Health and safety was listed first, possibly reflecting the recent Bangladesh factory disaster; ethical issues ranked second; and several environmental issues were also mentioned.

Failure to manage social, ethical, and environmental risk in supply chains can be very costly, managers have learned. One study looked at the impact on stock prices of disruptions in companies' supply chains. Over a three-year period bracketing publicly announced disruptions, these companies' stock underperformed that of their peers by 40 percent. Operating income, return on sales, and return on assets were all adversely impacted, the researchers found, and firms did not recover quickly.[22] For example, when the Norwegian public pension fund decided to sell its holdings in Walmart Stores in 2006 because of concerns about child labor in its supply chain, Walmart's stock dropped 11 percent over a six-week period.[23] A strike in 2014 by many of the 43,000 workers at Yue Yuen Industrial Holdings, an enormous shoe factory in China, disrupted supplies to Adidas, Asics, and Nike, all of which had contracts with the firm. The workers were upset by their employer's failure to make required payments on their behalf into a government social security program.[24] In an effort to get production back on track, Adidas later worked with labor rights groups in China to seek the release of two strike leaders who had been detained.[25] In the meantime, production was halted and the flow of shoes to customers stalled.

What happens in a company's supply chain can help its reputation—as well as hurt it. Exhibit 17.A profiles the use of technology to promote supply chain transparency and build brand loyalty.

[22] Kevin B. Hendricks and Vinod R. Singhal, "An Empirical Analysis of the Effect of Supply Chain Disruptions on Long-Run Stock Price Performance and Equity Risk of the Firm," *Production and Operations Management,* 14, no. 1 (March 2005), pp. 35–52.

[23] PwC, Table 3, "Cases of Risk Reduction," p. 13.

[24] "Strike at Nike, Adidas China Supplier Halts Output," *Bloomberg.com,* April 18, 2014.

[25] "How Adidas Supported Worker Rights in China Factory Strike," *The Guardian,* June 12, 2014.

Supply chain transparency means that what happens in a company's supply chain is fully disclosed to stakeholders—as if seen through a clear glass window. Some firms have realized that openly revealing supply chain information can enhance brand loyalty among consumers concerned about social, ethical, and environmental responsibility. Technology increasingly makes this possible at the point of purchase. Products have always been labeled, of course. But today, advances in so-called technology tags, genetic markers, mobile phone apps, and virtually unlimited cloud data storage make it possible for consumers to see how and where a product was made in startling detail. For example, Switcher, a Swiss clothing company that sources from Bangladesh, China, India, Portugal, Romania, Turkey, and Taiwan, provides a unique number on the label of each of its garments. When the customer inputs this number at the website Respect-Code.org, he or she can track every step of the specific garment's journey, from the farm where its cotton fibers were grown to the factory where the garment was sewn. The website provides maps, photographs, and information about the most recent audits and certifications. The mobile app GoodGuide allows shoppers to scan the barcode of more than 120,000 food, personal care, and household products to access a rating of 1 to 10 based on health, environmental, and social responsibility impacts (including human and labor rights). GoodGuide used a variety of sources, including licensed databases, in creating its ratings. Supply chain transparency can give consumers confidence in the positive impacts of products they buy.

Sources: Andreas Wieland and Robert Handfield, "The Socially Responsible Supply Chain," *Supply Chain Management Review,* September/October 2013; Steve New, "The Transparent Supply Chain," *Harvard Business Review,* October 2010; and Andrew K. Schnackenberg and Edward C. Tomlinson, "Organizational Transparency: A New Perspective on Managing Trust in Organization-Stakeholder Relationships," *Journal of Management,* March 10, 2014.

Private Regulation of the Business–Supplier Relationship

Who establishes the rules for social, ethical, and environmental issues in supply chains? In other words, who regulates businesses' relationships with their suppliers?

This simple question has a complex answer. As the manufacturing supply chain has become increasingly globalized, its regulation has become more fragmented and ineffective. In response, new institutions have arisen to fill the void created by the inability of governments in both developed and developing countries to police the far-flung operations of large transnational corporations and their global supply chains. Mutually agreed-on standards, developed by private firms—often working in collaboration with nongovernmental organizations and United Nations affiliates such as the International Labor Organization—have emerged to complement, and in some cases even substitute for, national-level regulation.

Private regulation, also called *private governance,* refers to nongovernmental institutions that govern—that is, enable and constrain—economic activities. It occurs when private companies or groups of companies voluntarily set rules of behavior for themselves and their business partners.[26] Private regulation often takes the form of company and industrywide codes of conduct that establish standards governing labor, human rights, environmental, and related practices within global supply chains. Since the 1990s and accelerating in the 21st century, private regulation has assumed increasing importance, for several related reasons.

- *Lack of jurisdiction of home country governments.* The authority of governments in the home countries of lead firms normally does not extend to supplier factories in other countries. For example, in the United States, the Department of Labor and the

[26] Frederick Mayer and Gary Gereffi, "Regulation and Economic Globalization: Prospects and Limits of Private Governance," *Business and Politics* 12, no. 3 (October 2010), pp. 1–25; and Richard M. Locke, op cit.

Occupational Safety and Health Administration (OSHA) establish rules governing wages, overtime, child labor, safety conditions, and other workplace matters. The reach of these regulatory agencies normally does not extend beyond their national borders, however. For example, if blocked fire exits threatened worker safety in a factory in Indonesia making clothes for an American retailer, OSHA would have no authority to intervene.

- *Weak regulatory capacity in developing countries.* Nations with growing export-oriented manufacturing sectors often lack the institutional capacity, resources, and staff to regulate their own workplaces adequately. In some cases, business elites are so politically powerful that they can effectively block regulation. In Bangladesh, for example, one in ten members of parliament (or their relatives) are themselves garment factory owners, and members of powerful trade associations in the garment and knitwear industries sit on important government committees. Although regulatory capacity varies greatly by country, of course, in some cases, government agencies simply do not have the clout or independence to constrain the actions of powerful transnational corporations and their local partners.

- *Limited enforcement power of transnational institutions.* The United Nations has several affiliates that are deeply concerned with labor and human rights; among them are the International Labor Organization (ILO), the United Nations Children's Fund (UNICEF), and the Global Compact. All of these have developed important global standards, promoted them globally, and sought to implement them. The ILO, for example, has developed a Better Factories initiative that has improved working conditions in dozens of countries. These institutions have moral authority, but lack enforcement power, and their influence is limited by companies' willingness to cooperate with them.

In the absence of effective public regulation, many companies and industries have written—and undertaken to enforce—their own voluntary **supply chain codes of conduct** that establish rules for their suppliers. One of the first companies to develop such a code was Levi Strauss, a U.S. apparel maker. After the company was accused of using an unethical contractor in Saipan in 1991, the company reviewed its procedures and adopted a wide-ranging set of guidelines for its overseas manufacturing.[27] Reebok, Boeing, Mattel, and other companies soon followed suit. Supply chain codes of conduct quickly spread, with the footwear, apparel, and electronics industries leading the way.[28] By 2014, 58 percent of the largest publicly held companies in the United States had adopted codes of conduct that set social and environmental standards for their suppliers. Forty-seven percent considered social and environmental criteria in procurement (sourcing) decisions, and 34 percent monitored supplier performance. All of these percentages had risen from just two years earlier, as shown in Figure 17.3.

Scholars have hypothesized that private governance is most likely to emerge in global supply chains under several conditions. These include:

- Large lead firms have leverage over smaller suppliers.
- Firms and products have highly visible brands, and are therefore more vulnerable to reputational damage.

---

[27] Karl Schoenberger, *Levi's Children: Coming to Terms with Human Rights in the Global Marketplace* (New York: Grove Press, 2000).

[28] "Supply Chain," in CERES, *Gaining Ground: Corporate Progress on the CERES Roadmap to Sustainability,* July 16, 2014. Based on a survey 613 large, publicly held U.S. companies.

FIGURE 17.3
Percentage of Large U.S. Companies with Supplier Codes of Conduct, 2012 and 2014

Source: CERES, *Gaining Ground: Corporate Progress on the CERES Roadmap for Sustainability,* July 2014, p. 49. Based on a sample of 613 large, publicly traded U.S. companies. Used by permission.

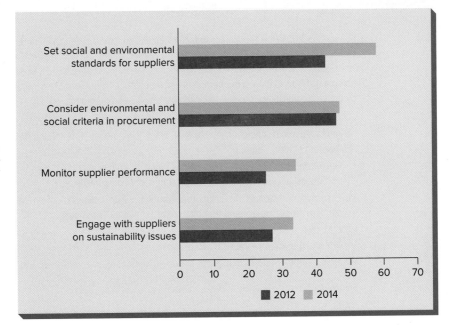

- Civil society is exerting pressure for responsible practices; for example, through campaigns, boycotts, or shareholder resolutions.
- A strong business case can be made for social and environmental responsibility.[29]

Although early codes of conduct were typically developed by and were specific to individual companies, the current trend is toward adoption of common standards within industries. In part, this reflects the influence of nongovernmental organizations and standard-setting associations that have provided templates. For example, the Fair Labor Association, the Council on Economic Priorities, and the Caux Round Table have all developed model codes. Common standards also reflect the efforts of groups of companies—sometimes with participation of government officials, NGOs, and worker and consumer representatives—to define industrywide standards that they can all agree to. For example, many leading high-tech companies joined forces as the Electronic Industry Citizenship Coalition (EICC) to establish a code of conduct that provided a uniform set of labor, health and safety, and environmental standards for their global supply chains. The EICC code is further described in Exhibit 17.B. Supporters of this industrywide approach argue that common standards improve compliance, since suppliers are not faced with myriad conflicting demands. It also can reduce the costs of monitoring, since brands can share audit results. (Supply chain auditing is further described in the following section.) A survey by the Stanford Global Supply Chain Management of 33 companies, almost all in the technology and apparel industries, found that 76 percent had adopted a standardized industry code of conduct.[30]

A 2013 survey of senior supply chain management executives in almost 800 companies around the world found that the leading reason why their firms had invested in supplier social responsibility was to create a positive customer image and enhance brand equity.

[29] Frederick Mayer and Gary Gereffi, "Regulation and Economic Globalization: Prospects and Limits of Private Governance," *Business and Politics* 12, no. 3 (October 2010), pp. 1–25.

[30] Barchi Gillai, Angharad Porteous, and Sonali Rammohan, "The Relationship between Responsible Supply Chain Practices and Performance," Stanford Global Supply Chain Management Forum, November 2013, Appendix 2, p. 9.

Founded in 2004, the Electronics Industry Citizenship Coalition (EICC) is made up of nearly 100 electronics companies, including such well-known firms as Hewlett-Packard, IBM, Apple, Dell, Intel, Lenovo, Oracle, Samsung, Sony, Microsoft, and Cisco. The coalition collaboratively developed a code of conduct and committed to enforce its terms in their own operations and in their tier-1 suppliers. Over 3.5 million employees are covered by the code, which includes the following provisions, among others:

- *Labor standards:* No forced labor, no child labor, workweek not to exceed 60 hours except under emergency situations, compliance with local wage laws, no harsh or inhumane treatment, no discrimination, freedom of association.

- *Health and safety:* Safe and healthy workplaces, with procedures to control hazards and prevent injury and illness; access to sanitation, clean water, and eating facilities.

- *Environmental standards:* Pollution prevention; waste minimization; proper handling of hazardous substances; proper control and treatment of water and air emissions.

- *Ethics:* Highest standards of integrity; fair business practices; no bribery; protection of intellectual property and privacy.

- *Management:* Systems in place to assure implementation, compliance, and improvement.

Source: The full code is available at *www.eiccoalition.org.*

Other reasons were to reduce costs, satisfy government regulations, avoid disruptions, increase sales, and allay public criticism.[31] These findings are shown in Figure 17.4.

Does private regulation make a difference? In an important recent book, *The Promise and Limits of Private Power,* Richard M. Locke argues that the most effective way to assure socially responsible practices in global supply chains is a *combination* of public and private regulation. Either, when used alone, is insufficient; they work best, he believes, when "layered" on top of each other in a kind of hybrid system. For example, private companies can rely on local laws to give legitimacy to demands for workplace changes, and government regulators can benefit from detailed workplace record keeping required by private companies' codes of conduct. Public and private regulators can also share the work. In the Caribbean nation of the Dominican Republic, for example, one study found that government inspectors (public regulators) and auditors for major North American brands (private regulators) had developed an informal division of labor, in which the former concentrated on firms producing for the domestic market, and the latter on firms producing for export.[32]

Companies can adopt their own code, or agree to one of the NGO or industrywide codes. But who is to say that they, and their suppliers, are actually living up to these rules? Many now conduct independent audits to determine if a code's standards are being met. This is discussed next.

Supply Chain Auditing

Once a company has developed its own code of supplier conduct, or agreed to comply with an industrywide or global code, it must undertake to enforce these rules. In a simpler time, when a firm operated its own manufacturing facilities in a limited geographical area, monitoring compliance with an established set of standards was straightforward. But in today's more complex world, obtaining this information can be extraordinarily difficult.

[31] SCM World, "The Chief Supply Chain Officer Report 2013: Pulse of the Profession," September 2013, Figure 7.

[32] Matthew Amengual, "Complementary Labor Regulation: the Uncoordinated Combination of State and Private Regulators in the Dominican Republic," *World Development* 38, no. 3 (2010), pp. 405–414.

FIGURE 17.4
Drivers of Social and Environmental Responsibility in Supply Chains
"What is your best judgment of your board's motivations for investing in SER [social and environmental responsibility]?"

Source: Supply Chain World, *The Chief Supply Chain Officer Report 2013,* Figure 7. Used by permission.

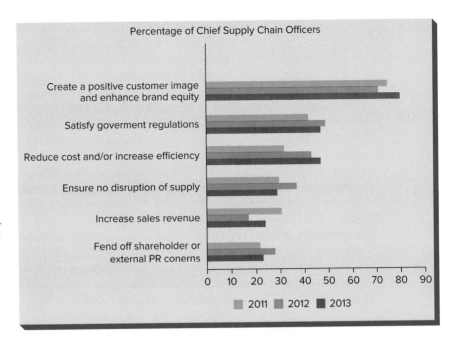

A lead firm's supplier code of conduct can require, for example, that all workers making its products are paid at least the minimum wage, but how can it assure that this is actually true? This assurance is usually obtained by conducting a **supply chain audit**. Such an audit monitors a supplier's performance to determine if it is in compliance with the relevant code of conduct. (Auditing is also discussed in Chapter 3.)

Companies have several choices in carrying out an audit. One is to hire and train its own staff of auditors whose job is to inspect factories—either its own or those operated by contractors—to determine whether or not they are in compliance. This is sometimes called an *internal audit.*

An example of a company that has conducted its own internal audits is Gap Inc. This specialty retailer of clothing, accessories, and personal care products adopted a code of vendor [supplier] conduct. In order to obtain a contract with Gap, suppliers had to agree to pay at least the minimum wage, respect human rights, and refrain from discrimination, among other commitments. To assure that suppliers were following the code, Gap hired more than 90 vendor compliance officers, or VCOs. These individuals came from the communities where they worked, so they would be able to communicate well and understand the culture of the contractors they audited. These VCOs visited thousands of factories annually in the 50 or so countries where Gap products were made. Their work was overseen by a chief compliance officer, who reported directly to the CEO.[33]

An advantage of an internal audit is that the company controls and manages the process. It can train its own compliance officers, determine what factories need to be audited, and learn immediately about any problems uncovered. On the other hand, a disadvantage is that stakeholders might view reports based on an internal audit as less credible, because the company would have an interest in casting itself and its suppliers in a favorable light.

[33] "Closing the Gap: Quality and Standards in Ethical Supply Chains," *International Trade Forum Magazine,* March 2010. Gap's corporate social responsibility reports are available at *www.gap.com.*

A second option is to hire another organization to carry out the audit and report back to the company. This is called an *external audit* or a *third-party audit,* because it is carried out by someone other than the company or the managers of the factories that produce its goods. The three largest publicly traded, for-profit monitoring companies are Bureau Veritas, Intertek, and SGS. Lead firms may also engage nonprofit organizations, such as Verité, the Fair Labor Association, or the Worker Rights Consortium. (An audit conducted for Apple by the Fair Labor Association is described in the discussion case at the end of this chapter.) Recently, a number of large accounting firms such as PricewaterhouseCoopers have developed specialized services in which they will conduct a social or environmental audit for clients (rather than a financial audit, which is their traditional specialty). The advantage of an external audit is that it is often perceived by stakeholders as more objective and reliable. Companies may find, however, that the information is delayed, and it does not directly control the quality of the audit.

An audit, whether conducted internally or externally, generally consists of a review of documentation (such as payroll and personnel records), a facility inspection, and interviews with workers and managers. Companies normally do not reveal what they spend on supply chain auditing. However, *The New York Times* estimated that the cost of a factory audit could range from $1,000 for a one-day, "check-the-box" audit to as much as $5,000 for a thorough, multi-day inspection.[34] A major firm can require hundreds of audits a year. For example, in 2013 Nike completed full assessments of 94 percent of its 785 supplier factories.[35]

While audits can provide considerable insight into conditions in supplier factories, they also have drawbacks. On-site inspections are expensive and time-consuming, and therefore cannot be scaled to cover a brand's entire supply chain, which might consist of thousands of factories. Audits are not always unannounced; in many cases, suppliers receive advance notice and are able to stage conditions to pass the inspection. Workers sometimes distrust auditors, not knowing if the inspectors represent the supplier, the brand, or an independent third party, and are therefore reluctant to share their experiences.

An emerging approach to auditing involves bypassing the factory inspection process entirely. Instead, a **crowd-sourced audit** gathers information about factory conditions directly from workers using their mobile phones. In this approach, rather than relying on inspectors—who may be deceived by factory managers who want conditions to appear better than they really are—workers provide information directly by responding to questions generated by a recorded voice on their mobile phones when they are away from work. For example, LaborVoices, a recently established social enterprise, has piloted such an approach in the garment industry in India and Bangladesh.[36] Workers must trust the process and participate widely for crowd-sourced data to be reliable and useful.

Increasingly, companies are working together to audit major suppliers and to share results. This avoids *audit fatigue,* in which supplier factories must endure audit after audit conducted by different buyers, and spares companies from duplicating efforts and incurring unnecessary costs. One such effort is the Sustainable Compliance Initiative (SCI).

In 2012, more than two dozen companies, working with the Fair Labor Association, announced the formation of a common auditing tool. The SCI audit tool included set of core questions that covered the minimum requirements for all participating companies' codes of conduct. The group planned to create an online data-sharing

---

[34] "Fast and Flawed Inspections of Factories Abroad," *The New York Times,* September 1, 2013.

[35] Nike, "FY12/13 Sustainable Business Performance Summary," *www.nikeresponsibility.com.*

[36] Ronald M. Roman, Anne T. Lawrence, and Chirag Amin, "LaborVoices: Bringing Transparency to the Global Supply Chain," *Case Research Journal* 34, no. 4 (Fall 2014). For more information, see *www.laborvoices.com.*

platform, to be operated by the Fair Factories Clearinghouse (FFC), which all participating companies could access. "The FFC is pleased to be able to offer this smart audit capability to its members, and we are expecting this new tool will see rapid adoption among industry leaders," said its executive director.[37]

Another cloud-based online platform for sharing data on labor, health and safety, environmental, and ethics practices in global supply chains is operated by Sedex Global, a nonprofit membership organization. A study of 33 companies by the Stanford Global Supply Chain Management Forum found that 52 percent shared audit results with other companies that used the same suppliers.[38]

What do companies do when an audit reveals a gap between their social, ethical, and environmental standards and a supplier's practices? Most audits turn up at least some instances in which a company's global operations are not in compliance. For example, inspectors may uncover underage workers, violations of environmental commitments, or discriminatory hiring practices. Sometimes, a company will terminate a supplier, if the supplier is unwilling to change or the deficiencies are egregious. For example, when Gap's auditors found an unauthorized, makeshift factory operated by a subcontractor in India, where children were embroidering a product for GapKids, the company immediately cancelled the order and banned the subcontractor from any future work. It also cooperated with a child welfare organization to care for the children and reunite them with their families. Forty-eight percent of companies in a recent survey said they would terminate a supplier in certain cases if violations were found.[39] But increasingly, firms try to work in a positive way with suppliers to help them improve their practices. This topic is discussed next.

Supplier Development and Capability Building

A growing trend is for lead firms to work collaboratively with their suppliers to help them improve their social, ethical, and environmental performance. The term **supplier development** refers to activities undertaken by companies to improve the performance of firms in their supply chains.[40] Rather than terminate or punish a supplier, a lead firm may choose instead to invest time and resources to build the supplier's capabilities. Such an approach starts from the premise that many suppliers wish to comply, but simply lack the managerial skill, technical knowledge, or resources to do so.

Why would lead firms decide to engage in **capability building**, rather than simply give their contracts to someone else—or even do the work themselves? One reason is that the cost of switching suppliers may be too high. A supplier may have critical capabilities, such as technical expertise in making a specific product, or other attributes that the lead firm values, such as relationships with other firms farther upstream in the supply chain. The lead firm may feel a moral obligation to the workers and local community not to cause job loss. Or, other suppliers may not be readily available to take over the contract.

[37] "Creating an Industry-Wide Audit Tool Together with Other Brands," p. 37 in Adidas Group, *Fair Play: Sustainability Progress Report 2013*, at *www.adidas-group.com*, and *www.fairfactories.org*.

[38] Barchi Gillai, Angharad H. Porteous, and Sonali V. Rammohan, "The Relationship between Responsible Supply Chain Practices and Performance," Stanford Global Supply Chain Management Forum, November 2103, Appendix 2, p. 9.

[39] Ibid., p. 12.

[40] Daniel R. Krause, Robert B. Handfield, and Beverly B. Tyler, "The Relationship between Supplier Development, Commitment, Social Capital Accumulation, and Performance Improvement," *Journal of Operations Management* 25 (2007), online at *www.sciencedirect.com*. See also Steven C. Dunn and Richard R. Young, "Supplier Assistance within Supplier Development Initiatives," *Journal of Supply Chain Management* (Summer 2004).

For many reasons, then, a lead firm may find it preferable to work with a supplier to improve its performance.

Supplier development may take several forms, including training, joint problem solving, and investing in equipment or infrastructure. An example of a company with a robust training program is Cisco Systems, which designs and markets networking equipment that is manufactured by more than 600 suppliers in Asia, the Americas, and Europe. To assure that these partners comply fully with its supplier code of conduct, Cisco has developed an online training library, run a series of webinars in English and Mandarin, and paired suppliers to share best practices.[41] Sometimes, technical assistance can be of great help. For example, a global apparel firm trained managers at a supplier factory in the Dominican Republic, where workers had complained repeatedly about excessive heat, how to install a new ventilation system, fans, and water coolers.[42] Following the catastrophic factory collapse in Bangladesh, mentioned earlier in this chapter, dozens of lead firms organized as the Accord on Fire and Building Safety inspected 1,100 supplier factories and found structural deficiencies in more than 100 of them. Under the terms of the accord, member brands committed to providing funds to correct these safety problems, either through loans or favorable contract terms.[43]

Some companies have invested directly in improving the lives and professional skills of their suppliers' workers.

Gap Inc., the apparel retailer, supports a program called Personal Advancement and Career Enhancement, or P.A.C.E., which has served more than 20,000 low-skilled women garment workers throughout its global supply chain. Created in collaboration with several NGOs—the International Center for Research on Women, CARE, and the Swasti Health Resource Centre (located in India)—P.A.C.E. provides up to 80 hours of free life skills and technical training. Classes have been held in India, Cambodia, Vietnam, Bangladesh, Sri Lanka, and China. An evaluation of the program showed that women who participated had a greater sense of self-worth and were better able to manage their work and professional lives. The program also decreased worker turnover, and women who completed the program were more likely to be promoted at work.[44]

This initiative went beyond the factory walls to empower women and build communities.

Lead firms can provide a variety of rewards or incentives to suppliers that collaborate to build capabilities. Cisco, for example, gives preference to otherwise qualified suppliers that meet certain sustainability standards. Starbucks offers farmers that achieve high marks in its CAFÉ (Coffee and Farmer Equity) program—which scores coffee producers on social and environmental criteria—a premium price for their coffee beans.[45] Research has shown that capability building initiatives work best where interactions between buyer and supplier are frequent and ongoing, and where the two parties have a long-term relationship.[46]

[41] 2013 Cisco CSR Report, "Supply Chain," pp. C1–19, *www.cisco.com/assets/csr/pdf/CSR_Report_2013.pdf*.

[42] Locke, op. cit., p. 91.

[43] "Inspections Highlight Flaws at Bangladesh Garment Factories," *The Wall Street Journal*, October 14, 2014.

[44] Priya Nanda, Anurag Mishra, Sunayana Walia, Shubh Sharma, Ellen Weiss, Jennifer Abrahamson,"Advancing Women, Changing Lives: An Evaluation of Gap Inc.'s P.A.C.E. Program," Washington, D.C.: International Center for Research on Women, 2013.

[45] "Starbucks C.A.F.E. Practices: Ensuring the Ethical Sourcing of Coffee," at *www.scsglobalservices.com/starbucks-cafe-practices*.

[46] Locke, pp. 101–102.

If suppliers are unconvinced they will benefit from more orders or higher margins, they are less willing to participate. On the other hand, they are more likely to engage when lead firms are prepared to offer them stable, long-term contracts, so they feel that investing in compliance is worthwhile.[47]

Effective supplier development often involves careful study to determine the underlying cause of repeated violations of particular code requirements or standards. This is known as **root cause analysis**. For example, Nike's supplier audits turned up repeated instances of excessive overtime in apparel manufacturing factories, particularly in China, despite rules prohibiting this practice. When the company studied the problem, it found that the biggest root cause was *style proliferation*—asking factories to make too many different styles and to switch frequently from one style to another. Each change reduced efficiency and required extra work hours. Nike also found other root causes, such as miscalculations in placing orders, last-minute changes in colors and fabrics, and poor forecasting of customer demand. In response, the company committed to reducing the number of styles contracted to each supplier.[48]

As this example implies, demands placed on suppliers may run at cross-purposes. If an electronics company places a rush, high-volume order for a popular new product, and at the same time prohibits excessive overtime, the supplier may be unable to fulfill both requirements at once. Or, a lead firm may pressure suppliers, on one hand, for ever-lower costs and, on the other hand, for compliance with expensive environmental standards. Suppliers are caught in a bind, not knowing which set of expectations is more important. These contradictory demands sometimes reflect divergent priorities within the lead firm itself. Departments of supply chain management or procurement may be focused on one set of goals, and departments of citizenship, sustainability, or social responsibility on another.

Some forward-thinking companies have directly addressed this problem. They have developed organizational mechanisms to resolve differences in priorities internally, and they have tried to communicate expectations more clearly to suppliers. One trend is the use of **integrated supplier scorecards** that rate suppliers on multiple dimensions, including both traditional measures (such as cost, quality, and timeliness) and newer measures of social, ethical, and environmental performance. For example, Nike has introduced a Manufacturing Index that measures and rewards suppliers on four dimensions—quality, on-time delivery, cost, and sustainability—each of which is weighted 25 percent. (The sustainability factor is broadly defined to include social, environmental, and health and safety issues.) "The [Manufacturing] Index enables us to reward contract factories that score consistently well across all categories," said Nike's vice president of sustainable business and innovation.[49]

Research shows that when companies invest in suppliers and their employees, exchange knowledge, and collaborate on improvements, they create **shared value** that benefits both parties.

---

[47] Locke, p. 104.

[48] Nike, Inc., "Corporate Responsibility Report, FY 07 08 09," online at *www.nikebiz.com.*

[49] Angharad H. Porteous and Sonali V. Rammohan, "Integration, Incentives, and Innovation: Nike's Strategy to Improve Social and Environmental Conditions in its Global Supply Chain," *Stanford Initiative for the Study of Supply Chain Responsibility,* November 9, 2013; and Hannah Jones, "Forum: Can Global Brands Create Just Supply Chains," May 21, 2013, at *www .bostonreview.net/forum/can-global-brands-create-just-supply-chains/new-conversation-responsibility.*

FIGURE 17.5
Lead Firm Responses to Supply Chain Audits of Social, Ethical, and Environmental Performance

Source: Created by the authors, based on a figure appearing in Gap Inc., *2011/12 Social and Environmental Responsibility Report*, p. 35.

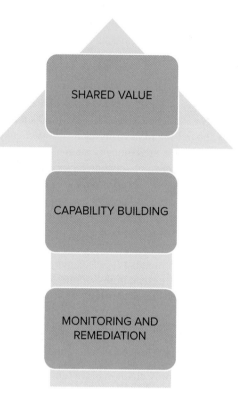

SHARED VALUE

CAPABILITY BUILDING

MONITORING AND REMEDIATION

One of the poorest countries in the world is Madagascar, an island nation off the east coast of the African continent. It is the source of about 80 percent of the global supply of vanilla—the world's most popular flavor. Vanilla comes from an orchid that is cultivated by farmers on small plots, using labor-intensive methods methods, often in remote villages. Two major companies—Unilever, the Anglo-Dutch multinational consumer goods company, and Symrise, a German supplier of flavors and fragrances—partnered with NGOs and aid organizations to train vanilla farmers in Madagascar to improve yields and diversify their crops. They also invested directly in local primary schools. The result was higher income and expanded opportunities for vanilla farmers and their children, and a more stable and higher-quality supply of vanilla for their business customers. "The comprehensive development program . . . is an opportunity to create value for all," said the CEO of Symrise.[50]

Supplier development, as shown in this example, can benefit both the lead firm and the supplier.

Figure 17.5 portrays interactions between lead firms and suppliers as a sequential process that begins with monitoring and remediation, and then moves upward through capability building, and finally to the creation of shared value. Firms continue activities at the lower levels, even as they progress through the next two, in cumulative steps.

---

[50] "Unilever, Symrise and GIZ Join Forces to Support Vanilla Farmers," January 29, 2014, at *www.unilever.com/mediacentre/pressreleases/2014/PrivatepublicpartnershipaimstoimprovelivelihoodsofvanillafarmersinMadagascar.aspx;* and Fairfood International, *Recipe for Change: The Need for Improved Livelihoods of Vanilla Farmers in Madagascar,* February 2014.

Summary

- A supplier is an organization that provides goods or services to another organization. Suppliers are important market stakeholders, since they provide critical inputs and often manufacture branded products. Although suppliers are diverse, they share a common interest in building long-term, stable relationships with buyers. Suppliers that provide unique skills, resources, or capabilities tend to have more power. As globalization has increased, supply chains have become increasingly complex.

- Many social, ethical, and environmental issues arise in global supply chains. These include low wages, unsafe conditions, child and forced labor, unethical sourcing from conflict areas, and adverse environmental impacts of resource extraction, production, and transportation. Companies that do not manage supply chain risks effectively can suffer financial and reputational damage; conversely, those that manage these risks well can benefit.

- Private regulation refers to nongovernmental institutions that establish rules in global supply chains. It generally takes the form of company and industrywide codes of conduct with which suppliers must comply. Private regulation tends to arise in situations where public regulation is weak, and lead firms carry significant reputational risk because of strong consumer brands.

- Lead firms and groups of firms use several methods to audit compliance with supply chain codes of conduct. These include internal audit, third-party (external) audits, and crowd-sourced audits. Increasingly, companies are working together to audit major suppliers and to share results, often on cloud-based platforms.

- A growing trend is for companies to engage collaboratively with suppliers to build capability. This benefits both the firm and supplier, creating shared value. Suppliers are more likely to engage with lead firms with which they have stable, long-term relationships.

Key Terms

capability building, *387*
child labor, *377*
crowd-sourced audit, *386*
human trafficking, *377*
integrated supplier scorecard, *389*
local sourcing, *379*
private regulation, *381*

root cause analysis, *389*
shared value, *389*
supplier, *373*
supplier development, *387*
supply chain, *373*
supply chain audit, *385*
supply chain codes of conduct, *382*

supply chain map, *375*
supply chain transparency, *381*
sweatshop, *376*
tier-1 and tier-2 suppliers, *373*

Internet Resources

www.scw-mag.com/	Supply Chain World
www.ism.ws/SR/	Institute for Supply Management: Social Responsibility
www.theguardian.com/sustainable-business/series/supply-chain	The Guardian Sustainable Business Supply Chain
www.gsb.stanford.edu/value-chain-innovation/research/responsible-supply-chains	Stanford University Value Chain Innovation Initiative
www.weforum.org/	World Economic Forum (reports on supply chain responsibility)
www.sourcingnetwork.org/	Responsible Sourcing Network

Discussion Case: *Apple's Supplier Code of Conduct and Foxconn's Chinese Factories*

In 2015, Apple released its ninth annual supplier responsibility report. In it, the company said that in the past year it had carried out 633 audits of factories in its global supply chain, covering 1.6 million workers in 19 countries—including the massive facilities operated by Foxconn in China, where most of its iPads and iPhones were made. Apple's own auditors had conducted these inspections, supported by local third-party experts.

The supply chain audits had turned up some persistent problems. Eight percent of work-weeks were not compliant with the company's 60-hour maximum standard, and auditors had also found instances of underage workers and excessive fees paid by foreign contract workers. As a result of the audits, workers were retroactively paid for unpaid overtime and refunded excessive fees. Where underage workers were found, the supplier was required to pay for the young person's safe return home, fund his or her continuing education, and continue to pay their wages—a stiff penalty that deterred the practice. In addition, Apple had trained more than 2 million workers on their rights under the code of conduct and local laws.

"We care deeply about every worker in Apple's global supply chain," said the company's senior vice president of operations. But, he acknowledged, "gaps still exist, and there is more work to do."

In 2015, Apple was the largest publicly traded company in the world, with a market capitalization in excess of $700 billion. The company directly employed almost 100,000 people and operated more than 450 stores in 16 countries, as well as its iTunes online music store. *Fortune* magazine had named Apple the most admired company in the world for eight years in a row.

Although Apple seemed to be making progress, its path to supplier responsibility had been lengthy and difficult. Since the 1990s, Apple had outsourced almost all of its manufacturing, mostly to China. The company's biggest supplier was the Taiwanese firm Foxconn, the largest contract manufacturer of consumer electronics in the world. Foxconn's facility in Shenzhen, China, operated like a good-sized city, with its own dormitories, cafeterias, hospital, swimming pool, and stores. In its complex of factories, 300,000 workers—many of them young women and men from rural areas—churned out electronics for Sony, Dell, IBM, and other major brands, as well as Apple.

In 2006, a British newspaper ran a story alleging mistreatment of workers at the Shenzhen facility. Apple investigated and found some violations of its supplier code of conduct, which it had introduced in 2005. In 2010, other developments focused a fresh spotlight on harsh conditions in Foxconn's factories. In a few short months, nine workers committed suicide by throwing themselves from the upper floors of company dormitories. (Foxconn responded by putting up nets to catch jumpers, raising wages, and opening a counseling center.) In 2011, two separate explosions at factories where iPads were being made (one was Foxconn's facility in Chengdu), apparently caused by a build-up of combustible aluminum dust, injured 77 and killed four. At Wintek, another Chinese supplier, 137 workers were sickened after using a toxic chemical called n-hexane to clean iPhone screens.

In January 2012, the public radio show *This American Life* broadcast a feature by monologist Mike Daisey about his interviews with workers leaving their shifts at Foxconn's Shenzhen facility, which related in dramatic fashion their disturbing stories. Although Daisey's piece was later criticized for not being entirely factual, it prompted some listeners to launch a petition drive on www.change.org that quickly garnered more than a quarter million signatures calling on Apple to protect workers that made their iPhones.

Just one week later, Apple announced it had joined the Fair Labor Association (FLA), the first electronics company to do so. The FLA, founded in 1999, was a nonprofit alliance of companies, universities, and human rights activists committed to ending sweatshop conditions. At Apple's request and with the company's financial support, the FLA immediately undertook the most extensive audit ever conducted of conditions in China's electronics supply chain. In its report, issued in March 2012, the FLA found a number of serious violations of Apple's supplier code of conduct, including excessive overtime, pay that was too low to meet workers' basic needs, and many workplace accidents and injuries.

Under intense public scrutiny and pressure from Apple, Foxconn made significant changes. According to one report, after the FLA issued its findings the company's CEO Terry Gou rushed to Shenzhen, where he told his managers emphatically, "The world is watching! We are going to fix this, right here!" The supplier worked to reduce overtime, cutting hours first to 60 a week and then to 49. It also raised wages, by as much as 50 percent in some cases, to offset fewer overtime hours. It replaced workers' stools with chairs with sturdy backs and put automatic shut-off devices on machinery to prevent injuries. (But, it also began introducing automation and moving some production away from the industrialized coast to less affluent, interior provinces.)

Whether its reforms had helped or hurt Foxconn remained an open question. In 2015, a Chinese NGO released data allegedly showing that Apple had begun shifting work from Foxconn to Pegatron, another supplier, in order to save money. Pegatron had an 8 percent cost advantage over Foxconn, mainly because it paid its workers less. "As two suppliers essentially compete over labor costs, to only demand that one side [Foxconn] improve labor conditions is no different than making it sacrifice market share," said the NGO.

Sources: "Supplier Responsibility 2015 Progress Report," available at *www.apple.com/supplier-responsibility;* China Labor Watch, "Analyzing Labor Conditions of Pegatron and Foxconn," February 2015, at *www.chinalaborwatch.org;* "Signs of Change Taking Hold in Electronics Factories in China," *The New York Times,* December 26, 2012; Ross Perlin, "Chinese Workers Foxconned," *Dissent,* Spring 2013; "Fair Labor Association Secures Commitment to Limit Workers' Hours, Protect Pay at Apple's Largest Supplier" [press release], March 29, 2012, at *www.fairlabor.org;* and reporting by *The New York Times, Bloomberg Businessweek,* and *www.abcnews.com.*

Discussion Questions	1. What were the interests and sources of power of Foxconn, Apple's supplier?
	2. What social, ethical, and environmental risks were present in Apple's supply chain?
	3. What were the advantages and disadvantages to Apple of using its own company-specific supplier code of conduct, rather than an industrywide code?
	4. What are the advantages and disadvantages to Apple of relying on its own internal audits, as contrasted with using an independent auditor like the Fair Labor Association?
	5. What more, if anything, could Apple do now to reduce supply chain risk and create shared value?

The Community and the Corporation

A strong relationship benefits both business and its community. Communities look to businesses for civic leadership and for help in coping with local problems, while businesses expect to be treated in fair and supportive ways by the community. As companies expand their operations, they develop a wider set of community relationships. Community relations programs, including corporate giving, are an important way for a business to express its commitment to corporate citizenship.

This Chapter Focuses on These Key Learning Objectives:

LO 18-1 Defining a community, and understanding the interdependencies between companies and the communities in which they operate.

LO 18-2 Analyzing why it is in the interest of business to respond to community problems and needs.

LO 18-3 Knowing the major responsibilities of community relations managers.

LO 18-4 Examining how different forms of corporate giving contribute to building strong relationships between businesses and communities.

LO 18-5 Evaluating how companies can direct their giving strategically, to further their own business objectives.

LO 18-6 Analyzing how collaborative partnerships between businesses and communities can address today's pressing social problems.

Salesforce.com, a cloud computing company based in San Francisco, develops software that helps companies and other organizations manage their relationships with customers and other stakeholders. Since its founding in 1999, the company has embraced what it calls the "1-1-1" model of integrated corporate philanthropy: it donates 1 percent of its stock, 1 percent of its employee time, and 1 percent of its products to its foundation, which in turn gives these assets to charitable causes. Over a decade and a half, the foundation has given more than $85 million in grants, almost a million dollars' worth of community service, and donations of software and other products to 25,000 nonprofits and higher education institutions. "Our industry has . . . done a phenomenal job creating value for the world through our technology," said CEO Marc Benioff. "But we are not really an industry known for giving that wealth back." Benioff set out not only to change that perception, but also to convince other technology companies to join Salesforce in taking the 1-1-1 pledge.[1]

One of the leading financial institutions in the world, ING has operations in more than 50 countries. Based in the Netherlands, the company provides insurance, banking, and asset management services throughout Europe, with a growing presence in the Americas and Asia. Recognizing that the needs of the many communities where it does business differ, the company has delegated responsibility for corporate citizenship programs to business unit managers, provided their decisions are consistent with the firm's core values. The result has been a remarkable diversity of community initiatives. In India, ING trained secondary school heads; in the United States, it ran financial literacy classes for teens; in Malaysia, it worked on the conservation of rain forests. Across the globe, ING employees participated in a worldwide fund-raising effort for Creating Chances for Children, the company's partnership with UNICEF, with a goal of positively impacting one million children by 2015.[2]

Whole Foods Market is a natural foods retailer with stores in many communities in North America and the United Kingdom. Founded in 1980 in Austin, Texas, the company believes that its business "is intimately tied to the neighborhood and larger community that we serve and in which we live." Whole Foods donates 5 percent of its net profit to charitable causes and operates a foundation that supports rural economic development, as well as projects that support animal welfare, organic production, and healthy nutrition. Each of the company's 367 stores hosts a community giving day three times a year, with 5 percent of the day's total sales revenue contributed to a worthy local nonprofit organization. Whole Foods also encourages its employees to volunteer their time and expertise to the community. Employees have been involved in a wide range of service projects, including organizing blood donation drives, raising money for breast cancer research, developing community gardens, renovating housing, and delivering "meals on wheels."[3]

Why do businesses as diverse as Salesforce.com, ING, and Whole Foods Market invest in community organizations, projects, and charities? Why do they contribute their money, resources, and time to help others? What benefits do they gain from such activities? This chapter explains why many companies believe that being an involved citizen is part of their basic business mission. The chapter also looks at how companies participate in community life and how they build partnerships with other businesses, government, and community organizations. The core questions that we consider in this chapter are: What does it mean to be a good corporate neighbor? What is the business case for doing so?

---

[1] "Salesforce Expands Its 'Pledge 1%' Philanthropic Model to New York Tech Companies," May 4, 2015, at *http://techcrunch .com/2015/05/04/salesforce-1-percent/*; and "Marc Benioff's Philanthropic Mission: San Francisco," *Bloomberg Businessweek*, December 23, 2014. The website of the Salesforce Foundation is at *www.ing.com/ING-in-Society.*

[2] Information on ING's community initiatives is available at *www.ing.com/ing-in-society.*

[3] See *www.wholefoodsmarket.com/mission-values/caring-communities/community-giving.*

The Business–Community Relationship

The term **community**, as used in this chapter, refers to a company's area of business influence. Traditionally, the term applied to the city, town, or rural area in which a business's operations, offices, or assets were located. With the rise of large, complex business organizations, the meaning of the term has expanded to include multiple localities. A local merchant's community relationships may involve just the people who live within driving distance of its store. A bank in a large metropolitan area, by contrast, may define its community as the both the central city and the suburbs where it does business. And at the far extreme, a large transnational firm such as ING, ExxonMobil, or H&M has relationships with numerous communities in many countries around the world.

Today the term *community* may also refer not only to a geographical area or areas but to a range of groups that are affected by an organization's actions, whether or not they are in the immediate vicinity. In this broader view, as shown in Figure 18.1, the *geographical* (sometimes called the *site*) community is just one of several different kinds of communities.

Whether a business is small or large, local or global, its relationship with the community or communities with which it interacts is one of mutual interdependence. As shown in Figure 18.2, business and the community each need something from the other. Business depends on the community for education, public services such as police and fire

FIGURE 18.1
The Firm and Its Communities

Source: Adapted from a discussion in Edmund M. Burke, *Corporate Community Relations: The Principle of Neighbor of Choice* (Westport, CT: Praeger, 1999), ch. 6.

Community	Interest
Site community	Geographical location of a company's operations, offices, or assets
Fence-line community	Immediate neighbors
Virtual communities	People who buy from or follow the company online
Communities of interest	Groups that share a common interest with the company
Employee community	People who work near the company

FIGURE 18.2
What the Community and Business Want from Each Other

Business Participation Desired by Community	Community Services Desired by Business
• Pays taxes	• Schools—a quality educational system
• Provides jobs and training	• Recreational opportunities
• Follows laws	• Libraries, museums, theaters, and other cultural services and organizations
• Supports schools	• Adequate infrastructure, e.g., sewer, water, and electric services
• Supports the arts and cultural activities	• Adequate transportation systems, e.g., roads, rail, airport, harbor
• Supports local health care programs	• Effective public safety services, e.g., police and fire protection
• Supports parks and recreation	• Fair and equitable taxation
• Assists less advantaged people	• Streamlined permitting services
• Contributes to public safety	• Quality health care services
• Participates in economic development	• Cooperative problem-solving approach

The professional sports franchise is one kind of business that has historically been particularly dependent on support from the community. Cities often compete vigorously in bidding wars to attract or keep football, basketball, baseball, hockey, and soccer teams. Communities subsidize professional sports in many ways. Government agencies build stadiums and arenas, sell municipal bonds to pay for construction, give tax breaks to owners, and allow teams to keep revenues from parking, luxury boxes, and food concessions. Some say that public support is warranted, because high-profile teams and sports facilities spur local economic development, offer wholesome entertainment, and build civic pride. But critics argue that subsidies simply enrich affluent team owners and players at taxpayer expense and shift spending away from other more deserving areas, such as schools, police and fire protection, social services, and the arts. In this view, this is a case in which the relationship between business and the community is deeply out of balance.

One of the most outrageous examples of this was the Paul Brown Stadium, built at an estimated cost to the public of $555 million to house the National Football League's Cincinnati Bengals after the team threatened to move to Baltimore. Hamilton County, where the stadium was located, issued bonds and raised its sales tax to pay for the new stadium, the most costly ever built at taxpayer expense. That was just the beginning, because the county had also agreed to pay for most operating expenses and capital improvements going forward. The Bengals got to keep the revenue from naming rights, advertising, tickets, suites, and most parking. The annual cost to the county was $35 million, about 16 percent of its budget, a huge strain as the region struggled under the weight of a weak economy. "It's the monster that ate the public sector," said the administrator of the juvenile courts, speaking of the stadium. The juvenile courts had just seen their funding slashed, and had been forced to cut its programs for troubled youth.

Sources: "As Super Bowl Shows, Build Stadiums for Love and Not Money," *Bloomberg Businessweek,* February 3, 2012; "A Stadium's Costly Legacy Throws Taxpayers for a Loss," *The Wall Street Journal,* July 12, 2011; and "Stadium Boom Deepens Municipal Woes," *The New York Times,* December 25, 2009. A website critical of public subsidies to sports facilities is *www. fieldofschemes.com.*

protection, recreational facilities, and transportation systems, among other things. In some cases, businesses receive financial support from a community to locate a facility there. In 2014, for example, the electric car company Tesla Motors negotiated a $1.3 billion package of tax breaks and other incentives from the state of Nevada to locate a lithium battery factory in Reno.[4] On the other side, the community depends on business for support of the arts, schools, health care, and the disadvantaged, and other urgent civic needs, both through taxes and donations of money, goods, and time. And, of course, business brings with it jobs and economic development.

Ideally, community support of business and business support of the community are roughly in balance, so that both parties feel that they have benefited in the relationship. Sometimes, however, a business will invest more in the community than the community seems to provide in return. Conversely, a community sometimes provides more support to a business than the firm contributes to the community. Exhibit 18.A discusses subsidies by communities to professional sports franchises, an instance in which the relationship between business and the community is sometimes perceived as out of balance.

The Business Case for Community Involvement

The term **civic engagement** describes the active involvement of businesses and individuals in changing and improving communities. *Civic* means pertaining to cities or communities, and *engagement* means being committed to or involved with something. Why should businesses be involved with the community? What is the *business case* for civic engagement?

[4] "Nevada Gets Musked," *The Wall Street Journal,* September 17, 2014.

The ideas of corporate social responsibility and citizenship, introduced in earlier chapters, refer broadly to businesses acting as citizens of society by behaving responsibly toward all their stakeholders. Civic engagement is a major way in which companies carry out their corporate citizenship mission. As explained in Chapter 3, business organizations that act in a socially responsible way reap many benefits. These include an enhanced reputation and ability to respond quickly to changing stakeholder demands. By acting responsibly, companies can also avoid or correct problems caused by their operations—a basic duty that comes with their significant power and influence. They can win the loyalty of employees, customers, and neighbors. And by doing the right thing, businesses can often avoid, or at least correctly anticipate, government regulations. All these reasons for social responsibility operate at the level of the community as well, via civic engagement.

Another specific reason for community involvement is to win local support for business activity. Communities do not have to accept a business. They sometimes object to the presence of companies that will create too much traffic, pollute the air or water, or engage in activities that are viewed as offensive or inappropriate. A company must earn its informal **license to operate**—or right to do business—from society. In communities where democratic principles apply, citizens have the right to exercise their voice in determining whether a company will or will not be welcome, and the result is not always positive for business.

> Walmart has encountered serious local objection to its plans to build superstores and distribution centers in a number of local communities. Although some towns have welcomed Walmart for the shopping opportunities and jobs it brings, others have mounted intense opposition to the company's plans to move in. For example, in 2013 local activists organized to protest the arrival of a Walmart store in Sherwood, Oregon, saying it would degrade the community's "small town feel." The problem of community opposition seems likely to grow more complex for Walmart as it continues its expansion into international markets.[5]

Through positive interactions with the communities in which its stores are located, Walmart is more likely to avoid this kind of local opposition.

Community involvement by business also helps build social capital. **Social capital** has been defined as the norms and networks that enable collective action. Scholars have also described it as "the goodwill that is engendered by the fabric of social relations."[6] When companies such as Whole Foods Market, described at the beginning of this chapter, work to address community problems such as blood shortages, hunger, and dilapidated housing, their actions help build social capital. The company and groups in the community develop closer relationships, and their people become more committed to each other's welfare. Many experts believe that high levels of social capital enhance a community's quality of life. Dense social networks increase productivity by reducing the costs of doing business, because firms and people are more likely to trust one another. The development of social capital produces a win–win outcome because it enables everyone to be better off.[7]

---

[5] "Sherwood Residents Opposed to Wal-Mart Fear Collapse of Small Town Environment," May 8, 2013, at *www.oregonlive.com*. For the company's perspective on its community relationships, see *www.walmart.com*.

[6] Paul S. Adler and S. W. Kwon, "Social Capital: Prospects for a New Concept," *Academy of Management Review* 27, no. 1 (January/February 2002), pp. 17–40. For a more general discussion, see Robert D. Putnam, *Bowling Alone: The Collapse and Revival of American Community* (New York: Simon and Schuster, 2000).

[7] Some benefits of social capital are described on the World Bank website at *www.worldbank.org*.

Community Relations

The organized involvement of business with the community is called **community relations**. Some corporations have established specialized community relations or community affairs departments; others house this function in a department of corporate citizenship or corporate responsibility.[8] The job of the **community relations manager** (sometimes called the community involvement manager) is to interact with local citizens, develop community programs, manage donations of goods and services, work with local governments, and encourage employee volunteerism. These actions are, in effect, business investments intended to produce more social capital—to build relationships and networks with important groups in the community. Community relations departments typically work closely with other departments that link the company to the outside world, such as public relations (discussed in Chapter 19), as well as internal departments such as human resources. All these roles form important bridges between the corporation and the community.

> An example of an executive with broad responsibility for building community relationships is Stanley S. Litow, vice president of corporate citizenship and corporate affairs at IBM Corporation and president of the IBM Foundation. Before joining IBM, Litow headed a nonprofit think tank and served as deputy chancellor of the New York City Public Schools. "Community consciousness and civic engagement is part of the company's value system," Litow explained. One of the initiatives he championed was the "smarter cities challenge," which sent teams of six IBM executives into 116 different communities, on the company payroll, to improve the way local governments delivered services. To celebrate the company's 100th anniversary, Litow organized a community service program that provided more than 3 million hours of employee volunteerism worldwide."[9]

Community relations departments are typically involved with a range of diverse issues. According to a survey of community involvement managers, education was viewed as the most important issue. Many companies had developed a specific focus on science, technology, engineering, and math (STEM) literacy among young people. Other critical issues included poverty and hunger, disaster relief, and environmental sustainability. Further down the list of issues, although still important, were education, health care, and the arts.[10] (Figure 18.5, which appears later in this chapter, shows the issues to which companies donate the most money.) Although not exhaustive, this list suggests the range of needs that a corporation's community relations professionals are asked to address. These community concerns challenge managers to apply talent, imagination, and resources to develop creative ways to strengthen the community while still managing their businesses as profitable enterprises.

Several specific ways in which businesses and their community relations departments have addressed some critical concerns facing communities are discussed below. The all-important issue of business involvement in education reform is addressed later, in the section on collaborative partnerships and in the discussion case at the end of the chapter, which describes an innovative partnership between Fidelity Investments and a nonprofit organization committed to after-school programs for middle-school children.

---

[8] Center for Corporate Citizenship, "Advancing From the Core: Profile of the Practice 2103 Highlights," *at http://ccc.bc.edu.*

[9] "Corporate Citizenship is Linked to Business Success, Says Stanley Litow, IBM Foundation," *The Economic Times,* February 13, 2015; and "Building a Smarter Planet," *Leaders Magazine,* 35(2), 2012.

[10] "Advancing from the Core," op. cit.

Economic Development

Business leaders and their companies are frequently involved in local or regional economic development that is intended to bring new businesses into an area or to develop workforce skills.

> When the Distinct 89 nightclub closed in downtown Newark, NJ, no one had much hope that the abandoned lounge would provide jobs any time soon. But that changed in 2014, when a startup called AeroFarms took over the space to test a technology called aeroponics that used LED lighting, fabric, and nutrient-rich mist to grow vegetables indoors. The experiment worked so well that the company leased a former steel mill in Newark's Ironbound district, where it planned to hire 70 people to produce nearly two million pounds of produce annually. The company choose its location because of strong community support, access to consumers, and a desire to support job creation. "We are very much focused on how we can drive economic development and job creation," said the company's cofounder.[11]

Housing

Another community issue in which many firms have become involved is housing. Life and health insurance companies, among others, have taken the lead in programs to revitalize neighborhood housing through organizations such as Neighborhood Housing Services (NHS) of America. NHS, which is locally controlled, locally funded, nonprofit, and tax-exempt, offers housing rehabilitation and financial services to neighborhood residents. Similar efforts are being made to house the homeless. New York City's Coalition for the Homeless includes corporate, nonprofit, and community members. Corporations also often work with nongovernmental organizations (NGOs) such as Habitat for Humanity to build or repair housing. Globally, businesses have also been active in housing issues, as illustrated by the following example.

> CEMEX, a global leader in the building materials industry that is based in Mexico, was a longtime supporter of affordable housing in developing countries. In 2014, the company extended this commitment by joining the Business Call to Action, an alliance of companies and governments supporting the United Nations' Millennium Development Goals. For its part, CEMEX committed to ensure that 150,000 low-income families had access to safe and affordable housing by 2016. It planned to meet this commitment through a range of programs that supported families with the training, materials, and microfinancing needed to construct their own low-cost housing safely and efficiently. "CEMEX is a company that is constantly striving to innovate so that our products, services, and strengths contribute to improve the quality of life, particularly of vulnerable families," said the company's director of corporate responsibility.[12]

Aid to Minority, Women, and Disabled Veteran-Owned Enterprises

Private enterprise has also extended assistance to minority, women, and disabled veteran-owned small businesses. These businesses often operate at an economic disadvantage. In some cases, they do business in economic locations where high crime rates, poor

---

[11] "Say Hello to the (Soon to Be) World's Largest Indoor Vertical Farm," *Bloomberg Businessweek,* March 17, 2015; and "Newark's Industrial Wasteland May Be the Next Farming Capital of America" [blog], April 21, 2015, at *http://collectively.org.*

[12] "Building the Link to Home Ownership, CEMEX Joins the Business Call to Action," press release, February 10, 2014, at *www.businesscalltoaction.org.*

transportation, low-quality public services, and a low-income clientele combine to produce a high rate of business failure. In others, they face competition from more established suppliers. Many large corporations now have supplier diversity programs that seek out partnerships with such enterprises.

> AT&T has operated supplier diversity programs for more than 40 years. In 2014, the company spent almost $17 billion procuring products and services from certified minority, women, and disabled veteran-owned businesses—more than a quarter of its procurement spending. An example of such a supplier is Group O Direct, an Illinois-based firm that provides fulfillment services for customer promotions. Group O Direct, which is owned by Mexican Americans, has many other high-profile clients in addition to AT&T, including Caterpillar, MillerCoors, and Microsoft, and annual revenues of $710 million.[13]

Disaster, Terrorism, and War Relief

One common form of corporate involvement in the community is disaster relief. Throughout the world, companies, like individuals, provide assistance to local citizens and communities when disaster strikes. When floods, fires, earthquakes, ice storms, hurricanes, or terrorist attacks devastate communities, funds pour into affected communities from companies.

> Businesses from all over the world responded with great generosity to the communities impacted by the massive earthquake that struck the mountainous nation of Nepal in 2015. Many companies gave cash either directly or through the Red Cross. Others drew on their own special expertise to lend a hand. Verizon, AT&T, Sprint, and T-Mobile offered its customers free unlimited calls and text message service between the United States and Nepal in the first weeks after the disaster, so family members and friends could reconnect. Facebook activated a "safety check" feature that enabled users to notify friends and family that they were safe. Health care companies Abbott, GlaxoSmithKline, and the Hospital Corporation of America sent medicines and supplies; PepsiCo sent bottled water; and Procter & Gamble sent water purification packets. The British construction equipment maker JCB donated 10 backhoe loaders to aid the reconstruction effort. The logistics company DHL sent a disaster response team to help organize relief supplies pouring into the Katmandu airport from all over the world.[14]

International relief efforts are becoming more important, as communications improve and people around the world are able to witness the horrors of natural disasters, terrorism, and war. Corporate involvement in such efforts is an extension of the natural tendency of people to help one another when tragedy strikes. It is also a way for companies to build brand loyalty, as people often develop lasting gratitude to those who helped them in times of great need.

In all these areas of community need—economic development, housing, aid to minority enterprise, and disaster relief—as well as many others, businesses around the world have made and continue to make significant contributions.

---

[13] AT&T's supplier diversity programs are described at *www.attsuppliers.com/sd.* The website of Group O is at *www.groupo.com.*

[14] "Nepal Earthquake: Corporate Aid Tracker," updated May 27, 2105, *www.uschamberfoundation.org;* and "DHL's Special Delivery for Nepal," May 9, 2015, *http://news.AsiaOne.com.*

Corporate Giving

An important aspect of the business–community relationship is **corporate philanthropy**, or **corporate giving**. Corporate philanthropy has been defined as the voluntary and unconditional transfers of cash or other assets by private firms for public purposes.[15] Every year, businesses around the world give generously to their communities through various kinds of philanthropic contributions to nonprofit organizations.

America has historically been a generous society. In 2014, individuals, bequests (individual estates), foundations, and corporations collectively gave more than $358 billion to churches, charities, and other nonprofit organizations, as shown in Figure 18.3. This figure had risen for the fifth year in a row, as the economy recovered from the Great Recession. Businesses were a small, but important, part of this broad cultural tradition of giving. In 2014, corporate contributions totaled $17.8 billion, or about 5 percent of all charitable giving. This amount included in-kind gifts claimed as tax deductions and giving by corporate foundations.

As U.S. firms have become increasingly globalized, as shown in Chapter 4, their international charitable contributions have also grown. A 2014 survey by the Conference Board found that international giving comprised more than one-fifth (22 percent) of all donations that were made the prior year by the 113 companies in the sample. Companies tended to give where they had operations or customers or in response to specific natural disasters. Global energy companies were particularly likely to focus their giving internationally. The Asia-Pacific region received the largest share (33 percent of international donations from manufacturing firms and 21 percent from service firms), probably reflecting the outpouring of aid to victims of Super Typhoon Hiayan in the Philippines.[16] To cite just one example, the Coca-Cola Foundation has donated millions of dollars to support education around the world. Its contributions have, among other projects, helped build schools in Chile, Egypt, and the Philippines.[17]

FIGURE 18.3
Philanthropy in the United States, by Source of Contributions, 2014 (in $ billions)

Source: Giving USA Foundation™ (formerly the American Association of Fundraising Counsel Trust for Philanthropy), *Giving USA 2015* (Indianapolis: Center on Philanthropy at Indiana University, 2015), p. 16. Used by permission.

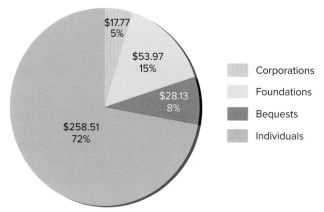

Total value of contributions was $358.38 billion.

[15] This definition is drawn from Arthur Gautier and Anne-Claire Pache, "Research on Corporate Philanthropy: A Review and Assessment," *Journal of Business Ethics,* February 2015, and is based on one developed by the Financial Accounting Standards Board.

[16] "International Giving," pages 20–21 in The Conference Board, *Giving in Numbers: 2014 Edition.*

[17] More information about Coca-Cola's contributions to education is available at *www.thecoca-colacompany.com/stories/education.*

FIGURE 18.4

Corporate Contributions in the United States, as a Percentage of Pretax Corporate Profits, 1972–2014

Source: Giving USA Foundation™ (formerly the American Association of Fundraising Counsel Trust for Philanthropy), *Giving USA 2015* (Indianapolis: Center on Philanthropy at Indiana University, 2015), p. 246. Used by permission.

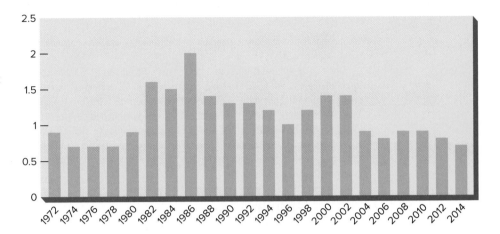

In the United States, tax rules have encouraged corporate giving for educational, charitable, scientific, and religious purposes since 1936. Current rules permit corporations to deduct from their taxable income all such gifts that do not exceed 10 percent of the company's before-tax income. In other words, a company with a before-tax income of $1 million might contribute up to $100,000 to nonprofit community organizations devoted to education, charity, science, or religion. The $100,000 in contributions would then reduce the income to be taxed from $1 million to $900,000, thus saving the company money on its tax bill while providing a source of income to community agencies. Of course, nothing prevents a corporation from giving more than 10 percent of its income for philanthropic purposes, but it would not be given a tax break above the 10 percent level.

As shown in Figure 18.4, average corporate giving in the United States is far below the 10 percent deduction now permitted. Though it varies from year to year, corporate giving has generally ranged between one-half of 1 percent and 2 percent of pretax profits since the early 1960s, with a rise that reached a peak at 2 percent in 1986. Corporate giving was 0.7 percent of pretax profits in 2014. A few companies, including a cluster in the Minneapolis–St. Paul area that has pledged to donate 5 percent annually, give much more than this. The top cash givers in 2013, relative to pretax profits, were Alcoa (12 percent), Safeway (7 percent), and UPS (6 percent).[18] One company, Newman's Own, the philanthropic corporation established by the late film star Paul Newman, gives *all* of its earnings to charity.

Exhibit 18.B describes the efforts of one company, Goldman Sachs, to increase its corporate philanthropy in the wake of the financial crisis. Some observers thought that the financial firm was motivated mainly by altruism, while others thought it was simply trying to rebuild its reputation.

In Europe, corporate philanthropy has lagged behind that in the United States, in part because tax breaks are less generous and differences in the law across countries make cross-border giving difficult. Greater spending on social welfare by governments has also reduced the need for private-sector donations. Europe-based multinational corporations remain active, however. To cite one example, Sanofi, a multinational pharmaceutical company based in France, launched the Sanofi Espoir ("hope") Foundation in 2010, with the mission of reducing health care inequalities throughout the world. The foundation trained midwives in Uganda, Mexico, and Cambodia. It worked to improve access to health care in some of the poorest and most vulnerable communities in France, and promoted early detection of childhood cancers in Paraguay, Pakistan, and the Philippines.[19]

[18] "Corporate Profits Surge But Cash Donations Creep Up Only 3%," *Chronicle of Philanthropy,* July 17, 2014.

[19] The website of the Sanofi Espoir Foundation is at *http://foundation_sanofi_espoir.com.*

Exhibit 18.B

What motivates companies to ramp up their charitable giving? A controversial case in point was the financial firm Goldman Sachs.

Since 2008—the year that the financial crisis hit full force—Goldman Sachs has contributed $1.6 billion to charitable causes. In 2013 alone, it gave away $262 million, an increase of almost 9 percent from the prior year; this amount was 2.3 percent of its pretax profits. (Before the crisis, Goldman had given less than 1 percent to charity.) During this period, the company launched several high-profile philanthropic initiatives, including *10,000 Women,* a five-year $100 million project to support underserved female entrepreneurs around the world. A 2014 study by Babson College researchers found that this project had enjoyed considerable success; participants in the program had increased their businesses' revenue, created jobs, and improved their leadership skills.

"Engaging wasn't just the right thing, it was necessary, especially in the wake of the financial crisis when people said we weren't doing enough," said the company's chief of staff.

Some praised Goldman's efforts. "I think Goldman's [philanthropic] programs are the best I've seen," said investor Warren Buffett (although he added that "I personally don't like the idea of giving away other people's money.") But others were skeptical of the company's motives, saying its philanthropy was just a way to buy back its tarnished reputation. A columnist for *The New York Times* offered this opinion: "Goldman Sachs helped to wreak havoc on the housing market, betting against the very investments it was pushing on clients. And then it took a sliver of its money and used it to provide money, mentorship and training to 'over 10,000 women.' But how many women saw their businesses implode or their pensions disappear because of the financial crisis Goldman helped to foster?"

Sources: "Philanthropy Starts after Profits Are Tallied," *The New York Times,* May 12, 2015; "Goldman Sachs: Buying Redemption," *The New York Times,* October 26, 2013; and "Investing in the Power of Women: Progress Report on the Goldman Sachs 10,000 Initiative," September 2014, Babson College. Goldman Sachs' philanthropic initiatives are further described at *www.goldmansachs.com/citizenship.*

Is the public generally aware of corporate giving? An intriguing 2014 study from the United Kingdom suggested that companies were not doing a good job of communicating their philanthropic efforts. The research showed that large companies in the United Kingdom had actually doubled their donations of cash, products, and employee time since 2007. But when people were asked what they knew about corporate philanthropy, the answer was: very little. Respondents thought that about a third of big companies gave to charity; the actual proportion was 98 percent. They thought consumer services and consumer goods companies were the most generous (perhaps because they were most familiar with these brands); but, in fact, these two actually ranked fifth and sixth among industries studied. "For public perceptions to change, consistent evidence of positive social impact needs to be published in an engaging and accessible manner," said a representative of the foundation that had conducted the study.[20]

Although many companies give directly, some large corporations have established non-profit **corporate foundations** to handle their charitable programs. This permits them to administer contribution programs more uniformly and provides a central group of professionals that handles all grant requests. To give just one example, the Wells Fargo Foundation, which donated $187 million in 2013, supports a wide range of community nonprofits, schools, and environmental initiatives. Seventy-nine percent of large U.S.-based corporations have such foundations; collectively, corporate foundations gave about $5.43 billion

[20] "New Survey Shows FTSE 100 Companies Have Increased Charitable Giving," *The Guardian,* August 14, 2014. The study is available at the website of the Charities Aid Foundation at *www.cafonline.org.*

in 2014.[21] Foreign-owned corporations use foundations less frequently, although firms such as Panasonic and Hitachi use sophisticated corporate foundations to conduct their charitable activities in the United States. Foundations, with their defined mission to benefit the community, can be a useful mechanism to help companies implement philanthropic programs that meet this corporate social responsibility.

Forms of Corporate Giving

Typically, gifts by corporations and their foundations take one of three forms: charitable donations (gifts of money), in-kind contributions (gifts of products or services), and volunteer employee service (gifts of time). Many companies give in all three categories.

> An example of a particularly generous cash gift was one made by Intel, the computer chip maker. Intel, together with its foundation, pledged $120 million over the 10-year period 2008 to 2017 to the Society for Science & the Public Interest. The purpose of the gift was to support this organization's Science Talent Search, a prestigious science competition for high school seniors. The gift also included funds for outreach to young people and mentoring for program alumni. As part of the competition, every year 40 finalists traveled to Washington, DC, to present their research to members of the scientific community. Awards included college scholarships and computers. Many former winners had gone on to distinguished careers in science and entrepreneurship. "I can't think of a more critical time to invest in math and science education," said Intel's vice president for corporate affairs.[22]

The share of all giving comprising **in-kind contributions** of products or services has been rising steadily for the past decade or so and has now surpassed cash contributions. Of U.S. corporate contributions in 2013, 19 percent were in-kind (noncash), 48 percent were cash, and the balance came in the form of contributions from affiliated foundations.[23] For example, high-technology companies have donated computer hardware and software to schools, universities, and public libraries. Grocery retailers have donated food, and Internet service providers have donated time online. Publishers have given books. The most generous industry, in terms of in-kind contributions, is pharmaceuticals. In 2013, for example, Pfizer contributed an extraordinary $3.1 *billion* to charity, almost all of it in the form of medicines and other products and services. Many of these donations were directed to underserved communities around the world.[24]

In-kind contributions can be creative—and they need not cost a lot. Frito-Lay, for example, donated publicity to Do Something—a nonprofit whose mission is to encourage young people to improve the world—by featuring photos of the organization's work on 500 million bags of Doritos chips. "It drove fabulous recognition for our organization and helped our Web traffic," said the grateful director.[25] The contribution was a low-cost one for Frito-Lay, which would have had to print its bags anyway.

Under U.S. tax laws, if companies donate new goods, they may deduct their fair-market value within the relevant limits. For example, if a computer company donated

[21] *Giving in Numbers,* 2014 ed., op. cit., p. 30; and *Giving USA 2015,* op. cit., p. 20.

[22] "Intel Encourages More Youth to Participate in Math and Science," press release, October 20, 2008, *www.intel.com/ pressroom.* The website of the Intel Science Talent Search is at *www.societyforscience.org.*

[23] *Giving in Numbers: 2014 Edition,* op. cit., p. 17.

[24] "Corporate Profits Surge, But Cash Donations Creep Up Only 3%," op. cit. Pfizer's philanthropic initiatives are reported at *www.pfizer.com/responsibility.*

[25] "Philanthropy: A Special Report: Firm Decisions: As Companies Become More Involved in Giving, Charities Are Glad to Get Aid Faster and with Less Red Tape," *The Wall Street Journal,* December 10, 2007.

$10,000 worth of new laptops to a local school, it could take a deduction for this amount on its corporate tax return, provided this amount was less than 10 percent of its pretax income.

Business leaders and employees also regularly donate their own time—another form of corporate giving. **Volunteerism** involves the efforts of people to assist others in the community through unpaid work. According to a report by the Department of Labor, about 25 percent of Americans aged 16 and older volunteered during the prior year, donating on average 50 hours of their time.[26] Many companies encourage their employees to volunteer by publicizing opportunities, sponsoring specific projects, and offering recognition for service. Offering such opportunities can benefit companies by attracting young employees, as new research shows.

> A 2014 survey by the consulting firm Achieve found that a company's volunteer policies had a big impact on where Millennials chose to work. One third of Millennials said that the opportunity to volunteer had influenced their decision to apply for a job, two-fifths said it had influenced their decision to interview, and more than half said it had influenced their decision to accept an offer. "Millennials are blending who they are, what they do, what they stand for, and the causes and things they care about into the workplace," said the president of the consulting firm. An example of a company that was acting on this insight was ExactTarget, a cloud marketing firm, which ran a program that matched the interests of employees with the needs of local nonprofits. The company's vice president for community programs reported she regularly received e-mails from employees saying, "It is so fantastic to be part of an organization that is committed to giving back." "That is all the evidence we need that we are doing the right thing," she concluded.[27]

An important trend is what is known as *skills-based volunteerism,* in which employee skills are matched to specialized needs. For example, American Express established a consulting program that sent expert teams into nonprofits to solve organizational problems, free of charge. At the Lower East Side Tenement Museum in New York City, AMEX consultants helped the museum learn how to better manage its relationships with visitors, significantly improving their engagement and loyalty.[28]

Another approach is for companies to provide employees with *paid* time off for volunteer service in the community. For example, Wells Fargo offers a volunteer leave program, under which employees can apply for a fully paid sabbatical of up to four months to work in a nonprofit organization of their choice. In recent years, Wells Fargo employees on paid leave have trained teachers in Afghanistan; built homes in Oaxaca, Mexico; and helped renovate a facility for the mentally ill. A 2014 survey found that 21 percent of U.S. employers allowed all or most of their employees to volunteer during regular work hours.[29] One country where this trend is particularly strong is Brazil: in just a two-year period between 2010 and 2012, the proportion of employers allowing volunteering on work time increased from 35 to 60 percent.[30]

---

[26] "Volunteering in the United States, 2014," U.S. Department of Labor, press release, February 25, 2015.

[27] "Millennials Are Drawn to Companies That Offer Chances to Volunteer," *Chronicle of Philanthropy,* July 17, 2014.

[28] "Key Trends to Watch: The Next Wave of Growth in Corporate Pro Bono Service: 2014 Report," Taproot Foundation, at *www.taprootfoundation.org.*

[29] "2014 National Study of Employers," at *http://familiesandwork.org.*

[30] Silicon Valley Community Foundation, *Global Employee Engagement Report: Brazil, China, India, South Africa, United Kingdom* (2015), at *www.siliconvalleycf.org.*

Many companies have turned to technology to improve the amount and effectiveness of employee volunteerism. "Technology is transforming the landscape," commented the executive director of the Mitsubishi Electric America Foundation. "The speed of communications enables us to quickly get information to and from our employees." Horizon Bank, for example, has linked Volunteer Match, a web-based service that enables nonprofits to post volunteer opportunities online, to its company intranet. The bank uses the service to track employee volunteer hours and makes a contribution to charities based on the number of hours its employees commit to them. Other providers of volunteer software include CyberGrants, Inc., MicroEdge LLC (AngelPoints), and JK Group. Some firms—among them, Oracle and IBM—have developed their own computerized systems to oversee their employees' volunteerism. Bank of America has developed a custom-designed website to measure and recognize employee volunteerism. BofA gives workers two hours a week of paid time to volunteer, and for every 50 hours contributed gives the organization a $250 contribution on the volunteer's behalf. Whether provided by outside vendors or in-house, software enables companies to better monitor the impact of their employees' work in the community. Commented the national director of community involvement for Deloitte, a large consulting firm, "We can be more strategic and more focused on social outcomes [and can more easily] answer questions about when and how we as a company [become] engaged."

Source: Center for Corporate Citizenship, "Community Involvement Technology Vendors: An Overview," 2013, at *http://ccc.bc.edu.*

Evidence shows that companies with robust volunteer programs reap benefits, even as communities gain from their workers' contributions of time and skill. For example, Green Mountain Coffee Roasters, a purveyor of specialty coffees and single-cup brewing systems based in Vermont, has an active volunteer program called Community Action for Employees (CAFÉ). Green Mountain employees can spend up to 52 hours per year of paid work time volunteering for nonprofits in their communities. The company's Dollars-for-Doers program provides a $250 grant to any organization to which an employee donates 25 hours or more in a year. Their 5,600 employees volunteer on average one day a year—and some much more. An academic study of the company's volunteer program found that employees who valued the program were more likely to be proud of their company and want to continue to work there. Moreover, their supervisors reported separately that these employees ranked higher than their peers in organizational citizenship. The researcher concluded the program had benefited Green Mountain directly through its impact on employees, quite apart from any impact it may have had on branding and consumer loyalty.[31]

The increasing use of technology to help organize and promote employee volunteering is profiled in Exhibit 18.C.

Priorities in Corporate Giving

Overall, what kinds of organizations receive the most corporate philanthropy? The distribution of contributions reflects how businesses view overall community needs, and how this perception has changed over time. As shown in Figure 18.5, the corporate giving "pie" is divided into several main segments. The largest share of corporate philanthropy goes to health and human services; the next largest share goes to education. Civic and community

---

[31] David A. Jones, "Does Serving the Community Also Serve the Company? Using Organizational Identification and Social Exchange Theories to Understand Employee Responses to a Volunteerism Programme," *Journal of Occupational and Organizational Psychology* 83, (2010); and "Employee Volunteerism," at *www.gmcr.com.*

FIGURE 18.5
Priorities in Corporate Giving (percentage of corporate cash and in-kind contributions to various sectors)

Source: *Giving in Numbers: 2014 Edition* (New York: The Conference Board, 2014), p. 5. All data are for 2013. Numbers do not add to one hundred because of rounding error. Used by permission.

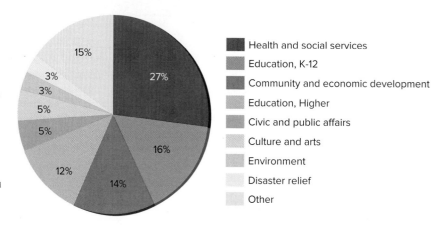

- Health and social services
- Education, K-12
- Community and economic development
- Education, Higher
- Civic and public affairs
- Culture and arts
- Environment
- Disaster relief
- Other

organizations and culture and the arts also receive large shares of business philanthropy. Of course, these percentages are not identical among different companies and industries; some companies tend to favor support for education, for example, whereas others give relatively greater amounts to cultural organizations or community groups.

Corporate Giving in a Strategic Context

Communities have social needs requiring far more resources than are normally available, and businesses often face more demands than they can realistically meet. This is particularly true in hard economic times, when funds may be less plentiful. Companies must establish priorities to determine which worthy projects will be funded or supported with the company's in-kind or volunteer contributions and which ones will not. What criteria should community relations departments apply in determining who will receive corporate gifts? These are often difficult choices, both because businesses may want to support more charities than they can afford, and because saying no often produces dissatisfaction among those who do not get as much help as they want.

One increasingly popular approach is to target corporate contributions *strategically* to meet the needs of the donor as well as the recipient. **Strategic philanthropy** refers to corporate giving that is linked directly or indirectly to business goals and objectives. In this approach, both the company and society benefit from the gift.

> For example, Cisco Systems, a manufacturer of hardware for the Internet, has established a Networking Academy to train computer network administrators. From a modest start in 1997 in a high school near the company's headquarters in San Jose, California, by 2015 the program had expanded to include more than 9,000 sites in all 50 states and 170 countries, and had trained more than a five million students. The academy initiative benefits communities throughout the world by providing job training for young people, many of whom go on to successful careers in systems administration. But it also benefits the company, by assuring a supply of information technology professionals who can operate Cisco's complex equipment. Companies and governments are more likely to buy from Cisco if they are confident skilled technicians are available.[32]

[32] More information about the Networking Academy is available at *www.cisco.com*.

A study in the *Harvard Business Review* identified four areas in which corporate contributions were most likely to enhance a company's competitiveness, as well as the welfare of the community.[33] Strategic contributions focus on:

- *Factor conditions,* such as the supply of trained workers, physical infrastructure, and natural resources. Cisco's Networking Academy is an example of philanthropy that helps the donor by providing skilled employees both for Cisco and for its corporate customers.

- *Demand conditions,* those that affect demand for a product or service. When Microsoft provides free software to libraries and universities, new generations of young people learn to use these programs and are more likely later to buy computers equipped with the company's products.

- *Context for strategy and rivalry.* Company donations sometimes can be designed to support policies that create a more productive environment for competition. For example, contributions to an organization such as Transparency International that opposes corruption may help a company gain access to previously unreachable markets.

- *Related and supporting industries.* Finally, charitable contributions that strengthen related sectors of the economy may also help companies. For example, when Starbucks contributes to programs that provide training and assistance to coffee farmers in developing countries, as described in Chapter 17, the company is not only helping farmers, it is helping itself assure a continuing supply of high-quality, ethically sourced coffee beans.

Of course, not all corporate contributions benefit their donors directly, nor should they. But most, if handled correctly, at least build goodwill and help cement the loyalty of employees, customers, and suppliers who value association with a good corporate citizen.

Specialists in corporate philanthropy recommend several other strategies to help companies get the most benefit from their contributions.[34]

- *Draw on the unique assets and competencies of the business.* Companies often have special skills or resources that enable them to make a contribution that others could not. For example, Google, Inc., provides free advertising on its search engine to nonprofit organizations in many countries. Donations to Direct Relief International, just one of many charities supported in this way, increased more than tenfold after it joined Google's program.[35]

- *Align priorities with employee interests.* Another successful strategy is to give employees a say in deciding who will receive contributions. An advantage of this approach is that it strengthens ties between the company and its workers, who feel that their values are being expressed through the organization's choices. For example, VMware, a software company, gives all new employees $25 on their first day at work to give to a charity of their choice. Each year they stay with the company, they are given more to give away; on their 12th year, for example, they are permitted to make a $12,000 grant. The company picks one or two top engineers every year and allows them to endow an $800,000 scholarship at a university of their choice. "We're giving our people the platform and the permission to express what they care about," said VMware's vice president for global community affairs.[36]

---

[33] Michael E. Porter and Mark R. Kramer, "The Competitive Advantage of Corporate Philanthropy," *Harvard Business Review,* December 2002.

[34] See, for example, David Hess, Nikolai Rogovsky, and Thomas W. Dunfee, "The Next Wave in Corporate Community Involvement: Corporate Social Initiatives," *California Management Review* 44, no. 2 (Winter 2002).

[35] "Google Grants Success Profile," *www.google.com/support/grants;* and "Google Starts Up Philanthropy Campaign," *The Washington Post,* October 12, 2005.

[36] "Power to the People: Companies Hand Grant Decisions to Employees," *Chronicle of Philanthropy,* July 17, 2014.

- *Align priorities with core values of the firm.* McDonald's Corporation, the fast-food giant, focuses its philanthropic contributions on children's programs. One of the company's major recipients is the Ronald McDonald House Charities, which operates facilities where families can stay in a homelike setting while their child receives treatment at a nearby hospital. The program operates 347 houses in 60 countries, including new programs in Thailand, Indonesia, and Uruguay. Since 2002, the company has raised $170 million at its McHappy Day events for the RMHC and related charities. McDonald's believes that this initiative is consistent with its mission to "make a difference in the lives of children."[37]

In short, businesses today are taking a more strategic approach to all kinds of corporate giving. They want to make sure that gifts are not simply made randomly, but rather are targeted in such a way that they are consistent with the firm's values, core competencies, and strategic goals.

Measuring the Return on Social Investment

A final important trend in corporate philanthropy is assessment of impact. Increasingly, companies are using standard business tools to measure the outcomes of their investments in the community, just as they would any other investment. The benefits that accrue to business and society are sometimes called **return on social investment.** Return on social investment is often more difficult to measure than other kinds of return. For example, return to shareholders may be readily gauged by changes in share price and dividends paid. Return on investment in new machinery may be readily gauged by increases in productivity. By contrast, the results of corporate donations and employee volunteerism may occur over longer periods of time and be less amenable to measurement. Nevertheless, community relations and corporate giving professionals have made significant advances in developing appropriate metrics. Figure 18.6 shows the four elements that are often measured in assessing the return on social investment.

Inputs are the resources companies provide. They may include cash contributions, employee time, products and services, or logistics support. For example, a pharmaceutical company that has committed to help address the HIV-AIDS epidemic in sub-Saharan Africa might measure the value of medicines donated, employee time to administer the program, and cash donated to partner nongovernmental organizations in receiving countries.

Outputs are measures of the activities that took place—usually numerical counts of people and communities served. In the same example, outputs might be the number of persons who received antiretroviral medications and doses provided, the number of clinics provisioned, or the number of medical professionals trained.

Impacts represent the difference the program made; that is, the actual benefits that accrued to the people and communities served. It is similar to outputs, except that it tries to capture the actual results of the gift. How many cases of mother-to-child transmission of infection were prevented? What were the impacts on the ability of HIV-positive individuals to continue to work and contribute to the economic and social health of their communities? Since most firms partner with nonprofit agencies and governments, measuring impacts of their gifts generally requires close collaboration with these organizations.

---

[37] "Worldwide Corporate Social Responsibility 2010 Report," *www.mcdonalds.com;* and "Our History" [Ronald McDonald House Charities] at *http://rmhc.org.*

FIGURE 18.6
Measuring the Return on Social Investment

Sources: Adapted from "Effective Community Engagement," *BCG Perspectives,* May 22, 2012, at *www.bcgperspectives.com;* and *Measuring the Value of Corporate Philanthropy: Social Impact, Business Benefits, and Investor Returns,* Committee Encouraging Corporate Philanthropy, 2010.

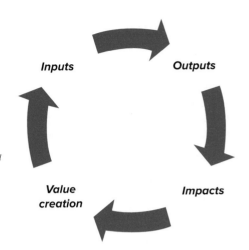

Inputs   *Outputs*

Value creation   *Impacts*

An example of a company that has worked hard to measure the impact of its social investments is Intel. The chipmaker's "Intel Teach" program has trained more than 15 million teachers in 70 countries. Its purpose is to help teachers use technology to promote students' problem solving, critical thinking, and collaboration skills. The company does more than simply count the number of teachers trained (outputs); it works with research organizations to measure how they actually use technology in their own classrooms and the impact of these efforts on student learning (impacts). "Intel is rigorously numerical," commented Wendy Hawkins, executive director of the Intel Foundation. "Measurement makes it more likely that our leaders will support and fund the philanthropy."[38]

Value creation represents the benefits to the business of the program. This is similar to the concept of enlightened self-interest, as presented in Chapter 3. Often this is the most difficult element to measure. In the same example used earlier, was the reputation of the pharmaceutical company enhanced? Did the firm develop new relationships and opportunities in developing countries? Did the program help it attract and retain the brightest scientists? Increasingly, companies are moving away from reliance on anecdotal evidence and trying to measure the business benefits quantitatively. As shown in Figure 18.6, when businesses benefit from their gifts (*value creation*), this enhances their ability to make further gifts (*inputs),* thus creating a kind of virtuous circle.

Research shows that 31 percent of companies measure the outputs of their community involvement efforts, and 23 percent measure the impacts. (This study did not examine the percentage that measured value creation.)[39]

Building Collaborative Partnerships

The term *partnership,* introduced in Chapter 4, refers to a voluntary collaboration among business, government, and civil society organizations to achieve specific objectives. The need for such **collaborative partnerships** is very apparent when dealing with community problems.

One arena in which collaborative partnerships among business, government, and communities have been particularly effective is education. As mentioned earlier in this chapter, community relations managers count education as the most critical challenge they face. Many school districts and colleges in the United States face an influx of new students from

---

[38] Updates on Intel's Teach Program are available at *www.intel.com.*
[39] "Focus on Results: The Community Involvement Index," (2011), op. cit.

the so-called echo boom generation, increasing class sizes and making it more difficult to give students the individual attention they need. Many schools are challenged to educate new Americans, immigrants from other parts of the world who often do not speak English as their native language. More children are living in poverty, and many come from single-parent homes. A fast-changing economy demands that the technological tools accessible to students be greatly expanded. All these challenges must be met in many states under conditions of extreme fiscal constraint, as tax revenues fall and budget crises loom. The difficulties faced by schools are of immediate concern to many companies, which rely on educational systems to provide them with well-trained employees equipped for today's high-technology workplace.

Business has been deeply involved with education reform in the United States for over two decades. A series of studies by The Conference Board identified four waves, or distinct periods, in corporate involvement in education reform from the 1980s to the present.[40] The first wave was characterized by *direct involvement* with specific schools. For example, a company might "adopt" a school, providing it with cash, equipment, and volunteer assistance, and promising job interviews for qualified graduates. The second wave focused on the *application of management principles* to school administration. Business leaders assisted schools by advising administrators and government officials who needed training in management methods, such as strategic planning and performance appraisal. The third wave emphasized advocacy for *public policy initiatives* in education, such as ones calling for school choice and adoption of national testing standards. The fourth wave, which is ongoing, focuses on *collaboration for systemic reform.* This involves collaborative partnerships among business organizations, schools, and government agencies. In such collaborations, all partners bring unique capabilities and resources to the challenge of educational reform. The result is often outcomes that are better than any of them could have achieved acting alone.[41]

A recent example of a successful collaborative partnership is IBM's work with P-TECH (short for Pathways in Technology Early College High School), a new high school in Brooklyn, New York, designed to track students into technology careers. The company partnered with the public school and city university systems to create the program in 2011. Once accepted into P-TECH, students—most of whom are minority and low-income—take a sequence of technically focused courses that lead, in six or fewer years, to a high school diploma, an associate's degree in applied science—and a job interview with IBM. The company also supported the school with volunteer mentors, structured workplace visits, and paid summer internships. In 2015, the school graduated its first cohort, and IBM hired its first P-TECH graduates. Since 2013, twenty more P-TECH schools have been created in New York, and the model has also spread to other cities (and companies). Said Stanley Litow of IBM (also mentioned earlier in this chapter), "In 2011, we and our partners had high hopes when we launched the P-TECH model. Now, just four years later, we have undeniable proof that it works."[42]

[40] Susan Otterbourg, *Innovative Public–Private Partnerships: Educational Initiatives* (New York: The Conference Board, 1998); and Sandra Waddock, *Business and Education Reform: The Fourth Wave* (New York: The Conference Board, 1994).

[41] For a discussion of the benefits of collaborative partnerships, see Bradley K. Googins and Steven A. Rochlin, "Creating the Partnership Society: Understanding the Rhetoric and Reality of Cross-Sectoral Partnerships," *Business and Society Review* 105, no. 1 (2000), pp. 127–44.

[42] Stanley S. Litow, "P-TECH: Tackling Youth Unemployment One Student at a Time", June 3, 2015, at *http://blogs.forbes.com;* "From High School Calculus Straight to a Job at IBM; Meet the First Graduates of P-TECH," *Fast Company,* June 18, 2015; and "Could Public-Private Collaboration Help Reduce Income Inequality?" February 11, 2015, at *ww2.kqed.org/news/2015/02/11/ could-public-private-collaboration-help-reduce-income-inequality..*

The success of P-TECH illustrates the potential of collaborative partnerships that allow business to contribute its unique assets and skills to a broader effort to solve significant community problems.

Communities need jobs, specialized skills, executive talent, and other resources that business can provide. Business needs cooperative attitudes in local government, basic public services, and a feeling that it is a welcome member of the community. Under these circumstances much can be accomplished to upgrade the quality of community life. The range of business–community collaborations is extensive, giving businesses many opportunities to be socially responsible.

Like education, other community challenges are, at their core, people problems, involving hopes, attitudes, sentiments, and expectations for better human conditions. Neither government nor business can simply impose solutions or be expected to find quick and easy answers to problems so long in the making and so vast in their implications. Moreover, neither government nor business has the financial resources on their own to solve these issues. Grassroots involvement is needed, where people are willing and able to confront their own needs, imagine solutions, and work to fulfill them through cooperative efforts and intelligent planning. In that community-oriented effort, government, nonprofit organizations, and businesses can be partners, contributing aid and assistance where feasible and being socially responsive to legitimately expressed human needs.

Summary

- The *community* refers to an organization's area of local influence, as well as more broadly to other groups that are impacted by its actions. Businesses and their communities are mutually dependent. Business relies on the community for services and infrastructure, and the community relies on business for support of various civic activities.

- Addressing a community's needs in a positive way helps business by enhancing its reputation, building trust, and winning support for company actions. Like other forms of corporate social responsibility, community involvement helps cement the loyalty of employees, customers, and the public.

- Many corporations have established community relations departments that respond to local needs and community groups, coordinate corporate giving, and develop strategies for creating win–win approaches to solving civic problems.

- Corporate giving comprises gifts of cash, property, and employee time. Donations currently average about 0.8 percent of pretax profits. Philanthropic contributions both improve a company's reputation and sustain vital community institutions.

- Many companies have adopted a strategic approach to philanthropy, linking their giving to business goals. Corporate giving is most effective when it draws on the unique competencies of the business and is aligned with the core values of the firm and with employee interests. Increasingly, companies are measuring the return on their social investment for both recipients and themselves.

- The development of collaborative partnerships has proven to be effective in addressing problems in education and other civic concerns. Partnerships offer an effective model of shared responsibility in which businesses and the public and nonprofit sectors can draw on their unique skills to address complex social problems.

Key Terms

civic engagement, *397*
collaborative partnerships, *411*
community, *396*
community relations, *399*

community relations manager, *399*
corporate foundations, *404*
corporate philanthropy (corporate giving), *402*
in-kind contributions, *405*

license to operate, *398*
return on social investment, *410*
social capital, *398*
strategic philanthropy, *408*
volunteerism, *406*

Internet Resources

www.bcccc.net	The Center for Corporate Citizenship at Boston College
www.pointsoflight.org	Points of Light Foundation
www.corporatephilanthropy.org	Committee Encouraging Corporate Philanthropy
http://philanthropy.com	Chronicle of Philanthropy
www.givingusa.org	Giving Institute and Giving USA Foundation
www.onphilanthropy.com	Resources for nonprofit and corporate professionals working in the philanthropic sector
www.communityactionpartnership.com	Community Action Partnerships
http://foundationcenter.org	Foundation Center
www.businessfightspoverty.org	Business Fights Poverty

Discussion Case: *Fidelity Investments' Partnership with Citizen Schools*

Roy Fralin stood in front of a roomful of active sixth and seventh graders in an inner-city public school in Roxbury, Massachusetts. The classroom walls were covered with flip chart paper, which were packed with diagrams, numbers, and terms like "savings," "budget," and "investment." A student stood at the front of the classroom. Fralin handed him a baseball cap to illustrate a loan with interest. "OK, when you give it back, you'll owe me how much?" Another student shouted out the answer. "Great!" exclaimed Fralin. They exchanged high fives. "Now, how much are we putting away for your 401(k)?" The students punched their handheld calculators.

Fralin was not a public school teacher, and teaching personal finance to middle schoolers was not his regular job. He was a vice president and investment advisor at Fidelity Investments, where he worked mostly with high net-worth clients. But here he was, every Wednesday afternoon for 10 weeks, teaching a curriculum that Fidelity employees had developed called "How to Invest Like a Millionaire." The program was part of a partnership between an innovative nonprofit called Citizen Schools and Fidelity Investments, one of its corporate partners. "I just don't see any downside," Fralin later reflected in a clip posted to YouTube about his experience as a citizen teacher. "I think this is going to be a success."

In June 2015, Fidelity Investments was one of the leading providers of financial services in the world, administering $5.2 trillion in assets for 24 million individual and institutional clients. The company, which was privately owned, offered investment management, retirement planning, portfolio guidance, brokerage, and benefits outsourcing services. It also operated its own family of mutual funds. Fidelity maintained its headquarters in Boston, but had 10 regional operating centers and about 180 retail locations. In 2015, the firm employed 41,000 associates.

In 2009, Fidelity set about rethinking its approach to community relations. For many years, the firm had been philanthropically active, giving to a wide range of charities in its home community and elsewhere. But the company had come to believe that it could have a greater impact by focusing on partnerships with a small number of what it called "best in class" nonprofit organizations. An issue of particular concern to Fidelity was education, especially the shocking dropout rates in many of the communities it served; nationally, 1.2 million students dropped out of high school every year, many of them as early as ninth grade. In researching various options for making a difference, the company learned that the middle school years were critical in determining whether or not students would go on to graduate from high school.

To focus its resources on this issue, Fidelity chose to partner with Citizen Schools (CS). Social entrepreneur Eric Schwarz had founded CS in 1995 in Boston to operate after-school programs for middle school students, aged 11 to 14, in disadvantaged communities. The nonprofit recruited volunteer professionals—"citizen teachers"—to offer after-school apprenticeships in subjects they were passionate about in schools in the CS network. As a culminating experience, students would present what they had learned to friends, family, and teachers at what CS called "WOW!" events. In 2015, Citizen Schools had active partnerships with 29 schools in low-income communities in seven states, serving more than 4,800 students.

Fidelity had contributed money to Citizen Schools since 1998, but in 2009 it significantly stepped up its commitment and the company went beyond charity, encouraging its employees, like Roy Fralin, to teach in Citizen School programs. By 2015, Fidelity volunteers had taught more than 180 apprenticeships in such wide-ranging topics as robotics, law, and financial literacy in 34 middle schools. More than 1,500 associates had volunteered over 20,000 hours of volunteer service. Several executives served on various advisory boards. The company also donated meeting space and equipment. For example, students who had learned about web design from a Fidelity employee were invited to use the Fidelity Center for Applied Technology for their WOW! event, presenting their work in a state-of-the-art facility.

An external evaluation commissioned by Citizen Schools showed that its programs had "successfully moved a group of low-income, educationally at-risk students toward high school graduation and advancement to college, and [had] set them up for full participation in the civic and economic life of their communities." Seventy-one percent of Citizen Schools alumni completed high school in four years, compared with 59 percent of matched peers. Sixty-one percent of students who had participated in their 8GA (8th Grade Academy) program five or more years earlier had enrolled in college, compared with 41 percent of low-income students nationally.

Fidelity indicated that in an internal survey, 89 percent of the company's employees who had participated in the Citizen Schools partnership reported feeling more connected to their colleagues, 78 percent reported improved team-building skills, and over three-quarters reported having improved communication skills. Most importantly though, Heidi Siegal, Fidelity's vice president for community relations, noted, "Our employees and our company enthusiastically support Citizen Schools because we know that they make a unique and significant impact on the lives of students in need."

Sources: Corporate Voices for Working Families, "Fidelity Investments" (case study), 2012, at *http://employmentpathwaysproject .org/wp-content/uploads/2014/04/Fidelity-and-Citizen-Schools-5.9.12.pdf;* "Fidelity Investments," at *www.citizenschools.org/ investors/current-investors/fidelity-investments;* "Teaching Kids to Invest Like Millionaires," [Roy Fralin], at *www.youtube.com;* "Guest Blog: At Citizen Schools, Volunteers Make STEM Relevant through Web design," at *www.educationnation.com;* and private correspondence with representatives of Fidelity Investments and Citizen Schools. The website of Citizen Schools is at *www.citizenschools.org.* The website of Fidelity Investments is at *www.fidelity.com.*

Discussion Questions

1. What evidence do you see in this case of the three kinds of corporate philanthropy discussed in this chapter: contributions of cash, in-kind products or services, and employee time?

2. What are the benefits and risks to Fidelity Investments of its partnership with Citizen Schools?

3. Do you consider Fidelity Investment's partnership with Citizen Schools to be an example of strategic philanthropy, as defined in this chapter? Why or why not?

4. If you were a community relations manager for Fidelity Investments, how would you evaluate the impact of this partnership? What kinds of impacts would you attempt to measure, and why?

CHAPTER NINETEEN

The Public and Corporate Reputation

How the general public perceives a business firm can have a major effect on its performance and its ability to remain in business. Therefore, building a positive public reputation for providing superior products or services is of great importance. Most companies employ many people to help establish and maintain a good reputation. Their job is to formulate a strategy that includes, at a minimum, the careful management of the brand, interaction with the media, managing key issues that may arise, and successfully responding to any unanticipated crises. Ultimately, maintaining a positive public reputation depends on acting in an ethical and socially responsible manner.

This Chapter Focuses on These Key Learning Objectives:

LO 19-1 Recognizing why the general public is an important organizational stakeholder.

LO 19-2 Understanding what constitutes a good corporate reputation and why it is important.

LO 19-3 Knowing the basic elements and activities of a firm's public relations department.

LO 19-4 Assessing how brand management can best manage a firm's reputation.

LO 19-5 Evaluating a firm's crisis management plan as an effective tool for handling an unexpected situation.

LO 19-6 Recognizing tactics that enable businesses to engage with the general public and other stakeholders to enhance the firm's reputation.

In 2014, Yahoo Inc. partnered with Yelp Inc., the online business review service, to incorporate Yelp ratings for businesses into Yahoo's search results. After Yahoo began including Yelp reviews, old reviews that had been cultivated by businesses on Yahoo Local suddenly vanished. While this new service might have been helpful for Yahoo users looking for ratings, many businesses found that years' worth of positive comments on Yahoo Local were suddenly erased. "It's a slap in the face that they took all those reviews down overnight," said Dan Tringale, owner of Colonial Hardwood Flooring in Lexington, Massachusetts. As for his business's online reputation, Tringale said Yahoo "just took away six or seven years of hard work." According to a 2014 study conducted by BrightLocal, roughly 95 percent of consumers said they used the Internet to search for local business listings and used ratings services, such as Yelp, 85 percent of the time. Having multiple reviews over a long period of time is essential for a business because it provides consumers with a set of diverse and trustworthy opinions that help to form the business's reputation over time.[1]

After a number of news outlets ran stories raising an alarm about "pink slime,"[2] many nutritionists and chefs—among them the TV celebrity chef Jamie Oliver—led a campaign to ban lean finely textured beef (LFTB). In response to the media attention, McDonald's and several national supermarkets, including Kroger and Safeway, banned LFTB from their processed food offerings. The dropping demand for LFTB soon became a huge problem for Beef Products Inc. (BPI), which had developed the process to create LFTB. BPI was forced to close three of its four LFTB facilities and layoff hundreds of employees. The founder of BPI, 69-year-old Eldon Roth, was heartbroken over the campaign against "pink slime." Roth had come up with the idea for LFTB in 1993 after four children died of *E. coli* poisoning from eating hamburgers purchased at a fast-food restaurant. He received government approval to treat meat with a puff of ammonium hydroxide after the fat was spun out helping to prevent the spread of disease. The editor of *Cattle Buyers Weekly* commented, "BPI has been in the forefront of food safety in the beef industry for a decade or more." A professor of dairy and animal science at the Pennsylvania State University also came to the defense of BPI. "This is a company with a long-standing reputation of doing things right, working with regulatory agencies and food safety people. From a technical or logical standpoint, these are the folks you'd hold up and say this is the way you do it."[3]

Both the Yahoo–Yelp and BPI examples illustrate the importance of maintaining a good reputation with the public. In an era when information travels at lightning speed through both conventional channels—television, radio, and newspapers—as well as social media outlets—blogs, websites, Twitter, e-mails, and others—reaching thousands, if not millions, of people, reputations can be lost in an instant. While businesses seek publicity and spend millions of dollars annually to improve their image and reputation, company executives must navigate many minefields as they compete for the hearts and minds of the consuming public. This chapter will define the general public as a stakeholder and present a variety of tools that businesses can use to build and protect their reputations and brands.

---

[1] "Report: Yahoo to Partner with Yelp on Search," *USA Today,* February 9, 2014, *www.usatoday.com;* and "Online Reputations List as Yahoo Switches to Yelp," *The Wall Street Journal,* April 10, 2015, p. B1.

[2] According to the U.S. Department of Agriculture (USDA) Food Safety and Inspection Service "pink slime" refers to lean finely textured beef (LFTB), a food product created by a process that recovers useful bits of meat from carcass trimmings. These bits are warmed, centrifuged to remove the fat, treated with ammonium hydroxide gas to kill germs, and then compressed into blocks that are frozen for later use. Although LFTB has never been sold directly to the public, it has been widely added to hamburgers and other prepared foods, and has been used in school lunches.

[3] "Pink Slime in Ground Beef: What's the Big Deal?" *CBS News,* March 14, 2012, *www.cbsnews.com;* "Backlash to the 'Pink Slime' Backlash," *Time Moneyland,* March 29, 2012, *www.moneyland.time.com;* and "The Sliming of Punk Slime's Creator," *Bloomsburg BusinessWeek,* April 12, 2012, *www.businessweek.com.*

The General Public

The **general public** is broadly defined as an organizational stakeholder comprising individuals and groups found in society. As described in Chapter 1, the general public does not deal with business organizations through an economic exchange with the firm, but does affect the firm through its opinions of the firm's activities or performance, which in turn help shape the firm's public image or reputation, as initially discussed in Chapter 3 and later in this chapter.

The public may utilize its own stakeholder networks—consumer advocacy groups, employee labor unions, or local community action groups—and engage with government agencies, special interest groups, or the media to demand a certain level of performance or to condemn or praise a firm. The public may react strongly against a business firm, even when its intentions are good, as the following story shows.

> Parents, consumer advocates, and health professionals joined together to address the issue of child obesity and nutrition, also discussed in Chapter 14. They called on the Academy of Nutrition and Dietetics, one of the world's largest groups of health professionals, to develop the "Kids Eat Right" program to spread the message that children need more calcium and vitamin D in their diets. Kraft Foods, an American producer and marketer of foods products, agreed to sponsor the Kids Eat Rights program, and in exchange was given permission to print the Kids Eat Right logo on packages of its Kraft American Singles packages. Some supporters of Kids Eat Right were outraged at the apparent attempt by Kraft to associate its brand with the program. They noted that Kraft Singles is a "pasteurized prepared cheese product" and not a good candidate for sponsorship of the Kids Eat Right program. Opponents also pointed out that the Academy and Kraft were in a financial partnership, in which Kraft agreed to provide a grant to support research or public education initiative undertaken by the academy.[4]

Companies should be aware of how their actions may be portrayed in the media. The media is understood as the collective means of communicating to an audience. It traditionally included television, radio, and newspapers, but has grown to include the emerging communication networks found on the Internet and through social media. Through the media, the firm can establish its reputation, repair a tarnished image, manage its public relations, address an organizational crisis, or engage with multiple stakeholders in a variety of ways. These topics will be addressed throughout this chapter.

What Is Reputation?

It may seem obvious that business organizations want to cultivate a good reputation. The term **corporate reputation** refers to desirable or undesirable qualities associated with an organization or its actors that may influence the organization's relationships with its stakeholders. It relies on the collective perceptions of past actions, results, and future prospects.[5]

> The importance of a good reputation is certainly obvious to Warren Buffet, owner of conglomerate Berkshire Hathaway. He reminds his managers each year in a now famous memo that their top priority must be to guard Berkshire's

---

[4] "'Eat Right' Meltdown for Kraft Singles," *Wall Street Journal,* March 23, 2015, *www.wsj.com.*

[5] Charles Fombrun and Cees Van Riel, "The Reputational Landscape," *Corporate Reputation Review,* 1 (1997), pp. 5–13.

reputation: "As I've said in these memos for more than 25 years," Buffet wrote, "we can afford to lose money—even a lot of money. But we can't afford to lose reputation—even a shred of reputation. It takes 20 years to build a reputation and five minutes to ruin it."[6]

Scholars have noted that reputation is related to corporate identity and corporate image and that these sometimes reinforce each other. **Corporate identity** refers to the way in which an organization presents itself to an audience, while **corporate image** refers to the way organizational members believe others see the organization.[7] For example, the way an organization presents itself to it stakeholders (identity) may influence the stakeholders' perceptions of the organization (image). Each of these concepts is important to keep in mind when crafting a reputation-building strategy.

Few companies start with a reputation of distinction, simply because such a reputation must be built over time. Firms may have name recognition—an identity—but that is not the same as having a good reputation. So, firms need a strategy for building a good reputation.

Building a reputation can be thought of as a step-by-step process beginning with the very product(s) or service(s) the firm offers. Therefore, managers must first strive to become a company that is perceived by its stakeholders to offer *significantly* better products and services than its competitors. This perception is largely based on image. For example, the success of Apple smartphones and tablets is based in large part on their reputation for superior performance.

Next, managers must aim to create and convey an *identity:* a consistent and compelling story about who the company is and what it stands for. This story needs to grab the attention of the news media, online media, and opinion leaders.

> The L.L. Bean company consistently tells the story that its products, designed for the outdoor enthusiast, are durable. Its policy of allowing consumers to return items, indefinitely, helps it uphold that reputational claim. One consumer has been returning her L.L. Bean backpacks for two decades whenever a zipper breaks. According to Steve Fuller, L.L. Bean's chief marketing officer, "If she believes her zippers should last a longer time, we'll respect that and we'll refund her money or give her a new product until she's happy," he said. Fuller believes that the real value of the policy is in how many times the woman tells people about her backpack returns.[8]
>
> REI, also a maker of outdoor clothing and gear, had the same policy but noticed that the amount of questionable returns was increasing after people talked about it on social media. In contrast to L.L. Bean, REI thought it was getting a reputation as a sucker. Nicknames like "Rental Equipment Inc.," "Rent Every Item," or "Return Every Item" began popping up on Facebook and Twitter. REI decided to change its policy to a one-year limit.[9]

These two different examples illustrate that a company's story must be a message that it can uphold and one that echoes the strong ethical values and beliefs of the company.

---

[6] "Warren Buffet on Ethics: We Can't Afford to Lose Reputation," *The Wall Street Journal,* May 31, 2011, *blogs.wsj.com.*

[7] See Reggy Hooghiemstra, "Corporate Communication and Impression Management: New Perspectives Why Companies Engage in Corporate Social Reporting," *Journal of Business Ethics* 27, (2000), pp. 55–68; Cees van Riel and C.B.M. van Riel, *Principles of Corporate Communication* (Harlow, England: Pearson Education, 1995); and The Reputation Institute at *www.reputationinstitute.com.*

[8] "10 Retailers That Will Let You Return Anything," *Business Insider,* September 23, 2013, *www.businessinsider.com.*

[9] "REI Return Policy Changes: Items Must be Returned within 1 Year," *The Denver Post,* June 4, 2013, *blogs.denverpost.com.*

Why Does Reputation Matter?

Academic researchers and practitioners share a consensus that organizations with strong positive reputations, such as L.L. Bean, outperform their competitors. Respected organizations are generally more successful because they (1) receive more opportunities to advance their interests, (2) are given the benefit of the doubt in uncertain circumstances, and (3) are generally more immune to the long-term effects of harsh criticism than their less respected counterparts. Research also shows that a sound reputation allows firms to charge premium prices; enhance their access to capital markets and investors; and obtain better credit, trust, and social ratings.[10] Likewise, stakeholders want to engage with respected companies.

In short, a good reputation can help firms gain a competitive advantage over other companies in the same industry. Unfortunately, numerous opinion polls like those conducted by *Edelman* (Trust Barometer), *Fortune* (World's Most Admired Companies), *Hill & Knowlton* (Corporate Reputation Watch), *Weber Shandwick Worldwide* (Safeguarding Reputation), and the *Reputation Institute* (Rep Trak) indicate that relatively few organizations have a reputation of distinction. As reported by the Harris Poll, the reputation of American businesses overall has increased somewhat since 2008. Figure 19.1 shows the results from a large sample of respondents when asked the question, "How would you rate the overall reputation of corporate America today?" The poll shows that the proportion of respondents rating the reputation of U.S. companies as "excellent" increased slightly, and the proportion rating it "very poor" had decreased slightly, since 2009.

However, surveys also reveal that although senior managers want to improve their companies' reputations, they lack confidence about how to go about doing so. Interestingly, while a majority of executives of global companies (76%) are confident that their corporate reputations are strong, according to the 2014 Reputation At Risk survey conducted by *Forbes* Insight, their confidence declines when it comes to protecting against reputational risks. Only 19 percent of these executives would award themselves an "A" grade for their ability to manage against such risks.[11]

FIGURE 19.1   **The Harris Poll's Reputation Quotient, 2009–2015**

Source: Adapted from the *Harris Poll 2015 Reputation Quotient Summary Report,* Harris Poll, *www.harrisinteractive.com.*

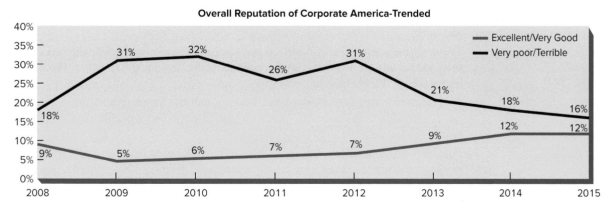

[10] Reggy Hoogheimstra (2000) and Charles Fombrun and Cees van Riel (1997), ibid.

[11] "Making the Grade When Stakeholders Rule: 2013 Annual Reputation Leaders Survey," *Reputation Institute,* 2013, *www.reputationinstitute.com;* and *2014 Global Survey on Reputational Risk,* Deloitte (October 2014), *deloitte.wsj.com.*

The task of building a corporation's reputation, and protecting it against various risks, is often entrusted to the firm's public relations department, as discussed next.

The Public Relations Department

Given the importance of the general public to business and the potential for business to significantly benefit or harm the public, firms often create public relations departments, appoint public relations officers, and develop public affairs strategies to manage their relationship with the public. Bill Nielsen, former corporate vice president of public affairs at Johnson & Johnson, clearly articulated the importance of an effective public relations approach for businesses:

> In today's increasingly global world of business, there is a clear and, I believe, pressing agenda for public relations. . . . The agenda is all about the critical components of reputation that have to do with values and trust—trustworthiness being the ultimate condition of public approval that we seek for our companies, our clients, and our profession—on a global scale and wherever in the world we operate.[12]

The role of the **public relations department** is to manage the firm's public image and, more generally, its relationship with the public. This department may also be called *media relations,* since much of its work involves interacting with the media. It does so through direct communications with the public (for example, through its website) and indirect communications with them through various media outlets. Most public relations officers have close links with top managers. According to a study by the Foundation for Public Affairs, nearly half of the public affairs executives surveyed report directly to the CEO, chairman of the board of directors, or company president, and another nearly 30 percent report to the company's general counsel. According to the report, because of this access, public affairs executives have been able to persuade CEOs to become increasingly involved in corporate public affairs activities.[13] The specific major activities carried out by public relations managers include:

- *Advertising:* Preparation, purchase, and placement of purposefully planned and executed messages in selected media to further the interest of an organization or person.
- *Corporate sponsorship:* Providing support to an event or a cause by devoting corporate resources in exchange for an opportunity to enhance goodwill, product image, and sales.
- *External communications:* Controlled and uncontrolled messages disseminated in the mass media as well as other communications media, including pamphlets, brochures, nonbroadcast videos, speeches, and so on.
- *Internal communications:* Planned messages disseminated to employees through a variety of communications channels, including newsletters, bulletin boards, payroll stuffers, posters, and so on.
- *Publicity:* Dissemination of purposefully planned and executed messages to selected media to further the interest of an organization or person without specific payment to media.[14]

---

[12] Bill Nielsen, "The Singular Character of Public Relations in a Global Economy," International Distinguished Lecture at the Institute for Public Relations, October 11, 2006, p. 1. Nielsen's entire address is available at *www.instituteforpr.com.*

[13] Foundation for Public Affairs, *The State of Corporate Public Affairs,* (Washington, D.C., Foundation for Public Affairs, 2014).

[14] "Public Relations Activities," *MediaMiser, www.mediamiser.com.*

Using Technology-Enhanced Channels for Public Relations

Historically, public relations officers worked mostly through contact with traditional media outlets. An organization worked to enhance its public image by seeking positive coverage in news reports and feature stories, or by paid advertisements via television, radio, magazines, newspapers, or billboards. Public relations may still utilize these interactions, but as new technologies have emerged, the variety of available channels of communication has grown dramatically. More and more people are finding their news, marketing, or other public relations information through Internet-related vehicles, such as blogs, e-mails, social networking, podcasts, cell phones, and other technology-based communication sources.

Many firms, from chocolate makers to pharmaceuticals, are using social networking to connect with their past or potential customers, prospective employees, and others in the communities where they operate as shown in these examples.

- Hershey's, the chocolate manufacturer, launched its Simple Pleasures line to provide a product without compromise: good taste and less fat. To share its newest creation with consumers, Hershey's launched a campaign with traditional media outreach to bloggers, newspapers, wires, and magazines; a custom Facebook tab where visitors could declare their Sweet Independence and receive a coupon; a road tour to 10 cities, where consumers could try the candy and declare "Sweet Independence" through a custom iPad app; a 70-blog tour through The Motherhood with a Twitter party that resulted in *#hsysimplepleasures* becoming the No. 1 trending topic on Twitter; and employee awareness by setting up stations for Hershey's staff to stop by and play games, listen to music, and declare Sweet Independence and enjoy chocolates. The campaign had upwards of 217 media hits, more than 25,000 likes on Facebook, and distribution of 13,500 samples. The initial sales of Simple Pleasures exceeded forecasts.

- Bristol-Myers Squibb wanted to bring attention to the important social issue of men contracting melanoma, a type of skin cancer. To hit its target market, this campaign identified NFL spokespeople to raise awareness; set up an interactive website with educational video and details on local screenings; attracted gamers through a football-themed game called Football Avenue; operated a mobile exam room at highly attended NFL events; and leveraged the NFL's digital reach through Facebook and Twitter. After attending events, 81 percent of respondents said they were more knowledgeable about melanoma; 42 million people were reached through NFL digital entities; and 176 million media impressions.[15]

Public relations strategies increasingly assume a global focus, since business interactions with the public through media channels frequently transcend national boundaries. Therefore, many businesses have extended their public relations strategies globally, as shown in the following example.

P&G (formerly Procter & Gamble), based in Cincinnati, Ohio, is the largest consumer packaged goods company in the world. P&G created a comprehensive, yet unified network of public affairs departments to address the flow of information from the company to and from its stakeholders around the world. At P&G, public affairs is broken down into functions (corporate communications, global marketing and consumer and marketing knowledge, corporate digital communications, and global business services), product lines (male grooming, female beauty and grooming, cosmetics, fine fragrances, oral care, feminine care, baby care, general health care, pet care and snacks), and geographical regions (North America contacts,

---

[15] "3 Examples of Integrated PR Campaigns," *CISION*, October 21, 2013, *www.cision.com.*

Ohio government relations, multicultural marketing public relations). Each contact point has its own set of contact information directing you to a person, location, office telephone number, mobile telephone number, and e-mail address.[16]

When public relations strategies take on a global perspective, new challenges emerge. For example, public relations managers must be sensitive to cultural disparities, as well as similarities, in crafting press releases and interactions with the media. The impact of the organization's public relations program could vary country to country given the culture, social mores, political system, or history. A public relations manager must be able to communicate with local media and other stakeholder groups in their native language and avoid embarrassing or misleading communication due to poor translations. All of the basic public relations tasks are more complex in an international business environment.[17]

Some businesses decentralize their global public relations programs and establish officers in each of the locations where they have operations. This helps to ensure that the local public relations strategy is in tune with local customs and emerging issues. "Forward thinking companies will become more decentralized in their . . . communications. They will increasingly put tools out there to arm influencers, peers, enthusiasts, customers, and prospects, as well as employees—and then get out of the way and let the magic happen," explained Bob Geller, senior vice president at Fusion Public Relations.[18]

Brand Management

Managers are very aware how important and how difficult it is to create a widely recognized brand; typically, the focus of the marketing team. **Brand management** uses techniques to increase the perceived value of a product line or brand over time.

Well-established brands must be managed as part of maintaining the firm's reputation. All brands have to re-establish themselves continually. Even luxury brands have begun to tout the number of their Facebook fans and Twitter followers. The *Brand Directory* publishes the value of the largest worldwide brands. In 2014, the U.S.-based Apple brand was valued at over $104 billion; Korea's Samsung brand was valued at $78 billion; and in the United Kingdom Vodafone's brand was estimated to be worth $29 billion.[19]

A recognizable brand is one that can immediately signal to stakeholders how the company is different from its rivals. For example, the company *3M* communicates innovation. But increasingly, a truly iconic brand fosters an emotional appeal that creates loyalty, even love, of the brand. Brand consultants, say that it is this emotional attachment that gives brands their market power. For example, the Apple brand (and its creator Steve Jobs) instilled such a strong emotional appeal that fans were moved to place hundreds of cards and flowers at numerous Apple stores around the world upon hearing of Jobs's death in 2012. Similarly, Harley-Davidson riders tattoo the brand name on their bodies. It is difficult to think of another brand that people would be willing to tattoo on themselves.

A corporation's reputation is captured in a recognized and trusted name. The company's name and logo act as its signature, a sign that says they can be trusted to deliver exceptional value to customers. Often, brand management involves conveying what the product

---

[16] See P&G's website at *news.pg.com/media_contacts.*

[17] For a thorough discussion of these issues, see Craig S. Fleisher, "The Development of Competencies in International Public Affairs," *Journal of Public Affairs* 3, no. 3 (March 2003), pp. 76–82.

[18] "Command and Control to a Decentralized Marketing Tool," *Flack's Revenge* blog, February 23, 2009, *www.flacksrevenge.com.*

[19] "Global 500 2014—The World's Most Valuable Brands," *Brand Directory, branddirectory.com.* See also "BRANDZ Top 100 Most Valuable Global Brands 2014," *MillwardBrown, www.millwardbrown.com.*

DHL = Documents Hopelessly Lost

Fiat = Fix It Again, Tony

Ford Motor Company = Fix Or Repair Daily

British Petroleum = Burning the Planet; Big Problems; Broken Pipelines; and Bloated Profits

Neiman Marcus = Needless Markup

REI = Rental Equipment Inc.; Rent Every Item; Return Every Item

Starbucks = Four Bucks

Taco Bell = Taco Hell; Toxic Bell

UBS (bank) = Used to Be Smart

Whole Foods = Whole Paycheck

Sources: "10 Best Company Nicknames," *Daily Finance,* August 30, 2010, *www.dailyfinance.com;* and Grahame R. Dowling, "Winning the Corporate Reputation Game" (Cambridge, MA: MIT Press, 2016).

or service offers—the benefits, solutions to problems, or simply an experience. This can be challenging, because the experience may not be an obvious feature of the product. Charles Revson, the founder of the *Revlon* cosmetics company, commented that "in the factory we make cosmetics; in the drugstore we sell hope."

When a company fails to meet the public's expectations, people can retaliate by ascribing a new meaning to a company's name, with devastating results for its reputation. Some examples of some unflattering corporate nicknames are shown in Exhibit 19.A.

Crisis Management

A critical function for any manager is *crisis management*. **Crisis management** is the process by which an organization deals with a major event that threatens to harm the organization, its stakeholders, or the general public.[20] Every organization is likely at some time to face a crisis that forces management and its employees to act quickly and without perfect information. A **corporate crisis** is a significant business disruption that stimulates extensive news media or social networking coverage. The resulting public scrutiny can affect the organization's normal operations and also can have a political, legal, financial, and governmental impact on its business. A crisis is any event with the potential to negatively affect the health, reputation, or credibility of the organization.[21] The Institute for Crisis Management breaks down corporate crises into four groups:

- "Acts of God"—earthquakes, tornados, violent storms, volcanic eruptions.
- Mechanical problems—breakdowns of or faulty equipment, metal fatigue.
- Human errors—through miscommunication, improper employee behavior.
- Management decision or indecision—often involving a cover-up or lack of urgency.[22]

[20] Paul Shrivastava, Ian I. Mitroff, Danny Miller, and Anil Miglani, "Understanding Industrial Crises," *Journal of Management Studies,* 25 (1988), pp. 285–304.

[21] For additional information on crisis management strategies, see "Handling a Corporate Crisis: The Ten Commandments of Crisis Management," *The Conference Board,* August 2012; Catherine H. Tinsley, Robin L. Dillon, and Peter M. Madsen, "How to Avoid Catastrophe," *Harvard Business Review,* April 2011, pp. 90–97; and for suggestions on what to avoid doing during a crisis, see Peter S. Goodman, "In Case of Emergency: What Not To Do," *The New York Times,* August 21, 2010, *www.nytimes.com.*

[22] From the Institute for Crisis Management's website, *www.crisisexperts.com.*

Exhibit 19.B

Excuse Me, There Is a Finger in My Chili!

On March 22, 2005, Denny Lynch, senior vice president for communications at Wendy's, one of the country's largest fast-food restaurant chains, received a shocking and unexpected call. A customer, Anna Ayala, claimed she had bitten down on a severed finger while eating a cup of chili purchased at a Wendy's restaurant in San Jose, California. Lynch knew that he had to act quickly, since this incident would certainly be the top story on the evening news and in the headlines of every major newspaper the next day.

Wendy's immediately assembled its crisis management team in its regional headquarters in Sacramento, California. Lynch prepared a statement for the press, instructed the company's website to be frequently updated, and began coordinating with the San Jose police department, which was already involved in the case. According to Lynch, "It went nonstop the next two or three days. Even when the Pope passed away, it still got coverage."

In the wake of the immediate crisis, Wendy's focused on trying to discover what had really happened. Through an internal investigation, Lynch learned that a 10-year veteran and trusted employee had prepared the chili for Ayala; he assured Lynch there was nothing improper in the food preparation.

While Lynch and his team worked furiously around the clock to discover the truth, Ayala, the woman who had made the accusation, was a guest on numerous morning and late night television shows. Yet, it was soon discovered that Ayala had a litigious history that included a settlement for medical expenses for her daughter, who had claimed she became sick at an El Pollo Loco restaurant in Las Vegas.

The break Lynch and Wendy's needed occurred exactly one month after the initial incident, when Anna Ayala was arrested in her Las Vegas home for attempted grand larceny, accused of trying to extort $2.5 million from Wendy's. The finger in her chili was all a hoax. "The true victims are Wendy's owners and operators," said San Jose chief of police Rob Davis. Forensic evidence proved that the finger was not cooked at 170 degrees for three hours—the typical preparation of Wendy's chili. It was later discovered that Ayala acquired the finger through her husband's workplace, where a fellow worker had lost part of his finger in an industrial accident.

Later that year, Ayala and her husband, Jaime Plascencia, pleaded guilty to attempted grand larceny and conspiring to file a false claim. Ayala was sentenced to 9 years in prison and her husband, who supplied the finger, was sentenced to 12 years and 4 months in prison.

Sources: "At CSI: Wendy's, Tracking a Gruesome Discovery," *The New York Times,* April 22, 2005, *www.nytimes.com;* "Finger in Chili Is Called Hoax; Las Vegas Woman Is Charged," *The New York Times,* April 23, 2005, *www.nytimes.com;* and "Stiff Sentences for Wendy's Chili-Finger Couple," *Bay City News,* January 18, 2006, *www.SFGate.com.*

A corporate crisis can take many different forms. It might be a terrorist attack, poor financial results, the death of a key executive or government official, employee layoffs, a charge of sexual harassment, or the filing of class-action lawsuits brought by injured customers. Or it might be something bizarre and unique, such as the crisis that confronted Wendy's, described in Exhibit 19.B. But crises, by definition, are often unique. To prepare for these unexpected events and sometimes tragedies, an organization must develop a crisis management plan before the crisis hits.

Some businesses or industries are more prone to corporate crises than others and therefore have greater need for a crisis management plan. According to the Institute for Crisis Management, medical and surgical manufacturers, pharmaceutical companies, and software manufacturers (because of the sophisticated technology found in their products and the potential for disruptive impact on consumers' lives) are at the top of a recent list of crisis-prone industries.

Most experts recommend that organizations develop a crisis management plan ahead of time, to deal with such unexpected events as the one that happened to Wendy's. Since the first 24 hours during a crisis are the most crucial, having a plan ready for implementation

when the crisis occurs is imperative, citing the biblical wisdom: Noah built his ark *before* it began to rain. These plans must include as many scenarios as possible and a variety of responses for multiple stakeholders.

> Randy Mastro, a partner at the law firm Gibson Dunn and cochair of the firm's crisis management practice group, explained that having procedures and protocols in place for reporting, decision making, investigative steps, public relations, disclosure obligations and crisis response actions helps mitigate crises when they actually hit. "There's a tendency to react spontaneously or emotionally to crisis situations," he said. "Having protocols in place helps eliminate problems down the road and reduces panic."[23]

According to experts, an effective crisis management plan must include these steps:

- *Get ready before the crisis hits* by creating an internal communication system that can be activated the moment a crisis occurs. Scenario-based press releases, key employees and discussion points, and procedures to activate the organization's website (to use the Internet to announce any news, product recalls, etc.) should be at the ready. Many organizations create a **dark site**, a website that is fully developed and uploaded with critical information, contacts for the media, and other useful details, ready to be activated at the moment it is needed. McDonald's holds "hater" sessions where they ask themselves the following question, "If we said X, how would someone who doesn't like us respond?" That way, when people criticize the company on social media, they're not surprised.[24]

- *Communicate quickly, but accurately.* Firms facing a crisis must communicate with the media and others promptly. Communications must always be honest and disclose fully what the company knows—even if it does not know the full story. Wendy's, for example, effectively communicated with the public even when it did not yet know how the finger got in the chili. The media have excellent resources and will find the truth whether the organization speaks it or not.

- *Use the Internet* to convey the message to minimize the public's fears and provide assistance. In addition to face-to-face press releases, Wendy's frequently updated its company website to communicate to the public and others what the company was doing about the crisis situation.

- *Do the right thing.* Often the true test of an organization is how it reacts in a time of crisis. Public relations managers should not try to minimize the seriousness of a problem or make excuses. It is possible for the organization to accept responsibility without accepting liability. It also is important that the organization be sympathetic. For example, Wendy's clearly expressed regret over its customers' fears and advised the public that it was doing everything possible to investigate.

- *Follow up* and, where appropriate, make amends to those affected. Seek to restore the organization's reputation. Wendy's relentless pursuit of the truth resulted in vindication for the company and assisted law enforcement in the prosecution of those making the false claims.

A *crisis management guide* describing a series of critical crisis management checkpoints is shown in Exhibit 19.C.

---

[23] "The GC's Guide to Corporate Crisis," *Inside Counsel,* January 28, 2013, *www.insidecounsel.com.*

[24] Jana Seijts, "When the Twitterverse Turns on You," *Harvard Business Review,* March 2014, pp. 117–21.

1. Create and document policies and procedures and circulate them widely.
2. Know the policies and procedures and follow them.
3. Be prepared with a continuity plan to provide for continuing operations during the crisis management phase.
4. Work as a team with assigned responsibilities and a clear leader and practice, practice, practice in mock drills.
5. Identify and understand the organization's vulnerabilities; most importantly, correct shortcomings.
6. Let your conscience be your guide, follow good ethical practice, and remember the "front-page test." (Or, better yet, consider: What would Grandma say?)
7. Beware of dangerous and distorted minds and protect coworkers and facilities.
8. Put all phases of the event under a microscope and track and record activities.
9. Handle all records, samples, information, materials, and evidence with care.
10. Know the media and how to handle it. NEVER lie, cover up, or obfuscate.
11. Keep your eyes on the law and contact legal counsel; don't make decisions simply to avoid lawsuits.
12. Provide timely updates to coworkers and provide follow-up meetings and counseling.

Source: FosterHyland & Associates, Inc., *www.fosterhyland.com.* Used with permission.

Engaging Key Stakeholders with Specific Tactics

In the past, building the corporate reputation was achieved mostly through contact with traditional media outlets, like newspapers, magazines, and television. While reputation management still involves these tactics, new technologies have emerged creating a much larger variety of available communication options. As the Internet has transformed how organizational stakeholders search for and find information, public relations managers have increasingly embraced social media as a platform for reaching the public.

Using all of these media outlets, companies strive to build a solid reputation by targeting the stakeholders who are important to their commercial success. Employees and customers are very important to the organization's success, as are many other market and nonmarket stakeholders listed in Chapter 1. Different tactics for communicating and enhancing the firm's reputation may be more appropriate for some stakeholders than others. For example, executive visibility and event sponsorship are most often targeted to employees. The other tactics, such as user-generated content, paid content, public service announcements, and image ads, discussed next in this chapter, can be used to target almost any type of stakeholder.

The most important element in establishing the firm's reputation is to win the trust of its key stakeholders. What media outlets are most trusted by the public? Both traditional media and online search engines are the highly trusted sources (65 percent), but hybrid, social, and owned media are also trusted, according to the 2014 Edelman Trust Barometer, as shown in Figure 19.2.

Executive Visibility

In today's business environment, the firm's overall reputation is clearly on the agenda for the board of directors because of its effect on the firm's products and profits (for more information on the board of directors and its role in the governance of the company

FIGURE 19.2
Most Trusted Media Outlets

Source: 2014 Edelman Trust Barometer, *www.edelman.com.*

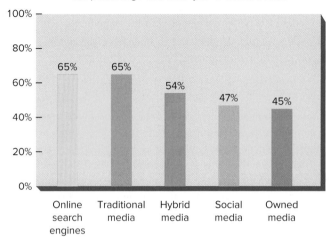

Level of trust in sources of information
Secondary header = In 2014, 27,000 people from 27 countries were asked: "Do you trust this source of information?" The percentage who said "yes" is shown below.

see Chapter 13). The growing importance of board-level attention toward a firm's reputation, combined with assuring damage control that a bad or failing reputation can cause, makes executive visibility a necessity. Specifically, executives need **media training** that focuses on helping them to interact with the public and media. This is especially true for those executives who are likely to have contact with the media, such as members of the board of directors, the CEO, CIO, CFO, general counsel, and directors of human resources, investor relations, and marketing. They are the ones who will tell the corporate story, and they must be well versed in all aspects of the story and aware of how their comments might affect the reputation of the company. Executives should make themselves visible and available to both their internal and external stakeholders in good times and in bad. Media training is necessary because communicating with the media is not as simple as talking with friends or coworkers.

> Emil Michael, Uber's senior vice president of business, learned the value of such training the hard way. At a 2014 dinner in New York that included Uber's CEO Travis Kalanick, celebrities, and some journalists, Michael expressed outrage at PandoDaily editor Sarah Lacy's recent column, which was critical of Uber. Michael said that he believed women were far more likely to get assaulted by taxi drivers than by Uber drivers, in contrast to Lacy's position. He said that Lacy should be held "personally responsible" for any woman who followed her advice in deleting Uber and was then sexually assaulted. According to *The Wall Street Journal,* Michael's comments led to a major backlash on Twitter, with many people saying they were uninstalling the app.[25]

Media communication experts generally give their clients the following advice.

- *Be honest.* Always tell the truth and explain why you cannot discuss a particular subject.
- *Be current.* The media wants to speak with you because of your up-to-date knowledge. If you do not have current information, promise to find out and get back to the media.

[25] "Is Uber's Biggest Rival Itself? A Collection of Controversy," *The Wall Street Journal,* November 18, 2014, *blogs.wsj.com.*

- *Be accessible.* A spokesperson is expected to be on-call and promptly respond to demands made by the media, as long as the demands are reasonable.
- *Be helpful.* If you do not know the answer to a question, say so and offer to find out. Try to make the media's job easier; they will print or broadcast anyway, so if you are helping them there is a better chance of your message being heard.
- *Be understanding.* Understand the needs of the media, their pending deadline or the importance of their acquiring background information.
- *Be cool, courteous, and professional.* You are representing your organization in the eyes of the media and the public. Remember, nothing is really ever "off the record."

Employees trained to interact with the media should know the basic message points that the organization wants communicated. These key points need to be reinforced with facts and statistics, whenever possible, and elaborated upon in an interview or press conference. Many times the audience is not aware or knowledgeable of the organization's operations or product or whatever is the focus of the press conference. Therefore, it is important to be clear and avoid jargon or technical language. Finally, the spokesperson should close the interview by reiterating the organization's key message.

Some of the best techniques to assist a spokesperson to stay on point when challenged by a reporter with a tough question are the following:

- *Hooking.* Grab the reporter's attention by making a statement that influences the next question. For example, "We are undertaking a program to correct the situation." Typically the reporter will follow up by asking about the organization's new program.
- *Bridging.* Answer the challenging question but quickly move on to the key message. For example, "Yes, but . . ." or "What I can tell you is . . ." or "While that is true, what is important to know is . . .".
- *Flagging.* Emphasize key points and guide the reporter to them. For example, "Your listeners may not know that . . ." or "This is important news because . . .".

Managers may also consider using not only the traditional press conference but also other media outlets—namely, user-generated content and well-heeled content distributors—all of which are useful tools to tell the company's story to maintain, or sometimes defend, its reputation.

User-Generated Content

User-generated content refers to sources of information provided by users through social media sites like Facebook, YouTube, Twitter, and Instagram. This information can be supportive or critical of business since the content is created by consumers, employees, investors—indeed, by anyone with access to a computer. Larry Weber, founder of Weber Shandwick Worldwide, a global communications company, suggests the communications world is dramatically moving in a digital direction. Managers who understand the growing importance of user-generated content will communicate much more effectively than those who do not. Weber, and coauthor Lisa Leslie Henderson, argue in their book, *The Digital Marketer,* that managers need to embrace a world where, "the 'digital genie' isn't going back into her bottle and neither is the consumer."[26]

---

[26] Larry Weber and Lisa Leslie Henderson, *The Digital Marketer: Ten New Skills You Must Learn to Stay Relevant and Customer-Centric* (New York: Wiley, 2014).

User-generated sites can be used effectively for brand, issue, and crisis management. An increasingly popular technique is to create a hashtag on Twitter, which is simply text placed in the beginning, middle, or end of a tweet by inserting a pound sign in front of a keyword. Hashtags are used to start an online dialogue with employees, consumers, media, and brand lovers creating buzz around a product or an issue. One effective example is Keurig Green Mountain's #keurig hashtag campaign, which is full of happy thoughts about this particular coffee maker and its coffee. A recent post on Twitter said it well:

> Say hello to my new bestfriend. #KeurigK45 **#KeurigCoffee** #KeurigKCups #HelloKeurig #Keurig #ImpulseBuy #Kcups
>
> —Annette Williams @LadyGemini71 Oct 15

However, these campaigns can sometimes result in the hashtag becoming what has been called a *bashtag* as McDonald's recently found out.

> When McDonald's promoted the hashtag #McDStories, hoping that customers would tweet about positive experiences with the company, they discovered that after just a few hours, the conversation was turning unexpectedly negative [For example, one person tweeted: "I'd pet a million stray pit bulls before I'd eat a single pink-slimy McBite. #3McDStories"]. In response, the company changed the hashtag to #MeettheFarmers, which had been successful earlier that day in soliciting positive posts, and they also stopped promoting the troublesome one. Within 15 minutes, the disparaging tweets were down to zero. So, managers need to be mindful that critics can take over and direct a firm's hashtag campaign.[27]

A similar situation occurred during JPMorgan Chase's #AskJPM in the spring of 2014, as described in the discussion case at the end of this chapter.

Paid Content

When firms pay to have online or print publishers create and distribute their content— also referred to as *content distribution*—they are using the tactic of **paid content**. This represents a major shift in the way firms manage their reputation because corporations now deliver directly to multiple stakeholders via the web, whereas traditional marketing and public relations relied on journalists to disseminate it. (A case at the end of the book, "Carolina Pad and the Bloggers," explores the ethical implications of companies paying bloggers to promote their products.)

Companies are increasingly paying to put information on a newswire or other distribution network. This tactic can reach almost any stakeholder with the same message. Creating high-quality content is very important for a firm's brand and image management, but its distribution is equally vital. There are many companies that provide distribution services for paid content. Perhaps best known are promoted feeds on Facebook, LinkedIn, and Twitter, but other less well-known options, like CSRWire, Outbrain, Taboola, Nativo, Nrelate, and Disqus, are also available.

> For example, CSRwire, perhaps one of the largest of these distributors, has a membership that includes corporations, NGOs, advertising agencies, and

---

[27] "How to Use Hashtags on Twitter: A Simple Guide for Marketers," *HubSpot Blogs,* April 24, 2012, *blog.hubspot.com.*

universities. These organizations pay CSRwire to communicate their corporate citizenship, sustainability, philanthropy, and socially responsible initiatives to not only this membership base but to its vast individual subscriber base. CSRwire's CEO Joe Sibilia stated recently, "All content is paid for now."

Outbrain, a similar content distributor, has a network that spans some of the largest publishers on the web, including CNN, Fox News, Hearst, Mashable, MSNBC, and Slate, along with premium sites like *NYTimes.com, CNN.com,* and a number of widely read blogs. These publishers pay a few cents per click, and Outbrain's marketing team claims the volume of traffic and relevancy of the topics generates 44 percent higher page views per session than search or social media referrals.[28]

Experts warn, however, understanding the nuances of the distribution process can be the difference between getting ignored or standing out.

Event Sponsorship

Another important tactic to reach consumers, the general public, employees, and the media is to sponsor an event with the company's name and logo, as mentioned earlier when Kraft added the Kid Eat Right logo to their cheese packages. The total value of sponsorships sold in North America was about $20 billion in 2013 and the rate of increase of spending in this medium is expected to continue to grow at about 5 percent annually.[29] Depending on the event, this is also an opportunity to gain some visibility for the firm's executive team.

However, sponsorship is not as simple as placing the company name on a colorful banner. According to Jeff Haden at *Inc.com,* "when you sponsor an event your focus should always be on the *quality* rather than the *quantity* of brand impressions." Therefore, Haden recommends that much emphasis be placed on choosing the right event. Haden also recommends that businesses ask the following questions:

1. What's in it for me?
2. What is unique about this opportunity over others?
3. How is my company directly engaging the audience at this event?
4. What kind of return could I see from sponsorship? (not necessarily monetary)
5. Do I like this event and does the audience fit my target audience?[30]

While sponsoring an event can be a real benefit for employees, having them volunteer at these events must be done by considering whether it adds value to the firm as would be the case for any comparable monetary donation. (This tactic is similar to strategic philanthropy—where corporate giving is linked directly or indirectly to business goals and objectives—and discussed in Chapter 18.) A good example of leveraging a sponsorship is Ford Motor Company's association with the Fuel for Business Council, which helps the more than 55 official NASCAR sponsorship partners get together to set up promotions and other programs aimed at boosting business.

---

[28] Information from a speech by CEO of CSRWire, Joe Sibilia, at the 10th Annual Bentley Global Business Ethics Symposium on Integrated Reporting. May 19, 2014; also see "6 Turnkey Tools for Content Distribution," *Mashable,* January 3, 2012, *mashable.com;* and "The Pros, Cons, and Costs of the Top 10 Content Distribution Platforms," *Contently,* April 10, 2014, *contently.com.*

[29] "Keys to Sponsorship Success," *TK Business Magazine,* November 14, 2013, *www.tkmagazine.com.*

[30] Jeff Haden, "Sponsoring an Event? Tips to Maximize Your Return," *Inc.,* September 25, 2012, *www.inc.com.*

As a sponsor of NASCAR's Fuel for Business Council (FFCB), Ford Motor Company sold more than 20,000 vehicles in 2012 and generated more than $200 million in sales as a result of its participation. According to Ford's research, 38 percent of potential car buyers say they are motorsports fans, and within that group, 86 percent say they follow NASCAR. Likewise, Ford said it sold more than 5,500 vehicles to other NASCAR sponsors through its Partner Recognition Program, which gives employees at those companies access to special discounts of Ford vehicles. Through the FFCB, Ford set up a promotion with Sprint telecommunications that gave consumers a chance to win a Ford Fusion car. Sprint is the title sponsor of the NASCAR Sprint Cup racing series.[31]

Public Service Announcements

Since 1942, the Ad Council has been the leading producer of **public service announcements** (PSAs), addressing critical social issues for generations of Americans and global citizens. The Ad Council has created some of the most memorable slogans, such as its inaugural campaign of "Loose Lips Sink Ships," promoting secrecy of military operations during World War II to the more recent "Friends Don't Let Friends Drive Drunk" and "A Mind Is a Terrible Thing To Waste."

More recently, PSA campaigns have ranged from disaster relief and energy efficiency to arts education and the prevention of childhood obesity. The longest running PSA in American history, introduced in 1944 and continuing today, features Smokey the Bear and his famous warning: "Only You Can Prevent Forest Fires." The forest fire prevention campaign has reduced the number of acres lost annually from 22 million to less than 10 million.[32]

Modeled after the actions taken by the Ad Council, businesses have discovered that public service announcements are an effective means for promoting various social issues or topics that resonate with the public, as demonstrated by the campaign by the Ad Council and *Teach.org* called "Make More, Teach."

> In 2014, the Ad Council and *Teach.org* partnered to create the TEACH campaign, which aimed to recruit the next generation of teachers by redefining teaching as a top career choice for the United States' most talented students. The campaign sought to change current perceptions of teaching and showcased the evolution and elevated stature of the teaching career. The ad was designed around some compelling statistics making for an effective PSA: "17 percent of the job openings in 2020 will be in teaching because half of those currently teaching will retire in the next decade."[33]

Image Advertisements

Image advertisements are used by business organizations to enhance their public image, create goodwill, or announce a major change such as a merger, acquisition, or new product line. These ads are different than issue advertisements, as discussed in Chapter 8, that focus on a public policy issue or piece of legislation. Image ads promote the image, or

---

[31] "Ford Says Winning NASCAR Races Still Drives Showroom Sales," *The Wall Street Journal,* March 8, 2013, *blogs.wsj.com.*

[32] See the Ad Council's website, *www.adcouncil.org.*

[33] See *www.psacentral.org.*

FIGURE 19.3
Brazil's Star Model's "Say No To Anorexia" Campaign is a good example of using ads to change the image of an industry.

Source: "Images of Brazil Say No to Anorexia, *bing.com/images.*

A poster from Brazil's Say No To Anorexia campaign (Picture: Star Models)

general perception, of a product or service, rather than promoting its functional attributes. They target the public's emotions and seek to influence the consumers' imaginations.

In 2014, Brazilian modeling agency Star Model created an anorexia ad campaign to help change the image of the modeling industry. Designers used software graphic techniques to turn real women into life-size versions of fashion illustrations, as shown in Figure 19.3. Showing what women would look like if they had the same measurements as the illustrations. Star Model's "Say No To Anorexia" campaign stated: "You are not a sketch." Mary George of the UK-based charity Beat Eating Disorders commented, "Although there are naturally thin individuals in the fashion world, the images certainly don't reflect the majority of us. A recent survey by the London College of Fashion shows the average UK woman to be size 14 to 16." The campaign went viral and George says, "We know the difference it would make to all young people's self-esteem and body confidence if they could be sure which of the images they see are natural and true to life." The aim was both to help young women form a positive body image and to create awareness that its agency was different by promoting such an image.[34]

The American Association of University Women and Pantene, a well-known maker of hair products, joined forces in 2014 on a new program designed to challenge women student leaders on college campuses throughout the country to initiate change and tackle biases and stereotypes that permeate our culture.[35] One of Pantene's more thought-provoking image ads aired in the Philippines in 2013, and as of late 2014 had received over 46 million views on YouTube. The ad dealt with gender bias and asked both male and female viewers to question their own inherited bias of themselves and others.

This chapter illustrates that managers, and particularly public relations managers, are in charge of safeguarding the story of the firm. By using information strategies and tactics that can apply broadly to managing the corporate reputation they may avoid some of that harm that can befall any company.

---

[34] "Why Brazil's 'Shocking Say No To Anorexia' Campaign May Be Self-Defeating," *Metro,* May 13, 2013, *metro.co.uk.*
[35] "This Pantene Commercial Calls Women Out for Saying 'Sorry' Too Often," *The Washington Post,* June 18, 2014, *www.washingtonpost.com.*

Summary

- The general public affects the firm through its opinions of the firm's activities or performance, which in turn help shape the firm's public image or reputation. The public may utilize its own stakeholder networks and engage with government agencies, special interest groups, or the media to demand a certain level of firm performance.

- A good corporate reputation conveys the desirable qualities associated with an organization in order to positively influence the organization's relationships with its stakeholders, on whom it depends to survive and thrive.

- Firms often create public relations (or media relations) departments, appoint public relations officers, and develop public affairs strategies to manage their relationship with the public. As new technologies have emerged, the variety of available channels of communication for the public affairs officer and departments has grown dramatically.

- Effective brand management helps increase the perceived value of a product line or brand over time and helps companies be more successful because they can charge premium prices, enhance their access to capital markets and funding, obtain better credit, trust, and social ratings.

- An effective crisis management plan is one that is ready to be implemented before the crisis occurs, enables the organization to quickly and accurately communicate to the media, utilizes the Internet to convey critical information to the public, and always remains focused on the organization's ethical responsibilities to its stakeholders.

- Business organizations can influence or change their reputation through a variety of tactics such as executive visibility, media training, user-generated or paid content, event sponsorship, public service announcements, and image advertisements.

Key Terms

brand management, *424*
corporate crisis, *425*
corporate identity, *420*
corporate image, *420*
corporate reputation, *419*
crisis management, *425*

dark site, *427*
general public, *419*
image advertisements, *433*
media training, *429*
paid content, *431*

public relations department, *422*
public service announcements, *433*
user-generated content, *430*

Internet Resources

www.icma-web.org.uk	International Crisis Management Association
www.crisisexperts.com	Institute for Crisis Management
www.pcma.com	Professional Crisis Management Association
www.prsa.org	Public Relations Society of America
www.adcouncil.org	The Ad Council
www.reputationinstitute.com	The Reputation Institute
www.fcc.gov	U.S. Federal Communications Commission
www.ftc.gov	U.S. Federal Trade Commission (FTC)

Discussion Case: *JPMorgan Chase's #AskJPM*

JPMorgan Chase & Co. is one of the largest banking institutions in the United States and a leader in investment banking, financial services for consumers and small businesses, commercial banking, and asset management. The company serves millions of customers in the United States and many of the world's most prominent corporate, institutional and government clients.

In 2008, many financial analysts credited the firm and its CEO, Jamie Dimon, with being instrumental in saving two important financial services companies, Bear Stearns and Washington Mutual. JPMorgan Chase purchased these firms at the request of U.S. Treasury Secretary Henry M. Paulson in order to stabilize a rapidly unraveling but highly interconnected international banking system. But, JPMorgan Chase's reputation took a turn for the worse a few years later.

In 2012, *Bloomberg News* reported that JPMorgan Chase was behind massive trades that were distorting the world financial and commodities markets. A JPMorgan Chase employee based in London, Bruno Iksil, had apparently made securities trades that were so large that his trades were driving significant price movements worldwide. His influence on the market was so great that Iksil became known colloquially as "the London Whale." In 2013, JPMorgan Chase was fined nearly $920 million due to Iksil's trading losses, one of the biggest financial penalties ever assessed on a financial institution. A year later, JPMorgan Chase reached a $13 billion settlement with the U.S. Department of Justice over bad mortgage loans previously made by its 2008 acquisitions of Bear Sterns and Washington Mutual.

Despite its legal troubles, JPMorgan Chase moved forward with plans to help Twitter underwrite its initial public offering. The firm was interested in the public's reaction to this event and opened up a social media channel. On the day that Twitter went public, a JPMorgan Chase employee managing the social media program tweeted on the account @jpmorgan, "What career advice would you ask a leading exec at a global firm? Tweet a Q using #AskJPM." The idea was intended to give college students an opportunity to communicate directly with Jimmy Lee, a senior executive, according to JPMorgan Chase spokesman Brian Marchiony.

The company was not expecting what happened next. Some of the tweets included:

What's your favorite type of whale? #AskJPM

Did you always want to be part of a vast, corrupt criminal enterprise or did you "break bad"? #AskJPM

My question: Why is JPMorgan Chase foreclosing on my neighbor after she's paid for her house 4 times over? #AskJPM Disgusting.

How many $jpm bankers does it take to screw in a lightbulb? None, they just foreclose on the house. #AskJPM

By early afternoon of the day @jpmorgan went live, the *Daily Beast* editor and columnist Daniel Gross tweeted, "Oh my lord, the #askjpm session. Will go down as case study in corporate use of social media."

Some think that in a social media climate, sarcasm rules, and as a result companies have much less control over how the public engages with their brand and how to manage its reputation. JPMorgan Chase was unprepared to deal with the public's negative view of the bank and its actions, especially in the wake of a recession that some believed was caused in part by JPMorgan Chase's irresponsibility. On November 13, 2013, a week after the original tweet by JPMorgan Chase, the company cancelled its original Q&A with Jimmy Lee and sent the following tweet to its followers:

Tomorrow's Q&A is cancelled. Bad Idea. Back to the drawing board.

In total, 1,661 people retweeted the message. CNBC had actor Stacy Keach, the voice from its television documentary series *American Greed,* read the message cancelling the Q&A verbatim. His reading of the posted tweet from the #AskJPM became very popular on YouTube.

Even though JPMorgan Chase managed through the 2008 financial crisis without posting a quarterly loss and was able to purchase the nearly bankrupt Bear Stearns and Washington Mutual's assets, some said that its reputation was tarnished. A business and law professor at the University of Michigan said, "It is a jolt of reality, and the reality for JPMorgan is ugly. The bank is highly visible and greatly disliked."

In December 2014, JPMorgan Chase released a report called "How We Do Business" that described not only its business standards and practices but also reviewed how it had addressed recent challenges resulting from the fallout of the 2008 financial crisis. The report highlighted some of the company's mistakes and its efforts to rearticulate and re-emphasize its cultural values and corporate standards—with the aim of ensuring that employees internalize and live by these standards. The report detailed many of the company's efforts to strengthen its internal controls through improved infrastructure, technology, operating standards, and governance.

Sources: Information for this case taken from JPMorgan Chase & Company's *How We Do Business—The Report,* 2014, available at *www.jpmorganchase.com;* "JPMorgan Trader's Positions Said to Distort Credit Indexes," *Bloomberg Business,* April 6, 2012, *www.bloomberg.com;* "JPMorgan to Pay $13 Billion in Deal with US," *MSN Money,* October 22, 2013, *www.msn.com;* "JPMorgan's Twitter Mistake," *The New Yorker,* November 16, 2013, *www.newyorker.com;* and "JPMorgan's #AskJPM Twitter Hashtag Backfires against Bank," *Bloomberg Business,* November 14, 2013, *www.bloomberg.com.*

Discussion Questions

1. What are the benefits and costs to JPMorgan Chase's reputation given its use of a stakeholder question-and-answer session on Twitter? How do its various stakeholders now think of JPMorgan Chase's image?

2. Develop a reputation management strategy for JPMorgan Chase to combat the bad publicity it encountered.

3. Would you define this incident as a crisis? Assume you are JPMorgan Chase's CEO and are conducting a press conference: what main points about the incident should you emphasize to the media and convey to the public?

4. What other tactics mentioned in this chapter could JPMorgan Chase use to improve the public's opinion of their products? Should it use Twitter again and, if so, how can it avoid a repeat of this embarrassment?

Cases in Business and Society

After Rana Plaza

Around nine in the morning on April 24, 2013, Rana Plaza, an eight-story building in Savar, Bangladesh, collapsed catastrophically in a hail of twisted concrete, steel bar, and sewing machinery. At the time, more than 3,000 garment workers were on duty in five separate factories, located on the building's third to eighth floors. Photographs of the scene showed hundreds of people—community members, workers from other nearby factories, and police and firefighters—furiously moving debris and pulling people out of rubble. When the rescue and recovery effort was finally suspended more than a week later, 1,134 workers, most of them women, had been found dead; 2,500 others had been hurt, many with amputations and severe head and back injuries.[1] Most of the victims were under 30, and a fifth of them were teenagers. They had earned in the range of $38 to $102 a month.[2] It was the worst industrial disaster in the history of the global garment industry.

The collapsed building was owned by Sohel Rana. Rana, 35, was described as a "gun-toting politician" who "traveled by motorcycle, as untouchable as a mafia don, trailed by his own biker gang." In 2007, he had obtained the permit to build the plaza directly from the mayor of Savar, a political ally, bypassing the standard procedure. The building, which was partly situated on a drained swamp, was initially permitted for five stories; Rana illegally added three more floors between 2008 and 2012 and was in the process of constructing another when the structure collapsed.[3] The architect later said the building had not been designed for industrial use. "If I had known that it was to be an industrial building, I would have taken other measures," he told an investigator.[4] Analysis showed that the building was carrying almost six times more weight than it was designed to bear. Poor-quality concrete and steel used in construction and uneven settlement on saturated soils may also have contributed to the structural failure.[5]

The day before, workers reported that large cracks had opened up in the building's walls. An engineer called in to inspect the cracks told Rana that the building needed to be

By Anne T. Lawrence. Copyright © 2015 by the author. All rights reserved. An earlier version of this case was presented at the 2014 annual meeting of the Western Casewriters Association.

[1] "Report on Deadly Factory Collapse in Bangladesh Finds Widespread Blame," *The New York Times*, May 22, 2013.

[2] Clean Clothes Campaign and the International Labor Rights Forum, *Still Waiting: Six Months after History's Deadliest Apparel Industry Disaster, Workers Continue to Fight for Compensation*, 2013.

[3] "The Most Hated Bangladeshi, Toppled from a Shady Empire," *The New York Times*, April 20, 2013; and "Bangladesh's Paradox for Women Workers," *Bloomberg BusinessWeek*, May 15, 2013.

[4] "Bangladesh: Rana Plaza Architect Says Building Was Never Meant for Factories," *Telegraph (U.K)*, May 3, 2013.

[5] "Analysis: Wake-Up Call for Bangladesh's Building Industry," *IRIN, UN Office for the Coordination of Humanitarian Affairs*, May 6, 2013; and "Bangladesh Building Collapse Due to Shoddy Construction," *National Geographic News*, April 25, 2013.

shut down immediately. Managers of a bank and retail shops operating on the first and second floors told their employees to stay home until the building was declared safe. But Rana himself dismissed the engineer's conclusion, saying, according to witnesses, "The plaster on the wall is broken, nothing more. It is not a problem."[6]

Managers of the five Bangladeshi-owned factories operating in rented space in the building—New Wave Style, New Wave Bottoms, Phantom Apparels, Phantom Tac, and Ether Tex—all of which manufactured apparel for export to Western firms, apparently agreed with Rana. The next morning, when garment workers arrived for work, they were greeted by a loudspeaker: "All the workers of Rana Plaza, go to work. The factory has already been repaired." Workers who objected were threatened with the loss of a month's pay. Shortly after the workday started, factory managers turned on large electric generators located on the third and fourth floors, a common occurrence because of regular power failures in the building. A government report later found that vibrations from the generators had shaken the building, triggering a massive structural failure as the already compromised concrete walls failed, floors began collapsing onto the ones below, and the entire building buckled outward.[7]

Several dozen well-known U.S. and European retailers and brands—including Walmart, Benetton, Primark, Children's Place, Loblaw, and Mango—were at the time or had recently sourced products from factories in Rana Plaza. The extensive news coverage of the disaster repeatedly mentioned these companies and displayed photos of their labels. One particularly gruesome photograph showed a dust-covered human corpse, partially buried in rubble, surrounded by clothing tags displaying the logo of the brand Joe Fresh, owned by the Canadian retailer Loblaw. "I am troubled," Galen Weston, the executive chairman of Loblaw, told reporters, "that despite a clear commitment to the highest standards of ethical sourcing, our company can still be part of such an unspeakable tragedy."[8] Now, Loblaw—and all the other companies that sourced apparel from suppliers in the low-wage and notoriously unsafe Bangladeshi garment industry—faced a stark and immediate challenge: What should they do now, after Rana Plaza?

The Emergence of Bangladesh's Garment Industry

At the time of the Rana Plaza collapse, Bangladesh was the site of one of the fastest-growing garment industries in the world.

Located between India on the west, north, and east and Burma (Myanmar) on the southeast, Bangladesh (meaning "the Country of Bengal" in the native Bengali language) sat on a vast delta formed by the confluence of the Ganges, Brahmaputra, and Meghna Rivers, which emptied into the Bay of Bengal. The country, which was predominantly Muslim, had become independent of Pakistan in 1971. With almost 164 million people in a country about the size of Iowa, Bangladesh in 2013 was one of the most densely populated nations in the world. It was also one of the poorest. The United Nations ranked the country 146th (out of 187) on its human development index. Fifty-eight percent of the population was estimated to live in multidimensional poverty, defined by the United Nations as "overlapping deprivation in health, education, and standard of living." Forty-three percent lived on $1.25 or less a day. In 2013, the country was still predominantly

[6] "The Most Hated Bangladeshi, Toppled from a Shady Empire," op. cit.

[7] "Report on Deadly Factory Collapse in Bangladesh Finds Widespread Blame," *The New York Times,* May 22, 2013.

[8] "Global Report: The Uncomfortable Truth about Bangladesh," *Canadian Business,* June 6, 2013.

rural; almost half of Bangladeshis lived off the land, mostly growing rice.[9] The low-lying nation was particularly vulnerable to natural disasters and regularly suffered punishing typhoons and floods.[10]

The Bangladeshi ready-made garment industry had its origins in the worldwide quota systems that emerged shortly after the country's independence. The Multi-Fibre Arrangement (MFA) of 1974 capped the volume of textile and apparel exports to the United States and other developed nations from various countries, especially in East Asia. One consequence of the MFA was a shift of manufacturing to other countries, like Bangladesh, that had no prior history of garment production and were therefore not covered by the quotas. In 1978, Desh Garments, headed by Bangladeshi businessman Noorul Quader, negotiated an agreement with Daewoo, a Korean firm, to teach the Bangladeshis how to manufacture apparel.[11] After training in Korea, Quader and his team returned to set up the first export-oriented garment factory in Bangladesh. Development of the industry was further spurred by structural reforms in the 1980s that privatized and deregulated markets, opened the nation to foreign investment, and permitted garment companies to take loans secured by contracts from foreign buyers.[12]

Once established, the ready-made garment industry in Bangladesh grew steadily. Entrepreneurs flooded into the industry, drawn by low capital requirements, readily available workers, and cheap industrial rents in communities, like Savar, on the outskirts of Dhaka and Chittagong. Large operators secured contracts with Western apparel companies, and small ones emerged to handle their overflow as subcontractors. By 2013, Bangladesh had become the largest garment exporter in the world, after China, employing 4 million workers in 5,600 factories, as shown in Exhibits A and B. Bangladesh exported more than $20 billion of garments annually, accounting for 10 percent of its GDP and more than three-quarters of its total exports by value. (Other exports included frozen shrimp, jute, and leather.) The United States and Canada were the destination of 25 percent of Bangladesh-made garments; more than half went to Europe.

Political Influence

The burgeoning garment industry wielded great political power in the developing nation. Employers were organized into a powerful trade association, the Bangladesh Garment Manufacturers and Exporters Association (BGMEA), founded in 1983. Almost every garment manufacturer joined, because only members were permitted to export garments. With control of the lion's share of exports, the trade association came to function almost as a branch of government. *The New York Times* reported that the organization performed many official functions, such as regulating and administering exports and collecting fees. BGMEA members sat on government committees on labor and security.[13] A similar organization, the Bangladesh Knitwear Manufacturers and Exporters Association (BKMEA), represented employers in factories making knitwear, such as sweaters.

[9] Nations Development Programme, *Human Development 2013.*

[10] "Bangladesh," *CIA Fact Book;* and World Bank, "Bangladesh Overview." The history of Bangladesh is recounted in Willem van Schendel, *A History of Bangladesh* (Cambridge, U.K.: Cambridge University Press, 2009).

[11] Zoe Chace, "Nixon and Kimchi: How the Garment Industry Came to Bangladesh," *Planet Money,* aired on National Public Radio December 2, 2013; and "History of Desh Group," at *www.deshgroup.com.*

[12] Although the Multi-Fibre Arrangement and its successor agreements expired in 2004, international trade rules continued to support the country's garment industry. Under the European Union's "everything but arms" rules, designed to benefit poor countries, all apparel imports from Bangladesh were duty-free. The United States also offered Bangladesh trade preferences on a number of products (although not apparel). See the testimony of Lewis Karesh, Assistant U.S. Trade Representative, June 6, 2012, before the Senate Foreign Relations Committee.

[13] "Garment Trade Wields Power in Bangladesh," *The New York Times,* July 24, 2013.

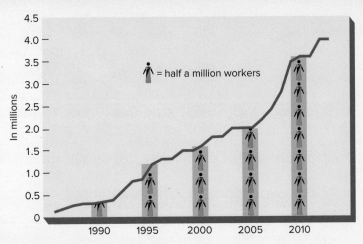

Factory owners also exercised political power directly. Sixty percent of the 300 members of Bangladesh's parliament were active in business, and 31 members or their family members owned garment factories.[14] A. K. Azard, president of the Bangladesh Chambers of Commerce and Industry and owner of one of Bangladesh's largest garment factories, also owned a newspaper and a television station.[15] Garment employers were major political donors. The director of Transparency International's (TI's) country office explained the reality this way: "Politics and business [are] so enmeshed that one is kin to the other. There is a coalition between the [garment] sector and people in positions of power."[16] In 2012, TI ranked Bangladesh next to last among 14 garment-exporting countries on their corruption perceptions index.[17]

Garment manufacturers were heavily favored by the government; tax breaks and subsidies to the industry were estimated to exceed tax revenues by $17 million a year. Speaking of garment factory owners, the secretary of the Bangladesh nonprofit Citizens for Good Governance stated, "They extract all kinds of subsidies. They influence legislation. They influence the minimum wage. And because they are powerful, they can do, or undo, almost anything, with impunity."[18]

Worker Safety

The tragedy at Rana Plaza, while exceptional in its death toll, was not an isolated event. The safety record in Bangladesh's garment industry was one of the worst in the world, with

[14] "Garment Trade Wields Power in Bangladesh," op. cit.

[15] "Export Powerhouse Feels Pangs of Labor Strife," *The New York Times,* August 23, 2012.

[16] Ibid.

[17] Transparency International, "Call on Clothing Companies to Tackle Corruption, Factory Safety" (press release), June 11, 2013. TI's annual corruption perceptions index is available at *www.transparency.org.*

[18] "Garment Trade Wields Power in Bangladesh," op cit.

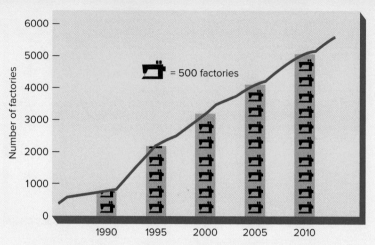

Source: Bangladesh Garment Manufacturers and Exporters Association, 2013. Graphic design by The Sketchy Pixel. © 2015. All rights reserved. Used by permission.

high numbers of both fires and building collapses. Between 2000 and 2012, at least 1,000 garment workers were killed and 3,000 injured in industrial accidents.[19] In November 2012, a fire at the nine-story Tazreen factory, located in a suburb of Dhaka, which began in a ground-floor storage area, killed at least 112. A reporter offered this description of the Tazreen fire:

> The fire alarm: waved off by managers. An exit door: locked. The fire extinguishers: not working and apparently "meant just to impress" inspectors and customers. That is the picture survivors painted of the garment-factory fire Saturday that killed 112 people who were trapped inside or jumped to their deaths in desperation.[20]

Eighty percent of factory fires in Bangladesh were believed to be caused by faulty electrical wiring.[21] Once a fire had broken out, the toll of deaths and injuries was driven higher—as at the Tazreen factory—by missing fire suppression equipment, barred windows and doors, and insufficient emergency exits. In 2005, the Spectrum factory collapsed, killing 64 workers. Like Rana Plaza, this factory was built on filled wetlands, and cracks had appeared in the walls in the days before the collapse.[22]

A major contributor to both fires and collapses was the inadequacy of the structures where manufacturing was taking place. The hectic growth of the industry and the lack of affordable land in densely populated urban areas meant that many nonindustrial buildings

---

[19] International Labor Rights Forum, *Deadly Secrets: What Companies Know about Dangerous Workplaces and Why Exposing the Truth can Save Workers' Lives in Bangladesh and Beyond,* p. 10.

[20] Farid Hossain, "Bangladesh Fire Alarm Ignored, Extinguishers Inoperable," *MSN News,* November 24, 2012.

[21] Clean Clothes Campaign/SOMO, *Fatal Fashion: Analysis of Recent Factory Fires in Pakistan and Bangladesh: A Call to Protect and Respect Garment Workers' Lives,* March 2013, p. 40.

[22] Clean Clothes Campaign, *Hazardous Workplaces: Making the Bangladesh Garment Industry Safe,* November 2012, p. 23.

were repurposed for use as factories. A study by a European NGO, the Clean Clothes Campaign, noted:

> The rapid expansion of the industry has led to the conversion of many buildings, built for other purposes, into factories, often without the required permits. Other factories have had extra floors added or have increased the workforce and machinery to levels beyond the safe capacity of the building. Many factories run day and night in order to meet production targets. The establishment of factories, or the conversions of other buildings into garment factories, has often been done as quickly and as cheaply as possible, resulting in widespread safety problems including faulty electrical circuits, unstable buildings, inadequate escape routes and unsafe equipment.[23]

The country's weak and often corrupt regulatory apparatus simply could not keep up. The director of Bangladesh's Housing and Building Research Institute said after the Rana Plaza disaster that the country's building codes were "good enough," but the problem was they were rarely enforced. An architect involved in drafting the codes commented, "Dhaka has limited space. Developers are in this market for money and want to squeeze as much as they can into any space. Yes, we have a law, but who is implementing it?"[24]

Bangladesh law established occupational health and safety standards and gave government inspectors the right to shut down any factory that presented an imminent danger to human life.[25] However, the country employed just 52 factory inspectors, and the maximum fine for noncompliance was just $309.[26] In early 2013, Bangladesh's commerce minister offered this explanation: "The ready-made garments industry grew in Bangladesh all of a sudden, at a very high pace. The industry grew out of proportion compared to our facilities or our controlling capacities."[27]

Workers and Labor Rights

Who were the workers toiling in these hastily converted factories? Eight-five percent were women, many of them immigrants from poor, rural areas to the major urban manufacturing districts around Dhaka and Chittagong. In a survey of garment workers in more than 40 factories, War on Want, a British NGO, found that almost nine in ten were between 18 and 32 years old. Just 22 percent had a high school degree. Many lived in "mess housing," shared accommodations for single people that had sprung up near the factories. Verbal and sexual abuse in the workplace was common. The War on Want survey found that 73 percent of workers reported being sworn at by managers. Forty-five percent had been beaten, 43 percent hit in the face, and 30 percent sexually harassed.[28]

Wages in the industry were the lowest in the world. In 2013, the legal minimum wage in the garment industry was $37 a month. (The average monthly wage, including overtime, was higher—about $91.) A great majority of garment workers put in overtime; the War on Want survey found that only 14 percent of garment workers worked less than 40 hours a week, and 80 percent started work at 9 a.m. and left the factory between 8 and 10 p.m.

[23] *Fatal Fashion*, op. cit.

[24] "Analysis: Wake Up Call for Bangladesh's Building Industry," op. cit.

[25] Bangladesh Labour Act, 2006, Section VI.

[26] Testimony of Lewis Karesh, Assistant U.S. Trade Representative, June 6, 2012, before the Senate Foreign Relations Committee, June 6, 2013.

[27] "The Hidden Cost of Fast Fashion," *Bloomberg BusinessWeek*, February 11–17, 2013.

[28] War on Want, *Stitched Up: Women Workers in the Bangladeshi Garment Sector*, July 2011.

at night.[29] Although conditions were often brutal, the garment industry offered one of the few socially acceptable jobs for women in the predominantly Muslim country. Many women sought jobs in the garment sector, preferring work as a sewing machine operator to domestic or farm labor. And, although low, wages for women in the garment industry were 14 percent higher than wages for women with comparable schooling and experience in other industries.[30]

The Bangladesh constitution guaranteed the right to join unions. If 30 percent or more of the workers in a factory joined a union, the employer was required to recognize and bargain with it; if more than one union was present, an election would be held to determine the workers' bargaining representative. As a practical matter, however, these rights were routinely ignored by factory owners and their political allies. The Ministry of Labor informed employers of the names of workers applying for union registrations; they were usually promptly fired. Worker strikes and protests were routinely met by riot police. The U.S. State Department concluded in a review of human rights in Bangladesh that although the law provided the right of citizens to form associations, "government action [makes] it nearly impossible to form new trade unions in many sectors, for example, in the ready-made garment [industry]."[31]

A labor union called the Bangladesh Garment and Industrial Workers' Federation (BGIWF) had organized committees in some factories and had participated in a successful campaign in 2010 to raise the minimum wage, but by 2013 had not succeeded in negotiating a single union contract. BGIWF's leaders had been persecuted, harassed, and even murdered. In 2012, the federation's president, Aminul Islam, disappeared from Savar (the industrial suburb of Dhaka where Rana Plaza was located), where he had been organizing workers. Four days later, his dead body was found, showing signs of torture. Garment manufacturers were believed to have colluded with the NSI (National Security Intelligence, the military intelligence agency) in his death.[32] After the Rana Plaza tragedy, Islam's successor as president of the BGIWF noted, "With collective bargaining power, tragedies like Rana Plaza would not happen, since owners would not be able to force workers to work in unsafe conditions."[33]

Nongovernmental organizations that sought to advocate for worker rights were also harassed. The Bangladesh Center for Worker Solidarity (BCWS), for example, an NGO run by former garment workers, was regularly monitored by intelligence agencies and subjected to government restrictions that impeded its work.[34]

The Rise of Fast Fashion

The rapid growth of the ready-made garment industry in Bangladesh in the decade before the Rana Plaza tragedy was intimately connected to retailing trends in the West, and in particular to the rise of "fast fashion."

Fast fashion referred to a garment retailing strategy characterized by low prices, high volume, and rapid turnover of inventory and styles.[35] Leading fast fashion brands included

---

[29] Ibid.

[30] "After Horror, Apologies," *Dollars and Sense,* September/October 2013.

[31] U.S. Department of State, *2012 Country Reports on Human Rights Practices: Bangladesh.*

[32] Ibid.

[33] "Bangladesh Opens Door to More Unions," *The Wall Street Journal,* May 13, 2013.

[34] Human Rights Watch, *Bangladesh Country Summary,* January 2012.

[35] Elizabeth L. Cline, *Overdressed: The Shockingly High Cost of Cheap Fashion* (New York: Penguin, 2012), Chapter 4.

H&M, Zara, Old Navy, Topshop, Forever 21, and Mango. For these retailers, fast fashion was a successful strategy: its purveyors enjoyed twice the average profit margins of traditional clothing stores. For example, H&M (which sourced about a quarter of its garments from Bangladesh) had enjoyed gross margins of over 50 percent in the decade preceding the collapse of Rana Plaza.

Shoppers at these establishments were drawn in by fast-breaking trends. Fashion cycles were incredibly short; trendy colors, styles, hem lengths, and embellishments would come and go almost on a weekly basis. Cobalt blue, for example, would be here today, gone tomorrow. Zara and H&M introduced new styles every two weeks.[36] "What is so astonishing today is the breakneck pace of change, which has shifted from seasonal and focused to constant and schizophrenic," commented author Elizabeth L. Cline in her book, *Overdressed: The Shockingly High Cost of Cheap Fashion.*[37]

Shoppers were also drawn in by low prices. Fast fashion was cheap; indeed, retailers pursued a strategy they sometimes called "extreme pricing." Customers could drop by the mall and pick up a shirt for $10, a pair of trousers for $15, or a jacket for under $30. Since 1998, women's clothing prices in the United States had fallen overall by 7 percent; men's, by 6 percent. In the United Kingdom, the drop was even sharper; there, prices had dropped 20 percent since 2005—at a time when the prices of many other consumer goods were rising.

Enticed by fast-changing styles and low prices, shoppers simply bought more. Americans purchased an average of 64 items of clothing a year, more than one a week. They spent $1,700 annually, making clothing the second largest consumer sector after food. The quality of much fast fashion was low; but this mattered little to the customer, who might wear and launder an item just a few times before discarding it. For many customers, particularly young people, clothes shopping became a favorite leisure activity. The average Zara's customer, for example, visited the store 17 times a year.

Most clothing customers in the United States and Europe were completely unaware of the conditions under which their clothing was made. Even in the wake of the extensive media coverage given the Rana Plaza collapse, most consumers seemed unconcerned; a study by America's Research Group a few days after the tragedy reported that it had observed "no consumer reaction to any charges about harmful working conditions."[38]

A very small number of clothing brands—among them, yoga-wear maker PrAna—had sought Fair Trade certification. American Apparel, which was based in Los Angeles and manufactured in the United States, sought a competitive advantage by advertising its products as "sweatshop free."[39] Overall, however, less than 1 percent of global fashions were explicitly marketed as ethically sourced. Although most garments had a tag showing the country of origin, customers had no way of knowing anything about the specific factory where the item was made. "For the consumer, it's virtually impossible to know whether the product was manufactured in safe conditions," commented the president of a retail consultancy.[40] Two organizations, Not for Sale and GoodGuide, rated apparel brands on their labor and human rights records and offered mobile phone apps that allowed a consumer to scan a barcode for more information. But, in 2013, these were not widely used.

---

[36] "The Hidden Cost of Fast Fashion," *Bloomberg BusinessWeek,* February 11, 2013.

[37] Cline, op. cit., p. 103.

[38] "Shoppers Face Hurdles in Finding Ethical Clothing," *Bloomberg BusinessWeek,* April 30, 2013.

[39] Ibid.

[40] Ibid.

The "Next Hot Spot"

As Western customers increasingly embraced fast fashion, brands and retailers continued to search the world for suppliers that could produce garments at low cost with fast turnaround and good-enough quality.

Bangladesh seemed perfectly positioned to meet their needs. Eighty-nine percent of chief purchasing agents in U.S. and European apparel firms, surveyed by McKinsey in 2011, named Bangladesh as one of their three "sourcing country hot spots" for the next five years, ahead of all other countries. One reason for the country's popularity was capacity: Bangladesh had more garment factories than Indonesia, Vietnam, and Cambodia combined. But the primary reason cited by the purchasing agents was price: it was simply cheaper to source garments from Bangladesh than from any other place in the world. Bangladesh offered clothing manufacturers the lowest labor costs in the world—at a time when costs in some other countries, particularly China, were increasing. For example, in 2011, monthly wages in the garment industry averaged $325 in China, $182 in Vietnam, $360 in Thailand, $359 in Honduras, and $150 in India—all major exporting countries. By comparison, monthly wages in Bangladesh averaged just $91.[41] (Wages, of course, did not represent the full cost of a finished garment. By one estimate, direct wages comprised just 2 percent of the retailer's cost; other expenses included materials, laundering and pressing, factory overhead, import duties, middleman fees, and transportation.)[42] McKinsey concluded that garment exports from Bangladesh would double by 2015 and nearly triple by 2020.[43]

Although the low cost of production in Bangladesh remained a powerful draw for Western apparel companies and retailers, even before Rana Plaza many were becoming increasingly concerned about the impact of poor working conditions on their reputations. In June 2012, the U.S. ambassador said in a speech to the Bangladesh Garment Manufacturers and Exporters Association that he had been called by the CEO of one of the industry's leading buyers—an unnamed retailer—to say that "the tarnishing Bangladesh brand may be putting his company's reputation at risk." The CEO also told the ambassador that his company's reputation was worth more than "saving a few cents per shirt from Bangladesh."[44]

Companies in the Crossfire

At the time of the Rana Plaza collapse, major U.S. and European retailers and brands sourcing apparel from Bangladesh, in addition to Loblaw, included the following:

Walmart, the multinational retailer, was the largest single buyer of garments from Bangladesh. More than 200 factories there produced more than $1 billion worth of jeans, sweatshirts, underwear, T-shirts, and other apparel for Walmart annually.

Marks & Spencer, the leading clothing retailer in Britain, had sourced from Bangladesh, where it had local buyers and a compliance office, for more than 10 years. It had contracts with 60 factories in Bangladesh.

Carrefour SA was a major multinational retailer, based in France. More than 50 percent of apparel sold by Carrefour in Europe was made in Bangladesh by more than 40 suppliers.

[41] Worker Rights Consortium, *Global Wage Trends for Apparel Workers, 2001–2011,* July 2011.

[42] "What Does That $14 Shirt Really Cost? Bangladesh Disaster Raises Tough Questions about Cheap Clothes," *Maclean's Magazine,* May 1, 2013. Data are from the O'Rourke Group.

[43] McKinsey & Company, *Bangladesh's Ready-Made Garment Landscape: The Challenge of Growth,* November, 2011.

[44] "Mozena Fears 'Perfect Storm' in Garment Sector," *The Daily Star* (Bangladesh), June 17, 2012.

MNG Holding SL, the Spanish company behind the Mango brand, contracted with 260 factories in Bangladesh.

Hennes & Mauritz, the second-largest clothing retailer in the world had contracts with 166 factories in Bangladesh and the Swedish-based H&M planned to increase production there in the future.

Inditex, the world's largest apparel company, made the popular Zara brand. The Spanish firm contracted with about 350 factories in Bangladesh.

Gap, the U.S. specialty retailer, which owned the Gap, GapKids, Banana Republic, and Old Navy brands, did business with 78 factories in Bangladesh.

As these companies, and others, faced the challenge of responding to Rana Plaza, they faced a complex set of issues.

By 2013, almost all brand-name clothing companies, including most of those doing business in Bangladesh, had adopted codes of conduct governing labor conditions in their global supply chains. These were typically based on labor standards adopted by the International Labour Organization (ILO) or developed by the Fair Labor Association (FLA), Worker Rights Consortium (WRC), Fair Wear Foundation, or Social Accountability International (SAI). Companies usually instituted internal processes and management systems to qualify new suppliers and assess their capabilities, and also monitored existing suppliers on an ongoing basis to ensure compliance. Many companies contracted with independent third-party auditors to assure compliance with both their codes of conduct and local laws in their supply chains.

While audits were often helpful, they also had disadvantages. On-site inspections were expensive and time-consuming, and therefore could not be scaled to cover a brand's entire supply chain. While companies usually had close ties with their direct suppliers, lower-tier suppliers, and subcontractors were often not directly accessible. Sometimes, companies did not even know where their products were being made. At Rana Plaza, for example, after the collapse Walmart had initially indicated that it did not produce at the ill-fated factory, but later had to correct itself, saying that one of its supplies had subcontracted work there without its knowledge.[45] Suppliers were sometimes resistant to cooperating with audits, particularly if they served multiple customers, each with their own distinct requirements. Audits were not always unannounced; in many cases, suppliers received advance notice and were able to stage conditions to pass inspection.

The exigencies of production often militated against compliance, even when suppliers were willing. As brands and retailers moved toward the fast fashion model, production cycles accelerated. Compelled to come up with something new every few weeks, companies like Inditex (the owner of Zara) learned to design, prototype, manufacture, and distribute clothing items in just two weeks. Brands often waited as long as possible before placing an order, to be more responsive to fickle consumer tastes. This pattern put tremendous pressure on suppliers, which were expected to respond to constant design changes and demands for rapid turnaround—even if it meant forced overtime and abusive supervision. "Flexible supply chains are great for multinationals and consumers," commented James Surowiecki, writing in *The New Yorker.* "But they erode already thin profit margins in developing world factories and foster a pell-mell work environment in which getting the order out the door is the only thing that matters."[46]

The owner of Plummy Fashions, a Bangladeshi garment supplier, told *Bloomberg BusinessWeek:* "It's like a chain reaction. Consumers always want new designs; they

---

[45] "Wal-Mart Fires Supplier after Bangladesh Revelation," *ABC News,* May 15, 2013.

[46] James Surowiecki, "After Rana Plaza," *The New Yorker,* May 20, 2013.

always want to stay in season. Clothing companies follow the new trend, and we pay the price."[47]

Moreover, relationships between brands and suppliers were often unstable, reducing incentives for the manufacturer. The Clean Clothes Campaign noted:

> Buyers shift orders continuously from supplier to supplier, blocking the economic security needed for suppliers to make investments in building safety. Instead of building stable trading relations with multi-year contracts and placing substantial orders, buyers generally look for the cheapest options and allow for the expansion of orders even when factories are knowingly unsafe, or when it can be reasonably expected that high production volumes will override the capacity of factories.[48]

The NGO noted that transitory relationships reduced the supplier's motivation to improve working conditions and safety, and reduced the buyer's leverage to force the supplier to do so.

A final problem facing the apparel companies was that most of their codes of conduct were missing a critical element—requirements for fire and structural safety. Codes typically required suppliers to comply with all relevant local laws and established standards for wages, hours of work, minimum age, and overtime. In most cases, however, the fundamental safety of the factory itself had simply been assumed to be the responsibility of the supplier. After Rana Plaza, this assumption no longer seemed valid. "Our audits align with those of industry around the world," Loblaw acknowledged in a public statement, after its clothing labels were found in the rubble of Rana Plaza. "But we recognize that these measures do not address the issue of building construction or integrity."[49]

Discussion Questions

1. Who was responsible for the collapse of Rana Plaza, and why do you think so? In your answer, please address the responsibility, if any, of the building owner, factory owners, Bangladeshi government, U.S. and European governments, Bangladeshi workers and their advocates, clothing customers, and apparel retailers and brands in the United States, Canada, and Europe.

2. What could be taken now to reduce the chances of a similar tragedy occurring in the future? In your answer, please consider what actions, if any, the various individuals and groups mentioned in question 1 could take.

3. Of the various options you mentioned in response to question 2, which do you think is most likely to be effective, and why?

4. Develop a typology of corporate strategies to prevent worker abuse by contractors in complex supply chains (e.g., put political pressure on local governments to develop stronger regulations; develop codes of conduct).

5. Under what conditions are different corporate strategies appropriate? Can you predict why different companies might respond in different ways?

---

[47] "The Hidden Cost of Fast Fashion," op. cit.

[48] *Fatal Fashion,* op. cit., p. 15.

[49] "Global Report: The Uncomfortable Truth about Bangladesh," op. cit.

Google and the Right to Be Forgotten

In 2009, Mario Costeja Gonzalez, a self-employed attorney living in a small town outside Madrid, Spain, casually "googled" himself and was startled by what came up on his computer screen. Prominently displayed in the search results was a brief legal notice that had appeared more than a decade earlier in a local newspaper, *La Vanguardia,* which listed property seized and being auctioned by a government agency for nonpayments of debts. Among the properties was a home jointly owned by Costeja and his wife.

Costeja immediately realized that this information could damage his reputation as an attorney. Equally troubling, the information was no longer factual. He had paid his debt nearly a decade earlier. Abanlex, Costeja's small law firm, depended on the Internet to gain much of its new business, which was often generated by a Google search. Potential clients might choose not to hire him, based on the old auction notice, he reflected. His mind then turned to the possible effects of this kind of information on other people's livelihoods. "There are people who cannot get a job because of content that is irrelevant," he thought.[1] "I support freedom of expression and I do not defend censorship. [However, I decided] to fight for the right to request the deletion of data that violates the honor, dignity and reputation of individuals."[2]

The next week, Costeja wrote to *La Vanguardia* and requested that it remove the article about his debt notice, because it had had been fully resolved a number of years earlier and reference to it now was therefore entirely irrelevant.[3] In doing so, he was making use of his rights under Spain's strong data protection policies, which recognized the protection and integrity of personal data as a constitutional right under Section 18 of the nation's Data Protection Act.[4] In response, the newspaper informed him that it had recently uploaded to the Internet all its past archives, dating back to 1881, to allow them to be searched by the public. It also noted that the auction notice had originally been publicly posted in order to secure as many bidders as possible. The newspaper refused Costeja's request, stating that the information was obtained from public records and had thus been published lawfully.[5]

To be sure, the real problem for Costeja was not that the notice had appeared in *La Vanguardia*'s digital library, but that it had shown up in the results of the most widely

[1] "Google Privacy Campaigner Praises Search Engine for Bowing to EU," *Financial Times,* May 30, 2014.

[2] "The Man Who Sued Google to be Forgotten," *Newsweek,* May 30, 2014.

[3] European Parliament. Judgment of the Court, May 13, 2014, at *http://curia.europa.eu/juris/document/document. jsf?docid=152065&doclang=EN.*

[4] "The Unforgettable Story of the Seizure to the Defaulter Mario Costeja González that Happened in 1998," *Derechoaleer,* May 30, 2014, at *http://derechoaleer.org/en/blog/2014/05/the-unforgettable-story-of-the-seizure-to-the-defaulter-mario-costeja-gonzalez-that-happened-in-1998.html.*

[5] "Will Europe Censor this Article?" *The Atlantic,* May 13, 2014, *www.theatlantic.com/international/archive/2014/05/europes-troubling-new-right-to-be-forgotten/370796/.*

used search engine in the world, Google, where potential clients might use it to judge his character.[6] Following this reasoning, Costeja then wrote to Google Spain, the firm's Spanish affiliate, only to be told that the parent company, Google Inc., was the entity responsible for the development of search results.[7] Costeja was taken aback by this development. "The resources Google has at their disposal aren't like those of any other citizens," he reflected.[8] Costeja felt he would be at a disadvantage in a lawsuit against an industry giant like Google.

In March 2010, after his unsuccessful attempts with the newspaper and Google Spain, Costeja turned to Spain's Data Protection Agency (SDPA), the government agency responsible for enforcing the Data Protection Act. "Google in Spain asked me to address myself to its headquarters in the U.S., but I found it too far and difficult to launch a complaint in the U.S., so I went to the agency in Spain to ask for their assistance. They said I was right, and the case went to court," he explained.[9] In a legal filing, Costeja requested, first, that the agency issue an administrative order requiring *La Vanguardia* either to remove or alter the pages in question (so that his personal data no longer appeared) or to use certain tools made available by search engines in order to shield the data from view. Second, he requested that the agency require that Google Spain or Google Inc. remove or conceal his personal data so that it no longer appeared in the search results and in the links *to La Vanguardia*. Costeja stated that his debt had been fully resolved.[10]

With these steps, a small-town Spanish lawyer had drawn one of the world's richest and best-known companies, Google, into a debate over the right to be forgotten.

Google, Inc.

Google Inc. was a technology company that built products and provides services to organize information. Founded in 1998 and headquartered in Mountain View, CA, Google's mission was to organize the world's information and make it universally accessible and useful. It employed more than 55,000 people and had revenues of $45 billion. The company also had 70 offices in more than 40 countries.

The company's main product, *Google Search,* provided information online in response to a user's search. Google's other well-known products provided additional services. For example, *Google Now* provided information to users when they needed it, and its *Product Listing Ads* offered product image, price, and merchant information. The company also provided *AdWords,* an auction-based advertising program and *AdSense,* which enabled websites that were part of the Google network to deliver ads. *Google Display* was a display advertising network; *DoubleClick Ad Exchange* was a marketplace for the trading display ad space; and *YouTube* offered video, interactive, and other ad formats.

Search Technology

In its core business, Google conducted searches in three stages: crawling and indexing, applying algorithms, and fighting spam.

[6] "The Unforgettable Story of the Seizure to the Defaulter Mario Costeja González that Happened in 1998," *Derechoaleer,* May 30, 2014, *http://derechoaleer.org/en/blog/2014/05/the-unforgettable-story-of-the-seizure-to-the-defaulter-mario-costeja-gonzalez-that-happened-in-1998.html.*

[7] B. Van Alsenoy, A. Kuczerawy, and J. Ausloos. "Search Engines after Google Spain: internet@liberty or privacy@peril?" ICRI Working Paper Series, September 6, 2013, at *http://papers.ssrn.com/sol3/papers.cfm?abstract_id=2321494.*

[8] "Spain's Everyday Internet Warrior Who Cut Free from Google's Tentacles," *The Guardian,* May 13, 2014, *http://www.theguardian.com/technology/2014/may/13/spain-everyman-google-mario-costeja-gonzalez.*

[9] "The Man Who Sued Google to Be Forgotten," op. cit.

[10] Court of Justice, Judgment in Case C-131/12 Google Spain SL, *Google Inc. v. Agencia Española de Protección de Datos, Mario Costeja González.*

Crawlers, programs that browsed the web to create an index of data, looked at web pages and followed links on those pages. They then moved from link to link and brought data about those web pages back to Google's servers. Google would then use this information to create an index to know exactly how to retrieve information for its users. Algorithms were the computer processes and formulas that took users' questions and turned them into answers. At the most basic level, Google's algorithms looked up the user's search terms in the index to find the most appropriate pages. For a typical query, thousands, if not millions, of web pages might have helpful information. Google's algorithms relied on more than 200 unique signals or "clues" that made it possible to guess what an individual was really looking for. These signals included the terms on websites, the freshness of content, the region, and the page rank of the web page.[11] Lastly, the company fought spam through a combination of computer algorithms and manual review. Spam sites attempted to game their way to the top of search results by repeating keywords, buying links that passed Google's PageRank process, or putting invisible text on the screen. Google scouted out and removed spam because it could make legitimate websites harder to find. While much of this process was automated, Google did maintain teams whose job was to review sites manually.[12]

Policy on Information Removal

Google's policy on the general removal of information was the following:

> Upon request, we'll remove personal information from search results if we believe it could make you susceptible to specific harm, such as identity theft or financial fraud. This includes sensitive government ID numbers like U.S. Social Security numbers, bank account numbers, credit card numbers and images of signatures. We generally don't process removals of national ID numbers from official government websites because in those cases we consider the information to be public. We sometimes refuse requests if we believe someone is attempting to abuse these policies to remove other information from our results.[13]

Apart from this general policy, Google Inc. also removed content or features from its search results for legal reasons. For example, in the United States, the company would remove content with valid notification from the copyright holder under the Digital Millennium Copyright Act (DMCA), which was administered by the U.S. Copyright Office. The DCMA provided recourse for owners of copyrighted materials who believed that their rights under copyright law had been infringed upon on the Internet.[14] Under the notice and takedown procedure of the law, a copyright owner could notify the service provider, such as Google, requesting that a website or portion of a website be removed or blocked. If, upon receiving proper notification, the service provider promptly did so, it would be exempt from monetary liability.

Google regularly received such requests from copyright holders and those that represented them, such as the Walt Disney Company and the Recording Industry Association of America. Google produced and made public a list of the domain portions of URLs that had been the subject of a request for removal, and noted which ones had been removed.

---

[11] Information on PageRank is available online at *http://infolab.stanford.edu/ backrub/google.html.*

[12] Information about Google search is available online at *www.google.com/insidesearch/howsearchworks/index.html.*

[13] http://www.google.com/insidesearch/howsearchworks/policies.html.

[14] Information about Digital Millennium Copyright Act ("DMCA") notice procedure is available at *www.fosterinstitute.com/ legal-forms/dmca-notice.*

As of July 2015, it had removed more than 600,000 URLs out of more than 2.4 million requests.[15]

Likewise, content on local versions of Google was also removed when required by national laws. For example, content that glorified the Nazi party was illegal in Germany, and content that insulted religion was illegal in India.[16] The respective governments, via a court order or a routine request as described above, typically made these requests. Google reviewed these requests to determine if any content should be removed because it violated a specific country's law.

When Google removed content from search results for legal reasons, it first displayed a notification that the content had been removed and then reported the removal to *www.chillingeffects.org,* a website established by the Electronic Frontier Foundation and several law schools. This website, which later changed its name to lumendatabase.org, collected and analyzed legal complaints and requests for removal of a broad set of online materials. It was designed to help Internet users know their rights and understand the law. Researchers could use the data to study the prevalence of legal threats and the source of content removals. This database also allowed the public to search for specific takedown notifications.[17]

Google removed content quickly. Its average processing time across all copyright infringement removal requests submitted via its website was approximately 6 hours. Different factors influenced the processing time, including the method of delivery, language, and completeness of the information submitted.

The Right to Be Forgotten

The right to be forgotten can be understood as peoples' right to request that information be removed from the Internet or other repositories because it violated their privacy or was no longer relevant. This right assumed greater prominence in the digital era, when people began finding it increasingly difficult to escape information that had accumulated over many years, resulting in expressions such as *"the net never forgets," "everything is in the cloud," "reputation bankruptcy,"* and *"online reputation."*[18] According to Jeffrey Rosen, professor of law at George Washington University, the intellectual roots of the right to be forgotten could be found in French law, "which recognizes *le droit à l'oubli*—or the 'right of oblivion'—a right that allows a convicted criminal who has served his time and been rehabilitated to object to the publication of the facts of his conviction and incarceration."[19]

Although the right to be forgotten was rooted in expunging criminal records, the rise of the Internet had given the concept a new, more complex meaning. Search engines enabled users to access information on just about any topic with considerable ease. The ease with which information could be shared, stored, and retrieved through online search raised issues of both privacy and freedom of expression. On the one hand, when opening a bank account, joining a social networking website, or booking a flight online, a consumer would voluntarily disclose vital personal information such as name, address, and credit card numbers. Consumers were often unsure of what happened to their data and were concerned that it might fall into the wrong hands—that is, that their privacy would be violated.

---

[15] Information about the removal process is available online at *www.google.com/transparencyreport/removals/copyright/*

[16] *http://www.google.com/insidesearch/howsearchworks/policies.html.*

[17] The Berkman Center for Internet & Society at *https://cyber.law.harvard.edu/research/chillingeffects.*

[18] "The Unforgettable Story of the Seizure to the Defaulter Mario Costeja González that Happened in 1998," op. cit.

[19] "Will Europe Censor this Article?" op. cit.

On the other hand, by facilitating the retrieval of information, search engines enhanced individuals' freedom to receive and impart information. Any interference with search engine activities could therefore pose a threat to the effective enjoyment of these rights.[20] As Van Alsenoy, a researcher at the Interdisciplinary Center for Law and Information Communication Technology, argued, "In a world where search engines are used as the main tool to find relevant content online, any governmental interference in the provisioning of these services presents a substantial risk that requires close scrutiny."[21]

Europe

Since the 1990s, both the European Union and its member states (such as Spain) had enacted laws that addressed the right to privacy and, by extension, the right to be forgotten.

A fundamental right of individuals to protect their data was introduced in the EU's original data protection law, passed in 1995. Specifically, the European Data Protection Directive 95/46 defined the appropriate scope of national laws relating to personal data and the processing of those data. According to Article 3(1), Directive 95/46 applied "to the processing of personal data wholly or partly by automatic means, and to the processing otherwise than by automatic means of personal data which form part of a filing system or are intended to form part of a filing system."[22] Article 2(b) of the EU Data Protection Directive 95/46 defined the processing of personal data as

> any operation or set of operations which is performed upon personal data, whether or not by automatic means, such as collection, recording, organization, storage, adaptation or alteration, retrieval, consultation, use, disclosure by transmission, dissemination or otherwise making available, alignment or combination, blocking, erasure or destruction.

Individual countries within the European Union also enacted their own laws, which were sometimes stronger than those of the EU. For example, in Spain, the protection of data was a constitutional right. The Spanish Constitution recognized the right to personal privacy, secrecy of communications, and the protection of personal data. These rights were protected through the Data Protection Act (the "Act"), passed in 1999, which incorporated the 1995 European Directive on data protection, and was enforced by the Spanish Data Protection Agency (SDPA). Created in 1993, this agency was relatively inactive until the passing of the Act, which gave it more powers and a mandate to enforce privacy rules in a wide range of situations.[23]

The Spanish agency exercised its powers broadly. For example, in 2013, it fined telecom firm Telefonica SA €20,000 for twice listing an individual's phone number in local phone books without the individual's prior consent. In 2008, the agency fined a marketing company €600 for using "recommend this to a friend" icons on websites, saying that senders of recommendation e-mails had to first request the recipient's permission. The agency had also successfully required anyone using security cameras to clearly mark their presence with a recognizable icon. Supporters of this move have highlighted the importance of transparency in protecting one's privacy.[24]

---

[20] Alsenoy et al., 2013.

[21] Alsenoy et al., 2013.

[22] Alsenoy et al., 2013.

[23] "Data Protection in Spain" June 24, 2010, at *www.i-policy.org/2010/06/data-protection-in-spain.html.*

[24] "Spanish Agency Behind the Google Ruling Lauded by Some, Hated by Others," *The Wall Street Journal,* June 26, 2014.

Over time, however, differences in the way that each EU country interpreted privacy rights led to an uneven level of protection for personal data, depending on where an individual lived or bought goods and services. This led the European high court to take a second look, in 2013, at the original law.[25] A European Commission memo at that time noted that the right "is about empowering individuals, not about erasing past events or restricting freedom of the press."[26] The changes were intended to give citizens more control over their personal data, making it easier to access and improve the quality of information they received about what happened to their data once they decided to share it. An unanswered question, however, was the latitude given to national courts and regulators across Europe to set the parameters by which these requests could be made.[27]

The United States

U.S. courts had taken a very different approach to privacy and to the right to be forgotten. A few U.S. laws recognized the right to be forgotten; the Fair Credit Reporting Act of 1970, for example, gave individuals the right to delete certain negative information about their credit—such as late payments, tax liens, or judgments—seven years from the date of the delinquency. But, for the most part, fundamental differences in legal philosophy made this right less likely to become widely supported in the United States. In an article published in the *Atlantic* in May 2014, Matt Ford suggested that in the U.S. context, one person's right to be forgotten logically imposed a responsibility to forget upon someone else, a notion that was alien to American law. The First Amendment to the Constitution barred the government from interfering with free speech. Law professor Rosen argued that the First Amendment would make a right to be forgotten virtually impossible, not only to create but to enforce. For example, the U.S. Supreme Court ruled in 1989 that penalizing a newspaper for publishing truthful, lawfully obtained information from the public record was unconstitutional.[28]

The Lawsuit and Court Decision

The main focus of Costeja's complaint before Spanish Data Protection Agency (SDPA) was his request that *La Vanguardia* remove the debt notice from its archives. In doing so, he was claiming his constitutional right to protect the integrity of his personal data. Costeja's request had two parts: that (1) *La Vanguardia* be required either to remove or alter the pages in question or to use certain tools made available by search engines in order to protect the data and (2) that Google Spain or Google Inc. be required to remove or conceal the personal data relating to him so that the data no longer appeared in search results.

In July 2010, two months after Costeja's original request, the SDPA ordered Google Spain and Google Inc. to take "all reasonable steps to remove the disputed personal data from its index and preclude further access," upholding that part of the complaint.[29]

[25] "What is the 'Right to Be Forgotten?'" *The Wall Street Journal*, May 13, 2014.

[26] European Commission, "LIBE Committee Vote Backs New EU Data Protection Rules", October 22, 2013, at http://europa.eu/rapid/press-release_MEMO-13-923_en.htm.

[27] "What is the 'Right to Be Forgotten?'" op. cit.

[28] "Will Europe Censor This Article?" op. cit.

[29] Audiencia Nacional. Sala de lo Contencioso, Google Spain SL y Google Inc., S.L.c. Agencia de Protección de Datos, paragraph 1.2, at *www.poderjudicial.es*.

However, the SDPA rejected Costeja's complaint as it related to *La Vanguardia,* because it considered that the publication by it of the information in question was legally justified.[30]

A year later, Google filed an appeal against the decision by the SDPA before the Audiencia Nacional in Madrid, Spain's highest national court. In March 2012, this court referred the case to the European Court of Justice, the EU's high court, for a preliminary ruling.[31]

In their briefs, Google Spain and Google Inc.'s argument hinged on the meaning of "personal data" and "crawling." Crawling, as noted above, was the use of software programs to find multiple websites that responded to requests for information online.[32] These programs were configured to look for information on the Internet, according to a set of criteria that told them where to go and when.[33] Once the relevant web pages had been copied and collected, their content was analyzed and indexed.[34] Google compared its search engine index to an index at the back of a textbook, in that it included information about words and their locations.[35]

Specifically, Google argued before the European Court of Justice that because it crawled and indexed websites "indiscriminately" (that is, without a deliberate intent to process personal data as such), no processing of personal data within the meaning of Article 2 (b) of the EU Data Protection Directive 95/46 actually took place. This absence of intent, the company argued, clearly distinguished Google's activities as a search engine provider from the processing of personal data as interpreted by the Court.

Google's other main argument was that the publisher of the information should be the sole controller of data, not the search engine. After all, its attorneys argued, Google's intervention was purely accessory in nature; it was merely making information published by others more readily accessible. If a publisher, for whatever reason, decided to remove certain information from its website, this information would (eventually) be removed from Google's index and would no longer appear in its search results. As a result, Google's counsel argued, the role of a search engine should be thought of as an "intermediary."

In May 2014, the European Court of Justice ruled against Google. The court found the Internet search provider was responsible for the processing of personal data that appeared on web pages published by third parties. It further required Google to remove links returned in search results based on an individual's name when those results were deemed to be "inadequate, irrelevant or no longer relevant, or excessive." At the heart of the court's logic was the process that Google used to produce its search results. The official ruling explained the court's rationale:

> The Court points out in this context that processing of personal data carried out by such an operator enables any Internet user, when he makes a search on the basis of an individual's name, to obtain, through the list of results, a structured overview of the information relating to that individual on the internet. The Court observes, furthermore, that this information potentially concerns a vast number of aspects of his

---

[30] "Spanish Agency behind the Google Ruling Lauded by Some, Hated by Others," *Wall Street Journal,* June 23, 2014 at *http://online.wsj.com/articles/spanish-agency-behind-the-google-ruling-lauded-by-some-hated-by-others-1403795717?cb=logged0.03531818146039811.*

[31] Van Alsenoy et al., 2013.

[32] See *http://answers.google.com/answers/threadview/id/33696.html.*

[33] Matt Cutts (Google Quality Group Engineer), *How Search Works,* s30–s44, available at *http://www.youtube.com/watch?v=BNHR6IQJGZs.*

[34] Alsenoy et al., 2013.

[35] More information about crawling is available online at *https://www.google.com/search/about/.*

private life and that, without the search engine, the information could not have been interconnected or could have been only with great difficulty.[36]

In essence, the Court ruled that an activity, "whether or not by automatic means" could be considered to be the "processing of personal data" within the meaning of Article 2(b), even if no intention to process such data existed.[37] The court's ruling applied to any search engine operators that had a branch or a subsidiary in any of the 28 member states of the EU.[38]

Costeja's lawyer, Joaquín Muñoz, was pleased with the ruling. "When you search for something in Google, they don't scour the entire Internet for you and then give you a result. They've stored links, organized them, and they show them based on a criteria they've decided upon."[39] As for Costeja, he expressed satisfaction with the result of his four-year legal crusade. Speaking of the court's decision, he said, "I think this is the correct move. You have to provide a path for communication between the user and the search engine. Now that communication can take place."[40]

Google's Application of the Ruling

For its part, Google—although disappointed with the ruling—set about complying with it. Soon after the court decision, it removed Costeja's disputed information from its search results. But, the company also took more general action.

The Court's decision recognized Google as a data controller, or the operator of the search engine and the party responsible for its data. As such, the court said, Google was required to police its links and put into place a mechanism to address individual concerns. Accordingly, shortly after the ruling was announced, Google set up an online form for users (from the European Union only) to request the right to be forgotten. The company website stated that each request would be evaluated individually and that Google would attempt to "balance the privacy rights of the individual with the public's interest to know and the right to distribute information."[41] Once an individual had filled out the form, he or she received a confirmation. Each request was assessed on a case-by-case basis. Occasionally, Google would ask for more information from the individual. Once Google had made its decision, it notified the individual by e-mail, providing a brief explanation if the decision was against removal. If so, the individual could request that a local data protection authority review Google's decision.

In evaluating a request, Google looked at whether the results included outdated or inaccurate information about the individual. It also weighed whether or not the information was of public interest. For example, Google generally retained the information if it related to financial scams, professional malpractice, criminal convictions, or a government official's public conduct.[42]

[36] Court of Justice. Judgment in Case C-131/12 Google Spain SL, *Google Inc. v Agencia Española de Protección de Datos, Mario Costeja González.*

[37] European Parliament. Judgment of the Court. May 13, 2014, at *http://curia.europa.eu/juris/document/document. jsf?docid=152065&doclang=EN.*

[38] European Commission, "Fact sheet on the Right to be Forgotten," at *http://ec.europa.eu/justice/data-protection/files/ factsheets/factsheet_data_protection_en.pdf.*

[39] "Spain's Everyday Internet Warrior Who Cut Free from Google's Tentacles," op. cit.

[40] "Google Privacy Campaigner Praises Search Engine for Following to EU," *Financial Times,* May 30, 2014.

[41] "Search Removal Request under Data Protection Law in Europe," at *https://support.google.com/legal/contact/ lr_eudpa?product=websearch.*

[42] Frequently Asked Questions, at *http://www.google.com/transparencyreport/removals/europeprivacy/ faq/?hl=en#how_does_googles_removals.*

At the same time, Google invited eight independent experts to form an advisory council expressly to "advise it on performing the balancing act between an individual's right to privacy and the public's interest in access to information."[43] The committee included three professors (two of law and one of ethics), a newspaper editorial director, a former government official, and three privacy and freedom of speech experts (including one from the United Nations). Google's CEO and chief legal officer served as conveners. The committee's job was to provide recommendations to Google on how to best implement the EU court's ruling.

The majority recommendation of the advisory council, published on February 6, 2015, was that the right to be forgotten ruling should apply only within the 28 countries in the European Union.[44] As a practical matter, this meant that Google was only required to apply removals to European domains, such as Google.fr or Google.co.uk, but not Google.com, even when accessed in Europe. Although over 95 percent of all queries originating in Europe used European domains, users could still access information that had been removed via the Google.com site.

The report also explained that once the information was removed, it was still available at the source site (e.g., the newspaper article about Costeja in *La Vanguardia*). Removal meant merely that its accessibility to the general public was reduced because searches for that information would not return a link to the source site. A person could still find the information, since only the link to the information had been removed, not the information itself.

The advisory council also recommended a set of criteria Google should use in assessing requests by individuals to "delist" their information (that is, to remove certain links in search results based on queries for that individual's name). How should the operator of the search engine best balance the privacy and data protection rights of the subject with the interest of the general public in having access to the information? The authors of the report felt that whether the data subject experienced harm from such accessibility to the information was relevant to this balancing test. Following this reasoning, they identified four primary criteria for evaluating delisting requests:

- First, what was the data subject's role in public life? Did the individuals have a clear role in public life (CEOs, politicians, sports stars)? If so, this would weigh against delisting.
- Second, what type of information was involved? Information that would normally be considered private (such as financial information, details of a person's sex life, or identification numbers) would weigh toward delisting. Information that would normally be considered to be in the public interest (such as data relevant to political discourse, citizen engagement, or governance) would normally weigh against delisting.
- Third, what was the source of the information? Here, the report suggested that journalistic writing or government publications would normally not be delisted.
- Finally, the report considered the effect of time, given that as circumstances change, the relevance of information might fade. Thus, the passage of time might favor delisting.

The advisory council also considered procedures and recommended that Google adopt an easily accessible and easy-to-understand form for data subjects to use in submitting their requests.

---

[43] The Advisory Council to Google on the Right to be Forgotten, February 6, 2015, at *https://drive.google.com/ file/d/0B1UgZshetMd4cEl3SjlvV0hNbDA/view?pli=1.*

[44] "Limit 'Right to Be Forgotten' to Europe, Panel Tells Google," *The New York Times,* February 6, 2015.

The recommendations of the advisory council were not unanimous. Jimmy Wales, the cofounder of Wikipedia and one of the eight group members, appended a dissenting comment to the report. "I completely oppose the legal situation in which a commercial company is forced to become the judge of our most fundamental rights of expression and privacy, without allowing any appropriate procedure for appeal by publishers whose work in being suppressed," Mr. Wales wrote. "The recommendations to Google contained in this report are deeply flawed due to the law itself being deeply flawed."[45]

Discussion Questions

1. In what ways has technology made it more difficult for individuals to protect their privacy?

2. Do you believe an individual should have the right to be forgotten, that is, to remove information about themselves from the Internet? If so, should this right be limited, and if so, how?

3. How does public policy with respect to individual privacy differ in the United States and Europe, and what explains these differences?

4. Do you think Google should be responsible for modifying its search results in response to individual requests? If so, what criteria should it use in doing so? Are there limits to the resources the company should be expected to expend to comply with such requests?

5. If you were a Google executive, how would you balance the privacy rights of the individual with the public's interest to know and the right to distribute information?

[45] Ibid.

General Motors and the Ignition Switch Recalls

In November 2004, Candice Anderson was driving her boyfriend, Gene Erickson, to pick up his car when her Saturn Ion swerved off the road at a slight curve and hit a tree, killing her passenger. The couple was not wearing seat belts, and the air bags did not deploy. The Texas State Police found traces of an antianxiety medication in Anderson's system, and she was fined and charged with criminally negligent homicide. Over the next 10 years, Anderson constantly relived the nightmare and wondered how she lost control on such an easy curve.

On a cloudy Wisconsin night in October 2006, Megan Ungar-Kerns was driving with her friends Amy Rademaker and Natasha Weigel in a 2005 Chevy Cobalt. The vehicle suddenly lost power and veered off the road into a utility pole and several trees. The air bags failed to operate, the driver was seriously injured, and both passengers died on the spot. The state police report noted that at the time of the crash the key was in "accessory" mode.

Brooke Melton was driving in Georgia on a rainy March evening in 2010. It was her 29th birthday. Her 2005 Chevy Cobalt suddenly stalled, slid into an oncoming vehicle, rolled, and dropped 15 feet into a creek. Melton was wearing her seat belt, but the air bags did not operate and she died on the way to the hospital. Police recorded driving too fast for conditions as the cause of the accident; she was going 58 mph in a 55 mph zone.

These tragic accidents had little in common except for three commonalities: in all of these cases (and, as it turned out, dozens more like them), the driver had for some reason lost control of the car, the built-in air bag protection systems had failed to deploy—and the vehicles were made by General Motors (GM).

In February 2014, nearly a decade after Gene Erickson died, GM began a series of recalls that eventually affected 2.6 million vehicles whose model years ranged from 2003 to 2011. The reason for the recalls was a faulty ignition switch that easily shifted the key from "run" into the "off" or "accessory" positions. When the key was not in "run," the cars lost power, including to the steering, braking, and protective air bag systems. This reduced the driver's control and increased the risk of injury in the event of an accident. In addition to facing individual and class action lawsuits, the company was under investigation by the National Highway Traffic Safety Administration (NHTSA), the U.S. Congress, and the

By Debra M. Staab and Anne T. Lawrence. Copyright © 2015 by the authors. All rights reserved. The authors developed this case for class discussion rather than to illustrate effective or ineffective handling of the situation. Materials in this case are drawn from testimony at the hearings on the GM ignition switch recall held by the Energy & Commerce Committee, Subcommittee on Oversight and Investigations, on April 1, 2014, and June 18, 2014; the GM study known as *The Valukas Report;* the General Motors website; the House of Representatives Committee on Energy and Commerce *Staff Report on the GM Ignition Switch Recall: Review of NHTSA;* and from articles in *The New York Times, The Wall Street Journal, Automotive News, About.com, NewWorldEncyclopedia.org, Bloomberg.com, gmignitioncompensation.com, nationallawjournal.com, fortune.com, money.cnn.com, Nasdaq.com;* and the NHTSA Recall Database. A full list of references appears in the instructor's manual that accompanies this book.

Justice Department. By May 2014, 47 accidents and more than a dozen fatalities had been linked to the ignition switch defect. But many questions regarding the decade-long delay in repairing the defective part remained unanswered.

General Motors

General Motors was America's largest automaker with a 2014 profit of $2.8 billion, 21,000 dealerships, and a workforce of over 200,000 across six continents. GM produced several well-known brands including Chevrolet (Chevy), Buick, GMC, Cadillac, Saturn, Saab, Pontiac, Oldsmobile, and Hummer. Founded in 1908 by William "Billy" Durant, the company motto was "a car for every purse and purpose." GM was known for innovative styling, exemplified by models such as the 1953 Chevrolet Corvette and the 1959 Cadillac El Dorado.

Over several decades, GM repeatedly changed with the times, enjoying a run of successes. During WWII, GM diverted 100 percent of its manufacturing to the production of $12 billion worth of airplanes, trucks, and tanks for the war effort. In the 1970s, GM responded to rising gasoline prices with engines that ran on unleaded fuel, offered air bags for protection, and introduced the first emission-reducing catalytic converter. In the 1980s, GM added Saab and Hummer to its product line and expanded its global footprint through joint ventures with China and India. GM partnered with Toyota in the NUMMI joint venture in the 1990s to cocreate trucks and SUV's that satisfied emerging consumer demand. By the mid-2000s, GM's push for innovation led to the development of the Chevy Volt, one of the first electric vehicles, as well as the concept of a hybrid vehicle that switched from electric to gasoline.

Still, GM was not as agile as the German, Japanese, and Korean automakers and began to lose market share, especially in fuel-efficient vehicles. The recession and credit crisis of 2008 significantly undermined GM's operating budget, and the firm, along with its financial arm GMAC, agreed to a government bailout. On June 1, 2009, the old General Motors Corporation filed for bankruptcy and transferred most of its assets to the new General Motors Company, whose major shareholders included the U.S. and Canadian governments and the United Auto Workers (UAW) medical trust fund. The new owners replaced then-CEO Rick Wagoner with Fritz Henderson, who was then almost immediately dismissed in favor of the chairman of the board, Ed Whitacre. They also demanded increased fuel efficiency levels to compete with foreign automakers, and required the firm to streamline operations. GM sold the Saab line, discontinued the Saturn and Hummer models, and restructured GMAC into Ally Financial.

The company became profitable once again by the end of 2009. In 2010, Whitacre stepped down and Dan Akerson became the CEO until Mary Barra, a 35-year veteran of GM and the first female CEO in the auto industry, took over in January 2014. The bailout, which also included Chrysler Motors, ended in December 2014 with a net loss to taxpayers of $9.2 billion, with only $1.3 billion attributed to Chrysler. Justification for the bailout hinged on the "too big to fail" concept, as the auto industry had contributed 3.6 percent of the total U.S. Gross Domestic Product (GDP), and every additional 30 percent decline in auto sales meant a corresponding 1 percent decline in GDP.[1]

The Ignition Switch Defect

The ignition switch at the center of the recall was first introduced in the late 1990s. Between 1997 and 2001, GM designed a new low-current switch, formally named the

---

[1] "Auto Industry Bailout (GM, Ford, Chrysler)," *About.com,* February 6, 2015.

Discrete Logic Ignition Switch (DLIS). Concurrently, GM implemented cost-saving manufacturing efficiencies through a baseline design, called a platform, which allowed the use of common parts across vehicle makes, models, and production years. The Delta Platform included the Saturn Ion, Chevrolet Cobalt, Chevrolet HHR, and the Pontiac G5, and the Kappa Platform included the Saturn Sky and Pontiac Solstice.

The recalled ignition switch, a part shared across the Delta and Kappa platforms, was embedded in the steering column and had four positions. The driver turned the key to "start" (technically referred to as "crank") to turn on the engine, and once started, the key automatically toggled into the "run" position to indicate that the vehicle had power. When the key was moved to "accessory," the system signaled an engine shutdown, which turned off the air bags, power steering, and power brakes, and left only small electrical features, like the radio, operable. In the "off" or "lock" position, the switch cut power to all vehicle functions. Inside the ignition switch, a plunger cap and coiled spring unit that fit into a small groove called a "detent" kept the key in the selected mode. The driver applied enough pressure, or torque, to move the key between positions. The longer the plunger and more tightly coiled the spring, the harder it was to shift key slots.

The DLIS ignition switches were manufactured for GM by another company, Eaton Corporation (acquired by Delphi Mechatronics in 2001). GM's switch specifications recommended a target amount of pressure that a driver would have to apply to toggle the key from "run" to "accessory." But, as early as 1999, the parts manufacturer reported that prototype switches did not meet GM's specifications. Subsequent mechanical tests conducted by Delphi in 2001–2002 also showed that switches within every sample set had a "torque problem," tending to slip out of position when inadvertently jostled.

Despite the test failures, the GM engineer in charge of the part authorized production of the switch in 2002, signing his approval e-mail as "Ray (tired of the switch from hell) DeGiorgio." DeGiorgio's decision was based on Delphi's advice that a fix for the torque problem, such as a longer plunger, would take time, add costs, and could compromise the switch's electrical components, which he had already redesigned several times. The GM engineer apparently believed that the torque issue did not pose a safety problem, because he later told an investigator that he had "no awareness that the below-specification torque would have an impact on the safe operation of the car."[2]

However, this was not the case. The ignition switch defect compromised safety because if the car lost power while in motion, as a result of the key slipping out of position, it went into what was called a moving stall. Drivers in a moving stall would be less able to navigate the car because they no longer had access to power steering or braking (although they retained manual control). Then, if an accident occurred, the air bags would not deploy, because they no longer had power. GM used special sensors to control the air bag system. To avoid accidental inflation, the sensors were programmed to shut down when the ignition switch moved to the "off" or "accessory" position. All GM vehicles in the Delta and Kappa platforms used the same air bag sensor systems.

The First Indications of a Problem and GM's Response

The 2003 Saturn Ion was the first GM vehicle to roll off the assembly line with the DLIS switch. Within the first year of its release, the Ion had logged over 200 warranty incidents related to its ignition switch. The two most common problems were the car stalling while in motion because the key slipped out of position, and the car refusing to start under cold

---

[2] "Report to Board of Directors of General Motors Company Regarding Ignition Switch Recalls (The Valukas Report)," *Jenner & Block*, May 29, 2014.

weather conditions. DeGiorgio, still in charge of the ignition switch, focused on finding a fix for the latter problem. In 2004, he approved use of a different type of grease within the ignition to resolve most of the nonstart issues. Despite several reports of moving stalls issued by both internal GM test teams and external drivers; however, company engineers made no effort to correct the key slippage problem.

Nonetheless, in February 2005, GM released a warning message to dealers, referred to as Preliminary Information, which identified possible stalls as a problem and suggested that drivers remove unnecessary items from the key ring to avoid weighing down the key and inadvertently knocking the ignition out of the "run" position. One such message stated that "there is potential for the driver to inadvertently turn off the ignition due to low key ignition cylinder torque/effort. The concern is more likely to occur if the driver is short and has a large heavy key chain."[3] Presumably, a short driver would be more likely to move the seat forward, increasing the risk of jostling the key with his/her knee or leg.

One month later, however, GM's related internal issue tracking report was closed with no action taken. In 2014, an investigative review of the decision to close the report without a fix disclosed significant finger-pointing within the organization. During repeated fact-finding interviews, GM managers folded their arms, hands together, and pointed their fingers outward in a gesture that suggested someone else was responsible; this behavior became known as the "GM salute."

By June 2005, the company had received multiple customer complaints about moving stalls in the Cobalt and the Solstice, which triggered a new non–safety-related defect report. This time, engineers recommended a plug that reduced the size of the key slot. This solution was sent out to dealers as an updated Preliminary Information notice.

But, even after this bulletin was released, complaints kept piling up, and several negative news articles decried the problem and GM's inadequate response. For example, journalist Gary Heller reported in *The Daily Item,* a Pennsylvania newspaper, "Unplanned engine shutdowns happened four times during a hard-driving test [of the Chevy Cobalt] last week. . . . I never encountered anything like this in 37 years of driving, and I hope I never do again." This quote was later picked up by *The New York Times.*[4]

As a direct result of the negative press, GM's Product Investigations (PI) team conducted tests that reproduced the moving stalls. In spite of these results, the PI team recommended the release of a Technical Service Bulletin (TSB) to dealers rather than a recall. The TSB applied to the 2005–06 Chevy Cobalt, 2006 Chevy HHR, 2005–06 Pontiac Pursuit, 2006 Pontiac Solstice, and the 2003–06 Saturn Ion. The bulletin repeated the message used in the Preliminary Information notice, including the key insert fix, with one notable difference: the word "stall" was removed from the text. During investigative interviews, GM quality manager Steve Oakley later stated that the term "stall" was not typically used in bulletins because it might sound like a safety issue and cause NHTSA to question why the company did not issue a recall. Oakley also revealed that he did not want to "push hard on safety issues" because the previous quality manager, Courtland Kelley, was demoted—allegedly due to a failed 2003 whistle-blowing lawsuit over a leaky fuel line in the Chevy Trailblazer.[5]

The TSB provided a solution for any customer who complained, but did not address switch defects in the production of new vehicles. When GM was unable to resolve price and quality disputes with their supplier of keys, they cancelled the plan to use a key designed

[3] "Engine Stalls, Loss of Electrical Systems, and No DTCs LSJ phantom #PIC3421," *General Motors,* February 28, 2005.

[4] "Making a Case for Ignitions That Don't Need Keys, *The New York Times,* June 19, 2005.

[5] "How GM Silenced a Whistle-Blower," *Bloomberg Business,* June 18, 2014.

with a small hole instead of a wide slot and continued to build new cars with the same defective key and switch parts. The 2014 investigations revealed that internal GM e-mails from 2005 noted that the cost per vehicle to increase the torque by 10 percent was $0.57 and to increase the torque by 50 percent was about $1.00 per vehicle.

The National Highway Traffic Safety Administration

The federal regulatory agency in charge of automobile safety issues such as those experienced by GM drivers was the National Highway Traffic Safety Administration (NHTSA). In 1966, U.S. legislators enacted the National Highway Traffic and Motor Vehicle Safety Act and the Highway Safety Act, and also created the Department of Transportation (DOT) reporting to the U.S. secretary of commerce. Through the subsequent Highway Safety Act of 1970, the NHTSA was established within the DOT. NHTSA's mission was to protect public safety by reducing deaths, injuries, and monetary loss associated with motor vehicle accidents. To accomplish their goals, NHTSA developed Federal Motor Vehicle Safety Standards (FMVSS) for new vehicle design, manufacturing, and performance as related to crash prevention (warning systems), crashworthiness (structural soundness), and postcrash survivability of the occupants. In 2000, the Transportation Recall Enhancement, Accountability, and Documentation Act (TREAD) was passed to expand the reporting requirements of auto manufacturers regarding potential safety concerns as well as establish penalties for noncompliance. NHTSA also maintained the public website *www.safercar.gov* to assist consumers with vehicle safety information.

One of the responsibilities of the agency was setting the rules governing air bags and other passive safety devices. These devices played an important role in protecting occupants; the agency reported that the risk of serious head injury in a crash was reduced by 83 percent when both seat belts and air bags were used.[6] The NHTSA first mandated the installation of driver-side air bags in motor vehicles for models produced after April 1, 1989; and in 1998, they further required advanced dual front air bags that used the size and position of each occupant to properly adjust the bag's inflation pressure. This feature was introduced to prevent injury or death caused by the opening force of the air bag itself.

Within NHTSA, the Office of Defects Investigations (ODI) was responsible for screening and investigating motor vehicle deficiencies that allegedly violated its regulations, as well as overseeing the recalls issued by automakers. Under ODI, the Defects Assessment Division (DAD) performed the screening step using data from the Early Warning Reporting (EWR) system that captured TREAD reports, direct customer complaints collected by the Correspondence Research Division (CRD), and data from the Special Crash Investigations (SCI) team who performed in-depth analysis of specific crash conditions. By 2014, NHTSA had overseen the recall of, on average, around nine million vehicle per year since 2000. The agency had also annually reviewed from 45,000 to 55,000 consumer complaints, around 6,000 death and injury reports, and had conducted between 100 and 125 special crash investigations. NHTSA's operations and research division employed 519 full-time equivalent workers and operated under a budget of $257.5 million.[7]

When one of the first reports of air bag nondeployment in the Cobalt was sent to NHTSA in 2005, the SCI conducted an investigation. The researchers concluded that the air bags failed because the vehicle had decelerated gradually by first impacting smaller

---

[6] "Air Bag," *New World Encyclopedia*, September 8, 2012.

[7] "FY2015 NHTSA Budget Justification," March 5, 2014, at *www.nhtsa.gov*.

trees prior to crashing into a large tree. No questions were raised as to why the power mode was in "accessory," and the case was closed with no further action. By 2007, NHTSA's Early Warning team noted high warranty claim rates for the Cobalt and the Ion and asked the DAD to review. The request mentioned 43 accidents that caused 27 injuries and four deaths, and indicated that the number of claims for the Cobalt were higher than other GM vehicles, and also greater than those of other automakers.

The DAD chose the Rademaker/Weigel case (from Wisconsin), but the packet of case documents related to the crash did not include some critical items, even though they were stored in the agency's own files. These included an earlier SCI study conducted by the Indiana University Transportation Resource Center, which had correctly linked the issues of low torque keys, power loss, and air bag failure, and the 2007 Wisconsin State Police report that had noted that the key had been in "accessory" mode. The packet also did not include GM's TSB related to the key slip problem. Failing to consider these reports, the team ultimately placed the blame for the Rademaker/Weigel crash on air bag non-deployment due to off-road conditions. Despite a recommendation from its associate administrator of enforcement to expand research, the ODI decided not to pursue a formal investigation. In 2014, the Energy and Commerce Committee's review of NHTSA's decision found no written documentation explaining why the agency had chosen not to pursue its GM study.

Over the next two years, the media published a number of reports criticizing the NHTSA for its lack of oversight regarding air bag failures. The *Kansas City Star* printed a series of scathing articles with headlines such as *Air Bag Recall Process Drags On, Crash Kills Another Driver,* and *Taking Air Bag Cases to Court Can be Tricky.* The NHTSA publicly complained to the editor that the paper "ignored warnings by the [NHTSA's] experts that the underlying premise of its recent air bag story was fundamentally flawed." Nonetheless, these news reports prompted NHTSA to further examine frontal crash safety, including another look at the Cobalt. But, the DAD examined minimal data and again concluded that there was no pattern of failure, which brought the investigation to a standstill. After declining three times to cite GM, the agency would not revisit the air bag nondeployment issue again until 2014, after the GM recalls started.

The GM Engineer's Secret Fix

As the NHTSA investigated—and failed to take action—the GM engineer in charge of the ignition switch, Ray DeGiorgio, apparently set about fixing the torque problem on his own, in secret, and without fully documenting his process.

General Motors followed a formal approval process for development of all vehicle parts, called the Production Part Approval Process (PPAP). This process required official sign-off from both the supplier and GM personnel. DeGiorgio had followed this process in 2004 when he approved a different type of grease to fix the cold start problem. But, in 2006, he worked secretly with the switch supplier, Delphi, to completely replace the short, problematic spring-plunger with a longer, more tightly coiled version, a design GM had originally rejected in 2001. DeGiorgio approved the low-cost plunger replacement as part of another electrical update for the cold start problem, but made no change to the part number and did not communicate the change internally. Under GM policy, a new part number should have been assigned.

During investigative interviews in 2014, DeGiorgio claimed that he did not remember approving the plunger-spring part change. Documents discovered in the supplier's files suggested otherwise. In one internal e-mail, sent in 2005, a Delphi engineer stated, "Cobalt is blowing up in their face in regards to turning the car off with the driver's knee."[8] The corrected switch was put into new vehicle production part way through the 2007 model year. The secret fix later confounded company investigators, as they tried unsuccessfully to research and document the ignition switch problem.

Victim Lawsuits and GM's Response

As the number of accidents caused by the defective ignition switch rose, victims and their families began filing lawsuits.

These lawsuits were dealt with internally by GM's legal department, which managed both product litigation and safety matters. The legal department worked, in turn, with the Field Performance Assessment (FPA) team, customer claim administrators, and outside counsel. A committee known as the "Roundtable" met weekly to review and approve claims where the payout was in the range of $100,000 to $2 million. For larger awards—those between $2 million and $5 million—a group called the Settlement Review Committee (SRC) convened on a monthly basis. Only the general counsel could approve payouts of more than $5 million.

By 2006, GM had received several wrongful death lawsuits related to nondeployment of air bags in Ions and Cobalts. The Roundtable determined that in cases lacking a frontal crash event, the air bags were not expected to deploy, and settled without admitting guilt. Throughout 2007 and 2008, GM continued to settle wrongful death cases without acknowledging any defects (although it did add the newer 2007 model to its technical service bulletin and added the Saturn Sky). On June 1, 2009, GM filed for bankruptcy and all pending litigation was placed on hold.

Bankruptcy notwithstanding, the FPA team continued researching why data recorded by the vehicles' sensors sometimes indicated that the ignition switch was in the "off" or "accessory" position just before a crash in which the air bags did not deploy. The team also noted one odd fact: no reports had emerged of air bag failures for the model year 2008 or later. But, they could find no part change records. Even when questioned directly, DeGiorgio stated that there had been no ignition switch alterations that would have addressed loss of power. The FPA research seemed to have run into a dead end.

By late 2010, some air bag-related lawsuits began blaming "sensing anomalies" as the cause of improper air bag operation. This implied a serious vehicle malfunction that would be difficult to defend and could lead to significant punitive damages. Consequently, the SRC requested more information from product investigators about this anomaly. But the PI team apparently felt no sense of urgency, because it set no timetable and never assigned responsibility to a specific individual. This behavior was later characterized by new CEO Mary Barra as the "GM nod," which she defined as "when everyone nods in agreement to a proposed plan of action, but then leaves the room with no intention to follow through, and the nod is an empty gesture."[9] The product investigation team's lack of commitment resulted in delays and incomplete work efforts for another year.

Finally, in May 2012, the PI team concluded from junkyard tests that the air bags had failed to deploy due to mechanical rather than electrical reasons and wondered if this was because the ignition switch had moved out of the "run" position. Once again, in June 2012,

---

[8] "Report to Board of Directors of General Motors Company Regarding Ignition Switch Recalls (The Valukas Report)," *Jenner & Block*, May 29, 2014.

[9] "Report to Board of Directors of General Motors Company Regarding Ignition Switch Recalls (The Valukas Report)," *Jenner & Block*, May 29, 2014.

DeGiorgio denied knowledge of any changes to the switch that would have affected rotational torque. Hence, in September 2012, the PI team requested help from a specialized group known as Red-X, which included experts in parts differentiation, to assess why the torque measurements differed between 2007 and 2008 Cobalt models. However, since the Red-X team had been instructed by the GM legal department that all cars in question were under quarantine, they were unable to secure a vehicle to evaluate. The study was cancelled, and the investigation was mired yet again.

In the meantime, Brooke Melton's parents were convinced that she had not been driving too fast for conditions, and that there must have been something wrong with her 2005 Cobalt. In fact, just days before the fatal accident, Brooke had taken her vehicle to a GM dealership to research a worrisome and unexpected moving stall. In 2010, her bereaved parents hired an independent engineer named Mark Hood to review the accident. Hood inspected the ignition with particular focus on the plastic and metal switch, to no avail. Next, he purchased a $30 replacement part from a GM dealer and repeated the inspection. To his surprise, the newer part had a longer plunger and a tighter spring, and required a notable increase in torque to rotate the key. The details of this study were presented to GM at a deposition for the Melton case in April 2013. During the deposition, DeGiorgio acknowledged the differences between the original plunger-spring and the replacement part, but again disavowed any knowledge of a change to the parts. The evidence was then presented to the SRC, and in September 2013, they authorized a $5 million settlement with the Meltons.

GM also hired an outside investigator to repeat Hood's research, and six months later in October 2013, the study concluded that there had been a definite design change in the ignition switch between 2006 and 2007, and that earlier versions of the switch did not meet GM specifications. Given this compelling evidence, the partmaker, Delphi, turned over documents that explicitly showed DeGiorgio's approval for the change in April 2006. Finally, GM understood that the ignition switch was defective, and when it slipped into a moving stall, the resulting lack of power disabled the air bags and risked the occupants' safety.

In December 2013, the SRC sent its conclusions regarding the flawed switch to the Executive Field Action Decision Committee (EFADC), which was responsible for considering a recall. Their first meeting on the topic was inconclusive and a decision was delayed for another six weeks. Finally, starting on February 7, 2014, EFADC ordered a succession of recalls that eventually included over 2.6 million defective vehicles.

Congressional Hearings

Congressional hearings followed the recalls, the first on April 1 and the second on June 18, 2014. GM CEO Mary Barra and NHTSA acting director David Friedman testified at the April hearing.

For his part, Friedman admitted shortcomings within NHTSA, but placed the blame on GM, stating that the automaker withheld critical information such as the failure to change the switch part number and the fact that defect discussions were covertly held with the supplier. Government interrogators suggested that NHTSA had ample information and might have been too soft on GM. Senator Claire McCaskill opined in the hearing that the agency was "more interested in singing Kumbaya with the manufacturers than being a cop on the beat." Representing GM, Ms. Barra promised full disclosure and indicated that the company and its board of directors had retained outside counsel, the law firm Jenner & Block, to conduct a full investigation.

In May, immediately following the hearings, Senator Ed Markey introduced stricter legislation related to the Early Warning system and commented:

> At almost every juncture for the past decade, whenever NHTSA was made aware of possible safety issues with the GM vehicles, it chose to take no action. As damaging as the "GM nod" that is said to have embodied the culture of ineptitude at the company, the "NHTSA shrug," when confronted by evidence of this fatal safety defect, was also responsible for keeping these deadly vehicles on the road. It is time to pass legislation to ensure that information about possible deadly defects is made public so American families can be protected even if NHTSA abdicates its responsibility to public safety again in the future.[10]

In May 2014, NHTSA slapped GM with the maximum $35 million penalty for failure to disclose the defect in a timely manner.[11] The same month, GM fired 15 employees, including engineer Ray DeGiorgio and several high-level lawyers, and disciplined five more.

The Valukas Report, named after its lead author Anton R. Valukas of Jenner & Block, was released on June 5. In preparing the 325-page report, Valukas and his team had reviewed over 41 million documents and interviewed 230 witnesses. The report concluded that the delayed recall was due to a pattern of "incompetence and neglect," a dysfunctional organization, and a culture driven by cost over safety. The report exonerated senior leadership, including the board of directors.

However, the Valukas report also described a culture of mixed messages from management. On one hand, management promoted a message of safety first, saying "when safety is at issue, cost is irrelevant;" while on the other hand, it also promoted a message of "cost is everything," seeming to suggest the opposite. A quality training course from 2004 instructed employees to demand excellence:

> The harsh reality is—we are competing in a new world, one that demands a culture where there is no tolerance for defects an any point during in [sic] the vehicle development and manufacturing process. Because the marketplace has zero tolerance for defects, this organization will have no tolerance for defects.

Yet, statements from GM workers indicated that cost-containment measures in the 2000s overshadowed the "zero tolerance" directive, noting that a cost-control focus "permeates the fabric of the whole culture." Leading up to GM's 2009 bankruptcy, the company was clearly concerned about costs when they instituted workforce reductions in 2006, 2008, and 2009 that shrank a 1979 peak headcount of around 468,000 to just 66,000.[12] The Valukas Report concluded by stating that there had been no intentional cover-up related to the ignition switch defect.

The June hearing included testimony from Ms. Barra and Mr. Valukas, who were both grilled by members of Congress over the findings of the Valukas Report. The hearings were opened by House Representative Tim Murphy, who suggested that the Valukas Report could have been subtitled "Don't Assume Malfeasance When Incompetence Will Do." Murphy went on to state that:

> Even when a good law, like the TREAD Act of 2000, is in place, it requires people to use common sense, value a moral code, and have a motivation driven by compassion for it to be effective. Here, the key people at GM seemed to lack all of these in

---

[10] "Markey on GM Recall: While GM Nods, NHTSA Shrugs," June 18, 2014, at *Markey.senate.gov.*

[11] "GM Gets Record Penalty for Failing to Report Defect," *The Wall Street Journal,* May 16, 2014.

[12] "GM Layoffs: Thousands of Factory Jobs Likely To Be Cut," *Huffington Post,* September 3, 2009.

a way that underscores that we cannot legislate common sense, mandate morality, nor litigate compassion, and at some point it is up to the culture of the company that has to go beyond paperwork and rules.

Congresswoman Diana DeGette pressed Mr. Valukas about management's role, saying:

The report singles out many individuals at GM who made poor decisions or failed to act, but it doesn't identify one individual in a position of high leadership who was responsible for these systemic failures. The report absolves previous CEOs, the legal department, Ms. Barra, and the GM Board from knowing about the tragedy beforehand. This is nothing to be proud of. That the most senior GM executives may not know—have known about a defect that caused more than a dozen deaths is, frankly, alarming and does not absolve them of responsibility for this tragedy.

Mr. Murphy went on to question Mr. Valukas about a possible cover-up:

Mr. Murphy: Does an employee who acts alone, or who hides or doesn't share information, a cover-up?

Mr. Valukas: If the individual knows that the information is a—for instance, a safety information, and understands that and deliberately decides to conceal that, that is a cover-up, yes, it is.

Mr. Murphy: I just find it hard to believe that of 210,000 employees, not a single one in that company had the integrity to say, I think we are making a mistake here. Not a single one. That is puzzling to me.

Despite the intense scrutiny, Ms. Barra remained composed and promised to turn the company around:

We are currently conducting, and I believe—what I believe is the most exhaustive comprehensive safety review in the history of our company. We are leaving no stone unturned, and devoting whatever resources it takes to identify potential safety issues in all of our current vehicles and on vehicles no longer in production. Our responsibility is to set a new norm and a new industry standard on safety and quality. I have told our employees it is not enough to simply fix this problem; we need to create a new standard, and we will create a new norm.

Discussion Questions

1. Who or what was responsible for the ignition switch defect and the resulting deaths and injuries? In your response, please consider the roles of General Motors and its managers and employees, U.S. auto safety regulators, and the drivers of the vehicles themselves and their representatives.

2. If you were a GM employee, what would you do if you had knowledge of a safety defect? If your manager told you to ignore the problem, would you go outside the company to blow the whistle? What might be the cost of keeping silent to the employee and the employer?

3. If you were the CEO of General Motors, what changes would you implement to avoid similar problems from arising in the future?

4. What actions do you recommend that policymakers and regulators take to avoid similar problems from occurring in the future?

5. As a consumer, what can you do to ensure safety in your own vehicle, before and after purchase?

Sustainability at Holland America Line

Holland America Line (HAL) was proud of its reputation as a sustainability leader in the global cruise industry. Bill Morani, vice president for safety and environmental systems, was responsible for ensuring that the company and fleet complied with both safety and environmental regulations and policies. In light of the maritime industry's significant environmental impacts and its complex and rapidly evolving regulatory environment, Morani was thinking about how to prioritize the company's current sustainability initiatives. His musings were interrupted as Dan Grausz, executive vice president for fleet operations, came into his office waving an article. The Stena Line, a ferry operator, had reduced fuel use on one of its vessels by installing two wind turbines on deck, the article reported. Grausz, who also served as leader of the company's fuel conservation committee, reminded Morani that wind turbines were one of 56 initiatives HAL was evaluating. It had been assigned a low priority, but Grausz asked Morani if he thought that should be reconsidered.

HAL, headquartered in Seattle, Washington, was founded as a shipping and passenger line in 1873 and offered its first vacation cruises in 1895. In 1989, HAL became a wholly owned subsidiary of Carnival Corporation. HAL maintained its own identity, operating its own fleet, and managing its marketing, sales, and administrative support. In 2011, HAL operated 15 mid-size ships, mostly in the premium segment, and expected to carry 750,000 passengers to 350 ports in 100 countries. The company had more than 14,000 employees.

HAL was widely recognized as a leader in the cruise industry in its environmental sustainability. In 2006, HAL had received the Green Planet Award, which recognized eco-minded hotels, resorts, and cruise lines for outstanding environmental standards. This award was based on the company's ISO14001 certification and the installation of shore power plug-in systems on three ships. In 2008, Virgin Holidays awarded HAL its Responsible Tourism Award based on its reduction of dockside emissions, increased use of recycling, and adoption of a training program to avoid whale strikes. In 2011, HAL was named the World's Leading Green Cruise Line at the World Travel Awards in London, and in both 2010 and 2012 the company had received the Gold Environmental Protection Award from the U.S. Coast Guard.

Morani was particularly proud of the progress HAL had made in improving fuel efficiency; the company had reduced its fuel use per passenger per nautical mile by 20 percent between 2005 and 2011. Burning less fuel meant lower emissions of carbon dioxide, sulfur

By Murray Silverman, San Francisco State University. This is an edited version of a longer case, "Protecting Our Oceans: Sustainability at Holland America Line," copyright © 2012 by Murray Silverman; all rights reserved. This version was edited, abridged, and used by permission of the author. A full set of footnotes is available in the longer case. The case was developed with the cooperation of Holland America and the support of the Center for Ethical and Sustainable Business at San Francisco State University and the Campbell Foundation. This case was prepared as a basis for class discussion rather than to illustrate the effective or ineffective handling of an administrative situation.

and nitrous oxides (SOX and NOX), and particulate matter (PM). These emissions were increasingly regulated, because of rising concerns about both their health and environmental impacts. According to Morani:

> Fuel conservation is our go-to strategy. It is a win–win. By consuming less fuel, we are not emitting as much exhaust containing greenhouse gases and other pollutants, while reducing HAL's fuel costs. And, by the way, the money saved through fuel conservation can help offset the increased cost of cleaner fuel.

Morani put aside his thinking about broader sustainability priorities in order to look into the wind turbine idea.

The Global Cruise Industry

Taking a cruise was very popular among tourists, and the cruise industry was one of the fastest growing sectors of the tourism industry. The modern cruise industry traced its beginnings to the early 1970s, when the industry began offering Caribbean cruises from Miami, Florida. As it evolved, the industry created a reasonably priced opportunity for many people to experience a resort-type vacation. Sometimes, cruise ships were referred to as floating hotels or marine resorts, because they had sleeping rooms, restaurants, entertainment, shops, spas, business centers, casinos, swimming pools, and other amenities, just like land-based resorts.

By the mid-2010s, cruise ships traveled in every ocean, frequently visiting the most pristine coastal waters and sensitive marine ecosystems. Among the most popular destinations were the Caribbean, the Mediterranean Sea, various European ports, the Bahamas, and Alaska. Worldwide, approximately 2,000 ports were capable of receiving cruise ships. Destinations varied from tropical beaches like Cozumel, to nature-based destinations such as Alaska, to historical and culturally rich locations such as Istanbul. The cruise product was highly diversified, based on destination, ship design, on-board and on-shore activities, themes, and cruise lengths; accommodations and amenities were priced accordingly. Classifications ranged from budget to conventional to premium and, lastly, to luxury. The passenger capacity of cruise ships tended to be larger in the budget and conventional categories and varied from a few hundred to over 5,000 passengers.

The popularity of cruising was reflected in its growth. Since 1980, the number of passengers had grown by an annual rate of 7.6 percent. Between 1990 and 2010, more than 191 million passengers took a cruise. Twenty-four percent of the American population had cruised at least once. Passengers were predominately Caucasian (93%), well educated, and married (83%). Their average age was 46, with an average household income between $90,000 and $100,000. The leading factors in the customer's selection of a cruise package were destination and price; industry executives believed that few customers considered a cruise line's environmental practices in their choice. As demand grew, the industry responded by building more cruise ships. As of 2012, 256 cruise ships plied global waters. Newer ships tended to be bigger, and they often included innovative amenities such as planetariums and bowling alleys.

Cruise lines were a $30 million a year global industry. In 2012, three major companies dominated the industry: Carnival Corporation (52 percent of passengers), Royal Caribbean Cruises Ltd. (21 percent), and Norwegian Cruise Line (7 percent). Each of these companies had a number of brands, allowing them to operate within various pricing segments. The industry was organized into the Cruise Line Industry Association (CLIA), whose membership included 22 of the world's largest cruise line companies and accounted for 97% of the demand for cruises.

The World's Oceans

HAL and the cruise industry as a whole relied on the oceans as their most important resource. The unspoiled waters and coral reefs at port destinations were a major attraction for passengers. Oceans, which covered 71 percent of the Earth's surface, provided many benefits for society. They were a source of food, in the form of fish and shellfish, and were used for transportation and recreation, such as swimming, sailing, diving, and surfing. They provided biomedical organisms that helped fight disease. And, the ocean played a significant role in regulating the planet's climate by absorbing carbon dioxide and heat.

Yet, in the mid-2010s, the oceans faced many environmental threats:

Overfishing: More than half the world's population depended on the oceans for their primary source of food, yet most of the world's fisheries were being fished at levels above their maximum sustainable yield. Furthermore, harmful fishing methods were unnecessarily killing turtles, dolphins, and other animals and destroying critical habitat.

Pollution: Eighty percent of all pollution in seas and oceans came from land-based activities. More oil reached the ocean each year as a result of leaking automobiles and other nonpoint sources, for example, than was spilled by the Exxon Valdez. An enormous amount of oil had been accidentally spilled from ships, destroying aquatic plant and animal life.

Eutrophication: Another serious ocean threat was algal blooms caused mainly by fertilizer and topsoil runoff and sewage discharges in coastal areas. As algae died and decomposed, water was depleted of available oxygen, causing the death of other organisms such as fish.

Ocean acidification: Carbon dioxide in the atmosphere, caused mainly by the burning of fossil fuels, was a well-known contributor to global warming. But, it also acidified the oceans. When absorbed in water, carbon dioxide was converted into carbonic acid, which in turn dissolved reefs needed by organisms such as corals and oysters, threatening their survival.

Ocean warming: Atmospheric warming also increased the temperature of the ocean, reducing the generation of plankton, the base of the ocean's food web, and leading to significant marine ecosystem change.

Tourism: While tourism generated vast amounts of income for host countries, it could also have adverse environmental impacts, especially in heavily visited coastal areas. Sewage and waste from resorts, hotels, and restaurants could find their way into bays and oceans. Careless diving, snorkeling and other tour activities could damage coral reefs.

Environmental Impacts of the Cruise Industry

In a number of ways, the cruise industry contributed to these threats to ocean health. The primary inputs for a cruise were food, packaging materials, fresh and sea water, and fuel. As these inputs were processed over the course of a cruise, they produced discharges or waste with environmental impacts on water, air, and land. These impacts are diagrammed in Exhibit A.

Discharges to Water

The primary discharges to water from a cruise ship were blackwater (sewage), graywater (from showers, sinks, laundry, and the galley), and bilge water (potentially oily water leaked from engines and equipment that accumulated in the bilges).

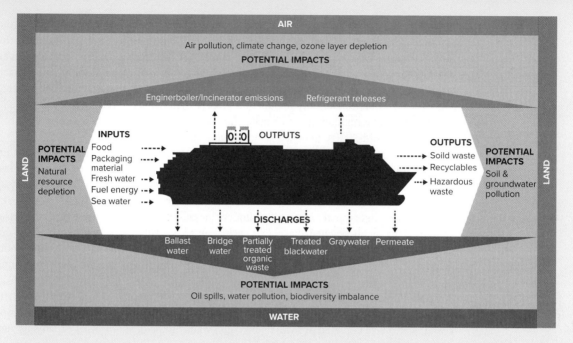

Source: Holland America Lines.

Blackwater contained pathogens, including fecal coliform bacteria, which could contaminate fisheries and shellfish beds, risking human health. On most cruise ships, sewage was treated using a marine sanitation device (MSD) that disinfected the waste prior to discharge. A newer technology, called advanced wastewater purification systems (AWWPS), was capable of producing water effluent as clean as or cleaner than that produced by many municipal treatment plants. International and U.S. regulations required that treated sewage be discharged at least 3 nautical miles from shore and untreated sewage at least 12 nautical miles from shore. All discharges were banned in certain sensitive zones.

Graywater could also contain pollutants, including oil, detergents, grease, suspended solids, nutrients, food waste, and small concentrations of coliform bacteria. U.S. regulations prohibited the discharge of graywater within three miles of the coast in California and Alaska. Voluntary industry standards specified a distance of at least four miles from the coast.

Bilge water. Regulators required that discharged bilge water contain less than 15 ppm (parts per million) of oil and could only be discharged while the vessel was en route and not operating in protected zones.

Solid and Hazardous Waste

Cruise ship waste streams could be either hazardous (e.g., chemicals from dry cleaning or photo processing, solvents, and paint waste) or nonhazardous (e.g., food waste, paper, plastic, and glass). Waste could be discarded either in the water or on land.

The potential impact from pollution by solid waste on the open ocean and the coastal environment could be significant, including aesthetic degradation of surface waters and coastal areas. Sea birds, fish, turtles, and cetaceans could be entangled in waste and injured or killed. The disposal of food wastes in restricted areas could cause pollution.

Air Emissions

Cruise ship engines were designed to generate the energy they needed both for propulsion and for operating lights, refrigeration, heating and cooling, and other onboard services. The main fuel used by cruise ships was the relatively dirty-burning heavy fuel oil (HFO). Distillate and low-sulfur fuel oil (LSFO) offered a cleaner alternative to HFO, but usually cost between 10 and 50 percent more. Fuel costs typically accounted for around 15 percent of operating costs on a cruise ship.

Engine exhaust was the primary source of air emissions; these included carbon dioxide, nitrous and sulfur oxides, and particulate matter. Around 2 to 3 percent of global carbon dioxide emissions came from maritime shipping, mostly from the 50,000 merchant ships plying the ocean. The 350 cruise ships contributed in a small way to this problem. The impact of shipping on SOX and NOX was greater: the maritime industry as a whole accounted for approximately 4 percent and 7 percent, respectively, of global SOX and NOX emissions, with cruise ships contributing part of this.

Regulation of the Maritime Industry

Regulations governing the maritime industry and its environmental impacts were complex and multilayered. Shipping activities were governed by a mixture of United Nations conventions, the international law of the sea, the laws of various nations, and voluntary rules established by industry trade associations.

Several formal institutions and instruments provided mechanisms for cooperation among national governments in managing the ocean commons. The International Maritime Organization (IMO), a specialized agency of the United Nations, regulated the international shipping industry. One of its most important initiatives was the IMO Convention for the Prevention for Pollution from Ships, known as MARPOL (for "marine pollution"). Ships operating under the flags of countries that had signed the MARPOL convention were subject to its rules. (Countries responsible for 99 percent of marine shipping had signed.) Other international agreements included the UN Convention on the Law of the Sea (UNCLOS), a comprehensive treaty establishing protocols for the use and exploitation of the ocean and its resources. The International Whaling Convention regulated the hunting of great whales. Overall, regulations of the maritime industry had become stricter over time, as concern about the ecological health of the oceans had grown. For example, international bodies had created special emission control areas, where discharges of airborne pollutants were sharply curtailed.

The country where a ship was registered, called the *flag state,* was obligated to ensure that its ships complied with regulations set down in international conventions to which the flag state was a signatory. Even if a ship was registered in a flag state that had not ratified a particular IMO convention, it had to obey rules adopted by any nations it visited. Since almost all cruise ship ports were in nations that had ratified the IMO regulations, as a practical matter, cruise ships were required to abide by IMO regulations.

Individual nations had also established their own regulations, and cruise ships had to follow the rules of any country they visited. For example, in 2009 the United States and Canada joined together to establish an Emissions Control Area covering all of North America, with the goal of reducing pollution in coastal waters. In situations where national rules were stricter than those of international conventions, the cruise industry had to follow the national rules.

In addition, the CLIA had developed its own waste management practices and procedures. In many instances, these voluntary environmental standards exceeded the requirements of both U.S. and international laws. For example, while regulations permitted the discharge of untreated blackwater 12 nautical miles from shore, CLIA standards called for treating all blackwater using advanced water purification systems, no matter how far from shore it was discharged. However, CLIA did not proscribe the manner in which the voluntary standards were to be implemented, nor impose penalties for failing to follow them.

Holland America Lines was committed to meeting or exceeding the standards established by all relevant international and national laws (including those of the Netherlands, where its ships were registered), as well as the CLIA standards.

HAL's Sustainability Practices

HAL operated its sustainability programs relatively independently of its parent firm, Carnival. The Safety and Environmental Management Systems (SEMS) Department oversaw HAL's programs in this area. Bill Morani served as vice president for SEMS; he, in turn, reported to Dan Grausz, executive vice president of fleet operations. SEMS was responsible for ensuring that all employees understood their roles and responsibilities. It also developed written environmental procedures, emergency preparedness plans, and performance targets and oversaw a rigorous environmental audit program. Onboard each ship, a safety, environmental and health (SHE) officer advised the captain's staff on compliance policies, processes, and environmental regulatory requirements.

In 2009, HAL released its first sustainability report covering activities from 2007–09; a second report was issued in 2012. Their sustainability reports used the Global Reporting Initiative's (GRI) G3 Guidelines as its organizing framework. The data in this baseline report was not independently verified, although this was not unusual among first-time GRI reporters. Their environmental management system (EMS) was recertified in 2009 and 2012 as meeting ISO 14001 environmental standards.

HAL's sustainability reports documented the company's progress in a number of areas. These included the following highlights:

- HAL was instrumental in developing advanced wastewater purification systems (AWWPS) technology for use in cruise ships, first installed on the MS Statendam in 2002. These systems used a combination of screening, maceration, biodigestion, ultra-filtration, and ultraviolet light to clean wastewater to a much higher standard that conventional systems. By 2012, 12 of HAL's 15 ships used AWWPSs (compared with 40 percent in the rest of the industry). HAL was also a leader in improving bilge water treatment prior to overboard discharge.

- HAL also had used various conservation strategies to reduce the amount of water used and discharged. In 2009, HAL used their environmental management system (EMS) to set a target of using 7 percent less water than in 2008. They exceeded the target using a number of approaches including low-flush toilets, low-flow showerheads and faucets, and specialized pool filters.

- HAL had taken steps to reduce its solid waste flow. Onboard, paper and cardboard were shredded and often incinerated to reduce the fire load carried by the vessel. Food waste was run through a pulper and discharged more than 12 nautical miles from shore. The company recycled much of its glass, paper, cardboard, aluminum, steel cans, and plastics on shore. It replaced highly toxic dry-cleaning fluids with a nontoxic technology, developed a paint and thinner recycling program, and implemented a list of approved chemicals to reduce the use of toxics. HAL donated many partially used products and reusable items (mattresses, toiletries, linen, clothing, etc.) to nonprofit organizations.

One supply issue that received special attention was the sustainability of seafood served on board. In 2010, Hal partnered with the Marine Conservation Institute (MCI) to protect marine ecosystems in a program called "Our Marvelous Oceans." MCI was a nonprofit organization working with scientists, politicians, government officials, and other organizations around the world to protect essential ocean places and the wild species in them. Under the terms of the partnership, HAL committed to purchasing sustainable seafood to be served on board. It also developed a series of video programs about the oceans to be shown to guests, and supported MCI grants to graduate students and young scientists in marine ecology. As part of the partnership, MCI staff evaluated the sustainability of over 40 species of fish. HAL committed to use best choice items where available and to discontinue purchase of not-sustainable species. When more information was needed, HAL went back to the suppliers, who in many cases were able to find sustainable alternatives (such as Dover sole caught with hook and lines). HAL's senior managers embraced this program, even though in some cases the cost of fish was higher.

Managing Fuel Conservation at HAL

As part of its overall sustainability initiatives, in 2005, HAL's parent, Carnival Corporation, set an ambitious goal of increasing fuel efficiency as measured by the amount of fuel used per lower berth per nautical mile by 20 percent by 2015. In order to meet this goal, HAL had established a cross-functional fuel conservation committee in 2007 that systematically identified and assessed fuel reduction opportunities, based primarily on projected fuel savings and return on investment (ROI). The committee had been very effective in adopting successful initiatives based on established financial criteria, and HAL reached the 2015 target in 2011. Exhibit B shows the company's improved fuel efficiency over time, as well as its mix of fuels used. It shows that although fuel use increased overall (due to an expanding fleet and more passengers), fuel used per lower berth steadily decreased.

HAL had reduced its fuel use through a variety of techniques, including:

- Using more energy-efficient equipment and ships.
- Conserving energy.
- Plugging into shore power when docked.
- Encouraging competition among vessels on energy efficiency.
- Sharing best practices from high-performing ships.
- Providing monetary incentives to senior shipboard staff to encourage fuel conservation practices.

In 2012, the fuel conservation committee was evaluating close to 50 initiatives to improve efficiency even further. These initiatives fell into five broad categories, most of which required capital investments in new and modified equipment:

- Sailing and maneuvering (6 initiatives), such as using software to optimize speed and maneuvering.
- Modifying or adding equipment (28 initiatives), such as upgrading air conditioner chiller control systems.
- Operational improvements (8 initiatives), such as running a seawater cooling pump while in port.

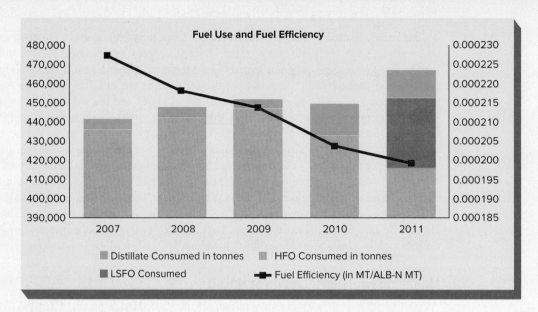

Source: Holland America Line.

Note: Fuel efficiency is measured as metric tons of fuel per lower berth/nautical mile.

- Monitoring various sources of energy consumption (10 initiatives), such as installing meters in electrical substations to monitor the energy consumption of various users.
- Waste heat recovery (4 initiatives), such as adding an additional heat exchanger to reuse high temperature waste heat for potable water heating.

The committee's spreadsheets included estimates of potential savings from each initiative and the cost per ship. Typically, the estimates of savings were measured in terms of percentage of overall fuel budget. For the 38 initiatives for which estimates had been made, 13 would probably save 0.25 percent of fuel or less, 16 would save between 0.26 and 0.99 percent, and 9 would save more than 1 percent. The committee also tracked whether each initiative was proven or assumed to be viable and its stage of implementation (study, funding required, implemented, or discontinued). Finally, based on all of this information, the committee assigned a priority (1, 2, or 3) to each initiative. Because the capital budget available to pursue fuel conservation projects was limited, even initiatives with a priority of 1 might not be implemented, or might not be implemented fleetwide. When the committee concluded that a proposed fuel conservation initiative should be implemented, it was pilot-tested on a single ship. Performance was tracked, and if the results met investment criteria, the initiative would be eligible to be rolled out to other ships.

Because of the unproven nature of the wind turbine initiative and skepticism on the part of HAL's engineering department, the fuel conservation committee had earlier assigned it a priority "3" and an estimated fuel savings of less than 0.25 percent. However, when Morani read the article about Stena Line (a ferry line providing service between Britain, Holland, and Ireland), he wondered if this option should be revisited. He learned that the two turbines installed on the Stena Jutlandica could generate about 23,000 kilowatt hours per year, equivalent to the annual domestic electricity consumption of four average homes or a reduction in fuel consumption of between 80 and 90 tons per year.

Morani began to inquire internally at HAL about the wind turbine idea. One of his direct reports had received unsubstantiated information that the Stena Line installation was projected to be very cost effective, and—contrary to intuition—the turbines actually reduced aerodynamic drag on the ferry. Morani also found another article describing how Hornblower Cruises planned to launch a hybrid vessel to take passengers on sightseeing, dinner, and social events in New York Harbor. This 600-passenger vessel would incorporate wind turbines, solar panels, and hydrogen fuel cells in addition to its diesel engine. The company believed the combination of alternative power generators would result in fuel savings that justified the investment.

Morani also consulted with Pieter Rijkaart, former director of New Builds, who had led the design and built most of HAL's current fleet. Rijkaart echoed the skepticism expressed by other engineers. For example, the engineers had noted that a cruise liner was much larger and more streamlined than a ferry, raising questions about the applicability of the Stena Line's performance results. Cost was also an issue. A pilot-test on one ship would require a large up-front investment in addition to the cost of the turbine, as it would have to be anchored to the deck and tied into the electrical grid on the ship. Rijkaart also voiced aesthetic concerns. Cruise ships were designed to be beautiful, and having bulky wind turbines on the deck could be an eyesore. Lastly, the amount of energy supplied by the wind turbines would account for an extremely small percentage of the ship's energy needs.

Morani wondered whether using wind turbines might bring intangible benefits. HAL had already demonstrated a proactive interest in alternative energy initiatives. For example, HAL had installed heat reflective film on windows to reduce the transfer of heat to the interior, thus reducing the load on air conditioners. At a cost of $170,000 per ship, and a projected fuel savings between 0.5 to 1.0 percent, three ships had already installed this technology, and other ships awaited funding. HAL had adopted an initiative involving the pumping of used cooking oil into the fuel line. This low-cost option had resulted in both the reduction of fossil fuel and avoidance of the disposal cost of drums of used cooking oil.

Wind turbines represented another opportunity for HAL to explore using alternative energy. While this could contribute to HAL's reputation as a sustainability leader in the industry, Morani did not believe that reputation should be factored into the decision. "We don't talk about whether something will get good press," he commented. While the turbines would produce only a very small amount of the electricity used on the boat, they would contribute to reduced fuel use. Morani did not have enough information to estimate ROI or payback. Given the dozens of other proposed initiatives, he wondered whether it made sense to expend effort on this particular initiative. On the other hand, he commented, "I would be concerned that we could be missing an opportunity." Morani was eager to pull together his thinking on the wind turbine initiative for the upcoming fuel conservation committee meeting.

Discussion Questions

1. What are the most significant environmental issues facing Holland America Line (HAL)?
2. In what ways has HAL gone "beyond compliance" in its environmental initiatives?
3. Do you consider HAL an ecologically sustainable organization (ESO), and why or why not? What additional steps would HAL need to take to become an ESO?
4. What are the advantages and disadvantages to HAL of its sustainability practices?
5. What action would you recommend Morani take with respect to the wind turbine initiative? If you are not sure, what additional information would be helpful?

The Carlson Company and Protecting Children in the Global Tourism Industry

Marilyn Carlson Nelson, in her seventh year as chief executive officer (CEO) of the Carlson Company, a global marketing, travel, and hospitality company, faced a major dilemma. In 2006, the company was considering a proposal to expand its luxury Regency accommodations and services to Costa Rica. The venture gave many indications of being strategically sound and highly profitable, and it would also provide a basis for future expansion throughout Latin America. However, during the feasibility study of a promising property located in Papagayo, a popular tourist destination along Costa Rica's northern coast, company executives learned that the surrounding area was notorious for child trafficking and prostitution. This was of particular concern to Carlson Nelson, because under her leadership Carlson had, in 2004, signed the *Code of Conduct for the Protection of Children from Sexual Exploitation in Travel and Tourism* (the Code). This global project brought together the travel and tourism industry and nongovernmental organizations to prevent sexual exploitation of children at tourist destinations.

As part of its obligations under the Code, Carlson had adopted a corporate ethics policy designed to eliminate any organizational association with sex trafficking. Carlson Nelson was confronted with the need to assess whether the proposed Regent resort could ensure compliance with the Code in an environment where sexual exploitation of children was often an integral part of doing business. Should Carlson Companies decide to abandon the

By Robyn Linde and H. Richard Eisenbeis. Copyright © 2011 by the *Case Research Journal* and the authors. Used by permission. All rights reserved. This case study was generously funded by the *United Front for Children Conference: Global Efforts to Combat Sexual Trafficking in Travel and Tourism*, held at the University of Minnesota in Minneapolis in April 2006. The Curtis L. Carlson Foundation was one source of funding for the conference. Interviews for the case study were conducted between 2006 and 2008 with Carlson Companies executives, including Marilyn Carlson Nelson, then president and chief executive officer of Carlson Companies; Deb Cundy, assistant dean of external relations at the Carlson School of Management at the University of Minnesota; Doug Cody, corporate vice president of public relations and communications; Kim Olson, vice president, chief communications officer; Tom Polski, vice president of global communications and external relations; Bill Van Brunt, executive vice president, Carlson Companies; and Jay Witzel, president and CEO of Carlson Hotels Worldwide. Carol Smolenski of *End Child Prostitution Child Pornography and Trafficking of Children for Sexual Purposes* (ECPAT) was an especially valuable resource during the many drafts of this case. Robyn Linde would additionally like to thank Sally Kenney, Holiday Shapiro, Kathryn Sikkink, fellow case writers in Professor Kenney's seminar on *Case Studies on Women and Public Policy* at the University of Minnesota, and the anonymous reviewers for their helpful comments on earlier drafts.

project, it would certainly lose a viable opportunity to become a major player in the high-end Central American tourism market.

Carlson Companies, Marilyn Carlson Nelson, and the Code

Carlson's history was one of the classic business success stories in the American free enterprise system. Starting in 1938 with an idea and a $55 loan, entrepreneur Curtis L. Carlson founded the Gold Bond Stamp Company in his home town of Minneapolis. He knew that grocery stores, drug stores, gas stations, and other independent merchants could use stamps to drive customer loyalty and to distinguish themselves from their competitors. During the 1950s and 1960s, Gold Bond and its sister company, Top Value Stamps, helped revolutionize the way retail goods were marketed. Trading stamps proved to be right for the times and swept the nation in a wave of dramatic growth.[1]

In the late 1960s, when the trading stamp market reached its peak, the Gold Bond Stamp Company expanded into the hospitality industry. In the 1970s, the company acquired dozens of additional businesses, including T.G.I. Friday's and Radisson. To reflect its diversification, Gold Bond changed its name to Carlson Companies in 1973. Based in Minneapolis, Minnesota, Carlson brands generated more than $31.4 billion in gross sales system-wide and employed about 188,000 people in more than 140 countries by 1999. In 2006, to demonstrate that they were one company serving a variety of needs, the firm became known as the Carlson Company.[2]

The company had long been involved in philanthropy through its Curtis L. Carlson Family Foundation. Established in 1959, the foundation was one of many avenues Carlson Companies chose to carry out its charitable work. Curtis Carlson, the son of Swedish immigrants, became widely recognized in Sweden for his success in business as well as for his charitable endeavors. His ancestral ties to Sweden eventually led to a lasting friendship between the Carlson family and the royal family of Sweden.

Marilyn Carlson Nelson, Curtis Carlson's eldest daughter, graduated with honors from Smith College with a degree in international economics and a minor in theater. She also attended the Sorbonne in Paris and the Institute Des Hautes Etudes Economiques Politiques in Geneva, Switzerland, where she studied political science and international economics. Carlson Nelson succeeded her father as president and CEO of Carlson Companies in 1998. In this role, she was responsible for the day-to-day operations of one of the largest privately held companies in the world. Carlson Nelson led the management of a global business portfolio encompassing Carlson's major operating groups, specializing in corporate solutions and consumer services: Carlson Hospitality Worldwide (hotels, restaurants, and cruise ships); Carlson Wagonlit Travel (business travel and leisure travel brand); Carlson Leisure Group (leisure travel agencies and tour operators); and Carlson Marketing Group (incentive and loyalty marketing). By 2006, under Carlson Nelson's leadership, Carlson's annual sales exceeded $37 billion and it employed over 150,000 people worldwide. She was widely recognized as one of the world's most influential women.[3]

---

[1] Based on "Company History," *www.carlson.com.*

[2] Based on "Our Founder and History," *www.clcfamilyfoundation.com.*

[3] Beverly Kopf and Bobbie Birleffi, "Not Her Father's Chief Executive," *U.S. News and World Report,* October 2006, *http://www.usnews.com/usnews/news/articles/061022/30nelson.htm,* last accessed February 24, 2011; Maggie Rauch, "Leading the Field: Marilyn Carlson-Nelson," *Incentive Magazine,* May 1, 2006, *http://www.incentivemag.com/News/Industry/Articles/Leading-the-Field—Marilyn-Carlson-Nelson/,* last accessed February 24, 2011; "Carlson Chair and CEO Named 'Businesswoman of the Year,'" *Travel Daily News,* April 2005; "Marilyn Carlson Nelson (Chairman & CEO, Carlson Companies)" *Ethisphere,* December 2007, *http://ethisphere.com/marilyn-carlson-nelson/,* last accessed February 24, 2011; "The Word's Most Powerful Women," *Forbes,* 2005, *http://www.forbes.com/lists/2005/11/PV8L.html,* last accessed February 24, 2011.

Carlson Nelson defined her role as president and CEO of Carlson as follows:

> A CEO has to train and operate like a jet pilot. Once the company's talented executive team is flying in formation, I'm usually raising peripheral vision issues—how a decision is going to impact other pieces of the business, how it's going to impact our shareholder relationships and our banking relationships. I really go through the various stakeholders in my mind. And I might try to impact the final outcome so that it will bring people the broadest possible ownership of the decision.

Carlson Nelson's general management style was described by other executives in the organization as being "collective." Kim Olson, vice president and chief communication officer, described Carlson Nelson as:

> . . . having a participative leadership style. When making decisions at the corporate level, we hear and discuss all points of view before arriving at a decision. We believe these collective decisions enhance our sense of global corporate citizenship.

Tourism and the Commercial Sexual Exploitation of Children

Although the commercial sexual exploitation of children occurred in countries worldwide, the growing popularity and declining cost of travel and the rise of new communication technologies had changed the nature of child exploitation by facilitating the rise of global sex tourism. The World Tourism Organization defined organized sex tourism as:

> Trips organized from within the tourism sector, or from outside this sector but using its structures and networks, with the primary purpose of effecting a commercial sexual relationship by the tourist with residents at the destination.

Prostitution, child prostitution, and sexual exploitation of children have existed throughout history. However, prior to the last quarter of the 20th century, the child segment had been confined largely to the poorer, more destitute countries of the world where selling female children for sex was often seen as an accepted means of family survival. By the 1990s, the survival dimension had changed dramatically. Trafficking children for sex had become a formidable international business and part of a multi-billion-dollar industry in which approximately two million children were exploited annually.

Basically, sex trafficking was a type of commercial trade in people, either across borders or within countries, whereby individuals were forced into sexual slavery. Children under the age of 18 made up a large portion of this trade and were trafficked for multiple reasons, including forced labor, criminal activity, and sexual exploitation. The travel and tourism industry facilitated the trafficking of children in two ways: (1) hotels, airlines, trains, and buses provided the means by which children were trafficked; and (2) more commonly, the industry transported the sex tourists to his/her destination and provided accommodations once there.

A few travel companies actually targeted sex tourists and actively sought their business. For example, an advertisement by Lauda Air, an Austrian airline, consisted of a picture of a partially clothed girl and captions reading, "From Thailand with Love," and "the tarts in the Bangkok Baby Club are waiting for us." Generally, however, companies in the travel and tourism industry downplayed their role in the sex trade and the sexual exploitation of children by turning a blind eye toward tourist industry practices that inadvertently exposed children around the world to sexual abuse and violence.

International and U.S. Law Regarding Sex Trafficking

International legal efforts to protect women and children from trafficking were first made at the beginning of the 20th century, when many conventions were established to end what was then referred to as "white slave traffic." Both international and U.S. enforcement officials had been unwavering in their condemnation of the trafficking of children. In addition, the International Criminal Court had declared it a crime against humanity, and a number of other international treaties and declarations had condemned the practice and called on states to prevent it. The most important and widely cited international agreement for the protection of children is the 1990 *Convention on the Rights of the Child,* which had been ratified by nearly every state in the international system. Article 35 of this convention provided that "States shall take all appropriate national, bilateral, and multilateral measures to prevent the abduction, sale, or traffic of children for any purpose or in any form."

Children's advocates had also targeted the demand side of child sex trafficking in hopes of curtailing the number of tourists who sexually exploited children while traveling. In 1994, the Child Sexual Abuse Prevention Act made it illegal for U.S. citizens and permanent-resident aliens to travel abroad to commit sexual acts with minors. As a result, the U.S. government was able to prosecute Americans for sexual acts with children even if those acts took place outside U.S. borders. Moreover, efforts to prosecute travel agencies that catered to sex tourists continued to increase.

Sex Trafficking and Child Sexual Exploitation in Costa Rica

By the late 1980s, Costa Rica had become one of the principal tourist destinations in Central America, and the expanding industry became the country's primary source of foreign capital. According to the U.S. Department of State, the boom in tourism had also resulted in Costa Rica becoming a "source, transit, and destination country" for sex trafficking.[4] Women and girls were trafficked into Costa Rica from Nicaragua, the Dominican Republic, Colombia, Guatemala, Russia, and Eastern Europe for sexual exploitation. Costa Rican women and girls were trafficked within the country as well as to other Central American countries, Mexico, and Japan. The problem of child prostitution in Costa Rica was so serious that one NGO, the National Institute for Children (PANI), put the number of child prostitutes at 3,000 in the capital, San Jose, alone. This group, along with other NGOs, had continued to fight against sex tourism and had condemned the practice in the West.

Nongovernmental organizations began to raise concerns about Costa Rica's problem with sex tourists and child exploitation in the late 1990s, but the Costa Rican government did not make concerted efforts to address the issue until 2006.[5] Not until 2009 did the

---

[4] Casa Alianza and ECPAT International, "Creating a Database as a Tool For Campaigning," San Jose (2002); ECPAT International, "Five Years after Stockholm," The Fifth Report on the Implementation of the Agenda for Action Adopted at the World Congress against Commercial Sexual Exploitation of Children, Sweden (2001); ECPAT International, "Informe Global de Monitoreo de las acciones en contra de la explotacion sexual comercial de ninos, ninas y adolescentes: Costa Rica" (2006); Michael B. Farrell, "Global Campaign to Police Child Sex Tourism," *The Christian Science Monitor,* April 22, 2004; Julia O'Connell Davidson and Jacqueline Sanchez Taylor, "Child Prostitution and Sex Tourism: Costa Rica," ECPAT International (1995); Susan Song, "Children as Tourist Attractions," Youth Advocate Program International Resources Paper, Washington, D.C. (2004); U.S. Department of State, "Trafficking in Persons Report" (2002); U.S. Department of State, "Trafficking in Persons Report" (2006); U.S. Department of State, "Trafficking in Persons Report" (2007); U.S. Department of State, "Trafficking in Persons Report" (2009); U.S. Department of State, "Trafficking in Persons Report" (2010); U.S. Department of State, Bureau of Democracy, Human Rights and Labor, Country Reports on Human Rights Practices, "Costa Rica" (2005).

[5] See U.S. Department of State "Trafficking in Persons Report"from 2002 to 2010 to see the evolution of Costan Rican efforts to curb child trafficking.

country make all forms of trafficking illegal: trafficking became punishable by prison terms of 6 to 10 years, which could be increased to 16 years if a minor was involved.[6] Despite these penalties, the U.S. Department of State determined that the government of Costa Rica did not meet the "minimum standards" for eliminating trafficking as endorsed by the United States.

The Marriott Incident

In 2002, a Marriott Resort Hotel employee in Papagayo, Costa Rica, was indicted for the aggravated pimping of minors in a case that involved a number of its hotel employees. The fallout for Marriott was next to catastrophic. The Interfaith Center on Corporate Responsibility, a coalition of faith-based investors that files shareholder actions against corporations in the name of social responsibility, organized a widespread shareholder campaign against Marriott. The First Swedish National Pension Fund (Första AP-fonde) also played a key role in drafting a shareholder resolution condemning Marriott for failing to adopt policies that would prevent similar exploitation from happening in the future. Marriott failed to respond. In 2005, immediately preceding its annual stockholder meeting, the resolution became public knowledge. Marriott was immediately subjected to severe and damaging criticism throughout the world. Although Marriott had been pressured prior to the litigation to adopt a strong policy against sexual exploitation of children, it had failed to do so. However, as a result of the international outrage stemming from the shareholder resolution, the firm undertook an internal review of its policies that eventually produced a human rights policy to combat child sex trafficking, somewhat placating its critics.[7]

Queen Silvia, the Code, and Carlson Company's Response

In 1998, in response to concerns about the ways in which the travel and tourism industry facilitated child trafficking and at the initiative of Queen Silvia of Sweden, an influential NGO (ECPAT—End Child Prostitution, Child Pornography, and Trafficking of Children for Sexual Purposes), the Scandinavian Tourism Industry, and the World Tourism Organization combined forces to create a Code of Conduct for companies in the industry. The Code was a voluntary commitment for travel and tourism companies to pledge their aid in combating child trafficking. Key elements of the code included:

1. Establishing an ethical policy regarding commercial sexual exploitation of children.
2. Training personnel in the country of origin and travel destinations.
3. Introducing a clause in contracts with suppliers, stating a common repudiation of commercial sexual exploitation of children.
4. Providing information to travelers by means of catalogs, brochures, in-flight films, ticket slips, and home pages, etc.

---

[6] Although 268 Costa Rican companies and organizations have become members to the code. See *www.thecode.org* for more information.

[7] Forsta AP-fonden, "Första AP-fonden Influences Marriott to Combat Child Sex Tourism," *http://www.ap1.se/en /Asset-management/Ethical-and-environmental-consideration-in-our-investments/Long-term-commitment-pays-off /Forsta-AP-fonden-influences-Marriott-to-combat-child-sex-tourism/*, last accessed February 24, 2011; Interfaith Centre on Corporate Responsibility, "Selling Innocence: Child Sex Tourisim," *http://www.docstoc.com/docs/66828019 /Accor-Hospitality-Asset-Management*, last accessed February 24, 2011; "Marriott Hotel Chain Combats Child Sexual Exploitation" (December 2006), *http://www.humantrafficking.org/updates/494*, last accessed February 24, 2011.

5. Providing information to local "key persons" at the destinations.
6. Filing annual reports to various monitoring bodies.

Companies that adopted the Code were required to submit annual reports on their corporate practices to international, transnational, and national monitoring bodies to demonstrate compliance with the Code, share information, build know-how about best practices, and identify problems. Companies that adopted the Code were also encouraged to monitor their employees and the practices of their contractors through documented spot checks.

As of November 2009, more than 947 companies in 37 countries had signed the Code, affecting millions of tourists who employed the services of these companies. However, only two U.S. companies had signed. The absence of signatories among U.S. companies presented a serious problem given that an estimated 25 percent of sex tourists outside of the United States were Americans who presumably utilized U.S. travel and tourism services. The majority of U.S. hoteliers, travel agencies, airlines, and tour companies had not signed the Code for fear of such consequences as:

1. Negative publicity that their adoption of the Code might generate.
2. The burden the Code imposed on companies to police their employees and contractors.
3. Litigation from trafficked children themselves.
4. Litigation initiated by guests who might witness trafficking while utilizing a company's travel and tourist services.
5. Absence of other corporate signatories.

Carlson Nelson and Queen Silvia of Sweden shared a long-held concern for at-risk children, which led to numerous collective projects over the years. Foremost among them was the establishment of the World Childhood Foundation, founded in 1999 by Queen Silvia along with 14 cofounders, including the Carlson Family Foundation. When asked by the Queen to become a signatory to the Code in 2004, Carlson Nelson enthusiastically committed. Carlson Companies thus became the first major North American travel and tourism company to sign, committing to the Code for all of Carlson's brands.[8] In signing the code, Carlson Nelson assured the tourism industry that all future decisions made by Carlson's executive team would take into consideration the next generation—"thinking about children and teens and the impact of the company's actions upon their welfare and development."

When asked about Carlson Companies' early adoption of the Code, Carlson Nelson remarked:

> We like to think that we play a leadership role on this particular issue. Sometimes
> I wish we weren't as far out in front as a leader because we had hoped that more
> travel and hotel companies would sign on to the Code.

However, initially there was not full agreement among executives within Carlson Companies that signing the Code was a good idea.[9] Concerns identified by Carlson executives essentially mirrored the concerns of other executives in the travel and tourism

---

[8] The other North American signatories at the time were the American Society of Travel Agents and Amazon Tours. Since then, three more companies have signed the Code: Millennium Hotel St. Louis, Delta Airlines, and Hilton Hotels.

[9] However, each Carlson executive interviewed made it clear to the researcher that signing the Code was Carlson Nelson's decision and that it was adopted as policy because she advocated for it. No different or alternative views were expressed during the course of the interviews.

industry. Doug Cody, corporate vice president of public relations and communications, further questioned:

> Why should Carlson get involved in something so ugly when there are so many other worthwhile causes that we could be involved with? . . . Do we really want to associate our name with such an ugly thing? No other major travel and tourism company has signed the Code in North America, and the issue of child trafficking is not widely discussed in the media. My primary concern is associating with it. Even though we are fighting against it, it could backfire and hurt you. People could misunderstand it or believe that somehow we were connected with it. There were a lot of reasons to say "no."

Cody's opinion about the public relations liability of the Code abruptly changed when Carlson Nelson invited him along to witness the signing of the Code at the United Nations with Queen Silvia. Upon seeing dozens of television cameras from around the world present to witness the signing, it occurred to Cody that the media exposure would prove very beneficial to the company—indeed "the eyes of the world were watching." Even so, Cody argued that other companies in the travel and tourism industry would be "steered away from the Code because of the legal ramifications if the Code is not followed once signed."

In retrospect, Tom Polski, vice president of global communications and external relations, said:

> The shift in thinking at Carlson Companies about the Code resulted from increased awareness of the whole issue through activities at the World Childhood Foundation. Carlson Companies and the travel and tourism industry are in the "happiness" business, and child trafficking is not very pleasant and people sometimes don't want to hear unpleasant things. I supported the Code because child exploitation is a reality in the travel and tourism business.

By many accounts, Carlson's corporate culture was noticeably affected by its newfound commitment to curtailing child trafficking. Jay Witzel, president and CEO of Carlson Hotels Worldwide, said:

> Once Carlson Companies signed the Code, the level of commitment to end child trafficking throughout the entire Carlson system rose to an unbelievable level where people actually started to say, "That is not going to happen here." Once you get to that position . . . the people on the staff have come to the conclusion that they can do something about it . . . it is not a hopeless situation. Signing the Code raised our diligence. It certainly raised our commitment and it raised the involvement of the greater community of Carlson hotels, their owners, operators, and employees to do something about it.

 ## The Dilemma

Within a few years after signing the Code, Carlson Companies began planning for development of a Regent Hotel and Resort in the Papagayo region of Costa Rica. Regent, Carlson's luxury brand, provided higher-end accommodations to its patrons than its Radisson brand, which was already established in the capital of San Jose. The venture would be Carlson's first luxury hotel and resort in Central America. It offered Carlson the opportunity to expand its luxury chain into Costa Rica's lucrative and rapidly growing high-end tourist market, as well as the potential for further expansion into Central and South America.

Initially, the proposed project was well received by Carlson executives, as its Radisson Hotel in San Jose was doing well.

It was Jay Witzel, president and CEO of Carlson Hotels Worldwide, who learned during the course of his research of the extensive problem of child sex trafficking in Costa Rica and immediately brought it to Carlson Nelson's attention. Witzel's concerns were well-founded. Between the opening of the first Radisson Hotel in San Jose in 1996 and the new opportunity in Papagayo, two important events had occurred that had a major impact on whether the project should be given the go ahead. First, Carlson had signed the Code of Conduct, creating new obligations within its companies in the fight against child sex trafficking. Concerns were raised about whether management would be able to fully enforce the Code once the resort became operational. If Carlson could not fully guarantee the protection of children within the resort complex, could or should this be considered a viable business opportunity? The second concern stemmed from the Marriott child sex trafficking case and its implications for Carlson's Regent resort. The fact that Carlson would face a similar environment in Costa Rica as Marriott was cause for alarm. Any plans to introduce the Regent brand to Costa Rica would have to be reassessed, especially in light of the proliferation of child sex trafficking in Costa Rica and new concerns over trafficking litigation.

However, the potential advantages of developing the hotel in Costa Rica were many. First, Carlson executives believed that it presented a lucrative business opportunity, one that they were hard-pressed to abandon. Additionally, the executives saw the opportunity to serve as a positive force and role model in the travel and tourism business, a prospect that was especially attractive to Carlson Nelson given her commitment to children. Witzel described his conversations about the Costa Rica project with Carlson Nelson as "robust." If they could succeed in meeting the challenges of socially responsible hotel management in a country rife with child sex trafficking, they could demonstrate the project's feasibility to others in the industry and the world.

But changes to the policies and practices of other travel and tourism companies were not the only positive externality that Carlson Nelson and her executives hoped for. They also believed that by empowering hotel employees to monitor and act against the exploitation of children in Carlson hotels, this vigilance would have a spillover effect, benefiting the communities to which the employees belonged. Carlson Nelson argued that:

> The more we train our employees, the better the potential that they will use their judgment and in a way, it becomes like a social anthropology and there is a higher likelihood that a culture will reject or self-correct around somebody who is acting inconsistently with our policy.

The goal was that the employees themselves would serve as agents of social change, improving the larger community of which they were a part.

Although the promises of both social change and increased revenue were certainly tempting, the project's disadvantages also caused Carlson management several concerns. The first arose as Carlson Nelson and the executive team watched the Marriott litigation. As the case unfolded, they became more and more aware of the impact the case would have on Carlson's future Costa Rica operations. They took special note of the Swedish National Pension Fund's blacklisting of the company and the very public international shaming of Marriott over the trafficking issue. It was disturbing that the actions of just a handful of Marriott employees brought that company international rebuke and a shareholder resolution against it. Second, there was the risk that the international community would associate Carlson's Regent Hotel with child sex trafficking simply because it was located in Costa Rica. A third concern was that the resort would fail to meet its obligations under the

Code and Carlson would risk public censure from the Code's monitoring body. Indeed, a variety of powerful stakeholders, including local politicians, corrupt law enforcement officers, travel agents, and others, would benefit substantially from child sex trafficking and could pressure employees to violate the Code.

Additionally, for the Code's implementation to be successful there had to be commitment from franchise owners—no easy task. Enforcement would require employees and contractors to monitor guests, business transactions, and one another in a way that might not be possible or even advisable. Was it worth the risk to place the reputation of Carlson, a highly respected international company, in the hands of franchise owners and untested local employees, some of whom might have multiple and conflicting loyalties? And, there was some doubt whether it would be possible for a hotel resort to create an environment intolerant of child sex trafficking without losing a significant portion of its high-end tourist trade. Was it possible that sex tourism constituted such a large share of tourism in Papagayo that by rejecting it in its hotel, Carlson would be unable to earn an acceptable return on its investment?

Yet, Carlson executives agreed that the biggest disincentive to developing the hotel was the fear of litigation, both from tourists who might witness child exploitation—despite efforts on Carlson's part to deter the practice—and from those who might be victimized by traffickers utilizing Carlson's services. If Carlson continued with the project, would it risk compromising its commitment to the Code and to eliminating the sexual exploitation of children? On the other hand, if Carlson abandoned the project, the company would forfeit a potentially lucrative business opportunity. Time was drawing near for the final decision. Should Carlson Nelson push forward with the project? Then again, were there other possible alternatives?

Discussion Questions

1. Why did the Carlson Company sign the Code of Conduct for the Protection of Children from Sexual Exploitation in Travel and Tourism? Do you agree with the company's decision, and why or why not?

2. What are the advantages and disadvantages to the Carlson Company of developing the hotel complex in Costa Rica?

3. What stakeholders would be affected by a decision to develop the hotel complex in Costa Rica, and how would they be affected? What are their interests and sources of power in this situation?

4. Would developing the hotel complex in Costa Rica be ethical, or not? Why do you think so?

5. If the Carlson Company decides to proceed with the hotel development, what steps can it take to assure that the company remains in compliance with the code of conduct it has signed?

Ventria Bioscience and the Controversy over Plant-Made Medicines

"Ventria is dedicated to leading the development of plant-made pharmaceuticals that promise affordable human health products for the global community."

Scott Deeter, president and CEO, Ventria Bioscience

It was a warm, sunny day in mid-July 2004—perfect conditions for growing rice in California's lushly irrigated Sacramento Valley. But *their* rice was not in the ground, thought Scott Deeter with mounting frustration. Deeter was the president and CEO of Ventria Bioscience, a Sacramento, California–based biotechnology firm. The 20-person start-up had developed an innovative process to produce pharmaceutical proteins in the seeds of genetically modified rice. Ventria believed that its first product—a medicine designed to lessen the severity of childhood diarrhea—held great promise for public health, particularly in the developing world. The company had tested its bioengineered rice in small test plots near its headquarters. That spring, it had sought to plant at least 120 acres to begin commercial-scale production. But in its effort to obtain the necessary permits, Ventria had been stymied at nearly every turn. Facing vigorous opposition from environmentalists, food safety activists, consumer advocates, and rice farmers, the California Secretary of Agriculture had denied the company's request to plant rice on a commercial scale. Now Deeter had to figure out the best way forward for the fledgling, venture capital–backed firm.

Ventria Bioscience

Ventria Bioscience (originally called Applied Phytologics) was founded in 1993 by Dr. Raymond Rodriguez, a molecular biologist on the faculty of the University of California–Davis. In the early 1980s, Rodriguez and his graduate students had embarked on an ambitious research program aimed at improving the productivity of rice, a crop he recognized as being of great importance to human nutrition worldwide. With the support of a state government grant to encourage the commercialization of basic scientific research, Rodriguez

By Anne T. Lawrence. Copyright © 2008 by the author. All rights reserved. An earlier version of this case was presented at the 2008 annual meeting of the North American Case Research Association. The author is grateful to Dr. Raymond Rodriguez for his assistance in the preparation of this case. The author also gratefully acknowledges research funding provided by the Don and Sally Lucas Foundation.

began to develop techniques to "express" medically useful proteins in rice plants, from which they could be extracted and purified. He explained,

> We were working on expression technology—taking a gene that encodes for a medical protein and using recombinant DNA technology to produce that protein in the plant. The key technology for Ventria was the ability to express a protein abundantly in a harvestable organ or tissue. That was the breakthrough. Roots or tubers like a potato, fruits like a tomato, ears of corn, or grains of rice—those are harvestable. Expressing the protein of interest in stems and leaves is a waste of effort and resources. If you can focus your overexpression technology on a harvestable organ, you are way ahead in terms of efficiency. Very few research labs or ag biotech companies could do this at that time.

In 1993, Rodriguez incorporated Applied Phytologics to commercialize his techniques for producing medical proteins in rice. In his search for funding, he approached Dr. William Rutter, the founder and board chairman of the Emeryville biotechnology firm Chiron, with whom he had earlier worked as a postdoctoral fellow at the University of California–San Francisco. Rutter was immediately attracted to the potential of the new venture. Rodriguez recalled,

> [Rutter and I] both like disruptive technologies. Neither of us was interested in incremental improvements in yield and cost efficiencies. We *were* excited, however, by the prospects of order-of-magnitude improvements—thousand-fold increases in yield with similar fold decreases in costs. For a technology-based industry, that's really critical. We wanted to revolutionize the biopharmaceutical industry by putting production on a metric ton scale instead of a gram or kilogram scale.

With the help of an early "angel" investment from Rutter, Rodriguez opened a lab in Sacramento in 1994 and recruited a small staff of scientists and technicians, including some of his former graduate students. Within a few years, the new company launched research on around 15 different medical and industrial proteins, filed dozens of patent applications, and continued to improve its core technology, which eventually became known as the "ExpressTec System." In the venture's early years, Rodriguez chaired the board, as well as overseeing the company's R&D activities.

As the venture continued its research and development, Dr. Rodriguez gradually built a board of directors of biotech leaders and seasoned entrepreneurs. Early board members included Dr. William J. Rutter and Dr. Pablo Valenzuela, cofounders of Chiron Corporation and early pioneers in biotechnology; William H. Rutter, an attorney and venture capitalist; Ron Vogel, president of Great Western Malting; and bioentrepreneur Dr. Roberto Crea. In 2000, Thomas N. Urban, the former chairman and CEO of Pioneer Hi-Bred International, Inc., a leading agricultural seed company, was recruited to chair the board. Melvin Booth, the former CEO of MedImmune, later became a director. So did William W. Crouse, a general partner of HealthCare Ventures, and David Dwyer, a general partner in Vista Ventures; both venture capital funds specialized in biotechnology. Members of the board and their organizations collectively provided more than 85 percent of the company's financing.

Overseeing the company's day-to-day operations was a management team consisting of Frank E. Hagie, Jr., president and CEO; Dr. Delia R. Bethell, a biologist and Ventria's vice president of clinical development; and Dr. Ning Huang, a molecular biologist and vice president of research and development. (Dr. Huang had received his Ph.D. from Dr. Rodriguez in 1990.) In 2000, Dr. Rodriguez resigned from the board to devote more time to his university research and teaching. As chairman emeritus, Dr. Rodriguez continued to support the company but did not participate directly in its day-to-day operations or governance.

Plant-Made Medicines

Designing plants to produce pharmaceuticals—the work that Rodriguez and his colleagues were pursuing—represented the second wave of agricultural biotechnology. The first wave concentrated on adding traits, such as insect resistance and herbicide tolerance, to edible crops—such as corn, canola, and soybeans—and to fiber crops such as cotton. For example, "RoundUp-Ready" soybeans, developed by Monsanto, were genetically engineered to be impervious to the herbicide RoundUp, allowing farmers to spray the field with weedkiller without hurting the soybean crop. "YieldGuard" corn plants were genetically engineered to resist the corn borer, a common insect pest. The second wave, of which Ventria was part, involved the use of genetic engineering to "phytomanufacture" protein pharmaceuticals and other commercially valuable compounds in plants.

Plant-made medicines, particularly those made in rice, held many real and potential benefits. First, it was too expensive to chemically synthesize anything but the smallest proteins. Most therapeutic proteins, therefore, were produced in mammalian or microbial cell cultures. This was costly and sometimes dangerous, as animal tissues could transmit viruses or prions (such as the infectious agents that caused "mad cow" disease). Second, plant-grown medicines could also be produced much less expensively than they could be using conventional, mammalian cell-culture technology. Third, rice and other agricultural crops could be stored at room temperature from months to years, allowing processing facilities to operate year-round and respond quickly to customer demand. Fourth, the well-established existing infrastructure for harvesting, storing, and milling rice could support the production of rice-based medical proteins. A final advantage of using rice was that medical proteins produced in food crops could be delivered orally without extensive purification. The hypoallergenic and hyperdigestible rice starch served as an ideal natural medium for the recombinant protein.[1]

On the other hand, the technology also carried potential risks. Most plant-made medicines were grown in crops also used for food, posing the danger that pharmacologically active plants might become mistakenly commingled with and contaminate the human or animal food supply. Pharmaceutical plants might crossbreed with wild plants or food crops, creating unwanted hybrids, or pose a threat to insects. Also, since the modified genes being transferred into plants often originated as human or animal genes, the potential ethical issues were profound. The public's reactions to plant-made pharmaceuticals were likely to be extreme, given the high benefits, potential risks, and deep moral quandaries posed by these new technologies.

One earlier incident, in particular, had highlighted the potential risk. In 2001, ProdiGene, a Texas biotech company, had planted a test plot of corn that had been genetically engineered to produce a pig vaccine. The following year, the same field was planted with conventional soybeans, which became contaminated by volunteer corn that had sprouted from the previous season's seeds. By the time this was discovered, the soybeans had been harvested and stored in a silo containing 500,000 bushels. The genetically modified corn tainted the entire lot of soybeans, which had to be destroyed. ProdiGene was fined $250,000 and had to pay for the cleanup. Although the contaminated soybeans never reached the food supply, some saw the incident as a warning of the possible risks of commingling.[2]

[1] Scott Deeter, "Prepared Remarks," House of Representatives, Small Business Committee, Hearing on Different Applications for Genetically Modified Crops, June 29, 2005.

[2] "Pharming Reaps Regulatory Changes," *http://pewagbiotech.org/buzz.*

In 2004, seven companies and research organizations in the United States held permits for field tests of genetically engineered pharmaceutical plants.[3] Most, like Ventria, were small, private firms that relied mainly on venture capital as they worked toward the goal of an initial public offering or acquisition by a larger firm. Many were thinly capitalized. In 2004, according to the Biotechnology Industry Organization (BIO), an industry trade association, 60 percent of all biotechnology firms had less than a two-year supply of cash on hand and 30 percent had less than a one-year supply. Reflecting a high concentration of professionals, wages in the biotechnology industry were relatively high, averaging $65,775 in 2004; top companies invested $130,000 per employee in research and development. With high wages and research costs, many of these firms had high burn rates. A successful product launch, according to BIO, could take 10 to 15 years and cost as much as $1 billion in private investment.[4]

Lactiva and Lysomin

In April 2002, Ventria's board appointed Deeter to succeed Hagie as president and CEO. Born in Kansas, Deeter had completed his undergraduate work in economics at the University of Kansas and had then gone on to earn an MBA at the University of Chicago and a Masters of Science at the London School of Economics. He had begun his career in the technology and life sciences group of the Wall Street investment bank Salomon Brothers. He then took a position with the agribusiness firm Cargill, where he worked on a joint venture with Hoffman LaRoche to make human health products from soybeans. From Cargill, Deeter moved to Koch Industries as vice president for agriculture, where he was involved in negotiations to buy Purina Mills in 1998. In 1999, Deeter left Koch to launch CyberCrops, a venture capital–backed website that hosted an online grain exchange service and provided news, weather, and other information to farmers. Deeter sold the business in April 2001, after the dot-com firm was unable to attract additional capital.[5]

Deeter's first task as the new CEO of Ventria was to help Rodriguez and the board winnow down the professor's long list of projects to one or two that had the greatest likelihood of successful commercialization. Deeter and his team analyzed some two dozen possible medically active proteins. They asked three key questions of each one. Did it meet a demonstrated need? Was another company already working on it? Could it be delivered orally or topically, as opposed to injected? Rodriguez later recalled,

> What we were looking for was a protein that was extremely valuable to human health and in extremely short supply, with no competition, that could be administered orally in a partially purified form.

---

[3] "Regulation of Plant-Based Pharmaceuticals," Congressional Research Service Report for Congress, March 8, 2005, p. 1. Other sources give a higher figure for the number of organizations involved in biopharming. See, for example, "Biopharming: The Emerging World Market of Plant-Based Therapeutics," *Theta Reports,* November 2002; "The Transgenic Plant Market—Profits from New Products and Novel Drugs," Drug and Market Development Corp., August 2002; and "World Agricultural Biotechnology: Transgenic Crops," Freedonia Industry Study, March 2002, cited in the *Federal Register* 68, no. 151 (April 6, 2003), p. 46435.

[4] "Biotechnology Industry Facts" and "Importation of Prescription Drugs," Biotechnology Industry Organization, *http://www .bio.org.* These figures provided by BIO are for the biotechnology industry as a whole, of which plant-made pharmaceuticals represent only a small fraction.

[5] Biographical information on Deeter appears at *http://www.ventria.com.*

The proteins Deeter and his team selected were *lactoferrin* and *lysozyme*, two compounds naturally found in human breast milk. Medical researchers had long recognized that breast-fed babies suffered less from diarrhea than did bottle-fed babies. They had hypothesized that lactoferrin and lysozyme—both considered "natural antibiotics"—conferred some protection against bacterial gastrointestinal illness. Rodriguez had developed a process for producing these compounds abundantly in the grains of genetically modified rice plants. Since the 1960s, the standard treatment for severe diarrhea had been oral rehydration solution (ORS), a mixture of salts and sugars that had been credited with saving the lives of millions. Ventria's scientists believed that adding lactoferrin and lysozyme to ORS would improve the effectiveness of this commonly used therapy for gastrointestinal illness. The company branded its lactoferrin and lysozyme products *Lactiva* and *Lysomin*, respectively.

The potential market for such a product was huge, the company reasoned. The World Health Organization estimated that the world's children suffered 4 billion episodes of diarrhea each year. Nearly 2 million of these children died annually from complications of the disease, chiefly dehydration and malnutrition. Just 65 acres of pharmaceutical rice could generate 1,400 pounds of lactoferrin, enough to treat 650,000 children with dehydration, the company estimated.[6] It also believed that these compounds might be of value in the treatment of diarrhea suffered by tourists and military personnel and in the treatment of inflammatory bowel disease.[7] The company believed early adopters might include infant formula companies, drug companies that produced ORS, and public health organizations like the Red Cross.

Regulation of Farmed Pharmaceuticals

In order to move forward with its plans to commercialize Lactiva and Lysomin, Ventria needed both federal and state regulatory approval. In 2004, the regulatory rules covering plant-made pharmaceuticals were complex and evolving. At the federal level, three agencies held partial jurisdiction over plant-made medicines.

FDA: The Food and Drug Administration (FDA) was responsible for the safety and effectiveness of food and medicines. Normally, a medicine produced in a genetically modified plant was subject to the same mandatory premarket approval procedures as any other medicine. However, Ventria had sought classification of Lactiva and Lysomin as "generally recognized as safe" (GRAS) food additives, which required a lower threshold for approval. A panel of scientific experts commissioned by the company had concluded that Lactiva and Lysomin met the GRAS standard, and the company had submitted these results to the FDA. In 2004, however, the FDA had not yet cleared Ventria's products for commercial sale. The FDA also maintained a "zero-tolerance" standard for pharmaceutical crop products in any food intended for animals or humans; any commingling of pharmaceutical crops and food crops was strictly forbidden. The FDA considered fields in which pharmaceutical crops were grown to be manufacturing facilities, and the agency had a right to inspect them. If necessary, it could condemn contaminated food and enjoin the manufacturer.

[6] "Tending the Fields: State and Federal Roles in the Oversight of Genetically Modified Crops," Pew Initiative on Food and Biotechnology, *www.pewtrusts.org/en/research-and-analysis/reports/0001/01/01/tending-the-fields*, p. 97.

[7] Scott Deeter, "Prepared Remarks," House of Representatives, Small Business Committee, Hearing on Different Applications for Genetically Modified Crops, June 29, 2005.

EPA: The Environmental Protection Agency (EPA) was responsible for the environmental safety of food crops genetically engineered to contain pesticides or other substances potentially harmful to the environment. The agency's rules required pesticides—including those engineered into a plant—to have "no unreasonable adverse impact on the environment." Pesticide-containing plants required experimental use permits for most field tests. Because Ventria's rice did not contain pesticides, these rules did not apply to it.

USDA: For its part, the U.S. Department of Agriculture's Animal and Plant Health Inspection Service (known as APHIS) had oversight of genetically modified crops being tested in fields. Plants that were genetically modified to produce pharmaceuticals always required an APHIS permit, which generally specified acceptable field testing, storage, transportation, chain of custody, and auditing requirements. APHIS forwarded its permits to the relevant state agency, which could add its own requirements. The service also conducted its own field inspections; it inspected all pharmaceutical field trials at least annually.[8] Since 1997, Ventria had applied for and received dozens of permits from APHIS to field-test its pharmaceutical crops.

In 1986, the federal government adopted a Coordinated Framework for the Regulation of Biotechnology, which proposed to use existing agencies and laws to regulate the products of biotechnology. Michael Rodemeyer, former executive director of the Pew Initiative on Food and Biotechnology, explained the complexities of this regulatory approach for both regulators and those they regulated:

> On one level . . . the Coordinated Framework is very easy to describe. The FDA is responsible for food safety, the EPA is responsible for microbes and pesticides, and APHIS is responsible for all plants. In practice, however, it is much more complex than that. Why? In part, because some products fall into multiple categories. For example, a corn plant that has been engineered to produce its own pesticide is a plant, a pesticide, and a food, so it falls under the purview of all three agencies. In addition, each of the three agencies uses different laws to govern the products of biotechnology, and most of these laws were passed well before the advent of biotechnology.[9]

The consequence of this system, for biotechnology firms, was a complex regulatory landscape with multiple, overlapping requirements.

California Rice Industry

In California, genetically engineered rice required the approval not only of federal and state regulators, but also indirectly of the rice industry itself.

California was home to a major rice industry. The state was the leading producer of short- and medium-grain rice in the United States and second only to Arkansas in total volume of rice produced. (Other major rice-producing states were Missouri, Texas, Louisiana, and Mississippi.) In 2003, California produced 1.75 million tons of rice on 507,000 acres. Almost all of the state's rice fields lay in a swath of land abutting the Sacramento River, a broad valley that relied on the river and its tributaries for irrigation. The crop generated annual sales of more than $500 million.

---

[8] "Regulation of Plant-Based Pharmaceuticals," CRS Report for Congress, p. 4.

[9] "Opportunities and Challenges: States and the Federal Coordinated Framework Governing Agricultural Biotechnology," Pew Initiative on Food and Biotechnology, May 2006, pp. 9–10.

Forty percent of California rice was exported, mainly to Japan, Taiwan, Korea, and Turkey. The rest was consumed domestically in food, pet food, and beer. Although the United States produced only 2 percent of the world's rice, it accounted for 14 percent of the international rice trade; the nation was second only to Thailand and Vietnam in rice exports.[10] However, the U.S. share of the world rice trade was declining; it had dropped from 28 percent in 1975 to 12 percent in 2003.[11]

Rice producers in California, as in much of the developed world, used highly sophisticated technology. Farmers used laser-guided grading equipment to position perimeter levees and level their fields precisely to enable an even covering of five inches of water during the growing season. From the fourth week in April to the second week in May, weather permitting, skilled pilots used low-flying, small aircraft guided by global positioning systems to deposit pregerminated seeds onto the flooded fields. Within a few days, the plants would emerge above the surface of the water, and within a few weeks the fields would be densely covered with bright green, grasslike stalks. The grains of rice—the plant's seeds—developed in late summer, when the rice was about three feet tall. When the rice matured in September and early October, farmers drained the fields and harvested the crop with combines, which separated the grain from the stalks. After the harvest, the rice was transported to a drying facility and from there to a mill. At the mill, the rice was processed to remove the inedible hull and then either sold as brown rice or further polished into white rice. Many mills used laser sorters to remove broken or immature grains.[12]

The two stages of rice production, farming and milling, defined the two major segments of the industry. California was home to more than 2,000 rice farmers, many of whom continued to operate as family-owned businesses. They were organized through their trade association, the Rice Producers of California. Rice mills, which required significant capital investment, tended to be owned by larger organizations. Leading millers in California included agribusiness giants ADM, Far West Rice, Pacific International, and Sun West. The Farmers Rice Cooperative, owned by a cooperative of 800 growers, also operated several mills.

To protect the interests of its rice industry, the California state government had established a body known as the California Rice Commission (CRC), declaring, "The production and milling of rice in this state is . . . affected with a public interest."[13] The commission's work was supported by an assessment on farmers and millers, based on their volume of production. The CRC was authorized by law to "promote the sale of rice, educate and instruct the wholesale and retail trade with respect to the proper handling and selling [of] rice, and conduct scientific research."[14]

In 2000, California had passed the Rice Certification Act (known as AB 2622), empowering the CRC to appoint an advisory board, which would have the right to review any varieties of rice "having characteristics of commercial impact," except for rice planted for research purposes on 50 or fewer acres. The enabling legislation stated,

> There is a growing need to maintain the identity of various types of rice to satisfy increasing consumer demand for specialty rices. This demand requires providing the industry with the ability to establish the terms and conditions for the production

[10] California Rice Commission Statistical Report, May 1, 2005.

[11] "Tending the Fields," p. 92.

[12] Information from the California Farm Bureau Federation, the U.S. Rice Foodservice, and personal observation.

[13] California Food and Agricultural Code, Section 71005.

[14] California Legislative Counsel's Digest, *http://www.leginfo.ca/gov.*

and handling of rice in order to minimize the potential for the commingling of various types of rice, and in order to prevent commingling where reconditioning is infeasible or impossible.[15]

By statute, the advisory board was composed of four producers (farmers), four handlers (millers), and four public representatives.[16] The job of the advisory board was to recommend to the Secretary of Agriculture "proposed regulations [on] planting, producing, harvesting, transporting, drying, storing, or otherwise handling rice . . . including, but not limited to, seed application requirements, field buffer zones, handling requirements, and identity preservation requirements." Once the secretary had received a recommendation from the advisory board, he was required within 30 days to issue the proposed regulation, decline and give the advisory board a written explanation, or request additional information.[17] Although the advisory board could not legally prohibit the production of any particular rice, including genetically modified rice, as a practical matter its recommendations to the secretary carried considerable weight. As the CRC itself pointed out, "No other commodity in the U.S. has a similar mechanism to protect its industry."[18]

The CRC Advisory Board Considers Ventria's Protocol

In 2003, as Ventria ramped up to commercial-scale production, Deeter and his team made plans to expand their acreage of rice planted. Their goal was to plant 120 acres during the 2004 growing season, an amount that, for the first time, exceeded the 50-acre rule and therefore fell under the CRC advisory board's authority. Accordingly, the company began discussions with members of the advisory board to develop an acceptable production protocol. During these talks, Ventria stipulated that its rice had a "commercial impact" and agreed to a number of provisions to address the rice industry's concerns. For example, the company agreed to establish buffer zones around its plots, to transport its rice in covered trucks, and to use dedicated processing equipment.

On Monday, March 29, 2004, the advisory board of the CRC held its regular meeting at the Best Western Bonanza Inn in Yuba City, in the heart of the Sacramento Valley rice belt. Heading the agenda was a discussion of Ventria's draft protocol. Discussion was animated. Members who had been involved in the discussions with Ventria recommended that the board approve the draft protocol. Several farmers, however, expressed concern that the presence of genetically modified rice in California posed a serious commercial threat, particularly to the state's export markets. Their concern seemed to be validated by the Japanese Rice Retailers Association, which wrote the advisory board:

> From the viewpoint of rice wholesalers and retailers in Japan, it is certain that the commercialization of GM [genetically modified] rice in the U.S. will evoke a distrust of U.S. rice as a whole among Japanese consumers, since we think that it is practically impossible to guarantee no GM rice contamination in non-GM U.S. rice. As you know, most Japanese consumers react quite negatively to GM

[15] Ibid.

[16] The public representatives were drawn, one each, from the California Crop Improvement Association, the California Warehouse Association, the California Cooperative Rice Research Foundation, and the University of California.

[17] Legislative Counsel's Digest.

[18] "California Rice Certification Act," California Rice Commission: *Serving the California Rice Industry* [newsletter], 6, no. 3 (March/April 2004).

crops. If the GM rice is actually commercialized in the U.S., we shall strongly request the Japanese government to take necessary measures not to import any California rice to Japan.[19]

Representatives from Californians for GE-Free Agriculture[20] and the Center for Food Safety both submitted written comments expressing opposition to the protocol.

After further debate and the passage of several amendments to strengthen the protocol—including a provision that Ventria plant its rice in southern California, far from the Sacramento Valley—the advisory board voted 6 to 5 to approve Ventria's protocols. Voting in favor were all four public members, one farmer, and one miller. Most of the farmers and millers voted "nay."[21] Whether for or against, all seemed to agree that the industry was moving into uncharted water. "There's a learning curve here for producers," said Ronald Lee, a farmer. "Some have some knowledge. Some have very little. We're entering new territory here."[22]

At the request of the company, the CRC recommended "emergency status" for Ventria's protocol review. This designation would give the California Secretary of Agriculture 10 days to approve or reject it, without a period of public comment, so the company could move forward in time for the spring 2004 planting season. Over the next 10 days, the Secretary of Agriculture was lobbied from both sides. The Biotechnology Industry Association expressed its support for the emergency status:

> [We] are writing to express strong support for your authorization of a protocol approved by the California Rice Commission. . . . Plant-made pharmaceuticals offer an exciting approach to scalable, economically attractive biopharmaceutical manufacturing, producing broad access to exciting new health products to address many of the most prevalent human diseases.[23]

Several environmental and consumer groups asked the secretary to deny the request for an emergency exemption. A number of rice farmers also spoke out in the press. "Consumers in Japan and many of California's other major rice export markets have already shown strong resistance to GM crops," said Greg Massa, a grower of organic rice. "Approval of this [Ventria] rice could shatter our years of hard work in building these markets and spell trouble for all California rice farmers."[24] Joe Carrancho, a grower and former president of the Rice Producers of California, commented, "If the Japanese have the perception— underline perception—that our rice has [genetically modified organisms] in it, then we're done. You can put a bullet in our head." He and environmentalists "may be apart on some issues, but on this one we're together," he said.[25]

On April 9, the Secretary of Agriculture rejected the recommendation for emergency status for the protocol review, saying, "It is clear that the public wants an opportunity to comment prior to any authorization to plant."[26] He called for more information about federal permits and asked the CRC to consult with affected groups.

[19] Quoted in Greg Massa, "Pharmaceutical Rice Is a No-Grow," *Sacramento Bee,* May 14, 2004.

[20] In this context, GE refers to "genetically engineered."

[21] Minutes of the March 29, 2004, AB 2622 Advisory Board, provided to the author by the president of the California Rice Commission.

[22] "State's Rice Farmers Fear Biotech Incursion," *San Francisco Chronicle,* April 8, 2004.

[23] Biotechnology Industry Association, letter to the Honorable A. G. Kawamura, April 5, 2004.

[24] "Plan Calls for Altered Rice Crops in State," *San Diego Union-Tribune,* March 27, 2004.

[25] "State's Rice Farmers Fear Biotech Incursion."

[26] "Modified Rice Won't Be Planted," *San Francisco Chronicle,* April 10, 2004; "Protein Rice Suffers Setback," *Sacramento Bee,* April 10, 2004.

Ventria's Opponents Mobilize

Even after the secretary's decision, the controversy continued to mount. In July, four advocacy organizations—Friends of the Earth, the Center for Food Safety, Consumers Union, and Environment California—produced a detailed report detailing their concerns about pharmaceutical rice in California. The groups submitted their report to the California Department of Food and Agriculture, the California EPA, and the California Department of Health Services, as well as to the public. In the document, the groups called for "a moratorium on the cultivation of Ventria's pharmaceutical rice and other pharm crops."[27]

The activist alliance made four arguments for a moratorium on pharmaceutical rice. First, it argued that contamination of food rice by genetically modified pharmaceutical rice grown outdoors was "inevitable," because of multiple potential pathways:

> Contamination of human foods with plant-made pharmaceuticals can occur through dispersal of seed or pollen. Wildlife, especially waterfowl, can transport seeds for long distances, as can extreme weather events such as floods or tornadoes. Harvesting equipment can carry seed residues to conventional fields, seeds can be spilled from trucks, or unharvested seeds can sprout as volunteers amid the following year's crop. Cross-pollination occurs at considerable distances in high winds or by insect, even with self-pollinating crops such as rice.[28]

The report argued that Ventria's protocols did not offer sufficient protection against contamination:

> The lack of detailed plans to prevent birds from spreading the pharm rice is particularly disturbing. California's Central Valley is one of the most important wintering areas for waterfowl in North America. Viable seed are known to pass through the gut of many waterfowl species, making waterfowl effective dispersal agents for many wetland plant species, including rice. . . .
>
> Ventria's protocol also does not deal with the possibility of seed dispersal through flooding. . . . Historical records show that floods of various magnitude occur not infrequently in the Sacramento Valley. . . .
>
> Ventria's . . . one-year fallow period following cultivation of its pharm rice means a greater likelihood of pharm rice volunteers contaminating a commercial rice crop grown subsequently in the same field. . . .
>
> The 100-foot isolation distance from food-grade rice . . . may not be adequate to prevent cross-pollination.[29]

What would happen if Ventria's rice did contaminate the food supply? Once commingling had occurred, the report continued, the potential for adverse impacts to human health was great. Possible consequences included infections, allergies, and autoimmune disorders:

> While human lactoferrin has antimicrobial properties, it paradoxically poses the potential hazard of exacerbating infections by certain pathogens capable of using it as a source of needed iron. Such pathogens include bacteria that cause

---

[27] "Pharmaceutical Rice in California: Potential Risks to Consumers, the Environment, and the California Rice Industry," Friends of the Earth, Center for Food Safety, Consumers Union, and Environment California, July 2004, p. 1.

[28] Ibid., p. 6.

[29] Ibid., p. 7.

gonorrhea and meningitis, as well as [those] implicated in causing ulcers and certain forms of stomach cancer. . . . Ventria's rice-expressed lysozyme and lactoferrin have two characteristics of proteins that cause food allergies: resistance to digestion and to breakdown by heat. . . . Pharmaceutical proteins generated by inserting human genes into plants . . . are usually different from their natural human counterparts. These differences may cause the body to perceive them as foreign, resulting in immune system responses.[30]

Finally, Ventria's rice could have serious environmental consequences if it crossbred with existing weed species, creating noxious "super weeds," the report argued:

Ventria's rice-produced pharmaceuticals have antibacterial and antifungal properties. If these traits are passed to related weed species such as wild and annual red rice, they could lend these weeds a fitness boost, promoting their spread.[31]

Moving Forward

In discussions with representatives of the CRC advisory board over the past year and a half, Deeter and his team had offered numerous concessions to address the concerns of rice farmers and others. The company had agreed to grow rice many miles away from any rice grown for food. It had promised to use dedicated equipment for field production, storage, and transportation and to use only processing equipment that was restricted to bio-engineered rice or had been thoroughly sanitized before reuse. The company had agreed to keep detailed logs and to allow third-party inspections. None of this, however, had been enough to satisfy the company's critics. In biotechnology, things always seemed to take longer, cost more, and face hurdles that could not have been anticipated when the company was started. Now another planting season had come and gone, and Ventria's investors appeared no closer to successful commercialization than they had been a year earlier.

Discussion Questions

1. What is the problem facing Scott Deeter and Ventria?
2. What groups have a stake in Ventria's actions? Identify the relevant stakeholders and for each, state its interests and sources of power.
3. What options might emerge from a dialogue between Ventria and its relevant stakeholders?
4. If Ventria chooses to employ a political action strategy, how might it go about influencing relevant regulators?
5. If Ventria chooses not to engage in dialogue or political action (or dialogue and political action are unsuccessful), what other options does the company have?
6. What do you think Ventria should do now, and why?

[30] Ibid., p. 3.
[31] Ibid., p. 3.

Moody's Credit Ratings and the Subprime Mortgage Meltdown

On October 22, 2008, Raymond W. McDaniel Jr. raised his right hand to be sworn as a witness before the U.S. House of Representatives Committee on Oversight and Government Reform. The topic of the day's hearing was the role of the credit rating agencies in the financial crisis on Wall Street. McDaniel, 50, was chairman and CEO of Moody's, one of the leading credit rating agencies in the world. The word "credit" came from the Latin verb *credere,* meaning to believe or to trust. Credit rating agencies, such as Moody's, had the job of evaluating bonds issued by governments, companies, and investment banks. The world's financial markets relied heavily on their assurances that various borrowers could be trusted to pay their debts on time. Now, however, Moody's and other credit rating agencies had come under strong criticism, as many questioned the accuracy of their ratings and their role in the widening financial crisis.

In late 2008, the world faced what many believed was the deepest financial crisis since the Great Depression of the 1930s. As the housing bubble burst and home prices began falling across the United States, billions of dollars' worth of securities backed by their mortgages had plummeted in value, straining the balance sheets of venerable Wall Street investment banks. Lehman Brothers, Bear Stearns, and Merrill Lynch had either failed or been sold off. Prominent commercial banks and mortgage lenders, including Washington Mutual, Countrywide, and Wachovia, had collapsed and been sold to the highest bidder. Now credit had seized up, as surviving banks became afraid to lend to businesses and individuals. Consumers were reining in their spending, and jobless rates were rising. Hundreds of thousands of homes bought with easy credit and an assumption of ever-rising values were in foreclosure. In a single year, investors had lost some $7 trillion, as the value of their stocks and bonds fell precipitously.

The causes of the financial crisis were complex, and many parties bore a share of the responsibility. But some analysts pointed to a critical role played by Moody's Corporation and other credit rating agencies. Over the previous several years, Moody's had rated thousands of bonds made up of bundles of "subprime" mortgages—home loans to people with low incomes and poor credit histories, who were buying houses they probably could not afford. Now many of these buyers were failing to make their monthly payments. Their loans were going bad at an alarming rate, and Moody's had downgraded its ratings on

By Anne T. Lawrence. Copyright © 2009 by the author. All rights reserved. This case was presented at the 2009 annual meeting of the North American Case Research Association. The author is grateful to Professors Thomas Nist and James Burnham of Duquesne University for their thoughtful comments on an earlier draft of this case.

many mortgage-backed bonds. Some blamed Moody's for having misjudged the risk inherent in these securities. Henry Waxman, the chair of the oversight committee, was one such critic. He opened the hearing with a broad condemnation. "The story of the credit rating agencies is a story of colossal failure," he told the hearing. "The credit rating agencies occupy a special place in our financial markets. Millions of investors rely on them for independent, objective assessments. The rating agencies broke this bond of trust, and federal regulators ignored the warning signs and did nothing to protect the public. The result," he added, "is that our entire financial system is now at risk."[1]

Moody's Corporation

The company that McDaniel had come to Congress to defend was the oldest credit rating agency in the world. Moody's had been founded in 1909 by John Moody, who got his start as an errand boy at a Wall Street bank. Observing the growing popularity of corporate bonds, the young entrepreneur recognized that investors needed a source of reliable information about their issuers' creditworthiness. Moody's first manual, on the safety of railroad bonds, proved highly popular, and by 1918 Moody and his firm were rating every bond then issued in the United States. By 2008, Moody's had become the undisputed "aristocrat of the ratings business."[2] The company was composed of two business units. By far the largest was Moody's Investors Service, which provided credit ratings; it earned 93 percent of the company's revenue. The other was Moody's KMV, which sold software and analytic tools, mainly to institutional investors. In 2007, Moody's reported revenue of $2.3 billion and employed 3,600 people in offices in 29 countries around the world.[3]

Moody's core business was rating the safety of bonds—debt issued by companies, governments, and public agencies. For example, if a state government issued a bond to build new classroom buildings at a public university, Moody's would evaluate the likelihood that the government would pay back the bondholders on time. (When a bond issuer was unable to make timely payments, this was known as a default.) Then Moody's would rate the bond according to a scale from Aaa—"triple A," with a very low chance of default—to C, already in default, with some 19 steps in between. (Credit ratings were technically considered opinions on the probability of default.) Moody's ratings, along with those of its competitors, enabled buyers to evaluate the risks of various fixed-income investments.

Over the years, Moody's business model had shifted. For many decades after its founding, Moody's had charged investors for its ratings through the sales of publications and advisory services. As a Moody's vice president explained in 1957, "We obviously cannot ask payment [from the issuer] for rating a bond," he wrote. "To do so would attach a price to the process, and we could not escape the charge, which would undoubtedly come, that our ratings [were] for sale."[4] In 1975, however, the Securities and Exchange Commission (SEC) changed the rules of the game. The SEC designated three companies—Moody's, Standard & Poor's (now a unit of the McGraw-Hill Companies), and Fitch (now a unit of Fimalac SA)—as Nationally Recognized Statistical Rating Organizations, or NRSROs. In effect, the government officially sanctioned these three rating agencies and gave them a

---

[1] Congress of the United States, House of Representatives, Committee on Oversight and Government Reform, "Credit Rating Agencies and the Financial Crisis," October 22, 2008, Opening Statement of Rep. Henry A. Waxman, p. 4.

[2] Michael Lewis, "The End," *Portfolio*, December 2008.

[3] *http://ir.moodys.com;* and various annual reports at *www.moodys.com.*

[4] Edmund Vogelius, writing in the *Christian Science Monitor*, quoted in "Debt Watchdogs: Tamed or Caught Napping?" *The New York Times,* December 8, 2008.

quasi-regulatory role. At this time, Moody's and the other two NRSROs began charging bond issuers to rate their products. (In 2008, Moody's market share was about 40 percent; S&P had 40 percent; and Fitch had between 10 and 15 percent.)

The new SEC rules changed the relationship between bond issuers and rating agencies. Because ratings strongly influenced the market value of the bond, issuers had a strong incentive to shop for the best possible ratings. For their part, rating agencies also had a strong incentive to compete for market share by catering to their clients. In 2000, Moody's was spun off from its parent, Dun & Bradstreet (which had acquired Moody's in 1962), becoming once again an independent, publicly owned firm. The spin-off further increased pressure on Moody's managers to increase revenues and improve shareholder returns. A former Moody's executive later recalled that in the early 2000s "things [became] a lot less collegial and a lot more bottom-line driven" as top executives sought to make the firm more responsive to clients.[5]

The Rise of Structured Finance

As Moody's business model was changing, so were the kinds of products the company was asked to evaluate. For many years, Moody's rated mainly plain-vanilla corporate and municipal, state, and federal government bonds. Wall Street investment banks, however, were becoming more innovative. Barriers to the global flow of capital were falling. New techniques of quantitative analysis permitted the creation of increasingly sophisticated financial products, known as structured finance. This term referred to the practice of combining income-producing assets—everything from conventional corporate bonds to credit card debt, home mortgages, franchise payments, and auto loans—into pools, and selling shares in the pool to investors. Instead of buying a simple IOU from a company, say, an investor would buy a share of income and principal payments flowing from a complex financial product made up of many loans.

One structured finance product that became particularly popular in the early 2000s was the residential mortgage-backed security, or RMBS. An RMBS started with a lender—a bank such as Washington Mutual or a mortgage company such as Countrywide Financial—that made home loans to individual borrowers. The lender (or another intermediary) would then bundle several thousand of these loans and sell them to a Wall Street investment bank such as Lehman Brothers or Merrill Lynch. (This gave the lender fresh cash with which to make more loans.) The Wall Street firm would then create a special kind of bond, based on a pool of underlying mortgage loans. Buyers of this bond would receive a share of the income flowing from the homeowners' monthly payments. (The investment banks also held some of these securities on their own books, a fact that contributed to their later difficulties.)

In order to make the RMBS more attractive to investors, the investment bank usually divided them into separate "tranches" (a French word meaning "slice"), with varying degrees of risk. If any homeowners defaulted on their loans, the lowest ("subordinated") tranches would absorb the losses first, and so on, up to the highest tranches. (The lower tranches earned higher interest, commensurate with their higher risk.) This is where the rating agencies, such as Moody's, came in: They were asked to rate the creditworthiness of various tranches of the mortgage-backed securities. Reflecting their greater complexity, Moody's charged more for rating structured products—around 11 basis points, or $11 for every $10,000 in value—compared with traditional corporate bonds (4.25 basis points).

[5] Jerome S. Fons, testimony before the House Committee on Oversight, October 22, 2008, p. 4; and Eliot Blair Smith, "Bringing Down Wall Street as Ratings Let Loose Subprime Scourge," *Bloomberg.com,* September 24, 2007.

	Year Ended December 31				
	2003	**2004**	**2005**	**2006**	**2007**
Total revenue	$1,246.6	$1,438.3	$1,731.6	$2,037.1	$2,259.0
Revenue from structured finance	474.7	553.1	708.7	883.6	885.9
Structured finance as % of revenue	38.5	34.1	40.9	43.4	39.2
Operating income	663.1	786.4	939.6	1,259.5	1,131.0
Operating margins (operating income as % of total revenue)	53.2	54.7	54.3	61.8	50.1

	Year Ended December 31			
	1999	**2000**	**2001**	**2002**
Total revenue	$564.2	$602.3	$796.7	$1,023.3
Revenue from structured finance	172.4	199.2	273.8	384.3
Structured finance as % of revenue	30.6	33.1	34.4	37.6
Operating income	270.4	288.5	398.5	538.1
Operating margins (operating income as % of total revenue)	47.9	47.9	50.0	52.6

Note: All amounts in millions of dollars, except for percentages.

Source: Moody's Annual Reports, 2001–2008. Where relevant, the most recently corrected figures have been used.

For example, to rate an RMBS worth $500 million, Moody's would receive about half a million dollars in fees.[6]

Credit ratings were especially important to investors in mortgage-backed securities, because these products were so difficult to understand. As a former managing director at Moody's explained,

> First, RMBSs and their offshoots offer little transparency around the composition and characteristics of the underlying loan collateral. Potential investors are not privy to the information that would allow them to understand the quality of the loan pool. Loan-by-loan data, the highest level of detail, are generally not available to investors. Second, the complexity of the securitization process requires extremely sophisticated systems and technical competence to properly assess risk at the tranche level. Third, rating agencies had a reputation, earned over nearly one century, of being honest arbiters of risk.[7]

In other words, investors had almost no way to assess independently the safety or security of these products, so they based their judgment wholly on the agencies' ratings.

Rating structured financial products, such as RMBSs, proved to be a highly lucrative business for Moody's. Exhibit A presents selected financial results for Moody's Investors

---

[6] Estimates of fees for rating various products are drawn from Smith, "Bringing Down Wall Street as Ratings Let Loose Subprime Scourge."

[7] Jerome S. Fons, testimony, p. 2.

Exhibit B

Comparison of Cumulative Total Return since December 31, 2001, Moody's Corporation, S&P Composite Index, and Peer Group Index

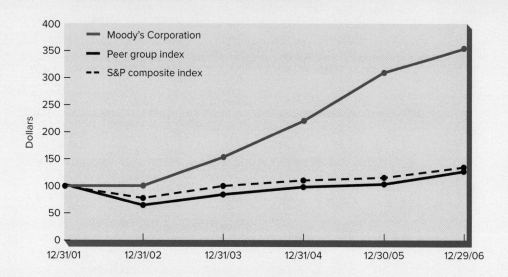

	Period Ending					
	12/31/2001	12/31/2002	12/31/2003	12/31/2004	12/30/2005	12/29/2006
Moody's Corporation	100	104.01	153.07	220.51	313.63	354.23
Peer group index	100	61.80	81.57	96.18	100.97	127.43
S&P composite index	100	77.90	100.25	111.15	116.61	135.03

Source: *Moody's Annual Report,* March 1, 2007, p. 13. The performance peer group is composed of Dow Jones & Company, Inc., The McGraw-Hill Companies, Pearson PLC, Reuters Group PLC, Thomson Corporation, and Wolters Kluwer nv. Figures assume reinvestment of all dividends.

Service for 1999 to 2007. Revenue from structured finance grew as a proportion of Moody's overall revenue throughout much of this period, peaking at 43 percent in 2006, contributing to the company's exceptional profitability. Operating margins (the percentage of revenue left after paying most expenses) during this period ranged from 48 to 62 percent, an unusually high level. In fact, for five years in a row, Moody's had the highest profit margin of any company in the S&P 500, beating even such consistently successful companies as Microsoft and Exxon.[8]

These stellar financial results rewarded Moody's shareholders with an outstanding total return in the early 2000s, relative to the company's peer group and to the broader stock market, as shown in Exhibit B. (Moody's financial results cannot be compared directly to those of S&P and Fitch, since the latter two are both part of larger companies that report consolidated results.)

[8] "Debt Watchdogs"; and Rep. Henry Waxman, statement.

Exhibit C

Value of Global Financial Assets, 1980–2007, by Asset Class, in Trillions of Dollars

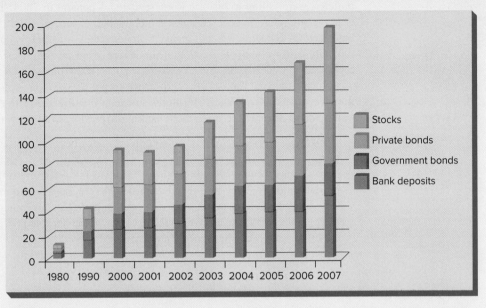

Legend:
- Stocks
- Private bonds
- Government bonds
- Bank deposits

Source: McKinsey Global Institute, *Mapping Global Capital Markets,* 5th Annual Report, October 2008, p. 9. Used by permission.

Reflecting the company's success, Moody's top executives were well compensated. In 2007, for example, Moody's chairman and CEO Raymond McDaniel earned total compensation of $7.4 million, according to *Forbes.*[9]

The Giant Pool of Money

In the 2000s, the total global volume of financial assets—money available worldwide to purchase stocks and bonds, as well as more complex structured financial products created by Wall Street—grew by leaps and bounds. As shown in Exhibit C, global financial assets grew from $94 trillion in 2000 to $196 trillion in 2007. Until the advent of the credit crisis, private bonds (fixed-income securities, including mortgage and other asset-backed securities) were one of the fastest-growing asset classes, growing 10 percent a year between 2000 and 2007, when their global value stood at $51 trillion.

Several factors contributed to the growth of what National Public Radio, on the program "This American Life," vividly dubbed this "giant pool of money." Big pension plans, private hedge funds, individuals saving for retirement, and foreign governments all sought safe investments with good returns. Emerging economies, including China, India, United Arab Emirates, and Saudi Arabia, built up substantial reserves selling oil and manufactured goods to the United States and other developed nations. China grew particularly rapidly; by 2007 it had become the third-largest financial market in the world.

At the same time that the pool of money was growing, many classes of assets were becoming less attractive to investors. In the early 2000s, the stock market was languishing in the wake of the bust of the high-tech bubble and the collapse of Enron and WorldCom.

[9] "Profile: Raymond W. McDaniel," *www.forbes.com.*

Interest rates, driven down by the U.S. Federal Reserve's very accommodative interest policies, were falling to historic lows, reaching 1 percent in 2004. This meant that investors' rates of return in U.S. Treasuries, money market accounts, certificates of deposit, and bank savings accounts were, to many, disappointingly low. In this context, RMBSs, which typically paid well above the federal funds rate, even for the investment grade (Moody's top 10 steps) tranches, became increasingly attractive to the world's investors.

Growing demand for asset-backed securities put pressure on investment banks to create more of them. Mike Francis, formerly an executive director in the residential mortgage trading department at the investment banking firm Morgan Stanley, told a reporter,

> [I]t was unbelievable. We almost couldn't produce enough [residential mortgage-backed securities] to keep the appetite of the investors happy. More people wanted bonds than we could actually produce. That was our difficult task, was trying to produce enough. They would call and ask, "Do you have any more fixed rate? What have you got? What's coming?" From our standpoint it's like, there's a guy out there with a lot of money. We gotta find a way to be his sole provider of bonds to fill his appetite. And his appetite's massive.[10]

No Income, No Jobs, No Assets

As the investment banking firms, such as Morgan Stanley, scrambled to produce enough asset-backed securities to meet global demand, they put pressure on mortgage originators to produce more loans. This, in turn, encouraged lenders to weaken the standards they used to qualify borrowers. Traditionally, when a person applied for a home loan, he or she would be required to have good credit, money for a down payment, and proof of income and assets—all indicators of creditworthiness. Increasingly, in the rush to make loans, lenders began overlooking these requirements—taking on borrowers with poor credit, low-paying jobs, few assets, and no money to put down. These borrowers—and the loans made to them—were known as *subprime*.

Lenders' willingness to weaken their underwriting standards appeared consistent with public policy. The administrations of both presidents Bill Clinton and George W. Bush had pursued policies designed to expand home ownership, particularly among minorities. In an effort to make housing more affordable, the government had helped first-time buyers with down payments and closing costs and allowed borrowers to qualify for federally insured mortgages with no money down. It also encouraged Freddie Mac and Fannie Mae, the two government-sponsored mortgage lenders, to buy RMBSs that included loans to low-income borrowers.[11]

The industry developed tongue-in-cheek acronyms for loans made to poorly qualified borrowers, such as NINAs—no income, no assets—and NINJAs—no income, no assets, and no job. Mike Francis, the former Morgan Stanley executive, described these loans:

> No income no asset loans. That's a liar's loan. We are telling you to lie to us. We're hoping you don't lie. Tell us what you make, tell us what you have in the bank, but we won't verify? We're setting you up to lie. Something about that feels very wrong. It felt wrong way back when and I wish we had never done it. Unfortunately, what happened . . . we did it because everyone else was doing it.

[10] National Public Radio, "The Giant Pool of Money," at *www.thislife.org/extras/radio/355_transcript.pdf*.

[11] "Don't Blame Bankers, It's Down to a Man Called Bill," *The Evening Standard (London)*, October 2, 2008; and "White House Philosophy Stoked Mortgage Bonfire," *The New York Times*, December 21, 2008.

The industry also began to write more nontraditional mortgages. Instead of fixed-rate loans, under which a borrower made a stable payment every month for many years, the industry developed products with lower monthly payments to allow less-qualified buyers to get into the market. These included adjustable-rate loans with low introductory "teaser" rates (which reset after three or five years at a much higher rate); interest-only loans (where the borrower was required to pay only the interest, not also a portion of the principal each month); and payment-option loans (where the borrower could choose to make a full payment, an interest-only payment, or a minimum payment that would actually cause the principal owed to increase). From 2003 to 2005, the subprime and low-documentation share of mortgage originations tripled from 11 percent to 33 percent. These loans were particularly popular in states where housing prices were going up the fastest—the so-called "sand states" of Nevada, California, Arizona, and Florida.[12]

Some banks and mortgage companies became particularly aggressive in pushing loans on poorly qualified borrowers. An investigative report for *The New York Times* examined the practices of one such lender, Washington Mutual (which later collapsed in the largest bank failure in U.S. history). WaMu, as it was known, operated a "boiler room" culture in which bank employees were under tremendous pressure to generate loan volume—and were rewarded handsomely if they did. *The New York Times* reported,

> WaMu pressed sales agents to pump out loans while disregarding borrowers' incomes and assets, according to former employees. The bank set up what insiders described as a system of dubious legality that enabled real estate agents to collect fees of more than $10,000 for bringing in borrowers, sometimes making agents more beholden to WaMu than they were to their clients.
>
> WaMu gave mortgage brokers handsome commissions for selling the riskiest loans, which carried higher fees, bolstering profits and ultimately the compensation of the bank's executives. WaMu pressured appraisers to provide inflated property values that made loans appear less risky, enabling Wall Street to bundle them more easily for sales to investors.
>
> "It was the Wild West," said [a founder of an appraisal company that worked with WaMu]. "If you were alive, they would give you a loan. Actually, I think if you were dead, they would still give you a loan."[13]

Of course, on the other side of each of these transactions was a borrower. The producers for *This American Life* interviewed one such individual—who had received a home loan for more than half a million dollars. At the time, this man was working three irregular part-time jobs and making around $45,000 a year. By the time he was interviewed, he had, not surprisingly, fallen behind in his payments, and his home was in foreclosure. The homeowner recalled,

> It's almost like you pass a guy in the street and say, [can you] lend me five hundred and forty thousand? He says, what do you do? Hey, I got a job. OK. It seems that casual . . . I wouldn't have loaned me the money. I know guys who are criminals who wouldn't loan me that and they break your knee-caps. I don't know why the bank did it . . . Five hundred and forty thousand dollars to a guy with bad credit . . . I'm not trying to absolve myself of anything . . . The bank made an imprudent loan. I made an imprudent loan. We're partners in this.[14]

---

[12] *FDIC Outlook,* Summer 2006, *www.fdic.gov.*

[13] Peter S. Goodman and Gretchen Morgenson, "Saying Yes, WaMu Built Empire on Shaky Loans," *The New York Times,* December 28, 2008.

[14] National Public Radio, *This American Life,* Program #355, transcript.

In many cases, the borrowers knew they were getting in over their heads—or ought to have. But in other cases, borrowers were misled by bank officers or mortgage brokers, did not understand their loan's terms, or simply believed that they would be able to sell or refinance in a year or two when, they assumed, their home would be worth more.

As the quality of mortgage loans deteriorated, some regulators tried to sound the alarm. In 2005, the Office of the Comptroller of the Currency (OCC), the arm of the Treasury Department that oversees most commercial banks, considered new regulations that would have limited risky mortgages and required clearer explanations to borrowers and warnings to buyers of RMBSs. Mortgage lenders and investment banks, however, lobbied strenuously against these rule changes, and federal regulators backed off.[15] Officials in North Carolina, Iowa, Michigan, Georgia, and other states attempted to rein in lenders, but were overruled by federal officials who argued that federal regulation pre-empted state regulation. The OCC brought only one enforcement action related to subprime lending between 2000 and 2006.[16]

 The Collapse

In 2006, the market for residential mortgage-backed securities began to unravel. Interest rates began to rise, and housing prices began to drop. As loans began to reset, homeowners found that they were unable to make the new, higher payments—or to refinance or sell their property. Increasing numbers of homeowners realized they were "under water"—that is, they owed more than their home was worth. Lenders coined a new term—"jingle mail"—to describe what happened when borrowers simply dropped the keys in the mail and walked away from their homes. As they did so, their mortgages became worthless—and the value of securities based on them swooned.

In July 2007, Ben Bernanke, chairman of the Federal Reserve, testified in the Senate that he anticipated as much as $100 billion in losses in the market for subprime-backed securities. That month, Moody's stopped rating new RMBSs and began a series of what *Barron's* magazine called "express train downgrades, since there are no stops between Blue Chip Land and oblivion."[17] By the following summer, Moody's had downgraded more than 5,000 mortgage-backed securities, with a value in the hundreds of billions of dollars, including 90 percent of all asset-backed securities it had rated in 2006 and 2007.[18,19]

In April 2008, Roger Lowenstein, reporting for *The New York Times,* took a close look at one of many poorly performing RMBSs that had been rated by Moody's and downgraded around this time. This particular security, which he called Subprime XYZ, was comprised of 2,393 mortgages collectively worth $430 million. A West Coast mortgage lender had issued these loans in early 2006, at the height of the housing bubble. All of the borrowers were subprime—people with poor credit histories and high debt-to-income ratios. Three-quarters of the borrowers had taken adjustable-rate mortgages with low initial rates, and almost half had provided no written proof of their incomes. By early 2007, just a year after this security was created, 13 percent of the loans were delinquent. By early 2008, 27 percent of these mortgage holders were no longer paying.[20]

[15] Matt Apuzzo, "Anatomy of the Lending Crisis," *San Francisco Chronicle,* December 2, 2008.

[16] Robert Berner and Brian Grow, "They Warned Us about the Mortgage Crisis," *BusinessWeek,* October 9, 2008.

[17] Jonathan R. Laing, "Failing Grade," *Barron's,* December 24, 2007.

[18] Gretchen Morgenson, "Debt Watchdogs: Tamed or Caught Napping?" *The New York Times,* December 11, 2008.

[19] Eliot Blair Smith, "Race to Bottom at Moody's, S&P Secured Subprime's Boom, Bust," *Bloomberg.com,* September 25, 2008.

[20] Roger Lowenstein, "Triple-A Failure," *The New York Times Magazine,* April 27, 2008.

As Moody's began downgrading bonds like Subprime XYZ, many institutional investors—whose holdings of mortgage-backed securities were suddenly worth much less—became irate. Mary Elizabeth Brennan, a Moody's vice president, got an earful when she called several RMBS investors in the summer of 2007, as the problem was beginning to become obvious. According to internal documents, a portfolio manager at Vanguard, a leading money management company, told Brennan that the rating agencies had "allow[ed] issuers to get away with murder." She added, "Rating agencies aren't helping me make the right decisions." A representative of Pacific Investment Management Company (PIMCO), another money management firm, told her that Moody's "doesn't stand up to Wall Street." "Someone up there just wasn't on top of it," he added. The chief investment officer of Fortis Investments took the initiative to phone Moody's with what the manager who took the call called a "few choice words":

> If you can't figure out the loss ahead of the fact, what's the use of your ratings? You have legitimized these things [subprime mortgage-backed securities] . . . leading people into dangerous risk. If the ratings are b.s., the only use in ratings is comparing b.s. relative to more b.s.[21]

A Slippery Slope

As criticism poured in and the downgrades continued—and Moody's own stock dropped in value—the company's executives began a tough reevaluation of Moody's own practices. On September 10, 2007, McDaniel convened a town hall meeting with his managing directors (top managers). As revealed in a transcript later released to a Congressional investigation, McDaniel started out by acknowledging the criticism that "the rating agencies got it wrong." The CEO offered the following explanation of the subprime mortgage crisis:

> Looking at the subprime crisis specifically . . . We had historically low [interest] rates. We had very easy credit conditions for a number of years. We had official and market-based support for adjustable-rate mortgages. It created what I think is an overdone condition for the U.S. housing [market]. This was a condition that was supported by U.S. public policy in favor of home ownership. And as I once said, once housing prices started to fall, we got into a condition in which people can't refi[nance], can't sell, can't afford their current mortgage.[22]

Later, during the question and answer period, McDaniel reflected on the industry environment in which Moody's had rated many RMBSs:

> What happens is, as long as things are going extremely well, no one cares . . . [It] was a slippery slope . . . What happened in '04 and '05 with respect to the subordinated tranches is that our competition, Fitch and S&P, went nuts. Everything was investment grade. It didn't really matter . . . We rated . . . 20 to 25 percent of that market. We tried to alert the market. We said we're not rating it. This stuff isn't investment grade. No one cared because the machine just kept going.[23]

After the meeting, McDaniel invited attendees to submit any additional comments they wished to make electronically. One managing director commented,

> Really no discussion of why the structured [finance] group refused to change their ratings in the face of overwhelming evidence they were wrong.[24]

---

[21] Quotations are drawn from internal e-mails, released to Congress on October 22, 2008.

[22] Moody's Investors Service, "Managing Directors Town Hall Meeting," September 10, 2007, transcript, pp. 6–8.

[23] Ibid., pp. 62–63.

[24] "Moody's Managing Director Town Hall Feedback," September 2007, p. 1.

Another managing director asked rhetorically,

> [W]hat really went wrong with Moody's subprime ratings leading to massive downgrades and potential more downgrades to come? We heard 2 answers yesterday: 1. people lied, and 2. there was an unprecedented sequence of events in the mortgage markets. As for #1, it seems to me that we had blinders on and never questioned the information we were given . . . As for #2, it is our job to think of the worst-case scenarios and model them . . . Combined, these errors make us look either incompetent at credit analysis, or like we sold our soul to the devil for revenue, or a little bit of both.[25]

A month later, on October 21, McDaniel made a confidential presentation to his board of directors, also later disclosed to Congress. The subject of his briefing was credit policy—the overall standards governing the rating process. With respect to ratings quality, McDaniel told the board,

> The real problem is not that the market [under weights] ratings quality but rather that, in some sectors, it actually penalizes quality . . . Unchecked, competition on this basis can place the entire financial system at risk. It turns out that ratings quality has surprisingly few friends: issuers want high ratings; investors don't want rating downgrades; short-sighted bankers labor short-sightedly to game the rating agencies for a few extra basis points on execution.

Under the topic heading "rating erosion by persuasion," he commented,

> Analysts and MDs [managing directors] are continually "pitched" by bankers, issuers, investors—all with reasonable arguments—whose views can color credit judgment, sometimes improving it, other times degrading it (we "drink the kool-aid"). Coupled with strong internal emphasis on market share and margin focus, this does constitute a "risk" to ratings quality.

He also noted the inherent tension between market share and ratings quality:

> Moody's for years has struggled with this dilemma. On the one hand, we need to win the business and maintain market share, or we cease to be relevant. On the other hand, our reputation depends on maintaining ratings quality (or at least avoiding big visible mistakes). For the most part, we hand the dilemma off to the team MDs [managing directors] to solve. . . . I set both market share and rating quality objectives for my MDs, while reminding them to square the circle within the bounds of the code of conduct.

Later in the meeting, he reflected,

> The RMBS and derivatives teams are comprised of conscientious bright people working long hours. They are highly desirous of getting the rating right. But a certain complacency sets in after a prolonged period of rating success. . . . Organizations often interpret past successes as evidencing their competence and the adequacy of their procedures rather than a run of good luck.[26]

---

[25] Ibid., p. 3.

[26] "Credit Policy Issues at Moody's," Raymond McDaniel, confidential presentation to the board of directors, October 21, 2007.

What Should Be Done?

Now, on October 22, 2008, the House of Representatives Committee on Oversight and Government Reform had convened a hearing to question executives of the top credit rating agencies about their role in the nation's financial crisis. Testimony at the hearing revealed broad disagreement over the culpability of the agencies, and what if anything should be done about them.

Jerome S. Fons, managing director for credit policy at Moody's until August 2007, testified,

> My view is that a large part of the blame can be placed on the inherent conflicts of interest found in the issuer-pays business model and rating shopping by issuers of structured securities. . . . A drive to maintain or expand market share made the rating agencies willing participants in this shopping spree. It was also relatively easy for the major banks to play the agencies off one another. . . . Originators of structured securities typically chose the agency with the lowest standards, engendering a race to the bottom in terms of rating quality. . . . [T]he business model prevented analysts from putting investor interests first.

Fons recommended a "wholesale change at the governance and senior management levels of the large rating agencies." He also proposed eliminating the SEC's NRSRO designations, an increased reliance on "common sense" in the rating process, and "taming the conflicts posed by the issuer-pays model."[27]

Raymond McDaniel, who addressed the hearing on behalf of Moody's, strongly disputed the view that the business model was to blame. He pointed out the investors—as well as issuers—had an interest in influencing bond ratings. "[J]ust as an issuer has an interest in the rating to improve the marketability of its bonds, investors seeking to improve their existing bond portfolio values or to establish new portfolio positions on more favorable terms have an interest in the rating of a bond," he said. He also noted that bond issuers, such as investment banks, were themselves also often investors, weakening the distinction between the two. Companies such as Lehman Brothers issued asset-backed securities, but also held them on their books. Finally, he argued, switching to an investor-pay model would deprive individual investors of access to ratings, because only big institutional investors could afford to pay.

Rather, Moody's favored various methods of actively managing potential conflicts. The company's code of conduct, McDaniel pointed out, already required that bonds be rated by a committee, rather than by an individual, who might be swayed by personal interest. Analysts were barred from owning stock in companies whose bonds they rated, and compensation was not based on revenue associated with entities analysts rated. McDaniel concluded,

> The events of the past 15 months have demonstrated that markets can change dramatically and rapidly. Such change brings important lessons. The opportunity to improve market practices, including credit analysis and credit rating processes, must be pursued vigorously and transparently if confidence in credit markets and their healthy operation are to be restored.[28]

---

[27] Jerome Fons, testimony, pp. 3–6.

[28] Testimony of Raymond W. McDaniel, House Committee on Oversight and Government Reform, October 22, 2008, p. 19.

**Discussion
Questions**

1. What did Moody's do wrong, if anything?
2. Which stakeholders were helped, and which were hurt, by Moody's actions?
3. Did Moody's have a conflict of interest? If so, what was the conflict, and who or what were the principal and the agent? What steps could be taken to eliminate or reduce this conflict?
4. What share of the responsibility did Moody's and its executives bear for the financial crisis, compared with that of home buyers, mortgage lenders, investment bankers, government regulators, policymakers, and investors?
5. What steps can be taken to prevent a recurrence of something like the subprime mortgage meltdown? In your answer, please address the role of management policies and practices, government regulation, public policy, and the structure of the credit ratings industry.

The Upper Big Branch Mine Disaster

On Monday, April 5, 2010, just before 3:00 in the afternoon, miners at Massey Energy Corporation's Upper Big Branch coal mine in southern West Virginia were in the process of a routine shift change. Workers on the evening shift were climbing aboard "mantrips," low-slung electric railcars that would carry them into the sprawling, three-mile-wide drift mine, cut horizontally into the side of a mountain. Many day shift workers inside the mine had begun packing up and were preparing to leave, and some were already on their way to the portals. At one of the mine's main "longwalls," one thousand feet below the surface, a team of four highly experienced miners was operating a shearer, a massive machine that cut coal from the face with huge rotating blades. The shearer had been shut down for part of the day because of mechanical difficulties, and the miners were making one last pass before the evening shift arrived to take their places.

Suddenly, a spark thrown off as the shearer's blades cut into hard sandstone ignited a small pocket of flammable methane gas. One of the operators immediately switched off the high-voltage power to the machine. Seconds later, the flame reached a larger pocket of methane, creating a small fireball. Apparently recognizing the danger, the four miners on the longwall crew began running for the exit opposite the fire. They had traveled no more than 400 feet when coal dust on the ground and in the air ignited violently, setting off a wave of powerful explosions that raced through the mine's seven miles of underground tunnels. When it was over three minutes later, 29 miners (including all four members of the longwall crew) were dead, and two were seriously injured. Some had died from injuries caused by the blast itself, others from carbon monoxide suffocation as the explosion sucked the oxygen out of the mine. It was the worse mining disaster in the United States in almost 40 years.

An evening shift miner who had just entered the mine and boarded a mantrip for the ride to the coal face later told investigators what he had experienced:

> All of a sudden you heard this big roar, and that's when the air picked up. I'd say it was probably 60-some miles per hour. Instantly black. It took my hardhat and ripped it off my head, it was so powerful.

This miner and the rest of his group abandoned the mantrip and ran for the entrance, clutching each other in the darkness. On the outside, stunned and shaken, they turned to the most senior member of their crew for an explanation. "Boys . . . , I've been in the mines a long time," the veteran miner said. "That [was] no [roof] fall. . . . The place blew up."[1]

By Anne T. Lawrence. Copyright © 2012 by the author. All rights reserved. This case was presented at the 2012 annual meeting of the Western Casewriters Association Annual Meeting.

[1] Governor's Independent Investigation Panel, *Report to the Governor,* p. 26. This account of the disaster is based on a reconstruction of the events of April 5, 2010, by federal and state investigators and by the United Mine Workers Union.

Massey Energy Corporation

At the time of the explosion, Massey Energy Corporation, the owner and operator of the Upper Big Branch mine, was one of the leading coal producers in the United States. The company, which specialized in the production of high-grade metallurgical coal, described itself as "the most enduring and successful coal company in central Appalachia," where it owned one-third of the known coal reserves. Massey extracted 37 million tons of coal a year, ranking it sixth among U.S. producers in tonnage. The company sold its coal to more than a hundred utility, metallurgical, and industrial customers (mostly on long-term contracts) and exported to 13 countries. In 2009, Massey earned $227 million on revenue of $2.7 billion. The company and its subsidiaries employed 5,800 people in 42 underground and 14 surface mines and several coal processing facilities in West Virginia, Kentucky, and Virginia.

Massey maintained that it brought many benefits to the nation as a whole and to the Appalachian region. The coal industry in the United States, of which Massey was an important part, provided the fuel for about half of the electricity generated in the United States, lessening the country's reliance on imported oil. The company provided thousands of relatively well-paying jobs in a region that had long been marked by poverty and unemployment. Economists estimated that for every job in the coal industry, around three and a half jobs were created elsewhere. The company donated to scholarship programs, partnered with local schools, and provided emergency support during natural disasters, such as severe flooding in West Virginia in May 2009. "We recognize that it takes healthy and viable communities for our company to continue to grow and succeed," Massey declared in its 2009 report to shareholders.

But critics saw a darker side of Massey. The company was one of the leading practitioners of mountaintop removal mining, in which explosives were used to blast away the tops of mountains to expose valuable seams of coal. The resulting waste was frequently dumped into adjacent valleys, polluting streams, harming wildlife, and contaminating drinking water. In 2008, Massey paid $20 million to resolve violations of the Clean Water Act, the largest-ever settlement under that law. In an earlier incident, toxic mine sludge spilled from an impoundment operated by the company in Martin County, Kentucky, contaminating hundreds of miles of the Big Sandy and Ohio rivers, necessitating a $50 million cleanup. Worker safety was also a concern. An independent study found that Massey had the worst fatality rate of any coal company in the United States. For example, in the decade leading up to the Upper Big Branch disaster, Peabody Coal (the industry leader in tons produced) had one fatality for every 296 million tons of coal mined; Massey's rate was one fatality per 18 million tons—more than 16 times as high.

Donald L. Blankenship

At the time of the Upper Big Branch mine disaster, the chief executive officer and undisputed boss of Massey Energy was Don Blankenship. A descendant of the McCoy family of the famous warring clans the Hatfields and the McCoys, Blankenship was raised by a single mother in a trailer in Delorme, a railroad depot in the coalfields of West Virginia. His mother supported the family by working 6 days a week, 16 hours a day, running a convenience store and gas station. Michael Shnayerson, who wrote about Blankenship in his book, *Coal River,* reported that the executive had absorbed from his mother the value of hard work—as well as contempt for others who might be less fortunate. "Anyone who didn't work as hard as she did deserved to fail," Shnayerson wrote. "Sympathy appeared to play no part in her reckonings."[2]

Blankenship graduated from Marshall University in Huntington, West Virginia, with a degree in accounting. As a college student, he worked briefly in a coal mine to earn money for tuition. In 1982, at age 32, he returned to the coalfields to join Massey Energy, taking a job as an office manager for a subsidiary called Rawls. Soon after, Massey announced it intended to spin off its subsidiaries as separate companies and re-open them as nonunion operations. The United Mine Workers, the union that then represented many Massey workers, struck the company. Jeff Goodell, a journalist who profiled Blankenship in *Rolling Stone,* described the young manager's technique for defeating the union at Rawls:

> Blankenship erected two miles of chain link fence around the facility, brought in dogs and armed guards, and ferried nonunion workers through the union's blockades. The strike, which lasted more than a year, grew increasingly violent—strikers took up baseball bats against the workers trying to take their jobs, and a few even fired shots at the scabs. A volley of bullets zinged into Blankenship's office and smashed into an old TV. . . . For years afterward, Blankenship kept the TV with a bullet hole through it in his office as a souvenir.[3]

The union's defeat at Massey (by 2010, only about 1 percent of Massey's workers were union members, all of them in coal preparation plants rather than mines) contributed to the overall decline of the United Mine Workers in the coalfields. In the 1960s, unions represented nearly 90 percent of the nation's mine workers; by 2010, they represented just 19 percent.

Blankenship quickly moved through the management ranks. In 1990, only eight years after he joined the company, he became president and chief operating officer of the Massey Coal Company and in 1992 was promoted to CEO and chairman. (The company was renamed Massey Energy in 2000 when it separated from its parent, Fluor Corp.) By some measures, he was a successful CEO. Between 2001, the first full year of Massey's independent operation, and 2009, annual revenue increased from $1.2 billion to $2.7 billion. During this period, employment rose from around 3,700 to 5,800. Blankenship more than doubled the company's coal reserves, mainly through acquisitions of smaller firms. Massey shareholders, like all investors, were buffeted by the extreme volatility of the stock market during the 2000s. Nevertheless, an investor who purchased $10,000 worth of Massey stock in December 2004 would have a holding valued at $12,800 in December 2010—a rate of return close to that of the coal industry as a whole during this period.[4]

As CEO, Blankenship developed a reputation as a hands-on, detail-oriented manager. He lived in the coalfields and ran the company out of a double-wide trailer in Belfry, Kentucky, just over the West Virginia line. He signed off on all hires, all the way down to janitors. One manager expressed amazement when he learned that the CEO would have to approve a tankful of gasoline for his truck. Managers were required to fax production figures to Blankenship every half hour. Red phones connected mine managers directly to the CEO. "If the report was late or the numbers weren't good, or the mine was shut down for any reason," Shnayerson reported, "the red phone would ring. The terrified manager would pick it up to hear Mr. B demanding to know why the numbers

[2] Michael Shnayerson, *Coal River: How a Few Brave Americans Took on a Powerful Company—and the Federal Government—to Save the Land They Love* (New York: Farrar, Straus, and Giroux, 2008), p. 155.

[3] Jeff Goodell, "The Dark Lord of Coal Country," *Rolling Stone,* December 9, 2010.

[4] Massey, 2009 Annual Report, "Shareholder Information," p. 23.

weren't right."[5] Blankenship told an interviewer, "People talk about character being what you do when no one else is looking. But the truth of the matter is character is doing that which is unpopular if it's right, even if it causes you to be vilified."[6]

As CEO, Blankenship maintained a laser focus on productivity. In 2005, he sent a memo titled "RUNNING COAL" to all Massey underground mine superintendents that stated:

> If any of you have been asked by your group presidents, your supervisors, engineers, or anyone else to do anything other than run coal (i.e., build overcasts, do construction jobs, or whatever) you need to ignore them and run coal. This memo is necessary only because we seem not to understand that coal pays the bills.

A week later, after this memo had been widely circulated, he followed up with another one which referred to the company's S-1, P-2 (safety first, production second) program. He wrote: "By now each of you should know that safety and S-1 is our first responsibility. Productivity and P-2 are second."

Executive Compensation

Blankenship was well compensated for running Massey. As shown in Exhibit A, his total compensation in 2009 was almost $18 million; this was up from $11 million in 2008 and $9 million in 2007. Blankenship's base salary in all three years was close to $1 million. By far the greatest proportion of his total pay came from a performance-based incentive system established by Massey's board of directors. In its filings with the SEC, the board described its philosophy of compensation this way:[7]

> We compensate our named executive officers in a manner that is meant to attract and retain highly qualified and gifted individuals and to appropriately incentivize and motivate the named executive officers to achieve continuous improvements in company-wide performance for the benefit of our stockholders.[8]

Accordingly, the compensation committee of the board established an incentive plan for Massey's CEO. (Similar plans were in place for other senior executives as well.) The plan set specific performance measures for "areas over which Mr. Blankenship was responsible and positioned to directly influence outcome." These areas, and the proportion of his incentive compensation based on them, are shown in Exhibit B.

By one estimate, in the 10 years leading up to the disaster Blankenship received a total of $129 million in compensation from Massey.[9] "I don't care what people think," he once said during a talk to a gathering of Republican Party leaders in West Virginia, speaking of

---

[5] Michael Shnayerson, quoted in United Mine Workers of America, *Industrial Homicide: Report on the Upper Big Branch Mine Disaster,* p. 80.

[6] Jim Snyder, "Q&A with Don Blankenship," November 16, 2009, *http://thehill.com.*

[7] At the time of the UBB disaster, Massey was governed by a nine-person board of directors chaired by Blankenship. The other members were Baxter Phillips, Jr., Massey's president; Stanley Suboleski, formerly Massey's chief operating officer and later commissioner of the Federal Mine Safety and Health Review Commission under President George W. Bush; Lady Judge, an attorney and former commissioner of the Securities and Exchange Commission; Bobby R. Inman, a retired naval admiral and former director of the National Security Agency; James Crawford, a former coal industry executive; Robert Fogelsong, president and executive director of the Appalachian Leadership and Education Foundation; Richard Gabrys, formerly vice chairman of Deloitte and Touche; and Dan Moore, a retired banker. In 2009, directors earned $39,600 in cash and $90,000 in stock, plus $2,000 for each meeting attended, plus extra compensation for special duties (e.g., lead director). (Massey, Form 8-K, November 2009).

[8] Massey Energy, 2010 Proxy, p. 25.

[9] David Roberts, "Grist" [blog], April 9, 2010, *www.grist.org.*

Year	Salary	Bonus	Stock Awards	Option Awards	Incentive Plan	Change in Pension Value	Other(*)	Total Compensation
2009	933,369	300,000	3,869,819	—	11,549,156	573,618	609,875	17,835,837
2008	1,000,000	300,000	390,000	2,160,000	6,022,447	691,415	357,129	11,020,991
2007	1,000,000	300,000	604,800	1,700,000	5,257,576	111,794	386,480	9,361,000

Source: Massey Energy 2010 Proxy, "Compensation Discussion and Analysis" and "Compensation of Named Executive Officers."

Note: "Other" includes personal use of company cars, aircraft (Challenger 601 corporate jet), housing, and related costs and services.

himself in the third person. "At the end of the day, Don Blankenship is going to die with more money than he needs."[10]

Government Regulation of Mining Safety and Health

Coal mining had always been a hazardous occupation. Methane gas, an odorless and colorless by-product of decomposing organic matter that was often present alongside coal, was highly flammable. Methane explosions had contributed to the deaths of more than 10,000 miners in the United States since 1920. To mine safely, methane levels had to be constantly monitored, and ventilation systems had to be effective enough to remove it from the mine. Coal dust itself—whether on the floor or other surfaces, or suspended in the air—was also highly flammable. The standard practice was to apply layers of rock dust (crushed limestone) over the coal dust to render it inert. In addition to the ever-present danger of fire, miners had long contended with the threat of collapsing roofs and walls, dangerous mechanical equipment, and suffocation. Miners often developed coal workers' pneumoconiosis, commonly called black lung, a chronic, irreversible disease caused by breathing coal dust. (Black lung was preventable with proper coal dust control.)

Health and safety in the mining industry had long been regulated at both the federal and state levels. Over the years, lawmakers had periodically strengthened government regulatory control, mostly in response to mining disasters.

- In 1910, following an explosion at the Monongah mine in West Virginia in which 362 men died, Congress established the *U.S. Bureau of Mines* to conduct research on the safety and health of miners.

- The Federal Coal Mine Health and Safety Act, known as the *Coal Act*—which passed in 1969 after the death of 78 miners at the Consol Number 9 mine in Farmington, West Virginia—greatly increased federal enforcement powers. This law established fines for violations and criminal penalties for "knowing and willful" violations. It also provided compensation for miners disabled by black lung disease.

- The 1977 *Mine Act* further strengthened the rights of miners and established the Mine Safety and Health Administration, MSHA (pronounced "Em-shah") to carry out its

---

[10] Goodell, op. cit.

The calculation of incentive plan compensation was based on achievement of specific targets in these areas:

EBIT (earnings before interest and taxes)	15%
Produced tons	15%
Continuous miner productivity (feet/shift)	5%
Surface mining productivity (tons/man-hour)	5%
Environmental violations (% reduction)	10%
Fulfillment of contracts	15%
Nonfatal days lost due to injury and accident (% reduction)	10%
Identification of successors	5%
Employee retention	15%
Diversity of members	5%

Source: Massey Energy 2010 Proxy.

Note: A "continuous miner" is a large machine that extracts coal underground.

regulatory mandates. The law required at least four full inspections of underground mines annually.

- Then in 2006, after yet another string of mine tragedies focused public attention on the dangers of mining, Congress passed the Mine Improvement and New Emergency Response Act, known at the *MINER Act.* This law created new rules to help miners survive underground explosions and accidents.[11]

States like West Virginia that had significant mining industries also had their own regulatory rules and agencies.

Although MSHA was empowered to inspect mines unannounced and to fine operators for violations, the agency had limited authority to shut down a mine if a serious problem was present or if the operator refused to pay its fines. Criminal violations of mine safety laws were normally considered misdemeanors rather than felonies.

Over time, fatalities in the industry had declined. At the turn of the 20th century, around 300 to 400 miners died every year in the nation's coal mines; by the 1980s, this number had dropped to less than 50. Injuries and illnesses had also dropped. In part, these declines reflected tougher government regulations. They also reflected the rise of surface mining (mostly in the western United States), which tended to be safer, and the emergence of new technologies that mechanized the process of underground mining. The unionization of the mining industry had also given workers a greater voice and the right to elect safety representatives in many workplaces.

The Upper Big Branch Mine

Massey had bought the Upper Big Branch mine in 1993 from Peabody Coal. It was a particularly valuable property because its thick coal seam produced the high-grade metallurgic coal favored by utilities and the steel industry. Two hundred employees worked there on three, round-the-clock shifts. In 2009, Upper Big Branch produced

---

[11] "History of Mine Safety and Health Legislation," Mine Safety and Health Administration, *www.msha.gov.*

1.2 million tons of coal, about 3 percent of Massey's total. The mine, like all of those operated by Massey, was nonunion.

The regulatory record revealed a widespread pattern of safety violations at the Upper Big Branch mine and an increasingly contentious relationship between its managers and government regulators. As shown in Exhibit C, government inspectors had issued an increasing number of violations over time, with a sharp spike upward the year before the disaster. These data also showed that around 2006, management had begun to contest regulatory penalties rather than pay them. The state investigation reported the story that at one point Massey's vice president for safety—an attorney—"took a violation written by an inspector, looked at her people, and said, 'Don't worry, we'll litigate it away.'" Appealing the citations not only allowed the company to delay or avoid paying; it also blocked tougher sanctions, such as shutting down the mine.

Miners testified that they were intimidated or disciplined if they complained about safety. When one foreman told his men not to run coal until a ventilation problem was fixed, he was suspended for three days for "poor work performance." Another miner, who was killed in the blast, had told his wife that a manager had told him when he complained about conditions, "If you can't go up there and run coal, just bring your [lunch] bucket outside and go home." The father of a young miner who was still a trainee when he was killed at Upper Big Branch related his son's experience to investigators. The young man had told his father that when he had expressed concerns about safety to his supervisor, he was told, "If you're going to be that scared of your job here, you need to rethink your career."[12] Miners who were hurt on the job were told not to report their injuries, so an NFDL (non-fatal day lost) would not be recorded. A former Massey miner who testified before a Senate committee explained, "If you got hurt, you were told not to fill out the lost-time accident paperwork. The company would just pay guys to sit in the bathhouse or to stay at home if they got hurt."[13]

Investigators found that the company had kept two sets of books at UBB, one for its own record keeping and the other to show inspectors. "If a coal mine wants to keep two sets of books, that's their business," the administrator for MSHA later commented. "They can keep five sets of books if they want. But they're required to record the hazards in the official set of books."[14] Conditions that were recorded in the company's own books—but not the official set—included sudden methane spikes, inoperative safety equipment, and other dangers.

The mine also had a system in place, set up by its chief of security, to warn underground managers that an inspector was on the way—a clear violation of the law. A miner who survived the explosion later told Congress, "The code word would go out we've got a man [government inspector] on the property. . . . When the word goes out, all effort is made to correct the deficiencies."[15] A surviving miner testified:

> Nobody shuts one of Don Blankenship's mines down. It has never happened. Everyone knows when mine inspectors are coming, you clean things up for a few minutes, make it look good, then you go back to the business of running coal. That's how things work at Massey. When inspectors write a violation, the company lawyers challenge it in court. It's just all a game. Don Blankenship does what he wants.[16]

[12] UMW, op. cit., p. 81.

[13] UMW, op. cit., p. 78.

[14] "Mine Owners Misled Inspectors, Investigators Say," *The New York Times,* June 29, 2011.

[15] UMW, op. cit., p. 77.

[16] Jeff Goodell, op. cit.

Exhibit C

Year	Number of Citations	Assessed Penalty ($)	Amount Paid ($)
2000	240	55,325	55,325
2001	398	48,761	48,761
2002	221	64,726	64,726
2003	175	41,934	41,405
2004	238	48,371	48,371
2005	143	32,577	32,576
2006	173	191,249	84,411
2007	271	253,984	61,745
2008	197	239,566	105,965
2009	515	897,325	292,953

Source: MSHA data, reported in the appendices of *Industrial Homicide: Report on the Upper Big Branch Mine Disaster.*

After the disaster, Blankenship stated, "Violations are unfortunately a normal part of the mining process. There are violations in every coal mine in America, and UBB was a mine that had violations."

Causes of the Disaster

In the months following the tragedy at Upper Big Branch, three separate investigations—conducted by the federal MSHA, a commission established by the governor of West Virginia, and the United Mine Workers—examined the causes of the fatal explosion. All came to the same conclusion: that a spark from the longwall shearer had ignited a pocket of methane, which had then set off a series of explosions of volatile coal dust that had raced through the mine. Such events could only have happened in the presence of serious, systematic safety violations. Among the problems cited by the investigators were these:

- *Rock Dust.* Investigators found that the company had failed to meet government standards for the application of rock dust. As a result, explosive coal dust had built up on surfaces and in the air throughout the mine.

The state commission reported that the Upper Big Branch mine had only two workers assigned to rock dusting, and they typically worked at the task only three days a week and were frequently called away to do other jobs. Moreover, their task was often impossible because the mine's single dusting machine, which was about 30 years old, was broken most of the time. Federal investigators later determined that more than 90 percent of the area of the mine where the explosion occurred was inadequately rock dusted at the time of the explosion. They also found that the area of the longwall where the explosion began had not been rock dusted a single time since production started there in September 2009. The presence of large amounts of floating coal dust in the mine was also suggested by medical evidence. Seventy-one percent of the autopsied victims showed clinical signs of black lung disease, caused by breathing airborne coal dust. Nationally, the rate of black lung disease in underground coal miners was around 3 percent.

- *Ventilation.* Investigators found that the Upper Big Branch Mine did not have sufficient ventilation to provide the miners with fresh, breathable air, and to remove coal dust as well as methane and other dangerous gases.

Upper Big Branch, like many mines, used a so-called push-pull system in which large fans at the portal blew fresh air into the mine, and a fan on the other end pulled air out. The state investigation found that this system did not work very well at Upper Big Branch. The fans were powerful enough, but the plan was not properly engineered.

> The push-pull ventilation system at Upper Big Branch . . . had a design flaw: its fans were configured so that air was directed in a straight line even though miners worked in areas away from the horizontal path. As a result, air had to be diverted from its natural flow pattern into the working sections. . . . Because these sections were located on different sides of the natural flow pattern, multiple diversionary controls had to be constructed and frequently were in competition with one another.[17]

Poor ventilation had likely caused methane to build up near the longwall shearer, providing the fuel for the initial fireball, investigators found.

- *Equipment Maintenance.* Investigators concluded that water sprays on the longwall shearer were not functioning properly, and as a result were unable to extinguish the initial spark.

After the disaster, investigators closely studied the longwall shearer where the initial fire had started. They found that several of the cutting teeth on the rotating blades (called "bits") had worn flat and lost their carbide tips, so they were likely to create sparks when hitting sandstone. The investigators also examined the water nozzles on the shearer, which normally sprayed water onto the coal face during operation to cool the cutting bits, extinguish sparks, and push away any methane that might have leaked into the area. They found that seven of the nozzles were either missing or clogged. Tests found that the longwall shearer did not have adequate water pressure to keep the surface wet and cool. As a result, any small sparks thrown off during the mining process could not be extinguished.

In short, a series of interrelated safety violations had combined to produce a preventable tragedy. The United Mine Workers called the disaster "industrial homicide" and called for the criminal prosecution of Massey's managers.

For its part, Massey had a completely different interpretation of the causes of the events of April 5. An investigation commissioned by the company and headed by Bobby R. Inman, its lead independent director, said that the explosion was caused by a sudden, massive inundation of natural gas through a crack in the mine's floor—an Act of God that the company could not have anticipated or prevented. The company report stated:

> . . . the scientific data that [Massey] has painstakingly assembled over the last year with the assistance of a team of nationally renowned experts so far compels at least five conclusions. *First,* a massive inundation of natural gas caused the UBB explosion and coal dust did not contribute materially to the magnitude or severity of the blast; *second,* although an ignition source may never be determined, the explosion likely originated in the Tailgate 21 entries, but certainly not as a result of faulty shearer maintenance; *third,* [the company] adequately rock dusted the mine prior to the explosion such that coal dust could not have played a causal role in the accident; *fourth,* the mine's underground ventilation system provided significantly more fresh air than required by law and there is no evidence that ventilation contributed to the explosion; and *fifth,* MSHA has conducted a deeply flawed accident investigation that has been predicated, in part, upon secrecy, protecting its own self-interest,

---

[17] Governor's Independent Investigation Panel, op. cit., p. 61.

witness intimidation, obstruction of [company] investigators, and retaliatory citations.[18]

In a conversation with stock analysts six months after the disaster, Blankenship stated that he had a "totally clear conscience" and that he did not believe Massey had "contributed in any way to the accident."[19]

Discussion Questions

1. What were the costs and benefits to stakeholders of the actions taken by Massey Energy and its managers?

2. Applying the four methods of ethical reasoning (utilitarianism, rights, justice, and virtue), do you believe Massey Energy behaved in an ethical manner? Why or why not?

3. Who or what caused the Upper Big Branch mine disaster, and why do you think so?

4. What steps could be taken now to reduce the chances of a similar tragedy occurring in the future? In your answer, please address the appropriate roles of mining companies (and their directors and managers), government regulators and policymakers, and the workers and their union in assuring mine safety.

---

[18] *http://www.usmra.com/download/MasseyUBBReport.pdf.*

[19] "CEO says Massey has 'Clear Conscience' over Upper Big Branch," *Charleston Gazette,* October 27, 2010.

Carolina Pad and the Bloggers

A few weeks before the start of the September 2009 Type-A Mom Conference in Asheville, North Carolina, April Whitlock received yet another pay-for-blog request. Whitlock had only been with Carolina Pad, a maker and distributor of school supplies, for nine months. As the company's first director of brand management, she had been hired for her knowledge of social media and innovative uses of the Internet. A major part of her Internet strategy was the creative use of blogs and bloggers, especially mommy bloggers.

Mommy bloggers were typically stay-at-home mothers who wrote about their lives and the products they used. Providing these individuals with products to review or occasionally to give away in contests on their blogs seemed like a reasonable way to release information to the public about new Carolina Pad designs and products. Mommy bloggers had traditionally disclosed on their blogs when they had received free samples for review. Their reviews then ranged from very positive to very negative.

With Carolina Pad's limited promotional budget (no money was budgeted for traditional media), Whitlock believed that blogs offered a tool for increasing exposure for Carolina Pad's product designs at a relatively low cost compared to advertising in traditional media. Carolina Pad was able to provide product samples to select bloggers for a few hundred dollars while the expenditure for many advertising options was cost prohibitive.

April received several requests from mommy bloggers for financial support to cover their travel expenses to attend the Type-A Mom Conference. These requests also contained specific commitments to promote Carolina Pad's products at the conference and to write blogs about Carolina Pad products. "What are the ethics of fulfilling such requests?" April wondered. She wondered if she should request additional funding to pay the bloggers or if she should refuse the requests. She believed bloggers' writings about Carolina Pad's products were effective, and she felt certain that competitors had received similar requests.

Carolina Pad

In 1945, Joseph (Joe) K. Hall Jr. and several business associates managed to scrape up enough money and equipment to start a school supply manufacturing company in Charlotte, North Carolina. Joe, a former teacher, principal, and coach, owned and operated Hall & Morris,

By Steven M. Cox, Bradley W. Brooks, S. Cathy Anderson, and J. Norris Frederick. Copyright © 2011 by the *Case Research Journal* and the authors. Used by permission. All rights reserved.

The authors of this case express sincere gratitude to two anonymous reviewers of the *Case Research Journal* and to Anne Lawrence, the editor of this special issue, for their particularly insightful and valuable comments and suggestions.

a school supply wholesale business in nearby Belmont, North Carolina. Hall & Morris transformed into a new company, Carolina Pad, that both manufactured and distributed school supplies.

As a manufacturer, Carolina Pad offered composition books, notebook paper, primary tablets, pencils, crayons, and other school supplies. To gain an edge over larger, more established counterparts, Joe sold products directly to schools in the Carolinas and Virginia—often out of the back of his truck.

When Clay Presley joined Carolina Pad as president in 2000, he quickly realized that business as usual was not an option. In the 1980s and 1990s, Carolina Pad, like many other paper product manufacturers, faced the twin challenges of declining profit margins and stiff competition from overseas. During Presley's first back-to-school season, sales had been very disappointing, revenues had declined, and margins had shrunk. In a pivotal staff meeting, Presley asked everyone, "What would the company look like if it started today?" The team decided it needed to move toward designing fashionable products and away from manufacturing traditional pads of paper. They decided to target high school–age girls. For the next back-to-school season, Carolina Pad added a plaid designer notebook to its traditional lineup. Retailers loved it. That season the new designs became the top seller at Wal-Mart Stores, Inc.

In 2003, Carolina Pad began outsourcing its manufacturing to locations in other countries at significantly lower costs. The resulting savings allowed Carolina Pad to invest more money in creative designs, branding, and marketing. That same year, Carolina Pad hired designer Jacqueline McFee to lead its creative design efforts. With a focus on the latest fads, the company developed new lines of stationery that included popular text messaging phrases to publicize environmentally friendly messages. A buyer at Family Dollar Stores, Inc., said Carolina Pad's designs had become a perennial bestseller. "Carolina Pad and Paper is the fashion and trend leader for this category," the buyer noted.[1]

Carolina Pad was widely credited with making fashion and design a key ingredient in the industry by creating a series of designs for its notebooks and binders intended to appeal to teenage girls. The company displayed the design name on the front of each notebook or binder and the Carolina Pad name on the back and/or the inside cover. (See Exhibit A for a description of the 2009 fashions and designs found on Carolina Pad's notebooks and pads.) Company sales grew from $30 million in 2000 to $104 million in 2008. By 2009, Carolina Pad products were sold in retail stores across North America and in parts of Europe and Asia.

April Whitlock

A Duke University graduate, April Whitlock was a marketing veteran with a variety of experiences. Prior to accepting a position with Carolina Pad, April had been responsible for developing the national brand and marketing strategy for Mom Corps, a company that recruited talented moms who had outstanding professional experience (especially lawyers, CPAs, MBAs, etc.) and had opted to stay at home as their children's primary caregiver. Mom Corps worked with companies to identify flexible contract or part-time opportunities for these women. Prior to Mom Corps, April had spent seven and a half years with

[1] Adam O'Daniel, "Carolina Pad's Strategy Takes It to the Head of the Class," *Charlotte Business Journal*, August 7, 2009. Retrieved from *http://charlotte.bizjournals.com/charlotte/stories/2009/08/10/story16.html?b=1249876800^1895 411.*

What better way to express yourself than with products that reflect your personality? Our 2009 designs are in the stores now and you'll be seeing fabulous updates of some of our most popular designs, as well as a few new ones. Whether you want trendy or timeless elegance, there's something for you in one of our collections.

WHAT'S YOUR STYLE?

Feeling Chic-y?

You might want to try Pearl Stripe, designs with subtle color palettes and simple elegance. Simply Chic offers classic houndstooth, pinstripe, and scroll designs paired with bold color.

INSPIRED BY NATURE'S BEAUTY?

We've updated Carolina Pad classics Whimsical Flower and Graphic in Nature with new color palettes and designs.

WANT TO LIVE OUT LOUD?

Want to be noticed? The hip and fun Hot Chocolate and Eye Candy might be the right designs to get that second look!

The Kendall Kollection gives you great eye-catching design and lets you give back. Each product sold benefits The Leukemia & Lymphoma Society's efforts to fight Leukemia.

ARE YOU ECO-LOGICAL?

Our new Sasquatch Brand's eco-friendly products are in stores now. Get product and where-to-shop information at the Sasquatch website.

THE BASIC

Do you just want great functionality and durability? Notebound Colors and MX keep it simple.

LendingTree, where she had led key business-to-business marketing efforts. In her new role with Carolina Pad, April worked directly with its marketing, sales, and creative teams to shape the brand identities for all products.

In her thirties, April belonged to the first generation to be considered Internet natives rather than immigrants. As a member of the Public Relations Society of America (PRSA), she understood the power of Internet-based publicity. Websites such as Facebook® and Twitter® were reporting huge numbers of users. Facebook recently had reported over 400 million active users (users who had returned to the site within the last 30 days). In addition, online product reviews posted by online product evaluators and users on sites such as Epinions, cnet, consumer search, and Amazon were playing a more important role in the information search and decision process of consumers. Knowing that Carolina Pad's target market, teen girls, were heavy users of Internet social media, an Internet-based promotional strategy seemed a natural choice.

Within weeks of April's arrival, Carolina Pad had a presence on several major social media sites, including Facebook and YouTube. In addition, Carolina Pad became actively discussed on several blog sites such as Auntie Thesis, Eighty MPH Mom, A Bookish Mom, and Classy Mom Blog. April had been key in the development of product packages for

bloggers to review, and several blog sites had sponsored contests where the prizes were Carolina Pad products that April had supplied.

History of Blogging

Modern blogging began in the mid-1990s as nothing more than individuals keeping online diaries of their personal lives. The term "blog" is a contraction of "web log" or "weblog." In the late 1990s, a number of online tools paved the way for modern blog sites. By 2001, blogging had become popular enough that researchers began identifying the differences between blogging and journalism. Bloggers began reporting on current events. Unfettered by traditional journalists' needs for multiple sources and accuracy, bloggers were free to address topics and events more quickly than the mainstream media could. A classic example occurred in 2002 when bloggers first broke the story of Senator Trent Lott honoring Senator Strom Thurmond by suggesting that the United States would have been better off if Thurmond had been elected president in 1948. The history of Thurmond's racial views created a flurry of comments, which eventually forced Lott to resign as majority leader.[2]

Recognizing the effect of blogs on public opinion, by 2004 many politicians, pundits, and opinion leaders were active bloggers. More recently, tweets (micro blogs in the form of text-based posts of up to 140 characters) from Iran were the first to break the story that the election of Mahmoud Ahmadinejad might have been rigged.[3] By 2008, the United States had an estimated 26.4 million blog sites accessed by 77.7 million unique visitors, and 77 percent of Internet users were reading blogs.[4]

Blogging and Business

This new word-of-mouth (WOM) method to share one's personal life and opinions caught the attention of marketers. Businesses increasingly embraced social media as many bloggers began reaching large audiences. Blog sites sold advertisements at rates that were often more attractive than traditional print media. *Forbes* magazine provided an example rate comparison in 2007:

> And while blog networks are quickly gaining scale, even their most coveted offerings are cost-competitive. To make a back-of-the-napkin comparison based on rate cards: A start-up looking to get attention will grab a third-of-a-page color ad in a magazine with a rate base of 600,000 and might pay $27,300; or it can pay $21,000 for 600,000 impressions for its ads on TechCrunch—a site covering start-ups represented by Battelle's Federated Media—assuming they take the priciest ad slot on one of tech's hottest sites.[5]

[2] Mark Glaser, "Trent Lott Gets Bloggered; Free Finance Sites Spoofed by WSJ.com Ads." Retrieved from *http://www.ojr.org/ojr/glaser/1040145065.php.*

[3] Lev Grossman, "Iran Protests: Twitter, the Medium of the Movement," *Time,* June 17, 2009. Retrieved from *http://www.time.com/time/world/article/0,8599,1905125,00.html.*

[4] Technorati.com, "State of the Blogosphere 2008" (2008). Retrieved from *http://readwrite.com/2008/09/22/state_of_the_blogosphere_2008.*

[5] Brian Caulfield, "Tech Boom, Media Bust," *Forbes,* July 17, 2009. Retrieved from *http://www.forbes.com/2007/07/16/redherring-print-blogs-tech-media-cx_bc_0716techmedia.html%20accessed%209-3-09.*

In addition to advertising, blog sites provided valuable publicity for consumer products. Bloggers reviewed products and made free products available to their readers for comments. Consumer product companies routinely provided sample products for blog site review, offered products for blog site contests, and provided advance information about new products and models.

Several sites had begun advertising their pay-for-blogging opportunities. ReviewMe.com, CreamAid.com, Bloggerwave.com, Smorty.com, Blogitive.com, and PayPerPost.com all were willing to compensate bloggers for comments on specific products. Two of these—ReviewMe.com and PayPerPost.com—provided the following information on their websites:

ReviewMe.com

1. Submit your site for inclusion into our ReviewMe publisher network. Begin by creating a free account using the link below.
2. If approved, your site will enter our ReviewMe marketplace and clients will purchase reviews from you.
3. You decide to accept the review or not.
4. You will be paid $20.00 to $200.00 for each completed review that you post on your site.

PayPerPost.com

> Get paid for blogging. You've been writing about Web sites, products, services and companies you love for years and you have yet to benefit from all the sales and traffic you have helped generate. That's about to change. With PayPerPost advertisers are willing to pay you for your opinion on various topics. Search through a list of Opportunities, make a blog posting, get your content approved, and get paid. It's that simple.

In addition, manufacturers went directly to bloggers to offer products and monetary compensation. Microsoft, for example, sent several bloggers a Ferrari 5000 computer preloaded with its Vista operating system. The estimated retail value of the computer and software was over $2,000. Microsoft did not require the return of the computer; it merely asked that the recipients review the Vista operating system.[6]

Kmart had an innovative approach to influence bloggers. They gave Chris Brogan (a well-known blogger) and a handful of other bloggers $500 gift cards to spend at Kmart with the request that they write about their experiences. They were also asked to invite their readers to enter a contest to win a comparable giveaway.[7]

Even book publishers participated in paying for blogs. Textbook publisher Reed Elsevier discovered an employee's "overzealous" attempt to generate buzz for its titles. The employee's e-mails announced that anyone writing a "five-star" review of any of Reed Elsevier's new textbooks on either Amazon's or Barnes and Noble's e-commerce sites would get a free copy of the book and a $25 Amazon gift certificate from the publisher.[8] Upon learning of the offer, the publisher immediately withdrew it.

[6] Vaughan-Nichols, "Anatomy of a Blogger Bribe," *Linux-Watch*, December 28, 2009. Retrieved from *http://www.linux-watch.com/news/NS4123497783.html*.

[7] PaulGillan.com, "Ethics and the $500 Gift Card," December 15, 2008. Retrieved from *http://paulgillin.com/2008/12/ethics-and-the-500-gift-card/*.

[8] Bookseller.com, "$25 Offer a Mistake, Admits Reed Elsevier," June 24, 2009. Retrieved from *http://www.thebookseller.com/news/89581-25-offer-a-mistake-admits-reed-elsevier.html.rss*.

Product Recommendations and Undisclosed Advertising

The music industry provided a historic example of undisclosed pay for promotion. In the 1950s, the practice of radio deejays taking payments from record companies to play specific songs was common. Radio listeners could perceive significant airplay as a measure of a song's popularity, which could then lead to higher ratings and additional sales. Deejays did not disclose the fact that they took money to play certain records, and most listeners were unaware that the music choices were not a result of the popularity of a song or artist.

In 1960, as a result of its hearings, Congress amended the Federal Communications Act, specifically sections 317 and 507, to outlaw under-the-table payments and to require broadcasters to disclose if airplay for a song had been purchased. Pay-for-play was legal only if disclosed. Since the year 2000, there had been only 13 Federal Communications Commission (FCC) enforcement actions for undisclosed pay-for-play in the record industry.[9]

Although the FCC was charged with regulating the airways, whether the Internet fell under its jurisdiction was unclear. Other related industries had become the subject of more recent debates. As DVRs and other new technologies allowed viewers to skip traditional TV ads, advertisers looked for new advertising avenues, including paying to have a product used as part of a storyline, either as product placement (use of product as a prop, such as characters drinking a Coke or Pepsi or using an Apple computer) or product integration (use of the product in the dialogue or plot). In 2003, Commercial Alert, a nonprofit organization that sought to "keep the commercial culture within its proper sphere,"[10] petitioned the FCC to require pop-ups announcing "advertisement" in movie or television show scenes where paid product placements appeared.

The Federal Trade Commission (FTC) was charged with safeguarding consumers against false or misleading claims within various media. The FTC, however, had not updated its guidelines since 1980, well before the advent of blogging.[11] As such, no laws existed to regulate payments to bloggers for promotional purposes. The world of blogging and social media had become an unregulated environment with an audience reach that could rival traditional, heavily regulated broadcast media. As a result, lawsuits had been the primary redress for Internet-related grievances; and defamation, product disparagement, and invasion of privacy lawsuits had grown along with the popularity of the blogosphere. In most of these lawsuits, individual judges had to decide the proper balance between protecting individuals and safeguarding free speech.

 The Incident

April's primary objective for her mommy blogger approach was to create a buzz about Carolina Pad. She hoped that buzz would lead to positive perceptions of the brand name, as well as positive perceptions of specific Carolina Pad design names. The target market—teenage girls—was very fashion-conscious, with fashion being dictated by peer groups. By generating positive consumer perceptions, Carolina Pad sought to be viewed as attractive to this group.

---

[9] Federal Communications Commission, "Payola and Sponsorship Identification," March 9, 2009. Retrieved from *http://www.FCC.gov/eb/broadcast/sponsid.html*.

[10] Commercial Alert, *http://www.commercialalert.org*.

[11] Elisabeth Eaves, "Marketing's Wild West Gets Civilized," *Forbes*, July 31, 2009.

For nine months her Internet strategy had been building momentum. By July 2009, April had established a good relationship with several mommy bloggers, and they had given Carolina Pad's new product line very positive reviews. The number of positive tweets, Facebook mentions, and blog entries had been growing every month. On March 10, for example, one blogger promoted a Carolina Pad product giveaway contest on the "Just Pure Lovely" blog site:

> Because of my obsession with all things that have to do with "paper" and "writing" and "organizing" (*oh, my*!), I am So. Very. Delighted to host this BIG ($150 value) giveaway from Carolina Pad for one of you. . . . The winner of this giveaway gets to choose which set to call her (his?) own! I know, I know. How can you ever choose? I'll leave that dilemma to the winner. I couldn't choose, so I own parts of both sets.[12]

Less than a week later, another blogger wrote of her experience receiving product supplies from Carolina Pad on the site "This Full House":

> . . . Quite frankly, the girls and I fought tooth and nail over all the awesome stuff inside! My 10-year-old son, not so much.[13]

In late May, another blogger wrote about Carolina Pad on the site "Three Boys and a Dog":

> If you know anything about me, you know I have an honest to goodness addiction . . . ok, a couple of them, but we are only going to address one today. I LOVE office supplies! ALL office supplies! I would rather have paper, pens, notebooks, and binders than shirts, dresses, or shoes! So, when I was given the chance to review Carolina Pad's Eye Candy line, I was super excited. Carolina Pad has a bunch of super adorable things and you can find them everywhere: Walmart & Target both carry their products.[14]

As Carolina Pad moved into the most important part of its selling season—the back-to-school season—the Internet strategy designed to create a buzz seemed to be working. The next conference where a significant number of mommy bloggers would be present was scheduled for September. "A positive response from these women," April thought, "would continue the momentum that Carolina Pad has been generating."

In July, she received e-mails from four mommy bloggers requesting financial assistance ranging from $75 to $1,000 to attend the upcoming bloggers conference. Although these e-mails specifically described how Carolina Pad would benefit in exchange for providing funding, none of the e-mails stated that the blogger would disclose that she had been sponsored for promotional purposes. Exhibit B through Exhibit E provide copies of these e-mails.

"I always thought of mommy-bloggers as women who commented on their lives and the products they used," April thought. "Selling their blogs and tweets seems inconsistent with the concept of blogging." Despite such innocent perceptions, the blogging industry had not adopted any formal code of conduct that would apply to making or receiving payments for

[12] Just Pure Lovely, "A BIG Giveaway! $150 Worth of Fashion Office Products," March 10, 2009. Retrieved from *www.freelyeducate.com/2009/03/a-big-giveaway-150-worth-of-fashion-office-line-products.html*.

[13] This Full House, "Carolina Pad Giveaway: Fashionable School Supplies and Stylish Office Supplies, OH MY!" March 16, 2009. Retrieved from *http://www.thisfullhouse.com/reviews/2009/03/carolina-pad-giveaway.html*.

[14] Three Boys and a Dog, "Carolina Pad Eye Candy Review," May 31, 2009. Retrieved from *http://3boysandadog.com/2009/05/carolina-pad-eye-candy-review/*.

I am attending the Type-A Mom Conference September 24–27th in Asheville, NC. The good news is that I live pretty close so I will be driving and don't need to pay for airfare. I don't, however, live close enough to drive back and forth each day, so I am hoping to find a sponsor for the hotel room while I'm there plus expenses. I am open to more than one company offering partial sponsorships and I will promote however many will contribute. This would be a great venue to promote Carolina Pad to a very specific target audience of Moms/Women. Women who are hip, business oriented and have children of all ages!

Type-A Mom Conference is a unique mom blogging conference designed to help you take it to the next level. The conference will feature some of the most influential, admired and insightful mom bloggers talking about topics like power social networking, branding, blogging, finding your voice, and turning your passion for blogging into a real paycheck.

I'll be blogging/Tweeting live all weekend from the Type-A Mom Conference.

WHAT'S IN IT FOR YOU? GOOD QUESTION!

$100 Sponsors will get:

- Top billing as a [*Blog Site Name*] sponsor in all posts about the conference during the weekend and afterward!
- I'll hand out your business card, flyers, product, etc. during the weekend.
- A blog post about your company and several Tweets about your company during the weekend.

$250 Sponsors will get:

- Top billing as a [*Blog Site Name*] sponsor in all posts about the conference during the weekend and afterward!
- I'll hand out your business card, flyers, product, etc. during the weekend!
- Representation at the Type A Mom Conference in September (I'll pass out cards, wear your teeshirts, whatever you want me to do to get you noticed)!
- Advertising at [*Blog Site Name*] for one full year (direct link or graphic)!
- A blog post about your company and several Tweets about your company during the weekend.

Sponsors of $500 or more will get:

- Top billing as a [*Blog Site Name*] sponsor in all posts about the conference during the weekend and afterward!
- A blog post about your company and several Tweets about your company during the weekend.
- I'll hand out your business card, flyers, product, etc. during the weekend.
- Representation at the Type A Mom Conference in September (I'll pass out cards, wear your teeshirts, whatever you want me to do to get you noticed)!
- Advertising at [*Blog Site Name*] for one full year (direct link or graphic)!
- A party hosted by me, sponsored by your company one night during the weekend!

If you are interested in getting your company/product noticed by hundreds of bloggers and companies and being represented by a blogger with a strong background in public relations, promotions and product placement, e-mail me and let's get connected!

[*Blogger Name*]
[*Blog Site Address*]

Hi April!

My name is [*Blogger Name*]. I am the founder and administrator of [*Blog Site Name*], a newly revamped women's e-magazine. I received your information from the girls at Blog Friendly PR.

My offer is a bit different than many others you have probably received since posting on Blog Friendly PR. I will be attending the Type-A Mom blog conference in September and am seeking sponsorship in return for several types of compensation. Because of the recent expansion of [*Blog Site Name*], this is a fantastic opportunity for you to be included with one of the newest and most talked about women's blogs on the net. I have included our newest press release and media kit for [*Blog Site Name*].

In return for a FULL sponsorship ($1,000), I will:

- Wear YOUR logo clothing RATHER than my own.
- Hand out samples of YOUR product, business cards, and other promotional products.
- Live Blog for YOU!
- Conduct video interviews of your choice.
- Network on YOUR behalf to exhibitor booths.
- Write five different posts about the Type-A-Mom Conference on [Blog Site Name] linking to YOU.
- For a year, every time I write about the Type-A-Mom Conference I will include a link to YOU.
- Tweet periodically about your product for a month.
- Review of YOUR products featured on my site.

In return for one of five partial sponsorships ($200 each) I will:

- Wear YOUR logo on my clothing along with my own.
- Hand out samples of YOUR product, business cards, and other promotional products.
- Network on YOUR behalf to exhibitor booths.
- Write a post about the Type-A-Mom Conference on [*Blog Site Name*] linking to YOU.
- Review of YOUR product featured on my site.

I am a passionate person who would have to say I have never met a stranger. I am super loyal to the people, companies, products, and services that in return are good to me. Most of all, I feel attending The Type-A-Mom Conference will further bond me with the blogging community making me more relevant and beneficial for a company who understands that **Mom Word of Mouth** is the most powerful kind of publicity.

Thank you for your consideration and thank you for taking the time to review my bid for sponsorship. I am looking forward to your reply and hopefully to the chance of working with you to get to the Type-A-Mom-Conference! ;)

[*Blogger Name*]
Founder/Administrator
[*Blog Site Address*]
Twitter: [*Twitter Link*]
Facebook: [*Facebook Link*]

Hi April,

I love the feedback I'm getting on my giveaway. People really seem to love the products!

I had so much fun with everyone at [*Blog Site Name*] that I'm making plans to attend the Typeamomconference.com in Asheville, NC for September 23–27. I am looking for a few premium sponsors to partner with, and because I have absolutely loved your product, I would love the opportunity to promote this at the conference.

In return, I'd like to offer advertising in the top spots on [*Blog Site Name*] and/or branding on my [*Second Blog Site Name*] page.

I'd like to promote your brand to my 1,000 subscribers, 3,800 twitter followers, and almost 300 friends on facebook before and during the conference, and will be happy to . . .

before the conference:

- Blog, facebook, and tweet about your product at the conference:
- Hand out samples
- Brand my laptop, and phone skins
- Hand out your cards

For $100, I will offer four months' advertising on [*Blog Site Name*] on the top spots above the fold.

For $75, I will offer branding for three months on my [*Second Blog Site Name*] page. Your ad will pop up for every one of my page views, even when I am included in stories of the other bloggers in attendance. ([*Second Blog Site Name*] is a photo, story telling application, check out the sample story here [*Link to Second Blog Site*] and you can see branding on the pages.) I'm looking for up to three sponsors for this spot, and the graphic would hold the logo of all 3.

With both of those advertising options, I will do all the promotions listed before and during the conference.

I'm also willing to brainstorm ideas for additional sponsorship. For my [*Blog Site Name*] sponsor, [*Current Company Sponsor*], we are working on a [*Contest Name Related to Current Company Sponsor's Product*] contest that we started during the conference, and are continuing with voting and prizes after.

Consider me your voice for the conference. Looking forward to hearing your thoughts!

[*Blogger Name*]
[*Blog Site Address*]
www.twitter.com/[*Blog Site Twitter Link*]

promotion within the blogs. Although many blog sites did carry advertising, the fact that they were paid advertisements was clearly disclosed. Promotions within the blogs—and the disclosure of any material relationships with a sponsor(s)—were solely up to the discretion of the blogger.

Despite the absence of an agreed upon industry code of conduct, one independent website offered its own policies for blogging conduct. In evaluating her alternatives, April considered the policies set forth by BlogWithIntegrity.com, a website that sought to promote seven blogging principles deemed to be of high integrity. One of these principles stated that a blogger would disclose any material relationship with a business. The website

Hello,

I found you through the blog friendly companies list. I am currently looking for a sponsor to send me to Type A Mom Conference in Asheville, North Carolina. http://typeamomconference.com/. I work with a lot of websites with large traffic and really think that I could offer you some great promotion. I am currently selling two sponsorship opportunities. One sponsorship for my flight to the conference ($310) and one sponsorship for my hotel stay ($390). I have included a list below of the benefits of being a sponsor. Please take a look and let me know if you have any questions! I would love to work with your company!

- One article write-up/review on [*Blog Site Name*] which receives over half a million views monthly
- One review/giveaway on [*Second Blog Site Name*] which receives over twenty thousand views monthly
- One article write-up/review on my personal blog [*Third Blog Site Name*] as well as free advertising for six months
- Free advertising on [*Fourth Blog Site Name*] for three months. The [*Fourth Blog Site Name*] receives over fifty thousand views monthly
- Wear your logo at Type A Mom Conference as well as pass out promotion materials
- Host a product giveaway at Type A Mom Conference
- Ten tweets about your products and/or promotions (currently have 691 followers)

I would be happy to hear any additional ideas you have for promoting your business. I look forward to hearing from you!

Thanks,

[*Blogger Name*]

had created a "Blog with Integrity" badge that it offered for websites of bloggers who agreed with its principles.[15] (The seven principles and a copy of the badge are presented in Exhibit F.) April had only seen this badge displayed on a few mommy blogger websites. Of the nine websites specifically represented within the four blogger requests she had received, none of them displayed this badge.

Although none of these requests was for more than $1,000, April felt that the amount was not really the issue. April firmly believed the promotional considerations these bloggers were offering could provide a significantly higher rate of return for Carolina Pad than the company could receive from other, more traditional forms of promotion, such as advertising. In addition, she realized that her competitors were likely receiving similar requests from these or other bloggers, and many of them were probably benefiting already from paying such requests. April did not think that the fact that others would make such payments made it inherently acceptable for her to do so. April spoke to Carolina Pad's vice president of marketing who agreed with her on this point, even though no one at Carolina Pad had previously faced this decision.

---

[15] Blog with Integrity, *http://www.blogwithintegrity.com*.

PRINCIPLES

1. By displaying the Blog with Integrity badge or signing the pledge, I assert that the trust of my readers and the blogging community is important to me.

2. I treat others respectfully, attacking ideas and not people. I also welcome respectful disagreement with my own ideas.

3. I believe in intellectual property rights, providing links, citing sources, and crediting inspiration where appropriate.

4. I disclose my material relationships, policies, and business practices. My readers will know the difference between editorial, advertorial, and advertising, should I choose to have it. If I do sponsored or paid posts, they are clearly marked.

5. When collaborating with marketers and PR professionals, I handle myself professionally and abide by basic journalistic standards.

6. I always present my honest opinions to the best of my ability.

7. I own my words. Even if I occasionally have to eat them.

April was torn as she thought about her decision. The bloggers had not promised favorable reviews, just reviews. So wasn't she just putting forth advertising dollars to get her product visible? And yet, she worried there was something dishonest about this: wasn't it implicit that the reviews would be favorable? Was this ethical? Was it like paying radio disc jockeys to play your records? Would the payments be in violation of Carolina Pad's Mission and Values Statement (see Exhibit G)? And if she declined the bloggers' requests while questioning their ethical standards, would her relationship with any of the bloggers become strained?

Whatever she decided to do, she needed to make a decision soon, as the conference was in September.

We will excite our customers by bringing extraordinary fashion and innovation to everyday products.

At Carolina Pad, our mission and tagline reflect the dedication and care we put in every product we design. We are passionate in our mission to deliver the best product at the best price to the consumer and our customers.

Our core value system defines who we are and what we do every day:

- Build brands that meet the needs and wants of today's consumer.
- Anticipate and exceed consumer and customer expectations.
- Strive for design excellence in every product.
- Deliver products with superior functionality and value.
- Foster and encourage innovation, creativity, and teamwork in our company.
- Promote a healthier and safer workplace, community, and environment.

Discussion Questions

1. What is April Whitlock's dilemma? In your answer, include the relevant facts that Whitlock must consider and the assumptions she has made.

2. What alternative actions could Whitlock take? That is, what are her options?

3. For each of these options, identify which stakeholders would be affected, and how they would be affected.

4. Apply the four methods of ethical reasoning—utilitarianism, rights, justice, and virtue—to this situation. What would each of these methods suggest Whitlock should do?

5. What do you think Whitlock should do, and why?

This glossary defines technical or special terms used in this book. Students may use it as a quick and handy reference for terms that may be unfamiliar without having to refer to the specific chapter(s) where they are used. It also can be a very helpful aid in studying for examinations and for writing term papers where precise meanings are needed.

A

acid rain   Rain that is more acidic than normal; occurs when emissions of sulfur dioxide and nitrogen oxides from utilities, manufacturers, and motor vehicles combine with natural water vapor in the air and fall to earth as rain or snow.

advocacy advertising   A political tool used by companies to promote their viewpoint through the media.

affirmative action   A positive and sustained effort by an organization to identify, hire, train if necessary, and promote minorities, women, and members of other groups who are underrepresented in the organization's workforce.

air pollution   When more pollutants, such as sulfur dioxide or particulates, are emitted into the atmosphere than can be safely absorbed and diluted by natural processes.

alternative dispute resolution   A method for resolving legal conflicts outside the traditional court system, in which a professional mediator (a third-party neutral) works with the two sides to negotiate a settlement agreeable to both parties.

anti-Americanism   Opposition to the United States of America, or to its people, principles, or policies.

antitrust laws   Laws that seek to preserve competition in the marketplace and prohibit unfair, anticompetitive practices by business.

auditing process   Systems used by a business to ensure compliance with an industry or global set of standards.

B

B corporation   A business that explicitly seeks to blend its social objectives with its financial goals.

behavioral advertising   Advertising that targets particular customers based on their observed online behavior.

big data   When business uses technology to assist in the collection of massive amounts of information about its stakeholders.

biodiversity   The number and variety of species and the range of their genetic makeup.

biotechnology   A technological application that uses biological systems or living organisms to make or modify products or processes for specific use.

blogs   Web-based journals or logs maintained by an individual containing commentaries, descriptions, graphics, and other material.

blowing the whistle   (See whistle-blowing.)

board of directors   An elected group of individuals who have a legal duty to establish corporate objectives, develop broad policies, and select top-level personnel for a company.

bottom line   Business profits or losses, usually reported in figures on the last or bottom line of a company's income statement.

bottom of the pyramid   The world's poor; also refers to creative business actions to develop products and services that meet the needs of the world's poor.

boundary-spanning departments   Departments, or offices, within an organization that reach across the dividing line that separates a company from groups and people in society.

brand management   When managers use techniques to increase the perceived value of a product line or brand over time.

bribery   A questionable or unjust payment often to a government official to ensure or facilitate a business transaction.

bundling   The collection of political contributions made by an organization's stakeholders to increase the organization's ability to influence a political agent.

business   An organization that is engaged in making a product or providing a service for a profit.

business and society   The study of the relationship between business and its social environment.

business ethics   The application of general ethical ideas to business behavior.

C

campaign finance reform   Efforts to change the rules governing the financing of political campaigns, often by limiting contributions made or received.

capability building When a firm chooses to invest time and resources to build their supplier's capabilities.

cap-and-trade Allows businesses to buy and sell permits that entitle the bearer to emit a certain amount of pollution. The government or international agency issues these permits and caps the total amount of pollution that may be produced.

carbon neutrality When an organization or individual produces net zero emissions of greenhouse gases.

carbon offsets (carbon credits) Investments in projects that remove carbon dioxide or its equivalent from the atmosphere.

carrying capacity The maximum population that the Earth's ecosystem can support at a certain level of technological development.

central state control (system) A socioeconomic system in which economic power is concentrated in the hands of government officials and political authorities. The central government owns the property that is used to produce goods and services, and most private markets are illegal.

CERCLA (Comprehensive Environmental Response, Compensation, and Liability Act). The major U.S. law governing the cleanup of existing hazardous-waste sites, popularly known as Superfund.

chief information officer Manager who has been entrusted with the responsibility to manage the organization's technology with its many privacy and security issues.

chief sustainability officer Manager responsible for the organization's sustainability activities and performance.

child care The care or supervision of another's child, such as at a day-care center; offered as a benefit by some employers to working parents.

child labor The hiring of children in a way that deprives them of their childhood, their potential, and their dignity, and is harmful to their physical and mental development.

Citizens United decision A U.S. Supreme Court ruling that allowed corporations and unions to contribute directly to candidates for public office.

civic engagement The active involvement of businesses and individuals in changing and improving communities.

civil society Nonprofit, educational, religious, community, family, and interest-group organizations; social organizations that do not have a commercial or governmental purpose. (See also nongovernmental organization.)

clean economy Sectors of the economy that produce goods and services with an environmental benefit.

climate change Changes in the Earth's climate caused by increasing concentrations of carbon dioxide and other pollutants produced by human activity.

codes of conduct Define acceptable and unacceptable behavior for corporations or their partners.

collaborative partnerships Voluntary alliances among business, government, and civil society organizations that draw on the unique capabilities of each to achieve special, often social, objectives.

command and control regulation A regulatory approach where the government "commands" business to comply with certain standards (such as amounts of particular pollutants) and often directly "controls" their choice of technology to achieve these standards.

commons Any shared resource, such as land, air, or water, that a group of people use collectively.

community A company's area of local business influence. Traditionally, the term applied to the city, town, or rural area in which a business's operations, offices, or assets were located. With the rise of large, complex business organizations, the meaning of the term has expanded to include multiple localities.

community relations The organized involvement of business with the communities in which it conducts operations.

community relations manager (or community involvement manager) Manager delegated to interact with local citizens, develop community programs, manage donations of goods and services, work with local governments, and encourage employee volunteerism.

competition A struggle to survive and excel. In business, different firms compete with one another for customers' dollars, employees' talents, and other assets.

competitive intelligence The systematic and continuous process of gathering, analyzing, and managing external information on the organization's competitors.

Comprehensive Environmental Response, Compensation, and Liability Act (CERCLA) (See Superfund.)

conflicts of interest Occur when an individual's self-interest conflicts with acting in the best interest of another, when the individual has an obligation to do so.

consumer affairs officer Manages the complex network of consumer relations.

consumer movement A social movement that seeks to augment the rights and powers of consumers. (Also known as consumerism.)

consumer privacy   A consumer's right to be protected from the unwanted collection and use of information about that individual for use in marketing.

consumer protection laws   Laws that provide consumers with better information, protect consumers from possible hazards, encourage competitive pricing, protect privacy, or permit consumer lawsuits.

consumer rights   The legitimate claims of consumers to safe products and services, adequate information, free choice, a fair hearing, competitive prices, and privacy.

consumerism   (See consumer movement.)

Convention on Climate Change   First negotiated in 1992, an annual conference hosted by the United Nations to negotiate agreements to cut fossil fuel emissions that cause global warming.

corporate citizenship   This term refers to the actions corporations take to put their commitments to corporate social responsibility into practice worldwide.

corporate crisis   A significant business disruption that stimulates extensive news media or social networking coverage.

corporate culture   A blend of ideas, customs, traditional practices, company values, and shared meanings that help define normal behavior for everyone who works in a company.

corporate foundations   Organizations chartered as nonprofits, and funded by companies, for the purpose of administering contribution programs uniformly and providing a central group of people that handles all grant requests.

corporate giving   (See corporate philanthropy.)

corporate governance   The process by which a company is controlled or governed.

corporate identity   The way an organization presents itself to an audience.

corporate image   The way organizational members believe others see the organization.

corporate philanthropy   The voluntary and unconditional transfer of cash or other assets by private firms for public purposes.

corporate political strategy   Those activities taken by an organization to acquire, develop, and use power to achieve a political advantage.

corporate power   The capability of corporations to influence government, the economy, and society, based on their organizational resources.

corporate reputation   Desirable or undesirable qualities associated with an organization or its actors that may influence the organization's relationships with its stakeholders.

corporate social reporting   The public reporting of information collected by the organization or another party during a social audit.

corporate social responsibility   The idea that businesses should act in a way that enhances society and their stakeholders and be held accountable for any of its actions that affect people, their communities, and their environment.

corporation   Legally, an artificial legal "person," created under the laws of a particular state or nation. Socially and organizationally, it is a complex system of people, technology, and resources generally devoted to carrying out a central economic mission as it interacts with a surrounding social and political environment.

cost-benefit analysis   A systematic method of calculating the costs and benefits of a project or activity.

crisis management   The process organizations use to deal with a major event that threatens to harm the organization, its stakeholders, or the general public.

crowd-sourced audit   Gathering information about factory conditions directly from workers using their mobile phones.

cyberchondriacs   People who leap to the most dreadful conclusions while researching medical matters online.

cybercrime   Criminal activity done using computers and the Internet.

cyberspace   A virtual location where information is stored, ideas are described, and communication takes place in and through an electronic network of linked systems.

D

dark money   Political contributions made to tax-exempt organizations that are not required to report the donor's name and size of contribution to the Federal Election Commission.

dark site   A website that is fully developed and uploaded with critical information but remains dormant or "dark" until activated by the firm when needed in response to a crisis.

debt relief   The idea that the world's richest nations should forgive poor nations' obligation to pay back loans.

deceptive advertising   An advertisement that makes false or misleading claims about the company's own product or its competitor's product, withholds relevant information, or creates unreasonable expectations; generally illegal in most countries.

democracy A form of government in which power is vested in the people and exercised by them directly or by their elected representatives.

deregulation The removal or scaling down of regulatory authority and regulatory activities of government.

digital divide The gap between those that have access to the Internet and those that do not.

digital medical records The electronic storing of a patient's medical records so that they are accessible by other medical providers.

Digital Millennium Copyright Act The U. S. law that made it a crime to circumvent antipiracy measures built into most commercial software agreements between the manufacturers and their users.

directors (See board of directors.)

discrimination (in jobs or employment) Unequal treatment of employees based on non-job-related factors such as race, sex, age, national origin, religion, color, and physical or mental handicap.

diversity Variation in the characteristics that distinguish people from one another, such as age, ethnicity, gender, mental or physical abilities, race, and sexual orientation.

diversity council A group of managers and employees responsible for developing and implementing specific action plans to meet an organization's diversity goals. (See also diversity.)

divestment Withdrawing and shifting to other uses the funds that a person or group has invested in the securities (stocks, bonds, notes, etc.) of a company. Investors sometimes have divested the securities of companies doing business in countries accused of human rights abuses.

dividend A return-on-investment payment made to the owners of shares of corporate stock at the discretion of the company's board of directors.

Dodd-Frank Act Legislation passed in the U.S. in 2011 in response to the financial crisis; extensively reformed the regulation of financial institutions such as banks and credit rating agencies, established a new consumer financial protection bureau, and changed corporate governance and executive compensation rules.

drug testing (of employees) The testing of employees, by the employer, for the presence of illegal drugs, sometimes by means of a urine sample, saliva, or hair follicle analyzed by a clinical laboratory.

E

e-business Electronic business exchanges between businesses and between businesses and their customers via the Internet.

ecological footprint The amount of land and water an individual or group needs to produce the resources it consumes and to absorb its wastes, given prevailing technology.

ecologically sustainable organization (ESO) A business that operates in a way that is consistent with the principle of sustainable development. (See also sustainable development.)

economic leverage A political tool where a business uses its economic power to threaten to relocate its operations unless a desired political action is taken.

economic regulation The oldest form of regulation in the United States, aimed at modifying the normal operations of the free market and the forces of supply and demand.

ecosystem Plants and animals in their natural environment, living together as an interdependent system.

egoist (See ethical egoist.)

elder care The care or supervision of elderly persons; offered as a benefit by some employers to working children of elderly parents.

electronic monitoring (of employees) The use by employers of electronic technologies to gather, store, and monitor information about employees' activities.

emissions charges or fees Fees charged to business by the government, based on the amount of pollution emitted.

employee assistance programs (EAPs) Company-sponsored programs to assist employees with alcohol abuse, drug abuse, mental health and other problems.

employee ethics training Programs developed by businesses to further reinforce their ethical expectations for their employees.

employment-at-will The principle that workers are hired and retain their jobs solely "at the will of" (that is, sole discretion of) the employer.

enlightened self-interest The view that holds it is in a company's self-interest in the long run to provide true value to its stakeholders.

environmental analysis A method managers use to gather information about external issues and trends.

environmental intelligence The acquisition of information gained from analyzing the multiple environments affecting organizations.

environmental justice   The efforts to prevent inequitable exposure to risk, such as from hazardous waste.

environmental partnerships   A voluntary, collaborative partnership between or among businesses, government regulators, and environmental organizations to achieve specific environmental goals.

Environmental Protection Agency (EPA)   The U.S. federal government agency responsible for most environmental regulation and enforcement.

environmental scanning   Examining an organization's environment to discover trends and forces that could have an impact on the organization.

environmental standards   Standard amounts of particular pollutants allowable by law or regulation.

equal employment opportunity   The principle that all persons otherwise qualified should be treated equally with respect to job opportunities, workplace conditions, pay, fringe benefits, and retirement provisions.

Equal Employment Opportunity Commission (EEOC)   The U.S. federal government agency charged with enforcing equal employment opportunity laws and executive orders.

ergonomics   Adapting the job to the worker, rather than forcing the worker to adapt to the job.

ethical climate   An unspoken understanding among employees of what is and is not acceptable behavior based on the expected standards or norms used for ethical decision making.

ethical egoist   A person who puts his or her own selfish interests above all other considerations.

ethical principles   Guides to moral behavior, such as honesty, keeping promises, helping others, and respecting others' rights.

ethical relativism   A belief that ethical right and wrong are defined by various periods of time in history, a society's traditions, the specific circumstances of the moment, or personal opinion.

ethics   A conception of right and wrong conduct, serving as a guide to moral behavior.

ethics and compliance officer   A manager designated by an organization to investigate breaches of ethical conduct, promulgate ethics statements, and generally promote ethical conduct at work.

ethics policies or codes   A written set of rules used to guide managers and employees when they encounter an ethical dilemma.

ethics reporting mechanisms   A program that enables employees, customers, or suppliers to report an ethical concern directly to someone in authority in an organization.

European Union (EU)   The political and economic coalition of countries located in the greater European region.

executive compensation   The compensation (total pay) of corporate executives, including salary, bonus, stock options, and various benefits.

extended product responsibility   The idea that companies have a continuing responsibility for the environmental impacts of their products and services, even after they are sold.

external stakeholder   Individuals or groups that may have important transactions with a firm but are not directly employed by the firm, such as customers or suppliers.

F

family-friendly corporation   A company that fully supports both men and women in their efforts to balance work and family responsibilities.

family leave   A leave of absence from work, either paid or unpaid, for the purpose of caring for a family member, such as an elderly relative.

Federal Communications Commission   The U.S. federal government agency created in 1934 to regulate interstate and international communications; specifically regulates business advertisement.

fiscal policy   The patterns of government collecting and spending funds intended to stimulate or support the economy.

527 organizations   Groups organized under section 527 of the Internal Revenue Service tax code for the purpose of donating money to candidates for public office and influencing elections.

flextime   A plan that allows employees limited control over scheduling their own hours of work, usually at the beginning and end of the workday.

focal organization   The organization from whose perspective a stakeholder analysis is conducted.

foreign direct investment   When a company, individual, or fund invests money in another country.

fraud   Deceit or trickery due to the pursuit of economic gain or competitive advantage.

free enterprise system   A socioeconomic system based on private ownership, profit-seeking business firms, and the principle of free markets.

free market   A model of an economic system based on voluntary and free exchange among buyers and sellers. Competition regulates prices in all free market exchanges.

G

general public   Broadly defined as individuals or groups in society.

general systems theory   A theory that holds that all organisms are open to, and interact with, their external environments.

genetic engineering   A process by which scientists insert virtually any gene into a plant or other living organism in order to create a new crop or an entirely new species.

genetically modified foods   Food crops grown from genetically engineered seeds or food processed from such crops.

glass ceiling   An invisible barrier to the advancement of women, minorities, and other groups in the workplace.

glass walls   An invisible barrier to the lateral mobility of women, minorities, and other groups in the workplace, such as from human resources to operations, which could lead to top management positions.

global action network   A collaborative, multisector partnership focused on particular social issues or problems in the global economy.

global corporate citizenship   Refers to putting an organization's commitment to social and environmental responsibility into practice worldwide.

global warming   The gradual warming of the earth's climate, believed by most scientists to be caused by an increase in carbon dioxide and other trace gases in the Earth's atmosphere resulting from human activity, mainly the burning of fossil fuels.

globalization   The movement of goods, services, and capital across national borders.

greenhouse effect   The warming effect that occurs when carbon dioxide, methane, nitrous oxides, and other gases act like the glass panels of a greenhouse, preventing heat from the Earth's surface from escaping into space.

grey hatters   Hackers working on their own, often seeking media attention, but inclined to share their hacking exploits with the businesses they hacked.

H

hackers   Individuals, often with advanced technology training, acting alone or in groups, who, for thrill or profit, breach a business's information security system.

hacktivist   Individual or group that invades a secure computer network and releases the information stored there to embarrass or gain leverage against the organization.

hazardous waste   Waste materials from industrial, agricultural, and other activities capable of causing death or serious health problems for those persons exposed for prolonged periods. (See also toxic substance.)

hedge funds   Pools of private capital, so-called because of the aggressive strategies used to earn high returns for their investors.

honesty tests   Written psychological tests given to prospective employees that seek to predict their honesty on the job.

human genome   Strands of DNA developing a unique pattern for every human.

human rights   An ethical approach emphasizing a person or group's entitlement to something or to be treated in a certain way, such as the right to life, safety, or to be informed.

human trafficking (or forced labor)   The illegal recruitment and movement of people against their will, usually to exploit them for economic gain.

I

ideology   A set of basic beliefs that define an ideal way of living for an individual, an organization, or a society.

image advertisements   Used by businesses to enhance their public image, create goodwill, or announce a major change, such as a merger, acquisition, or new product line.

inclusion   Policies and practices that tap into the diverse perspectives, life experiences, and approaches that every individual brings to the workplace.

industrial ecology   Designing factories and distribution systems as if they were self-contained ecosystems, such as using waste from one process as raw material for another.

information phase   The fifth phase of technology; emphasizes the use and transfer of knowledge and information rather than manual skill.

in-kind contributions   Corporate charitable contributions of products or services, rather than cash.

innovation   Creating a new process or device that adds value.

insider trading   Occurs when a person gains access to confidential information about a company's financial condition and then uses that information, before it becomes public knowledge, to buy or sell the company's stock; generally illegal.

institutional investor   A financial institution, pension fund, mutual fund, insurance company, university endowment, or similar organization that invests its accumulated funds in securities offered for sale on stock exchanges.

integrated reporting   The combining of legally required financial information with social and environmental information into a single report.

integrated supplier scorecard   When suppliers are rated on multiple dimensions including traditional measures (costs, quality, timeliness) and newer measures (social, ethical, and environment performance).

intellectual property   Ideas, concepts, and other symbolic creations of the human mind that are recognized and protected under a nation's copyright, patent, and trademark laws.

interactive social system   The closely intertwined relationships between business and society.

internal stakeholder   Individuals who are employed by the firm, such as employees and managers.

international financial and trade institutions   Institutions, such as the World Bank, International Monetary Fund, and World Trade Organization, that establish the rules by which international commerce is transacted.

International Monetary Fund   An international financial institution that lends foreign exchange to member nations so they can participate in global trade.

Internet   A global network of interconnected computers, enabling users to share information.

Internet censorship   Government control of Internet access or content often on political, security, or religious grounds.

iron law of responsibility   The belief that those who do not use their power in ways that society considers responsible will tend to lose their power in the long run.

issue advertisements   A technique used by businesses to influence the public's opinion of a political or legislative issue of concern to the company.

issue management   The active management of public issues once they come to the attention of a business organization.

issue management process   A five-step process where managers identify the issue, analyze the issue, generate options, take action, and evaluate results.

J

justice   An ethical approach that emphasizes whether the distribution of benefits and burdens among people are fair, according to some agreed-upon rule.

K

Kyoto Protocol   An international treaty negotiated in 1997 in Kyoto, Japan, that committed its signatories to reduce emissions of greenhouse gases, such as carbon dioxide.

L

labor force participation rate   The proportion of a particular group, such as women, in the paid workforce.

labor standards   Conditions affecting a company's employees or the employees of its suppliers or subcontractors.

labor union   An organization that represents workers on the job and that bargains collectively with the employer over wages, working conditions, and other terms of employment.

laws   Society's formal written rules about what constitutes right and wrong conduct in various spheres of life.

legal challenges   A political tool that questions the legal legitimacy of a regulation.

legal obligations   A belief that a firm must abide by the laws and regulations governing the society.

license to operate   The right to do business informally conferred by society on a business firm; must be earned through socially responsible behavior.

life-cycle analysis   Collecting information on the lifelong environmental impact of a product in order to minimize its adverse impacts at all stages, including design, manufacture, use, and disposal.

living wage   A wage that enables workers, paid for a standard work week, to support half of the basic needs of an average-sized family based on local prices near the workplace.

lobbying   The act of trying to directly shape or influence a government official's understanding and position on a public policy issue.

local sourcing   When a company seeks to use nearby suppliers when practical.

M

marine ecosystems   Oceans and the salt marshes, lagoons, and tidal zones that border them, and well as the diverse communities of life that they support.

market-based mechanism   A form of regulation, used in environmental policy, based on the idea that the market is a better control than standards imposed on corporate behavior.

market failure   Inability of the marketplace to properly adjust prices for the true costs of a firm's behavior.

market stakeholder   A stakeholder that engages in economic transactions with a company.

material sustainability issues   Issues that are particularly relevant to an evaluation of a particular company or industry's sustainability practices.

m-commerce   Commerce conducted by using mobile or cell phones, allowing consumers to use their mobile or cell phones as electronic wallets.

media training   The education of executives and employees, who are likely to have contact with the media, in how to communicate effectively with the press.

microfinance   Occurs when financial organizations provide loans to low-income clients or a community of borrowers who traditionally lack access to banking or related services.

military dictatorship   A repressive regime ruled by a dictator who exercises total power through control of the armed forces.

mobile telephones (or cell phones)   Communication devices that use radio technology to enable users to place calls from random locations.

monetary policy   Government actions that affect the supply, demand, and value of a nation's currency.

monopoly   Occurs when one company dominates the market for a particular product or service.

Montreal Protocol   An international treaty limiting the manufacture and use of chlorofluorocarbons and other ozone-depleting chemicals. (See also ozone.)

moral development stages   A series of progressive steps by which a person learns new ways of reasoning about ethical and moral issues. (See stages of moral development.)

morality   A condition in which the most fundamental human values are preserved and allowed to shape human thought and action.

N

natural capital   The world's natural assets, including its geology, soil, air, water, and all living things.

natural monopolies   Where a concentration of the market is acquired by a few firms due to the nature of the industry rather than because of company practices.

negative externalities (or spill-over effects)   When the manufacture or distribution of a product gives rise to unplanned or unintended costs (economic, physical, or psychological) borne by consumers, competitors, neighboring communities, or other business stakeholders.

nongovernmental organizations (NGOs)   Organizations that do not have a governmental or commercial purpose, such as religious, community, family, and interest-group organizations. Also called civil society or civil sector organizations.

nonmarket stakeholder   A stakeholder that does not engage in direct economic exchange with a company, but is affected by or can affect its actions.

nonrenewable resources   Natural resources, such as oil, coal, or natural gas, that once used are gone forever. (See also renewable resources.)

O

Occupational Safety and Health Administration (OSHA)   The U.S. federal government agency empowered to set and enforce worker safety and health standards.

occupational segregation   The inequitable concentration of a group, such a minorities or women, in particular job categories.

omnichannel   The idea that every distribution channel must work together to deliver a unified and consistent customer experience.

ownership theory of the firm   A theory that holds that the purpose of the firm is to maximize the long-term return for its shareholders. (Also called the property or finance theory of the firm.)

ozone   A bluish gas composed of three bonded oxygen atoms. Ozone in the lower atmosphere is a dangerous component of urban smog; ozone in the upper atmosphere provides a shield against ultraviolet light from the sun. (See also Montreal Protocol.)

P

paid content   When a business pays to have online or print publishers create and distribute information.

parental leave   A leave of absence from work, either paid or unpaid, for the purpose of caring for a newborn or an adopted child.

pay gap   The difference in the average level of wages, salaries, and income received by two groups, such as men and women (called the gender pay gap) or whites and persons of color (called the racial pay gap).

performance–expectations gap   The perceived distance between what a firm wants to do or is doing and what the stakeholder expects.

philanthropy   (See corporate philanthropy.)

phishing   The practice of stealing consumers' personal identity data and financial account credentials by using fake e-mails.

political action committee (PAC)   An independently incorporated organization that can solicit contributions and then channels those funds to candidates seeking political office.

predatory pricing   The practice of selling below cost to drive rivals out of business.

privacy   (See right of privacy.)

privacy rights   Protecting an individual's personal life from unwarranted intrusion by the employer.

private equity firms   Organizations that manage pools of money invested by very wealthy individuals and institutions.

private property   A group of rights giving control over physical and intangible assets to private owners. Private ownership is the basic institution of capitalism.

private regulation (also private governance)   Nongovernmental institutions that govern—that is, enable and constrain—economic activities; occurs when private companies or groups of companies voluntarily establish codes of conduct governing working conditions, human rights, and environmental practices within global supply chains.

privately held corporation   A corporation that is privately owned by an individual or a group of individuals; its stock is not available for purchase by the general investing public.

product liability   The legal responsibility of a firm for injuries caused by something it made or sold.

product recall   Occurs when a company, either voluntarily or under an agreement with a government agency, takes back from its distribution channels all items found to be dangerously defective.

profits   The revenues of a person or company minus the costs incurred in producing the revenue.

proxy   A legal instrument giving another person the right to vote the shares of stock of an absentee stockholder.

proxy access   Changes in the nomination process for a company's board of directors that allows stockholders to nominate their own candidates.

proxy statement   A statement sent by a board of directors to a corporation's stockholders announcing the company's annual meeting, containing information about the business to be considered at the meeting, and enclosing a proxy form for stockholders not attending the meeting to vote.

public   (See general public.)

public affairs department   Manages an organization's interactions with government at all levels to promote the firm's interests in the political process.

public issue   An issue that is of mutual concern to an organization and its stakeholders, sometimes called a social or sociopolitical issue.

public policy   A plan of action undertaken by government officials to achieve some broad purpose affecting a substantial segment of a nation's citizens.

public relations   A program that sends a constant stream of information from the company to the public and opens the door to dialogue with stakeholders whose lives are affected by company operations.

public relations department   Manages the firm's public image and, more generally, its relations with the public.

public service announcements (PSAs)   Advertisements that address critical social issues.

publicly held corporation   A corporation whose shares of stock are available for purchase by the general investing public (as contrasted with a privately held firm).

Q

quality management   All measures taken by an organization to assure quality, such as defining the customer's needs, monitoring whether or not a product or service consistently meets these needs, analyzing the quality of finished products to assure they are free of defects, and continually improving processes to eliminate quality problems.

questionable payments   Something of value given to a person or firm that raises significant ethical questions of right or wrong in the host nation or other nations.

R

race to the bottom   When businesses move operations from one country to another seeking to pay workers the lowest wages possible or to avoid strong government regulations.

racial harassment   Harassment in the workplace based on race, such as ethnic slurs, derogatory comments, or other verbal or physical harassment that creates an intimidating, hostile, or offensive working environment or that interferes with an individual's work performance. (See also sexual harassment.)

rain forest   Woodlands that receive at least 100 inches of rain a year. They are among the planet's richest areas in terms of biodiversity.

regulation   The action of government to establish rules by which industry or other groups must behave in conducting their normal activities.

renewable resources   Natural resources, such as fresh water or timber, that can be naturally replenished. (See also nonrenewable resources.)

reputation   The desirable or undesirable qualities associated with an organization or its actors that may influence the organization's relationships with its stakeholders.

reregulation   The increase or expansion of government regulation on activities, especially in areas where the regulatory activities had previously been reduced.

return on social investment   Benefits of a business's social actions that accrue to both business and society.

revolving door   The circulation of individuals between business and government positions.

right (human)   A concept used in ethical reasoning that means that a person or group is entitled to something or is entitled to be treated in a certain way.

right of privacy   A person's entitlement to protection from invasion of his or her private life by government, business, or other persons.

right to be forgotten   The phrase used by Internet users when requesting that their personal information be removed from Google search results, supported by the European high court.

root cause analysis   Analysis undertaken to determine the underlying cause of repeated violations of particular code requirements or standards in global supply chains.

S

salience   Causes a stakeholder to stand out as important and to receive managers' attention; based on the stakeholder's power, legitimacy, and urgency. (See stakeholder salience.)

Sarbanes-Oxley Act   U.S. law enacted in 2002 that greatly expanded the powers of the SEC to regulate

information disclosure in the financial markets and the accountability of an organization's senior leadership regarding the accuracy of this disclosure. (See also Securities and Exchange Commission.)

say-on-pay   U.S. regulation requiring public companies to hold an advisory shareholder vote on executive compensation at least once every three years; also required in several other countries.

Securities and Exchange Commission (SEC)   The U.S. federal government agency whose mission is to protect stockholders' rights by making sure that stock markets are run fairly and that investment information is fully disclosed.

semantic phase   A phase of technology that began around 2000; characterized by the development of processes and systems to enable organizations and people to navigate through the expanding amount of links and information available on the Internet.

sexual harassment   Repeated, unwanted, and uninvited sexual attention or when on-the-job conditions are hostile or threatening in a sexual way. (See also racial harassment.)

shared value   Benefits created when the company invests in suppliers and employees, exchanges knowledge, and collaborates on improvements.

shareholder   A person, group, or organization owning one or more shares of stock in a corporation; the legal owners of the business. (Also investor or stockholder.)

shareholder lawsuit   A lawsuit initiated by one or more shareholders to recover damages suffered due to alleged actions of the company's management.

shareholder resolution   A proposal made by a stockholder or group of stockholders and included in a corporation's notice of its annual meeting that advocates some course of action to be taken by the company.

social assistance policies   Government programs aimed at improving social welfare in such areas as health care and education.

social audit   A systematic evaluation of an organization's social, ethical, and environmental performance.

social capital   The norms and networks that enable collective action; goodwill engendered by social relationships.

social contract   An implied understanding between an organization and its stakeholders as to how they will act toward one another.

social enterprise   A business that adopts social benefit as its core mission and uses its resources to improve human and environmental well-being.

social investment   The use of stock ownership as a strategy for promoting social, environmental, and governance objectives. (Also called socially responsible investment or sustainable, responsible, and impact investment, or SRI.)

social networking   A system using technology to enable people to connect, explore interests, and share activities around the world.

social regulation   Regulations aimed at important social goals such as protecting consumers and the environment, promoting equal employment opportunity, protecting pension benefits, and providing health care for citizens.

social responsibility   (See corporate social responsibility.)

social responsibility shareholder resolution   A resolution on an issue of corporate social responsibility placed before shareholders for a vote at a company's annual meeting.

society   Refers to human beings and to the social structures they collectively create; specifically refers to segments of humankind, such as members of a particular community, nation, or interest group.

soft money   Unlimited political contributions made to a political party by individuals or organizations, but not by businesses or labor unions, to support party-building activities.

software piracy   The illegal copying of copyrighted software.

sound bite   Information, often 30 seconds or less, used by the media in its broadcast to the public.

spam   Unsolicited e-mails (or junk e-mails) sent in bulk to valid e-mail and mobile accounts.

spirituality (personal)   A personal belief in a supreme being, religious organization, or the power of nature or some other external, life-guiding force.

stages of moral development   A sequential pattern of how people grow and develop in their moral thinking, beginning with a concern for the self and growing to a concern for others and broad-based principles.

stakeholder   A person or group that affects, or is affected by, a corporation's decisions, policies, and operations. (See also market stakeholder and nonmarket stakeholder.)

stakeholder analysis   An analytic process used by managers that identifies the relevant stakeholders in a particular situation and seeks to understand their interests, power, and likely coalitions.

stakeholder coalitions   Alliances among company's stakeholders to pursue a common interest; generally are not static relationships.

stakeholder dialogue   Conversations between representatives of a company and its stakeholders about issues of common concern.

stakeholder engagement   An ongoing process of relationship building between a business and its stakeholders.

stakeholder interests   The nature of each stakeholder group, its concerns, and what it wants from its relationship with the firm.

stakeholder map   A graphical representation of the relationship of stakeholder salience to a particular issue.

stakeholder materiality   Adaptation of an accounting term that focuses on the importance or significance of stakeholders for the firm.

stakeholder networks   A connected assembly of concerned individuals or organizations defined by their shared focus on a particular issue, problem, or opportunity.

stakeholder power   The ability of one or more stakeholders to make an event happen or to secure a desired outcome in their interactions with a company. The five types are voting power, economic power, political power, legal power, and informational power.

stakeholder salience   A stakeholder's ability to stand out from the background, to be seen as important, or to draw attention to itself or its issue. Stakeholders are more salient when they possess power, legitimacy, and urgency. (See also salience.)

stakeholder theory of the firm   A theory that holds that the purpose of the firm is to create value for society.

stem cell research   Research on nonspecialized cells that have the capacity to self-renew and to differentiate into more mature cells.

stock option   A form of compensation. Options represent the right (but not obligation) to buy a company's stock at a set price (called the strike price) for a certain period of time. The option becomes valuable to its holder when, and if, the stock price rises above this amount.

stock screening   Selecting stocks based on social or environmental criteria.

strategic philanthropy   A form of corporate giving that is linked directly or indirectly to business goals or objectives.

strict liability   A legal doctrine that holds that a manufacturer is responsible (liable) for injuries resulting from the use of its products, whether or not the manufacturer was negligent or breached a warranty.

Superfund   A U.S. law, passed in 1980, designated to clean up hazardous or toxic waste sites. The law established a fund, supported mainly by taxes on petrochemical companies, to pay for the cleanup. (Also known as the Comprehensive Environmental Response, Compensation, and Liability Act [CERCLA].)

super PAC (political action committee)   An organization that raises and spends money focusing on political issues but is not directly affiliated with any political campaign; also called an independent expenditure-only committee.

supplier   An organization that provides goods or services to another organization.

supplier development   Activities undertaken by companies to improve the performance of firms in their supply chain.

supply chain   The multiple steps involved in the movement of a product or service from the most distant supplier to the customer.

supply chain audit   An assessment of a supplier's performance to determine if it is in compliance with a relevant code of conduct.

supply chain codes of conduct   Company- or industry-established rules for suppliers.

supply chain map   Graphically depicts the movement of a product or service along the supply chain.

supply chain transparency   Occurs when a company's supply chain is fully disclosed to its stakeholders.

sustainability report   A single report integrating a business's social and environmental results.

sustainable development   Development that meets the needs of the present without compromising the ability of future generations to meet their own needs; ensuring a better quality of life for everyone, now and for generations to come.

sweatshops   Factories where employees—sometimes including children—are forced to work long hours, at low wages, and often under unsafe working conditions.

T

technology   A broad term referring to the practical applications of science and knowledge to commercial and organizational activities.

technology cooperation   Long-term partnerships between companies in developed and developing countries to transfer environmental technologies to attain sustainable development.

The Business Roundtable   Founded in 1972, an organization of chief executive officers from leading corporations involved in various public issues and legislation.

tier-1 suppliers (or contractors)   Organizations hired to manufacture products for or provide services directly to a company.

tier-2 suppliers (or subcontractors)   Organizations hired to manufacture products for or provide services to tier-1 suppliers (contractors).

tissue engineering   The growth of tissue in a laboratory dish for experimental research.

toxic substance   Any substance used in production or in consumer products that is poisonous or capable of causing serious health problems for those persons exposed. (See also hazardous waste.)

tradable permits   A market-based approach to pollution control in which the government grants companies "rights" to a specific amount of pollution (permits), which may be bought or sold (traded) with other companies.

trade association   A coalition of companies in the same or related industries seeking to coordinate their economic or political power to further their agenda.

transnational corporation   Corporations that operate and control assets across national boundaries.

transparency   Clear public reporting of an organization's performance to various stakeholders.

triple bottom line   The measurement of an organization on the basis of its economic results, environmental impact, and contribution to social well-being.

U

undocumented immigrant workers   Noncitizens employed by businesses without having the legally required work documents.

U.S. Corporate Sentencing Guidelines   Standards to help judges determine the appropriate penalty for criminal violations of federal laws and provide a strong incentive for businesses to promote ethics at work.

U.S. Foreign Corrupt Practices Act   Federal law that prohibits executives of U.S.-based companies from paying bribes to foreign government officials, political parties, or political candidates.

user-generated content   Sources of information provided by users through social media sites that can be supportive or critical of a business.

utilitarian reasoning   An ethical approach that emphasizes the consequences of an action and seeks the action or decision where the benefits most outweigh the costs.

V

values   Fundamental and enduring beliefs about the most desirable conditions and purposes of human life.

virtue ethics   Focuses on character traits to define a good person, theorizing that values will direct a person toward good behavior.

volunteerism   The efforts of people to assist others in a community through unpaid work.

W

Wall Street   A customary way of referring to the financial community of banks, investment institutions, and stock exchanges centered in the Wall Street area of New York City.

water pollution   When more wastes are discharged into waterways, such as lakes and rivers, than can be naturally diluted and carried away.

whistle-blowing   An employee's disclosure of alleged organizational misconduct to the media or appropriate government agency, often after futile attempts to convince organizational authorities to take action against the alleged abuse.

white hatters   Individuals employed by businesses or governments to hack their own information security systems deliberately to discover possible vulnerabilities.

workforce diversity   Diversity among employees, a challenge and opportunity for business. (See also diversity.)

World Bank   An international financial institution that provides economic development loans to member nations.

World Trade Organization   An organization of member nations that establishes the ground rules for trade among nations.

BIBLIOGRAPHY

Part One: Chapters 1–4

Ackerman, Robert. *The Social Challenge to Business*. Cambridge, MA: Harvard University Press, 1975.

Albrecht, Karl. *Corporate Radar: Tracking the Forces That Are Shaping Your Business*. New York: American Management Association, 2000.

Bader, Christine. *The Evolution of a Corporate Idealist: When Girl Meets Oil*. Brookline, MA: Bibliomotion, 2014.

Barth, Regine, and Franziska Wolff (eds.). *Corporate Social Responsibility in Europe—Rhetoric and Realities*. Cheltenham, UK: Edward Elgar Publishing, 2009.

Bhagwati, Jagdish. *In Defense of Globalization*. New York: Oxford University Press, 2007.

Boutilier, Robert. *Stakeholder Politics: Social Capital, Sustainable Development, and the Corporation*. Sheffield, UK: Greenleaf Publishing, 2009.

Bowen, Howard R. *Responsibilities of the Businessman*. New York: Harper, 1953.

Carroll, Archie B.; Kenneth J. Lipartito; James E. Post; and Patricia H. Werhane. *Corporate Responsibility: The American Experience*. Cambridge, UK: Cambridge University Press, 2012.

Chamberlain, Neil W. *The Limits of Corporate Social Responsibility*. New York: Basic Books, 1973.

Clarkson, Max B.E. (ed.). *The Corporation and Its Stakeholders: Classic and Contemporary Readings*. Toronto: University of Toronto Press, 1998.

Crane, Andrew; Dirk Matten; and Jeremy Moon. *Corporations and Citizenship*. Cambridge, UK: Cambridge University Press, 2008.

Elkington, John. *Cannibals with Forks: The Triple Bottom Line of 21st Century Business*. London: Thompson, 1997.

Fombrun, Charles. *Reputation*. Boston: Harvard Business School Press, 1996.

Frederick, William C. *Corporation Be Good!* Indianapolis, IN: Dog Ear Publishing, 2006.

Freeman, R. Edward. *Strategic Management: A Stakeholder Approach*. Cambridge, UK: Cambridge University Press, 2010.

Jamali, Dima; Charlotte Karam; and Michael Blowfield (eds.). *Development-Oriented Corporate Social Responsibility: Multinational Corporations and the Global Context*, Volume 1. Sheffield, UK: Greenleaf Publishing, 2015.

Jamali, Dima; Charlotte Karam; and Michael Blowfield (eds.). *Development-Oriented Corporate Social Responsibility: Locally-led Initiatives in Developing Economies*, Volume 2. Sheffield, UK: Greenleaf Publishing, 2015.

Kolb, Robert W. (ed.). *Encyclopedia of Business Ethics and Society*. Thousand Oaks, CA: SAGE Publications, 2008.

Korten, David C. *When Corporations Rule the World*, 2nd edition. San Francisco, CA: Berrett-Koehler, 2001.

Lawrence, Paul R., and Nitin Nohria. *Driven: How Human Nature Shapes Our Choices*. San Francisco, CA: Jossey-Bass, 2002.

Leipziger, Deborah. *The Corporate Responsibility Code Book*, 3rd edition. Sheffield, UK: Greenleaf Publishing, 2015.

Lindgreen, Adam; Philip Kotler; Joelle Vanhamme; and Francois Maon. *A Stakeholder Approach to Corporate Social Responsibility*. Farnham, UK: Gower Publishing, 2012.

Orlitzky, Marc, and Diane Swanson. *Toward Integrative Corporate Citizenship: Research Advances in Corporate Social Performance*. New York: Palgrave Macmillan, 2008.

Phillips, Robert. *Stakeholder Theory and Organizational Ethics*. San Francisco: Berrett-Koehler Publishers, Inc., 2003.

Phillips, Robert A., and R. Edward Freeman (eds.). *Stakeholders*. Northampton, MA: Edward Elgar Publishing, 2010.

Porter, Michael. *The Competitive Advantage of Nations*. New York: Basic Books, 1991.

Post, James E.; Lee E. Preston; and Sybille Sachs. *Redefining the Corporation: Stakeholder Management and Organizational Wealth*. Palo Alto, CA: Stanford University Press, 2002.

Scherer, Andreas Georg, and Guido Palazzo (eds.). *Handbook of Research on Global Corporate Citizenship*. Northampton, MA: Edward Elgar Publishing, 2008.

Svendsen, Ann. *The Stakeholder Strategy: Profiting from Collaborative Business Relationships*. San Francisco: Berrett-Koehler Publishers, 1998.

Vogel, David. *The Market for Virtue: The Potential and Limits of Corporate Social Responsibility*. Washington, DC: Brookings Institution Press, 2005.

Waddell, Steve. *Global Action Networks: Creating Our Future Together*. New York: Palgrave Macmillan, 2011.

Waibel, Piera. *Putting the Poor First: How Base-of-the-Pyramid Ventures Can Learn from Development Approaches*. Sheffield, UK: Greenleaf Publishing, 2012.

Yankelovich, Daniel. *The Magic of Dialogue: Transforming Conflict Into Cooperation.* New York: Simon & Schuster, 1999.

Yaziji, Michael, and Jonathan Doh. *NGOs and Corporations: Conflict and Collaboration.* New York: Cambridge University Press, 2009.

Yunas, Muhammad. *Building Social Business: The New Kind of Capitalism that Serves Humanity's Most Pressing Needs.* Philadelphia: Perseus Books Group, 2010.

Part Two: Chapters 5–6

Callahan, David. *The Cheating Culture.* Orlando: Harcourt, 2004.

Cavanaugh, Gerald F. *American Business Values: With International Perspectives*, 6th edition. Upper Saddle River, NJ: Prentice-Hall, 2009.

Colby, Anne, and Lawrence Kohlberg. *The Measurement of Moral Judgment: Volume I, Theoretical Foundations and Research Validations.* Cambridge, MA: Harvard University Press, 1987.

Comer, Debra R., and Gina Vega. *Moral Courage in Organizations: Doing the Right Thing at Work.* Armonk, NY: M.E. Sharpe, 2011.

Cortright, S.A., and Michael J. Naughton (eds.). *Rethinking the Purpose of Business: Interdisciplinary Essays from the Catholic Social Tradition.* Notre Dame, IN: University of Notre Dame Press, 2002.

Dempsey, Alison. *Evolutions in Corporate Governance: Towards an Ethical Framework for Business Conduct.* Sheffield, UK: Greenleaf Publishing, 2013.

Donaldson, Thomas, and Thomas W. Dunfee. *Ties that Bind: A Social Contracts Approach to Business Ethics.* Cambridge, MA: Harvard Business School Publishing, 1999.

Fluker, Walter Earl. *Ethical Leadership: The Quest for Character, Civility, and Community.* Minneapolis, MN: Augsburg Fortress, 2009.

Gentile, Mary C. *Giving Voice to Values: How to Speak Your Mind When You Know What's Right.* New Haven, CT: Yale University Press, 2010.

Hamington, Maurice, and Maureen Sander-Staudt (eds.). *Applying Care Ethics to Business.* New York: Springer, 2011.

Jackall, Robert. *Moral Mazes: The World of Corporate Managers.* New York: Oxford University Press, 1988.

Kochan, Nick, and Robin Goodyear. *Corruption: The New Corporate Challenge.* New York: Palgrave Macmillan, 2011.

Payne, Brian K. *White-Collar Crime.* Thousand Oaks, CA: Sage, 2012.

Price, Terry L. *Leadership Ethics: An Introduction.* New York: Cambridge University Press, 2008.

Rawls, John. *A Theory of Justice.* Cambridge, MA: Harvard University Press, 1971.

Singh, Nitish, and Thomas J. Bussen. *Compliance Management: A How-to Guide for Executives, Lawyers and other Compliance Professionals.* Santa Barbara, CA: Praeger, 2015.

Stone, Christopher D. *Where the Law Ends: The Social Control of Corporate Behavior.* Prospect Heights, IL: Waveland Press, 1975.

Werhane, Patricia H., and R. Edward Freeman. *The Blackwell Encyclopedic Dictionary of Business Ethics*, 2nd edition. Malden, MA: Blackwell, 2005.

Part Four: Chapters 7–8

Coen, David; Wyn Grant; and Graham Wilson (eds.). *The Oxford Handbook of Business and Government.* New York: Oxford University Press, 2011.

Epstein, Edwin M. *The Corporation in American Politics.* Englewood Cliffs, NJ: Prentice-Hall, 1969.

Foundation for Public Affairs. *The State of Corporate Public Affairs 2014–2015.* Washington, DC: Foundation for Public Affairs, 2014.

Harris, Phil, and Craig S. Fleisher (eds.). *Handbook of Public Affairs.* Thousand Oaks, CA: Sage Publications, 2005.

Healy, Robert. *Corporate Political Behavior: Why Corporations Do What They Do in Politics.* New York: Routledge, 2014.

Lodge, George C. *The New American Ideology.* New York: Alfred A. Knopf, 1978.

_____. *Comparative Business-Government Relations.* Englewood Cliffs, NJ: Prentice-Hall, 1990.

_____, and Ezra F. Vogel (eds.). *Ideology and National Competitiveness.* Boston: Harvard Business School Press, 1998.

Miller, Brian, and Mike Lapham. *The Self-Made Myth: And the Truth About How Government Helps Individuals and Businesses Succeed.* San Francisco: Berrett-Koehler, 2012.

Parker, Christine, and Vibeke Lehmann Nielsen (eds.). *Explaining Compliance: Business Responses to Regulation.* Northampton, MA: Edward Elgar Publishing, 2011.

Sorkin, Andrew Ross. *Too Big to Fail: The Inside Story of How Wall Street and Washington Fought to Save the Financial System—and Themselves.* New York: Viking, 2009.

Vogel, David. *Kindred Strangers: The Uneasy Relationship between Politics and Business in America.* Princeton, NJ: Princeton University Press, 1996.

Wilson, Gregory P. *Managing to the New Regulatory Reality: Doing Business under the Dodd-Frank Act.* Hoboken, NJ: John Wiley & Sons, 2011.

Yadav, Vineeta. *Political Parties, Business Groups and Corruption in Developing Countries*. New York: Oxford University Press, 2011.

Part Five: Chapters 9–10

Anderson, Ray C., with Robin White. *Business Lessons from a Radical Industrialist*. New York: St. Martin's Griffin, 2011.

Cline, Elizabeth L. *Over-dressed: The Shockingly High Cost of Cheap Fashion*. New York: Penguin, 2012.

Daly, Herman E. *Beyond Growth: The Economics of Sustainable Development*. Boston: Beacon Press, 1996.

Dunphy, Dexter; Suzanne Benn; and Andrew Griffiths. *Organisational Change for Corporate Sustainability*. New York: Routledge, 2003.

Ehrenfeld, John R., and Andrew J. Hoffman. *Flourishing: A Frank Conversation About Sustainability*. Stanford, CA: Stanford Business Press, 2013.

Esty, Daniel C., and Andrew S. Winston. *Green to Gold: How Smart Companies Use Environmental Strategy to Innovate, Create Value, and Build Competitive Advantage*, revised edition. Hoboken, NJ: John Wiley & Sons, 2009.

Foreman, Jr., Christopher H. *The Promise and Perils of Environmental Justice*. Washington, DC: Brookings Institution, 2000.

Frederick, William C. *Natural Corporate Management: From the Big Bang to Wall Street*. Sheffield, UK: Greenleaf Publishing, 2012.

Friedman, Frank B. *Practical Guide to Environmental Management*, 11th edition. Washington, DC: Environmental Law Institute, 2011.

Friedman, Thomas L. *Hot, Flat, and Crowded: Why We Need a Green Revolution—and How It Can Renew America*. New York: Farrar, Strauss, and Giroux, 2008.

Hammond, Allen. *Which World? Scenarios for the 21st Century*. Washington, DC: Island Press, 1998.

Hart, Stuart L. *Capitalism at the Crossroads: The Unlimited Business Opportunities in Solving the World's Most Difficult Problems*. Philadelphia, PA: Wharton School Publishing, 2005.

Hawken, Paul; Amory Lovins; and L. Hunter Lovins. *Natural Capitalism: Creating the Next Industrial Revolution*. Boston: Little Brown, 1999.

Hoffman, Andrew J. *Competitive Environmental Strategy: A Guide to the Changing Business Landscape*. Washington, DC: Island Press, 2000.

Kurucz, Elizabeth C.; Barry A. Colbert; and David Wheeler. *Reconstructing Value: Leadership Skills for a Sustainable World*. Toronto, Canada: University of Toronto Press, 2013.

Laszlo, Chris, and Judy Sorum Brown. *Flourishing Enterprise: The New Spirit of Business*. Stanford, CA: Stanford Business Press, 2014.

Russo, Michael V. *Companies on a Mission: Entrepreneurial Strategies for Growing Sustainably, Responsibly, and Profitably*. Stanford, CA: Stanford University Press, 2010.

Schendler, Auden. *Getting Green Done: Hard Truths from the Front Lines and Sustainability Revolution*. New York: Foundation for Public Affairs, 2009.

Speth, James Gustaveth, *The Bridge at the Edge of the World*. New Haven, CN: Yale University Press, 2008.

Stead, Jean Garner, and W. Edward Stead. *Management for a Small Planet*, 3rd edition. Armonk, NY: M.E. Sharpe, 2009.

Stoner, James A.F., and Charles Wankel (eds.). *Managing Climate Change, Business Risks and Consequences: Leadership for Global Sustainability*. New York: Palgrave Macmillan, 2012.

Visser, Wayne. *Sustainable Frontiers: Unlocking Change through Business, Leadership and Innovation*. Sheffield, UK: Greenleaf Publishing, 2015.

Waddock, Sandra, and Malcolm McIntosh. *SEE Change: Making the Transition to a Sustainable Enterprise Economy*. Sheffield, UK: Greenleaf Publishing, 2011.

Winston, Andrew S. *The Big Pivot: Radically Practical Strategies for a Hotter, Scarcer, and More Open World*. Boston: Harvard Business Press, 2014.

Worldwatch Institute. *State of the World 2015: Confronting Hidden Threats to Sustainability*. Washington, DC: Island Press, 2015.

Part Six: Chapters 11–12

Baram, Michael, and Mathilde Bourrier. *Governing Risk in GM Agriculture*. New York: Cambridge University Press, 2011.

Heinberg, Richard. *Cloning the Buddha: The Moral Impact of Biotechnology*. San Juan Capistrano, CA: Quest Books, 1999.

Horn, Tom, and Nita Horn. *Forbidden Gates: How Genetics, Robotics, Artificial Intelligence, Synthetic Biology, Nanotechnology, and Human Enhancement Herald the Dawn of Techno-Dimensional Spiritual Warfare*. Crane, MO: Defender Publishing, 2010.

Levy, Steven. *Hackers: Heroes of the Computer Revolution*. Sebastopol, CA: O'Reilly Media, 2010.

McClure, Stuart; Joel Scambray; and George Kurtz. *Hacking Exposed: Network Security Secrets and Solutions*. New York: McGraw-Hill, 2009.

Muller, Hunter. *The Transformational CIO*. Hoboken, NJ: John Wiley & Sons, 2011.

Park, Alice. *The Stem Cell Hope: How Stem Cell Medicine Can Change Our Lives*. New York: Hudson Street Press, 2011.

Rader, William C. *Blocked in the USA: The Stem Cell Miracle*. Malibu, CA: Nanog Publishing, 2010.

Rosen, Larry D. *Understanding our Obsession with Technology and Overcoming Its Hold on Us*. Hampshire, UK: Palgrave Macmillan, 2012.

Safko, Lon, and David K. Brake. *The Social Media Bible: Tactics, Tools and Strategies for Business Success*. New York: John Wiley & Sons, 2009.

Schneider, Bruce. *Data and Goliath: The Hidden Battles to Collect Your Data and Control Your World*. New York: W.W. Norton, 2015.

Weasel, Lisa H. *Food Fray: Inside the Controversy over Genetically Modified Food*. New York: American Management Association, 2009.

Part Seven: Chapters 13–19

Andvliet, Luc, and Mary B. Anderson, *Getting It Right: Making Corporate-Community Relations Work*. Sheffield, UK: Greenleaf, 2009.

Bainbridge, Stephen M. *Corporate Governance after the Financial Crisis*. New York: Oxford University Press, 2012.

Bebchuk, Lucian A., and Jesse M. Fried. *Pay without Performance: The Unfulfilled Promise of Executive Compensation*. Cambridge, MA: Harvard University Press, 2004.

Bugg-Levine, Antony, and Jed Emerson. *Impact Investing: Transforming How We Make Money While Making a Difference*. San Francisco: Jossey-Bass, 2011.

Carter, Colin B., and Jay W. Lorsch. *Back to the Drawing Board: Designing Corporate Boards for a Complex World*. Boston: Harvard Business School Press, 2004.

Coombs, W. Timothy. *Ongoing Crisis Communication*. Thousand Oaks, CA: Sage, 2012.

Dine, Philip M. *State of the Unions: How Labor Can Strengthen the Middle Class, Improve Our Economy, and Regain Political Influence*. New York: McGraw-Hill, 2008.

Dorff, Michael B. *Indispensable and Other Myths: Why the CEO Pay Experiment Failed and How to Fix It*. Berkeley, CA: University of California Press, 2014.

Eccles, Robert G., and Michael P. Krzus. *The Integrated Reporting Movement: Meaning, Momentum, Motives, and Materiality*. Hoboken, NJ: John Wiley & Sons, 2015.

Fagan, Colette; Maria Gonzalez Menendez; and Silvia Gomez Anson (eds.). *Women on Corporate Boards and in Top Management*. New York: Palgrave Macmillan, 2012.

Ferracone, Robin A. *Fair Pay, Fair Play: Aligning Executive Performance and Pay*. San Francisco, CA: Jossey-Bass, 2010.

Gordon, Averill Elizabeth. *Public Relations*. New York: Oxford University Press, 2011.

Grant, Peter. *The Business of Giving*. New York: Palgrave Macmillan, 2011.

Greenhouse, Steven. *The Big Squeeze: Tough Times for the American Worker*. New York: Anchor Books, 2009.

Herman, R. Paul. *The HIP Investor: Make Bigger Profits by Building a Better World*. Hoboken, NJ: John Wiley & Sons, 2010.

Hilts, Philip J. *Protecting America's Health: The FDA, Business, and One Hundred Years of Regulation*. New York: Alfred A. Knopf, 2003.

Jordan-Meier, Jane. *The Four Stages of Highly Effective Crisis Management*. Boca Raton, FL: Taylor & Francis Group, 2011.

Kalleberg, Arne L. *Good Jobs, Bad Jobs: The Rise of Polarized and Precarious Employment Systems in the United States, 1970s to 2000s*. New York: Russell Sage Foundation, 2013.

Kelly, Marjorie. *The Divine Right of Capital: Dethroning the Corporate Aristocracy*. San Francisco: Berrett-Koehler Publishers, Inc., 2003.

Lakin, Nick, and Veronica Scheubel. *Corporate Community Involvement: The Definitive Guide to Maximizing your Business' Societal Engagement*. Sheffield, UK: Greenleaf, 2010.

Lewis, Michael. *The Big Short: Inside the Doomsday Machine*. New York: W.W. Norton, 2010.

Locke, Richard M. *The Promise and Limits of Private Power: Promoting Labor Standards in a Global Economy*. New York: Cambridge University Press, 2013.

Lorsch, Jay W. *The Future of Boards: Meeting the Governance Challenges of the Twenty-First Century*. Boston: Harvard Business Review Press, 2012.

Miceli, Marcia P.; Janet Pollex Near; and Terry M. Dworkin. *Whistle-Blowing in Organizations*. London: Routledge, 2008.

Mitroff, Ian I. *Managing Crisis Before They Happen*. New York: American Management Association, 2005.

Monks, Robert A. G., and Nell Minow. *Corporate Governance*, 5th edition. Hoboken, NJ: John Wiley & Sons, 2011.

Piketty, Thomas. *Capital in the Twenty-First Century*. Cambridge, MA: The Belknap Press of Harvard University Press, 2014.

Rivoli, Pietra. *The Travels of a T-Shirt in the Global Economy: An Economist Examines the Markets, Power, and Politics of World Trade,* 2nd edition. Hoboken, NJ: John Wiley & Sons, 2015.

Rosen, Jeffrey. *The Unwanted Gaze: The Destruction of Privacy in America.* New York: Random House, 2000.

Rotenberg, Marc; Julia Horwitz; and Jeramie Scott (eds.). *Privacy in the Modern Age: The Search for Solutions.* New York: The New Press, 2015.

Schlosser, Eric. *Fast Food Nation: The Dark Side of the All-American Meal.* New York: Perennial, 2002.

Schneider, Bruce. *Data and Goliath: The Hidden Battles to Collect Your Data and Control Your World.* New York: W.W. Norton, 2015.

Siegel, Lucy B. (ed.). *Public Relations Around the Globe: A Window on International Business Culture.* New York: Bridge Global Strategies, 2012.

Stout, Lynn. *The Shareholder Value Myth: How Putting Shareholders First Harms Investors, Corporations, and the Public.* San Francisco, CA: Berrett-Koehler, 2012.

Ton, Zeynap. *The Good Jobs Strategy: How the Smartest Companies Invest in Employees to Lower Costs and Boost Profits.* Boston: Houghton Mifflin Harcourt, 2014.

Weil, David. *The Fissured Workplace: Why Work Became So Bad for So Many and What Can Be Done to Improve It.* Cambridge, MA: Harvard University Press, 2014.